MOON

JAMAICA

OLIVER HILL

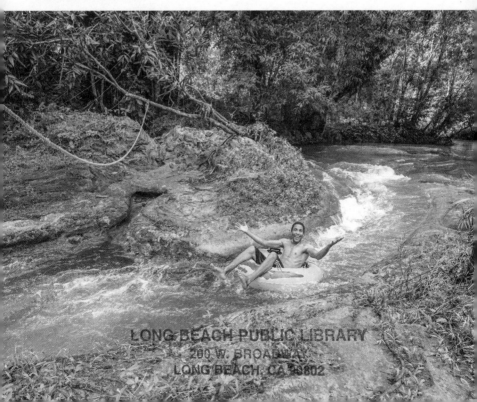

Contents

Discover Jamaica **6**
　7 Top Experiences 10
　Planning Your Trip 16
　The Best of Jamaica 20
　• Boutique Spas 21
　Musical Roots and Culture 23
　• Adrenaline Rush 25
　Hidden Beaches and Hillside Hikes ... 26
　• Top Beaches 27
　• Jamaican Cuisine 29

Negril and the West Coast **30**
　Sights 35
　Beaches 35
　Recreation 37
　Entertainment 41
　Shopping 44
　Food 44
　Accommodations 49
　Information and Services 57
　Transportation 58
　Northeast of Negril 59
　Southeast of Negril 65

Montego Bay and the Northwest
Coast **72**
　Sights 78

Beaches 82
Recreation 83
Entertainment 88
Shopping 91
Food 93
Accommodations 98
Information and Services 102
Transportation 103
East of Montego Bay 104
North Cockpit Country 114

Ocho Rios and the Central North
Coast **117**
　Ocho Rios 122
　West of Ocho Rios 143
　Runaway Bay 148
　Discovery Bay 153
　Nine Mile 155
　St. Mary Parish 157

Port Antonio and the East
Coast **166**
　Port Antonio 170
　Upper Rio Grande Valley 188
　West of Port Antonio 190
　East of Port Antonio 191
　Morant Bay 197

**Kingston and the Blue
    Mountains** **200**
    Sights 205
    Entertainment.................. 218
    Shopping 229
    Recreation..................... 232
    Food 235
    Accommodations 246
    Information and Services 249
    Transportation.................. 251
    Around Kingston................ 253
    The Blue and John Crow Mountains . . 263

The South Coast **276**
    Mandeville..................... 280
    North of Mandeville 284
    South of Mandeville 286
    Treasure Beach 288
    Black River and South Cockpit Country 298

Background **305**
    The Landscape 305

Plants and Animals 307
History......................... 312
Government and Economy......... 315
People and Culture 318
The Arts....................... 322
Sports 326

Essentials **328**
    Transportation.................. 328
    Visas and Officialdom 331
    Food 331
    Accommodations 333
    Conduct and Customs 334
    Travel Tips 335
    Sustainable Tourism 337
    Health and Safety 339
    Information and Services 340

Resources **343**
    Glossary....................... 343
    Suggested Reading.............. 347
    Internet Resources 349

JAMAICA

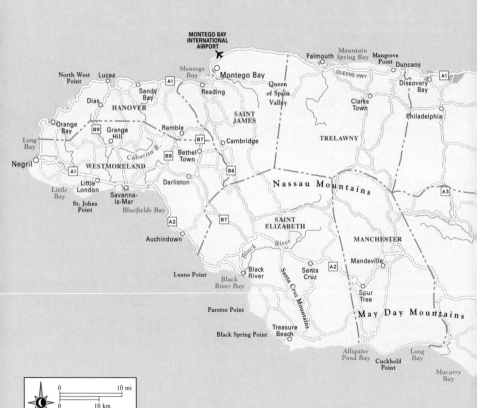

CARIBBEAN
SEA

MONTEGO BAY
INTERNATIONAL
AIRPORT

Montego
Bay

Montego Bay

Falmouth   Mountain   Mangrove
Spring Bay   Point   Duncans

QUEENS HWY   Discovery   A1
Bay

North West   Lucea   Reading   Queen   Philadelphia
Point   of Spain   Clarks
Valley   Town

Sandy   SAINT
Bay   JAMES
Dias   HANOVER   Ramble
Orange   Cambridge   TRELAWNY
Bay   B9   Grange   B7
Hill   Bethel   Nassau Mountains
Long   B8   Town
Bay   Cabarita R.   B6   A3
Negril   A1   WESTMORELAND   Darliston
Little   Little   SAINT
Bay   London   B7   ELIZABETH   Santa Cruz Mountains   MANCHESTER
St. Johns   Savanna-   Mandeville
Point   la-Mar   Black   River   A2
Bluefields Bay   Spur
Auchindown   A2   Santa   Tree
Luana Point   Black   Cruz   May Day Mountains
Black   River
River Bay   Alligator   Long
Parotee Point   Treasure   Pond Bay   Cuckhold   Bay
Black Spring Point   Beach   Point   Macarry
Bay

0   10 mi

0   10 km

© MOON.COM

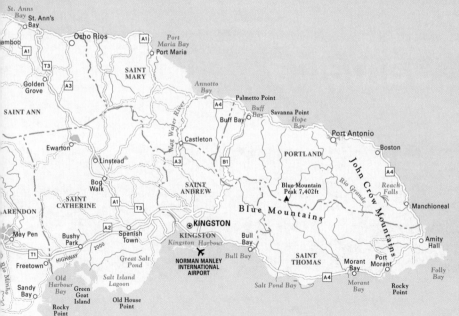

I t's hard to argue when Jamaicans assert that their island is blessed. Simple luxuries abound, like picking a mango from a tree for breakfast, watching hummingbirds flit about tropical flowers, or bathing in a crystal-clear waterfall on a hot day. It's no wonder that for more than a century visitors have come to Jamaica to escape cold northern winters and bask in the island's tropical climate and calm Caribbean waters.

Jamaica's resorts have supplemented these simple pleasures with luxury: hot stone massages, candlelit gourmet dinners, soft reggae music, and lapping waves are just the beginning. Many resorts have perfected the art of indulgence to such a degree that it's entirely possible to miss the depth and color of the country's culture beyond their walls.

Outside the hotel gates you'll find the tenacious evolution of a nation approaching 60 years old, where preachers—religious, musical, and political—lend vibrancy to everyday life. Jamaica's vibrant culture and resilient spirit can be felt throughout the country, from small villages to bustling urban centers like Kingston.

Clockwise from top left: The "Grammy Kid" Damian Marley at Reggae Sumfest; a guide at Nine Mile; a Carnival dancer in Kingston; fern trees and misty peaks in the Blue Mountains; a Chukka catamaran cruise; beach at Bloody Bay

Ironically, it wasn't the tropical climate or endless natural beauty that brought worldwide attention to Jamaica in the 20th century. It was a young man growing up with the odds stacked against him in the ghetto of Trench Town, who managed to make his truthful message heard above the din of political violence and clashing Cold War ideologies of the 1970s. Bob Marley, along with band members Peter Tosh and Bunny Wailer, became a beacon of hope, not just for disenfranchised Jamaicans, but for the oppressed the world over. Today, countless singers keep Marley's legacy alive and fuel Jamaica's music industry, one of the most prolific on the planet.

Whether you're seeking to explore the country's rich history, soak in the sunshine and the clear warm waters of the Caribbean, or just go with the flow, you'll come to understand what makes this island and its inhabitants so exceptional.

Clockwise from top left: Miss T's Kitchen in Ocho Rios; Blue Ridge on a hillside coffee farm in the Blue Mountains; a flaming torch blossom; Bluefields Villas

7 TOP
EXPERIENCES

1 **Climb a Waterfall:** Gradually ascend to the top of 600-foot **Dunn's River Falls** (page 122), the most popular attraction in Jamaica. To avoid the crowds, scale the beautiful **Konoko Falls** (page 125) instead.

2 **Feel the Rhythm:** Music is the pulsating cultural milieu that shapes Jamaican society. Explore the legacy of the legendary Bob Marley (page 156) while also experiencing the ever-evolving music scene of today (page 224).

3 **Taste Local Flavors:** Jamaican food is reason enough to visit the island. The culinary trend is Pan-Caribbean fusion, which brings creative flourishes to traditional staples (page 29).

>>>

4 **Chase Adrenaline:** Jamaica is known for being laid-back, but that doesn't mean it can't get your heart pounding (page 25). The especially adventurous might consider **cliff jumping** at Rick's Café (page 37).

5 Relax on a Beach: Find your zen on less touristy beaches and soak up some real Jamaican vibes (page 27).

6 **Float in the Blue Hole:** In this world-famous lagoon, ice-cold spring water mixes with the warm, salty sea to create a magical hue (page 176).

7 **Hike Blue Mountain Peak:** Take in the best views from the country's highest peak (page 273).

Planning Your Trip

Where to Go

Negril and the West Coast

Jamaica's westernmost parish has the country's **most popular beach resort town,** Negril. Once a quiet fishing village, Negril is known as the capital of casual, where recreational activities like **water sports** and **cliff jumping** complement the inactivity of **relaxing in the sun.**

Montego Bay and the Northwest Coast

Known the island over as Mobay, Jamaica's leading resort town offers **beaches, great house tours,** and the world-famous **Reggae Sumfest** musical showcase each July. Rivers along the eastern and western borders of St. James offer **rafting,** and Mobay has an active yacht club with a lively social calendar. Neighboring Trelawny encompasses a rugged inland terrain known as **Cockpit Country,** riddled with caves and underground rivers and a handful of postcard-perfect **beaches** along the coast.

Ocho Rios and the Central North Coast

Throngs of travelers disembark cruise ships each week in Ocho Rios, many headed for Jamaica's most popular attraction, **Dunn's River Falls.** Less trafficked river gardens abound, and **world-class hotels and villas** dot the coast to the east and west. Contrasting bustling Ocho Rios, **St. Mary** is laid-back, with **quiet hills, hidden waterfalls,** and **sleepy fishing villages.**

Port Antonio and the East Coast

Portland's parish capital and the biggest town in the east, Port Antonio has **Old World charm** lingering in **luxurious villas** and **hilltop resorts.** Despite its claim as the first Caribbean tourist destination, it has, for better or worse, been spared from large-scale development, and the area's **natural beauty** remains its principal draw, with singular **beaches, lush forests,** and **waterfalls.**

Kingston and the Blue Mountains

The boisterous capital city has **remarkable restaurants, pulsating nightlife,** and **historical treasures.** There's no sugarcoating the juxtaposition of poverty and wealth, but their coexistence inspires a prolific **music industry** and **vibrant arts scene.** Spectacular views and cool air are just a short drive away in the Blue Mountains, where visitors can enjoy the **world's finest coffee, hiking,** and **bird-watching.**

The South Coast

The South Coast defines **off-the-beaten-track,** where **waterfalls, crocodile-infested wetlands,** and **seafood** are the main attractions. **Treasure Beach,** a string of bays and fishing villages, is a favored destination for those wary of crowds and looking to get away from it all, while **Mandeville's cool highland air,** historic **golf course,** and **fine restaurants** represent a chance to experience the island's quiet interior.

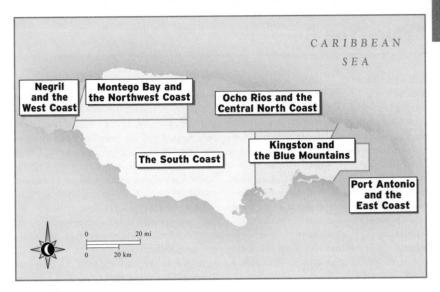

When to Go

Jamaica has typically been marketed as a destination for escaping the winter blues, but it can be just as good, or better, in the summer, when temperatures are comparable or even cooler than in places as far north as New York, especially at higher elevations and along the coast.

Jamaica's **hurricane season,** with regular low-pressure systems accompanied by rain, runs **June through October.** In the absence of a large tropical storm, or in the worst-case scenario a full-fledged hurricane, rainfall usually lasts only a few minutes and shouldn't be cause for concern in planning a trip.

The high season and low season should be of more concern in planning a trip, as many establishments set rates according to demand. **High season** runs **December 15 to April 15,** when accommodations can be twice as expensive as during the low season. Some establishments set their own specific dates, and others vary pricing throughout the year, raising them for Easter, Thanksgiving, or the week between Christmas and New Year's. If escaping the winter blues is not your first priority, visiting during the **low season** can be much more cost-effective. Check with each establishment when planning a trip to see how prices vary seasonally.

The Jamaican calendar is filled with **annual events,** many of which are worth considering in planning a trip. A music festival like Rebel Salute or Sumfest is one of the best ways to jump out of the tourism box and appreciate Jamaica's culture alongside Jamaicans from all walks of life. If music isn't your thing, there are several other annual events, like the Calabash Literary Festival, Blue Mountain Coffee Festival, Jamaica Rum Festival, and fishing tournaments.

Before You Go

Passports and Visas

Jamaica requires **passports** for all visitors, including those from the United States and the United Kingdom. A **tourist visa** is required for many nationalities. A listing of visa requirements and vaccination requirements by country can be found on the website of the Consulate General in New York (www.congenjamaica-ny.org/visas/requirements-2). Visitors must also be able to demonstrate sufficient funds to cover their stay and be in possession of an onward or return ticket or itinerary. It helps to know where you will be staying on arrival, as immigration officials tend to detain visitors on entry until they can provide an address.

Vaccinations

The Jamaican government requires documentation demonstrating visitors arriving from certain countries have been vaccinated against measles, rubella, polio, and yellow fever. Officials sporadically enforce these requirements at the main ports of entry. Countries with a risk of yellow fever transmission can be found on the World Health Organization website (www.who.int). Ensure you can provide documentation for required vaccinations upon entry. Check with the **Jamaica Tourist Board** (tel. 876/929-9200, www.visitjamaica.com) or **Passport Immigration and Citizenship Agency** (PICA, 25C Constant Spring Rd., Kingston, tel. 876/754-7422, www.pica.gov.jm) for current requirements.

Mosquito-borne illnesses, including dengue fever, chikungunya, and Zika, have affected Jamaica in recent years, and the U.S. Centers for Disease Control and Prevention (CDC) has on occasion issued alerts for travel to many parts of the Caribbean. Check the CDC website (https://wwwnc.cdc.gov) for the latest advisories when planning a trip. As a general practice, travelers should take every precaution to avoid mosquito

a red-billed streamertail, Jamaica's national bird

Secrets St. James Resort at Montego Bay

bites: Use insect repellent and wear protective clothing when venturing outdoors, and use a fan or mosquito net at night if your accommodation isn't screened.

What to Pack

Most Jamaican **ATMs** will dispense cash with foreign debit cards. The best exchange rates are found at foreign exchange traders like FX Trader. **Banks** accept traveler's checks but typically have long lines and offer less competitive rates.

Where **clothing** is concerned, what to take depends entirely on the nature of your trip. Most all-inclusive hotels have semiformal dress codes (a collared shirt, dress shoes) for their fine-dining restaurants.

Jamaicans take great care and pride in their attire. Tourists aren't held to the same standard, however; shorts, T-shirts, and flip-flops are the norm in the tourism centers. Some resorts, like Couples and Hedonism, have designated areas for nudists. Beyond beach resort towns like Negril, entering a place of business without a shirt will be frowned upon, if it's permitted at all.

Cool, light-colored cotton apparel is best for the heat and humidity, and of course, bring your favorite bathing suit or two. For cool evenings, pack a long-sleeved shirt and long pants.

Many travelers to Jamaica are surprised to find that Jamaicans rarely wear shorts on a normal day, while jeans and full suits are common everyday attire. It is not necessary to buy an entire wardrobe of Hawaiian shirts before your trip, and in a pinch plenty are sold in gift shops across the island with the requisite "Jamaica, no problem" printed across the front.

You'll definitely want to bring some flashy clothes if you're planning a **night on the town.** At clubs and street dances, women and men are dressed to the nines: men in their best shoes and a "criss" jacket to "flex" in the corner till the dance floor heats up and they've built the vibes sufficiently to bust a move.

For **hiking** and overnights in the higher elevations of the Blue Mountains, you'll want a sweater or sweatshirt, parka, boots, and warm socks.

I-Octane at Rebel Salute

a rope swing at YS Falls

The Best of Jamaica

Most people spend 3-5 days in Jamaica, but to get a true taste, 10 days is ideal. It provides enough time to relax on the beach while also venturing beyond the sun and sand for a mix of adventure and culture. Highlights include the cliff jumping and scrumptious food of Negril's West End, the culture and nightlife of Kingston, coffee plantations in the Blue Mountains, and the beaches of Portland. For shorter stays, combine one or two of the regions below to create your own custom trip.

Montego Bay

DAY 1

Arrive at the airport in **Montego Bay** and check in for two nights at **Wharf House.** Splurge for dinner at **The Sugar Mill** or **The HouseBoat Grill,** or keep it casual and affordable at **Scotchies** for some authentic roadside jerk. Hit up **Mobay Proper** for an evening drink to gauge the scene along the **Hip Strip.**

DAY 2

Tour **Rose Hall Great House** in the morning, then spend the afternoon lazing at **Doctors Cave Beach**. Dine at **Day-O Plantation,** followed by a play at **Fairfield Theatre** or a night out at **Pier 1** or **Margaritaville.**

Negril

DAY 3

Head west to **Negril** for **cliff jumping** on the West End or a splash at Brighton's **Blue Hole Mineral Spring** by late morning. Head to **Miss Lily's at Skylark** for lunch and soak up some rays before taking a sunset stroll down **Seven-Mile Beach.** Try some jerk or seafood at **Island Lux Beach Park** or **Pushcart Restaurant and Rum Bar** for dinner before checking out some live reggae on the beach.

DAY 4

In the morning, drive to **Savanna-la-Mar** and then turn inland to **Mayfield Falls** or **Blue Hole**

Boutique Spas

Jamaica has world-class spas, based predominantly at the high-end resorts. These spas strike the right balance between high-end and rootsy: even the most expensive among them draw from Jamaica's panoply of natural products and soothing vibes.

NEGRIL

- **Rockhouse Spa** offers massage treatments in clifftop cabanas; signature foot ceremonies, detox pedicures, and revitalizing scrubs in a temple-like garden pavilion; and deep-soak baths seaside, utilizing indigenous mind-, body-, and soul-stimulating ingredients (page 55).

- **The Spa Retreat** draws on the vast experience of one of Canada's leading day-spa operators, with a full range of pampering and invigorating treatments as well as educational couples massage sessions that can enhance a relationship with practical skills (page 56).

- **The Spa at The Caves** is the only place where you can get a massage inside a cavern glowing with candles and sprinkled with flower petals. Follow that with a relaxing soak in the private whirlpool-tub chamber carved into the cliff side while gazing out to sea (page 56).

- **Kiyara Spa on the Cliff,** located at The Cliff on Negril's West End, prides itself on offering natural herbal remedies made from seasonal local ingredients applied in treatment rooms near the water's edge to the tune of crashing waves. Or opt for the convenience and privacy of in-room treatments (page 56).

MONTEGO BAY

- **Fern Tree Spa** at Half Moon Resort, Montego Bay's leading boutique hotel and villa complex, pulls out all the stops, offering massage in a gazebo overhanging the soothing surf and facials, manicures, and pedicures in a state-of-the-art treatment room surrounded by rejuvenating plunge pools (page 100).

OCHO RIOS

- **The FieldSpa** at Goldeneye is uniquely situated overhanging a magical lagoon, where guests are pampered with products and

bubbling plunge pools at Fern Tree Spa

treatments not even Ian Fleming enjoyed when he sought solitude at this seaside estate to pen his James Bond classics. The spa is located on the wooded lagoon banks in and around a cozy two-story cottage with soaking tubs and massage tables hidden amid the tropical foliage (page 162).

BLUE MOUNTAINS

- **The Strawberry Hill Field Spa** marries deep-tissue treatments and ayurvedic healing philosophies. The spa features five treatment rooms, hydrotherapy, a sauna, a yoga deck, and a plunge pool with spectacular panoramic views of the Blue Mountains surrounded by lush cloud forests and rejuvenating mountain air that naturally promotes health and tranquility (page 270).

THE SOUTH COAST

- **Jake's Driftwood Spa** features seaside cabanas facing the water where the surf lulls visitors into a trance as they receive treatments that merge holistic techniques and philosophies from around the globe into a potent blend of Caribbean concoctions (page 291).

Gardens. Spend the morning exploring the falls and gardens, grab lunch at Guangos Jerk in Sav, then stop at Eldin Washington Ranch for Reggae Horseback Riding in the afternoon on the way back to Negril.

South Coast

DAY 5

Leave Negril and drive east to YS Falls in Middle Quarters for a splash in the river and an adrenaline-fixing zip-line canopy tour. Grab some jerk chicken at YS before heading to nearby Appleton Estate to sample Jamaica's best rum. Continue on to Treasure Beach in the late afternoon to check in for the night and sample the conch soup and fried fish at Jack Sprat Motel.

DAY 6

Wake up with a dip at one of the area's best beaches in Great Bay before a mid-morning stroll to Back Sea Side. In the afternoon catch a canoe boat to Black River to spot alligators and birds or head straight to Pelican Bar, a one-of-a-kind watering hole and ramshackle fried fish joint built on stilts 1.5 kilometers (1 mile) offshore, for some snorkeling and Red Stripe. Cruise back to Treasure Beach for a second night.

Kingston and the Blue Mountains

DAY 7

Leave early for Kingston to get there by late morning. Sightsee downtown with a visit to the National Gallery followed by a stroll along Ocean Boulevard and around Coronation Market. Grab lunch at Gloria's Seafood City along the waterfront before stopping by Bob Marley's first Kingston residence at Culture Yard, followed by a tour of his Tuff Gong Recording Studio or the Bob Marley Museum. Pick up some souvenirs and chow down at La Pizzeria, followed by ice cream at Devon House, a historic home with boutiques and restaurants, before a night on the town.

DAY 8

Head up to the Blue Mountains before the late morning clouds roll in for a coffee tour at Craighton Estate. Continue over the hills to Portland to reach Port Antonio in time for an afternoon dip at Winnifred Beach or Frenchman's Cove before dinner at Craft Village on East Harbour and a night out at Cristal Night Club.

Ocho Rios

DAY 9

Depart for Ocho Rios, stopping at Firefly on the way to check out playwright Noël Coward's island digs. Lunch at Chris Café in Oracabessa and then head up to Mystic Mountain for a bobsled run and zip-line tour through the canopy. Take a late-afternoon dip in the White River before dinner at Miss T's Kitchen.

DAY 10

Get on the road early to beat the crowds for a climb up Dunn's River Falls before heading west toward Montego Bay for an afternoon departure. Stop by Green Grotto Caves or Greenwood Great House on your way, time permitting.

reggae artist Sizzla

Musical Roots and Culture

Delve into the pulsating cultural milieu that shapes and defines Jamaican society. The roots of Jamaican popular music will become vivid with this tour, designed to immerse visitors in the island's singular musical gold mine. Keep tabs on the weekly events calendars in Kingston and Negril to plan your time in these areas.

Day 1

Arrive in **Montego Bay** for one night at the **S Hotel Jamaica.** If you arrive in the morning, visit **Rose Hall Great House** or **Bellefield Great House** for a step back in time with a stop at **Scotchies** for jerk either before or after the tour. Visit the **Gallery of West Indian Art** for some inspiration before dinner at **Pier 1** or **The HouseBoat Grill.** Hit up **Margaritaville** to mingle and "wine" with visitors and locals if you still have the energy before bed.

Day 2

Head to **Doctors Cave Beach** in the morning and then to **Negril** in the afternoon, stopping at **Island Lux Beach Park** for a bite before catching sunset and dinner on the cliffs at **Tensing Pen** or **Pushcart Restaurant and Rum Bar.** Check out the night's live reggae band on the beach or hit **The Jungle** nightclub.

Day 3

Make a loop from Negril to **Blue Hole Gardens** or **Mayfield Falls** to experience one of Jamaica's natural treasures before swinging back around to **Half Moon Beach** along the Hanover coast. Head back to Negril for dinner at **Miss Lily's at Skylark** or **Zest Restaurant** at The Cliff.

Day 4

Leave for the four-hour drive to **Kingston** bright and early, stopping in Belmont to pay respects to a reggae legend at **Peter Tosh Memorial Garden** and take a quick dip in the turquoise waters across the road. Make a pit stop in **Middle Quarters** for pepper shrimp, and then take a break at **Scott's Pass,**

dancers onstage for Bacchanal Fridays in Kingston

Clarendon, to meet the Rasta elders at the headquarters of the **Nyabinghi House of Rastafari** before continuing on to Kingston for the night.

Day 5

Hit Kingston's cultural sights, or any combination of the **Bob Marley Museum, Tuff Gong Recording Studio, Culture Yard,** and the **National Gallery.** Visit **Cap Calcini** to pick up some oldies reggae vinyl before heading out to **Hellshire Beach** for an early supper of fried fish, festival, and bammy at **Shorty's,** or dine at **Gloria's Seafood Restaurant** in **Port Royal** or **Gloria's Seafood City** on the Kingston waterfront before a night out on the town at **Reggae Mill Bar, Skydweller Ultra Lounge,** or at a street dance.

Day 6

Leave in the morning for **Jamnesia Surf Camp** in **Bull Bay** to ride waves with Billy "Mystic" Wilmot and his family, followed by dinner and an overnight stay in one of their bungalows. Time your stay to fall on the last Saturday of the month to witness the musical talents of the host family and friends riffing at **Jamnesia Sessions.**

Day 7

Spend the morning sampling the ritualized Rasta life at **Bobo Hill** if you're in the mood for some serious worship. Visit **Cane River Falls** (near Bull Bay) or **Reggae Falls** (a bit farther east in St. Thomas) in the afternoon before heading back to town. Dine on Indian cuisine at **Pushpa's** or **Tamarind** and then head up to Skyline Drive for some roots music and a drink at Gabre Selassie's **Kingston Dub Club,** especially lively on Sunday.

Day 8

Leave in the morning for **Port Antonio,** checking in at **Great Huts, Drapers San Guest House,** or **Goblin Hill.** Spend the afternoon at **Reach Falls** or on the beach with a quick visit to **Folly Mansion,** a dilapidated old structure located between the Folly Oval cricket field and the sea.

Day 9

Depart first thing for **Ocho Rios,** stopping in **Charles Town** on the way to take in some Maroon history, hiking, and swimming at **Asafu Yard.** In Ocho Rios, visit **Konoko Falls** to check out the iguanas and take an evening dip before dinner at the **Ocho Rios Fishing Village.**

Adrenaline Rush

Jamaica is known for being laid-back, but that doesn't mean it can't be thrilling enough to get your heart pumping. Zip-line tours abound, and between cliff jumping in Negril, learning to windsurf or kiteboard outside Montego Bay, and the breathtaking views of the Blue Mountains, there's plenty to keep your heart racing.

CLIFF JUMPING

- Cliff jumping on Negril's West End is the cheapest adrenaline fix in Jamaica. Several locations are suitable for jumping into the azure waters, but **Rick's Café** is the most famous for having the highest cliffs around, about 18 meters (60 feet) above the water (page 37).

WHITE-WATER RAFTING

- Raft the Rio Bueno in Montego Bay with **Braco Rapids Adventures** (page 113).

- **Chukka Caribbean** offers rafting on the Great River in St. James and tubing down the White River in St. Ann, as well as a more languid river experience along the Martha Brae at Good Hope in Trelawny (page 87).

ZIP-LINING

- **Mystic Mountain** in Ocho Rios offers canopy zip-line tours and a thrilling "bobsled" monorail (page 124).

- **Chukka Caribbean** also offers canopy zip-line tours at Good Hope Plantation in Montego Bay (page 114) and YS Falls in St. Elizabeth (page 300).

KITEBOARDING

- **Kitesurf Jamaica,** based in Montego Bay, offers kiteboarding and windsurfing lessons for

kiteboarding

the uninitiated and gear rentals for the experienced (page 84).

SURFING

- **Jamnesia Surf Camp,** east of Kingston in Bull Bay, has professional surfing equipment and respectable waves on a good day. A skateboard park entertains when the seas are flat (page 257).

- **Boston Bay** and **Long Bay** in Portland are both frequent destinations for the **Jamnesia crew;** Boston Bay also has surfboard rentals on-site (page 193).

Day 10

Visit **Calby's River Hidden Beauty** on the White River for swimming and a bit of light hiking in the morning before making your way to **Montego Bay** for an evening departure. Stop by **Burwood Beach** in **Trelawny** on the way for a quick dip, time permitting.

Hidden Beaches and Hillside Hikes

Hikes, wildlife-watching, secluded beaches, and mangrove tours are indispensable to a greater appreciation of Jamaica's natural wonders.

Transportation is an important consideration when planning, as many of the less-visited sights are remote and require a **rental car** or car and driver. Excursions into remote parts of Cockpit Country and the Blue Mountains require a **4WD vehicle**, but for most places, SUVs are not necessary and the extra expense is not justified.

Day 1

Arrive in **Montego Bay** and head directly to check in at **Silver Sands** in **Duncans**. Spend a few hours at **Burwood Beach** in Bounty Bay or at **Harmony Cove** in nearby Braco before a relaxing dinner back at the ranch.

Day 2

Explore **Cockpit Country** on horseback in the morning or go tubing down the river with **Chukka Caribbean,** followed by lunch back in Falmouth. Head to **Burwood Beach** in the afternoon for **kiteboarding** before a casual dinner at **Far Out Fish Hut** in nearby **Greenwood.**

Day 3

Depart in the morning for **Negril,** stopping at **Half Moon Beach** for lunch and a dip. Continue on to **Tensing Pen** to spend the afternoon **cliff jumping** and **relaxing by the pool.**

Day 4

Depart for **Belmont,** stopping at **Blue Hole Mineral Spring** in Brighton before heading to **Blue Hole Gardens** for another refreshing

Konoko Falls at Ocho Rios

Top Beaches

Jamaica has fantastic beaches, from extensive stretches of sand in Negril to little coves far from the crowds in the northeast. Most resorts are located beachfront, enticing guests to stay nearby, but it's worth venturing farther afield to experience some of the island's other offerings. Hitting less touristy beaches outside the heavily trafficked destinations also affords the opportunity to hang with locals and soak up some real Jamaican vibes.

NEGRIL

- **Seven-Mile Beach** is full of Negril's quintessential beach town vibes, with fine white sand and gentle surf (page 35).

- **Bluefields Beach** is a tranquil spot practically unvisited by tourists but popular with locals on the weekends (page 68).

MONTEGO BAY

- **Doctors Cave Beach** is the heart and soul of Montego Bay's Hip Strip, where visitors and locals alike enjoy fine sand, clear waters, and good service from the bar and restaurant on-site (page 82).

- **Burwood Beach** in Bounty Bay is one of the best places for kiteboarding, free of coral and shallow enough to stand 100 meters (330 feet) out (page 107).

- **Silver Sands** in Duncans is ideal for families, as it's reserved for guests of the gated community and completely free of hustlers (page 111).

- **Harmony Cove** in Braco is one of Jamaica's best-kept secrets (page 111).

OCHO RIOS

- **Laughing Waters,** just west of Ochi, has a breathtaking waterfall that cascades onto its gentle surf (page 129).

PORT ANTONIO

- **Frenchman's Cove** in San San has a chilly

Harmony Cove

meandering river that meets the formidable warm surf, creating an invigorating mix (page 175).

- **Boston Beach** consistently gets some of the best waves for surfing, with boards for rent on-site (page 193).

- **Long Bay Beach** has nice breakers for boogie boarding and surfing and a few kilometers of fine white sand (page 194).

KINGSTON

- **Lime Cay,** offshore Port Royal, is a sandbar barely rising above sea level that's popular with boaters and bathers, especially on weekends (page 254).

SOUTH COAST

- **Great Bay** in Treasure Beach, protected by Great Pedro Bluff, has one of the safer beaches on the South Coast, with gentle surf and fine golden sand (page 291).

dip and walk to see the many bubbling springs nearby. Catch sunset at **Bluefields Beach** and overnight in **Belmont** at the **Luna Sea Inn.**

Day 5

On your way to the **Blue Mountains,** make a stop in **Black River** for a morning kayak or pontoon boat safari to see the crocs, and then stop by **YS Falls** for an early afternoon dip. Push on through past Kingston to overnight at **Forres Park Guest House** in **Mavis Bank,** or **Lime Tree Farm** in the hills above, both prime locations for birding.

Day 6

Rise early to hike up to **Blue Mountain Peak.** Descend by early afternoon, stopping at **Crystal Edge** for lunch before checking in at **Woodside,** a 12-hectare (30-acre) coffee farm with hummingbirds aplenty, for your last two nights.

Day 7

Hike the trails of **Holywell National Park** or up to **Cinchona Gardens** in the morning. Afterward, drop in at David Twyman's **Old Tavern Coffee Estate** to pick up some beans to carry home. Enjoy home-cooked food back at Woodside before settling in for the night.

Day 8

Rise early for the drive back to **Montego Bay,** stopping in Ocho Rios for a dip in the **White River** or at **One Love Trail** by the roadside, or take a garden tour at **Konoko Falls.** Leave Ochi in time for an evening departure from Mobay's Sangster International Airport.

YS Falls

Jamaican Cuisine

Jamaica offers tantalizing food options that reflect the country's history and potpourri of cultures, with a wide variety of tropical ingredients, many of them unknown to the uninitiated. From ackee and saltfish, the national dish, to mannish water, a broth made with every imaginable goat part, to fish tea and conch soup, the offering will keep adventurous eaters salivating.

JAMMIN' JERK

Jamaica's best-known seasoning is made with scallion, ginger, molasses, scotch bonnet pepper, and pimento (called "all spice"), and is used to marinate all types of meat and seafood, giving them a rich, spicy flavor.

- Montego Bay: The original **Scotchies** (page 94) in Iron Shore serves mouth-watering jerk chicken, pork, and roast fish in a laid-back, open-air setting under thatch and zinc roofs.

- Ocho Rios: The satellite location of Montego Bay's renown restaurant, **Scotchies Too** (page 144) stays true to the original serving jerk chicken, pork and roast fish with rustic seating under zinc and thatch roofs in a garden setting replete with hibiscus.

- Kingston: **Jo Jo's Jerk Pit and More** (page 238) is a haven for locals and expats, serving scrumptious jerk chicken, pork, lamb, steam fish, conch and lobster from an extensive menu in an open-air setting where local bands, karaoke, and lively banter keep patrons thoroughly entertained.

- The South Coast: **All Seasons Restaurant Bar & Jerk Centre** (page 282) offers dependable and moderately spicy jerk chicken and pork half-way up Spur Tree Hill commanding a panoramic view of Manchester and St. Elizabeth.

POWERFUL PATTIES

A quick-fix meal on the go, Jamaican patties are baked bread pockets stuffed with curried chicken, minced beef, cheese, or veggies. Gourmet versions have curry goat, fish, shrimp, or lobster.

- Island-wide: **Juici Patties** is a ubiquitous fast-food chain serving excellent patties as well as more substantial meals for breakfast, lunch, and dinner.

- Kingston: **Devon House Bakery** (page 242) serves gourmet patties filled with atypical ingredients, like creamy lobster, fish, shrimp, or

curry goat, in addition to the more conventional chicken filling.

DELECTABLE CURRY GOAT

Curried goat is a favorite meal for many Jamaicans that draws on the country's rich heritage fusing African and Indian traditions. Typically served with white rice for Sunday dinner or other special occasions, the dish is flavored with scallion, ginger, pimento, and Indian curry powder, with its distinct yellow turmeric.

- Port Antonio: **Soldier's Camp** (page 182) is part kitchen, part bar, and 100 percent vibes, drawing an eclectic mix of locals and tourists who feast of specialties that include janga (crayfish) soup, curry goat, and steam fish. It is especially lively on Friday nights.

- The South Coast: **Claudette's Top Class** (page 282) at the top of Spur Tree Hill is renowned for its curry goat, cooked to perfection and best enjoyed with white rice.

SUMPTUOUS SEAFOOD

As an island nation, it's only logical that seafood should play a big part in the Jamaican diet. Fish dishes are typically prepared steamed and seasoned with pimento and scotch bonnet pepper, or fried with a dressing of tangy escoveitch sauce.

- Negril: **Dervy's Lobster Trap** (page 63) is a ramshackle joint on the waterfront that is a favorite rootsy spot for lobster with guests of the ultra-luxurious Round Hill Resort nearby, as well as other visitors and locals in the know.

- Ocho Rios: **Ocho Rios Fishing Village** (page 135) was recently spruced up, bringing order to what was once an eyesore and a stomping ground for hustlers. Today it is home to several seafood restaurants with modern and clean facilities, cooking up some of the best fresh fish, conch, and lobster in Ocho Rios.

- Port Antonio: **Cynthia's** (page 182) on Winnifred Beach is the go-to seafood restaurant in Port Antonio on the area's only free public beach, where the lovely proprietor makes guests feel at home with delicious seafood dishes as well as other Jamaican staples.

- Kingston: **Shorty's** (page 263) is one of the most trusted fish shacks at Hellshire Beach, where the founders' daughter Judith carries on the legacy of her parents with each plate of scrumptious escoveitch snapper and garlic lobster.

Negril and the West Coast

Sights 35

Beaches 35

Recreation 37

Entertainment 41

Shopping 44

Food 44

Accommodations 49

Information and
Services 57

Transportation 58

Northeast of Negril 59

Southeast of Negril 65

Negril is Jamaica's most popular beach town, embodying the "Jamaica No Problem" spirit plastered on T-shirts sold in souvenir shops across the island. It's a place where visitors and locals alike quickly forget what day of the week it is.

Live music blasts from beachfront bars virtually every night—and once in a while, one of the island's top-ranking artists passes through town to perform. Negril is split topographically between the iconic Seven-Mile Beach, with its fine white sand stretching from the Negril River to Point Village, and the limestone cliffs running along the West End, which lend themselves to thrill-seekers and romantics who flock in droves for adrenaline rushes and glowing sunsets from any number of lofty perches. It's as much a raucous beach town for mass tourism

Highlights

Look for ★ to find recommended sights, activities, dining, and lodging.

★ **Blue Hole Mineral Spring:** Cool off with a jump into this popular swimming hole a short drive from Negril (page 35).

★ **Seven-Mile Beach:** Jamaica's longest patch of sand is great for long walks into the sunset (page 35).

★ **Cliff Jumping on the West End:** Negril's West End runs along limestone cliffs with many locations ideally suited for thrilling leaps into the turquoise sea (page 37).

★ **Half Moon Beach:** Escape to this crescent-shaped cove with fine sand, pristine coastline, and Calico Jack's, a beach bar and grill on a small cay just offshore (page 60).

★ **Mayfield Falls:** Spend an afternoon at one of the best waterfall attractions in Jamaica. Take a dip in the river or walk upstream along a series of gentle cascades and pools (page 66).

★ **Blue Hole Gardens:** Visit one of Jamaica's most picturesque swimming holes and enjoy surreal turquoise water, lush gardens, and the 13 bubbling wellheads of Turtle River (page 66).

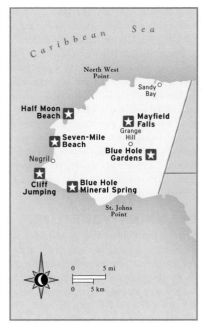

as it is a secluded enclave for the well-heeled vacationer. While Negril seems tailor-made for parties and relaxation, travelers seeking serenity may be disappointed by an abundance of loud motorbikes zooming up and down Norman Manley Boulevard and West End Road and by incessant music blasting from stacks of speakers at all hours.

After the Jamaican government decriminalized marijuana in 2015, the spliff-infused, Red Stripe-soaked, laid-back lifestyle espoused by so many in this coastal community has finally been officially embraced; the Cannabis Cup joined the line-up of annual events that year, before morphing into a locally produced annual event representative of Jamaica's cultural heritage, the Rastafari Rootz Fest and the concurrent Ganjamaica Cup. While smoking the sacramental herb, whether for recreation or on religious or medicinal grounds, can no longer get you locked up, possessing more than two ounces without authorization from the Cannabis Licensing Authority (CLA) is still a criminal offense.

Enterprising travelers who like to get out and about will find Negril to be a good base for exploring Westmoreland and neighboring parishes, with spectacular sunsets to come back to in the evening. If being surrounded by other travelers isn't your thing, sleepy coastal communities like Little Bay, Bluefields, Belmont, and Whitehouse offer fewer distractions and a variety of lodging options, from rustic clapboard cottages to boutique hotels and luxury villas.

PLANNING YOUR TIME

Negril is the ultimate place to kick back on the beach with plenty to do by day or night, and for many, it's the only destination they'll visit during their stay in Jamaica. If Negril is but one stop among several on your itinerary, two or three nights are sufficient to feel the vibes. The area has many worthwhile attractions that make great day trips and can

help break up long hours under the sun, avoid overexposure, and provide a glimpse of the "real" Jamaica—with all the allure of its languid countryside lifestyle and lush scenery. Most visitors to Negril come specifically to laze on the beach in the dead of winter, but there are special events throughout the year to be considered if you're planning a trip with flexibility. Apart from the Christmas and New Year's period, when it can be difficult to find accommodations, Negril is completely overrun by local and international visitors during the first week of August for Dream Weekend, a party series straddling national holidays that fall on the 1st and the 6th.

ORIENTATION

Life in Negril is centered along the west-facing coastline divided between **Seven-Mile Beach** and the cliffs along the **West End.** Seven-Mile Beach runs the length of **Long Bay,** from a small peninsula separating it from **Bloody Bay** on its northern end to the mouth of the Negril River at the southern end. There are three main roads that meet at the roundabout in the center of Negril: **Norman Manley Boulevard,** which turns into the A1 road as it leaves town heading northeast toward Montego Bay; **West End Road,** which continues south from the roundabout, hugging the cliffs well past the lighthouse, until it eventually turns inland, rejoining the main South Coast road (the A2) in the community of Negril Spot; and **Whitehall Road,** which extends eastward inland from the roundabout toward the golf course, becoming the A2 as it passes the Texaco gas station.

Whitehall Road turns south just before the Texaco station, climbing a hill and passing the ruins of Whitehall Great House. It passes through the communities of Mount Airy and Orange Hill before rejoining the A2 in Negril Spot. A sharp turn south between Orange Hill and Negril Spot leads to Brighton and Little Bay. From there, the road continues eastward,

---

Previous: The Caves; a glass bottom boat at Seven-Mile Beach; Blue Hole Gardens

The West Coast

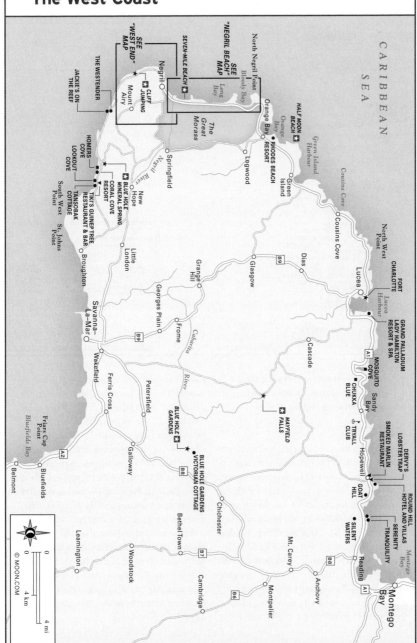

West End

MI YAAD
CANOE RESTAURANT
THE SPA RETREAT
HOME SWEET
HOME RESORT
SAMSARA
XTABI ON
THE CLIFFS
Westlands
3 DIVES
JERK CENTRE
PUSHCART GRILL
ROCKHOUSE
HOTEL
HUNGRY LION
Pirates Cove
TENSING PEN
RESORT — RAS RODY
CATCHA FALLING STAR
BANANA GARDENS
BANANA SHOUT — VILLAS SUR MER
CLIFF JUMPING — LTU PUB
CITRONELLA — CAN JAM RETREAT/
WAKE N BAKE CAFE
THE CAVES HOTEL — CLANDESTINO VILLA
AT THE CAVES
THE SANDS
NEGRIL
LIGHTHOUSE
THE CLIFF — JUST NATURAL
HIDE AWHILE
TINGALAYA'S RETREAT

Negril

SEE DETAIL

Whitehall

Mount
Airy

To Long
Bay
SWEET SPICE
RESTAURANT
ACKEE TREE
RESTAURANT

WHITEHALL
GREAT HOUSE

To
Springfield

0   0.5 mi
0   0.5 km
© MOON.COM

LLANTRISSANT
BEACHCLIFF VILLA
SEAVIEW
BAR & GRILL
SCOTIABANK
WEST END RD
NEGRIL
BUS PARK
SEAVIEW HOUSE
CHINESE RESTAURANT
VALUE
MASTER
POLICE
STATION
HAMMOND'S
BAKERY

passing Jamwest before rejoining the A2 in Little London and continuing toward the parish capital, Savanna-la-Mar.

SAFETY

As Jamaica's foremost tourism mecca, Negril attracts some of the island's most aggressive hustlers. Many will feign friendship and generosity only to demand, often with aggression and intimidation, exorbitant compensation for whatever good or service is on offer, whether it's a CD of one of the countless "up-and-coming artists," a marijuana spliff handed to you as someone extends their hand in greeting, or a piece of jewelry. As a general rule, avoid accepting anything you don't actually want and clarify the expected compensation if you do want it before allowing anyone to put something in your hand or mouth. Though not commonplace, it's not unheard of for hustlers to draw a knife to intimidate, and there's generally little fear of repercussions from the police, who tend to be slow-moving, if responsive at all. The police are unlikely to be sympathetic, especially if a quarrel or skirmish involves drugs, even if the mix-up was unprovoked. Do your best to stay in well-trodden areas and try to avoid unsolicited approaches from strangers. Marijuana is decriminalized and touted openly along the beach and in bars and clubs at night, though its legal sale is restricted to licensed dispensaries. A list of licensed retailers is supposed to be available on the website of the Cannabis Licensing Authority (www.cla.org.jm), though it may be incomplete.

Sights

WHITEHALL GREAT HOUSE

Little more than the ruins of a former mansion, **Whitehall Great House** (unmanaged, free) is on the old Whitehall Estate on the ascent to Mount Airy. It's a great vantage point for a panoramic view of Seven-Mile Beach and the large swampy expanse known as the Negril Morass. To get here, take a right immediately before the Texaco Station on Whitehall Road heading east from the Negril roundabout toward Savanna-la-Mar. The ruins are about 1.5 kilometers (1 mile) up the hill on the left. One of the largest cotton trees in Jamaica stands on the property.

NEGRIL LIGHTHOUSE

Negril Lighthouse is located near the westernmost point of Jamaica on West End Road, just past The Caves. The lighthouse dates from 1894 and stands 30 meters (100 feet) above the sea. The site is seldom visited by travelers as it falls outside the typical tour bus circuit, making it a more tranquil alternative to Rick's Café for a dip, though the cliffs are not as high. The entrance gate is typically left open, and a rusty old ladder offers access to the sea. The active lighthouse building is not accessible to the public.

★ Blue Hole Mineral Spring

A deep swimming hole located a few minutes' drive inland from Little Bay in Brighton and about 15 minutes from Negril, **Blue Hole Mineral Spring** (Brighton, U.S. tel. 954/353-5392, cell tel. 876/860-8805, info@blueholejamaica.com, www.blueholejamaica.com, 10am-6pm Mon.-Thurs., 9am-2am Fri.-Sun., US$10) is about five meters (15 feet) below the surface, and daredevils can climb the overhanging tree to add another three meters (10 feet) of adrenaline to the drop. An adjacent swimming pool is fed with mineral water from the spring, and a bar keeps visitors refreshed, even if they're not inclined to jump into either pool. Jerk chicken is served hot off the grill. The property also offers no-frills accommodations (US$150 d including breakfast, US$250 d with three meals) in 10 rooms furnished with bamboo canopy beds. Amenities include cable TV, private baths, and complimentary Wi-Fi throughout.

Beaches

★ SEVEN-MILE BEACH

Jamaica's longest stretch of golden sand, **Seven-Mile Beach** is no more the undisturbed fishing spot it was in the 1960s, but there are plenty of benefits that have come as a result of the unbridled development of the last several decades. The sand is fine, the water crystal clear, and a cold Red Stripe is never more than a stone's throw away at one of the myriad bars that line the waterfront. Every kind of water sport is offered by determined captains and their countless freelance promoters. Expect come-ons from all manner of peddler and hustler until your face becomes known and your reaction time to these calls for attention slows to island speed.

The northern end of the beach is monitored by private security guards in front of several all-inclusive resorts, while at the southern end the Negril River forms a natural border by the fishing village and craft market. At the southern end of the beach is **Norman Manley Sea Park Beach,** where dances and daytime events are often held. The sand is interrupted about three-quarters of the way up Seven-Mile Beach above Long Bay Beach Park

Negril Beach

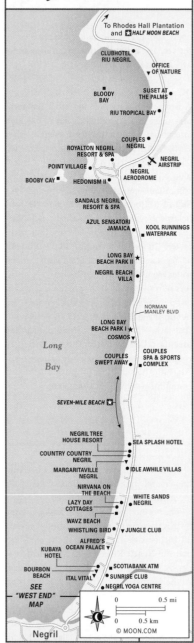

To Rhodes Hall Plantation and ✚HALF MOON BEACH

CLUBHOTEL RIU NEGRIL

OFFICE OF NATURE

BLOODY BAY

SUSET AT THE PALMS

RIU TROPICAL BAY

COUPLES NEGRIL

ROYALTON NEGRIL RESORT & SPA

NEGRIL AIRSTRIP

POINT VILLAGE

NEGRIL AERODROME

BOOBY CAY

HEDONISM II

SANDALS NEGRIL RESORT & SPA

AZUL SENSATORI JAMAICA

KOOL RUNNINGS WATERPARK

LONG BAY BEACH PARK II

NEGRIL BEACH VILLA

NORMAN MANLEY BLVD

LONG BAY BEACH PARK I

COSMOS

Long

COUPLES SWEPT AWAY

COUPLES SPA & SPORTS COMPLEX

Bay

SEVEN-MILE BEACH

NEGRIL TREE HOUSE RESORT

SEA SPLASH HOTEL

COUNTRY COUNTRY NEGRIL

MARGARITAVILLE NEGRIL

IDLE AWHILE VILLAS

NIRVANA ON THE BEACH

LAZY DAY COTTAGES

WHITE SANDS NEGRIL

WAVZ BEACH

WHISTLING BIRD

JUNGLE CLUB

ALFRED'S OCEAN PALACE

KUBAYA HOTEL

BOURBON BEACH

SCOTIABANK ATM

ITAL VITAL

SUNRISE CLUB

SEE "WEST END" MAP

NEGRIL YOGA CENTRE

0   0.5 mi

0   0.5 km

© MOON.COM

Negril

by a small stretch of mangrove. Beyond that, the sand continues northward all the way to Negril Point past Island Lux Beach Park and a handful of all-inclusive resorts.

BLOODY BAY

Bloody Bay is just north of Negril Point, the peninsula jutting out toward Booby Cay that is home to Hedonism II, Point Village, and Royalton Negril. All-inclusive resorts dominate the waterfront, beginning with Royalton at the southern end, then Couples Negril, Riu Tropical Bay, Sunset at the Palms, and Riu Negril to the north. The beach on Bloody Bay is accessible to the public at several points along the road, most easily just past the fenced-off beach reserved for guests of Sunset at the Palms. Here you can buy lobster and fish at the **Office of Nature** (11am-sunset daily, US$10-30) or hire **Ackee** (Roydel Reid, cell tel. 876/868-7312) for snorkeling excursions (1.5 hours, 2-person minimum, US$25 pp) and glass-bottomed boat tours.

LONG BAY BEACH PARK

Just past Cosmos restaurant, about three-quarters of the way up Seven-Mile Beach, south of Island Lux Beach Park, the four-hectare (10-acre) **Long Bay Beach Park** (tel. 876/957-3159 or 876/957-5260, longbaybeachpark@udcja.com, 9am-5pm daily, US$3 adults, US$1 ages 4-11) is where the unspoiled coastline is dotted with sea grape trees and lifeguards keep watch.

Island Lux Beach Park (cell tel. 876/322-9639 or 876/531-2805, info@islandlux.com, www.islandluxbeachparkja.com, 10am-11pm daily, no entry free, water sports from US$30) has culinary attractions that include Pimentoz jerk pit and seafood restaurant Little Negril, along with an outpost of Devon House I-Scream. Island Lux offers water sports like wakeboarding, water skiing, standup paddle boarding, tube rides, sailing, parasailing, scuba diving, snorkeling, and kayaking. Plush cushioned beach loungers are available for rent (US$5 per day), and there's a floating obstacle course (US$20 per hour).

Recreation

★ CLIFF JUMPING

One of the most unique activities on offer in Negril, afforded by the exceptional topography along the West End, is cliff jumping. While Rick's Café is the most famous venue for it, many properties boast cliffs of suitable height to get the adrenaline pumping. These include Xtabi, Rockhouse, Tensing Pen, Catcha Falling Star, and The Caves. Caution should always be taken to ensure proper clearance of the craggy rocks and that your point of entry in the water is sufficiently deep. Swimming along the West End is particularly dangerous when the sea is rough, as the waves crash into the cliffs with a lot of force, and currents can pull you under and out to sea, even if you do avoid being smashed into the rocks. Always seek the advice of hotel staff rather than jumping blindly into the sea.

Thanks to the tall precipice jutting out over a protected cove with deep turquoise water, **Rick's Café** (tel. 876/957-0380, info@rickscafejamaica.com, www.rickscafejamaica. com, noon-10pm daily, free) buzzes with visitors every afternoon, especially just before sunset. Cliff jumping is showcased as an art form by local daredevils who solicit tips to dive into the sea from the tallest possible point in an overhanging tree. Adrenaline junkies can choose to jump from three different heights: 3 meters (10 feet), 7.5 meters (25 feet), and 10.5 meters (35 feet). A pool area surrounded by lounge chairs and cabanas (US$120 per day, plus minimum US$75 food or alcohol purchase, up to 15 guests) is suitable for children and those with no appetite for heights. Live bands belt out reggae classics throughout the evening. The café serves beer, spirits, and bar food, and the gift shop sells T-shirts and souvenirs. This is a mandatory stop for every tour bus and sunset catamaran cruise in Negril.

WATER SPORTS
Diving
Dream Team Divers (Sunset on the Cliffs, tel. 876/957-0054 or 876/831-0435, info@ dreamteamdiversjamaica.com, www.

parasailing in Negril

dreamteamdiversjamaica.com, 8am-4pm daily) has English- and German-speaking dive instructors and offers free pickup and drop-off from any lodging in Negril. Dream Team visits dolphin dive sites and locations not visited by others. Rates range from the Discover Scuba intro course (US$80) to dive master certification (US$600). Certified divers can rent equipment (US$5 per dive) and suits (US$6) and tank up (from US$40).

Sun Divers (Travelers Beach Resort, tel. 876/405-6872, seabossdivers@yahoo.com, US$55, US$65 with equipment, 2-tank dive US$100) offers a great intro class for beginners lasting about three hours, with classroom and pool time and one open-water dive.

Snorkeling

Captain Junior's Glass Bottom Boat Tours (cell tel. 876/849-2301, juniorkirlew@gmail.com, US$30 pp) takes guests on a clean boat on 1.5-hour snorkel trips to reefs about 15 minutes offshore or along the coast. Junior docks his boat next to Negril Palms Hotel on Norman Manley Boulevard, but he can pick you up from your hotel anywhere along Seven-Mile Beach.

Parasailing

Parasailing (8-10 minutes in the air US$60 single, US$100 double, US$150 triple), tubing (10-15 minutes US$30 pp) and glass-bottomed boat tours (US$25, US$30 with snorkeling gear) are on offer from **Premium Water Sports** (Norman Manley Blvd., next to Foote Prints, tel. 876/957-3928, Trevor Forbes cell tel. 876/383-2906, premiumairparasail@hotmail.com). **Negril Treehouse Resort** (Norman Manley Blvd., tel. 876/957-4287) has a water sports center offering parasailing (US$40), Jet Skis (US$50 per half hour), and fishing trips (US$150 up to 4 people).

Fishing

The waters off Negril are severely overfished, according to surveys conducted by the Negril Area Environmental Protection Trust. Nevertheless, farther offshore in deeper waters, the problem isn't as stark, and it's possible to catch wahoo, tuna, mahimahi, and even marlin. Billfish should be caught and released to minimize the impact of sportfishing on the marine ecosystem.

A professional trolling outfit offering a good mix of options, **Stanley's Deep Sea Fishing** (tel. 876/957-6341, cell tel. 876/818-6363, deepseafishing@cwjamaica.com, www.stanleysdeepseafishing.com) has half-day (US$500), three-quarter-day (US$750), and full-day trips (US$1,000) for up to four people. The boat will hold up to eight (US$50-100 per additional person). Stanley's also offers the option of charter sharing on four-hour half-day excursions, where individuals can team up with others to fill the boat (US$150 pp) rather than charter exclusively. Transport from anywhere in Negril to the boat is included. Billfish are tagged and released, but other fish can be taken for dinner.

Kool Runnings Waterpark

Located across from Sensatori Hotel, **Kool Runnings Waterpark** (tel. 876/957-5400 or 876/618-0780, info@koolrunnings.com, www.koolrunnings.com, 11am-5:30pm Tues.-Sun. May 21-Aug., US$40 over 122 centimeters/4 feet tall, US$28 under 122 centimeters/4 feet, free under age 2 with US$9.50 purchase of swim diaper) has several slides, a wave pool, a lazy river for gentle tubing, and a kiddie pool. Three restaurants serve Jamaican dishes (about US$6), and a juice bar serves natural smoothies. Outside food is not permitted.

Activities at the park include the **Kool Kanoe Adventure** (US$48 for 1 or 2 people), which takes visitors on a guided tour of the Great Morass, Jamaica's largest wetland area, in the water park's back yard. Visitors share a large inflatable "kanoe" for a guided tour through canals of the morass. **Jamboo Rafting** (US$48 single or double) is similar, but on a bamboo raft. Those favoring a more independent experience can opt for

---

1: cliff jumping at Rick's Café 2: Negril Lighthouse 3: 3 Dives Jerk Centre at twilight

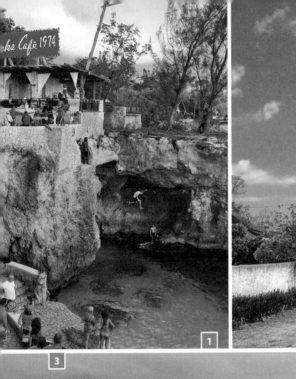

the **Kayaking Adventure** (US$20 double) through the morass or rent a paddleboard (US$20). You are likely to encounter yellow snakes, land crabs, mongooses, turtles, and many endemic and visiting bird species, including the West Indian whistling duck, the yellow-breasted crake, and the shiny cowbird.

With a 2,500-person capacity, the water park regularly hosts events that include wild parties during Emancipation-Independence celebrations in early August. The in-house DJ provides entertainment throughout the season, and there are Soldier Crab Derbies that allow visitors to bet on the winners, a snake show, **Paintball** (US$25), **Laser Tag** (US$20), a human gyroscope (US$8), and **Go-Kart Racing** (3 minutes US$8).

HORSEBACK RIDING

Five minutes northeast of Negril toward Montego Bay, **Rhodes Beach Resort** (tel. 876/957-6422, cell tel. 876/431-6322, info@rhodesresort.com, www.rhodesresort.com) has good horseback riding (US$70, US$35 under age 12) that takes riders through the coconut groves, a mangrove swamp with crocodiles, up the hill for a panoramic view of Negril, and back to the beach.

Based at Eldin Washington Ranch on the main road from Negril to Savanna-la-Mar, **Reggae Horseback Riding** (contact Paul Washington, cell tel. 876/881-6917, paul@reggaehorsebackriding.com, www.reggae-horsebackriding.com, 1 hour US$60 pp, 2 hours US$80, US$50 ages 6-10, including transportation from Negril) features horseback riding on a 365-hectare (900-acre) farm populated by peacocks, ostriches, donkeys, and goats. Schedule a tour with up to 15 riders. The two-hour ride ends on a 1.6-kilometer (1-mile) stretch of private beach.

Jamwest Motorsports and Adventure Park (tel. 876/957-4474, cell tel. 876/475-7588, info@jamwest.com, www.jamwest.com) is a short drive from Negril in Old Hope, Little London, offering ATV tours (US$115), safari tours (US$89), zip-line tours (US$115), horseback riding (US$89), a driving experience on a racetrack (US$250), and combo packages (from US$139).

In Sandy Bay, Hanover, **Chukka's Horseback Ride 'N' Swim** (tel. 876/953-5619, montegobay@chukkacaribbean.com, US$73) offers two-hour rides through forest and along the shore before swimming on horseback. Remember to bring a change of clothes and a waterproof camera if you

Long Bay Beach Park

don't want to buy photos from Chukka. The Sandy Bay location also offers two-hour ATV tours (over age 15, US$115 pp) and dune buggy tours (over age 15 to drive, US$130 single, US$230 double). Canopy zip-line tours (US$79), river tubing (US$65), and kayaking (US$70) are staged from Chukka's Montpelier location in St. James, about 45 minutes from Sandy Bay.

GOLF

Negril Hills Golf Club (Sheffield, east of the roundabout along the A2, tel. 876/957-4638, www.negrilhillsgolfclub.com, 7:30am-3pm daily) has reasonable rates for nonmembers on a quiet course. Greens fees are for 9 holes (US$29) or 18 holes (US$58), and carts (US$17-35), caddies (US$7-14), and clubs (US$18-40) are available.

Entertainment

The great thing about Negril is that no matter the season, you can forget what day of the week it is in a hurry. Weekends remain going-out nights and important acts that draw large Jamaican audiences generally perform on Friday or Saturday, but big artists also perform Monday, Wednesday, and Thursday nights. Because Negril is so small, the handful of clubs that monopolize the regular live entertainment market have a tacit pact that each takes a night or two of the week so that the main clubs are guaranteed a weekly following and it's easy to know where to go on any particular evening.

NIGHTLIFE
Bars and Venues

Negril has an overwhelming number of bars and grills. This section covers establishments recommended as nightlife spots rather than for food.

Negril's only off-the-water club, in an old bank toward the middle of the beach on the morass side of Norman Manley Boulevard, **The Jungle** (Norman Manley Blvd., tel. 876/954-4005, cell tel. 876/997-5750, thejunglenegriljamaica@gmail.com, www.thejungle-negril.com) is generally only open two nights a week: Thursday Ladies Night (women free before midnight, US$10) and Inclusive Saturdays (US$15), when patrons can opt to upgrade to top-shelf spirits (US$30).

With complimentary round-trip transportation from any hotel in Negril,

Margaritaville (Norman Manley Blvd., tel. 876/957-4467, www.margaritavillecaribbean. com) hosts a beach party (5pm-9pm Wed.) and a drinks-inclusive night (10pm-2am Fri., US$55). Margaritaville has been a venue for spring-break parties for a number of years and is one of the most successful bar chains on the island; the Jimmy Buffet franchise also has locations in Montego Bay and Ochi.

Live Music

Live performances on Monday and Wednesday nights are at **Roots Bamboo Beach Resort** (Norman Manley Blvd., tel. 876/957-4479, denise.plummer64@hotmail. com). The Wednesday shows have featured some of Jamaica's top musicians, from Freddie McGregor to Luciano and the late John Holt.

Bourbon Beach (Norman Manley Blvd., tel. 876/957-4432, info@bourbonbeachjamaica.com, www.bourbonbeach.com) features live music on Monday, Tuesday, and Saturday nights with up-and-coming acts from all over Jamaica. Bounty Killa and Marcia Griffiths are among the internationally acclaimed artists to have graced the stage. Bourbon Beach serves mouthwatering jerk from mid-morning until 2am.

Live music Sunday, Tuesday, and Friday features predominantly local acts and some bigger names at **Alfred's Ocean Palace** (Norman Manley Blvd., tel. 876/957-4669 or 876/957-4375, info@alfreds.com, www. alfreds.com). The beach bar and restaurant

(8am-10:30pm daily high season, 8am-9pm daily low season, US$10-15) serves Jamaican and international cuisine, including chicken, shrimp, and fish dishes. Alfred's also has eight double and triple rooms (US$60).

FESTIVALS AND EVENTS

The weekends around Emancipation Day (Aug. 1) and Independence Day (Aug. 6) bring party animals to Negril en masse for **Dream Weekend** (tel. 876/631-6623, www. jamaicadreamweekend.com), a series of parties typically sponsored by a brewery or spirits brand held over the course of several days. Promoters from "yaad" (home) and abroad draw partygoers from near and far to indulge in booze, ganja, general debauchery, and a few stage shows. It's the only time of year when Negril is almost completely taken over by Jamaicans, who make spring breakers appear tame in comparison.

A charity event held the second Sunday in February each year to finance community projects, **Rotary Club of Negril Donkey Races** (held at Wavz Entertainment Centre, contact Richard Warren, cell tel. 876/437-3735, US$6) sees local organizations sponsor 25 donkeys dressed to compete in a number of categories for trophies and prizes. The family-friendly fun day features local food vendors and games.

The first weekend in March, **Stepping High Festival** (Cayenne Beach, tel. 876/957-0186, cell tel. 876/296-1719 or 876/549-5606, info@steppinghighfestival.com, www.steppinghighfestival.com, US$20-200) is a celebration of Rastafarian culture aimed at building the ganja nation, featuring the sacred herb in great bounty, ital food, the requisite irie music, and crafts. Events include concerts, workshops, and ganja exhibitions.

An annual cultural event series held in late April-early May at multiple venues around Negril, **Tmrw Tday Festival** (connect@tmrwtday.com, www.tmrwtday.com,

US$12.50-120) is part retreat, part music festival, with events to encourage participants to slow down, relax, enjoy the tropical setting, and feed the mind, body, and spirit with yoga, meditation, healthy food, and great music. Musical performances have featured the likes of Protoje and Beenie Man, while medical marijuana symposia have featured high-profile ganja activists like Montel Williams.

Western Consciousness (contact Worrel King, cell tel. 876/849-8426 or 876/821-8853, kingofkingspro@hotmail.com) is a not-to-be-missed roots reggae show, held off and on as an annual event in April or May, usually in the vicinity of Savanna-la-Mar.

Held annually on the last Saturday in June, **Painted Negril** (Cayenne Beach, Norman Manley Blvd., tel. 876/528-5527, info@blackgoldjamaica.com) has high-energy soca, EDM, and dancehall music. Paint, water, and debauchery add to the music.

The first Saturday in December, the **Reggae Marathon, Half Marathon, and 10K** (Alfred "Frano" Francis, tel. 876/922-8677, racedirector@reggaemarathon.com, or Diane Ellis, frandan@cwjamaica.com, www.reggaemarathon.com) is a popular event drawing locals and expats for a race on a mostly flat IAAF-certified route starting at Long Bay Beach Park on Seven-Mile Beach. Registration and package pickup begins on Thursday, continuing on Friday with a pasta party and village bash. Races start at dawn Saturday, with a ceremony later in the day. Prizes total US$10,000. You must be age 18 to run the marathon (US$120) and at least age 10 for the 10K (US$85). Fees are lower if you register earlier.

The **Rastafari Rootz Fest** (www.rastafarirootzfest.com) was quick to celebrate the Jamaican government's move to decriminalize ganja by hosting the **Cannabis Cup Jamaica** in partnership with *High Times,* now an annual affair held in mid-December at Long Bay Beach Park alongside the Ganjamaica Cup, bringing friendly competitiveness, crafts, and wares as well as great music to the Negril waterfront.

1: The Jungle nightclub 2: Branzo, one of Negril's foremost wood carvers

Shopping

CRAFTS

Run by Abdel, a.k.a. Branzo, **One Stop Branzo Wood Sculptures** (cell tel. 876/867-4246, 8am-8pm daily), can be found on the beachfront at Wavz Entertainment Centre. Branzo is one of the most talented woodcarvers around and also sells the work of other woodworkers in his little shop. **Negril Crafts Market** (between Norman Manley Sea Park and the Negril River) has a wide variety of crafts, some better and more authentic than others. Sadly, an increasing proportion of the products on sale are made in China rather than locally produced. **Errol Allen** (cell tel. 876/385-5399) is a talented local artist who makes unique silhouette sculptures and oil paintings. Allen's sculptures can be seen on the grounds of Whistling Bird.

Next to the aerodrome just before the Petcom gas station, heading northeast toward Montego Bay, is **Rutland Point Craft Centre.** Find a mix of Rasta knit hats and "Jamaica No Problem" T-shirts among a plethora of crafts and trinkets at **Kosmic Gift Shop & Boutique** (on the beach next to Cosmos restaurant, Norman Manley Blvd., tel. 876/957-3940). **Octavious Art** (Negril Beach Club, tel. 876/429-4387, 9am-5pm Mon.-Sat.) is an art gallery that showcases carvings from the roots of cedar trees and acrylic paintings.

APPAREL

On Norman Manley Boulevard across from Bourbon Beach, **Time Square Mall Plaza** (tel. 876/957-9263, 9pm-7pm daily, Mon.-Sat.) is a duty-free shopping center with jewelry, Cuban cigars, crafts, liquor, watches, and trinkets. Next to Scotiabank by the roundabout, **A Fi Wi Plaza** has crafts and T-shirts from Sun Island.

Food

SEVEN-MILE BEACH
Breakfast and Cafés

A wide variety of welcome options to start the day off right are at ★ **Sunrise Club** (tel. 876/957-4293, www.sunriseclub.com, breakfast 8am-noon daily, US$10-35), including omelets or eggs and bacon, Jamaican breakfast (ackee and saltfish, callaloo, and fried dumpling), crepes, pancakes, french toast, fresh-squeezed orange juice, and proper Italian coffee made in a quality espresso machine.

Hammond's Bakery (at the roundabout, tel. 876/957-4734, 8am-6pm Mon.-Sat., US$3-10) serves patties, cakes, and deli sandwiches.

Jerk and Jamaican

Pimentoz Jerk (Island Lux Beach Park, tel. 876/957-4556, 10am-11pm daily, www.islandluxbeachparkja.com, US$5-30) serves a variety of jerked meat dishes with open-air beachfront seating.

Sun Beach Restaurant Bar and Jerk Hut (tel. 876/957-9118, 9am-9pm daily, US$6-32) serves seafood and Jamaican-inspired cuisine. The cozy beachfront bar and restaurant treats guests to live reggae every Thursday evening.

The first Jamaican outpost of a popular New York eatery specializing in haute Caribbean cuisine, ★ **Miss Lily's at Skylark** (tel. 876/957-4364, www.skylarknegril.com) has a team of top-rated chefs and a jerk smokehouse and barbecue grilling station that create a unique culinary experience, featuring seasoned chicken, pork, and fish as well as traditional dishes like curried goat, oxtail, and whole grilled fish. The design of the venue couldn't be more Jamaican, with stacks of speakers encompassing the bar, a loving nod to Kingston's sound-system culture.

With a small seating area roadside and a bar, **Best in the West** (Norman Manley Blvd., across from Idle Awhile, contact Devon James, cell tel. 876/383-3981, 10:30am-11pm daily) is the most dependable spot on the boulevard for jerk chicken (quarter pound US$7, half pound US$12) and pork (half pound US$9), served with bread and salad.

Vinnie's Colie Shop Bar N Grill (Norman Manley Blvd., tel. 876/353-2741, 11am-9:30pm daily, US$6-30) serves seafood dishes like grilled lobster, garlic conch, and steamed fish along with pan jerk chicken for lunch and dinner.

Rainbow Arch (between Charela Inn and White Sands, contact Joy James, cell tel. 876/423-6760, tel. 876/957-4745, 10am-10pm daily, US$10-30) specializes in curry shrimp and curry goat, fish and lobster dishes, and jerk chicken.

Sonia's (across from Roots Bamboo, cell tel. 876/377-7069, 8am-9pm daily, US$5-10) is well recognized for her delicious Jamaican cuisine and homemade patties.

Woodstock Negril (tel. 876/550-8079, 7am-11pm Mon.-Sat. US$3-15) serves a variety of grilled and seafood dishes. This is a

great place to bring the family, with free live band entertainment on Thursday, different themed cocktails each night, and karaoke Saturday night.

Within the Island Lux Beach Park, in a location shared with Pimentoz Jerk restaurant, The Gallery Restaurant, Ital Island Restaurant, and Beach House Sweet Eats (Devon House I-Scream), **Little Negril Seafood** (tel. 876/322-9639, info@islandlux. com, www.islandluxbeachparkja.com, 10am-10pm daily, US$7-50) serves seafood dishes in a cozy thatch-covered, rustic, beachfront restaurant.

★ **Sweet Spice** (Whitehall Rd., tel. 876/957-4621, 8:30am-10:30pm daily, US$5-25) is the best place along the main road heading toward Savanna-la-Mar for typical Jamaican fare at local prices. It is popular with locals for real-world value in a town where prices are usually on par with U.S. cities. Dishes like fried chicken, coconut curry, or escoveitch fish, conch, and lobster are representative of Jamaica's traditional cuisine.

Frequented by artists in the know, **Ackee Tree Restaurant** (Whitehall Rd., across from the Texaco station, cell tel. 876/871-2524, 8am-8pm daily, US$5-8) serves vegetarian dishes

Jamaican gungo pea soup

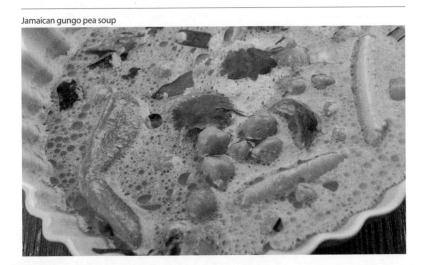

like steamed vegetables and the best ital stew around.

A mixed crowd weighted toward locals is testament to the reasonable prices and tasty Jamaican home-style cooking at ★ **Cosmos Seafood Restaurant and Bar** (next door to Beaches Negril, tel. 876/957-4330, 9am-10pm daily, US$5-43), serving excellent Jamaican seafood dishes, including conch soup, shrimp, and fried fish, in addition to other local dishes like curry goat, stewed pork, fried chicken, and oxtail. The beach out front is wide and good for swimming.

Kuyaba (Norman Manley Blvd., tel. 876/957-4318, 7am-11pm daily, US$12-27) has consistently decent, but pricey, international and Jamaican fusion cuisine, including pork kebab, brown stew conch, peppered steak, and seafood linguine lobster for main courses.

The garlic lobster gets rave reviews at **The Boat Bar** (between Rondel Village and Mariposa, tel. 876/957-4746, 8am-10pm daily, US$10-30), a favorite that has been serving chicken, fish, shrimp, goat, pork, and steak since 1983.

International

The setup at **Kenny's Italian Café** (Norman Manley Blvd., tel. 876/957-4032, kennykjohnson@yahoo.com, 7am-2am daily) is inviting, with bamboo thatch ceilings, hanging lanterns, and padded stools with seating for up to 200. A DJ spins mostly house music nightly. Complimentary appetizers are offered 4pm-7pm daily. The menu is Kenny's take on Italian, absorbed from his wife and trips to the motherland, with salads, pasta dishes, seafood, and pizza. Entrées range from spaghetti with olive oil (US$9) to a mixed seafood platter ($55) with whole lobster, fish fillets, calamari, and shrimp.

The only place in Negril to get Mexican-inspired dishes, **Nikki's Taco** (across Norman Manley Blvd. from Bar-B-Barn, cell tel. 876/490-0838, 11am-9pm daily, US$4-10) has tacos, burritos, and quesadillas as well as chips and salsa with guacamole.

Fine Dining

Owned and operated by Italian expat Luca, ★ **The Lobster House** (Sunrise Club, beside Coral Seas Garden, tel. 876/957-4293, noon-11pm daily) serves Italian and Jamaican fare such as pasta with tomato sauce (US$8), gnocchi (US$12), wood-fired pizza (US$10-16), and grilled lobster (US$26). Wines are about US$24-26, and great coffee is served.

Lounge chairs and wireless internet are free to customers of **Chill Awhile** (Idle Awhile Resort, tel. 876/957-3303, 7am-9pm daily). The charming beachfront deck restaurant serves light items for lunch, including club sandwiches, burgers, fish-and-chips (US$6-8), and jerk chicken (US$10). For dinner, international and Jamaican-style entrées include grilled chicken breast with peanut or Jamaican sauce (US$9), coconut-breaded snapper with tartar sauce (US$13), lobster thermidor (US$24), or a seafood platter with grilled lobster and coconut shrimp (US$25). There is a bar next to the restaurant.

WEST END
Breakfast and Cafés

Located just past Rick's Café, **Canjam Wake N Bake Café** (West End Rd., across from Citronella, cell tel. 876/536-6642, 7:30am-3pm daily high season, US$10-15, ganja edibles mid-Apr.-Sept.) serves fresh fruit juices and breakfast items, as well as famous ganja cookies that pack a punch far beyond their weight.

Located on the side of One Love Drive on West End Road, **Patsy's Coffeeshop** (tel. 876/841-3388, enquiries@patsyscoffeeshop.com, www.patsyscoffeeshop.com, 8am-10pm Mon.-Fri., 9am-10pm Sat.-Sun., US$2-18) serves local coffee, breakfast, lunch, cocktails, and desserts. Some of its specialties include tasty homemade waffle cones, shakes, and ganja ice cream.

1: 3 Dives Jerk Centre, home to the Negril Jerk Festival **2:** Ital Vital pushcart along Norman Manley Boulevard **3:** Tensing Pen

Jerk and Jamaican

★ **Seaview Bar & Grill** (West End Rd., around the bend from Scotiabank, tel. 876/957-9199, 4pm-2:30am daily) does the best steam roast conch (US$4) in Jamaica, as well as steam roast fish (US$12), conch soup (US$2), and jerk or fried jerk chicken (US$5), among other local favorites.

Jamaican breakfast, pancakes, french toast, and eggs to order are at **Canoe Beach Bar & Grill** (across from MX3, tel. 876/957-4814, Kirby's cell tel. 876/878-5893, canoebeachbar@gmail.com, 7am-10:30pm daily, US$10-30). Chicken, shrimp, lobster, and vegetarian dishes are served for lunch and dinner in a dining room overlooking the beach.

Breakfast, lunch, and dinner at **Motions HQ Bar & Grill** (West End Rd., cell tel. 876/532-1078, 7am-11pm daily, US$8-20) includes dishes ranging from ackee and saltfish to seasoned shrimp, fish, and curry goat. A billiards table and bumping reggae provide entertainment.

Blue Mahoe Restaurant (Negril Spa Retreat, West End Rd., cell tel. 876/399-3772, info@thespajamaic.com, US$10-30) is at Negril Spa Retreat but welcomes non-guests, serving breakfast, lunch, and dinner seven days a week. The menu features a mix of Jamaica-inspired dishes like jerk fish tacos and jerk chicken pesto as well as more traditional Jamaican fare like braised oxtail and beans, curried chicken, and curried goat. International standards include burgers, sandwiches, and pizzas. The large indoor dining area extends outside onto the cliffs.

The place to get jerk on the West End is ★ **3 Dives Jerk Centre** (contact Lloydie, tel. 876/957-0845 or 876/782-9990, noon-midnight daily), offering a quarter chicken with bread (US$3.50) or with rice-and-peas and vegetables (US$5), half chicken with rice-and-peas and veggies (US$8), steamed or curried shrimp (US$17), and grilled lobster (US$34). Located right on the cliffs, the open-air restaurant has a nice outdoor barbecue vibe.

Bringing Jamaican street food to one of the West End's most exclusive resort enclaves, **Pushcart Restaurant and Rum Bar** (West End Rd., next door to Rockhouse, tel. 876/957-4373, www.rockhousehotel.com, 3pm-10pm daily, US$10-30) serves entrées that include peppered shrimp, homemade jerk sausage, curry goat, and oxtail. The menu is inspired by the pushcarts used by Jamaican street vendors across the island, selling produce or cooked food in open-air markets. A local mento band provides live entertainment several nights during the week. Pushcart offers casual dining in a breathtaking cliff-side setting made famous in the films *20,000 Leagues under the Sea* and the Steve McQueen classic *Papillon*. Pushcart has great spots for cliff jumping with smaller crowds than at Rick's Café.

The food is cooked in a jerk pan grill with open-air seating on picnic tables under a zinc roof at **Kool Vybes Bar & Jerk Centre** (across from Tensing Pen, cell tel. 876/489-6487, 11am-11pm daily, US$5-30), serving jerk chicken and pork as well as pepper shrimp, curry goat, lobster, and fish.

The Sands Bar (tel. 876/957-0270 or 876/618-1081, 4pm-7pm Wed. and Fri.-Mon.) is one of the best bars for sunset cliff jumping away from the gawking crowds that convene at nearby Rick's Café each evening. Located inside The Caves, an exclusive boutique resort operated by Chris Blackwell's Island Outpost. The Sands Bar fires up a jerk pan each afternoon, when nonguests are welcome to enjoy the 12-meter (40-foot) jump and the best view of Negril's lighthouse, right next door.

International

Decent Chinese food is on offer at **Seaview House Chinese Restaurant** (Cotton Tree Place, between Vendors' Plaza and the post office, tel. 876/957-4925, 10am-10pm daily), with vegetable dishes (US$7-10), chicken (US$10), seafood (US$18), and roast duck and lobster variations (US$27).

LTU Pub & Restaurant (tel. 876/957-0382, 7am-11pm daily, US$10-30) has good Jamaican and international food in a laid-back setting perched on the cliffs. Specialties include crab quesadilla, stuffed jalapeño, and crab ball appetizers, plus schnitzel, surf-and-turf, pasta, chicken, and seafood dishes like grilled salmon and the snapper papaya boat. Free Wi-Fi is available for customers.

At The Cliff, past the lighthouse on West End Road, **Zest Restaurant** (tel. 876/632-0919, 7am-10pm daily) showcases the creative hand of internationally acclaimed executive chef Cindy Hutson. Try singular starters like the shrimp ceviche with fried plantain and bean dip or mains like sautéed snapper with a side of cashew and jackfruit spiced rice. The dining area is split between a chic interior and clifftop alfresco, with crashing waves as a soundtrack. Reservations are required for guests not staying at the property.

Vegetarian

The ital (vegetarian) roadside food shop **RasRody Organics** (across from Tensing Pen, cell tel. 876/283-1421, truelove@gmail.com, 10am-6pm daily) specializes in red pea soup (US$3-10) and other vegetarian specialties of the day, such as steamed vegetables.

iNi Vegan Rastarant (tel. 876/326-8514, 9am-11pm daily, US$5-10) is a dab bar specializing in Rastafarian ital food. iNi offers indoor and outdoor seating, takeout options, and is wheelchair accessible. A few dishes and beverages offered include Rasta Pasta, ital patties, veggie sandwiches, bush tea, coffee, and ganja tea.

One of the best spots in Negril for ital vegetarian food is **Royal Kitchen** (just before Samsara, contact chef Errold Chambers, cell tel. 876/775-0386, by reservation only, US$5-8), where the signature dish is broad bean stew, veggie chunks, and tofu. Fresh juices (US$3) like pumpkin punch, beet, and cucumber as well as natural ginger beer accompany the meal.

Just Natural (Hylton Ave., past the lighthouse off West End Rd., tel. 876/957-0235, cell tel. 876/354-4287, 8am-9pm daily late Nov.-Apr., 8am-8:30pm Mon.-Sat., 8am-6pm Sun. May-Oct., US$3-15) serves breakfast, lunch, and dinner with items like callaloo or ackee omelets and fresh juices. Vegetarian dishes and seafood items are served for lunch and dinner.

Accommodations

Negril has something for everyone, from couples-only all-inclusive resorts and exclusive villas to hip inexpensive independent cottages by the sea. Low-season and high-season rates apply, as at other tourism centers on the island. Some establishments increase rates in the middle of the low season for special events like Independence weekend at the beginning of August, when Jamaicans flock for a torrent of nonstop parties that last for days on end.

Accommodations are listed geographically from Negril's roundabout, which distinguishes properties on Norman Manley Boulevard from those on West End Road. Within each price category, accommodations are organized from north to south. Seven-Mile Beach starts at the mouth of the

Negril River and stretches the length of Long Bay, which is separated from Bloody Bay by an outcropping of land known as Negril Point, home to Hedonism II, Point Village, and the Royalton Negril Resort & Spa. A multitude of small hotels face the beach on Long Bay, with the all-inclusive resorts concentrated to the northern end and on Bloody Bay further north.

SEVEN-MILE BEACH
Under US$100
Also known as The Little Oasis, **Negril Yoga Centre** (tel. 876/957-4397, negrilyoga@cwjamaica.com, www.negrilyoga.com, US$30-75) has simple, clean rooms with single and double beds. The center is tasteful and secure,

with a decent restaurant that specializes in vegetarian food cooked to order. The property boasts, "There is no bar, no pool, and no dance club at the Centre, which keeps our prices low and our ambience low-key."

Pure Garden Resort Negril (tel. 876/957-4767, info@purenegril.com, US$55) is a cozy 31-room family-friendly hotel. Each room has two double beds and a private bath as well as Wi-Fi and cable TV.

A collection of 14 well-appointed rooms with wood furnishings, **Sunrise Club** (tel. 876/957-4293, cell tel. 876/422-1818, info@sunriseclub.com, www.sunriseclub.com, from US$90) has air-conditioning, safes, private baths, and verandas. B&B and all-inclusive plans are also available. The full-service on-site restaurant serves the best breakfast and Italian dishes in Negril.

A no-frills hotel with five categories of rooms on either side of Norman Manley Boulevard, **White Sands** (tel. 876/957-4291 or U.S. tel. 305/503-9074, info@whitesandsnegril.com, from US$60 low season, US$78 high season) has mini fridges, air-conditioning, and small balconies or porches. The hotel has a bar and dining area beachfront with a TV. A four-bedroom villa sleeps up to eight on the morass side of the road, with a full kitchen, a living area, and a private pool. One-bedroom apartments also have kitchens.

A modern, minimalist 28-room boutique hotel that wouldn't be out of place on Miami Beach, ★ **Skylark Negril Beach Resort** (Norman Manley Blvd., tel. 212/807-0868, info@skylarknegril.com, www.skylarknegril.com, from US$95 low season, US$175 high season) draws creative inspiration from Jamaica's singular culture and musical heritage. The beach club vibe begins in the airy lobby, where leafy wallpaper and bamboo ceiling panels add organic elements. Rooms feature contemporary four-poster beds, simple desks, effective blackout curtains, and a cork board in place of a TV. The baths have subway-tile walls and prewar-style sinks.

High-pressure showers and Starfish toiletries, produced in Jamaica, help wash off the salt and sand. All rooms have air-conditioning, stocked mini fridges, and a snack basket, with consumption tallied at check-out. The restaurant/bar beachside features creative renditions of local favorites, like jerk pork hash with eggs any style, traditional Jamaican fare, and coconut-topped pancakes. An outpost of the popular New York Jamaican eatery Miss Lily's operates next to the beachfront bar.

Indika Negril (Norman Manley Blvd., contact Bill Blauer, U.S. tel. 617/529-1534, info@indikanegril.com, www.indikanegril.com) has a spacious four-bedroom main building called Devon House (US$150 low season, US$225 high season) that sleeps up to seven, and another large structure with three bedrooms called Dolton House, which also sleeps seven. Also on the property is a self-contained cottage with a full kitchen and two beds (US$40 low season, US$60 high season), as well as two rustic cabins (US$30 low season, US$50 high season), each with two beds, a small fridge, a shower, and a standing fan. Dolton House bedrooms have exterior entrances and can rent separately (US$50 low season, US$65 high season) and share the kitchen and living area. Airport transfers (up to 4 people from Montego Bay US$120 round-trip) are offered by the caretaker, Devon.

US$100-250

Directly on captivating Seven-Mile Beach, famous for its beautiful white sand, **Ayurveda Resort** (Norman Manley Blvd., cell tel. 876/889-6761, lorenzomaieli@gmail.com, www.ayuresortnegril.com, from US$101) has activities for guests, such as windsurfing, golfing, and bicycle rental, at an additional charge, and tours. Services and amenities offered include wedding planning, spacious meeting halls and saunas, a restaurant, a bar with premium drinks, a private beach, and easy access to seaside activities.

A studio apartment located in the Point Village complex at the end of Seven-Mile Beach, **Cortina's Cottage** (cell tel.

1: Rockhouse Hotel 2: Coral Cove in Little Bay

876/382-6384, www.carolynscaribbean-cottages.com, US$100) is a good option for independent travelers. The apartment is tastefully decorated with plenty of curtains. **Yard Beach House** (Norman Manley Blvd., tel. 876/957-4041, info@yardbeachhouse.com, www.yardbeachhouse.com, from US$110) is an adults-only boutique resort with 21 suites, a restaurant, and a bar. The hotel sits facing Seven-Mile Beach and has a swimming pool and a jetted tub. The restaurant serves Jamaican cuisine 24-7 and is open to nonguests.

On the beach, **Kuyaba** (Norman Manley Blvd., tel. 876/957-4318 or 876/957-9815, kuyaba@cwjamaica.com, www.kuyaba.com) is a handful of tasteful cottages. The more rustic cottages (US$56-64 low season, US$70-77 high season) hold true to Negril's original rustic hippie vibe, while newer, more elegant cottages (US$77-85 low season, US$97-106 high season) have been added in recent years. All have ceiling fans, air-conditioning, and private baths with hot water. A restaurant on the property has good food.

With 32 cottages on the beach side of Norman Manley Boulevard and two self-contained apartments on the morass side, ★ **Country Country** (Norman Manley Blvd., tel. 876/957-4273, countrynegril@gmail.com, www.countryjamaica.com, US$170-250 low season, US$215-350 high season) cottages are sufficiently dispersed in the lush garden setting to allow privacy. Rooms have air-conditioning, flat-screen TVs with cable, spacious private baths with hot water, and porches. The superior and premium rooms are close to the beach. Rates include breakfast and Wi-Fi.

The Boardwalk Village (Norman Manley Blvd., tel. 876/957-4633, cell tel. 876/878-4308, www.theboardwalkvillagenegril.com, from US$137 low season, US$157 high season) offers standard rooms with two double beds, deluxe rooms with a king bed, and one-bedroom apartments with kings and kitchenettes. All rooms have air-conditioning, Wi-Fi, and cable.

Eight deluxe rooms and five suites on the beach side of the road, plus three suites across the road on the morass side, are at ★ **Idle Awhile Resort** (Norman Manley Blvd., tel. 877/243-5352 or 876/957-3302, from US$216 low season, US$312 high season). All rooms have king beds, while suites also have day beds in the living areas and functional kitchenettes. It is one of the more inviting options along Seven-Mile Beach, with contemporary decor,

Llantrissant Beachcliff Villa

white linen curtains and wooden blinds, and a beachfront restaurant and bar, Chill Awhile, built on a wooden deck.

Villas

Centrally located, with 90 meters (300 feet) of private sand on Seven-Mile Beach, an ideal option for families and small groups is **Idle Awhile Villas** (U.S. tel. 800/621-1120, info@ moondancevillas.com), which has an assortment of one- to five-bedroom villas (4-night minimum, US$600-1,500 low season, US$700-1,900 high season). Rates include a chef, a bartender, a housekeeper, security, internet access, a private pool and jetted tub, and airport transfers, with an unlimited food option (US$115 pp daily).

Llantrissant Beachcliff Villa (U.S. tel. 305/321-7458, info@beachcliff.com, www. beachcliff.com, from US$768 low season, US$960 high season) is a one-hectare (2-acre) beachfront estate with a quaint colonial cottage that harks back to when it was the sole house in Negril. The property juts into the sea just west of the roundabout with an uninterrupted view of Seven-Mile Beach. A clay tennis court and two private beaches make the property unique, as do the 15-meter (50-foot) veranda, enormous cotton trees, and the colonial-era double canopy beds in the two ground-level master suites. Upstairs, the attic is partitioned into three rooms that share a bath, with a king on the southern end, a single in the middle, and two single beds on the northern side of the house overlooking the bay. A friendly and committed staff includes housekeepers, a groundskeeper, and night watchmen.

Negril Beach Villa (tel. 876/957-3500, www.negrilbeachvilla.com, minimum 3 nights, US$800) is a secluded three-bedroom villa with a private pool on 0.6 hectare (1.5 acres), with 120 meters (400 feet) of beachfront facing Bloody Bay. Rooms have king beds, air-conditioning, and private baths.

All-Inclusive Resorts

A 222-room resort with exclusive butler service in its top room category, **Sandals Negril** (Long Bay, www.sandals.com, US$818-2,454, 65% discount for 3 or more nights) has a Red Lane Spa and two-story loft suites with spiral staircases. A pro sports complex offers racquetball, squash, and tennis. There are two pools, whirlpool tubs, and a scuba certification pool. Swim-up river suites have stairs descending from the veranda doors into a lazy river with views to the sea, and plantation suites have private plunge pools, outdoor showers, and private balconies. Wi-Fi, cable TV, and air-conditioning are standard.

Toward the northern end of Seven-Mile-Beach, ★ **Couples Swept Away** (U.S. tel. 800/268-7537, tel. 876/957-4061, from US$413 d low season, US$602 d high season) is an exceptional all-inclusive resort. A newer wing on the south end of the compound has a wet bar, a grill, and a tastefully decorated lounge. The four-hectare (10-acre) sports complex and spa has state-of-the-art fitness facilities, 10 tennis courts, squash, racquetball, and a basketball court. Eight-hour day passes (US$100) allow nonguests access to everything on the property.

Sister property **Couples Negril** (U.S. tel. 800/268-7537, tel. 876/957-5960, from US$408 d low season, US$590 d high season) is located towards the southern end of Bloody Bay and has comparable amenities.

Boutique adults-only all-inclusive property ★ **Sunset at the Palms** (Bloody Bay, tel. 876/957-5350, www.thepalmsjamaica. com) features cozy one-bedroom treetop deluxe bungalows (US$385 low season, US$600 high season per couple) and one-bedroom suites (US$620 low season, US$895 high season) spread out across lush, well-manicured grounds. The food offering is a mix of buffet style and à la carte meals at Lotus Leaf restaurant. Inside the bungalow-style cottages, dark wooden furniture and plush bedding accompany his-and-her showerheads. Baths and balconies have day beds and views over the lush gardens and wetlands area known as the Great Morass. A private beach with a bar and grill is located across the road, two minutes from the lobby on foot. The water sports center offers catamarans and windsurfing equipment. The property's tennis court and weight room are on the morass side of the property, along with the swimming pool, heated whirlpool, and a lounge.

A 420-room all-inclusive resort on Bloody Bay, **Club Hotel Riu Negril** (tel. 876/957-5700, www.riu.com, from US$252 d all-inclusive) has a large main building and four two-story annexes. The resort has a gym, a jetted tub, and an over-18 sauna. Rooms have minibars, kings or two double beds, and a balcony or terrace. Four restaurants offer à la carte and buffet options, with bars spread across the property. The resort has two hard-surface tennis courts, table tennis, volleyball, and a variety of water sports. The hotel has Wi-Fi throughout. The Renova Spa offers a variety of massages and treatments at additional cost.

Family-friendly all-inclusive resort **Royalton Negril** (Negril Point, tel. 876/632-7401, infonegril@royaltonresorts.com, www.royaltonresorts.com, from US$422 low season, US$460 high season) has nine room categories, five of them reserved for Diamond Club guests. An open-concept design between the bedrooms and baths of the junior suites

and wistful decor over the headboards help meld the modern look and feel of the suites, with the natural environment outside brought closer with ample use of large windows and glass sliding doors. The resort's beach is protected from the prevailing winds and overlooks Bloody Bay.

WEST END
Under US$100

Italian for "Fabio's Place," **Da Fabio** (Good Hope district, cell tel. 876/247-3125, info@dafabio.net, www.dafabio.net, US$70 d) offers eight bedrooms with queen beds, mini fridges, and en suite baths in a house in the hills overlooking Seven-Mile Beach. Proprietor Fabio offers a package with breakfast and dinner and round-trip shuttle service to Seven-Mile Beach (US$35 pp). The house has a pool and Wi-Fi.

An unpretentious and well-situated cliff-top resort, **Xtabi** (tel. 876/957-0121, xtabi-resort@cwjamaica.com, www.xtabinegril.com) has economy rooms (US$49 low season, US$65 high season) with fans, while spacious suites (US$59 low season, US$90 high season) have air-conditioning and TV. More stylish cliff-top cottages (US$120 low season, US$210 high season) offer a step up. The restaurant

boat off Seven-Mile Beach

and bar, also on the cliffs, serve some of the best lobster (US$25) in Negril, and the conch burger is highly acclaimed.

A tasteful retreat with five quaint self-contained cottages surrounded by lush vegetation, ★ **Banana's Garden** (across West End Rd. from Rick's Café, tel. 876/957-0909, cell tel. 876/353-0007, bananasgarden@gmail.com, US$85-135 low season, US$100-165 high season) has unique hand-carved wood detailing, ceiling fans, louvered windows, hot water, and kitchenettes in each cottage, making the property ideal for those seeking independence and the modest back-to-basics vibe that first put Negril on the map. A pool keeps guests cool without having to jump off the cliffs across the street or go to the beach. Rates include continental or Jamaican breakfast. Banana's Garden is ideal for small groups looking to book the entire property, for which discounts can be negotiated. The Solar Wellness Spa on the property offers massage and a variety of treatments.

US$100-250

One of the top hotels in Negril thanks to its quality service, well-maintained grounds, and competent management, ★ **Rockhouse** (tel. 876/957-4373, info@rockhousehotel.com, www.rockhousehotel.com) has beautiful villas (US$295-350 low season, US$355-425 high season) perched on the cliffs with views out to sea. The 34 rooms include standards (US$125 low season, US$160 high season) and studios (US$150 low season, US$185 high season). **Rockhouse Restaurant** has a great vibe with tables overlooking the water and a lounge area tucked away in the back with bamboo furniture and coffee tables with chess and backgammon boards. The signature coconut-battered shrimp are a must; the delectable menu also features jerk grilled calamari and crab quesadillas for starters, and mains such as blackened mahimahi, seared snapper with garlic shrimp, and grilled tenderloin. Breakfasts are solid, and vegetarians are covered with a dedicated menu and an inspiring juice bar. A large pool perches

at the edge of the cliffs, and the eight-room **Rockhouse Spa** offers massage, wraps, scrubs, herbal poultice massage, reflexology, and holistic treatments using natural local ingredients. Treatment rooms surround a courtyard with a fountain in the middle of a lotus pond.

The West End's crown gem is **Tensing Pen** (tel. 876/957-0387, tensingpen@cwjamaica.com, www.tensingpen.com, from US$145 low season, US$193 high season). Luxurious, thatch-roofed, bungalow-style cottages adorn the cliffs above turquoise waters. You won't find TV in the rooms, a deliberate choice aimed at putting guests in a state of relaxation in tune with the surroundings. Instead, expect details like hibiscus flowers on the pillows and cool water at the bedside. A nine-meter (30-foot) saltwater infinity pool in front of the dining area offers respite from the heat, even when the sea is too rough for a dip.

The cliff-top grounds are well maintained with neat walkways and verdant gardens that make **Catcha Falling Star** (tel. 876/957-0390, stay@catchajamaica.com, www.catchajamaica.com, US$95-175 low season, US$135-350 high season) one of the choice properties on the West End. There are 17 units, including five one-bedroom cottages and two two-bedroom cottages, and Ivan's Bar & Restaurant offers oceanfront dining for guests and nonguests.

Banana Shout (tel. 876/957-0384, cell tel. 876/350-7272, milo@bananashoutresort.com, www.bananashoutresort.com, US$80-100 low season, US$150-200 high season) is an assortment of rustic one- and two-bedroom cottages atop the cliffs with cozy furniture and an artsy vibe. A live band performs classic reggae covers every evening at Rick's Café next door for an earful of music to set the mood for sunset.

A boutique hotel straddling both sides of West End Road, **Villas Sur Mer** (134 West End Rd., tel. 876/957-0342, cell tel. 876/390-4843, reservations@villassurmer.com, www.villassurmer.com, from US$170) has a six-bedroom villa (from US$1,400) overhanging the crashing waves at the top of the cliff, with a private pool and bedrooms with sea views. On the other side of the road, one-, two-, and three-bedroom cottages are laid out around a large pool and bar area. Rooms have kitchenettes with polished cement countertops, queen beds, built-in sofas in the lounge areas with a flat panel TV, Wi-Fi, air-conditioning, ceiling fans, and screened louvered windows. A cave under the road leads to a lookout with a ladder into the sea for snorkeling.

The Westender Inn (tel. 876/957-4991, U.S. tel. 800/223-3786, cell tel. 876/473-8172, westenderinn@yahoo.com, www.westender-inn.com, from US$90) is a low-key lodging a bit farther out from Jackie's on the Reef, deep on the West End. Rooms are comfortable, with a variety of bed sizes and layouts in studios, one-bedrooms, and ocean-side suites. The hotel has a raised pool deck with a restaurant and bar where nonguests are welcome.

Over US$250

The place to go for a yoga retreat with no disturbances or distractions is **Jackie's on the Reef** (tel. 876/957-4997 or 718/469-2785, jackiesonthereef@rcn.com, www.jackieson-thereef.com, from US$300, including breakfast, dinner, and yoga). The hotel is one of the farthest out along West End Road, where there's less development and it's easy to meditate undisturbed.

A luxurious adults-only boutique on the cliffs with expert pampering and great food at the Blue Mahoe Restaurant is **The Spa Retreat** (cell tel. 876/399-3772, info@thespajamaica.com, www.thespajamaica.com, from US$250). The 18 rooms are comfortably dispersed along cut stone paths atop the cliffs on Negril's West End, all with air-conditioning, fridges, safes, Wi-Fi, Serta mattresses, room service, and cell phones. Garden Stone Cottages and Rooftop Stone Cottages have king beds and sleep up to four; Seaside Stone Cottages and Bridal Suites accommodate two queens or a king. It's best known for its outstanding Spa and treatments include manicures, pedicures, organic facial treatments, body wraps, body scrubs, reflexology,

and massage. Couples massage classes are also offered.

★ **The Caves** (West End Rd., tel. 876/957-0270 or 876/618-1081, reservations@island-outpost.com, www.islandoutpost.com, from US$615) epitomizes Negril's rootsy vibe. Thatch-roofed contoured cottages are seamlessly integrated with the cliffs. Conducive to spiritual relaxation, the hotel has a sophisticated African motif, soft music, and hot tubs carved into the cliffs. Vault into the crystal-clear water up to 18 meters (60 feet) below. Everywhere you turn are platforms for sunbathing or diving. At night, a large grotto just above water level is strewn with bougainvillea petals and lit with candles to create the most romantic dining room imaginable. **The Spa at The Caves** offers massage, scrubs, body wraps, facials, manicures and pedicures, and hair and scalp treatments as well as a sauna. A variety of packages offer combos up to two hours. Rooms are all unique, with king beds, African batik, classic louvered windows, and well-appointed baths. Love seats are nestled into the surroundings. The cottages are decorated with an assortment of Jamaican carvings and paintings. Every detail is consciously designed to put guests in relax mode—to the point of entrancement. Open bars (some staffed, some self-serve) dot the property, and a snack bar has gourmet food ready whenever you're hungry.

A secluded upscale boutique hotel and villa complex just past Negril's lighthouse, **The Cliff** (U.S. tel. 800/213-0583, www.thecliffja-maica.com, from US$407 low season, US$470 high season) has 33 spacious rooms, 22 in a hotel block and the rest in villas, wrapped around a large open garden peppered with palm trees and crisscrossed by an enormous multilevel swimming pool and meandering paths. Zest Restaurant, the dining facility on property, also caters to nonguests (by reservation), with some of the most inspiring meals in Negril and indoor and alfresco seating areas atop the limestone cliffs, with a bar located just below. Rooms have cushy sofas inside and simple wicker furniture on the balconies. Soft tones create a relaxing ambiance, encouraging romance. Soft cotton linens, firm mattresses, and fluffy pillows ensure peaceful rest in four-poster mahogany beds. Baths have rain showerheads and handmade Jamaican soaps. The Wi-Fi signal is strong, and the bedrooms have flat-screen TVs. All rooms have a mini fridge and air-conditioning. The KiYara Spa on the property offers a variety of treatments, including deep tissue, balancing and hot stone massage, scrubs, wraps, and masks as well as half-day and full-day wellness packages and daily yoga.

Cottages

Negril's most exclusive and luxurious private villa complex, **Hide Awhile** (West End Rd., tel. 877/243-5352 or 876/957-3302, www.idleawhile.com, from US$228) is away from the hustle and bustle. Three villas feature a duplex layout with a spacious master bedroom upstairs. Amenities include all the details expected in a high-end property, from flat-screen TVs to a fully equipped kitchen, plush bedding, and a relaxing porch. The property is best if you have a car. Wireless internet is available.

The eight tasteful cottages and bungalows at **Tingalayas Retreat** (tel. 876/957-0126, reservations@tingalayasretreat.com, from US$122 low season and US$170 high season) make a good place for groups and families, with accommodations for up to 14 people. Amenities include ceiling fans, hot water, wireless internet, and a combination of queen and bunk beds. Breakfast is included, and resident Rasta cook Jubey does excellent lobster, jerk chicken, and rice-and-peas to order.

Somewhere West (cell tel. 876/789-4309 or 876/278-0691, www.somewherewestnegril.com, US$100 low season, US$175 high season) has four apartments with a 16-person maximum capacity located past the lighthouse on West End Road. The property faces the sea atop low coral cliffs with a saltwater pool.

Information and Services

EMERGENCIES

The Negril **police station** (tel. 876/957-4268, emergency tel. 119) is on Whitehall Road just east of the roundabout next to the Negril Transport Centre. The police advise travelers to stay away from dark secluded areas at night, as people have had bags snatched. Don't leave valuables on the beach while swimming.

BANKS AND ATMS

Banking can be done at **NCB** (Sunshine Village, tel. 876/929-4622), with ATMs at Plaza Negril and Petcom, or **Scotiabank** (Negril Square, across from Burger King, near the roundabout, tel. 876/957-4236), with an ATM at the Petcom next to the airstrip across from the Royalton. Scotiabank also has an ATM at the Times Square shopping plaza. **FX Trader** (tel. 888/398-7233, 9am-5pm Mon.-Thurs., 9am-5:30pm Fri.-Sat.) has a branch at Hi-Lo supermarket in Sunshine Village Plaza by the roundabout.

The Negril **post office** (tel. 876/957-9654, 8am-5pm Mon.-Fri.) is on West End Road between Cotton Tree Hotel and Samuel's Hardware, just past Vendor's Plaza.

VISITOR INFORMATION

The **Negril Chamber of Commerce** (Vendors Plaza, West End Rd., tel. 876/957-4067, www.negrilchamberofcommerce.com) has visitor information, including a regularly updated brochure full of ads for hotels and attractions.

MEDICAL CLINICS

Long Bay Medical & Wellness Centre (Norman Manley Blvd., tel. 876/957-9028) is run by Dr. David Stair. **Omega Medical**

Centre (White Swan Plaza and Sunshine Plaza, tel. 876/957-9307 or 876/957-4697) has two branches run by husband-and-wife team

Dr. King and Dr. Foster. **Dr. Grant** (Sunshine Plaza, West End, tel. 876/957-3770) runs a private clinic.

Transportation

GETTING THERE
By Air

Negril's Aerodrome, a small airstrip just inland from Negril Point, can accommodate small private aircraft and charters. **AirLink Express** (Sangster International Airport, Domestic Terminal, tel. 876/940-6660, reservation@flyairlink.net, www.flyairlink.net) offers charter service flying Cessna 206 aircraft between any two airports or aerodromes on the island. **TimAir** (Sangster International Airport, Domestic Terminal, tel. 876/952-2516, timair@usa.net, www.timair.net) offers a similar service. Airfare between Montego Bay and Negril is about US$300 for up to two passengers each way.

By Land

Negril can be reached by several means, depending on your budget and comfort requirements. Most accommodations offer airport

transfers at additional cost, and a host of private taxi operators generally charge around US$60 for two people, plus US$20 pp for extra passengers.

Knutsford Express (tel. 876/971-1822, www.knutsfordexpress.com, 8am-10pm daily) offers bus service between Negril and Montego Bay (US$15), Ocho Rios (US$23), and Kingston (US$30), among other routes, with onboard Wi-Fi and a lavatory. Reserve online in advance for discounted fares.

The **Jamaica Union of Travelers Association** (JUTA) is the best option for budget-minded travelers booking an airport pickup or drop-off. Drivers use any kind of vehicle imaginable: sedans, vans, or buses carrying up to 45 passengers. JUTA's **Negril Chapter** (Norman Manley Blvd., tel. 876/957-4620 or 876/957-9197, info@jutatoursnegrilltd.com, www.jutatoursnegrilltd.com) offers the most affordable transfers to Negril

Seven-Mile Beach

from Montego Bay's Sangster International Airport, US$20 pp from the beach and US$25 from the cliffs. Reservations made by email get a US$2 discount. JUTA drivers take visitors on excursions to popular attractions across the island.

Alfred's Taxi and Tour Company (tel. 876/854-8016 or 876/527-0050, U.S. tel. 646/289-4285, alfredstaxi@aol.com, negriltracy@aol.com, US$50 for 2 people), led by proprietor Alfred Barrett, has a 15-seat vehicle for larger groups using his "Irie Airport Rides and Vibes" service, previously only offered in his tinted Toyota Corolla station wagon.

If you're on a budget and don't mind a more roundabout route, **minibuses** run between Montego Bay and Savanna-la-Mar (US$2), and **route taxis** travel between Savanna-la-Mar and Negril (US$2). It is also possible to take a route taxi from Montego Bay to Hopewell (US$2), then another from Hopewell to Lucea (US$2), and then a third from Lucea to Negril (US$2), but these cars leave when full and don't have much room for luggage.

Negril has two main **taxi** stands: one next to Scotiabank in Negril Square, where taxis depart for points along the West End following the cliffs; the other in the main park next to the police station on Whitehall Road, where taxis and buses depart for points along Norman Manley Boulevard and east toward Little London and Savanna-la-Mar.

GETTING AROUND

Route taxis run up and down the coast from the beach to the West End, generally using the plaza across from Burger King by the roundabout as a connection point. Some negotiating will generally be required, as the route taxis always try to get a higher fare from visitors, especially at night when everyone is charged extra. From anywhere on the West End to the roundabout should never be more than US$2 during the day or US$4 at night. From there to the beach should also not cost more than US$2. Excursions beyond the beach and the West End can be arranged with private taxi and tour operators.

Car and Motorcycle Rentals

Happy World Bike/Car Rental (opposite Idle Awhile, Norman Manley Blvd., tel. 876/957-4004, cell tel. 876/336-4795, happyworldnegril@yahoo.com, www.carrentalnegril.com, 8am-6pm daily) rents Toyota Corolla (US$105), Suzuki Vitara (US$152), and BMW X5 (US$210) vehicles (deposit US$1,500) and Suzuki mopeds and Yamaha dirt bikes (US$41 per day, US$300 deposit).

Jah B's Bike Rentals (Norman Manley Blvd., tel. 876/957-4235 or 876/353-9533, 8am-6pm daily) rents 125-cc mopeds and scooters, 175-cc Yamahas (US$40), and 600-cc Honda Shadows (US$50). Deposit is US$200 on the smaller bikes, US$500 for the larger ones. The sign on the road says "JB Bike Rental."

Tykes Bike Rental (West End Rd., across from Tensing Pen, just before Rick's Café, tel. 876/957-0388, cell tel. 876/441-2260, tonyvassell@yahoo.com, 8am-6pm daily) rents 21-speed cruiser bicycles (US$10) as well as 100-cc Activer (US$35) and 120-cc Suzuki scooters (US$45). A US$500 deposit is required for the scooters.

Northeast of Negril

Several attractions have cropped up along the busy route between Montego Bay and Negril in recent years, bringing outposts of attractions popular in the vicinity of Ocho Rios closer to Negril. These include Dolphin Cove, where visitors can interact with dolphins, pet sharks, and snorkel with stingrays. Tour operators have set up outposts around Lucea near Jamaica's largest all-inclusive resort, Grand Palladium Lady Hamilton, about halfway between Negril and Montego Bay. History buffs will enjoy the ruins of Fort Charlotte, which protected the once busy port in Lucea, and Kenilworth, an old sugar estate that had its heyday in the early 1800s.

Closer to Negril, Rhodes Beach Resort offers horseback riding on a large seaside estate, and Half Moon Beach just past Green Island is a quiet little cove devoid of hustlers with a beach bar and grill offering relaxation and quick boat rides to Calico Jack's, a little island just offshore. Golfers unimpressed by the club in Negril will surely find the greens at Tryall Club up to par. Closer to Montego Bay, Old Steamer Beach is a popular hangout for locals, with fine golden sand and ample shade under sea grape trees.

GREEN ISLAND
★ Half Moon Beach

Located in Orange Bay, just west of Green Island, Hanover, **Half Moon Beach** (Andrew Marr, cell tel. 876/809-6041 or 876/531-4508, halfmoonbeachja@gmail.com www.half-moonbeachjamaica.com) is a quiet little private beach park preserved close to how nature made it. The beach bar and grill is set back from the pristine strip of white sand, its eight rustic cottages hidden on the far side of the

property. A canoe boat takes visitors to Calico Jack's, a second bar and grill, on a small cay five minutes offshore at the center of the bay. Half Moon is a great place to come for a more low-key alternative to Negril's often crowded Seven-Mile Beach.

FOOD

Breakfast, lunch, and dinner are served at **Half Moon Beach Bar & Grill** (9am-9pm daily, US$7-20), a laid-back beach shack setting with typical Jamaican favorites as well as creative international fusion dishes like coconut-crusted shrimp, Green Island coconut chicken served in a pineapple bowl, and grilled lobster.

A ramshackle bar and grill on a little island just offshore from Half Moon Beach, **Calico Jack's** (11am-sunset daily, US$6-20) serves grilled lobster, jerk chicken, veggie kebabs, and escoveitch fish. The bar serves pirate's rum punch and beer. Calico Jack's hosts a Pirates Party (4pm-6pm Sat.).

ACCOMMODATIONS

Accommodations at Half Moon Beach are offered in a number of cabins (cash only). **Coconut Cabin** (US$65) is a one-bedroom with a bath, a ceiling fan, and a mini fridge.

Half Moon Beach

Blue Moon Cabin (US$75) has two bedrooms that share a bath, sleeping up to four, plus ceiling fans and a mini fridge. Seagrape I (US$65) and Seagrape II (US$65) each have one bed and a bath with ceiling fans; they share a balcony. Half Moon Beach is one of the few places in Jamaica ideal for camping (US$15) for those with their own tents.

On a 223-hectare (550-acre) estate adjacent to Orange Bay, Rhodes Beach Resort (tel. 876/957-6422, cell tel. 876/431-6322, info@ rhodesresort.com, www.rhodesresort.com, from US$144 low season, US$180 high season) is far enough from the hustle of Negril to feel neither the bass thumping at night nor the harassment during the day, and it has enough outdoor activities to feel like you're not missing anything. Inflatable speedboats take you to cruise Seven-Mile Beach in no time. Other activities include horseback riding, hiking, birding, and snorkeling. Modern, comfortable rooms, suites, and villas all have verandas with sea views. Satellite TV, air-conditioning, cell phones, queen beds, and hot water are standard. Ignore the floral bedcovers and focus on the woodwork and bamboo detailing, much of which is handcrafted from materials sourced on the property. Rates vary depending on room size and amenities; the largest villa has three baths, a full kitchen, a dining room, and a whirlpool tub. Rates include breakfast and Wi-Fi.

LUCEA

Lucea, Hanover's capital, is located on a horseshoe-shaped harbor a few kilometers from the Dolphin Head Mountains. Dolphin Head is a small 545-meter (1,788-foot) limestone mass that overlooks some of the most biologically diverse forestland in Jamaica, with the island's highest concentration of endemic species. A few kilometers away, Birch Hill, at 552 meters (1,811 feet), is the highest point in the parish. The small range protects Lucea Harbour from the dominant easterly winds. Both Lucea and Mosquito Cove are used as hurricane holes for small yachts.

Lucea is a quiet town with little to see beyond Fort Charlotte. The fort was built to protect a town that was busier than Montego Bay in its heyday, exporting molasses, bananas, and yams. The large Lucea yam, exported to Jamaican laborers in Cuba and Panama during the construction of railroads and the canal, is still an important product grown in the area, though the center of the island, from Trelawny to Manchester, grows more today.

The clock tower atop the historic 19th-century courthouse was meant to be destined for St. Lucia, but after a logistics mix-up brought it to Jamaica, the town's residents refused to give it up in favor of the less ornate version they had commissioned from the same manufacturer in Great Britain.

Sights

On the point of Lucea Harbour, the most intact fort in western Jamaica is Fort Charlotte (site is unmanaged, supervised by Jamaica National Heritage Trust, tel. 876/922-1287), with three cannons in good condition sitting on the battlements. It was built by the British in 1756, with 23 cannon openings to defend their colony. Originally named Fort Lucea, it was renamed during the reign of King George III after his wife. The Barracks, a large rectangular Georgian building next to the fort, was built in 1843 to house soldiers stationed at Fort Charlotte. It was given to the people of Jamaica in 1862 by the English War Office; it became the town's education center and is now part of the high school complex.

One of Jamaica's leading sugar estates of the mid-1700s to early 1800s was Kenilworth, which later produced cattle, pimento (allspice), and wood, growing to over 1,000 hectares (2,500 acres) at its height. Previously known as the Maggoty Estate, the ruins of the industrial mill-house have stood the test of time, with the masonry and cut stone largely intact and round window openings that were an atypical architectural feature at the time. A boiler house occupied one of the two outlying buildings, and a small burial ground is behind the ruins, where a slab pays homage to Thomas Blagrove, believed to be the father of John Blagrove, the owner of Maggoty Estate, according to the earliest crop records in 1757. The property is now home to a branch of HEART Academy, a vocational training school. To get here, look out for the sign reading "HEART Trust NTA Kenilworth." Turn inland and look for the ruins behind the institute building, which is painted blue and white.

Dolphin Cove Negril (Lucea, Hanover, tel. 866/393-5158, 876/974-5335, 876/618-0900, or 876/618-0901, www.dolphincoveja.com, 9am-5pm daily) offers three options: the Encounter program (US$99), consisting of a dolphin caress and a kiss in knee-deep water; the Swim Adventure program (US$149 adults, US$99 under age 13), where guests are pulled by a dolphin belly-to-belly; and the Royal Swim (US$199 adults, US$99 under age 13), where the guest is given a foot push or dorsal pull by two dolphins. Guests can also interact and snorkel with stingrays, pet camels and ostriches, and watch a shark show.

Dolphin Head Eco Park and Trail

Dolphin Head Eco Park and Trail can be explored with the help of guides arranged by Project Manager Norma Gilzene (cell tel. 876/364-6699 or 876/798-5470, normasten-nett@yahoo.com, dolphinhead.lfmc@gmail.com). A US$10 pp contribution to the guide is appreciated. A trail that takes about an hour round-trip leads to a few lookout points on the northern slopes of the range, where hikers can see views of Lucea, Montego Bay, and Negril.

Accommodations

Fiesta Group, a Spain-based hotel chain, runs the 1,054-room **Grand Palladium Lady Hamilton** (tel. 876/620-0000, www.fiesta-hotelgroup.com, from US$304 d), the largest resort in Jamaica by room count. The massive all-inclusive just west of Lucea encompasses the beautiful natural Molasses Beach and dozens of standalone blocks of suites across an expansive property along a rocky shoreline on the eastern flank of Lucea Harbour.

Food at the resort is quite good by all-inclusive standards, especially the Jamaican dishes. The island's largest rooftop solar plant meets a significant part of the resort's electricity needs, giving it bona fide green credentials despite its large footprint. Several large swimming pools and above-average service make the only all-inclusive resort between Montego Bay and Negril a worthwhile option.

HOPEWELL AND TRYALL

Just west of Montego Bay, the Great River marks the border of St. James and Hanover. The area is an enclave of high-end tourism. Round Hill is one of Jamaica's most exclusive club hotels, and Tamarind Hill and the surrounding coastline are dotted with luxury villas, most of them fetching upward of US$20,000 per week in the high season.

The town of Hopewell is not especially remarkable beyond its status as an active fishing community. There's a Scotiabank ATM, a small grocery store, and a few hole-in-the-wall restaurants in the heart of town for typical Jamaican fare. Sound systems and tipsy partygoers can bring traffic through the small town to a snarl Friday evenings, which precede a busy market day on Saturday; if you're staying in the vicinity, it's worth a stop.

A few kilometers farther west of Round Hill and Hopewell is Tryall, a former sugarcane plantation destroyed during the Christmas Rebellion of 1831-1832. The old waterwheel, fed by an aqueduct from the Flint River, can be seen as you round the bend approaching from the east, but little else remains as a reminder of its past as a sugar estate. Today the hotel and villa complex, which fans out from the historic great house, sits on one of the Caribbean's premier golf courses.

Beaches

Old Steamer Beach (unmanaged, free), named for the rusty remains of a scuttled steamboat sitting just offshore, is a popular beach for locals in the area. There's not much in the way of services or vendors, so bathers are advised to bring a picnic and beverages.

Food

★ **Dervy's Lobster Trapp** (cell tel. 876/535-3367, www.lobstertrapp.com, by reservation, lunch noon-3pm daily, dinner 6pm-10pm daily, US$20-35), owned by the charismatic Dervent Wright and operated by the whole family, prepares delicious grilled lobster, served alfresco with a view of Round Hill from its vantage point on the Hopewell waterfront. Be sure to call ahead to make reservations. Reach it by taking the second right in Hopewell, heading west down Sawyer's Road to the water's edge. A sign for "Lobster Trapp" indicates the turnoff from the main road. Shrimp and fish (in garlic sauce, steamed, or roasted) are served along with the lobster specialty, best enjoyed grilled.

Smoked Marlin (Hopewell, tel. 876/609-4181, noon-9pm Tues.-Thurs., noon-10pm Fri.-Sat., 10am-9:30pm Sun., US$5-20) has an affordable and well-conceived menu featuring smoked marlin on toast, of course, as well as other appetizers like shrimp cocktail, chicken satay, and wings. Soups include crayfish bisque, fish tea, and red pea, with mains like snapper, jerk conch, grilled lobster, lobster thermidor, and pasta dishes. Local dishes include stew pork, oxtail, and curry chicken.

The waterfront location makes a nice venue for a romantic sunset dinner.

Accommodations

Just west of the Great River, ★ **Round Hill Hotel and Villas** (U.S. tel. 800/972-2159, tel. 876/956-7050, reservations@roundhill-jamaica.com, suites from US$553) is an exclusive hotel and villa club on meticulously manicured grounds. In the Pineapple House, 36 oceanfront rooms feature plush Ralph Lauren lounge furniture, bamboo four-poster beds, and en suite baths with rain showerheads and his-and-her sinks. Large louvered windows in the second floor oceanfront rooms have a panoramic view of the infinity pool and the sea beyond, perfectly aligned for dreamy sunsets. Baths feature glass enclosures and large standalone bathtubs. Just above the hotel suites, villas dot the hillside, each surrounded by a maze of shrubs and flowers, ensuring utmost privacy. Next to the small, calm beach is a charming library with a huge TV (to make up for their absence in the rooms) and an open-air dining area; a short walk down the coast leads to the spa, based in a renovated plantation great house. The 27 **Villas at Round Hill** (US$1,294-7,122 low season)

Dervy's Lobster Trapp in Hopewell

can be booked through the hotel reservations office. Cottages 16, 18, 20, and 21 are among the finest at Round Hill and in all of Jamaica.

Tryall Club (tel. 876/956-5660, U.S. tel. 800/238-5290, reservation@tryallclub.com, www.tryallclub.com) has one-bedroom suites (US$395 low season, US$550 high season) adjoining the main house as well as villas scattered throughout the property that are pooled and rented through the club reservation office. **Tryall Villas** are priced in classic (from US$630 low season, US$1,185 high season), deluxe (from US$785 low season, US$1,572 high season), and luxury (from US$1,430 low season, US$2,143 high season) categories. Most suites and villas have a one-week minimum stay during high season, reduced to three or four nights in the low season. Villas are privately owned, and owners establish their own seasonal rates and discounts.

Tryall Club has one of the best golf courses on the island, sitting on an 890-hectare (2,200-acre) estate that extends deep into the Hanover interior. Tennis and golf are offered to nonmembers (greens fees US$115 low season, US$150 high season, carts US$30, caddy US$45, recommended minimum tip US$20 pp). Tryall members and overnight guests pay substantially lower greens fees (US$75 low season, US$105 high season). There are nine tennis courts, two with lights. The cushioned courts are less slippery than the faux clay. Courts are only for members and in-house guests and are included in the stay. Hitting partners are at hand (US$30 per hour), as well as club pros (US$50-70). A US$10 per hour fee for a ball boy is mandatory. At night, courts cost US$25 per hour for use of the lights.

The Spa at Round Hill

Southeast of Negril

As you leave Negril heading southeast toward Savanna-la-Mar, the trappings of Jamaica's booming tourism industry quickly fade, replaced by low-key communities of Jamaicans going about their daily lives. Many visitors who head in this direction are seeking just that, the Jamaican iteration of normalcy. Look no farther than the first seafront community to the southeast, Little Bay, where Bob Marley famously sought solace and relaxation.

The fishing village has a few accommodations catering to off-the-beaten-track travelers. Savanna-la-Mar, another 20-minute drive in the same direction, is the Westmoreland parish capital, a congested little town teeming with shoppers and students. Mayfield Falls, one of Jamaica's many waterfall attractions, is located about 40 minutes north of Savanna-la-Mar, and Blue Hole Gardens, a swimming hole surrounded by lush vegetation, is about half that distance to the northeast. Paradise Park, just a few minutes from Savanna-la-Mar along the coast, has a great picnic area along a meandering river, as well as a spectacular virgin beach. From there, the A2 turns northeast to Ferris Cross and then southeast toward the quiet seafront community of Bluefields.

LITTLE BAY AND AROUND

Broughton Beach

Broughton Beach is a secluded eight-kilometer (5-mile) stretch of sand located due east of Little Bay. To get there, turn south at the gas station in Little London, followed by a left at the T junction. Keep left at the Y junction, and drive to the parking lot of the old Lost Beach Hotel. Mostly used by fishers to launch their boats, it has fine white sand and an open expanse free of peddlers and hustlers.

Food

Tiki's Guinep Tree Restaurant & Bar (Little Bay, tel. 876/438-3496, 10am-9pm daily,

US$5-10), run by Vernon "Tiki" Johnson, is a favorite with locals. It serves dishes like stew conch, fried fish, fried chicken, and jerk pork, accompanied by rice-and-peas or french fries.

Accommodations

Three tastefully appointed double rooms a few meters from the water's edge in Little Bay are at **Tansobak** (Little Bay, U.S. tel. 608/873-8195, littlebaycottages@gmail.com, www.littlebaycottages.com, from US$120). It has simple comfortable decor, louvered windows, tiled floors, and hot water. Air-conditioning is available by request. A small saltwater pool overlooks the sea at the edge of the cliff.

A secluded family-owned and -operated boutique resort on the sea, ★ **Coral Cove Beach Resort & Spa** (Little Bay, U.S. tel. 217/649-0619, cell tel. 876/457-7594, coralcovejamaica@gmail.com, www.coralcovejamaica.com, from US$179) has tasteful bamboo furniture and wood-frame beds. The 17 rooms are naturally ventilated with louvered windows and ceiling fans. The resort offers bed-and-breakfast or all-inclusive plans sleeping up to 40 for large groups and weddings. Wi-Fi covers most of the two-hectare (5-acre) property, which has 400 meters (1,300 feet) of ocean frontage. Coral Cove puts an emphasis on fine cuisine and attentive service, and is also very ganja-friendly; a recent partnership with the Bobo Ashanti house of Rastafari led to the establishment of an award-winning growing operation on-site.

On a 1.5-hectare (3.5-acre) seafront estate with a tennis court and lush gardens, **Lookout Cove** (Little Bay, U.S. tel. 800/755-2693, www.lookoutcove.com, from US$3,850 weekly low season, from US$4,950 weekly high season) has a three-bedroom villa and a two-bedroom cottage sleeping up to four. It's an ideal retreat for families or groups of friends looking for peace and tranquility.

SAVANNA-LA-MAR AND THE WESTMORELAND INTERIOR

Savanna-la-Mar, or simply "Sav," as it is commonly referred to by locals, is the bustling parish capital of Westmoreland, which most visitors experience only in passing. The annual Curry Festival, held behind Manning's School in July, makes Sav a worthy destination for the day, and if you've got some time to kill, the decaying wharf along the waterfront is worth a romp. Another worthwhile event held in the general vicinity is Western Consciousness, a sometimes annual one-night roots reggae festival organized by veteran promoter Worrel King (cell tel. 876/849-8426).

Sights

MANNING'S SCHOOL

The most architecturally appealing building in Savanna-la-Mar, **Manning's School** is one of Jamaica's oldest educational institutions, established in 1738 after local proprietor Thomas Manning left land to 13 enslaved people as the endowment for a free school. Now considered the area's top high school, the attractive wooden structure, built in late-colonial style in 1910 on the site of the original school, stands in front of several newer, less stylish concrete buildings set around a large field. The annual **Westmoreland Curry Festival** (westmorelandcurryfestival@gmail.com, last Sun. in Apr.) is hosted in this field and is definitely the best time to stop for a visit.

★ MAYFIELD FALLS

One of the best waterfall attractions in Jamaica, **The Original Mayfield Falls** (cell tel. 876/792-2074, mayfieldfalls@hotmail.com, www.originalmayfieldfalls.com, US$20) was developed with minimal impact to the natural surroundings. It's a great place to spend an afternoon meandering up the river and cooling off. Five-hour tours (US$85 pp) include round-trip transportation from Montego Bay or Negril, the entry fee, and a guided hike up the river, followed by lunch.

To get to Mayfield Falls from the North Coast, turn inland before crossing the bridge at Flint River on the eastern side of Tryall Estate and follow Original Mayfield signs. From the South Coast, turn inland in Sav, keeping straight ahead at the stoplight by the gas station on the eastern side of town rather than turning right toward Ferris Cross, and head straight toward the communities of Strathbougie, then take a left off Petersfield main road at the four-way intersection toward Hertford. From Hertford, head toward Williamsfield and then to Grange before making a right in the square to continue for about 10 minutes to the settlement of Mayfield. You'll see a sign on the right indicating the entrance to Mayfield Falls. The road from the north passes through Flower Hill before you see the Original Mayfield sign on the left.

JAMAICA GIANTS

Local entrepreneur Rick Jackson established the sculpture park and gallery **Jamaica Giants** (Moreland Hill, cell tel. 876/597-5736, info@jamaicagiants.com, www.jamaicagiants.com, 9am-5pm daily, US$20) in 2016 to "give a forward," or lend support, to sculptor-in-residence Fitzroy "Fitzy" Russell and painter-in-residence Bruce Allen. The showcase of local works features carved wood and stone sculptures set amidst a replanted tropical forest.

★ BLUE HOLE GARDENS

A lush riverine garden with diverse vegetation springing from manicured grounds, **Blue Hole Gardens** (Petersfield/Roaring River, US$15 adults, free under age 13) surrounds a natural spring-fed pool brimming with surreal turquoise water most of the year. It's a great destination for swimming, relaxing in the shade, and hiking around to the dozen other wellheads that feed the Turtle River. Most of these springs have pools big enough to serve as natural jetted tubs. In the drier months, the water level falls in the largest pool at Blue Hole Gardens itself. It's definitely worth a visit for an afternoon splash, and for those who can't get enough, **Blue Hole Victorian Cottage** (contact Sharna, cell tel. 876/370-8033, from US$220), on the same property, can accommodate up to eight guests. The rocky dirt road to Blue Hole Gardens passes Roaring River, an attraction downstream, before passing through an impoverished rural community straddling the banks of the Turtle River.

RastaSafari Experience (US$130, tel. 876/822-5333, tours 9am and 1pm Mon.-Fri., 11:30am and 2:30pm Sat.-Sun.) provides a sightseeing discovery tour of the western mountains on ATVs. The tour takes visitors to a natural mineral pool and a ganja field. The cost includes round-trip transportation from Negril, a welcome drink, bottled water, an ital (vegetarian) meal, and the guide.

PARADISE PARK

A few kilometers east of Savanna-la-Mar in Ferris Cross, **Paradise Park** (tel. 876/955-2675, paradise1@cwjamaica.com, US$10 adults, US$5 under age 13) offers a picnic area with a gazebo, charcoal grills, and restrooms shaded by magnificent guango trees as well as a river fit for a cool dip.

Food

The best spot to eat out in Savanna-la-Mar, ★ **Guangos Jerk** (Smithfield Rd., beside the Petcom gas station, tel. 876/955-4099, 11:30am-11pm Sun.-Thurs., 11:30am-midnight Fri.-Sat., US$7-25) has a well-prepared menu featuring Jamaica's favorite seasoned meat. The jerk chicken is served with perfectly crispy skin, the festival is just the right consistency and sweetness, the red pea soup delicious, and the beer cold. Fish is also served in brown stew, fried, steamed, or roasted. Specials include oxtail, stew peas, curry goat, and mannish water.

Dex Tasty Spot Restaurant (Barracks Rd., beside the bus park, tel. 876/882-5568, 8am-10pm Mon.-Thurs., 8am-11pm Fri.-Sat., US$5-8) serves fried chicken, curry chicken, brown stew chicken, and other local dishes on a rotating basis. A second location (42b

Beckford St., cell tel. 876/799-1584, 10am-10pm Mon.-Thurs., 10am-noon Fri.-Sat., 11am-9pm Sun.) serves the same menu and is open on Sunday.

Patties and deli sandwiches as well an assortment of Jamaican sweets and pastries (US$1-4) are at **Hammond's Pastry Place** (18 Great George St., tel. 876/955-2870, 8am-6:30pm Mon.-Fri., 8am-8:30pm Sat.). A second location (54 Beckford St., tel. 876/955-3399, 7:30am-6:30pm Mon.-Thurs., 7:30am-8pm Fri., 7:30am-7:30pm Sat.) sells the same baked goods as well as cooked food items like fried chicken with rice-and-peas, potato salad, pasta, and vegetables.

Accommodations

Offering a variety of tour packages combining accommodations and culinary and cultural experiences, **Zimbali Retreat** (Little London, tel. 876/252-3232, mark@zimbaliretreats.com, www.zimbaliretreats.com, from US$250 d) is off the beaten path, along a winding road in the hills 10 minutes from the square in Little London and about 30 minutes by car from Negril. Built in traditional rootsy Jamaican country style, the retreat offers an assortment of guest cottages surrounding a central kitchen and lounge area where farm-to-table meals are prepared as a culinary show following a tour of the gardens.

A three-bedroom, three-bath hillside cottage that can accommodate up to eight guests, **Blue Hole Victorian Cottage** (contact Sharna, cell tel. 876/370-8033, from US$220), located at Blue Hole Gardens, includes both the gardens and the cottage. A stay at the Victorian Cottage offers a unique rural experience without sacrificing the comfort of soft linens and broadband.

A six-room eco-resort located on the banks of the Cabarita River near Mayfield Falls, **Camp Cabarita** (Glenbrook, U.S. cell tel. 414/531-4414, campcabarita@gmail.com, www.campcabarita.com, from US$270 d, including three meals, snacks, and nonalcoholic beverages) has rooms in three wooden cottages adorned with local artwork. A variety of room layouts can accommodate different-size groups. The property has 120 meters (400 feet) of riverfront with a three-meter-deep (10-foot) turquoise swimming hole as the featured attraction. Herbal salt foot baths and self-administered coffee scrubs are included, while Japanese soaking tubs and wrap treatments (US$85) are offered by appointment at extra cost.

BLUEFIELDS AND BELMONT

The stretch of Westmoreland coast between Sav-la-Mar and Whitehouse is as laid-back and "country" as Jamaica gets, with excellent lodging options and plenty of seafood. Bluefields Beach Park has more locals on it than foreign visitors, with vendors selling jerk chicken, fried fish, beer, and the ubiquitous herb.

Sights

About 400 meters (0.25 mile) inland from the police station, **Bluefields Great House** was the home of many of the area's most distinguished temporary inhabitants, including Philip Henry Goss, an English ornithologist who resided in Jamaica from 1844 to 1846, subsequently completing the work *The Birds of Jamaica*.

Peter Tosh Memorial Garden (10am-5pm daily, US$15), where the remains of this original Wailer lie, is worth a quick stop, if only to pause amid the ganja seedlings to remember one of the world's greatest reggae artists. The entrance fee is assessed when there's someone around to collect it; otherwise the gate is unlocked, and a quick visit usually goes unnoticed. In mango season the yard is full of locals fighting over the heavily laden branches. Peter Tosh was born in nearby Grange Hill before making his way to Kingston, where he became one of the original three Wailers, along with Bob Marley and Bunny Livingston.

Beaches

A popular local hangout that sees relatively few foreign visitors is **Bluefields Beach Park** (tel. 876/957-5159). It has fine white sand and is lined with vendors. Music is blasted on weekends when the beach gets more crowded. There's no entry fee to use the beach, which is owned by the Urban Development Corporation.

Sports and Recreation

This Bluefields-Belmont area is perfect for activities like hiking, swimming, snorkeling, and relaxing. Nobody is touting parasailing or Jet Skis, and the most activity you will see on the water is fishing boats and an occasional yacht moored off the Luna Sea Inn or Bluefields Villas.

Fishing excursions can be organized by Lagga or Trevor, who can be contacted through Carolyn Barrett of Barrett Adventures (tel. 876/382-6384, info@barrettadventures.com). **Reliable Adventures Jamaica** (cell tel. 876/421-7449, rajtoursjm@gmail.com, www.jamaicabirding.com) organizes nature walks, community tours, birding, hiking, and marine excursions with local fishers led by Wolde Kristos. One-day bird tours (US$95 pp) include lunch. Transportation is available at additional cost.

Food

Delish crab backs, curried crab in the shell, grilled lobster, chicken, steam and escoveitch fish, curried or garlic conch, and stew pork are at ★ **Dor's Crab Shak** (Belmont Sands, cell tel. 876/471-4984, 8am-10pm daily, US$4-15). Desserts include bread pudding, sweet potato pudding, and ice cream. Occasional karaoke nights start at around 8pm Friday and Sunday evening. Proprietor Doretta Hibbert is a much beloved fixture in Belmont, as she founded the **Belmont Crab Festival** (Belmont Community Centre, last Sun. in May).

The Cracked Conch (Luna Sea Inn, tel. 876/955-8099, 9am-9pm daily, US$5-15) serves creative takes on Jamaica's favorite green, like callaloo bundles or callaloo sticks, and classics like conch fritters and conch chowder. Mains include crab cakes, fish-and-chips, jerk chicken quesadillas, and pan-seared mahimahi. For dessert, try the bananas foster crepes or Dr. Linda's cheesecake.

Accommodations

UNDER US$100

Brian "Bush Doctor" Wedderburn, also known locally as Rasta Brian, runs **Nature Roots** (cell tel. 876/384-6610, info@nature-roots.de, www.natureroots.de, US$30), with basic rooms in a shared cottage. Brian leads hiking excursions (US$15-25) into the hills to learn about local flora and fauna. Wi-Fi and a shared kitchen are available to guests.

Across the road from the water along a little lane adjacent to Sunset Paradise Bar & Grill, **Rainbow Villas** (tel. 876/955-8078, cell tel. 876/861-4701, www.rainbowvillas-jamaica.com, US$50 d) has spacious and clean rooms with ceiling fans and kitchenettes, hot water, and air-conditioning. A spa (US$60 per hour) on the property specializes in deep tissue and Swedish massage and reflexology.

A cut-stone bar overlooking the water in the heart of Belmont, **Belair** (Belmont, across from Peter Tosh Memorial, cell tel. 876/437-7220 or 876/437-7593, info@belairjamaica.com, www.belairjamaica.com) has three guest rooms, two with double beds and one with a king, each with private bath. **Good Hope Retreat** (Cave Mountain Rd., cell tel. 876/391-3775, goodhoperetreat@gmail.com, from US$59) is a hilltop collection of three wooden cabins with outstanding views of the coast and surrounding hills set in natural beauty. The cabins have kitchenettes and desks, simple furnishings, and queen beds.

US$100-250

Two perfectly situated wooden cottages on Bluefields Bay are **Horizon Cottages** (cell tel. 876/382-6384, info@barrettadventures.com, www.carolynscaribbeancottages.com, 3-night minimum, US$110), which define rustic comfort. Each cottage is tastefully decorated with local artwork and has classic wooden louvered windows, queen beds, soft linens, attached baths with private outdoor showers, and cute functional kitchens. The porch steps of **Sea Ranch** cottage descend to the small, beautiful, private white-sand beach, and a pier off the manicured lawn makes the perfect dining room and cocktail bar. **Rasta Ranch** is a slightly larger cottage set farther back. Kayaks and snorkeling gear are on hand for excursions to the reef just offshore.

Luna Sea Inn (Belmont Main Road, tel. 876/955-8099, U.S. tel. 561/768-0280, cell tel.

the gazebo at Luna Sea Inn

876/383-6982, lchidester@lunaseainn.com, www.lunaseainn.com, from US$175, including breakfast) is a 10-room boutique hotel. The property juts into the sea with a raised gazebo on the point. A small pool is in the courtyard. Rooms have en suite baths with showers and hot water, air-conditioning, cable TV, and Wi-Fi.

VILLAS

A collection of extravagant vacation homes, ★ **Bluefields Villas** (U.S. tel. 877/955-8993, vacations@bluefieldsvillas.com, www.bluefieldsvillas.com, 5-night minimum low season, 7-night minimum high season, from US$6,561 weekly for 2, includes food and beverages) is set on prime seafront estates hugging the coast along Bluefields Bay. Each villa has a private pool and its own unique character and history, all impeccably appointed with antique furnishings, fine china, and silver. At San Michele in Belmont, a large gazebo stands by the pool for open-air dining; another gazebo sits on a small island just offshore, ideal for sunset cocktails. Across the bay, the remaining villas are joined by a romantic sea walk leading down to Bluefields Beach, where fine white sand, lounge chairs, and kayaks await. Sundecks, pools, and luxurious linens

make guests feel like royalty. Wi-Fi coverage is strong throughout. Great care goes into the preparation of lavish meals that set a high bar with quality ingredients, culinary competence, and impeccable service.

WHITEHOUSE

A quiet seaside town, Whitehouse has developed into a favored community for Jamaicans returning from years of working abroad thanks to a few developers who've built subdivisions targeting that market. The nicest beach in the area, Whitehouse Beach, is found at Sandals South Coast and requires a day pass to fully enjoy. However, the end of the beach closest to the road can be accessed along a short footpath through the bush from the base of the hill in Culloden district. The public beach along the waterfront in Whitehouse is known as Top Beach and can be reached by turning down the narrow lane toward the sea from Whitehouse Square.

Food

A few small supermarkets in Whitehouse Square sell basic groceries. Produce can be bought from any of several vendors lining the lane down to the waterfront from the square, and an open-air seafood market at Top Beach sells the daily catch,

Pelican Lookout on the waterfront in Whitehouse

including all manner of fish, conch, octopus, lobster, and occasionally shrimp.

Funky beachfront restaurant and bar ★ **Pelican Lookout** (Top Beach, tel. 876/963-5392, info@pelicanlookout.com, 10am-10pm Mon., 10am-10pm Wed.-Sat., 1pm-10pm Sun.) has brightly painted picnic tables and humorous catchphrases like "Eat yuh food" and "Rasta run di worl" hand-painted on little signs throughout. The kitchen serves light bar food items like wings, chicken fingers, and onion rings, as well as typical Jamaican meat dishes from curry, jerk, and brown stew chicken to curry goat and oxtail, while specializing in seafood with escoveitch, steamed and roast fish, conch, lobster, and shrimp prepared any style. Pizza and pasta dishes are also on offer. It's a great place to watch the sunset and watch the fishers bring in their catch.

Jimmyz Restaurant and Bar (tel. 876/390-3477, 6am-7pm Mon.-Sat., US$3.50-11), next to the supermarket in Whitehouse Square and run by George "Jimmy" Williams, serves Jamaican breakfast items like ackee and saltfish accompanied by yam and boiled banana, with lunch and dinner dishes that include chicken and seafood staples. Fresh juices are also served.

Accommodations

At the former home of the Culloden Café, ★ **Culloden Cove** (contact Andy McLean, tel. 876/472-4608, info@jamaicaholidayvilla.com, www.jamaicaholidayvilla.com, 2-5 bedrooms US$3,300-4,200 per week low season, US$3,950-5,100 high season) was renovated under new ownership in 2008. The property comfortably sleeps six in the villa and four in a separate cottage. An infinity pool is located seaside, at the bottom of a sloping lawn extending from the main house, with a gazebo at the water's edge.

A massive resort at the high end of the all-inclusive group's many properties, **Sandals South Coast** (U.S. tel. 800/726-3257, from US$790, 65 percent discount for 3 nights or more) features premium drinks, a multitude of dining options, a beautiful cabaret bar, and best of all, a fantastic beach exclusively for the hotel's guests. Rooms have all the luxurious amenities you could ask for. The property is stunning, if somewhat out of place in its European village-themed design, with a large central courtyard and an enormous pool with a wet bar. If you're not staying on property, day passes and evening passes are sold to enjoy the beach and water sports or the dining and entertainment.

Getting There and Around

Route taxis ply the coast all day long from Savanna-la-Mar (US$2) and Black River (US$2) to Whitehouse. **Karl** (cell tel. 876/368-0508) is a JUTA-licensed driver based in the area who offers tours and taxi service.

Montego Bay and the Northwest Coast

Sights 78
Beaches 82
Recreation 83
Entertainment 88
Shopping 91
Food 93
Accommodations 98
Information and
   Services 102
Transportation 103
East of Montego Bay . . . 104
North Cockpit Country . 114

Commonly referred to as "Mobay," Jamaica's second-largest city has the highest concentration of golf courses and all-inclusive resorts in the country, as well as a smattering of great restaurants and pulsating clubs.

Mobay is also home to Reggae Sumfest, arguably the best showcase of Jamaican music on the planet, held over two nights each July. The city buzzes with cruise ships and international flights loaded with visitors. Many spend barely a day on land before climbing aboard to depart for the next port. While Mobay can't boast the island's best public beaches, it's a central base for day trips in western Jamaica, from Ocho Rios to Negril and along the South Coast, all about 1.5 hours away on well-paved single-lane highways.

Highlights

Look for ★ to find recommended sights, activities, dining, and lodging.

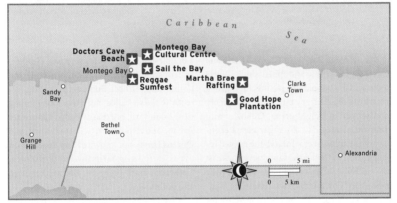

★ **Montego Bay Cultural Centre:** Check out historical and contemporary exhibits at the National Museum West and National Gallery West (page 78).

★ **Doctors Cave Beach:** At the center of Mobay's Hip Strip, this beach is the best spot to see and be seen on weekends. It's also the site of a monthly live reggae series (page 82).

★ **Sail the Bay:** Get out on the open water on a sailboat for half-day, full-day, or multi-day charter from the Montego Bay Yacht Club (page 83).

★ **Reggae Sumfest:** For two nights each July, the "Best Reggae Show on Earth" delivers both up-and-coming and legendary stars of Jamaica (page 90).

★ **Martha Brae Rafting:** Take a relaxing and romantic journey down a meandering river (page 109).

★ **Good Hope Plantation:** Chukka Caribbean offers culinary and adventure tours at this scenic citrus farm (page 114).

Mobay in One Day

As Jamaica's primary international gateway, Montego Bay is likely to be a part of many a Jamaican itinerary, even if it's just in passing. For those stepping off a cruise ship for a matter of hours, it may be the only part of Jamaica to be seen. Here are some suggestions for how to spend one day in and around Jamaica's "second city."

- **Hit the beach: Doctors Cave Beach,** located on Jimmy Cliff Boulevard, has a fine stretch of white sand and The Sand Bar. For a more local scene, try the free alternative, **Dead End Beach,** at the end of Kent Avenue, where you can watch the planes swoop in to touch down at Sangster International Airport.

- **Charter a yacht: Lark Cruises** offers day-sail charters on a 40-foot Jeanneau or 42-foot Catalina, and **Jamaica Water Sports** sails a 51-foot trimaran, both departing from Montego Bay Yacht Club.

- **Visit a great house:** No visit to Jamaica is complete without stepping back in time to experience what life was like when the island was a colony of the British Empire. **Rose Hall Great House,** perhaps the best-known and most foreboding, was the home of Annie Palmer, fearfully known as the White Witch of Rose Hall. Legend has it she murdered several lovers and ruled the plantation with an iron fist. Many visitors touring Rose Hall claim to feel the presence of spirits.

- **Take a Stroll Downtown:** There's no better way to get a feel for the real Jamaica than to take a stroll around **Sam Sharpe Square** and poke your head into the **Montego Bay Cultural Centre.** An **open-air market** and the city's largest collection of craft vendors are located a few blocks away.

The Montego Bay Yacht Club is a lively hub of activity for sailing and sportfishing. Rivers in the area are popular for rafting, tubing, or a refreshing dip. History buffs will find plenty to discover in neighboring Trelawny and Hanover, strategic to the sugar-based economy of the colonial era. Inland, the rugged region known as Cockpit Country stretches east beyond Bob Marley's birthplace at Nine Mile in St. Ann. The rough-hewn limestone landscape gave refuge to the indomitable Maroons, and lush valleys are home to working plantations offering adventure and family-oriented tours.

ORIENTATION

Montego Bay has several distinct tourist zones that are somewhat remote from the bustling and congested maze of downtown. Three roads lead from the roundabout as you exit Sangster International Airport: the A1, a double-lane highway leading past Flankers to Ironshore, Rose Hall, Greenwood, and points east; Sunset Boulevard, leading directly to the so-called **Hip Strip** along Jimmy Cliff Boulevard, previously called Gloucester Avenue and also known as Bottom Road; and Queens Drive, also known as Top Road, which bypasses the Hip Strip toward downtown, Catherine Hall, Freeport, Bogue, Reading, and points west.

Most of the city's budget and mid-range hotels, as well as a few all-inclusive resorts, are concentrated along **Jimmy Cliff Boulevard,** as are many restaurants and bars catering to foreign visitors. The Hip Strip is overrun with souvenir shops. Extending north from the Hip Strip is Kent Avenue, which terminates at one end of the airport runway along the popular public Dead End Beach.

New life was breathed into the Hip Strip with the reopening of Coral Cliff, a massive

---

Previous: Doctors Cave; former rivals Beenie Man and Bounty Killa at Sumfest 2019; the Montego Bay Cultural Centre and National Gallery West

The Northwest Coast

Darliston

Bethel Town

B8

Montpelier

B7

B6

Anchovy

Cambridge

Johns Hall

Spring Mount

Maroon Town

Queen of Spain Valley

Adelphi

Wakefield

Warsop

Albert Town

B5

Ulster Town

B10

B11

Stewart Town

Clark's Town

Duncans

B10

Sherwood Content

Sherwood

WINDSOR RESEARCH CENTER

PANTREPANT

GOOD HOPE POTTERY AND GALLERY

GOOD HOPE PLANTATION

MARTHA BRAE RAFTING VILLAGE

MARTHA BRAE RAFTING

Martha Brae

Falmouth

A1

Reading

WHARF HOUSE

MVP SMOKEHOUSE

BELLEFIELD GREAT HOUSE

MONTEGO BAY CULTURAL CENTRE

Montego Bay

Montego Bay

"MONTEGO BAY" MAP

SEE "MONTEGO BAY" MAP

SANDALS ROYAL CARIBBEAN RESORT & PRIVATE ISLAND

HOTEL RIU PALACE JAMAICA

SANDALS MONTEGO BAY

HYATT ZILARA/HYATT ZIVA

FERN TREE SPA

HALF MOON RESORT/ HALF MOON EQUESTRIAN CENTRE

ZOETRY MONTEGO BAY

SCOTCHIES

SUGAR MILL RESTAURANT

MONTEGO BAY CONVENTION CENTRE

ROSE HALL GREAT HOUSE

DOLPHIN COVE AT HALF MOON

HALF MOON GOLF CLUB

JEWEL GRANDE

HILTON ROSE HALL

SEACASTLES

St. Bran's Burg

IBEROSTAR GRAND HOTEL ROSE HALL/ IBEROSTAR ROSE HALL SUITES

DRESSEL DIVERS CLUB

GREENWOOD GREAT HOUSE

KITEBOARDING JAMAICA

CHILL-OUT HUT

FAR OUT FISH HUT & BEER JOINT

GLISTENING WATERS RESTAURANT AND MARINA

FISHERMAN'S INN

BLUE WATERS BEACH CLUB

OCEAN SONG

ROYALTON WHITE SANDS RESORT

LEROY'S BEACH BAR

SILVER SANDS PUBLIC BEACH

BURWOOD BEACH

CAPTAINS COVE

VILLA VICTORIA

VILLA KELSO

Duncans

SILVER SANDS

MANGO POINT BEACH

HARMONY COVE

BRACO STABLES

Rio Bueno

MELIA BRACO VILLAGE

YEOW REST STOP

LOBSTER BOWL

CARIBBEAN SEA

© MOON.COM

0   4 km
0   4 mi

Montego Bay

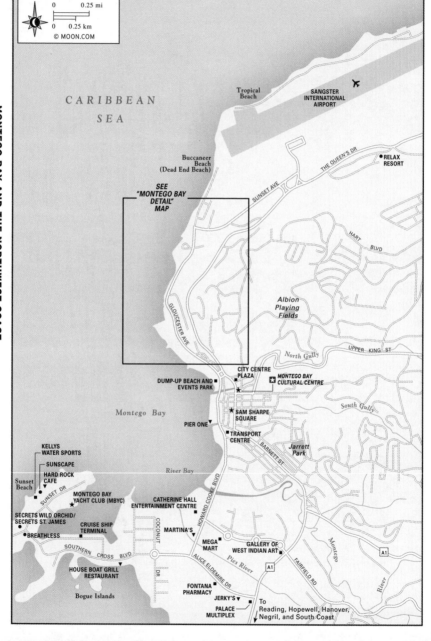

0   0.25 mi
0   0.25 km
© MOON.COM

CARIBBEAN
SEA

Tropical
Beach

SANGSTER
INTERNATIONAL
AIRPORT

Buccaneer
Beach
(Dead End Beach)

● RELAX
RESORT

THE QUEEN'S DR

SEE
"MONTEGO BAY
DETAIL"
MAP

SUNSET AVE

HART
BLVD

GLOUCESTER AVE

Albion
Playing
Fields

UPPER KING ST

North Gully

CITY CENTRE
PLAZA

DUMP-UP BEACH AND
EVENTS PARK

MONTEGO BAY
CULTURAL CENTRE

South Gully

Montego Bay

SAM SHARPE
SQUARE

PIER ONE

TRANSPORT
CENTRE

BARNETT ST

Jarrett
Park

KELLYS
WATER SPORTS

SUNSCAPE

HARD ROCK
CAFE

River Bay

HOWARD COOKE BLVD

Sunset
Beach

SUNSET DR

MONTEGO BAY
YACHT CLUB (MBYC)

CATHERINE HALL
ENTERTAINMENT CENTRE

COCONUT DR

SECRETS WILD ORCHID/
SECRETS ST. JAMES

● Breathless

CRUISE SHIP
TERMINAL

MARTINA'S

MEGA
MART

GALLERY OF
WEST INDIAN ART

Montego

SOUTHERN CROSS BLVD

ALICE ELDEMIRE DR

Pies River

A1

FAIRFIELD RD

A1

River

HOUSE BOAT GRILL
RESTAURANT

Bogue Islands

FONTANA
PHARMACY

JERKY'S

PALACE
MULTIPLEX

To
Reading, Hopewell, Hanover,
Negril, and South Coast

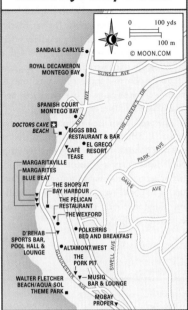

Montego Bay Detail

0   100 yds
0   100 m
© MOON.COM

SANDALS CARLYLE

ROYAL DECAMERON
MONTEGO BAY
SUNSET AVE

SPANISH COURT
MONTEGO BAY

DOCTORS CAVE
BEACH

BIGGS BBQ
RESTAURANT & BAR
EL GRECO
CAFÉ   RESORT
TEASE

MARGARITAVILLE
MARGARITES
BLUE BEAT

THE SHOPS AT
BAY HARBOUR
THE PELICAN
RESTAURANT
THE WEXFORD

POLKERRIS
BED AND BREAKFAST
ALTAMONT WEST

D'REHAB
SPORTS BAR,
POOL HALL &
LOUNGE

THE
PORK PIT

WALTER FLETCHER
BEACH/AQUA SOL
THEME PARK

MUSIQ
BAR & LOUNGE
MOBAY
PROPER

resorts, and a handful of middle- and upper-income residential developments.

Heading inland along Alice Eldemire Drive from the junction with Howard Cooke Highway leads past Fairview Shopping Centre to the junction of Barnett Street and Bogue Road. Barnett leads back into the city, and Bogue Road heads south and turns into the A1 as it turns westward, passing through Reading toward Negril.

East of the airport along the A1, **Ironshore** is a middle-class area that covers a large swath of hillside in subdivisions and oversize concrete mansions. Farther east, **Spring Garden** is the most exclusive residential neighborhood in Mobay, bordering **Rose Hall Estate,** where many of the area's all-inclusive resorts are wedged between the sea and the city's top golf courses.

PLANNING YOUR TIME

Sangster International Airport is an ideal point of entry if you're planning to spend most of your time in western Jamaica. A night or two in Montego Bay, especially on a weekend, can be a good way to enjoy some local culture before heading off to a more tranquil resort area. Ideally, the area deserves three days, split between beaches, historical sites, natural attractions, and fine dining and entertainment around the city.

Mobay makes a good base for exploring nearby areas. Negril (Jamaica's foremost beach town) and attractions on the South Coast and in the neighboring parishes of Trelawny and Hanover are only a few hours away. Several great house and plantation tours closer to town make excellent half-day excursions, and if you prefer to relax on the beach, a few good options right in town and along the coast in either direction are within easy reach.

Historical places of interest include **Sam Sharpe Square** downtown, as well as **Bellefield, Rose Hall,** and **Greenwood Great Houses**—at least one of which should be seen on a trip to Jamaica—and the Georgian town of **Falmouth.** All of these are close enough for half-day trips; tours and

gaming complex opposite Margaritaville; the arrival of S Hotel Jamaica, a smart upscale resort facing Doctors Cave Beach; the launch of a Usain Bolt's Tracks and Records franchise next door; and the opening of Island Strains, the city's first legal marijuana dispensary.

Queens Drive turns into Howard Cooke Highway as it bypasses the city center. The congested heart of Montego Bay is fraught with confusing one-way streets centered around **Sam Sharpe Square,** where a statue of the slave rebellion leader surrounded by a handful of followers stands to one side of a roundabout in front of the **Montego Bay Cultural Centre.**

A few stoplights south, Howard Cooke Highway meets Alice Eldemire Drive, which runs the length of **Freeport,** a peninsula jutting into the sea separating Bogue Lagoon to the south and the harbor to the north. Freeport is home to the city's cruise ship terminal, the yacht club, a few all-inclusive activities around Falmouth can easily consume the better part of an unhurried day. Natural attractions in the region include the **Martha Brae River, Windsor Caves,** and the **Great River.**

Mobay fills to the brim in mid-July for the island's premier music festival, **Reggae Sumfest.** The festival spans an entire week, culminating in two nights of live music on the weekend.

SAFETY

Montego Bay has many residential areas where it's not advisable to venture unless you know where you're going. Exercise particular caution in Canterbury, Clavers Street, Flankers, Hart Street, Norwood, and Rose Heights. As a rule of thumb, keep to well-heeled parts of town and be wary of overly friendly invitations and solicitations. If you've rented a vehicle, keep the doors locked while you're driving and don't let strangers inside the car. Stories abound of seemingly friendly residents offering to assist travelers with directions before entering vehicles without an invitation to "show the oblivious travelers the way," only to push overpriced ganja or otherwise lead new arrivals off course to extract money.

The downtown area around Sam Sharpe Square and the Montego Bay Cultural Centre are well policed and safe, as is the Hip Strip. Nonetheless, expect to be offered every product or service imaginable; you're best off not taking the bait. Women should avoid walking alone in poorly lit and desolate areas, especially at night.

Sights

RICHMOND HILL INN

Richmond Hill Inn (Union St., tel. 876/952-3859, info@richmondhillinnja.com, www.richmondhillinnja.com) is a great place for a sunset cocktail at the poolside terrace, which provides the best panoramic view of Mobay. As sun sets, the lights of the city begin to shimmer, the sea and sky merge into darkness, and cruise ships sail over the horizon. Nonguests are welcome to visit Richmond Hill from 7am to 7pm daily to enjoy the view (admission US$3).

The hotel has an illustrious history, and ancient relics pepper the property, many dating as far back as the 1600s. Columbus is said to have stayed here for a year around 1500 while stranded in Jamaica. A palatial abode was built on the property by John Dewar of Scotch whisky fame in 1804.

★ MONTEGO BAY CULTURAL CENTRE

The **Montego Bay Cultural Centre** (Sam Sharpe Square, tel. 876/971-3920, operationsmanager4mbcc@gmail.com, www.montegobayculturalcentre.com, 10am-5pm Tues.-Sun., US$8 adults, US$2 students and seniors) houses the National Museum West and the National Gallery West, showcasing Jamaica's history and contemporary arts scene, while the building itself is a Georgian relic worth visiting.

National Museum West, at ground level, features a permanent exhibit covering a history of St. James and Jamaica with a collection of artifacts spanning the Taino to postcolonial periods in the southern wing and temporary exhibits in the northern wing. **National Gallery West,** upstairs in an adjoining building, is an offshoot of the National Gallery in Kingston and showcases early, modern, and contemporary art in rotating exhibits. Special events, including occasional dance performances, are held in the town hall ballroom, and performing arts space is upstairs in the main building.

1: Old Steamer Beach **2:** White Witch Golf Course **3:** Rose Hall Great House

Sam Sharpe, National Hero

Sam Sharpe was the central figure of the Christmas Rebellion of 1831-1832, which many point to as the beginning of the end of slavery in Jamaica, officially granted in 1838. Sharpe was a Baptist deacon, respected across the deep societal divides of the time. Despite this, he was executed in a public hanging on May 23, 1832, in what is now Sam Sharpe Square in the heart of Montego Bay. Over 300 enslaved people were also executed for their role in the rebellion. Sharpe had originally envisioned and promoted a peaceful rebellion of passive resistance, whereby the slaves would stage a sit-down strike until the planters agreed to pay them for their labor, in accordance with what was perceived as a royal decree from England being withheld in Jamaica.

The rebelling slaves were swept up in the excitement of the hour as Sharpe's lieutenants swept across the western parishes to the sound of war drums in slave villages. Only 16 white people were killed during the rebellion, but around 20 large estates were torched, and the rebellion struck fear into the heart of the plantocracy. Sharpe took responsibility for the rebellion, relieving the white missionaries of the blame that was focused on them by the established powers of the day, including the Anglican Church. With few isolated exceptions, the Anglican Church backed the landed elite, even organizing terror squads to target Baptist missionaries who had made it their charge to foment discontent among the enslaved population. The Christmas Rebellion was consequently also known as the Baptist War.

A freedom monument stands at the back of the building, honoring those sentenced here when the building was used as a courthouse. The names of condemned enslaved people appear alongside the punishment meted out: whipping, striping, or death. **The Cage,** just in front of the Cultural Centre in Sam Sharpe Square, was once used to lock up misbehaving slaves and sailors.

CHURCHES

St. James Parish Church (Church St., tel. 876/971-2564) is one of the most attractive buildings in town. It's set on large grounds that house a small cemetery. It's worth a quick stop if you're passing by.

Burchell Baptist Church (23 Market St., tel. 876/952-6351) is also a historic chapel and where Sam Sharpe used to preach as a deacon. His remains were interred here before a relative had them removed and shipped to England. A plaque on the wall provides a brief history of the national hero. Services are at 7am and 10am Sunday.

ESTATE GREAT HOUSES

Each of the area's historic estate great houses is worth visiting, and each is distinct from the others, providing a glimpse of the island's glorious and tumultuous past. Jamaica's great houses sat at the center of vast sugar plantations, the grandeur of their construction representing the degree of wealth accumulated by their colonial landowners on the backs of enslaved Africans. The colonial period is presented on these tours as a simple fact rather than taboo. Despite decorating national heroes who helped transcend slavery, this dark period is ingrained in the national psyche, and Jamaica has yet to recover from the systematic destruction of the family unit, which scholars point to as the root of many modern ills.

Bellefield Great House

Five minutes from Mobay at Barnett Estate, **Bellefield Great House** (Fairfield Rd., tel. 876/952-2382, info@bellefieldgreathouse. com, www.bellefieldgreathouse.com) offers a 45-minute tour (10am-3pm Mon.-Thurs., US$33) of the great house and gardens and a demonstration of the how an old sugar mill works with a donkey walking around the chattanooga to press cane. The restaurant offers breakfast, lunch, and dinner. Visitors can wander the grounds freely, but the Great House is only accessible on an official tour.

To get to Bellefield, take Fairfield Road from Catherine Hall, keeping right where the road splits at a Y intersection. Go up the hill until you reach the Granville Police Station and take a right on Bellefield Road. Proceed until you see the great house on the left.

Rose Hall Great House

Rose Hall Great House (just past the Montego Bay Convention Centre, 20 minutes east of the airport, tel. 876/953-2323, greathouse@rosehall.com, www.rosehall.com, day tours 9:15am-5:15pm daily, night tours 6:30pm-9pm daily, US$25 adults, US$10 ages 4-11) offers one-hour tours in the former home of Annie Palmer, remembered as the White Witch of Rose Hall in Herbert de Lisser's novel of that name. It's the most formidable and foreboding renovated great house on the island today, with bone-chilling history. The tour through the impeccably refurbished mansion is informative and entertaining. The night tour is a bit more spooky, as actors in period dress jump out at unexpected moments. A tour of **Cinnamon Hill Great House** (US$25), the Jamaican residence of the late American singer Johnny Cash, located on the same estate, is also offered. Book online for a US$5 discount.

Rose Hall was built in 1770 by John Palmer, who ruled the estate with his wife, Rosa. The property ended up in possession of John Rose Palmer, who married the infamous Annie in 1820. A slight woman not more than 152 centimeters (5 feet) tall, Annie is said to have practiced Voodoo or black magic and killed several husbands and lovers, starting with John Rose. Annie ruled the plantation brutally and was much feared by the estate's enslaved workers. She would ultimately taste her own medicine, as she was killed during the Christmas Rebellion of 1831.

Rose Hall was virtually abandoned with the decline in the sugar economy until an American businessman, John Rollins, bought the estate in the 1960s and restored the great house. Rose Hall Great House forms the historic centerpiece of the vast Rose Hall Estate, which encompasses three 18-hole golf courses; the Hyatt Zilara and Hyatt Ziva, Half Moon Resort, and Hilton Rose Hall; and the most desirable residential district of Montego Bay, Spring Farm. Rose Hall is also the site of the Montego Bay Convention Centre.

To get to Rose Hall from downtown Montego Bay, head east for 10 minutes along the A1 and turn inland, up the hill, at the stoplight immediately after passing the Montego Bay Convention Centre.

PLANTATION TOURS

Several plantations in the area offer visitors a chance to learn about Jamaica's principal agricultural products—from those that were historically important to crops adapted to the modern economy.

John's Hall Adventure Tour (tel. 876/971-7776 or 876/952-0873, johnshalltours@hotmail.com, www.johnshalladventuretour.com) offers a three-hour **plantation tour** (US$75 pp, includes jerk lunch and fruit) with a historical and contextual commentary by the guides. Stops along the way include the St. James Parish Church and Sam Sharpe Square. Once at the farm, visitors learn about Jamaica's fruits and vegetables, see animals including a peacock, a goat, a pig, and a donkey, and have lunch. Also offered is the **Jamaica Rhythm Tour** (by reservation, US$75, includes dinner), a musical show held at John's Hall featuring old-time heritage, from maypole dancing and limbo to mento. Both tours include transportation from Mobay hotels.

Beaches

★ DOCTORS CAVE BEACH

Doctors Cave Beach (Jimmy Cliff Blvd., tel. 876/952-2566, drscave@cwjamaica.com, www.doctorscavebathingclub.com, 8:30am-5:30pm daily, US$6, US$3 under age 12) is a private bathing club located at the center of Montego Bay's Hip Strip. The beach is well maintained, the sand is soft and white, and the water is crystalline. Beach chairs (US$6), umbrellas (US$6), and towels (US$5) are also available. There's ample shade under almond and coconut trees. The beach is as popular among locals as it is for tourists. A yearly membership (US$150) grants access to the clubhouse, with its TV lounge, billiard table, and clean restrooms with showers.

The Sand Bar, an on-site restaurant, offers fish, burgers, and other light fare, and hosts a live music series, We Are Reggae (US$25, US$20 in advance), the last Saturday of each month. Gates open at 8pm and shows start at 10pm with a local act opening for a major artist like Freddie McGregor, Sizzla Kalonji, and Romaine Virgo.

OTHER BEACHES

Walter Fletcher Beach is on the Hip Strip, facing the harbor, across from The Pork Pit. It is the location of **Aquasol Theme Park** (Jimmy Cliff Blvd., tel. 876/979-9447 or 876/940-1344, 9am-6pm Mon.-Thurs., 9am-10pm Fri.-Sun., US$5 adults, US$3 under age 12), on a protected cove, with go-karts (US$3 single-seat, US$7 double), two tennis courts (Steve Nolan, cell tel. 876/364-9293, 6:30am-10pm daily, US$6 per hour), billiard tables (US$0.50 per game), a video game room, glass-bottomed boat excursions to the coral reef (30-minute tour, US$25 pp), and personal watercraft like Jet Skis ($75 for 30 minutes). There's also a sports bar with satellite TV and the Voyage restaurant (US$5-10), serving fried chicken, fried fish, and jerk.

Dead End Beach is the best free public beach in close proximity to the Hip Strip, at the heart of Mobay's tourism scene. Sandals Carlyle faces the beach, which borders the end of the runway at the airport. The beach is located on Kent Avenue, better known as Dead End Road.

Freeport splits the Montego Bay Marine Park down the middle.

Tropical Bliss Beach (9 Kent Ave., tel. 876/479-4193, tropicalblisstours@gmail. com, US$5) is a secluded beach with entertainment, food, and ambiance. The private beach club rents chairs (US$5); cabanas (US$120) that include a six-pack of beer or a bottle of wine, four beach chairs, and a personal butler; kayaks; water trampolines; and hammocks. Brian Thelwell (brian.tropicalblisstour@gmail.com) is the manager. The beach can be quite crowded when cruise ships are in port.

One Man Beach, also called Old Hospital Park Beach, is an underrated public beach located across from the Wexford Hotel on the Hip Strip. It's similar to Walter Fletcher Beach but doesn't have services and charges no admission. Dump-Up Beach, located across from KFC and Mobay's central roundabout, hosts occasional events and is being redeveloped into a waterfront park with a band shell.

Old Steamer Beach is 90 meters (100 yards) past the Shell gas station heading west out of Hopewell, Hanover. An embankment leads down to the skeleton of the USS *Caribou,* a steamer dating from 1887 that washed off its mooring in Mobay. You can hang your towel on the skeleton ship and take a swim at one of the nicest beaches around, which only gets busy on weekends when locals come down in droves to stir the crystal-clear waters.

Recreation

WATER SPORTS
★ Sailing

If you arrive in Jamaica on a private vessel, the Montego Bay Yacht Club (9am-midnight daily, tel. 876/979-8038, mbyc@cwjamaica. com, www.mobayyachtclub.com) has competitive docking fees (US$1.25 per foot per day up to 30 days), which are reduced for longer stays (US$0.90 per foot). Utilities are metered and charged accordingly, while boats at anchor can use the club facilities for the regular daily membership fee (US$10 pp). Mobay's mangrove areas in the Bogue Lagoon are often used as a hurricane hole for small vessels. The club has a small swimming pool, and the yacht club is a warm, family-friendly environment with a pool table, Ping-Pong, and a great bar and restaurant, Steakhouse on the Bay. Social and sailing membership (US$303 per year) grants members access to the Royal Jamaica Yacht Club in Kingston as well.

The Mobay Yacht Club is the finish line of the Pineapple Cup Race (www.montegobayrace.com), which covers 1,305 kilometers (810 miles) from its starting point in Fort Lauderdale, Florida. This classic race—a beat, a reach, and a run—is held in February every odd-numbered year. Other events include the annual Jamin J-22 International Regatta, each December, and the Great Yacht Race, which precedes the Easter Regatta, a fun-filled, competitive, yet friendly multiclass regatta. The International Marlin Fishing Tournament is held every fall, normally in September. Sailing camps for children are held during the summer, and courses are offered to adults based on demand.

The Lark Cruises (contact Captain Carolyn Barrett, cell tel. 876/382-6384, info@barrettadventures.com, www.barrettadventures. com) operates half-day (US$400 for up to 3 people, US$100 per additional person, up to 15) and full-day (US$600 for up to 3, US$150 each additional person, up to 10) cruises out of Mobay, with stops for snorkeling at reefs near the entrance to Bogue Lagoon or offshore from Doctors Cave Beach. A Jamaican lunch is included in the full-day charter. Weekly charters (US$5,000-8,000 for up to 4, excluding provisions) are also offered, inclusive of a captain and a cook. Charter destinations include Negril, Port Antonio, or even Cuba, contingent on favorable weather conditions. Guests are responsible for their own transportation to the yacht club.

Dreamer Catamaran Cruises (contact Donna Lee, tel. 876/979-0102, reservations@dreamercatamarans.com, www.dreamercatamarans.com, reservations required, 10am-1pm and 3pm-6pm Mon.-Sat., US$75 pp) has two three-hour cruises daily on its two 53-foot and three 65-foot catamarans, departing from Doctors Cave Beach. The excursion includes an open bar and use of snorkeling gear during a 45-minute stop in the Montego Bay Marine Park. The cruises also stop at Margaritaville for lunch (not included). A five-hour cruise (12:30pm Wed. and Sun., US$150 pp adults, US$120 under age 13) goes to Rick's Café in Negril; the trip ends with an hour of cliff jumping (or watching) and includes lunch of jerk chicken, festival, veggie pasta, and an open bar. The return journey by bus takes an additional two hours.

Jamaica Water Sports (cell tel. 876/381-3229 or 876/995-2912, dptgonefishing@hotmail.com, www.jamaicawatersports.com) offers sailing charters (2-hour sails US$600 for up to 10 people) on the 51-foot trimaran *Freestyle* for sailing and snorkeling around the Montego Bay Marine Park.

Kiteboarding

Kitesurf Jamaica (tel. 876/586-4877, bws@gorge.net, www.kitesurfjamaica.com) offers three-hour kiteboarding and windsurfing lessons (from US$85) for all levels as well as windsurfer (from US$60 per day) and kiteboard (from US$100 per day) rentals.

Scuba Diving

Kelly's Water Sports (Sunscape Splash, Freeport, cell tel. 876/893-2859 or 876/406-9380, kellyswatersports@gmail.com, kellyswatersportsjm.com) offers courses starting with the Discover Scuba Diving intro (US$120) and dives for certified divers, starting with a single tank (US$60) plus equipment rental (US$20).

Fishing

Ezee Sport Fishing (Denise Taylor, cell tel. 876/381-3229 or 876/995-2912, dptgonefishing@hotmail.com, half-day US$650 for up to 6, full-day US$1,300) operates *Ezee*, a 39-foot Phoenix sportfisher for deep-sea trolling, providing a good chance of catching big game like wahoo, blue marlin, or dorado, depending on the time of year. The crew assists in reeling them in with finesse.

Lucky Bastard Fishing Charters (cell tel. 876/572-0010, reservations@fishinginjamaica.com, www.fishinginjamaica.com, from US$250 for 2 people) boasts high catch rates on four-hour and eight-hour excursions deep-drop fishing, trolling, or a combination of both. Deep-drop fishing is done in around 300 meters (1,000 feet) of water and trolling from 60 meters (200 feet). *Lucky Bastard I* is a 30-foot cigarette boat converted for fishing; *Lucky Bastard II* is 28-foot Anacapri Flybridge.

Snorkeling

Montego Bay Marine Park (Pier 1, tel. 876/952-5619, mbmptmanager@gmail.com, www.mbmpt.org) covers the entire bay from the high-tide mark on land to 100 meters (330 feet) depth from Reading on Mobay's western edge to just east of the airport. The marine park encompasses diverse ecosystems that include mangroves, islands, beaches, estuaries, sea-grass beds, and coral reefs. The best way to see the marine park is with a licensed tour operator for a snorkeling trip or on a glass-bottomed boat tour. All the snorkeling, diving, and glass-bottomed boat operations in Montego Bay take guests into the Montego Bay Marine Park. Groups of at least 15 can book boat tours (US$35 adults, US$25 under age 12) of the marine park with the park rangers at the Marine Park office.

C-Jay's Watersports (Pier 1 Marina, tel. 876/632-5824, cell tel. 876/881-7585 or

---

1: an Island Routes catamaran **2:** Chukka's sedate river tubing tour at Good Hope Plantation **3:** Doctors Cave Beach

876/324-6065, contactus@cjwatersportsjm. com, www.cjwatersportsjm.com) offers glass-bottomed boat tours (US$25 adults, US$20 children), scuba diving (from US$110), parasailing (from US$60), waterskiing (US$30), wakeboarding (US$20), and tubing (US$25) as well as deep-sea fishing (4 hours, US$700 for 4 people). Snorkeling excursions (US$35 pp, minimum 2 people) last an hour, taking guests to the reef about 500 meters (550 yards) off Doctors Cave Beach, to the mouth of Bogue Lagoon, or to the reef just offshore the Decameron resort.

Reefs stretch from the mouth of Bogue Lagoon around Freeport and from Doctors Cave Beach east along Ironshore, Rose Hall, and continue along much of the North Coast. In most places around Montego Bay, it's easiest to snorkel off a boat, since the best reefs are located several hundred meters offshore, and the tour operators know exactly where to find them.

BIRD-WATCHING

Rocklands Bird Sanctuary and Feeding Station (just before Anchovy, St. James, tel. 876/952-2009, 11am-5:30pm daily, US$20 pp) was created by the late Lisa Sammons, popularly known as "the bird lady," who died in 2000 at age 96. Sammons had a way with birds, summoning them to daily feeding sessions, even after going partially blind later in life. The feeding sessions have continued, and visitors can sit on the patio and hold hummingbird feeders that entice the birds to perch on their fingers. A nature trail meanders through the property for bird-watching. More than 20 species can be seen on any given day. Guided tours through the forest (US$20 pp) are offered. To get to Rocklands, head up Long Hill from Reading and turn left off the main road at the big green "Rocklands Bird Sanctuary" sign. Follow the abominable road to the top of the mountain and down the other side, about 100 meters (330 feet), turning right at the first driveway on the descent.

GOLF

Montego Bay is the best base for golfing in Jamaica, with the highest concentration of courses on a nice variety of terrains, some with gorgeous rolling hills, others seaside, all within the immediate vicinity. The recommended minimum caddy tip is US$15-20 per player for courses across Jamaica.

White Witch Golf Course (Rose Hall, tel. 876/632-7444 or 876/632-7445, www.whitewitchgolf.com, 6:30am-9pm daily) is the most spectacular 18-hole course in Jamaica for its views and rolling greens. The course has a special rate for Hyatt, Iberostar Grand, and Riu guests. The course is also open to nonguests (greens fees, cart, and caddy US$139, US$119 after 10:30am, US$99 after 1:30pm, not including gratuity). Last tee time is at 4:30pm.

Cinnamon Hill Golf Course (Rose Hall, tel. 876/953-2650) is an 18-hole course operated by Hilton Rose Hall Resort & Spa and offers special rates to Hilton, Half Moon, and Sandals guests (greens fees, cart, and caddy US$141). After 1:30pm, the club offers a Twilight Special (US$99), in addition to the standard nonguest rate (greens fees, cart, and caddy US$160); club rental (US$40-50) is available. Cinnamon Hill is the only course in Jamaica that's on the coast, with holes 5 and 6 at the water's edge. A waterfall bubbles at the foot of Cinnamon Hill Great House, owned by Johnny Cash until his death.

Half Moon Golf Course (Rose Hall, tel. 876/953-2560, www.halfmoon.com) is a Robert Trent Jones Jr.-designed 18-hole course, with reduced rates for Half Moon guests (7am-noon 9 holes US$85, 18 holes US$159, afternoon 9 holes US$75, 18 holes US$139). Rates for nonguests are slightly higher (9 holes US$100, 18 holes US$189) but also include greens fees, a cart, and a caddy, but not club rentals. Half Moon is a walkable course. Rates go up in the winter months.

Kevyn Cunningham (cell tel. 876/361-3330, www.kevyngolf.com, office@kevyngolf.com) offers tailored golf-centric concierge services and lessons for all levels. Kevyn is a great resource for golfers of all levels and knows Mobay inside and out.

HORSEBACK RIDING

Half Moon Equestrian Centre (Half Moon Resort, tel. 876/953-2286, r.delisser@cwjamaica.com, www.horsebackridingjamaica.com) has the most impressive public stable in Jamaica, suitable for beginning to experienced riders. The center offers a pony ride for children under age six (US$20) and a 40-minute beginner ride (US$60) suitable for children over age six. A beach ride (US$80) includes a horseback swim for riders over age eight, and 30-minute private lessons for any experience level can include basic dressage, jumping, and polo.

Chukka Caribbean (www.chukkacaribbean.com) is Jamaica's leading adventure tour operator, taking visitors on horseback for its trademark Ride 'N' Swim (from US$80) at several locations across the island. The signature tour combines a low-key ride over land with a horseback swim at the end. Chukka has three locations in the vicinity of Montego Bay: at Good Hope Plantation in Trelawny, at Montpelier in St. James, and at Chukka Blue in Hanover.

TOURS

Tour packages typically include roundtrip transportation from your hotel, but rates are markedly lower if you have your own transport.

Chukka Caribbean (U.S. tel. 877/424-8552, tel. 876/656-8026, info@chukka.com, www.chukka.com) offers a host of activities for thrill seekers and adventure lovers, including catamaran cruises, canopy zip lines, cliff jumping, white-water rafting along the upper reaches of the Great River in Lethe, tubing on the White River along the St. Ann-St. Mary border, zip lines, and off-roading on ATVs and dune buggies in several locations, as well as trips to Bob Marley's birthplace at Nine Mile by old country Zion Bus or open-air Land Rover safari vehicles. The greatest number and variety of Chukka tours are offered at

Good Hope, a citrus plantation crisscrossed by the Martha Brae River, with jitney rides, food and rum tasting, tubing, horseback riding, and zip lines.

Bamboo Rafting (US$20 per raft) is offered on long bamboo rafts along the lower reaches of the Great River and out onto the tranquil Great River Bay where it spills into the sea. Immediately after crossing the Great River, turn inland and back to the river's edge, where several rafts are tied up under the bridge and where several raft captains can be found waiting to take visitors out on the water. The informal tours begin and end at the same spot. This part of the river typically has enough water to sustain the tours year-round.

Barrett Adventures (contact Carolyn Barrett, cell tel. 876/382-6384, info@barrettadventures.com, www.barrettadventures.com) is a tour company based in Mobay offering tailored itineraries anywhere in Jamaica. Veteran adventurer Carolyn Barrett will ensure anything you could want to do gets done in the allotted time.

Jamaica Tour Society (cell tel. 876/357-1225, info@jamaicatoursociety.com, www.jamaicatoursociety.com) is based in Montego Bay and offers all manner of off-the-beaten track tours across Jamaica, with a special expertise on Falmouth and Trelawny.

SPAS

Montego Bay has an abundance of high quality spas, the best ones located within the high-end resorts. Guests not staying on the properties are welcome to come and use the spa facilities.

The Irie Baths and Spa (tel. 876/979-0000, 8am-7pm daily) is a subterranean wellness center with plunge pools underneath the S Hotel on Jimmy Cliff Boulevard. Four treatment rooms offer an array of services: manicures, pedicures, facials, massages, body scrubs, waxing, and skin-care using Sothys and locally made products. A 24-hour fitness facility offers cardio machines and free weights.

Fern Tree Spa (Half Moon Resort, tel. 876/953-2211, www.halfmoon.com) is at the center of one of Montego Bay's most luxurious resorts, offering body treatments, therapeutic massage, facials, and salon services (from US$165). Spa appointments grant access to all spa facilities, including a steam room, sauna, terraced plunge pools, and a larger pool in front of the relaxation room. The Ital Café at the spa serves unprocessed vegan food. **Secrets Spa by Pavona** (Secrets St. James, Freeport, tel. 876/953-6600, ext. 8203) offers facials, deep tissue and Swedish massage (US$115 for 25 minutes, US$235 for 80 minutes), aromatherapy (from US$209), body treatments that include wraps and scrubs (from US$175), manicures (from US$59), pedicures (from US$69), haircuts for him and her (from US$59), makeup (US$79), and waxing (US$55-99).

Entertainment

BARS AND CLUBS

For an early evening drink, the **Montego Bay Yacht Club** (Freeport, tel. 876/979-8038, www.mobayyachtclub.com, 10am-10pm daily) is a popular spot among the upscale crowd, especially on a Friday.

The HouseBoat Bar (Southern Cross Blvd., Freeport, tel. 876/979-8845, www.thehouseboatgrill.com, 6pm-11pm Tues.-Sun., bar from 4:30pm, happy hour 5:30pm-7pm) is also a popular early evening spot.

Hard Rock Café (Sunset Dr., Freeport, tel. 876/953-6016, info@hrcmobay.com, www.hardrock.com, 10am-11pm Sun.-Thurs., 10am-2am Fri.-Sat.) has a decent beach accessible to patrons free of charge. Beach chairs (US$8) are available for rent. The beach itself faces the open sea, but unless it's stormy, waves tend to be mild, with boulder breakwaters on either side. The massive venue is designed like a beach club, with a large pool surrounded by a deck and bars inside and out. Food selections include continental meat fare with a Jamaican twist. Think burgers, wings, ribs, and jerk chicken with sides of rice-and-peas and coleslaw.

100 (MegaMart Plaza, Catherine Hall, tel. 876/665-0008, 11am-2am daily, contact@onehundredja.com, www.onehundredja.com, US$8-23) is a gaming lounge with a restaurant and bar that hosts occasional live music and live sports. The restaurant serves hotel lobby-quality pasta alfredo, steak, salmon, curried crab, and oxtail, in addition to bar bites like samosas and wings.

A popular local bar that has a happening scene almost every night of the week is **Mobay Proper** (44 Fort St., tel. 876/940-1233, 11:30am-1am daily, US$2-15). There are a few billiard tables and gaming machines, with indoor and outdoor seating areas serving local fare like oxtail, stew pork, curry goat, fried chicken, escoveitch, steam fish, and smoked pork.

Musiq (72 Jimmy Cliff Blvd., 4pm-1am daily) features an in-house DJ Thursday-Sunday playing R&B, hip-hop, reggae, and dancehall. A chic setting with musical motif lends itself to chilling out and watching passersby along the Hip Strip.

D'Rehab Lounge, Sports Bar & Pool Hall (32 Jimmy Cliff Blvd., tel. 876/620-9826, 5pm-2am daily) has a handful of billiard tables (US$0.50 per game) and two bars, and often hosts parties. The lounge only charges a cover (US$5-10) when hosting a party.

Recently renovated **Coral Cliff Gaming + Entertainment** (165 Jimmy Cliff Blvd., tel. 876/979-8149, www.coralcliff.com, US$9-22) has a ground-floor video arcade, a second-floor gaming lounge, a restaurant specializing in chicken dishes (try the honey butter), and a bar with a small stage for live music (9pm Wed.-Sun.). A sky bridge leads to Margaritaville.

Wildly popular restaurant and bar **Margaritaville** (Jimmy Cliff Blvd., tel.

876/952-4777, restaurant 10am-10pm daily, club until 2am Sun.-Wed., 4am Thurs., and 5am Fri., cover US$10) has a waterslide dropping off into the sea and giant trampoline inner tubes just offshore for patrons' enjoyment. The restaurant serves cheeseburgers, jerk chicken and pork, and lobster (US$10-35). The large open area on the ground level serves as Montego Bay's go-to nightclub, drawing crowds, especially on Saturday. Margaritaville has other locations in Ocho Rios, Negril, and the departure terminal at Sangster International Airport.

Blue Beat (Jimmy Cliff Blvd., tel. 876/952-4777, 6pm-2am daily, no cover) is Margaritaville's more sophisticated and upscale cousin, located in an adjacent building under the same ownership. The laid-back club features a resident DJ every night and live jazz (10pm-2am Wed.-Thurs. and Sun.).

Island Strains (Casa Blanca, Jimmy Cliff Blvd., tel. 876/418-7656, islandstrains@gmail.com, www.islandstrains.com) is a waterfront medical marijuana dispensary located next to Blue Beat that hosts occasional live music events.

Hilites Sky Bar and Grill (19 Queens Dr., tel. 876/775-3152, jamaica_flamingo_ltd@hotmail.com, 8:30am-6pm daily) has a great view over the harbor and airport from its perch on Top Road and is a good spot for an early evening drink or to watch the planes take off from the airport.

Facebaar (1139 Morgan Rd., Triangle Mall, Ironshore, cell tel. 876/496-1525, 5pm-midnight Sun.-Thurs., 8pm-2am Fri.-Sat., US$5) attracts a wide range of guests with three dance floors and VIP space, with an R&B and hip-hop vibe out front. Ladies Night is on Thursday; Latin night on Saturday.

LIVE MUSIC

The live music scene in Mobay is experiencing a revival, with several venues outside the all-inclusive hotels showcasing live music on a regular basis. **Coral Cliff,** a massive two-story video arcade and gaming lounge across from Margaritaville on the Hip Strip, has live music Wednesday-Sunday in the upstairs restaurant. Hard Rock Café features live performances on Saturday. When major acts are in town for one-off shows, they typically use the grounds of Pier 1.

Live jazz is performed on occasion at **Day-O Plantation,** as well as at **Blue Beat,** next to Margaritaville. For world-class music, the best time to visit is during Reggae Sumfest in mid-July. **Catherine Hall Entertainment**

the "Grammy Kid" Damian Marley at Reggae Sumfest 2018

Complex (Howard Cooke Blvd.), the main venue for the live performances at Sumfest, occasionally hosts other concerts and festivals.

FESTIVALS AND EVENTS

★ Reggae Sumfest

Organizers aren't being presumptuous when they claim **Reggae Sumfest** (www.reggae-sumfest.com) is the greatest reggae show on earth. Held over two nights in mid-July, with preceding events starting the prior weekend, live performances kick off on Friday for Dancehall Night (US$60, US$90 VIP, US$130 ultra VIP), featuring Jamaica's top acts of the moment and stalwarts of the genre, from Sizzla Kalonji to Rygin King and Popcaan. International Night (US$65-130) follows, with the more established acts on Saturday, including the like of Damian "Jr. Gong" Marley, Maxi Priest, and Beres Hammond. The performances typically start around 9pm and run well past daylight the next morning. Crowds pack Catherine Hall Entertainment Centre, a large open-air venue with VIP booths and smaller stages that erupt during set changes with dance shows and smaller live acts.

Other events in the lead-up to the live performances include Colorfest at Tropical Bliss Beach (US$35) on the preceding Sunday, a street dance on the Hip Strip on Monday (free), the All White Party (US$35) at Pier 1, the All Black Edition (US$70) at Hard Rock Café, and World Clash (US$45) on Thursday, back at the grounds of Pier 1, where rival sound systems from Jamaica and abroad duke it out. Tickets are slightly cheaper in advance than at the gate, and the season pass provides access to all the events throughout the week. Tickets are also sold at the entrance to each event.

The **Montego Bay Yacht Club** (tel. 876/979-8038, mbyc@cwjamaica.com,

www.mobayyachtclub.com) has its share of events, including three regattas: the Jamaica International Regatta held the first week in December, the Easter Regatta, and the All-Comers Regatta. The biannual Pineapple Cup is held every other February, and the Marlin Tournament is each October.

Trelawny Yam Festival (www.stea.net) is a highlight of the year, held around Easter in Albert Town, Trelawny. It's a family-friendly fun day centered on one of the island's most important staple foods, with tugs-of-war, beauty competitions, and, of course, music.

THEATER

Fairfield Theatre (Fairfield Rd., contact Inlen Johnson, cell tel. 876/384-5299 or 876/813-2057, US$15, students US$10) is the only venue in the Mobay area for theatrical productions that strive to professional standards. Performances run seasonally (June-Aug., Nov.-Jan., Feb.-Apr.), typically at 8pm Friday-Saturday and 7pm Sunday. The theater features traditional Jamaican roots plays and other family-friendly genres. The Montego Bay Little Theatre Movement sprang from the Little Theatre Movement in Kingston, formed by Jamaican cultural icons, among them Louise Bennett and Paul Methuen.

The theater performs contemporary works from leading Jamaican and Caribbean playwrights as well as classics by Shakespeare, Noël Coward, Peter Schaefer, Lorraine Hansberry, and Neil Simon. Caribbean writers such as Derek Walcott, Errol Hill, and Douglas Archibald have been produced to critical acclaim, but greater audience appeal has been found with the current crop of Jamaican playwrights that includes Basil Dawkins, Trevor Rhone, Patrick Brown, David Heron, and more recently, David Tulloch.

Shopping

Montego Bay's shopping scene is either geared toward the tourist market, with myriad souvenir shops selling generic trinkets and a slew of duty-free jewelry and watch outlets, or, in shops concentrated downtown, toward the local market, where authentic brand-name apparel and shoes are often crowded out by cheap knock-offs. The city isn't known as a production center for any products per se, but if you look hard enough, you'll find an array of authentic crafts made in Jamaica and worthy of carrying home. If not, there's always rum and coffee.

ARTS AND CRAFTS

Visiting Mobay's open-air markets requires a strong constitution, haggling skills, and a watchful eye. While these markets are heavily trafficked and generally safe, it's best to carry only the cash you intend to spend and keep your wits about you.

Wedged between Market Street, Howard Cooke Highway, and Harbour Street is **Harbour Street Craft and Cultural Village,** the largest craft market in the city and the place to go to find carvings and paintings, among other souvenirs. Market Street dead-ends one block east of the craft market at the Montego Bay Civic Centre, before beginning again on the opposite side of Sam Sharpe Square.

Mobay's largest open-air market is **Charles Gordon Market,** on Fustic Road 100 meters (110 yards) east of Lower Bevin Avenue. A bona fide cultural experience, it has stalls upon stalls of vegetable and fruit vendors and pushcarts overflowing with yams and dasheen (taro). Makeshift storefronts built of little more than a few sticks covered in blue tarpaulin spill out onto Fustic Road, along with that heady mix of pungent ripeness found only in Jamaica.

The Gallery of West Indian Art (Catherine Hall, 11 Fairfield Rd., tel. 876/952-4547, cell tel. 876/871-8103, nikola@cwjamaica.com, www.galleryofwestindianart.com, 10am-5pm Mon.-Fri.) is one of the most diverse galleries in Jamaica, featuring a curated collection of Jamaican art and pieces from neighboring islands, especially Haiti and Cuba. Look for work by Jamaican artists Delores Anglin and the late Gene Pearson, a renowned sculptor who specialized in magnificent bronze heads.

SHOES AND APPAREL

Schatzie (shop 7, next to Old Joe, Fairview, cell tel. 876/383-0992, katrin@schatzie-ltd.com, www.wrightinstyle.com, 10am-6pm Mon.-Sat.) retails linen and cotton resort wear (US$40-200).

Leroy Thompson (cell tel. 876/386-7718) is the head craftsman at **Klass Traders** (44 Fort St., tel. 876/952-5782) and produces attractive handmade leather sandals from a workshop adjacent to Mobay Proper.

Lloyd's (26 St. James St., tel. 876/952-3172; shops 24-25, Fairview Shopping Centre, tel. 876/979-8320) has a great selection of trendy urban and roots wear.

David & Subs Outfitters (Whitter Village, tel. 876/953-9386, 10am-8pm Mon.-Thurs., 10am-9pm Fri.-Sat., 1pm-4pm Sun.) is a local favorite apparel retailer selling trendy casual and formal clothing with name brands like American Eagle, Calvin Klein, Armani, Old Navy, and Gucci.

JEWELRY AND WATCHES

The Shoppes at Rose Hall (tel. 876/953-3245, www.theshoppesatrosehall.com) is a complex located across from the Montego Bay Convention Centre that is home to a few dozen duty-free stores selling jewelry and watches as well as boutiques with apparel, cigars, and sunglasses. You won't find much that's made in Jamaica, but if you're in the market for a brand name watch duty-free, you'll find

plenty of options: **Bijoux Jewelers** (shop 4, tel. 876/953-9530) boasts being the oldest duty-free jewelry store on the island. It carries a few dozen renowned brands of watches and jewelry. **Jewels in Paradise** (shop 26, tel. 876/953-9372 or 305/735-3076, www.jewelsinparadise.com, 9am-5pm Mon.-Sat.) carries high-end jewelry and watches.

BOOKS

Sangster's Book Stores sells all kinds of books and magazines and has two locations in Montego Bay: 2 St. James Street (tel. 876/952-0319, 8:30am-6pm Mon.-Sat.), and 9 King Street (tel. 876/979-2134, 8:30am-5:30pm Mon.-Sat.).

MUSIC

Tuff Gong Trading (commercial concourse of the departures terminal at Sangster International Airport, tel. 876/953-4409) has a decent selection of reggae CDs in addition to official Marley apparel and paraphernalia.

Food

Mobay has a smattering of great restaurants, from mouthwatering jerk pits and barbecue joints to a few venues that easily fall within the fine-dining category.

JAMAICAN

★ **Pier 1 on the Waterfront** (Howard Cooke Blvd., tel. 876/952-2452, info@pieronejamaica.com, www.pieronejamaica.com, 11am-11pm Mon.-Thurs. and Sat., 11am-4am Fri., noon-midnight Sun.) is a popular restaurant and entertainment venue. Seafood all day Sunday offers shrimp specials, discounts on beer, and a retro DJ. Pier 1 hosts the Pier Pressure party until 4am Friday, Star Struck Wednesday, a fashion and talent show, and occasional large events. Appetizers include crunchy conch (US$5), chicken wings (US$8), and shrimp cocktail (US$10), while entrées include chicken and mushrooms (US$12), bracelet steak (US$25), whole snapper (US$16 per pound), and lobster (US$28).

★ **Steakhouse on the Bay** (Montego Bay Yacht Club, Freeport, tel. 876/979-8038, 10am-10pm daily, US$6-25) offers a range from burgers, sandwiches, and salads to entrées like lobster and shrimp thermidor, snapper, lamb chops, seafood pasta, coconut curry chicken, zucchini pasta, and the best steak in Montego Bay. A popular buffet dinner (US$14) with a rotating menu is served on Friday.

Mobay Proper (44 Fort St., tel. 876/940-1233, 11:30am-midnight daily, US$5-15) is the in spot for Mobay's party-hearty youth. The food is a good value, with dishes like fried or curried chicken, fish done to order, steamed, escoveitch, brown stew, or curried. This is a good place to get a beer (US$2) and play some billiards (US$1 per game).

Sweet Spice (shop 3, Westgate Shopping Centre, tel. 876/952-3199, 8:30am-9pm Mon.-Sat., 8:30am-6pm Sun.) serves Jamaican breakfast dishes like callaloo and codfish, ackee and saltfish, kidney and onion, and brown stew chicken. The lunch menu includes items from curry goat to escoveitch fish.

Get Jamaican staples like fried chicken, curry goat, and oxtail buffet-style as well as shrimp, lobster, conch, and veggie chunks to order at **Nyam 'n' Jam** (shop 28, City Centre Bldg., tel. 876/971-1181, cell tel. 876/829-8373, 7am-midnight daily; 17 Harbour St., tel. 876/952-1922, 7am-11pm daily, US$3-10). Breakfast items include ackee and saltfish, callaloo and saltfish, brown stew chicken, yam, boiled bananas, and fried dumpling.

Find Jamaican specialties like stew pork,

1: Reggae star Capleton **2:** The Gallery of West Indian Art **3:** Pablo Plummer at Falmouth Jerk Center and Ganja Bar curried goat, oxtail, baked chicken, fresh whole fish, fillet fish, conch, and shrimp at **Martina's** (1 Howard Cook Blvd., tel. 876/953-6557, cell tel. 876/784-1687, cell tel. 876/856-3086, msaunders06@yahoo.com, 11am-midnight Mon.-Sat., 1pm-11pm Sun., US$6-30). Guest DJs spin (4pm-midnight Fri.-Sun.), and an ice cream shop (1pm-10pm daily) on the property sells Devon House ice cream in cones and cups (US$3-4). Patrons can also access a plant nursery, an aviary, and a playground with a swing set, a slide, and a seesaw.

The Sand Bar (Doctors Cave Beach, tel. 876/631-4952 or 9am-6pm daily, US$10-35) is popular with locals and visitors alike. It serves a wide range of bar food alongside Jamaican staples liked steamed or escoveitch fish with bammy, jerk chicken and pork, curried shrimp and lobster tail. Lighter fare includes pulled pork, chicken, and fish sandwiches. The restaurant's location on Doctors Cave Beach is unbeatable. The restaurant hosts a monthly "We Are Reggae" series on the last Saturday of each month. Doors open at 9pm, performances start at 10pm, and the venue closes at 1am.

Usain Bolt's Tracks and Records (St. James Plaza, 7 Jimmy Cliff Blvd., tel. 876/971-0000, www.tracksandrecords.com, 11:30am-midnight daily, US$10-40) offers a Jamaican sports bar concept, boasting "lunch in 9.58 minutes, or it's free." The restaurant serves bar food with a Jamaican slant and locally inspired entrées like escoveitch fish, curried mutton served in a crock pot, fried chicken, and jerk pork, in addition to international comfort food like pizza, quesadillas, pasta dishes, wings, and burgers.

JERK

Local bar and kitchen ★ **Smokeez by the Sea** (cell tel. 876/368-4669, 11am-11pm daily) is along the waterfront in Ironshore, specializing in roast conch, steam fish, jerk chicken, and pork with sides that include festival, yam, and boiled green banana (US$6-15). Those who happen by find down-to-earth Jamaican

hospitality, where strangers have been known to buy strangers a drink and time slows down enough to enjoy some old school reggae and honest conversation with newfound friends.

Consistently preparing the best jerk pork and chicken in Jamaica, ★ **Scotchies** (Carol Gardens, tel. 876/953-3301, 11am-11pm daily, US$4-11) also serves steam roast fish fillets, chicken sausage, pork sausage, and a soup of the day. Sides include breadfruit, festival, sweet potato, and yam. The legendary jerk pit was founded after Tony Rerrie began occasionally bringing a master jerk chef from Boston Bay in Portland, where locals claim jerk originated. Fans begged him to make the jerk offering a regular thing, and Scotchies was born when Tony pieced together a few cinder blocks, some bamboo poles, and a few sheets of zinc roofing. The minimalist ambiance remained true to its origins, as the jerk joint grew with franchises in Ochi and Kingston.

The Pork Pit (27 Jimmy Cliff Blvd., tel. 876/940-3008, 11am-11pm Sun.-Thurs., 11am-midnight Fri.-Sat., US$5-12) is Mobay's original jerk joint, serving mouthwatering jerk chicken, shrimp jerk pork, and ribs, with sides of festival, rice-and-peas, fries, bammy, and sweet potato. **Jerky's** (29 Alice Eldemire Dr., tel. 876/684-9101, 11am-midnight Sun.-Fri., 11am-late Sat. for karaoke, US$3-10) has jerk chicken, steamed fish, escoveitch fish, ribs, conch, shrimp, and fried fish. There is a large bar where beer costs US$2.50.

MVP Smokehouse (Bogue Rd., Reading, tel. 876/622-7198, info@mvpsmokehouse. com, www.mvpsmokehouse.com, noon-9pm Tues.-Thurs., noon-10pm Fri.-Sun., US$5-25) specializes in smoked meats and seafood with creative twists that go beyond jerk. Weekly specials include stew peas and pig's tail on Tuesday, curry chicken roti on Wednesday, and conch prepared your way on Friday. Oldies blast 3pm-close Sunday. It's a dependable option for an affordable rack of ribs, but the jerk chicken can be hit or miss. Sides include mac and cheese, bammy, and festival.

BREAKFAST AND CAFÉS

One of the few places outside the hotels where you can find a satisfying continental breakfast, ★ **Café Mocha** (shop 13, the Shops at Bay Harbour, Jimmy Cliff Blvd., next to Burger King, cell tel. 876/433-8848, 7:30am-10pm daily) serves a selection of hot and cold beverages, breakfast, and sandwiches.

Café Blue (www.jamaicacafeblue.com) has three locations in Montego Bay, at Rose Hall (shop 28, Shoppes at Rose Hall, tel. 876/953-4646, cafebluerosehall@coffeetradersjamaica.com, 9am-5pm Mon.-Sat.); inside Fontana Pharmacy (Fairview, tel. 876/622-9849); and at Sangster International Airport, all serving coffee and tea and light savory dishes and pastries. Try the Blue Mountain Fog iced coffee and smoked marlin sandwich.

INTERNATIONAL

Debut (shop 15, Bay Harbour, Jimmy Cliff Blvd., tel. 876/971-6566, 11am-10pm daily, US$3-15) serves brick oven pies in a pleasant interior pizza parlor-style dining area or alfresco on the balcony. Traditional Jamaican breakfast items are on offer in the late morning, including peanut porridge, ackee, and saltfish in addition to scrambled egg burritos and ham, or lox eggs benedict. Lunch and dinner fare includes chicken and shrimp skewers and fried calamari.

Some of Montego Bay's best Chinese food and great-value buffet combo lunch specials (US$5) are at **King Palace Chinese Restaurant** (shop 62, City Centre, Alice Eldemire Dr., Bogue, tel. 876/940-2104, 11:30am-9:30pm Mon.-Sat., 1pm-9:30pm Sun., US$9-15).

Dragon Court (Fairview Shopping Center, Alice Eldemire Dr., Bogue, tel. 876/979-8822 or 876/979-8824, 11:30am-10pm Mon.-Sat., US$5-18) has good dim sum every day. The shrimp dumplings are a favorite.

China House Restaurant (32 Jimmy Cliff Blvd., tel. 876/979-0056, 10am-10pm daily, US$3-23) serves Chinese, Mongolian, Thai, and Jamaican cuisine, as does its neighbor, **Golden Dynasty Chinese Restaurant** (39

Jimmy Cliff Blvd., tel. 876/971-0459, 11am-10pm Mon.-Sat., noon-10pm Sun., US$2-20). China House serves dim sum on Sunday.

Authentic Indian dishes in an atmosphere as transporting as the flavors are at **Mystic India Restaurant** (shop 13, Whitter Shopping Village, tel. 876/953-9460 or 876/630-4043, 11am-10pm daily, US$15-35). The soft color palette juxtaposes with mouthwatering dishes that would be just as convincing in Delhi or New York. *Pakodas*, risotto infused with cardamom, and a wide variety of curried vegetables, chicken, mutton, and shrimp dishes will leave even the most demanding palate satisfied.

From the same owners as Mystic India, ★ **Mystic Thai** (unit B11, Fairview Town Centre, tel. 876/633-6535, noon-9:45pm daily, US$10-25) takes care with the food's presentation and with the delectable fusion of fresh aromatic flavors from basil, lemongrass, spicy chili paste, and tangy dips. Staples like pad thai (US$10-14) are complemented with more adventurous entrées like the maple chili pork ribs with wilted spinach and kidney bean mash. A foray into Japanese cuisine fills a gap in Mobay's culinary scene with rolls, sushi, and tempura.

FINE DINING

On Montego Bay's Bogue Lagoon, ★ **The HouseBoat Grill** (Southern Cross Blvd., Freeport, tel. 876/979-8845, houseboat@cw-jamaica.com, www.thehouseboatgrill.com, 6pm-11pm Tues.-Sun., bar from 4:30pm, happy hour 5:30pm-7pm, US$12-38) is an unparalleled setting for a romantic dinner with vistas in every direction. Splurge for the signature surf and turf with garlic-butter lobster pulled live from a tank in the boat's hull, served alongside beef tenderloin. Other highlights include the peel-and-eat shrimp with scotch bonnet beurre blanc and char-grilled octopus. Reservations are recommended.

★ **The Sugar Mill Restaurant** (across the highway from Half Moon Shopping Village, tel. 876/953-2314 or 876/953-2228, 6pm-10pm daily) is one of the area's high-end establishments, specializing in Caribbean fusion cuisine with openers like pumpkin or conch soup (US$10), spring rolls, smoked marlin or conch in fritters, salad, or jerked (US$13-15). Entrées range from coconut-crusted or escoveitch fish to lobster tail (US$35-50).

Marguerite's (Jimmy Cliff Blvd., adjacent to Margaritaville, tel. 876/952-4777, 6pm-10:30pm daily, US$20-50) is the fine-dining wing of Mobay's popular Margaritaville, serving dishes ranging from Caribbean-style chicken to seafood penne and sugarcane-seared drunken lobster tail.

A favorite for weddings and other events that require the finest setting around a gorgeous pool, **Day-O Plantation** (Fairfield Rd., tel. 876/952-1825, cell tel. 876/877-1884, dayorest@yahoo.com, info@dayoplantationja.com, www.dayoplantationja.com, US$5-35, lunch by reservation, dinner 6pm-11pm Tues.-Sun.) was formerly part of the Fairfield Estate, which at one time encompassed much of Mobay. It is perhaps the most laid-back and classy place to enjoy a delicious dinner. Entrées range from typical chicken dishes (US$25) to grilled spiny lobster (US$40). A beer costs US$5. On a good day owner Paul will bring out his guitar and impress diners with his talent. Other professional musicians who have played at the restaurant's dinner shows include guitar legend Ernest Ranglin, jazz artist Martin Hand, and steel pan artist Othello Molineaux.

The Pelican Grill (Jimmy Cliff Blvd., tel. 876/952-3171, pelican@cwjamaica.com, www.pelicangrillja.com, 7am-10:30pm daily, US$10-40) is a Mobay institution serving a mix of local and international dishes, including Jamaican favorites like stewed peas (US$10), curry goat (US$15), steamed or brown stew fish (US$15), and lobster (US$45). It's Jamaica's answer to comfort food in the kind of casual, homely environment sitcoms are made of. International staples like cordon bleu (US$20) and hamburgers (US$12) match booths reminiscent of a 1980s diner. The milk shakes are a draw for locals and visitors alike.

VEGETARIAN

Chabad Kosher Hot Spot (shop 1, Shops at Bay Harbour, 1-3 Jimmy Cliff Blvd., tel. 876/894-6323, 11am-7pm Mon.-Thurs., 10am-8:30pm Fri., 10am-2:30pm Sat., 11am-8:30pm Sun.) serves falafel in pita or as a salad as well as pastries. Shop and restaurant **Adwa Nutrition for Life** (shop 2, West Gate Plaza, tel. 876/952-6554, US$4-10) is the best place in town for natural vegetarian food. The store sells nutritional supplements, books, juices, and vegan food. Dishes include curried tofu, peppered veggie steak, and red pea soup, with beverages like cane juice, fruit smoothies, and carrot juice. **Wright Life** (Fairview Town Centre, cell tel. 876/376-8708, 10am-6pm Mon.-Sat., US$5-15) is an eatery serving salads, juices, and natural products in an impeccably clean minimalist restaurant beside Fontana pharmacy.

SWEET SPOTS

Devon House I Scream (shop 7, Bay West Centre, tel. 876/940-4060, 10am-8pm daily) serves Jamaica's signature ice cream, produced at Devon House in Kingston. **Martina's** (1 Howard Cook Blvd., tel. 876/953-6557, cell tel. 876/784-1687, cell tel. 876/856-3086) has an ice cream shop (1pm-10pm daily) selling Devon House ice cream in cones and cups (US$3-4).

1: Scotchies, a popular jerk pit in Montego Bay **2:** surf and turf at the Houseboat Grill **3:** Steakhouse on the Bay

Accommodations

Options range widely, with cheap dives, mid-range B&Bs, guesthouses, luxury villas, world-class hotels, and all-inclusive resorts. In the center of town, on Queens Drive (Top Rd.), and to the west in Reading are several low-cost options, while the mid-range hotels are concentrated around the Hip Strip along Jimmy Cliff Boulevard (a.k.a. Bottom Rd.) and just east of the airport. Rose Hall is the area's most glamorous address, with several resorts in the vicinity of the city's top-notch golf courses. Also on the eastern side of town is Sandals Royal Caribbean, easily the chain's most luxurious property, complete with a private island. Along the Hip Strip, several mid-range hotels provide direct access to Mobay's nightlife, a mix of bars and a few clubs. Guesthouses farther afield offer great rates.

Mobay is the principal entry point for most travelers arriving on the island, many of whom stay at one of the many hotels in and around the city. The old Ironshore and Rose Hall estates, east along the coast, are covered in luxury and mid-range hotels.

UNDER US$100

Palm Bay Guest House & Restaurant (Reading Rd., Bogue, tel. 876/952-2274, www. palmbayguesthouse.com) has basic, clean rooms (from US$65) with air-conditioning and hot water in private baths. It is not the most glamorous location in town, opposite Mobay's biggest government housing project, Bogue Village, built to formalize the squatters of Canterbury, but Palm Bay is quiet, safe, and removed from the bustle along the Hip Strip. A restaurant (7am-10pm daily, US$8-20) on premises specializes in jerk, and Wi-Fi reaches most of the rooms.

US$100-250

Deja Resort (92 Jimmy Cliff Blvd., tel. 876/940-4173 or 876/971-5543, www.dejaresort.com, from US$168 low season, US$195 d

high season, all-inclusive) is a 93-room hotel at the heart of Montego Bay's Hip Strip directly across from Doctors Cave Beach, where guests have access included. Step outside for easy access to the beach, bars, and restaurants and a quick taxi ride to anything Montego Bay has to offer. Rooms are equipped with flat-panel TVs, air-conditioning, safes, irons, and either two double beds or one king bed; rooms with king beds feature private balconies.

With a total of 10 rooms in two villas on opposite sides of the road, ★ **Polkerris Bed & Breakfast** (13 Corniche Rd., tel. 876/877-7784, www.polvista.com, from US$134) has king, queen, or two doubles in each room, all with en suite baths, air-conditioning, and flat-screen TVs. Hidden on a quiet residential street, the villas seem far from the bustle of the Hip Strip but are only a five-minute walk away, striking the perfect balance between seclusion and proximity.

A bed-and-breakfast at the highest point in downtown Mobay, **Richmond Hill Inn** (tel. 876/952-3859, www.richmond-hill-inn.com, from US$153) has the best view in town from the large terraced swimming pool area. While the rooms fall short of luxurious, the sheets are clean, and the unmatched view and free Wi-Fi make Richmond Hill a decent value.

Facing the protected marine sanctuary Bogue Lagoon, ★ **Wharf House** (Bogue Rd., Reading, contact Nicky, cell tel. 876/839-9001, or Stefan, tel. 876/871-8103, tarah@cw-jamaica.com or prohaska@cwjamaica.com, rooms US$170, whole house US$640 for up to 8 guests bed-and-breakfast, add US$60 per day for a private chef) is an impeccable 300-plus-year-old collection of stone-hewn buildings. Gun slits in the 45-centimeter (18-inch) walls were once used to protect the sugar and rum warehoused here. The property has been remodeled into a rustic luxury lodging with a TV and sound system in the central living room and Wi-Fi throughout.

Bedrooms have air-conditioning, and common areas have plush inviting furniture and delightful artwork from across the Caribbean. Meals can be enjoyed on the large deck overhanging the water or in the formal dining room. A tiled pool is set back from the lawn and beach. Guests typically advise the owners of their food preferences or shop themselves to provide ingredients for the chef to prepare. The kitchen is reserved for staff use.

A 125-room boutique hotel is ★ **S Hotel Jamaica** (7 Jimmy Cliff Blvd., tel. 876/979-0000, reservations@shoteljamaica.com, www.shoteljamaica.com, rooms from US$209 d), built from the dilapidated shell of the old Superclubs Montego Bay into a gleaming resort that couples rootsy Jamaican culture with high-class sophistication. A swanky pool sits on an elevated deck between the rooms and the beach. Amenities include air-conditioning, ceiling fans, safes, big plasma TVs, USB outlets, mini fridges, Wi-Fi, a functional workspace, and Bluetooth speakers. Spa Suites have large showers and balconies overlooking Doctors Cave Beach. Two twins combine to make a king bed in the Essential City View rooms, while Deluxe rooms offer two doubles or a king. The Junior Suites have a king and a pull-out twin sofa bed. Spa suites

have 50 square meters (540 square feet) of living space, tall ceilings, views of the sea and coastline, and oversize baths with free-standing soaking tubs. The 93-square-meter (1,000-square-foot) Signature Sky Suite takes luxury through the roof, with a 6-meter (20-foot) ceiling, a fully equipped kitchen, and a loft bedroom with a king bed. The sky deck offers the best view, with its glass-walled pool and bar. The hotel has two restaurants and several bars.

OVER US$250

One of the more upscale resorts in Jamaica, ★ **Half Moon Resort** (Rose Hall, tel. 876/953-2211, reservations@halfmoonclub.com, www.halfmoon.com, US$250-1,250 low season, US$400-1,800 high season) is an assortment of rooms, cottages, and villas with private pools. Set on a 162-hectare (400-acre) estate, the resort has 33 staffed villas with 3-7 bedrooms, 152 suites, and 46 hotel rooms; an expansion added a new restaurant. The cottages are tastefully furnished and cozier than the villas, which can feel cavernous due to their immense size and vary considerably in decor, based on the taste of their individual owners.

Half Moon attracts golfers to its

Wharf House on Bogue Lagoon

championship par-72 Robert Trent Jones Sr. course and tennis players to its 13 lighted courts. A range of water sports includes a dolphin lagoon. Seagrapes is the main restaurant on the property, located off the lobby adjacent to Il Giardino's, an Italian restaurant, and a jerk shack on the beach. Other dining options include the Ital Café at the spa and The Sugar Mill Restaurant, across the road by the golf club. Also on the resort is the recently renovated **Fern Tree Spa,** among the best in the Caribbean. The crescent-shaped Half Moon Beach is one of the finest private beaches in the Mobay area, for exclusive use by Half Moon guests.

ALL-INCLUSIVE RESORTS

Zoetry Montego Bay (Rose Hall, tel. 876/953-9150, www.zoetryresorts.com, from US$400) is a 46-room, five-star, all-inclusive boutique property on a private white-sand beach 10 minutes east of the airport. The hotel has three seafront à la carte restaurants, a tapas bar, and unlimited top-shelf spirits. Zoetry features swim-out pools from ground-level rooms, a wrap-around infinity pool, and a 230-square-meter (2,500-square-foot) spa with plunge pools.

A budget-minded all-inclusive resort, **Royal DeCameron Montego Beach** (2 Jimmy Cliff Blvd., tel. 876/952-4340 or 876/952-4346, ventas.jam@decameron.com, www.decameron.com, US$116 low season, US$240 high season) is the chain's second property in Jamaica.

Next to one another on the southwestern tip of the Freeport peninsula, **Secrets St. James** and **Secrets Wild Orchid** (tel. 876/953-6600, reservations.sesmb@secretsresorts.com, www.secretsresorts.com, from US$188 pp low season, US$326 pp high season) have a combined 700 suites, all with a similar layout, with whirlpool tubs and either a balcony or a patio. The food is on par with the better mid-range all-inclusive resorts, with a varied breakfast buffet spread and

dining options showcasing French, Italian, and Japanese cuisines.

Breathless Montego Bay Resort & Spa (Sunset Dr., Freeport, tel. 876/953-6600, info@breathlessresorts.com, www.breathlessresorts.com, US$460-700) is adults-only and geared toward a younger set, with modern design, tablets for ordering from the rooms, and a rooftop pool and bar. The Breathless format touts a combination of luxurious relaxation and excitement, while access to restaurants, bars, and beaches at the adjoining all-inclusive resorts greatly expands the options for dining and offers a change of scene.

Sunscape Splash Montego Bay (tel. 876/979-8800, www.sunscaperesorts.com, from US$280 low season, US$365 high season) has a casual, family-friendly atmosphere with tennis courts, a water park, and a private beach. The 430-room resort is located in Freeport, facing west. Rooms are divided between a main building and smaller structures on the opposite side of a large pool area and face out to sea or toward central Montego Bay. Unlimited food, along with local and international beverages, is available 24 hours a day in several restaurants and bars across the property. The hotel is about 10 minutes by cab to the Hip Strip or central Montego Bay.

The most opulent Sandals hotel in Montego Bay, ★ **Sandals Royal Caribbean** (Mahoe Bay, Ironshore, tel. 876/953-2231, srjmail@grp.sandals.com, 3-night minimum, from US$473 d) has 197 rooms and suites well deserving of the chain's "Luxury Included" motto. The suites are over-the-top, with wood paneling, large flat-screen TVs, and tiled baths with standing showers and tubs. Balconies look over the courtyard and out to sea, with steps off ground-floor suites leading directly into a large pool. The private island at Sandals Royal Caribbean is the trademark feature, where boats shuttle guests out for dinner or to laze on the fine-sand beach. Five over-the-water villas (from US$2,938 d) have king beds, tubs, glass floors, and infinity pools for two on large private balconies.

In Ironshore, near the end of the

airport runway, next door to Sandals Royal Caribbean, **Riu Montego Bay** (tel. 876/940-8010, www.riu.com, US$115-160) is a 680-room all-inclusive resort with standard double and suite rooms and an immense swimming pool. Suites have hydro-massage tubs and lounge areas. All rooms have a minibar, satellite TV, air-conditioning, balconies, and en suite baths. The resort offers a host of activities, including water sports and tennis on two hard-surface courts. The gym has a weight room, a sauna, and a whirlpool tub.

Hyatt Ziva Rose Hall (U.S. tel. 888/763-3901, tel. 876/618-1234, www.rosehall.ziva.hyatt.com, US$830-970 d) is a 387-room all-inclusive resort catering to families. The best rooms are at ground level, with swim-out pools. Food options include buffet and à la carte restaurants: Di Roza serves pizzas from a wood-fired oven, and Fuzion is an Asian-style restaurant with a chef station as its centerpiece doing noodles in a wok. Calypzo is a beachfront grill, and other options include a deli, a grill, and an English pub. An enormous pool with two hot tubs is in the expansive courtyard facing the beach. **Hyatt Zilara** (US$886-1,060 d, www.rosehall.zilara.hyatt.com) is a 234-room resort adjoining the Hyatt Ziva catering to couples only. The hotel also features swim-up pools in some ground floor suites and two lighted tennis courts that are shared with guests of Hyatt Ziva.

Jewel Grande Montego Bay Resort & Spa (Rose Hall, from US$350 d low season, US$470 d high season, www.jewelgrande.com) is a waterfront complex with two massive towers originally built as condominiums. The spacious one- to three-bedroom suites and villas have a view of either the sea or the hills. The property has four restaurants as well as a café and juice bar.

Hilton Rose Hall Resort & Spa (Rose Hall, tel. 876/953-2650, U.S. tel. 800/445-8667, rosehallroomscontrol@luxuryresorts.com, www.rosehallresort.com, from US$148 pp) is a 489-room, seven-floor property that boasts sleek South Beach design. Food is excellent, with indoor and outdoor seating in

buffet and à la carte formats, and a seaside bar and grill by the Olympic-size pool in front of the hotel. The Sugar Mill Falls Water Park on the property boasts an 85-meter (280-foot) water slide for a thrilling ride on tubes, spilling into a freeform pool with a swim-up bar, a lazy river, waterfalls, and hot tubs in a lush garden setting. The beach, located below the main pool and grill area, has fine white sand along a respectable stretch of coast.

Iberostar (tel. 876/680-0000, U.S. tel. 305/774-9225, reservations@iberostar-hotel.com, www.iberostar.com) has three all-inclusive hotels in three price categories. Guests staying at the more expensive hotels can use the restaurants and facilities of the lower categories, but guests of the lower hotels are not permitted on the more expensive properties. The quality of the food varies by price point. The **Iberostar Rose Hall Beach** (from US$190 low season, US$309 high season) is a 366-room property that caters to the lower end. Standard rooms have either one or two beds and overlook the gardens; junior suites have either ocean or garden views. **Iberostar Rose Hall Suites** (from US$235 low season, US$363 high season) has 319 rooms, two pools with swim-up bars, and a lazy river meandering across the lawn. All rooms are suites with living rooms and minibars and have soaking tubs. **Iberostar Grand Rose Hall** (from US$336 low season, US$472 high season) has 295 suites, all with living areas, verandas with a swing, jetted tubs, rain showers, and minibars. The property has four pools with one swim-up bar. The food is excellent, with buffet and à la carte options, with top-of-the-line dishes like lobster and steak.

VILLAS

While not for the budget-minded traveler on a shoestring, staying in a villa can actually be quite affordable compared to mid-range resorts and the all-inclusive options when traveling as a group. On a per-person basis, staying in a villa can work out to be more affordable than booking several rooms in a hotel, even if villa rates don't include food and beverages. Many visitors who stay repeatedly at villas in Jamaica cite the familiar interaction with staff, exclusivity, and well-prepared meals as the main reasons they prefer this type of lodging. Jamaica has several discreet villa enclaves: in Portland, Discovery Bay, Runaway Bay, Mammee Bay, Ocho Rios, and Oracabessa in St. Ann and St. Mary; at Silver Sands in Trelawny; on the South Coast in Treasure Beach and Bluefields; and above all, in the west between Hanover and Montego Bay. Just a smattering are on offer in Negril.

Information and Services

BANKS AND MONEY

As elsewhere in Jamaica, the easiest way to get funds is from an ATM with your debit card. Nevertheless, you can get slightly better rates at the *cambios*, or currency trading houses, that can be found all over town. **FX Trader** is an exchange house that gives the best rates around, with locations at Hometown FSC (19 Church St.), Medi Mart (shop 1, St. James Place, Jimmy Cliff Blvd.), and Hometown Overton (shop 9, Overton Plaza, Union St.).

Global Exchange is an international currency trader that operates at Sangster International Airport. The rates are not as good as at *cambios* outside the airport, but if you need local currency on arrival and don't exchange a lot, the difference is negligible and the cost won't amount to much more than ATM fees if you're not exchanging more than US$100. It definitely beats using U.S. dollars on the streets of Jamaica, where egregious exchange rates are common.

NCB has locations at 93 Barnett Street (tel. 876/952-6539), 41 St. James Street (tel. 876/952-6540), and Harbour Street (tel. 876/952-0077), with ATMs at the airport and at the junction of Kent Avenue and Jimmy Cliff Boulevard. **Scotiabank** has an ATM along the Hip Strip on Jimmy Cliff Boulevard and branch locations at 6-7 Sam Sharpe Square (tel. 876/952-4440), 51 Barnett Street (tel. 876/952-5539), Westgate Shopping Plaza (tel. 876/952-5545), and Fairview II.

GOVERNMENT OFFICES

Jamaica Tourist Board (Montego Bay Convention Centre, tel. 876/952-4425, 8:30am-4:30pm Mon.-Fri.) has information on attractions across the region and throughout Jamaica. The JTB also has an information desk at Sangster International Airport (tel. 876/952-2462).

MEDICAL SERVICES

Hospiten Mobay Medical Center (across from Half Moon, Rose Hall, tel. 876/953-3981) is considered the best private hospital in Jamaica. **Soe-Htwe Medicare** (Jimmy Cliff Blvd., tel. 876/979-3444) is one of the best private clinics in town, centrally located on the Hip Strip next to the Pork Pit. **Fairview Medical and Dental Suite** (shop 5, Farview Office Park, tel. 876/953-6264) is a welcoming general practice.

PHARMACIES

City Centre Pharmacy (shop 30, City Centre Plaza, tel. 876/632-6918, cell tel. 876/427-2600, 9am-7pm Mon.-Fri.) is conveniently within easy walking distance of the Hip Strip and downtown Mobay. **Fontana** (Fairview Shopping Centre, tel. 876/952-3866, www.fontanapharmacy.com), the leading pharmacy chain in Jamaica, is a full-service pharmacy selling everything imaginable in addition to prescription drugs.

Transportation

AIR

Sangster International Airport (MBJ, tel. 876/952-3133, www.mbjairport.com) is the primary point of entry for most travelers to Jamaica, catering to over 4 million passengers a year. The airport is located near the Flankers district, a few minutes east of the Hip Strip and about 10 minutes from downtown and Rose Hall.

Sangster is served by most North American carriers, including American, JetBlue, Delta, United, Air Canada, Southwest, WestJet, and Spirit as well as regional operators Copa Airlines, Caribbean Airlines, Cayman Airways, InterCaribbean, and Aerogaviota. European airlines with regular service include Virgin Atlantic, Condor, and Eurowings, in addition to several charter carriers.

Most accommodations in western Jamaica offer transportation from Sangster International Airport. Knutsford Express, Jamaica's leading coach service, has several departures daily from the airport to Kingston, Ocho Rios, and Negril, among other destinations. Those with deep pockets can opt to charter small prop planes from Sangster to aerodromes across the island, including a 15-minute flight to Negril or a 30-minute flight to Boscobel, Treasure Beach, or Kingston. **InterCaribbean Airways** (U.S. tel. 888/957-3223 or 649/946-4999, res@intercaribbean.com, www.intercaribbean.com), a regional airline based in Turks and Caicos, operates the only regularly scheduled domestic flights in Jamaica in addition to flights from Providenciales to destinations in Cuba, Haiti, the Dominican Republic, and the eastern Caribbean. InterCaribbean flights for Kingston depart at 7:30am daily from the domestic terminal. To get there, take a left just inside the main entrance to the airport before reaching the gas station.

AirLink Express (Sangster International Airport, Domestic Terminal, tel. 876/940-6660, reservation@flyairlink.net, www.intlairlink.net) offers charters from its base in Montego Bay to Negril (US$350 for 2 people, US$150 pp, up to 4) and any other aerodromes on the island (US$765 for up to 4 to Boscobel/St. Mary, US$1,050 to Kington). **TimAir**

performance at Sangster International Airport

(Sangster International Airport, Domestic Terminal, tel. 876/952-2516, timair@usa.net, www.timair.net) also offers charter air taxi service to Negril (US$300 for 2, US$600 up to 4), Boscobel (US$750), and Kingston (US$1,580 for up to 4).

BUSES AND ROUTE TAXIS

Knutsford Express (tel. 876/971-1822, www.knutsfordexpress.com, 8am-10pm daily) offers bus service between its terminals at Sangster International Airport and Pier 1 in Montego Bay and Negril (1.5 hours, US$15), Ocho Rios (1.5 hours, US$15), Mandeville (3 hours, US$20), Port Antonio (5 hours, US$28), and Kingston (3.5 hours, US$25), among other routes, with onboard Wi-Fi and a lavatory. Reserve online in advance for discounted fares.

Buses and **route taxis** run between Mobay and virtually every other major town in the neighboring parishes, most notably Savanna-la-Mar, Westmoreland (1.5 hours, US$3), Hopewell, Hanover (15 minutes, US$2), Falmouth, Trelawny (US$2), and Runaway Bay in St. Ann (US$5). The bus terminal on Market Street is a dusty and bustling place where it's important to pay attention to your surroundings. Buses to any point on the island, including Kingston, never exceed US$20. Schedules are not adhered to, and buses depart as they fill up; you can generally count on a bus departing at least every 45 minutes to the more popular destinations. Get there before 7pm for routes outside the parish of St. James.

CAR RENTALS

Island Car Rentals (tel. 876/952-7225, icar@cwjamaica.com, 8:30am-10pm daily) is Jamaica's largest rental-car agency. It has an outlet in the international terminal at Sangster International Airport and offers Toyota, Mitsubishi, Nissan, and Suzuki vehicles, with sedans, SUVs, and vans at competitive rates (from US$60 per day all-inclusive).

With an office at the airport (tel. 876/952-3838, 8am-10pm daily) and in Ironshore (tel. 876/953-0534, 8am-5pm Mon.-Fri.), **Budget** (customerservice@budgetjamaica.com, www.budgetjamaica.com) offers Suzuki Swift, Mitsubishi Lancer, BMW sedan, Mitsubishi Pajero, and Toyota Hiace vehicles. A local licensee with locations at the airport, on Queens Drive, and at Fairview, **Hertz Jamaica** (Sangster International Airport, tel. 876/979-0438) has a wide range of vehicle makes and models, including Suzuki Swifts, Toyota Corollas and Camrys, BMW 3 Series, and Mercedes C-class, offering after-hours drop-off.

Enterprise (9 Queens Dr., 8am-5pm Mon.-Fri., 8am-2pm Sat.-Sun.; Sangster International Airport, 8am-10pm daily) offers intermediate-size vehicles (from US$60 per day all-inclusive), including Honda Citys, Honda Civics, and Kia Ceratos; and full-size vehicles (from US$85 all-inclusive), including Honda Accords, Kia Optimas, Honda CRVs, and Kia Sportage SUVs (from US$80). Operating from the airport, **Sixt** (tel. 876/952-1212, 8am-8pm daily, www.sixt.global) has Toyota and Mitsubishi compact cars, sedans, SUVs, and vans. The larger vehicles available from Sixt in Jamaica include the Suzuki Vitara and Mitsubishi Grandis minivan.

East of Montego Bay

East of Montego Bay, Ironshore and Rose Hall cover the coast with hotels and housing developments that range from middle-class to super-luxury before reaching Greenwood, a small community once part of the Barrett estate that borders the sea and the parish of Trelawny. The Trelawny coast has a smattering of tourism development concentrated in the area just east of Falmouth along the bay, while the inhabited parts of Trelawny's interior are covered in farming country, where yams, sugarcane, and citrus fruit are major crops. The early morning mist rises from dew-covered cane fields, making a trip through the interior from Rock in Trelawny to St. Ann a magical alternative to the coastal route at this time of day.

Three roads lead from the North Coast Highway into Falmouth: One is from the east, where the old highway used to run; another, Market Street, is a straight shot to Martha Brae; and the third, Rodney Street or Foreshore Road, runs from the west toward Mobay.

GREENWOOD
Greenwood Great House

Greenwood Great House (Greenwood, tel. 876/953-1077, greenwoodgreathouse@cwjamaica.com, www.greenwoodgreathouse.com, 9am-5pm daily, US$20) is one of the best examples of a living great house, built in the late 1600s by one of the wealthiest families of the British colonial period. The Barretts first landed in Jamaica on Cromwell's voyage of conquest, when the island was captured from the Spanish in 1655. Land grants immediately made the family a major landholder, and its plantations grew over the next 179 years to amass 2,000 enslaved people on seven estates

by the time of emancipation. Greenwood Great House boasted the best stretch of road in Jamaica as its driveway. Little upkeep has been performed over the past four centuries, apparently, and today the 1.5-kilometer (1-mile) road requires slow going, but the panoramic views from the house and grounds are still as good as ever.

Interesting relics like hand-pump fire carts and old wagon wheels adorn the outside of the building. Inside the house is one of the best collections of colonial-era antiques in Jamaica, including obscure musical instruments, Flemish thrones, and desks with secret compartments from the 17th century. An in-laid rosewood piano belonged to King Edward VII, and a portrait of poet Elizabeth Barrett Browning's cousin hangs on the wall. Another historical treasure at the great house is the will of Reverend Thomas Burchell, who was arrested for his alleged role in the Christmas Rebellion.

Greenwood Great House is unmissable from the A1 as you travel through the community of Greenwood. To get here, turn inland at the only stoplight in the area and follow the road straight up the hill. Greenwood is about 15 minutes by car or taxi due east of Rose Hall.

Greenwood Great House

Hampden Sugar Estate

Hampden Sugar Estate (Wakefield, tel. 876/482-4632, tours@hampdenrumcompany.com, www.hampdenrumcompany.com, tours 10am and 11am Mon.-Fri., US$50), a historic sugarcane plantation and rum distillery dating to 1753, offers two-hour tours for between 2 and 20 guests, where visitors learn about the distillation process and Jamaica's history with sugar and rum. Hampden produces its Rum Fire white rum for the local market and Hapdem Gold for export, both offered for tasting on the tour, along with lunch of jerk chicken or pork (or quiche for vegetarians). Be sure to wear enclosed footwear, a requirement at the working distillery.

Food

A popular waterfront watering hole and seafood joint serving steam, fried, escoveitch snapper and garlic butter, jerk or thermidor lobster, **Chill-Out Hut** (Greenwood, tel. 876/620-8720, 10am-11pm daily, US$7-38) also serves oxtail, curried goat, fried chicken, wings, jerk chicken, spare ribs, pizzas, and pastas. **Far Out Fish Hut & Beer Joint** (Greenwood, tel. 876/954-7155, 9am-10:30pm daily) serves seafood a variety of ways, with fish either fried (US$15 per pound) or steamed (US$12 per pound), lobster (US$14 per pound), shrimp (US$16 per pound), conch (US$12 per pound), and octopus (US$15 per pound) along with a side of bammy, bread, or plantain.

Getting There

Greenwood Great House is 20 kilometers (12 miles) east of Mobay on the A1. To get there, turn inland at the only stoplight in Greenwood and follow the bumpy road straight up to the Great House, sitting on the hillside overlooking the sea. Route taxis and minibuses depart from the bus park downtown, and those destined for Falmouth, will stop at Greenwood on request. A chartered car will cost about US$40 round-trip.

FALMOUTH

Trelawny's capital, Falmouth, is a run-down shadow of what it was in its short-lived Georgian prime. Nevertheless, noble efforts are underway to dust off years of neglect and shine a spotlight on the town's glorious past by restoring its architectural gems, especially after Royal Caribbean dredged the harbor and built a private cruise ship pier in 2011. The pier is chock-full of duty-free shops.

Today, with somewhat decent roads and proximity to resort areas in Montego Bay, the town is attracting a growing population once more. Thanks to the efforts of a nongovernmental organization known as **Falmouth Heritage Renewal** (www.falmouthjamaica.org), the town has become a laboratory for architectural restoration. The group has been working for several years to revitalize the architectural heritage of Jamaica's most impressive Georgian town by training local youth in restoration work. The organization also offers guided tours of Falmouth Historic District (fhrj@falmouthjamaica.org, 10am-2pm Mon.-Fri.). The **Georgian Society** (www.georgianjamaica.org) in Kingston has a wealth of information on Falmouth.

Most people who visit Falmouth do so off a Royal Caribbean cruise ship. The cruise line has exclusive use of the private port in the small town. Others come for the architecture, beaches, or Jewish heritage. Its location just 30 minutes east of Montego Bay makes Falmouth a convenient stopping point en route to the North Coast.

Sights

Originally constructed as the town's Masonic Temple in 1780, **Baptist Manse** (Market St.) was sold in 1832 to the Baptist Missionary Society, which had lost many buildings in raids of reprisal following the slave rebellion of 1831, in response to the Baptists' fiery abolitionist rhetoric. The building was home to several Baptist missionaries before it was destroyed by fire in the 1950s, to be reconstructed as the William Knibb School in 1961.

Today the building serves as headquarters for Falmouth Heritage Renewal.

One of the most impressive Anglican churches in Jamaica is **Trelawny Parish Church of St. Peter the Apostle** (Duke St.), built in typical Georgian style in 1795 on land donated by estate owner Edward Barrett, whose descendent, Elizabeth Barrett Browning, would become a well-recognized poet of the Romantic movement. The parish church is the oldest public building in town and the oldest house of worship in the parish.

Other historic churches in Falmouth include the **Knibb Memorial Baptist Church** (King St. and George St.), named after abolitionist missionary William Knibb, who came to Jamaica in 1825 and established his first chapel on the site of the existing structure, erected in 1926, and the **Falmouth Presbyterian Church** (Rodney St. and Princess St.), built by Scottish people in 1832. Knibb's first chapel was destroyed by the nonconformist militia after the Baptist War, also called the Christmas Rebellion of 1831-1832. Later structures were destroyed by hurricanes. A sculpture relief inside Knibb Memorial depicts a scene (repeated at several Baptist churches across the island) of a congregation of enslaved people awaiting the dawn that granted full freedom in 1838.

Built in 1815 in classic Georgian style, then destroyed by fire and rebuilt in 1926, **Falmouth Courthouse** stands prominently on a little square facing the water just off the main square at the center of town. **Falmouth All Age School** sits on the waterfront in a historic building and makes a good destination for a stroll down Queens Street from the square.

Beaches

A few minutes' drive east of Falmouth, **Burwood Beach** (free) in Bounty Bay is one of the best public beaches on the North Coast, with shallow water extending far off the shore and a reef a few hundred meters out that breaks the surf. It's a favorite spot among locals for windsurfing and kiteboarding.

A private beach club with over 180 meters (600 feet) of beach frontage adjacent to Excellence Oyster Bay, **Blue Waters Beach Club** (Cooper's Pen, cell tel. 876/405-2976, bluewatersfalmouth@gmail.com, www.bluewatersbeachclub.com, US$10, 9am-5pm days when a ship is in port at Falmouth, or by reservation) offers guests lounge chairs (included) and complimentary Wi-Fi. The restaurant serves Jamaican favorites like jerk chicken, festival, and rice-and-peas (US$10). The bar serves Red Stripe.

Recreation

Rois Kayak Adventure (Rois Lagoon, a.k.a. Jerk Island, Green Side, Falmouth, cell tel. 876/430-2827, roislagoon@gmail.com, reservation required, US$40) takes visitors on an hour-long kayak ecotour of Rois lagoon to explore mangroves and spot marinelife. After kayaking, guests are taken to Blue Waters Beach Club to relax and swim. An Appleton Estate Rum Seminar (by reservation 10am-4pm Tues.-Sat.) includes a sampling of three spirits.

Animal park and petting zoo **Jamaica Swamp Safari Village** (Foreshore Rd., Falmouth, next to Better Price Hardware, tel. 876/617-2798, cell tel. 876/775-3111, falmouthzoo@gmail.com, www.jamaicaswampsafari. com, 9am-4pm daily, US$25 adults, US$13 children) has an 80-minute guided walking tour with basic information on the barn owl, Jamaican iguana, coney, yellow snake, and American crocodile. Guests can handfeed the birds in the aviary. Scenes from the James Bond film *Live and Let Die* were filmed with Swamp Safari's founder, the late Ross "Kananga" Heilman, who acted as stunt double for Roger Moore.

Falmouth Heritage Walks (cell tel. 876/407-2245, www.falmouthheritagewalks. com) works closely with Falmouth Heritage Renewal and the Georgian Society of Jamaica to offer three tours for groups of 4-12, by reservation only: Heritage (US$25 adults, US$15 under age 12), Food (US$45 adults, US$25 under age 12), and Jewish Cemetery (US$15 adults, US$10 under age 12). The longer tours last approximately two hours; the Jewish Cemetery tour is about an hour on its own, or it can be incorporated into the Heritage tour. The food tour incorporates five local food stands and corner shops.

Shopping

Artist and crafts producer **Isha Tafara** (cell tel. 876/610-3292 or 876/377-0505) lives in Wakefield, near Falmouth, farther inland from Martha Brae. Tafara makes sandals as well as red, green, and gold crocheted hats, Egyptian-style crafts, handbags, belts, and jewelry with a lot of crochet and fabric-based items. Tafara works from her home, which can be visited by appointment, and supplies Things Jamaican and Sandals boutiques, among other retailers.

Falmouth is famous for its weekly **Bend Down Market** (8am-8pm Wed.), on Rodney Street next to Falmouth All-Age School. From the court square, pass Scotiabank and head toward the ocean. The market sells mainly produce. It was first organized by enslaved people who brought their excess produce for sale to supplement their meager rations.

Food

Decent food and good value are at **Donna's** (23 Market St., tel. 876/617-5175, 8am-11:30pm daily, US$5-15), serving seafood and Jamaican staples like oxtail, shrimp, quesadillas, burgers, wings, and sandwiches. Customers can use free Wi-Fi.

Pepper's Jerk Centre (20 Duke St., tel. 876/617-3427, clintrennie2014@gmail.com, 10am-10pm Mon.-Sat., US$5-6) serves jerk chicken, pork, fish, and lobster with sides like festival, bammy, and rice as well as a rotation of Jamaican favorites like baked, curried, and brown stew chicken, curry goat, oxtail, and roast fish.

Falmouth Jerk Center and Ganja Bar (lot 306, Foreshore Rd., tel. 876/572-2858 or 876/891-6077) serves jerk chicken, pork, fish, conch, lobster, and octopus (US$5-25). The ganja bar at the same location serves mixed drinks as well as herb brownies and ganja spread, in a hassle-free herb-friendly environment.

A rotating menu with items like fried chicken, curried beef, stewed peas, and barbecue pork is offered at **Rock Wharf Restaurant & Bar** (Rock District, Falmouth, tel. 876/617-2074, 11:30am-10pm daily, US$5-10). Snapper, escoveitch, and steamed or brown stew are prepared to order (US$15-22). **Jerk Island** (entrance to Rois Lagoon, Green Side, Falmouth, tel. 876/533-9363, jerkisland-falmouth@gmail.com, 11am-4pm Sat.-Sun. and days when cruise ships are in port) serves jerk chicken and pork accompanied by festival, fries, and rice-and-peas, along with rum ribs and jerk burgers.

Catering mostly to locals with brown stew fish, fried chicken, curry goat, and brown stew pork, **Aunt Gloria's** (Rock District, cell tel. 876/353-1301, 6am-8:30pm Mon.-Sat., US$3-5) jerk center opens on Friday and sometimes Saturday for the best jerk pork and chicken in town. Breakfast items include ackee and saltfish, kidney, dumpling, yam, and banana.

Tastee Patties (25 Market St., tel. 876/617-5150) has a restaurant in the center of Falmouth, on the square.

Spicy Nice (Water Square, tel. 876/954-3197) sells patties, breads, pastries, and other baked goods.

Services

Scotiabank has a branch with an ATM, built in replica Georgian style, next to the courthouse. **FX Trader** (U.S. tel. 888/398-7233) has a branch at Big J's Supermarket on Lower Harbour Street (8:30am-4:30pm Mon.-Wed. and Fri.-Sat., 8:30am-12:30pm Thurs.).

Free internet access is available at **Trelawny Parish Library** (Rodney St., entrance on Pitt St., tel. 876/954-3306, 9am-6pm Mon.-Fri., 9am-4pm Sat.). The **Falmouth Police** (tel. 876/954-3073) are based along the waterfront on Rodney Street.

Getting There

Falmouth is about 30 minutes from Montego

Bay by car. There are three well-marked exits off the highway that all lead to the town center. Buses and route taxis depart from the bus park downtown Montego Bay, arriving in the square in Falmouth.

MARTHA BRAE

Martha Brae River is one of Jamaica's longest and is navigable for much of its 32 kilometers (20 miles), running from the deep interior of Trelawny beyond Chris Blackwell's Pantrepant farm and Good Hope Plantation, where it wells up out of the earth near Windsor Cave. Legends surround the Martha Brae, likely owing to its important role in the early colonial years, when the Spanish used the river to reach the North Coast from their major settlement of Oristan, near present-day Bluefields.

★ Martha Brae Rafting

The only organized bamboo rafting attraction in western Jamaica, **Martha Brae Rafting** (tel. 876/940-6398 or 876/940-7018, or contact Marie Barrett, cell tel. 876/775-3111, info@jamaicarafting.com, www.jamaicarafting.com, 9am-4pm daily) has 84 CPR-trained and licensed raft captains. Rafts hold two passengers in addition to the captain, who guides the vessel down the normally lazy Martha Brae. The five-kilometer (3-mile) raft ride (US$65 per raft for 1-2 people) takes about 90 minutes. The excursion will not get your adrenaline pumping; it's a relaxing and romantic experience and includes a nonalcoholic welcome drink. Round-trip transportation can be arranged from Mobay (minimum 4 people, US$15 pp) and from Ochi (minimum 4, US$25 pp) and Negril (minimum 6, US$35 pp).

To reach the departure point on the Martha Brae River, exit left off the highway ramp after passing the first turnoff for Falmouth heading east. Turn inland (right) through the underpass, continuing into the small village of Martha Brae. At the intersection in the town, turn left, and then right after the second bridge. It's about 30 minutes' drive from Montego Bay.

GLISTENING WATERS

Glistening Waters, just east of Falmouth, is home to the Luminous Lagoon, one of Jamaica's most interesting natural phenomena.

The Luminous Lagoon

One of Jamaica's most touted attractions, the **Luminous Lagoon** owes its luminosity to

bamboo rafting on the Martha Brae River

the microscopic unicellular dinoflagellate *Pyrodinium bahamense,* which glows when the water is agitated. The organism photosynthesizes sunlight using chlorophyll during the day and then emits the energy at night. Four tour operators offer boat tours of the Luminous Lagoon.

Boat tours (every 30 minutes 7pm-9pm daily) that last half an hour are available from **Glistening Waters Restaurant & Marina** (tel. 876/954-3229, info@glisteningwaters.com, www.glisteningwaters.com). Virtually identical outings (7pm daily, US$15 pp) are organized by **Fisherman's Inn** (tel. 876/954-4078 or 876/954-3427, fishermansinn@cwjamaica.com). **Rock Wharf** (Stratty King, cell tel. 876/399-8686 or 876/617-2074, kingstrats@live.com, US$25) offers a 30- to 45-minute daily tour, starting at nightfall until about 9:30pm, that includes a boat ride around the lagoon and a brief history of the area.

Based at Fisherman's Inn on the Luminous Lagoon, **Luminous Lagoon Tours** (contact Captain David Muschett, cell tel. 876/276-9885, awahoo2@yahoo.com, US$25 pp) also offers one-hour night excursions on the lagoon. A bit more expensive than the competitors, it offers a more intimate experience for smaller groups (minimum 6 people). David also offers paintball (Fri.-Sun., or by appointment, US$30 pp, includes gear and 100 balls) on his farm in Martha Brae on the way to Good Hope Plantation, as well as deep sea fishing excursions (4 hours US$650, 8 hours US$1,200) on the same 35-foot Cabo used for the Luminous Lagoon Tours.

Getting There

Glistening Waters is located 32 kilometers (20 miles) east of Montego Bay along the A1. Route taxis traveling between Mobay and Falmouth (US$2) can be convinced to continue on to Glistening Waters after dropping off other passengers in Falmouth, or take the long route back to Montego Bay on the return for a few dollars more.

Recreation

FISHING

Glistening Waters Restaurant & Marina (directly off the A1, tel. 876/954-3229, info@glisteningwaters.com, www.glisteningwaters.com) offers fishing charters (US$600) from the marina on a 46-foot sport fisher with a capacity of eight people. A smaller 32-foot boat (4 hours, US$400) carries five people. Two complimentary drinks are included on fishing excursions. The marina also welcomes visiting yachts (US$1 per foot per day) and can accommodate boats of up to 86 feet. Boaters should call ahead for special instructions on entering the lagoon. Longer stays can be negotiated.

Based at Rock Wharf on the Luminous Lagoon, **Luminous Lagoon Tours** (contact Captain David Muschett, cell tel. 876/276-9885, awahoo2@yahoo.com) has excursions on the lagoon, trolling and deep-drop deep-sea fishing, and snorkeling day trips to the private beach at Harmony Hall aboard a 35-foot Cabo with an eight-person capacity. Fishing trips (half-day US$600, 8 hours US$1,100) for up to eight passengers chase marlin, kingfish, barracuda, sailfish, and wahoo and include bait and tackle.

Food and Accommodations

A 12-room hotel and restaurant on the Luminous Lagoon, **Fisherman's Inn** (just off the A1, Rock District, Falmouth, tel. 876/954-4078 or 876/954-3427, from US$95 d) includes the Hopscotch Jerk Centre, which serves jerk chicken (US$4), jerk pork (US$5), and fish (US$10-15). The hotel offers clean, spacious rooms overlooking the lagoon and a small marina, with private baths and hot water, TV and air-conditioning, and a mini fridge in most. The inn organizes outings on the lagoon (7pm daily, US$25 pp, US$20 for guests) led by informative and jovial Captain Michael Currie to see the phosphorescent microbes light up the water.

Glistening Waters Hotel & Marina (tel. 876/617-4625, info@glisteningwaters.com, www.glisteningwaters.com, US$112 d, extras US$50) has food ranging from lobster, shrimp, conch, pork, chicken, and pork. The seafood platter comes with lobster, fish, and shrimp served with rice-and-peas, bammy, or potato and steamed or raw veggies. The 28-room hotel offers a variety of room layouts, some with king beds, others with queens, and others with a combination of two singles or a king and a single. Guests get a 50 percent discount on Luminous Lagoon tours. Breakfast and Wi-Fi are included; the pool is exclusively for guests.

A 352-room all-inclusive resort with a variety of layouts, **The Royalton White Sands** (Burwood Beach, Coopers Pen, Falmouth, U.S. tel. 888/774-0040 or 305/774-0040, reservations2@vacstre.net, www.royalton-whitesandsresort.com, US$420-500) has rain showerheads, Wi-Fi, minibars, and balconies or terraces. Some rooms can interconnect for larger groups.

Excellence Oyster Bay (tel. 876/617-0200, www.excellenceresorts.com, from US$570 d) is an all-suites adults-only property on 3.2 kilometers (2 miles) of unspoiled beach on a peninsula just east of Falmouth. Four types of junior suite and seven Excellence Club categories offer a range of rates and amenities; the more expensive units have pools and ocean views. The all-inclusive resort offers 10 à la carte dinner options, 2 à la carte lunch options, and 10 bars with 24-hour room service. The property has three swimming pools and four outdoor whirlpool tubs along with non-motorized water sports, including windsurfing, kayaking, paddleboarding, and sailing, as well as introductory scuba diving.

DUNCANS
Jacob Taylor Bathing Beach
Just below the small hillside community of Duncans, **Jacob Taylor Bathing Beach** is a local hot spot where low-key craft vendors sell their goods and anglers park their canoes

to while away the days playing dominoes in the shade. The beach extends for a few kilometers to the west, and while not immaculately swept and maintained like the beach at Silver Sands, the sand is fine, the water's clear, and there's no entry fee. You can't miss the entrance to Jacob Taylor Bathing Beach, marked by a large sign by the road that leads downhill toward the sea to the left of the gated entrance to Silver Sands.

Silver Sands Beach
The gated community of Silver Sands has a restaurant, a bar, and a small grocery store within the complex—and what is considered by some to be the island's finest beach. **Silver Sands Beach** (tel. 876/954-2518, day use US$15 pp) has fine white sand and crystal-clear water with fixed umbrellas providing shade and a pier with a gazebo at its tip. It's necessary to call ahead to gain access to Silver Sands so they expect you at the gate.

About one kilometer (0.6 mile) east of Silver Sands, a private estate house facing a small beach lies in ruins, also with fine white sand and crystal-clear water. To get here, turn right off the main road down to Silver Sands through a green gate and drive along a rough, sandy, marl road through the dense scrub forest until you reach the coast.

A 20-minute walk farther east along low coral bluffs leads to **Harmony Cove,** one of Jamaica's few remaining virgin beaches and the future site of a massive hotel and casino, according to government plans. Harmony Cove can also be reached by turning off the North Coast Highway next to a cell phone tower five minutes' drive east of Duncans; from there, follow the dirt road around as it takes a wide sweep toward the coast and back inland until you see a wide sandy beach, at the end of a grassy road, off to the right. A dirt track just inland from the beach follows the coast west leading to Harmony Cove. It's about 20 minutes' walk from the east as well. Contact Harmonisation (tel. 876/954-2518) for information about the property.

FOOD

The local bar and restaurant **Leroy's** (cell tel. 876/447-2896 or 876/447-5414, US$3-12) is seaside at Jacob Taylor Bathing Beach and serves fish and Jamaican staples. Leroy can usually be found in the kitchen while his step-daughter Cameika "Chin" Wallace works the bar. The Silver Lights Band performs live reggae (8pm-late Sat.) during the winter months. The no-frills restaurant and bar is notable for its relaxing atmosphere that draws a healthy mix of locals and visitors, appreciably devoid of hustlers to interrupt the quiet seaside landscape.

Accommodations

Silver Sands (www.mysilversands.com) is a gated community of 44 rental cottages and villas that range considerably in price and comfort, from rustic to opulent. Even at the higher end, Silver Sands villas are among the best value to be found in Jamaica.

A charming three-bedroom at the top of the stairs leading down to Silver Sands' fine white beach in the gated community is **Cannon Cottage** (contact Karen Sangster, cell tel. 876/831-2221, U.S. tel. 305/482-6925, ksangster@cwjamaica.com, minimum 3 nights low season, 4 nights high season, 2 bedrooms US$250 low season, US$300 high season, 3 bedrooms US$300 low season, US$360 high season). The villa has a housekeeper, a cook, and a gardener to do the shopping, cooking, and cleaning. A courtyard has a jetted tub that fits six with a little waterfall and outdoor furniture for dining amid lush foliage. Two rooms have king beds, one with an additional single, and the third has a queen. The screened rooms have air-conditioning and ceiling fans. Flat-screen TVs with cable are in the queen room and the living room. A stay of a week or more includes round-trip airport transfers.

Windjammer (tel. 876/929-2378 or 876/926-0931, dianas@cwjamaica.com or bookings@windjammerjamaica.com, www. windjammerjamaica.com, from US$720) is a four-bedroom villa with a private pool,

internet access, a large veranda with a sea view, and a built-in barbecue. Two bedrooms have king beds, one has a queen, and the fourth has two twins.

A three-bedroom cottage a few steps from the shore at Jacob Taylor Bathing Beach is **Sea Rhythm** (contact caretaker Cardella Gilzine, cell tel. 876/857-0119, US$200). The master bedroom has a king bed and air-conditioning, with a double bed and fan in the second room and two twins in the third. Each room has a private bath with hot water, and there's a fully equipped kitchen. Meals are prepared to order.

Castaways Villa (294 Queens Dr., Duncans Bay, U.S. tel. 717/578-0136, castawaysjamaica@yahoo.com, from US$90 d) offers budget accommodations within walking distance of Jacob Taylor Bathing Beach. While not really a villa in the traditional sense, the guest house has decent rooms with cable TV, air-conditioning, and a pool, as well as a bar and restaurant serving Jamaican-style dishes, pizza, and pasta.

Getting There

Duncans is roughly 45 minutes east of Mobay by car with two exits off the A1. The first exit you come to heading east is the most convenient to get to Silver Sands and Jacob Taylor Bathing Beach, the other entrance being on the eastern side of town and requiring you pass through the often-congested little square.

RIO BUENO

The first community in Trelawny across the border from St. Ann, Rio Bueno is considered by historians to have been the actual landing point of Christopher Columbus on his second voyage, although that claim is also made for Discovery Bay. The port at Rio Bueno was an important export point, as can still be seen by the dilapidated warehouses and wharves along the waterfront. Today the small village is undergoing some renewal, with the new North Coast Highway bypassing the community entirely, which could ultimately enhance its picturesque appeal.

Sights

The riverbank along the Rio Bueno is great for a stroll; visitors can see ruins of the **Baptist Theological College,** the first of its kind in the western hemisphere. Other ruins in town include **Fort Dundas,** behind the school. The **Rio Bueno Baptist Church** was originally built in 1832 before being destroyed by the Colonial Church Union, whose mostly Anglican members organized militias to terrorize the abolitionist Baptists, who were upsetting the status quo. The church was quickly rebuilt, twice as large, in 1834, and the present structure was built in 1901. While the roof is largely missing, services are still held downstairs. The **Rio Bueno Anglican Church** was built at the water's edge in 1833 and remains there today.

The extensive **Gallery Joe James** (tel. 876/954-0048, cell tel. 876/401-0484, 10am-8pm daily), on the grounds of the Lobster Bowl and Rio Bueno Hotel, displays artwork by its late proprietor, Joe James, among other selected Jamaican artists. The gallery extends throughout the restaurant, bar, and hotel and makes for a surreal waterfront setting.

Recreation

Braco Stables (tel. 876/954-0185, bracostables@cwjamaica.com, www.bracostables.com, US$60, US$70 with transportation from Mobay or Runaway Bay) offers tame horseback riding tours traversing the Braco estate and a private beach in Braco, Trelawny. **Braco Rapids Adventures** (tel. 876/954-0185, info@bracotours.com, www.riverrapidsja.com, 10:30am and 1:45pm daily) offers 105-minute white-water river rafting, tubing, river boarding, kayaking, and waterfall explorer tours at Bengal Falls on the Rio Bueno, which runs down the border of Trelawny and St. Ann. The tour operation is based in Braco, five kilometers (three miles) east of Duncans. Round trip transportation is provided from hotels and cruise ship piers along the North Coast.

Food and Accommodations

With more than enough seating for the sparse crowds that trickle by, **The Lobster Bowl Restaurant** (tel. 876/954-0048, cell tel. 876/401-0484, 9am-8pm daily, US$18-40) serves shrimp, chicken, fish, and lobster dishes. Outside seating extends out on a dock along the waterfront as well as inside a large dining hall.

Rio Bueno Hotel (tel. 876/954-0048, galleryjoejames40@hotmail.com, from US$100) is a rustic 20-room place with balconies overlooking the sea, ceiling fans, TVs, and hot water in private baths. The ground-floor rooms are larger and geared toward families, with three double beds. The vibe of the place is of a bygone era.

Meliá Braco Village (Braco, tel. 876/678-0582 or 888/956-3542, melia.jamaica@melia.com, www.melia.com, from US$225 low season, US$486 high season) is an all-inclusive resort located seafront in the Braco area of Rio Bueno. The suites are modern, with flat-panel TVs, broadband internet, and double queens or kings. Some rooms have balconies with sea views. The hotel has five restaurants, including buffet and à la carte, and offers babysitting services, a fitness and wellness center, basketball courts, a football pitch, and a business center.

North Cockpit Country

Some of the remotest countryside in Jamaica is in the Trelawny interior known as Cockpit Country, with its cockpit karst topography, home to myriad caves, sinkholes, and subterranean springs, stretching from the St. James border in the west to St. Ann at the heart of the island. Hiking and exploring this region can be riveting, but adequate supplies and a good guide are essential. The Queen of Spain Valley, only a few minutes' drive inland, is one of the most picturesque farming areas in Jamaica, where the morning mist lifts to reveal a magical countryside of lush pitted hills.

Cockpit Country has some of the most unusual landscape on earth, where porous limestone geology created what is known as karst topography, molded by water and the weathering of time. Cockpit Country extends all the way to Accompong, St. Elizabeth, to the south and to Albert Town, Trelawny, to the east. Similar topography continues over the inhospitable interior as far as Cave Valley, St. Ann, even farther east.

Two routes lead into Trelawny's interior from Martha Brae, both requiring a vehicle with high clearance. The first route follows the Martha Brae River through Sherwood Content to Windsor. The second route passes through Good Hope Plantation, leading to Chris Blackwell's private estate, Pantrepant.

★ GOOD HOPE PLANTATION

The 810-hectare (2,000-acre) **Good Hope Plantation** (cell tel. 876/469-3443, goodhope1@cwjamaica.com, www.goodhopejamaica.com), located in the Queen of Spain Valley, is one of the most picturesque working estates on the island. Citrus has today replaced the cane of the past, while the plantation's great house and a collection of its historic buildings have been converted into the most luxurious countryside villas.

Chukka Caribbean (U.S. tel. 877/424-8552, tel. 876/656-8026, www.chukka.com, US$25-185), offers a number of tours of the estate, with dune buggies and ATVs, zip lines, river tubes and kayaking, a challenge course, a bird aviary, a swimming pool, gem mining, a great house tour, and Appleton Estate rum

Good Hope Plantation

tasting among the different tours on offer. Multiple activities are packaged together for combo tours. The tour operator built a waterfall and pool attraction around the old packing houses to create a water park, a restaurant, and a bar next to the meandering Martha Brae River. Tour package prices typically include transportation from Falmouth, Montego Bay, Ocho Rios, or Negril.

Located on the estate, **David Pinto's Ceramic Studio** (8 kilometers/5 miles north of Falmouth, cell tel. 876/886-2866, dpinto@ cwjamaica.com, www.jamaicaclay.com, 8am-4pm Mon.-Fri. or by appointment) is run by a Jamaican-born potter who studied ceramics during high school in the United Kingdom and later at Rhode Island School of Design before practicing in New York City. He returned to Jamaica in 1992 to establish this studio on Good Hope Plantation, where he runs retreats led by internationally acclaimed guest master potters. Pinto's work includes both functional and decorative pieces and is on display in the permanent collection at the National Gallery in Kingston.

To get to Good Hope Plantation, bypass the town of Martha Brae to the right when heading inland from the highway, and take a left less than 1.5 kilometers (1 mile) past the town, following well-marked signs. Continuing on the road past the turnoff to Good Hope ultimately leads to Wakefield, where the B15 heads back west to Montego Bay.

WINDSOR GREAT CAVE

Windsor Great Cave (www.cockpitcountry. com) is one of the top draws in the area. The caves are best visited with Franklyn (Dango) Taylor (US$20), the sanctioned warden for the Jamaica Conservation and Development Trust (JCDT) and the official guide, although experienced cavers may prefer to go alone. All visitors should check in with Dango and sign the guestbook, which serves to monitor visits and provide records in emergencies. Dango runs a little shop selling drinks and snacks. The source of the Martha Brae River is located nearby, affording a great spot for a dip to cool off.

The Windsor Caves are rich in both geological history and animal life, with up to 11 bat species emerging to feed in the evenings in large swarms. The geological formations inside the caves should not be touched, and a minimal-impact policy should be observed, which starts with visitors staying on the established path. Shining flashlights on the ceiling disturbs the resting bats. Michael Schwartz, of nearby Windsor Great House, warns of a chronic respiratory ailment afflicting cavers, caused by a fungus that grows on bat dung.

To get to Windsor, head inland from Falmouth to Martha Brae, take a left at the stop sign, crossing the bridge to the east, and turn right to follow the valley south into the hills. On the way, the road passes through the small farming communities of Perth Town and Reserve. Once the road leaves the banks of the Martha Brae, it heads to Sherwood Content, Coxheath, and finally Windsor, ultimately petering out at The Last Resort near Windsor Caves.

Hiking and Caving

Southern Trelawny Environmental Agency (STEA, cell tel. 876/393-6584, www. stea.net) and its eco-tourism arm, Cockpit Country Adventure Tours, led by Hugh Dixon, is based in Albert Town, a little hamlet at the edge of Cockpit Country. The STEA organizes spelunking (caving), hiking, and bird-watching for individuals and groups. Tourists are typically taken to Rock Spring Cave, which is not an active bat habitat, keeping guano and potentially dangerous airborne diseases at bay.

For more in-depth spelunking of lesser-known attractions, **Jamaica Caves Organization (JCO)** (info@jamaicancaves. org, www.jamaicancaves.org) knows Cockpit Country literally inside and out. It can arrange guides for hiking as well as caving. A good circuit is mapped out on the JCO site for a driving tour of Cockpit Country for those less interested in exercise. For those with a serious interest in hiking, the **Troy Trail** is one of the most interesting and arduous hikes in western Jamaica, traversing Cockpit Country from Windsor to Troy, which takes about eight hours over a rugged 19 kilometers (12 miles). The JCO can provide guides and maps for a reasonable fee that goes toward helping maintain the organization.

FOOD AND ACCOMMODATIONS

The Last Resort (Ivor Conolley tel. 876/931-6070, cell tel. 876/700-7128, iscapc@cwjamaica.com) is the remotest option in Cockpit Country. It's the headquarters for the Jamaica Caves Organization, and facilities were recently renovated but remain rusti,c with 20 bunk beds (US$15 pp) and a common bath. One private room has a queen bed. Expect intimacy with the surrounding environment—bug repellent is essential. To get to The Last Resort, turn right at Dango's shop in Windsor, continuing for about 1.6 kilometers (1 mile).

Windsor Great House (cell tel. 876/997-3832, windsor@cwjamaica.com, www.cockpitcountry.com) was built by John Tharp in 1795 to oversee his vast cattle estate, which included most of the land bordering the Martha Brae River. Today the great house has rustic lodging and a weekly "Meet the Scientists" dinner (US$40). A left turn at Dango's shop leads to Windsor Great House. A vehicle with good clearance is recommended, but the route is traveled frequently by vehicles with low clearance, driven with caution.

★ **Good Hope Carriage House** (contact Tammy Hart, cell tel. 876/881-6869, tammyhart3@me.com, www.goodhopejamaica.com, weekly US$6,325 low season, US$7,700 high season) is a six-bedroom villa offering luxurious accommodations at the center of a working citrus plantation where Chukka Caribbean offers a dozen tours and attractions. Antique furnishings, flat-screen TVs, Wi-Fi, and top-notch cuisine prepared by attentive staff make this the best option in the area. In the Queen of Spain Valley, Good Hope is one of the most picturesque working estates on the island, with the characteristic rolling limestone hills of the Cockpit Country interior. Citrus has today replaced the cane of yesteryear, while the plantation's great house and a collection of historic buildings have been modernized. Good Hope features Old World luxury, and the villa is staffed with a chef, housekeepers, and gardeners. This is an ideal base for family retreats, birding, hiking, mountain biking, and horseback riding, still the best means of exploring the surrounding countryside. The inviting swimming pool and a brimming river make for relaxation.

Ocho Rios and the Central North Coast

St. Ann is chock-full of rivers, waterfalls, and gar-dens, earning it the well-deserved moniker "the garden parish." Ocho Rios, or "Ochi" as the tourism hub is known locally, is the most developed town in St. Ann, its name a derivation of the Spanish name for bubbling cascades, Los Chorrillos, given to the area in the 1500s by the first Spanish settlers.

River gardens and cascades that attract many to the area include Dunn's River Falls, the most popular; Konoko Falls; Turtle River Falls; Shaw Park Gardens, closer to the center of town; and the White River, running down the parish border between St. Ann and St. Mary. Beaches are also a strong draw to Ocho Rios. Waterfalls spill onto the sand as they meet the sea along the entire stretch between

Ocho Rios 122
West of Ocho Rios. 143
Runaway Bay 148
Discovery Bay. 153
Nine Mile 155
St. Mary Parish 157

Highlights

Look for ★ to find recommended sights, activities, dining, and lodging.

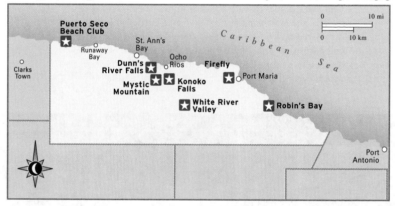

★ **Dunn's River Falls:** Climb a waterfall at the most visited attraction in Jamaica, best visited in the early morning to avoid the throngs (page 122).

★ **Mystic Mountain:** This thrilling attraction has a high speed monorail, a waterslide, and zip lines in the hills overlooking Ocho Rios (page 124).

★ **Konoko Falls:** This waterfall attraction has a botanical garden and a small historical exhibit as well as endemic and exotic birds and reptiles (page 125).

★ **White River Valley:** Go tubing down the White River, bathe in the shadow of a

historic Spanish bridge, or enjoy a picnic riverside at Calby's (page 127).

★ **Puerto Seco Beach Club:** This resort has it all: a jerk pit, a restaurant and bar, VIP cabanas, a Wibit marine obstacle course, and water sports (page 154).

★ **Firefly:** This one-time home of both pirate Henry Morgan and playwright Noel Coward has a majestic view of the northeast coast (page 158).

★ **Robin's Bay:** Immerse yourself in Jamaica's languid country life at the working farm on Green Castle Estate, discover hidden waterfalls, or loaf on the beach (page 163).

Ocho Rios and Old Fort Bay, five kilometers (3 miles) west. The mouth of Dunn's River Falls, Laughing Waters, Pearly Beach, Turtle Beach, Mahogany Beach, and Bamboo Beach are among the options for enjoying sun, sea, and sand.

Prospect Plantation, a few minutes' drive east of the town center, is home to Yaaman Adventure Park, offering a variety of tours by camel, jitney, or ATV as well as tours of the historic Prospect Great House. Mystic Mountain, just west of town, takes visitors by chairlift to the summit, where there are tours of the canopy by zip line or on a riveting monorail "bobsled." At nearby Dolphin Cove, awe-inspiring marine mammals, sharks, stingrays, and exotic birds entertain visitors in scores.

The next major settlement west of Ocho Rios is the parish capital, St. Ann's Bay, just east of where the Spanish established Sevilla la Nueva, or New Seville, in the early 1500s. Marcus Garvey, father of the pan-African movement, was born here in 1887. New Seville is now an archaeological site with a great house museum, where heritage events are held throughout the year. Farther west along the coast are two languid beach towns: Runaway Bay, with an 18-hole golf course, and Discovery Bay, one of Jamaica's high-end villa enclaves, newly reinvigorated by the reopening of the Puerto Seco Beach Club.

Neighboring St. Mary, the parish immediately east of Ocho Rios, has a reputation as Jamaica's best-kept secret. Hustlers are few and most people live oblivious to the tourism industry. The parish has a rocky coastline exposed to the prevailing northeast winds, punctuated by beaches, some with golden sand protected by coral, others with black sand or pebbles. Forested hills drop sharply to the sea. With its abundance of birdlife, St. Mary was the preferred corner of Jamaica for literary legends Ian Fleming and Noël Coward, who built their island homes here.

Fleming's home is now the centerpiece of the island's leading luxury retreat, Goldeneye, and Coward's is preserved as a museum and event venue.

PLANNING YOUR TIME

Unless your goal is to simply loaf on the beach, or you happen to be staying at a destination resort or villa too comfortable to leave, Ochi is not a place to spend more than a few days. It's the most practical base for a number of key attractions, however, most packaged into organized tours sold at hotel concierge desks or bookable online. If you're driving yourself or chartering a taxi, there's more flexibility to fit a string of activities into a single day, and there's no reason you can't spend the morning at a waterfall and go horseback riding or swim with dolphins in the afternoon.

As one of Jamaica's most active cruise ship ports, Ocho Rios is inundated with transient visitors several days a week. If you want to avoid the crowds, schedule visits to area attractions on days when there's no ship in town, or get an early start. Check Cruise Port Insider (www.cruiseportinsider.com) for ship schedules. An early start is recommended especially for Dunn's River Falls, Jamaica's most popular tourist attraction. By getting there as soon as the gates open, you'll have the place almost to yourself and can enjoy climbing the cascades and taking photos (with a waterproof camera) without bumping into strangers. The beach at the bottom of the falls is an attraction in its own right.

Cruise ship visits tend to encourage a more anxious grab for cash from retailers and street hustlers in Ocho Rios, which gives St. Ann's largest town a less-than-tranquil vibe, especially in the immediate vicinity of the port. Venture westward or eastward along the coast and you'll find a more laid-back attitude among locals, who don't seem as desperate to make a buck in the seafront communities of Priory, Runaway Bay, and Discovery

Previous: a secluded fountain at Konoko Gardens; English playright Noel Coward immortalized in bronze at Firefly; the ruins of a massive windmill at Green Castle Estate

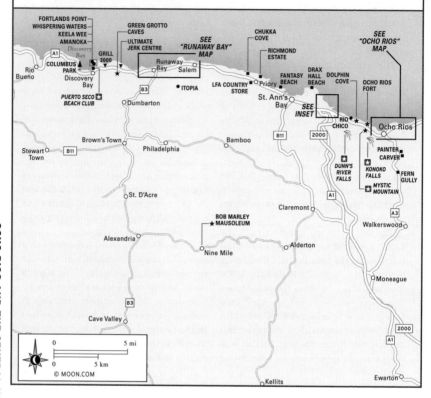

The Central Coast

Bay, or in Robin's Bay and Oracabessa in St. Mary. Strawberry Fields Together offers tours through the bush or by sea to a waterfall and desolate black-sand beach. The Strawberry Fields property has a small beach fit for swimming, protected from the crashing waves by reefs, along with a bar and restaurant, making it a nice day-trip destination from Ocho Rios or Kingston.

Several annual events make a stay along the North Coast all the more worthwhile. One of Jamaica's top reggae festivals, Rebel Salute, is held in mid-January. Around Easter, Jamaica's carnival season is in full swing with Bacchanal Beach J'Ouvert and several other parties held in and around Ochi. The Ocho

Rios Jazz Fest spices things up in June, and Emancipation Jubilee kicks off in Seville at the end of July. The area is party central again in mid-October for Heroes Weekend.

SAFETY

The Ocho Rios Police blame a high incidence of harassment in the area on large informal settlements around town. St. Ann, like Jamaica on a whole, is riddled with poverty. Hustlers tend to be more aggressive than in other parishes owing to the abundance of short-term visitors who make easy prey. Greet unsolicited advances with a smile, followed by clear communication demonstrating your lack of interest. Ignoring advances is

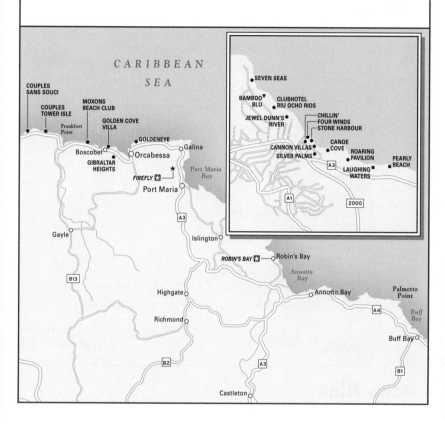

unwise as it can elicit an aggressive response. It's common for hustlers to quickly befriend and follow visitors, touting every kind of service, tour, or drug. Behind the theatrics used to get the attention of visitors, there's typically a down-to-earth Jamaican sincerity that will often surface by entertaining such overtures with a respectful, "No, thank you," or "I'm all set, thanks."

Common sense precautions should be taken, especially at night: Avoid dimly lit side streets and don't take the bait if a stranger attempts to lure you off the beaten path. Rural areas are less rife with hustlers, but precautions should be taken nonetheless: Don't stray off alone, especially at night, and leave valuables in a safe at your hotel. Carry only the cash you intend to spend.

Marijuana was decriminalized in Jamaica in 2015, allowing individuals to carry up to two ounces for personal use. Sale is restricted to licensed retailers, however, and engaging in transactions outside the regulated industry is prohibited. The list of licensed retailers continues to grow, with the first, Kaya Herb House, established in Drax Hall, just west of Ocho Rios, in 2017. Consult the Cannabis Licensing Authority (www.cla.org.jm) for a list of authorized retailers. Hard drugs are illegal in Jamaica and should be avoided.

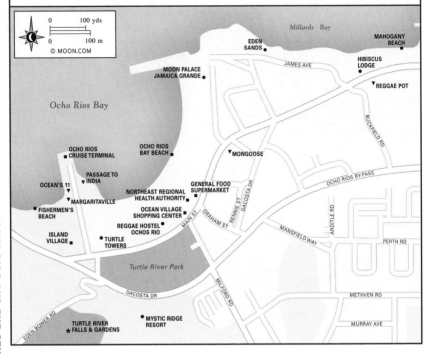

Ocho Rios

0 100 yds
0 100 m
© MOON.COM

Millards Bay

MAHOGANY BEACH

EDEN SANDS

HIBISCUS LODGE

JAMES AVE

REGGAE POT

MOON PALACE JAMAICA GRANDE

Ocho Rios Bay

BUCKFIELD RD

OCHO RIOS CRUISE TERMINAL

OCHO RIOS BAY BEACH

MONGOOSE

PASSAGE TO INDIA

OCEAN'S 11

GENERAL FOOD SUPERMARKET

OCHO RIOS BY-PASS

NORTHEAST REGIONAL HEALTH AUTHORITY

RENNIE ST

DACOSTA DR

ARDITLE RD

MARGARITAVILLE

OCEAN VILLAGE SHOPPING CENTER

MAIN ST

GRAHAM ST

MANSFIELD WAY

PERTH RD

FISHERMEN'S BEACH

REGGAE HOSTEL OCHOS RIO

ISLAND VILLAGE

TURTLE TOWERS

Turtle River Park

DACOSTA DR

MILFORD RD

METHVEN RD

EDEN BOWER RD

TURTLE RIVER FALLS & GARDENS

MYSTIC RIDGE RESORT

MURRAY AVE

Ocho Rios

Ocho Rios is the biggest town in St. Ann Parish and along the entire Central North Coast. The town limits extend west along the coast as far as the unimpressive Ocho Rios Fort and east to the St. Mary Parish border, marked by the White River, and inland southward to Fern Gully.

SIGHTS AND ATTRACTIONS

TOP EXPERIENCE

★ Dunn's River Falls

Dunn's River Falls (tel. 876/974-5944, www.dunnsriverfallsja.com, 8:30am-4pm daily, when cruise ships are in port 7am-4pm daily, US$23 adults, US$15 ages 4-12) is the most highly trafficked attraction in Jamaica, receiving over 300,000 visitors a year. Visitors start the climb from the beach at the mouth of the river and gradually ascending a 180-meter (600-foot) waterfall, which takes between 45 minutes and an hour. On the golden-sand beach, the river's cool spring water blends with the warm Caribbean Sea for exhilarating swimming. The falls themselves are climbable by anyone at least 90 centimeters (36 inches) tall. As long as you're steady on your feet, it's not too much of a challenge, provided the water level isn't too high. Handrails have been installed at the most challenging stretch just before an underpass beneath the road.

To avoid crowds scrambling up the cascades, Dunn's River is best visited on days when there's no cruise ship in the port of Ocho Rios, usually Sunday but easy to determine by taking a look at the pier or consulting the port arrivals schedule. Groups are also brought from cruise ships docking in Falmouth and Montego Bay, and every hotel on the island offers tour packages to the falls, so it's hard to avoid the crowds any day. Arriving as the park opens at 8:30am is the best way to find relative solitude among the cascades.

The rocks up the falls are slippery, and water booties are recommended. These can be rented (US$10) on-site and are also sold (US$20). The park recommends visitors climb the falls accompanied by one of the many guides. You'll likely be corralled and assigned a guide if you're with a group. The guides expect to be tipped; US$5 to US$10 pp is reasonable. Neither guide nor booties are compulsory, but first-timers may find a steady hand and some riverbed knowledge useful for the ascent.

Dunn's River is located two kilometers (1.2 miles) west of Ocho Rios, about five minutes by car. Route taxis pass the entrance to the falls on their way to St. Ann's Bay and will stop at Dunn's River by request. A private taxi chartered from Ocho Rios shouldn't cost more than US$10 each way, though the hard-hustling Ochi cabbies will likely start much higher. Don't be afraid to haggle, and remind the driver it's only a few kilometers. It's about 10 minutes by route taxi from St. Ann's Bay; you'll need to alert the driver where you'd like to get out.

On the subject of haggling, for those who enjoy it, the craft market that visitors are subjected to on the way to the park's exit provides ample opportunity to engage with aggressive vendors who lose no time making friends with, "How was it?" "Where're you from?" "Come here, let me show you something." For those who don't enjoy extreme shopping, keep left for the express route through the maze of shops and food concession stands as you exit.

Dolphin Cove

Dolphin Cove (on the A1, just before Dunn's River heading west from Ocho Rios, tel. 876/974-5335, cell tel. 876/296-5586-0900, www.dolphincoveja.com, reservations required, 8:30am-5:30pm daily), operated by Mexico-based Dolphin Discovery, offers a variety of programs where visitors interact with dolphins to varying degrees of intimacy, depending on the price—starting with the **Encounter Program** (US$99), where you get to touch the dolphins' snout in knee-high water and kiss a dolphin, to the **Swim Adventure** (US$149 adults, US$99 ages 6-12), where you're pulled belly-to-belly with the dolphin through the lagoon, to the **Royal Swim** (US$199 adults, US$99 ages 6-12) with two dolphins, being pulled by dorsal fins and then getting a foot push where the dolphins use their snouts to push you into the air.

In the **Shark Program** (US$99), guests snorkel with, hold, and feed nurse sharks 2.5-4 meters (8-14 feet) in length. Basic admission (US$49 adults, US$30 ages 6-12) includes a jungle trail, a lovebird aviary, glass-bottomed kayaking, snorkeling with debarbed stingrays, and a 12-meter (40-foot) monster slide that empties into a pool next to a heated whirlpool. For those who can't get enough, Dolphin Cove offers educational half-day (US$440) and full-day (US$660) **sea keeper programs,** providing children and adults a more in-depth experience from a caretaker's perspective. Dolphin Cove is a short drive from Ocho Rios and shouldn't cost more than US$10 by taxi. Route taxis plying the main road between Ocho Rios and St. Ann's Bay are easy to flag down and cost substantially less (US$1.50 pp).

Ocho Rios Fort

Built in the late 17th century, **Ocho Rios Fort** is beside the old Reynolds bauxite installation on the western end of town, just past Island Village. The fort is not managed as an attraction, and there's little to see beyond a row of cannons facing the sea, two originally from Ocho Rios Fort and two that defended the

Ocho Rios and Vicinity

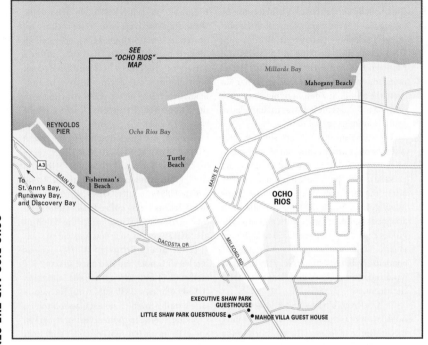

town of Mammee Bay. A plaque next to the fort offers a history of the site.

★ Mystic Mountain

Mystic Mountain (tel. 876/618-1553 or 876/618-1558, hotelres@mysticmountain. com, www.rainforestadventure.com, 9am-3pm daily) is located on 40 hectares (100 acres) of forest west of town, just before Dunn's River Falls and Dolphin Cove. The tour includes a 15-minute ride up to the peak of Mystic Mountain on the Sky Lift (US$47 pp), a chairlift similar to what you'd find at ski resorts. The ride and summit afford stunning views over Ocho Rios, and once at the peak, there's an exhibit of Jamaican history and culture, a gift shop, and a bar and restaurant in a wooden replica of an old Jamaican train station. A water slide descends into an

infinity pool in front of the building overlooking the sea.

The Bobsled Tour (US$69, including sky lift) is a two-seat tram that travels through the forest on suspended rails, an exhilarating five-minute blast of adrenaline, but only as gut-wrenching as the person in front, controlling the brakes, decides. The canopy tour (US$115, including sky lift) consists of a ride on a series of five zip lines through the forest. All three rides can be packaged for US$138 pp. Additional bobsled runs cost US$22; a family pack (US$44) is five rides. There is no additional charge for use of the pool and water slide. **Mystic Dining** (9pm-5pm daily, US$5-15) offers soups, sandwiches, burgers, pasta, and à la carte jerk chicken and pork in a large dining room with windows open to the view.

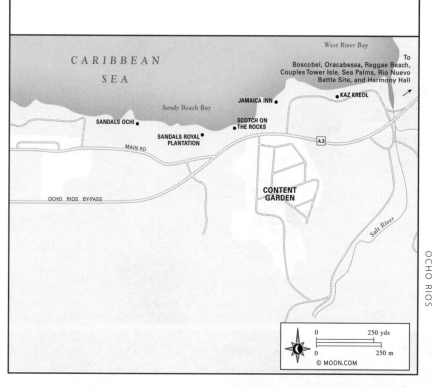

Shaw Park Gardens

Shaw Park Gardens (end of Shaw Park Rd., cell tel. 876/429-3424, or contact manager Andrew Reid, tel. 876/819-5686, l.andrew@cwjamaica.com, 8am-5pm daily, US$10, US$5 under age 12, 30- to 90-minute guided tour US$10 extra) is a river park whose glory days are long past. Nonetheless, the park makes a pleasant venue for a stroll or a picnic, with a large waterfall and two adjacent river-fed pools at the bottom of the property, and stairs and paths meandering back up to the parking area. The pools are often empty of water unless a special request has been made for them to be filled. Climbing the waterfall is not permitted. The 10-hectare (25-acre) property sees only a trickle of visitors and is a great place to escape the crowds, whether accompanied by one of the knowledgeable guides or on your own.

TOP EXPERIENCE

★ Konoko Falls

Konoko Falls (Shaw Park Rd., tel. 876/622-1712, cell tel. 876/408-0575, www.konokofalls.com, 8am-5pm daily, US$20 adults, US$10 under age 12) was once a banana stand on Shaw Park Estate before becoming the riverine botanical garden on the Milford River it is today. Visitors can see native yellow-billed and black-billed parrots, iguanas, and snakes as well as a pair of American crocodiles, a turtle, and a couple of macaws among a host of other endemic and exotic birds housed in an aviary and on display tethered or in contained areas between the historical exhibit and the falls.

Visitors can climb the waterfalls, where unobtrusive guides are on hand to help if needed. Tipping the guides is at your discretion. A few

small pools have enough space for a couple of people to be fully submerged and splash around. A Romanesque pavilion next to a bar and restaurant above the falls is used for events and weddings. A small museum features a history of the Taino people, Jamaica's earliest inhabitants, and a display covering the local watershed. Ysassi's Lookout Point, named after the last Spanish governor of Jamaica, has a view over Ocho Rios and the bay. The entire park can be traversed in about 15 minutes.

To get to Konoko, turn right opposite the Anglican church heading south toward Fern Gully on Milford Road (the A3), keeping right at the Y immediately thereafter and following the signs. The park entrance is on the left. A taxi from the center of Ocho Rios shouldn't cost more than US$10 for the 10-minute ride.

Turtle River Falls & Gardens

A six-hectare (14-acre) river park with 14 cascades, a walk-in aviary, and a swimming pool is at **Turtle River Falls & Gardens** (Eden Bower Rd., tel. 876/974-5114 or 876/974-8508, turtleriverfallsandgardens@gmail.com, US$20 adults, US$10 under age 12). The optional guided tour (included) lasts an hour and 15 minutes. Tipping is at visitor discretion; US$5-10 pp is sufficient. A snack bar serves drinks, and patrons are permitted to bring their own food. A path alongside the river leads to the largest cascade at the top of the park, where there's a deep pool fit for splashing around and where visitors can climb the falls. This is the best river park option in Ochi if you actually want to swim, thanks to its large swimming pool.

Turtle River Park

Ocho Rios is known for its lush gardens, though some are better maintained than others. **Turtle River Park** (tel. 876/795-0078, 7am-8pm Mon.-Fri., 8am-9pm Sat.-Sun., free) is near the center of town, straight ahead as

---

1: Dolphin Cove 2: Jamaica's leading tourist attraction, Dunn's River Falls

you descend from Fern Gully at the junction of Milford, Main Street, and DaCosta Drive. There's also a pedestrian entrance on Main Street across from Sandcastles. Ponds in the park have koi, butterfly koi, tilapia, and turtles. Within easy walking distance from downtown Ochi, Turtle River Park is great for a stroll, to sit and read a book, or to carry your takeout and have an alfresco picnic.

Prospect Plantation

Prospect Plantation (contact Dolphin Cove, tel. 876/994-1058, 8am-4pm Mon.-Sat.) is a 405-hectare (1,000-acre) working plantation bought by Sir Harold Mitchell in 1936. Mitchell entertained all manner of dignitaries here in the great house and the area's most luxurious villas. A tradition was that his guests would plant a tree on the grounds to mark their visit. The most notable of these tokens of remembrance is the giant mahogany planted by Winston Churchill in 1953. It stands in the driveway behind the great house.

Nestled among the groves of tropical hardwoods below the great house is a beautiful chapel built by Mitchell to mark the passing of his wife, Mary Jane Mitchell Greene, known as Lady Mitchell. The chapel was constructed completely with hardwoods and stone found on the plantation.

Tours of the Prospect Plantation at **Yaaman Adventure Park** (cell tel. 876/296-5586, www.yaamanadventure.com, US$59 adults, US$79 children) range from cooking lessons to rides on camels, horseback, jitneys, Segways, and mud buggies. A tour of the great house is included with each. The Yaaman Full Hundred package (US$149 adults, US$99 children) offers access to all the tours on property, along with a lunch of jerk chicken, bean stew, salad, and corn on the cob with fruit juice. To get to Yaaman, take a route taxi from the bus park or downtown by the clock tower (US$1.50). A charter will cost around US$10.

★ White River Valley

The White River Valley runs along the St. Ann-St. Mary border. The waterway was an important topographical feature for the Spaniards, who built the first road from the South Coast to the North Coast along its banks. The oldest **Spanish Bridge** on the island can still be seen at the river's upper reaches, just above the site where Chukka Caribbean's River Tubing Safari begins. Several river parks and gardens dot the banks. To get to the White River Valley, turn right at the first stoplight heading east from Ocho Rios along the A3, just after the second gas station. Follow the road for four kilometers (2.5 miles) and turn left at the intersection in Lodge, the second community, and then make a right along the rough dirt road adjacent to an electrical substation. Cars with low clearance may bottom out along sections of the rocky road.

Forty-minute tours down the lower reaches of the White River on bamboo rafts (2 people, US$55) and rubber inner tubes (1 person, US$25) are on offer from **Calypso River Rafting** (contact Judi Marsh, cell tel. 876/817-8433, yasanadi@yahoo.com, or Bobby Marsh, cell tel. 876/995-3220, bobmarcon@yahoo.com).

The popular **Blue Hole River** features a series of waterfalls and natural pools along the White River. Locals keep the banks clean and guide visitors to the different pools suitable for swimming for US$10 pp. The area is the first set of swimming holes you'll reach after turning right at the electrical substation. You'll see a parking area on the left as you come around the first bend in the rocky road.

A riverside park and chill spot along the White River, **Calby's River Hidden Beauty** (cell tel. 876/858-8771, 9am-5pm daily, US$10, US$5 under age 13) has a rope swing and areas where the limestone riverbed has been formed into smooth slides by gushing water. Tubes, guides, and life jackets are included. A bar and restaurant serve beer, jerk chicken, and pork with rice-and-peas and festival.

Take a well-organized serene ride down a five-kilometer (3-mile) stretch of the White River with **Chukka Caribbean's River Tubing Safari** (tel. 876/972-2506, ochorios@chukkacaribbean.com, www.chukkacaribbean.com, US$65), starting at the historic Spanish Bridge, an attraction in itself built in the 17th century. Tubers float over the limestone riverbed, sometimes lazily, sometimes fast as the banks narrow, creating mild rapids. The tour lasts about two hours.

Blue Hole at White River Valley

BEACHES

Most of the resorts in town and along the coast have cordoned off their seafront beach areas in their best attempt to make them private. Despite the fact that all beaches in Jamaica are accessible to the public up to the high-water mark, private landowners along the coast can apply for exclusivity permits, a clause in the law that most hotels take advantage of.

One of the best beaches in the vicinity, previously known as Reggae Beach, is **Bamboo Beach Club** (2 minutes east of White River, St. Mary, tel. 876/975-5122, info@bamboobeachclub.com, www.bamboobeachclub.com, 8am-6pm Mon.-Thurs., 9am-midnight Fri.-Sun., day pass from US$11). The private enclave caters mostly to cruise ship passengers with admission fees ranging from US$11 for entry and beach chair only to US$39 inclusive of food and drink. Pricier packages cover multiple beverages (US$59), a massage (US$69), transportation from area hotels (US$49 pp), and tours at other attractions.

Managed by the operators of Cool Runnings, a catamaran cruise outfit, **Mahogany Beach** (Main St., free) is east of the town center, just past Bibibip's. It's a decent place to soak up the local scene and is also the departure point for the catamaran booze cruises. The sand is not as plentiful nor is the sea floor as clean as at other beaches in the area.

Ocho Rios Bay Beach (Main St. at Ocho Rios Fishing Village, US$5), also known as Turtle Beach, dominates the shorefront area in the heart of town. Moon Palace Jamaica Grande has roped off a large piece of the beach on the eastern side of the bay, while Turtle Towers and Fisherman's Point share the western end with the public beach park and marina at the end.

Fishermen's Beach (Main St., free) is the newly renovated home to a number of seafood restaurants and craft vendors. The beach itself is crowded with colorfully painted fishing boats, or canoes, as they're known in Jamaica, and swimming is better on the other side of the little gully separating Fishermen's Beach

from the beach in front of Margaritaville. Fishing boat owners will charter their boats for snorkeling excursions to the reef or to Pearly Beach and Laughing Waters, a few kilometers west of Ocho Rios. A round-trip boat ride to Laughing Waters shouldn't cost more than US$20 pp.

One Love Trail, located about one kilometer (0.6 mile) west of Island Village shopping center heading out of town, leads down to a beautiful waterfall spilling onto a small beach protected by a reef just offshore. Caretaker Goshford Dorrington "Histry" Miller (cell tel. 876/893-1867) takes tips for keeping the place clean and sells artwork and natural jewelry. **Margaritaville Beach** (free) is a nice beach in front of Margaritaville that can be accessed through Island Village or just past Island Village heading down to the cruise ship terminal.

James Bond fans may be on the lookout for the beaches that appeared in the 1963 film *Dr. No*. **Pearly Beach** and adjacent **Laughing Waters** served as Crab Cay, the fictitious island that was home to villainous Dr. No, where the first "Bond girl," Ursula Andress, famously emerged from the sea to meet 007. Both beaches are privately managed by the St. Ann Development Corporation (SADCo) and aren't accessible unless rented exclusively. Pearly Beach can be booked through hotel concierge desks for large groups (75 people minimum, US$10 pp), and Laughing Waters can be booked through Janice Chong at SADCo (tel. 876/974-5015, chong@udcja.com, from US$1,000 for 75 people to US$2,500 for 250 people, plus US$500 deposit).

RECREATION
Water Sports

From the marina at Fisherman's Point there are a few boats available for charter for sailing and snorkeling. **Island Dog Water Sports** (Ocho Rios Marina, cell tel. 876/367-8342, shaltonwhyte@hotmail.com) offers deep-sea fishing and snorkeling excursions.

Garfield Diving Centre (Ocho Rios Bay

Beach, cell tel. 876/395-7023, www.garfield-diving.com, garfielddiving@hotmail.com) offers introductory diving tours (US$115) as well as PADI certification courses (US$475). The dive center also offers glass-bottom boat tours (US$30 pp per hour), deep-sea fishing (half-day US$600) on *Magic Time,* a 38-foot boat, or larger vessels up to a 53-footer accommodating up to 12 guests (US$1,200).

A recent addition to the Ocho Rios watersports scene is **Bluefish Dive Center** (Ocho Rios Marina, U.S. tel. 204/996-2756, tel. 876/575-5395, dive@bluefishdivecenter.com, www.bluefishdivecenter.com), offering PADI certification courses and introductory dives (from US$100).

With three catamarans and a trimaran, **Cool Runnings Catamarans** (1 Marvins Park, tel. 876/974-2446 or 954/434-5125, www.coolrunningscatamarans.com) operates cruises to Dunn's River Falls (12:30pm-4pm Mon.-Sat., US$86 plus transfer) that include an open bar and patties, snorkeling gear, and the entrance fee to the falls. A Taste of Jamaica evening cruise (5pm-8pm Thurs., US$75 pp) offers an open bar and Jamaican food like jerk pork, chicken, rice-and-peas, festival, and bammy. Other cruises offered are by charter, including the clothing-optional Wet and Wild cruise (minimum 15 people, from US$136). The boats depart and return to Mahogany Beach. The open bar serves beer, rum, and soft drinks.

Tours

The host of activities for thrill seekers and adventure lovers offered by **Chukka Caribbean** (U.S. tel. 877/424-8552, tel. 876/656-8026, www.chukka.com) includes catamaran cruises from the Ocho Rios Marina, canopy zip-line tours, cliff jumping, white-water rafting, river tubing, horseback riding, and off-roading on ATVs and dune buggies as well as trips to Bob Marley's birthplace at Nine Mile. Chukka offers guests transportation from wherever they are staying. Quintessential Chukka Chukka tours include tubing down the White River from the old Spanish Bridge

(U$65), canopy zip lines at a number of locations across the island, and the classic horseback ride and swim.

Konoko Bike Safari and Blue Mountain Bicycle Tours (121 Main St., tel. 876/974-7075, www.bmtoursja.com, from US$75) runs a downhill bike tour in the hills above Ocho Rios. Another tour takes groups of up to 20 riders to Cascade, above Buff Bay in the Blue Mountains, where the route descends for about an hour, with a stop for lunch, before continuing for another hour to the Fish Dunn waterfall above Charles Town. The entire excursion runs 8am-4:30pm from hotel pickup to drop-off.

Golf

A *Golf Digest* 3.5-star course in the hills above Ochi, **Sandals Golf and Country Club** (tel. 876/975-0119, www.sandals.com, 7am-5pm daily, greens fees US$100) is compact and very walkable, but carts (US$40) are also available. Clubs (US$30-45) can be rented, and players are obliged to use a caddy (US$17 plus US$10 pp minimum tip). A patio restaurant and bar serves burgers, hot dogs, and chicken sandwiches (US$7). The driving range offers baskets of 40 balls (US$4). Sandals guests don't pay greens fees, and special rates apply for guests of several other area lodgings.

ENTERTAINMENT
Bars and Nightclubs

Ochi's most popular club with visitors is **Margaritaville** (Island Village, tel. 876/675-8800, 9am-4am Mon., Wed., and Sat., 9am-10pm on Sun., Tues., and Thurs.-Fri.). It sees a lot of debauchery, and the pool party on Wednesday attracts a large crowd.

Ocean's 11 Watering Hole (Cruise Ship Pier, tel. 876/974-8444, manbowen@cwjamaica.com, 10am-midnight daily, 8am-midnight daily when ships are in town) is a café, bar, and restaurant serving a full menu

1: Yaaman Adventure Park offers ATV tours at Prospect Plantation 2: Ziplining at Mystic Mountain 3: Daybreak breakfast party

of steak, fish, lobster, salmon, conch, and ribs. It's a favorite local hotspot when hours are extended to 2am for karaoke on Tuesday, for an after-work jam Friday, and for the weekly retro party on Saturday. Live bands play until 1am on Sunday. Coffee is sold by the cup (US$3-6) and by the pound.

Each night features a different theme, with Cups Friday and Vybz Saturday, at **Gen-X Sports Bar & Night Club** (38 Island Plaza, Main St., tel. 876/974-4369). There is a large dance floor and a separate bar area, and the club attracts a decent crowd on a good night; otherwise it can be completely empty.

Amnesia (70 Main St., tel. 876/974-2633, cell tel. 876/588-2385, 9:30pm-4:30am Wed.-Sun., US$5-10) is a longstanding nightclub located in the heart of Ocho Rios. The club runs Beer Wednesday, Ladies Night on Thursday (US$10 high season, US$5 low season), Hangover Fridays (US$5), live music on select Saturdays (cover from US$10), and the big night, Sippin' Sunday (US$5).

On the top floor of Beecham Plaza overlooking Main Street Ocho Rios, **8 Rivaz Ultra Lounge** (Beecham Plaza, 76 Main St., cell tel. 876/838-6381, 5pm-2am Sun.-Thurs., 5pm-4am Fri.-Sat., US$5-10) is a modern club with an outdoor deck and hookah lounge. Ladies Night on Tuesday features free shots and specials all night, with R&B on Wednesday and Dancehall on Thursday. Glo Friday has patrons dancing with glow sticks, and International Night on Saturday features in-house and guest DJs spinning a mix of dancehall, reggae, hip-hop, and pop. Back-to-Back Sunday goes retro with dancehall from the 1980s and 1990s. Food from a bar menu is served 5pm-midnight and until 1am on weekends.

Festivals and Events

Jamaica can be a tough place when it comes to continuity, and some of the more obscure annual events wane with the passing years, while others regroup and come back stronger. There are several events held each year along the North Coast that are worth planning for.

The **Ocho Rios Jazz Festival** (U.S. tel. 323/857-5358, tel. 876/927-3544, www.ochoriosjazz.com) is held at various venues in Kingston, Ocho Rios, and Port Antonio over the course of seven days, starting at the end of May or the first week of June. The festival features a few dozen local and international jazz acts. Moon Palace has hosted music as part of the Ocho Rios Jazz Festival in recent years, along with FDR Resort in Runaway Bay and the Hope Gardens band shell in Kingston.

The largest annual music festival in the region, **Rebel Salute** (www.rebelsalutejamaica.com) is held in mid-January at Grizzly Plantation on Richmond Estate just west of Priory. Founded by iconic reggae artist Tony Rebel, the festival is held over two nights and features reggae artists and vendors selling ital (vegetarian) cuisine and crafts.

On the long Heroes weekend, **Frenchmen** (www.frenchmenparty.com), Jamaica's longest standing band of party promoters, hosts three parties at Pearly Beach that draw patrons from across the globe: Rise Up, an early-morning swimwear-clad beach party; Nitecap, a pajama and lingerie themed soirée; and Foreplay, on Sunday afternoon.

The Network Jam, another Kingston-based group of promoters, hosts a competing series at nearby Grizzly Plantation, dubbed **The Great Weekend,** consisting of a breakfast party, Daybreak, on Saturday morning; a party sunset cruise that evening; and Allure the following day. Allure returns to St. Ann again the last weekend in May.

On the third Saturday in April, **Bacchanal Jamaica** (www.bacchanaljamaica.com) brings the carnival vibes to the North Coast with Bacchanal Beach J'Ouvert at Grizzly Plantation, a full day of flying paint and debauchery.

SHOPPING

Ocho Rios is a duty-free shopping haven with countless shops hawking watches, jewelry, sunglasses, beachwear, and rootsy reggae apparel to short-stay visitors concentrated in the vicinity of the cruise ship pier. At the lower end of **Fern Gully,** a handful of wood carvers and painters patiently await patrons whose visits have slowed to a trickle now that most of the traffic between Kingston and Ocho Rios has shifted to the North-South Highway, completely bypassing the area. For a real Jamaica experience, there's nothing better than a stroll through the **Ocho Rios Market,** a seemingly endless maze of tarpaulin-covered stalls that stretches from the clock tower in the center of town to the transport center bordering the bypass.

Island Village Shopping and Entertainment Centre (www.island-villageja.com) is a complex housing Margaritaville, Cove Theatre cinema, an ice cream parlor, and a number of shops. **Bijoux Jewelers** (tel. 876/675-5220, bijouxja@cw-jamaica.com) claims to be Jamaica's longest-standing retailer of jewelry, with quality brands of watches, earrings, bracelets, and necklaces, including Michael Kors, Fossil, and Pandora. **Casa de Oro** (tel. 876/675-8999) sells duty-free jewelry and designer watches from the likes of Cartier, Tissot, Tag Heuer, and Dior as well as diamonds. **Tuff Gong Trading** (tel. 876/631-8484) retails authentic apparel, most of it depicting the image of reggae legend Bob Marley. **Hemp Heaven** (tel.

876/675-8969) retails hemp apparel, footwear, and arts and crafts.

A stately Georgian great house with a gallery on the second floor, **Harmony Hall** (Tower Isle, tel. 876/975-4222, www.harmonyhall.com, 10am-5pm Tues.-Sun.) features works by the likes of Cecil Cooper, Susan Shirley, and Graham Davis, among other contemporary painters. A bookshop in the gallery has cookbooks by local authors. Check the website for temporary exhibitions and craft fairs. The colonial-era building is five minutes east of Ochi along the main road in Tower Isle.

One of the brilliant artists associated with the defunct Wassi Art collective, which once produced some of Jamaica's most recognized hand painted ceramics, is **Homer Brown** (cell tel. 876/417-8916). Homer has carried on the tradition and now sells ceramics out of his home studio.

Fern Gully

Fern Gully is an old riverbed that was planted with ferns in the 1880s and later paved over as part of the main thoroughfare (the A3) between the North and South Coasts. The North-South Highway now takes most of the traffic, and Fern Gully is quiet but for locals,

the Ocho Rios Market

making it much more enjoyable as a shady stop for paintings and carvings from the few vendors located at the base of the hill.

Owned and operated by oil painter Owen Marsh, **Fern Gully Art Studio** (cell tel. 876/781-8999, 8am-5pm daily, US$50-1,500) is in an unmistakable octagonal building with wheels as windows at the base of Fern Gully, a five-minute drive from the stoplight by the gas station along the Ocho Rios bypass. A cab shouldn't cost more than US$10 round-trip from the clock tower in the center of town. Next door, **Ralph Cameron** (cell tel. 876/881-7050, 7am-7pm daily US$10-1,000) sells a wide variety of wood carvings made by himself and other local carvers.

FOOD

Ocho Rios has a smattering of great restaurants, including a couple of jerk pits, quality home-style Jamaican kitchens, and ital vegetarian joints, as well convincing Italian and Indian offerings and ample sports-bar fare.

Breakfast and Cafés

Typical Jamaican food for breakfast, lunch, and dinner is at **Nice-and-Nuff** (shop 8, Simmon's Plaza, 73 Main St., tel. 876/489-2190, 7am-7pm Mon.-Sat., US$3-4), with items like ackee and saltfish, oxtail, curry goat, and fried chicken. Food is served in foam boxes ready for takeout.

In a blue building across from the police station, toward the clock tower, **Mom's Restaurant** (7 Evelyn St., tel. 876/974-2811, 8am-10pm Mon.-Sat., US$5-13) is a local favorite for local dishes, starting the day right with ackee and saltfish, corned pork, mackerel rundown, and liver before moving on to staples like oxtail, brown stew fish, and baked or fried chicken on the lunch and dinner menu.

Jamaican

Ocho Rios Jerk Centre (16 DaCosta Dr., tel. 876/974-2549, 10am-11pm daily, US$5-13) serves pork, whole and half chicken, conch, and ribs and fish by the pound, accompanied by breadfruit, sweet potato, bammy, and

festival. It's located between Mystic Ridge and the stoplight at the junction of DaCosta and the road to Fern Gulley.

The real deal local Jamaican dive **Simply the Best Restaurant** (Shades Lane, look for the sign beside the entrance to Shades Night Club, Content Garden, 7am-3am Mon.-Thurs., 7am-5am Fri.-Sat., tel. 876/974-7268, US$4-8) serves brown stewed pork (US$4), curried goat, fried chicken, and escoveitch fish fillet late into the night. Daily specials include barbecue, baked, or jerk chicken, stew peas, stew beef, and mackerel rundown, among many others.

On an unassuming lane opposite Ochi's open-air market in the heart of Ocho Rios, ★ **Miss T's Kitchen** (65 Main St., tel. 876/795-0099, misstskitchen@gmail.com, www.misstskitchen.com, 9am-10pm daily, US$8-36) offers scrumptious home-style Jamaican food. Colorful paintings, vintage Marley photos, hanging gourd and wicker lamps, and musical instruments adorn the walls. Starters include stamp-and-go (saltfish fritters) spiced with fresh herbs and a Thai chili sauce, crab backs paired with fruit salsa, and oxtail sliders served on mini cocoa bread. The creamy coconut curry lobster served in the shell with sides of rice-and-peas and steamed veggies is guaranteed to satisfy. The signature house dish is Miss T's Famous Oxtail: mouthwatering meat simmered with butter beans, spinners, and carrot. For vegetarians, the Chickpea Stack is curried in coconut milk with ripe plantain, and Vegetable Rundown is pumpkin, greens, and plantain simmered in coconut sauce. Wash it all down with fresh-squeezed limeade or beer.

Offering guests a bespoke culinary experience on top of the world, **Miss T's @ Murphy Hill** (by reservation) has a panoramic view and a creative rotating menu that fuses Jamaican culinary traditions with inspirations from the master chef's travels abroad. To get there, take Milford Road to Shaw Park Road and then keep left at the Y intersection to Parry Town. From Parry Town continue on Parry Town Main Street to Pimento Walk and turn left across from the playground up to Murphy Hill. It's about 25 minutes from the center of Ochi.

On a hill overlooking Ocho Rios just outside the old Shaw Park Hotel and Gardens, **Oceans on the Ridge** (Shaw Park Rd., tel. 876/974-6290, cell tel. 876/878-4444, 9am-2am Mon.-Sat., 9am-11pm Sun., mikef@ oceansontheridge.com, www.oceansontheridge.com, US$8-30) boasts a panoramic view of Ocho Rios, the bay, and the Caribbean beyond. A large open-air deck has plentiful seating at tables and around the bar. The restaurant serves sandwiches, burgers, dogs, wraps, and Jamaican seafood and meat dishes like curry goat, jerk chicken, steamed and escoveitch fish, and lobster.

The menu changes daily at **My Favorite Place Restaurant** (shop 7, Ocean Village, tel. 876/795-0480, 7:30am-7:30pm Mon.-Sat., US$2-6), serving typical Jamaican dishes like fried chicken, curry goat, escoveitch fish, brown stew, and baked chicken.

Hashtagz (cell tel. 876/401-3868, 11am-midnight daily) is a food truck operated by Quincy Smith since 2016 in the Total gas station in Clock Tower Square. A couple of stools serve as the dining room, where patrons wolf down lasagna, kebabs, and buffalo wings on the go.

Mongoose Jamaica Restaurant & Lounge (52 Main St., tel. 876/622-6942, 9:30am-1am Sun.-Thurs., 9:30am-3am Fri.-Sat., US$10-35) serves well prepared and nicely presented starters like chicken wings, coconut breaded shrimp, and salads, and main courses that include the signature Mongoose burger with smoked bacon, grilled pineapple, and sautéed onion with ginger wine glaze. Other entrées include local dishes like curry chicken or goat, oxtail, and jerk chicken.

Seafood

A clean and sleek waterfront concourse replaced the ramshackle seafood shacks at the old Fishermen's Beach as the sparkling new restaurants of ★ **Ocho Rios Fishing Village.** The entrepreneurs who had businesses at the beach were provided space in the renovated space. A walkway from Island Village next door makes the Fishermen's Beach complex an accessible stroll. At times different music blasts from the competing businesses, but overall it has a good vibe, where children play in the sand as the food is being prepared, often on island time.

Formerly the Tropical Beach seafood restaurant, **Tropical Buzz** (Garwin Davis, tel. 876/550-0027, 9am-11pm daily, US$8-20) now occupies a unit three-quarters of the way down the boardwalk to the beach, serving fish, octopus, conch, shrimp, and the traditional Jamaican breakfast of ackee and saltfish in the morning.

Whalers Seafood Restaurant (upstairs, cell tel. 876/290-5817, orvillebgrant@gmail.com) serves fish, shrimp, conch, and lobster (US$10-25).

Sharing the second level with Whalers, **Lobster Dave** (upstairs, tel. 876/585-5385 or 876/568-0982, 10am-11pm daily, later on weekends, US$6-20) has indoor and balcony seating for air-conditioned and alfresco dining. The kitchen pumps out crab, lobster, fish, and conch.

Reggae Kitchen (shop 3, Fishermen's Beach, tel. 876/822-0984, noon-10pm daily, US$8-22) is a seafood and Jamaican fare specialist serving steamed or escoveitch snapper in addition to vegetable chunks, chicken, oxtail, and steamed veg.

Fancy Seafood (3 James Ave., tel. 876/974-4402, 9am-10pm daily, US$6-20), run by the congenial Alicia Archer, serves curry goat, fried chicken, shrimp, escoveitch, brown stew, and fried jerk fish.

International

The only place in town for falafel or a Greek sandwich is ★ **Little Santurini Grill** (Kaz Kreol, White River, 7am-10pm daily, tel. 876/974-4613, US$10-20). Both are convincingly prepared and affordably served beachside on a gorgeous stretch of coast by the mouth of the White River.

Almond Tree Restaurant (83 Main St., Hibiscus Lodge, tel. 876/974-2676 or 876/947-2813, 7:30am-10:30am, noon-2:30pm, and 6pm-9:30pm daily) serves a mix of Jamaican and international dishes like lobster (US$50), a variety of chicken (US$35), fish (US$40), lamb chops (US$30), and butterfly shrimp (US$35). A full bar in the restaurant serves beer (US$3) as well as mixed drinks. Indoor and outdoor dining areas overlook the water.

An Italian restaurant serving lobster, steak, and pasta dishes, **Evita's** (Eden Bower Rd., tel. 876/974-2333, noon-11pm daily, US$20-40) lacks an upscale edge, but the view is excellent and worth a trip. To get there, turn up Eden Bower Road from the Ocho Rios bypass; you'll see the sign after the first deep corner.

Rasta Taco Jamaica (Island Village, cell tel. 876/893-3155, jamaica@rastataco.com, www.rastatacojamaica.com, 11am-8pm daily, US$6-18) serves tropicalized Mexican-Caribbean fusion, including tacos, burritos, wraps, and salads, both vegetarian and for meat eaters.

Relocated from Kingston, **Caffé Da Vinci** (Island Village, tel. 876/630-7025, www.caffedavincija.com, noon-10pm daily) has Italian specialties that include rosemary chicken (US$15), shrimp linguine (US$23), and a seafood platter (US$55). The tagliatelle is homemade and served with shrimp, lobster, and calamari served in a bolognese, alfredo, or herb sauce (US$25).

Hong Kong International Restaurant (3 Champion Plaza, Dacosta Dr., tel. 876/974-0588, 10am-10pm Mon.-Fri., later Sat.-Sun., from US$7) is one of the better places for Chinese food in Ochi, serving chicken, beef, shrimp, seafood, and pork with noodles and rice. It lacks ambience, making takeout a good option.

In a breezy waterfront location at Fisherman's Point, overlooking the town's marina, **Passage to India Restaurant & Bar** (shop 2, Fisherman's Point Resort, next to Ocho Rios Cruise Ship Pier, 11am-11pm daily, US$11-26) serves authentic north Indian *palak paneer, mala kofta,* chicken vindaloo, lamb, lobster, and shrimp. It shares the premises with **Bottles & Chimney,** a Jamaican bar and cook shop under the same management.

Taste of India (Sonis Plaza, 50 Main St., tel. 876/795-3182, 10am-10pm Tues.-Sun., US$12-22) serves north Indian cuisine with dishes like *palak paneer, mala costa,* chicken vindaloo, lamb, lobster, and shrimp.

Mainland China (Landmark Plaza, tel. 876/974-8899, 11am-midnight Wed.-Mon., US$10-30) serves a mix of Jamaican, Indian, and Chinese cuisine and is considered one of the most dependable restaurants in Ochi by locals. Jamaican dishes range from curry goat, oxtail, and fried or jerk chicken with sides that include bammy, festival, yam, boiled corn, or rice-and-peas, while Indian offerings include marinated leg of lamb and tandoor and chicken kebab. The Chinese menu includes fried rice, garlic noodle, chop suey, chow mein, lo mein, pepper shrimp, butter garlic, black bean, ginger scallion, or Szechwan lobster.

Fine Dining
Spring Garden Seafood & Steakhouse
(Ocho Rios Bypass, tel. 876/795-3149, café. spring@yahoo.com, 11am-11pm daily) serves well-prepared seafood, steak, and chicken (US$10-40) with indoor and alfresco dining.

Christopher's Restaurant (Hermosa Cove, U.S. tel. 855/811-2683, tel. 876/974-3699, 7am-8:30pm daily, US$20-45) serves casual gourmet dishes in an open-air dining area with ocean views, a great way to experience one of the boutique resorts in the area, with worldly dishes like curried goat ravioli and pimento smoked beef tenderloin. The **Broken Rudder** is the beachside grill at the same property, offering a more casual dining experience for lunch.

Vegetarian
Healthy Way Vegetarian Kitchen (shop 54, Ocean Village, tel. 876/974-9229, 9am-6pm

1: a tasty dish at Stush in the Bush 2: Reggae Pot Restaurant

Mon.-Sat., US$1.50-5) serves escoveitch tofu; hominy, peanut, plantain, carrot, and bulgur porridge; steamed cabbage with banana; and fried dumplings.

Calabash Ital Restaurant (7 James Ave., 8am-10pm Mon.-Sat., 8am-8pm Sun., US$4-5) serves vegan dishes like ackee, veggie stew, and tofu on a rotating menu along with natural juices like beet, cane, and june plum (US$2).

Natural seasonal juices are prepared at ★ **Reggae Pot Rastaurant** (86 Main St., cell tel. 876/296-3591, 9am-9pm Mon.-Sat., 10am-8pm Sun., US$3-5), serving vegetarian ital food on a rotating menu with dishes like brown stew, curried or stir-fry tofu, and split peas with veggie chunks.

Bakeries

Golden Loaf Baking Company (72 Main St., tel. 876/974-2635, pizzeria tel. 876/974-7014, glb@cwjamaica.com, 8am-8:30pm Mon.-Sat.) makes bread, pastries, pizzas, stewed and jerk chicken and pork, oxtail, curry goat, stewed beef, and turkey neck.

Ice Cream

Local ice cream is sold at **Scoops Unlimited** (shop 11, Island Village, tel. 876/675-8776, 9am-8:30pm Mon.-Fri., 10am-10pm Sat.-Sun.).

ACCOMMODATIONS

As one of the original resort towns in Jamaica, Ocho Rios has developed a wide array of lodging options. Nevertheless, at the lower end, conditions tend to be consistently shabby, while there are several good mid-range and high-end options.

Under US$100

Located a few steps from the beach, the backpacker-friendly **Reggae Hostel Ocho Rios** (19 Main St., tel. 876/974-2607, www.reggaehostel.com, from US$20) has two dormitories with shared baths, one with six bunk beds, the other with eight, and private rooms with en suite baths, one category sleeping two

(US$65), the other four (US$100). Included are complimentary Wi-Fi, coffee and tea, parking, a communal kitchen, and a roof bar and lounge. The private rooms have air-conditioning and TVs.

Reasonably priced and with a common balcony overlooking the water, **Carleen's Villa Guest House** (85-A Main St., tel. 876/974-5431) has seven no-frills rooms (US$40) equipped with ceiling fans, two twin beds, TVs, and hot water in private baths. There's no pool and no food, but it's five minutes away from Mahogany Beach, Ochi's most popular with locals.

One of the original and less-attractive apartment-style options, **Turtle Beach Towers** (tel. 876/954-7807, admin@mysilversands.com, www.turtlebeachtowers.com, from US$75) is a cluster of gray towers, at the base of Fisherman's Point, that resemble government housing projects. Do not book here without first seeing the room in person, as individual owners decorate the apartments according to their tastes (or neglect, as the case may be), and the decor and amenities vary greatly from unit to unit. Reduced rates can be negotiated for longer stays.

US$100-250

A large condo complex on a hill overlooking Ocho Rios, **Columbus Heights Apartments** (Columbus Heights, tel. 876/974-9057 or 876/974-2940, columbushgts@cwjamaica.com, www.columbusheights.com, US$100-200 low season, US$120-220 high season) affords great views. Studios and one- and two-bedroom apartments have air-conditioning and hot water. Longer stays garner reduced rates.

The sister property to the Ocho Rios hilltop theme park, Mystic Mountain, **Mystic Ridge Resort** (17 DaCosta Dr., tel. 876/974-9831 or 876/618-1998, info@mysticridgejamaica.com, from US$118) offers guests discounted tour rates and complimentary transport. The stratified complex has standard rooms, loft suites, and one- and two-bedroom apartments. The furnishings and linens are modern and tasteful. Flat-panel TVs, Wi-Fi, kitchenettes, private baths, and balconies feature in the apartments. Rates include a complimentary breakfast buffet in the poolside Zedoj Restaurant. A mobile spa offers room service for a variety of treatments.

Run as individual apartment owners pooling their units, **Fisherman's Point** (Cruise Ship Wharf, contact Charmaine Annikey for bookings, U.S. tel. 877/211-6313, cell tel. 876/798-7647, accounts@selfcateringapartmentsjm.com, www.fishermanspoint.net, US$100 low season, US$125 high season) has some of the nicer self-contained units available in Ocho Rios, and while decor and furnishings vary considerably, there is much better oversight of the conditions than at neighboring Turtle Beach Towers. All units are fully furnished, with hot water, living rooms, equipped kitchens, TV, air-conditioning, and phones. There is a nice pool at the center of the complex, with Turtle Beach access two minutes away.

SuperClubs' answer to the demand for a dependable room-only option in Ochi is **Rooms on the Beach** (Turtle Beach, Main St., tel. 876/974-6632 U.S. tel. 877/467-8737, info@superclubs.com, US$105-141). Located beachfront in the heart of town, Rooms has a pool and all the fixtures of an all-inclusive without the all-inclusive. The rooms are clean, with TV, air-conditioning, phones, and hot water. The property is a short walk from all the restaurants and nightlife in downtown Ocho Rios.

With air-conditioning, TVs, and private baths with hot water, the comfortable rooms at **Hibiscus Lodge** (83 Main St., tel. 876/974-2676, www.hibiscusjamaica.com) are either garden view (US$135 low season, US$147 high season) or ocean view (US$147 low season, US$159 high season) and have two twins or a queen. Rates include breakfast, and the hotel is within easy walking distance of the heart of Ochi and Mahogany Beach.

Kaz Kreol (Shaw Park, tel. 876/974-4613, kazkreoljamaica@gmail.com, US$98, including breakfast) is a waterfront hotel located on a beautiful beach along White River Bay, adjacent to the Shaw Park Beach Hotel. Rooms have queen or king beds, cable, Wi-Fi, air-conditioning, and private baths with hot water.

Seaside ★ **Te Moana** (Main Street, Ocho Rios, tel. 876/974-2870, www.hamonyhall.com) has two modest and art-filled independent one-bedroom units, Garden Cottage (US$130) and Seaside Cottage (US$200), the latter slightly larger and closer to the water. Both units have queen beds, single daybeds, full kitchens, Wi-Fi, cable, and water access off a wooden deck for swimming along the craggy shore.

A quaint B&B run by Elise Yapp and her Chinese-Jamaican family, who live on the premises, ensuring attentive service and with home-cooked meals, **The Blue House** (White River Estates, tel. 876/994-1367, elise@thebluehousejamaica.com, www.thebluehousejamaica.com, 3-night minimum, US$180-260) is in a small subdivision five minutes east of downtown Ocho Rios past the White River and opposite Couples Sans Souci. A well-appointed ground-floor bedroom can accommodate up to five on a king, two twins, and a queen, with a bath across the hall. Three bedrooms on the second level each have a king and an en suite bath, and there is a cottage around back with a porch surrounded by lush gardens. The property has a small pool, but it doesn't compare to a refreshing dip in the White River, a five-minute walk away. Accessibility is the only drawback, as the innkeepers don't provide guests with a key to the front entrance or gate, but staff is on call into the wee hours to let guests in.

Over US$250

★ **Jamaica Inn** (Main St., tel. 876/974-2514, U.S. tel. 855/441-2044, reservations@jamaicainn.com, from US$362 d) has 60 percent repeat guests, among them Jamaican and foreign dignitaries, including Winston Churchill, who stayed in the signature White Suite, and Marilyn Monroe. Since then the amenities have only improved. You won't find

clocks or TVs in the bedrooms, but Wi-Fi covers the entire property. Rooms are appointed with dark mahogany furnishings, white-washed walls, and open living rooms facing the sea. One of Jamaica's finest private beaches is dotted with thatch umbrellas, its wide expanse of fine golden sand extending 20 meters (65 feet) from the water's edge to the beach bar, pool, and croquet pitch that separate the great house from the sea.

A quaint two-bedroom beachfront cottage that sleeps up to eight, **Eden Sands** (16 James Ave., cell tel. 876/865-2366, nathanbless@hotmail.com, www.edensandsvilla.com, US$350) features cable TV, air-conditioning in the bedrooms, a live-in handyman, security, and a housekeeper. The distinguishing feature is a private beach on Ochi's Riviera, the finest stretch of coast around.

All-Inclusive Resorts

★ **Couples** (www.couples.com) has two all-inclusive resorts just east of Ochi across the White River in St. Mary. One is **Couples Tower Isle** (Tower Isle, tel. 876/975-4271, all-inclusive from US$354 d), with 226 double-occupancy rooms with king beds, large flat-panel TVs, air-conditioning, and a modern sleek South Beach feel. Balconies overlook the private beach with a private island within swimming distance, reserved for nudists. Cuisine features local fruit and produce, a delicious mix of local and international cuisine, details like black pepper grinders at each table, and top shelf drinks and liquor.

The other is **Couples San Souci** (tel. 876/994-1353, all-inclusive from US$502 d), a sprawling gem with 150 suites a five-minute drive west of Couples Tower Isle. Two large beaches include a west-facing one reserved for nudists, with a large pool and bar on the lawn. The larger north-facing beach is at the center of the resort, facing a crescent-shaped bay. On the western side of the property, the pool and spa sit atop low limestone cliffs in front of room blocks facing the large cove. Seven room categories vary by size and the time since they were last renovated. All are more than comfortable with air-conditioning, stocked mini fridges, and ceiling fans. En suite baths are large and clean with Gilchrist & Soames toiletries.

An upscale all-butler property with champagne and caviar available at C-Bar, **Sandals Royal Plantation** (tel. 876/974-5601, U.S. tel. 305/284-1300, www.royalplantation.com, from US$1,384 low season, US$1,482 high season, 65 percent discount for 3 nights or more) has five restaurants that include French and Mediterranean cuisine. Some of the six room categories include whirlpool tubs and French balconies; one-bedroom suites have two walk-out balconies with lounge chairs and a huge living room area. Royal Plan guests have greens fees and transportation to the Sandals Golf Course included. All bedrooms have king beds. Open to nonguests as well, **Red Lane Spa** (tel. 876/670-9015, www.redlanespa.com) is one of the most comprehensive on the island, with 14 full-time employees and 8 full-time therapists offering a wide variety of services, from hot stone massage to nails and facials.

A 529-room property covering land on both sides of Main Street and the bypass, **Sandals Ochi** (Main St., tel. 876/974-5691, U.S. tel. 305/284-1300, www.sandals.com, US$1,108 low season, US$1,234 high season, 65 percent discount for 3 nights or more) is exclusively for couples. It features two resorts amid a 40-hectare (100-acre) seaside estate. High-end villas are nestled among lush foliage and have private pools at The Butler Village & Great House. A small white-sand beach hugged by a wraparound pier dotted with gazebos, dubbed the Grande Promenade, is the prominent feature at The Caribbean Riviera. Amenities include four-poster king beds, flat-screen TVs, stocked fridges, en suite baths, and air-conditioning. Wi-Fi is included in rooms and public areas. Guests can choose from 16 restaurants, 10 bars, 7 pools, and 22

1: water slide at Mystic Ridge Resort **2:** room at the Jamaica Inn whirlpools, as well as get complimentary access to the Sandals Golf & Country Club.

The most prominent hotel on Turtle Beach is **Moon Palace Jamaica Grande** (Main St., tel. 876/974-2200, www.jamaicagrande.com, from US$466 low season, US$652 high season), occupying the prime piece of real estate on the point of the bay. The resort boasts its own Dolphin Cove, a surf pool, a discotheque, and buffet and à la carte dining. Rooms are modern and well-appointed with Wi-Fi throughout.

INFORMATION AND SERVICES

The **St. Ann Chamber of Commerce** (tel. 876/974-2629) has tourism booklets that advertise the area's businesses and attractions. **DHL** (shop 3, tel. 876/974-8001, 9am-5pm Mon.-Sat.) is at Ocean Village Plaza.

Banks and Money

NCB Bank (40 Main St., tel. 876/974-2522) is next to Island Plaza/BK and across from the craft market. **Scotiabank** (tel. 876/974-2311) has a branch on Main Street, three buildings west of NCB. **Nancy's Cambio** (Taj Mahal, 4 Main St., tel. 876/974-2414; 50 Main St., tel. 876/795-4285, 9am-5pm Mon.-Sat.) offers slightly better exchange rates than the banks. Traveler's checks are accepted with two forms of ID. Money transfers are also possible at the St. Ann's Bay MoneyGram outlet. **FX Trader** has locations at Ocean Village Shopping Centre (Main St., shop 3, 9am-5pm Mon.-Sat.) and at H&L Rapid True Value (105 Main St., Pineapple Place).

Health Care and Pharmacies

Dr. Pavel Chang at **Medical Care and Surgical Centre** (110 Main St., tel. 876/974-6339, cell tel. 876/843-8109, 8am-5pm Mon.-Sat.) is a recommended general practitioner and surgeon. Sr. Sonali Thakurani at **Complete Care Medical Centre** (16 Rennie Rd., tel. 876/974-3357, cell tel. 876/579-5789) is also recommended. **St. Ann's Bay Hospital** (Seville Rd., tel. 876/972-2272) is the most important in the region, with people coming from kilometers around. However, better service can be obtained at private health centers in Ocho Rios.

Fontana Pharmacy (Eight Rivers Town Centre, tel. 876/974-8889, 9am-8pm Mon.-Thurs., 9am-9pm Fri.-Sat., 10am-6pm Sun.) is the best full-service pharmacy chain on the island, similar to the large-format stores found in the United States. **Pinegrove Pharmacy** (shop 5, Ocho Rios Mall, tel. 876/974-5586, 9am-8pm Mon.-Sat., 10am-3pm Sun.) is east of the clock tower on Main Street.

TRANSPORTATION

Getting There

With the completion of the North-South Toll Road in 2016, Ocho Rios is only a little over an hour from Kingston (tolls US$10 one-way). The two-lane highway descends from the hills to the coast a few kilometers west of Dunn's River Falls. The drive between Ocho Rios and Montego Bay takes about the same amount of time. Oracabessa can be reached in about 30 minutes, and Port Antonio is about 1.5 hours farther east.

Route taxis and **buses** leave for Kingston and points east and west along the coast from the lot just south of the clock tower in downtown Ocho Rios. Buses travel between Ochi and downtown Kingston (US$5) as well as to Montego Bay (US$5), while route taxis ply every other route imaginable: to Brown's Town (US$4), Moneague (US$2), and east and west along the coast to Oracabessa (US$3) and St. Ann's Bay (US$2). **Knutsford Express** (tel. 876/971-1822, www.knutsfordexpress.com) offers a more comfortable ride with air-conditioning and Wi-Fi, departing from the Ocho Rios Jerk Centre to Montego Bay (US$16), Kingston (US$16), and Port Antonio (US$17).

Ian Fleming International Airport (OCJ, Boscobel, 15 minutes east of Ochi, www.ifia.aero, tel. 876/787-0169 or 876/797-0114) caters to small private aircraft from overseas and domestic charter operators from Kingston, Montego Bay, Negril, or Port Antonio. **TimAir** (tel. 876/952-2516, timair@ usa.net, www.timair.net) offers fixed-wing flights for two passengers from Montego Bay to Boscobel (US$630), to Kingston's Tinson Pen (US$856) and Norman Manley International (US$878), Port Antonio (US$943), and Negril (US$294). TimAir's Cessna 206 aircraft can hold up to four passengers with luggage. **AirLink Express** (tel. 876/940-6660, timair@usa.net, www.timair. net) offers fixed wing service between any two points in Jamaica.

CAR RENTALS
Caribbean Car Rentals (99-A Main St., tel. 876/974-2513, 8:30am-5pm Mon.-Fri., 9am-2pm Sat., 9am-noon Sun., caribcars@ usa.net, www.caribbeancarrentals.net) has Toyota Yaris (US$350), Corolla (US$420), and Suzuki Jimny (US$300) and Vitara (US$500) vehicles as well as a 15-seater Hiace minibus (US$620). Taxes and insurance are extra, with a US$1,500-2,000 security deposit.

Getting Around
Route taxis are the most economical way of getting around if you don't mind squeezing

in with several other people. Taxis leave from the rank by the clock tower and can also be flagged down by the roadside if there is any room. Route taxis display their destination and origin in painted letters on the side of the car and are typically white Toyota Corollas. Overcrowding has been somewhat reduced in recent years with increased oversight from the authorities. It is impossible to walk the streets of Ocho Rios without being offered a chartered taxi; bear in mind that these drivers will quote any figure that comes to mind. Haggling is very much a part of hiring a local charter, and be sure not to pay the total in advance if you hope to see your driver stick around.

Dependable transport operator **Karandas Tours** (10 Balivard Ave., Buckfield, tel. 876/974-2063, cell tel. 876/775-8724, karandasstours@gmail.com, www.karandastours. com) offers charter taxis and tours across the island in comfortable cars, vans, and Coaster and coach buses, which include wheelchair accessible vehicles.

An authorized JUTA driver, **Dean "Johnny Kool" Johnson** (cell tel. 876/314-8713) is based in Ochi with an eight-seater Toyota Voxy van.

West of Ocho Rios

As you head west from Ocho Rios, the North Coast Highway hugs the waterfront, passing Dolphin Cove, Dunn's River Falls, and Laughing Waters before reaching a cluster of villas and resorts in adjacent Old Fort Bay and then Mammee Bay.

Continuing west, the next community is St. Ann's Bay, a busy town with one of the few hospitals on the North Coast and a few attractions worth stopping for, including Seville Great House and Heritage Park and a Marcus Garvey Statue at the Parish Library.

Still farther west, the small community of Priory sits along a dusty stretch of highway with few passersby stopping there, except on

Sunday when the community's public Fantasy Beach comes alive for family fun days, partying and dancing into the night.

From Priory westward the highway passes Richmond Estate, used as a venue for several annual events; a few subdivisions in various stages of construction; and Chukka Cove, the home base for Chukka Caribbean, the island's leading tour outfit. The next community of any size is Runaway Bay, where several hotels straddle the highway and waterfront. From Runaway Bay the highway continues west to Discovery Bay, the last settlement of any size before the Trelawny parish border.

Discovery Bay is one of Jamaica's most

upscale destinations, and the eastern side of the bay is dotted with luxury villas. In the center of the bay, a bauxite wharf feeds ships from an immense domed storage facility and wharf made famous as Dr. No's lair in the film based on Ian Fleming's first 007 novel.

OLD FORT BAY AND MAMMEE BAY

Old Fort Bay and Mammee Bay are contiguous to one another a few minutes west of Ocho Rios. Both bays have gated communities where visitors can rent condos and villas. Mammee Bay has two large hotels on its eastern side, ClubHotel Riu Ocho Rios and Jewel Dunn's River Beach Resort, adjacent to one another. Apart from these two all-inclusive resorts, accommodations in the area tend to the high end, with little in the mid-range.

Food

Bamboo Blu (Mammee Bay, contact Bunny Williams, tel. 876/974-9983, cell tel. 876/375-0417, info@bambooblujamaica.com, www.bambooblujamaica.com, 10am-10pm daily, by reservation only, US$12-40) is a beachfront bar and restaurant serving soup, breadfruit chips, saltfish bammy bruschetta, crab wontons, spicy shrimp, and heavier dishes like grilled lobster, coconut rundown snapper, and fish-and-chips. To get here, go through the gate marked Mammee Bay Estate adjacent to the entrance to Riu; the entrance is about one kilometer (0.6 mile) in on the right.

An outpost of Jamaica's most respected jerk center, ★ **Scotchies Too** (Drax Hall, beside the Epping gas station, tel. 876/794-9457, 11am-11pm Mon.-Sat., 11am-9pm Sun., US$4-11) consistently grills up the best pork, chicken, and roast fish, accompanied by breadfruit, yam, and festival.

Angler's (55 Windsor Rd., tel. 876/794-8449, US$12-35) serves shrimp, conch, octopus, fish, lobster steam, brown stew, and grilled shrimp kebab. Try the seafood combo for a taste of almost everything on the menu, or shrimp feast or lobster feast platters to feed nine or so.

In an unassuming seaside lot adjacent to Fantasy Beach Club at Priory Beach, **Seaside Dutchie** (adjacent to Fantasy Beach, 11am-11pm daily, tel. 876/383-4858, fatchef106@yahoo.com, US$3-20) has an extensive menu that adds flair to Jamaican favorites like steamed fish and red pea soup, all served in traditional aluminum Dutch pots. Starters include conch fritters, ackee and saltfish spring rolls, and blackened sprat. Whole fish is filleted and prepared steamed or fried, the head-to-tail deep fried and plated in swimming position. Other menu items include vegetarian pasta, curried goat, and fried chicken. Burgers, pork sandwiches, and grilled cheese are among the items from Dutchie's "Sub Bar." A raised wooden deck overlooks the beach, and a cozy indoor dining room provides cover when needed. The covered bar has ample seating. Patrons can use the beach, which is well maintained and good for swimming.

Seaside, opposite the turnoff to St. Ann's Bay, the **Roxborough Restaurant Bar & Grill** (Roxborough Beach, St. Ann's Bay, cell tel. 876/562-6725 or 876/460-9041, 10am-10pm daily) specializes in reasonably priced seafood like brown stewed conch, steamed fish, or grilled lobster (US$16-25) served with sides of festival, rice-and-peas, fries, bammy, or creamed potatoes.

Inspired vegetarian and seafood farm-to-table lunches and dinners at **Stush in the Bush** (Free Hill, contact Lisa and Christopher Binns, cell tel. 876/562-9760, www.stushinthe-bush.com, by reservation only Sun.-Fri., from US$55) include a tour of the hosts' Zionites Farm and medicinal plants. Quarterly moonlight dinners and yoga brunches are held throughout the year.

Accommodations
UNDER US$100

A 35-room property, **Seacrest Beach Hotel** (Richmond Cove, Priory, tel. 876/972-1594 or 876/972-1547, cell tel. 876/824-0702,

---

1: delicious island favorite at Seaside Dutchie **2:** slabs of smokey pork at Scotchies Too in Drax Hall

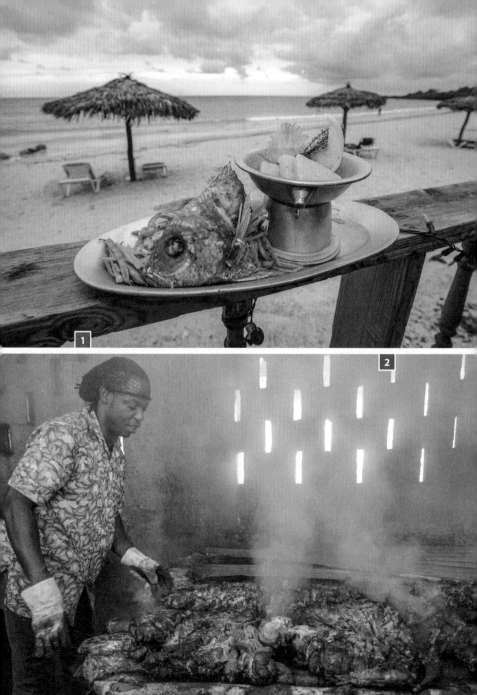

seacrestresort@cwjamaica.com, www. seacrestresorts.com, from US$81 low season, US$91 high season, including breakfast) has no-frills standard rooms with air-conditioning, private baths with hot water, cable TV, and private balconies with sea views. There's a pool and bar on the property. Honeymoon suites and one- and two-bedroom cottages are more spacious and separate from the main building.

OVER US$250

The six four-bedroom cottage-style villas at **Cannon Villas** (Old Fort Bay, tel. 876/754-1623 or 876/618-5948, cell tel. 876/298-5047, sgms_ltd@hotmail.com, www.cannonvillasja.com, US$560 low season, US$600 high season) share a lawn and a private beach, accommodating up to eight guests each. Amenities include air-conditioning, cable TV, and Wi-Fi. A housekeeper is assigned to each villa to prepare meals as needed.

A 12-unit townhouse complex near the beach, **Chillin'** (Old Fort Bay, tel. 876/754-1623 or 876/618-5948, cell tel. 876/298-5047, sgms_ltd@hotmail.com, www.chillinja.com, US$310-560 low season, US$352-600 high season) is set on 0.6 hectare (1.5 acres) with a pool and a whirlpool. Units have either two or four bedrooms each. A housekeeper is assigned to each unit, all of which have cable, Wi-Fi, stereos, air-conditioning, ceiling fans, full kitchens, and balconies.

ALL-INCLUSIVE RESORTS

The seven room categories at **Jewel Dunn's River Beach Resort & Spa** (Mammee Bay, U.S. tel. 855/617-2114, tel. 876/972-7400, reservationsdunnsriver@jewelresorts.com, www.jewelresorts.com, from US$309 low season, US$410 high season) all have four-poster king beds and either inland or sea views. Wi-Fi, available throughout the property, is included, as are greens fees at Runaway Bay Golf Club. The resort has two large pools with swim-up bars, a small water park, a nine-hole pitch-and-putt golf course, basketball, volleyball, tennis courts, and nonmotorized water sports.

A massive 865-room resort facing the sea in Mammee Bay, **ClubHotel Riu Ocho Rios** (Mammee Bay, tel. 876/972-2200, U.S. tel. 888/748-4990, www.riu.com, from US$291 low season, US$346 high season, 3 night minimum) has clean and well-appointed rooms with replica furniture and either one king, a king and a double, or two doubles. Riu is among the least expensive of the all-inclusive hotels, but it's hard to see the value when obtaining reservations at one of the three "premier dining" restaurants requires standing in a long line 10am-noon; after all that, the cuisine tends to disappoint. In the buffet dining room, where no reservations are required, the food quality is decent, albeit overwhelmingly imported. There is little inside the purple-painted buildings to remind guests that they are in Jamaica.

Transportation

The gated entrance to Old Fort Bay is immediately west of the roundabout at the end of the North-South Highway toll road. Mammee Bay Estate is just west of Old Fort Bay. Both are a 10-minute drive west of Ocho Rios and about the same distance east of St. Ann's Bay. From Runaway Bay it's about 15 minutes east by car to Mammee Bay and Old Fort Bay, and about 25 minutes to Ocho Rios, while Discovery Bay is about 10 minutes farther west of Runaway Bay. Route taxis ply the road between all these towns on the North Coast all day.

ST. ANN'S BAY

The parish capital, St. Ann's Bay, is a small bustling town at the foot of the hills that lead into the interior along rough potholed roads.

Sights

In a park area a few hundred meters off the highway about 1.5 kilometers (1 mile) before the main junction to turn off to St. Ann's Bay, **Fire River** is named for flammable gas that rises from a pool in the river and can be set ablaze. While locals tell legends of the history and significance of the spot, a large housing subdivision just through the trees raises the question of whether the gas is actually methane from the area's septic systems. Still, claims are made that the phenomenon predates the adjacent urbanization. The attraction is not managed, and can be reached by turning off the highway by the easternmost entrance to St. Ann's Bay and taking an immediate left after the dog clinic, off the road along a dirt track leading to the river.

Marcus Garvey is remembered with a statue in front of the St. Ann parish library (tel. 876/972-2660, 9:30am-5:30pm Mon.-Fri., 9:30am-3pm Sat.) just above the center of town. Garvey's bust stands in remembrance of the man whose ideas were suppressed by the powers of his day but whose teachings nonetheless made serious ripples, inspiring black power movements the world over. The library has several computers free to use for half-hour intervals.

The centerpiece of Seville Heritage Park, where rolling lawns command a panoramic view of the North Coast, **Seville Great House** (tel. 876/972-2191 or 876/972-0665, seville@anbell.net, 9am-4pm Mon.-Fri., US$15 adults, US$6 under age 13) is a UNESCO World Heritage Site, as it was the first major Spanish settlement in Jamaica and the first colonial capital of the island. An on-site museum offers a tour highlighting the area's history and a selection of artifacts. A large waterwheel along the driveway below the great house is a remnant of the old sugar works. Seville hosts the **Emancipation Jubilee** each July 31, celebrating Jamaica's heritage and culture through song, dance, drumming, theater, food, and crafts. The event culminates in musical performances in the evening followed by a reading of the Emancipation Proclamation at midnight.

Transportation

Getting to any of the coastal areas west of Ocho Rios is a straight shot along the A1 by car. Charter taxis will charge whatever they can; route taxis run between St. Ann's Bay and Ocho Rios (US$2) to the east and to Discovery Bay (US$2). Route taxis are regulated and charge a fixed fare, so there's no need to haggle. They also tend to cram as many passengers as possible into their vehicles. Route taxis are a good option for traveling between towns on a budget without luggage, but not convenient for carrying more than a small handbag.

PRIORY

Priory is a small community with one stoplight along the main road that is noteworthy only for its popular beach, a few pan chicken vendors, and a couple of seafood restaurants. The community hosts Jamaica's best roots reggae festival, Rebel Salute, held the second weekend in January each year.

LFA Country Store (Richmond Estate, tel. 876/794-8562, 8am-8pm daily) has groceries, a welcoming deli with a living wall covered with plants, and a pharmacy.

Fantasy Beach

Just east of the stoplight in Priory, **Fantasy Beach** (free) is one of the most popular beaches for locals on the North Coast. A beach bar and restaurant serves local dishes and blasts dancehall throughout the day. Sunday is typically the most crowded day at Fantasy Beach.

Marcus Garvey: Black Power Prophet

Marcus Mosiah Garvey was born in St. Ann's Bay in 1887 to humble but educated parents. After completing elementary school, he moved to Kingston, where he worked in a print shop and became increasingly interested and engaged in organized movements aimed at improving conditions for black Jamaicans. While free from the bonds of slavery since 1838, black Jamaicans were far from equal to their white compatriots and were denied the right to vote, among other basic rights. In 1907 Garvey was elected vice president of the Kingston Union, which cost him his job at the printer when he got involved in a strike. At age 23 Garvey left the island to work in Central America, as many Jamaicans in search of opportunity did at the time. His travels around the region gave Garvey an awareness of the common plight faced by blacks, seeding in him what would become a lifelong struggle to unite people of African origin of all nations under one common aim. In 1912 Garvey traveled to England, and in 1914 he returned to Jamaica and founded the first chapter of the United Negro Improvement Association (UNIA), whose motto, "One God! One Aim! One Destiny!" summed up the broad goal of the organization to improve the lives of black people through solidarity and self-determination.

While Garvey's message was well received by his followers in Jamaica, it was in the Harlem Renaissance in New York City that he was first lauded as a prophet. Garvey is credited as the father of the Black Power movement, which would take Harlem and the rest of the United States by storm and eventually lead to the Civil Rights Movement of the 1960s. Garvey sought to enfranchise black people by generating black-owned businesses that would be linked on an international level. To facilitate this project, he established the Black Star Line, an international shipping company.

Garvey's followers numbered four million worldwide in 1920, a movement large enough to get the attention of both the U.S. and British governments. When Garvey began to sell the notion of

Runaway Bay

The waterfront along Runaway Bay has several fine sand beaches that are protected by offshore reefs. A slew of all-inclusive resorts occupy prime property on the waterfront. A few shopping plazas dot a stretch of road near the waterfront, where hole-in-the-wall restaurants, grocery stores, and a multitude of small dive bars decorated with strands of colored lights attract a mix of locals and visitors.

BEACHES

In Salem district, just as you pass the first stoplight heading into Runaway Bay from the east, **Sharkies** has a long stretch of fine golden sand and gentle waves. There's no admission fee, but visitors are encouraged to patronize the restaurant. **Runaway Bay Public Beach,** better known as **Flavours,** has a grill that serves fried chicken, local dishes, beer,

and spirits and is a popular hangout that attracts throngs on weekends with loud music. The beach itself is free and has fine clean sand with a reef just offshore.

Adjacent to Jewel Runaway Bay, **Cardiff Hall Property Owners Association** (CHPOA, cell tel. 876/563-8804, chpoat93@ yahoo.com) has a small, well-maintained beach park (9am-sunset, admission US$5) that sees few visitors and tends to be quieter than the more popular and free Flavours Beach. The beach has sea grape trees for shade and a few round stone tables suitable for a picnic. There's a bar and kitchen that can be used for functions. Restrooms are available. **Swallow Hole Fisherman's Beach** (tel. 876/870-7331), about one kilometer (0.6 mile) west of Jewel Runaway Bay, is a quiet fishermen's beach shaded by sea grapes.

a mass return to Africa, however, he met resistance at the highest levels of government. He was convicted of mail fraud in the United States and imprisoned for five years on what his followers considered trumped-up charges. After two years, he was released on an executive pardon and deported back to Jamaica. Local authorities were not happy to see Garvey continue agitating for increased rights by forming the People's Political Party (PPP) in an effort to bring reform to Jamaica's colonial system. Garvey ran for a seat in parliament and lost; later he won a seat on the Kingston and St. Andrew Corporation, the local government, from a jail cell, where he'd been placed for contempt of court. At the time, voting was limited to landowners, a class to which many of Garvey's followers did not belong, and his political support was accordingly stifled. Frustrated by the slow pace of change in Kingston, Garvey returned to London in 1935, where he would remain until his death in 1940. In 1964 Garvey was declared a national hero in Jamaica, and his remains were reinterred at Heroes Memorial in Kingston.

Garvey's legacy has been mixed in Jamaica, to say the least. Perhaps the greatest disservice to his ideas lies in the fact that his pleas for universal education have never been answered at an institutional level. At the same time, there is no doubting the impact he has made in certain circles. Rastafarians claim Garvey repeatedly iterated the call, "Look to the east for the crowning of a black king." It was one of Garvey's followers, Leonard Howell, who first cited the crowning of Ethiopian emperor Haile Selassie on November 2, 1930, as a fulfillment of that prophecy, leading to the birth of the Rastafarian movement. Even today, it is the Rastafarian community both in Jamaica and abroad that has embraced Garvey's teachings to the greatest extent, often comparing him to John the Baptist.

RECREATION

Jamaica Scuba Divers (Runaway Bay, cell tel. 876/381-1113, www.scuba-jamaica.com, US$55, US$65 with equipment, 2-tank dive US$100) offers a beginners class lasting about three hours, with classroom and pool time and one open-water dive. The dive outfit is owned by Christian Rance, who also runs Sun Divers in Negril.

A five-star PADI dive facility operating out of Royal Decameron in Runaway Bay, **Resort Divers** (Salem Beach, contact Everett Heron, cell tel. 876/881-5760, heron@resortdivers. com, www.resortdivers.com) offers snorkeling, glass-bottomed boat tours, banana boat rides, drop-line and deep-sea fishing, and parasailing in addition to its core dive services, which include full certification. Runaway Bay dive highlights include canyons, crevices, and flats, with popular sites being Ricky's Reef, Pocket's Reef, a Spanish Anchor, the wreck of a 100-foot freighter, two airplanes, and a car. Resort Divers also

operates Sharkies Seafood Restaurant at Salem Beach.

With discounts for golfing on consecutive days, **Runaway Bay Golf Club** (Runaway Bay, tel. 876/973-7319, greens fees US$80, JGA members US$25, caddy US$16, cart US$35, clubs US$20-30, gratuity US$10 or more pp) is an 18-hole championship course. Guests at Jewel Resorts have greens fees waived.

Horseman Riding Stable (contact Robert Taylor, cell tel. 876/892-3663) offers horseback-riding tours led by Robert's nephew, ranging from US$65 for a 45-minute beach ride to US$85 for a mountain trail ride. Up to eight guests can ride at a time.

NIGHTLIFE

Runaway Bay has a down-to-earth bar scene with a few options for late night drinks and occasional dances. **Light House Lounge & Grill** (Salem district, contact Ricardo "Bumpy" McIntish, cell tel. 876/894-3388, 11am-4am daily) hosts dances in the

Runaway Bay

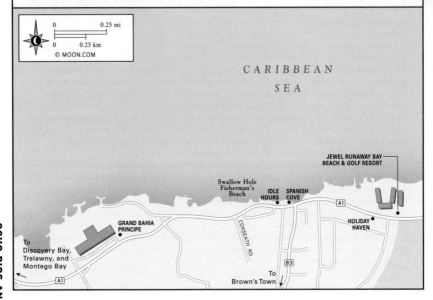

CARIBBEAN SEA

JEWEL RUNAWAY BAY BEACH & GOLF RESORT

Swallow Hole Fisherman's Beach

IDLE HOURS

SPANISH COVE

A1

HOLIDAY HAVEN

GRAND BAHIA PRINCIPE

COXSEATH RD

To Discovery Bay, Trelawny, and Montego Bay

A1

To Brown's Town

B3

open-air yard every other weekend on Friday or Saturday. Inside the bar, two billiards tables and karaoke on Wednesday entertain patrons. It's on the left when you're heading west, just past the stoplight as you enter Runaway Bay.

A popular hangout for locals and tourists alike, **Just 1 More Bar** (Main St., Salem, noon-4am daily, cell tel. 876/568-3599, just-1moreja@gmail.com) has karaoke madness on Saturday nights, which often carries on until 6am. Two billiards tables (US$0.50), indoor and outdoor seating, and unadulterated beer and spirits keep the good vibes flowing.

Tucked away on the western end of town amidst a beautifully planted garden, **A Mi Fi Tell Yuh** (next door to Jewel Runaway Bay, cell tel. 876/892-3663, www.takemetojamaica.com, noon-midnight daily) is an alfresco bar and grill where regulars gather in the evenings for a few drinks. Proprietor Robert Taylor can always be found on-site manning the bar or preparing steam fish with crackers. Diners require a reservation.

FOOD

Decent cooking, the fresh breeze off the sea, and sand underfoot make ★ **Sharkies** (Salem Beach, cell tel. 876/881-5760, 8am-10pm daily) the most popular seafood restaurant in Runaway Bay, serving fried, roasted, and steamed fish (US$7-10), fritters, stewed, or curried conch (US$5-7), and lobster (US$15).

A hole-in-the-wall cook shop specializing in pan chicken and Jamaican staples, **Tru-Look Restaurant Lounge & Bar** (Salem, next door to Salem Resort, tel. 876/847-5066, 6am-midnight daily) has bare-bones decor, including rum posters and hand-painted plates of food, adorning the walls. But the price is right, the rum flows, and a billiards table and oldies reggae provide ample entertainment. Sweet and sour chicken, ackee and saltfish, curry goat, and oxtail are among the items offered.

A recent addition to Runaway Bay's food offerings, **Milestone Sports Bar & Grill** (Salem, next door to Tru-Look, cell tel.

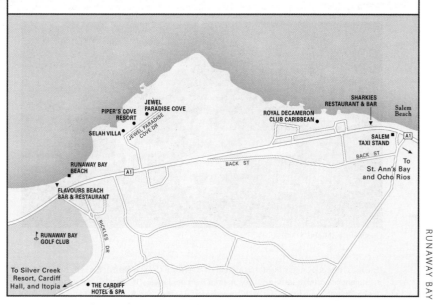

876/518-7316, 11am-11pm Sun.-Thurs., 11am-midnight Fri.-Sat.) is on the second level of a modern built-to-purpose plaza. Openers include chicken wings, kebabs, or shrimp cocktail, while mains are pasta alfredo (US$12), chicken cordon bleu, grouper fillet, and lobster curried, grilled, or in garlic sauce (US$25).

Specializing in, you guessed it, jerk chicken and pork, **Jerkie's Northern Restaurant** (Northern Shopping Complex, Salem, tel. 876/973-7365, jerkysnorthernrestaurant@yahoo.com, 7am-midnight daily) also has fried and baked chicken, cow foot, oxtail, fish, and pepper steak as well as breakfast items like ackee and saltfish, stew chicken, salt mackerel with boiled dumpling, steamed vegetables and kidney, and liver and callaloo (US$4).

The most authentic French restaurant in Jamaica is ★ **L'Escargot** (Main St., tel. 876/973-5652, tel. 876/973-5589, cell tel. 876/368-5883, lescargot70@gmail.com, www.lescargotja.com), however out of place it might feel in the center of Runaway Bay.

The dimly lit dining room has a baby grand piano gracing the entrance. Start with the signature escargot sautéed in garlic butter, herbs, and white wine, smoked marlin topped with mousse (US$12) or pâté de foie gras (US$9). For mains, try the coq au vin (US$18), the porc aux champignons, lamb chops, filet mignon, giant prawns in orange curry sauce, or stuffed grilled eggplant (US$14-35). The wine list relies exclusively on French vintages (US$26-78), and desserts are scribbled on a chalkboard alongside the daily specials.

On Runaway Bay's public beach, **Flavours Beach Bar & Restaurant** (tel. 876/973-5457, 10am-10pm daily) is a popular local hangout specializing in seafood, burgers, and local dishes (US$5-40). You won't find a more lively beach scene anywhere in Jamaica, with locals mingling with foreign visitors throughout the day and into the evening to the sound of reggae blasting from stacks of speakers.

★ **Luvinya Foods** (10 Main St., tel. 876/505-0117, luvinyafoods@gmail.com) is a vegan café (US$5-10) and juice bar (US$3-5)

Rebel Salute

Queen Ifrica at Rebel Salute 2019

The most popular annual music event held on the North Coast is **Rebel Salute** (www.rebel-salutejamaica.com). It started out commemorating the January 15 birthday of reggae icon Tony "Rebel" Barrett, who shares the birthday with Martin Luther King Jr., he's quick to point out. Held annually since 1994, the event currently occupies two nights at Richmond Estate, just west of Priory. The performances tend to stretch well past sunrise each morning.

Rebel demands adherence to a strict no alcohol, no meat, no degrading lyrics policy for the event, but patrons burn herb freely throughout the night, raising lighters in the air when their favorite artists "buss" a big tune. The show typically starts in the evening with the most popular crowd pleasers typically scheduled later in the morning.

The mission, says Rebel, is to preserve the healthy aspects of reggae music and to support community tourism. The annual event, held the Friday and Saturday closest to January 15, draws thousands of reggae fans from Jamaica and abroad, and typically features the more conscious artists of the genre, often allowing more hard-core artists from the dancehall to reinvent themselves for a night as they reveal their progressive side.

at Eastern Container Plaza. Dishes include mixed platters with ackee rundown, coconut curry plantain, steamed veg, and vegan omelets with garbanzo bean flour substituted for eggs. Raw food dishes include plantain carrot salad, beet seaweed salad, or raw okra salad as well as veggie burgers and vegan egg sandwiches.

ACCOMMODATIONS
Under US$100

The six studios (US$95) and 14 one-bedroom apartments (US$116) at **Piper's Cove** (tel.

876/973-7156, piperscove@msn.com, www.piperscoveresortjamaica.com) have air-conditioning, cable TV, Wi-Fi, and utilitarian kitchenettes. The dated furnishings can be overlooked given the affordability. Some apartments have sea views. A restaurant and bar on the property serves breakfast, lunch, and dinner.

US$100-250

A condo complex offering standard rooms as well as one- and two-bedroom suites with kitchen, living, and dining areas, **Holiday**

Haven Condo Resort (tel. 876/973-4893, www.holidayhavenresort.com, from US$100) is across the road from the shore, a short walk to Fisherman's Beach.

Overlooking the golf course run by Jamaica's HEART training institute, The Cardiff Hotel and Spa (tel. 876/973-6671, www.thecardiffhotel.com, US$114 low season, US$137 high season) has 44 rooms with tiled floors and balconies spread across four two-story blocks. Junior suites (US$137) have kings, ultra-deluxe rooms (US$123) are on the second level, and standard rooms (US$114) are on the ground floor with two double beds. The north-facing rooms overlook the golf course and the bay. Amenities include cable TV, air-conditioning, and private baths with hot water. Wi-Fi covers the property. A pool is just off the lobby, bar, and restaurant. Rates include breakfast.

All-Inclusive Resorts

Some of the 183 pleasant rooms at Royal DeCameron Club Caribbean (tel. 876/973-4802, ventas.jam@decameron.com, from US$127 pp) are in the main block; others are either beachfront or garden cottages with king beds, air-conditioning, TVs, and hot water. The property has two pools and a private beach and offers guests bicycles, which can be useful for navigating Runaway Bay's spread-out strip.

Jewel Resorts (www.jewelresorts.com) has two properties in Runaway Bay: Jewel Paradise Cove (from US$299 low season, US$526 high season), with 210 rooms, 15 junior suites, 6 restaurants and bars, and a pool; and Jewel Runaway Bay (from US$299 low season, US$526 high season), with 266 rooms and 3 swimming pools, including 44 suites with private plunge pools. Rooms are spacious with complete amenities. Staying at either property includes greens fees at Runaway Bay Golf Club.

SHOPPING

L&M Meats (8:30am-6pm Mon.-Thurs., 8:30am-7pm Fri.-Sat.) is a small grocery store in Salem with a Scotiabank ATM in the parking lot.

TRANSPORTATION

Runaway Bay is 15-20 minutes west of Ocho Rios by car, depending on traffic, and 10 minutes east of Discovery Bay. Route taxis ply the highway between Discovery Bay and St. Ann's Bay throughout the day and stop along the route when flagged down, provided they have space. Minibuses depart from the crossing next to the police station in Runaway Bay for Ochi (US$1.50) and Montego Bay (US$5).

Discovery Bay

Originally named Puerto Seco (Dry Harbor) by Christopher Columbus, Discovery Bay was renamed to reflect the debated assertion that this was the first point in Jamaica where the explorer made landfall. Experts believe the actual first landing was in Rio Bueno, a few kilometers farther west, where Columbus would have sought freshwater. Irrespective of this disputed detail, Discovery Bay has played an important role in Jamaica's recent history, first as a bustling port where barrels of sugar and rum departed for Europe, and then, from the early 20th century, as a bauxite port. It remains one of the few active bauxite facilities in Jamaica following the global economic downturn of 2009, when half the island's alumina and bauxite operations went idle. The industrious port is the curious backdrop for perhaps Jamaica's staunchest enclave of old Jamaican money, with several of the country's wealthiest families owning beachfront villas facing the bay.

SIGHTS

Jamaica's most popular underground, Green Grotto Caves (tel. 876/973-2841 or

876/973-3217, 9am-4pm daily, US$20 adults, US$10 children) is on a 26-hectare (64-acre) property between Runaway and Discovery Bays. While tamer than the experiences farther west in Cockpit Country, Green Grotto, also known as Runaway Cave or Hopewell Cave, is a well-conceived tour. The 45-minute tour descends to an underground lake, and well-versed guides give a history of the caves, their formations, and their importance to the Taino people and the Spanish. A drink is included. Green Grotto is on the eastern edge of Discovery Bay, across the highway from Ultimate Jerk Centre. Route taxis traveling between Discovery Bay and St. Ann's Bay will stop here on request.

Just west of the public beach in Discovery Bay, around the bend from the gas station, is **Old Folly,** a district covering the narrow valley containing the bauxite plant and export terminal, overlooking the stretch of sand on the opposite side of the bay that is home to some of Jamaica's most luxurious villas. **Quadrant Wharf** is the old sugar terminal, where an old winch lies rusting. A plaque on the wall facing the road tells of the importance of the location, from Columbus's landing to the export of sugar, arms, and bauxite.

Just around the bend from the bauxite terminal in Old Folly, **Columbus Park** (free) hugs the steep slope rising from the western side of the bay. The park consists of an open-air museum wedged between the highway and the slope descending to the water, with a mural depicting the arrival of Christopher Columbus and several relics from the colonial period scattered around.

★ PUERTO SECO BEACH CLUB

Puerto Seco Beach Club (tel. 876/670-0128, 8:30am-5pm daily, US$20 adults, US$10 ages 5-11, free under age 5) has transformed the quiet town beach into a destination attracting beachgoers from far and wide. Admission includes access to the beautiful white-sand beach and use of the 46-meter (150-foot) pool, as well as Wi-Fi and shade under large beach huts on a first-come, first-serve basis. Beach chairs (US$5) and umbrellas (US$5) are available for rent if the shade under the thatch is full. Groups of up to six can opt for private cabanas (US$150), which come with a six pack of beer, juice and water, a fruit plate, and personal butler.

Water sports include Jamaica's only Wibit

Columbus Park

floating obstacle course (US$10 pp), a challenging load of fun. Glass-bottomed boat tours, snorkeling, paddleboards, kayaks, and diving are also offered (from US$10). Dolphin Discovery established its fifth location in Jamaica here.

The restaurant serves burgers, fish, and bar food, and a Walkerswood-branded jerk pit grills chicken and pork. Larger groups can pre-book buffet-style meals (US$15-20 pp). The service at Puerto Seco is top notch, and lifeguards with watchful eyes abound.

Next door, wedged between Puerto Seco Beach Club and the first of many luxury villas, is the **Discovery Bay Fishermen's Beach** (free), where a couple of ramshackle bars serve beer, rum, and fried fish.

FOOD

Popular for locals to congregate to take in a cricket match, eat jerk, and vibe out, ★ **Ultimate Jerk Centre** (10 minutes west of Breezes, approaching Discovery Bay, tel. 876/973-2054, 9am-10:30pm Sun.-Fri., 9am-midnight Sat., US$1-5) does stewed chicken and pork, curry goat, stewed conch, potato, festival, bammy, fritters, rice-and-peas, and french fries. The bar serves a variety of liquor, and an oldies party is held the last Saturday of the month. The jerk is the best in the area and doesn't linger on the grill thanks to a steady flow of traffic.

Coconut Tree Restaurant & Bar (Dairy Pen, tel. 876/973-9781, 8am-8pm daily) serves Jamaican fare, including curried goat, jerk and fried chicken, escoveitch fish, and patties at honest prices (US$5-10). **Niesha's Cook Shop** (Old Folly, contact Antonio, cell tel. 876/588-7792, 11:30am-9pm daily) is a cook shop serving Jamaican staples like fried chicken, turkey neck, and stew beef (US$3-6) on the western side of town, across from the bauxite shipping terminal.

On the sea side of the road as you round a bend approaching Rio Bueno from Discovery Bay, opposite the derelict Bay Vista Resort, **Coconut Lagoon Bar and Restaurant** (Queen's Hwy., tel. 876/899-1245, 8am-9:30pm daily, US$5-12) is a popular pit stop serving typical Jamaican fare and fish dishes.

ACCOMMODATIONS

Set back from the highway in a quiet subdivision, **Paradise Place** (54 Bridgewater Garden, Poinciana Dr. at Sunflower Dr., contact Paul Shaw, tel. 876/973-9495, cell tel. 876/862-2095, shawtop@aol.com, www.paradiseplace54.com) offers two-bedroom apartments (US$100) and two stand-alone rooms (US$60), all with pine furniture, air-conditioning, microwaves, and fridges. There are front and back verandas, with sea views from the back, and a hot tub in a gazebo in the yard.

Nine Mile

The interior of St. Ann Parish is farm country, with few attractions compelling visitors to leave the coast. One major draw is the hillside hamlet of Nine Mile, the birthplace and final resting place of Bob Marley.

BOB MARLEY MAUSOLEUM

The **Bob Marley Mausoleum** (Nine Mile, contact Harry Shivnani, cell tel. 876/843-0498, harry.reggaeking@yahoo.com, 9am-5pm daily, US$25 adults, US$13 ages 5-11) is one of Jamaica's most popular tourist sites, drawing scores of fans to pay their respects to the late, great King of Reggae. As you arrive in Nine Mile, the Cedella Marley basic school looms in red, gold, and green splendor just before the Marley family home. Outside the official gated parking area, countless hustlers offer ganja and parking, in hopes of luring visitors to spend a few bucks outside the sanctioned attraction. There is no cost to park inside the

Bob Marley: King of Reggae

Bob Marley has become synonymous with all things good about Jamaica and its people, carrying the country's cultural torch decades after his death in 1981. The good will Marley brought the world through his intoxicating music and its uplifting messages is hard to quantify. Born Robert Nesta Marley on February 6, 1945, in Nine Mile, St. Ann, to Cedella Malcolm Marley Booker and Norval Sinclair Marley, Bob grew up a country boy in the small agricultural community before moving with his mother to Trench Town, a ghetto in central Kingston. His father, a white English naval officer and plantation overseer, was a scarce presence who died in 1955 at the age of 60. Bob's racial mix set him apart from his peers and often made him a target, but his heritage afforded him a perspective to approach issues of race and justice, and infused his music with universal appeal.

In Trench Town he teamed up with Peter McIntosh and Bunny Livingston to form the Wailin' Wailers. Trench Town in the 1960s was the creative epicenter of Jamaican music, where fledgling composers and musicians listened attentively to radio broadcasts of American music and reinterpreted classics on their ramshackle instruments, sparking a swing away from traditional Jamaican music like mento that led to the birth of ska, rocksteady, and reggae. Bob's early career spanned the development and evolution of these genres, but it was reggae that became his vehicle. When Bob traveled to London and recorded his first full album, *Catch a Fire*, on Chris Blackwell's fledgling Island Records label, he gained international recognition. Blackwell nurtured the Wailers and helped create a sound that had wide international appeal without watering down the message.

After recording several albums on Island Records, Bob established his own label, Tuff Gong, using his street name. Tuff Gong remains a symbol of artistic independence, a departure from

gate at the mausoleum, however, and visitors should resist calls to park outside.

The massive Bob Marley Mausoleum complex engulfs the humble one-bedroom country house where the world's foremost reggae superstar was born. Marley's mother, Cedella, was laid to rest in a similar mausoleum next door, and a small chapel was constructed across the path. Tours of the mausoleum start at the gift shop, where visitors pay the entry fee before heading upstairs to another gift shop and bar, where more encouragement is offered to spend some cash. From there, a guide is assigned to take visitors up another flight of steps to the mausoleum and Bob's small house. In and around the house are countless details the guides claim to be the literal inspiration for a multitude of songs from Marley's discography, including the single bed referred to in "Is This Love" and the rock pillow from "Talkin' Blues." Below the mausoleum, a clubhouse-style building with contemporary Rasta styling has a restaurant and lounge on the second floor and great views from the balcony over the quiet hills of the St. Ann interior.

Getting There

The shortest route from the North Coast to Nine Mile is via the B3, which heads inland from the stoplight by the police station in Runaway Bay and leads along 11 kilometers (7 miles) of winding country road to Brown's Town. From Brown's Town, continue along the B3 out of town for 12 kilometers (8 miles) south toward Alexandria. In Alexandria, turn east for 8 kilometers (5 miles) to Nine Mile.

Brown's Town is the closest town of any size to the Bob Marley Mausoleum and is famous for its bustling market (Wed., Fri., and Sat.). If you're heading to Nine Mile via route taxi, Brown's Town is the connection point from Runaway Bay or Priory via Bamboo.

the days when musicians were paid measly sums to play on studio recordings while the producers reaped the rewards. Bob's larger-than-life persona outgrew the Wailin' Wailers, creating resentment in Bunny Livingston, known as Bunny Wailer, and Peter McIntosh, or Peter Tosh, both of whom left to pursue successful solo careers. Following the departure of his bandmates, he renamed his band Bob Marley and the Wailers and went on to tour the world, filling stadiums until his untimely death at age 36 from cancer. Bob's popularity has only grown since his passing, with his posthumous *Legend* album going platinum several times over.

- **Tuff Gong Recording:** Bob Marley's production base offers a tour that shows the entire music production process and includes a visit to the studio and record-printing shop (page 209).

- **Bob Marley Museum:** The spirit of Jamaica's most revered son has been preserved at his former residence, where rooms full of newspaper clippings and personal effects stand as a shrine to the man and his music (page 216).

- **Culture Yard:** This Trench Town Development Association project offers a museum tour around Bob Marley's former home and the slums of Trench Town, which have retained the dire conditions that gave birth to songs like "Concrete Jungle" and "No Woman No Cry" (page 209).

- **Bob Marley Mausoleum:** The remote hillside hamlet of Nine Mile draws large numbers of fans looking to see the humble country house where the reggae superstar was born and to tour his final resting place (page 155).

St. Mary Parish

One of the least visited corners of Jamaica, St. Mary is considered the most attractive parish for its proximity to Kingston, Ocho Rios, and Portland; for its vast wilderness areas; and for its people, who don't exhibit the same hustler mentality rampant in more touristed areas. St. Mary is one of the best places in Jamaica for birding and farm tours, with Green Castle Estate standing out among the large plantations of the area.

ORACABESSA

A half hour's drive east of Ocho Rios, Oracabessa is a secluded enclave of high-end tourism where Ian Fleming's Goldeneye has become the benchmark for sophisticated, hip, and casual luxury tourism in Jamaica. Oracabessa has fostered a number of artists whose crafts are more original and far less expensive than in the markets of Ochi, Montego Bay, or Negril. The small community offers some decent beaches and picturesque countryside for those looking to get off the beaten track.

Oracabessa experienced a brief boom as a banana port in the early 1900s. Today the community is experiencing a different kind of boom, thanks to entrepreneur Chris Blackwell's luxury villa development at Goldeneye, which has cemented the area's reputation for exclusivity.

The area from Oracabessa to Port Maria has one of the nicest stretches of coast in Jamaica, where cliff-side villas were built by the likes of Ian Fleming, Noël Coward, and in more recent times, record magnate Chris Blackwell. The districts of Race Course, Galina, and Little Bay have small quiet communities where discreet tourism accommodations blend so well with the landscape that they're easy to miss.

Chris Blackwell and Island Records

One of the world's foremost music producers and founder of Island Records, London-born Chris Blackwell is credited with having introduced reggae music to the world. He built his early career first by selling record imports to the Jamaican market and then by bringing international attention to the budding careers of artists like Millie Small, whose "My Boy Lollipop" topped the charts in England in 1964, giving Island its first hit. Blackwell signed a slew of early English rock artists like Jethro Tull, King Crimson, Robert Palmer, and Cat Stevens. Then came Bob Marley, whose 1973 *Catch a Fire* album would be the first of many for Bob on the Island label. The deal was a huge hit and brought world recognition to a genre that was gaining popularity in Jamaica but unheard of elsewhere.

Blackwell bought some of Jamaica's most beautiful properties, including Strawberry Hill and Goldeneye, eventually forming Island Outpost to market them to luxury travelers without hype. His grand vision has set in motion a transformation in Oracabessa with the new villa development on a private island next to Ian Fleming's Goldeneye.

Blackwell was inducted into the Rock and Roll Hall of Fame in 2001 for his contributions to the music industry. He sold Island Records in 1989 and left the company in 1997, going on to establish Palm Pictures, a film production and distribution company based in New York. Blackwell's first foray into film was by backing Perry Henzell's cult hit *The Harder They Come* in 1971, which brought fame to Jimmy Cliff, before going on to produce other Jamaican classics like *Countryman* as well as successful Hollywood films. Blackwell's eye for talent and opportunity has made him one of the world's most creative and successful businessmen.

James Bond Beach

James Bond Beach (cell tel. 876/371-1528, marshall.bailey@jamesbondbeach.com, 9am-5pm daily, US$5) has two private beaches along with a bar and restaurant serving fish, lobster, shrimp, burgers, and chicken. The beach park occasionally hosts events and live performances.

James Bond Beach hosts the Bicycle Bash kickoff of the **Fat Tyre Festival** (www.singletrackjamaica.com), held each year around the second week in February. This festival was created for mountain biking enthusiasts and showcases much of the talent of the St. Mary Off-Road Bicycling Association. The kickoff features BMX races, stunts, and displays of unusual and pimped-out bikes, followed by several days of competitive and sometimes grueling rides, mostly along single track through the hills of St. Mary.

★ Firefly

Firefly (Island Outpost, tel. 876/975-3677, or caretaker Victor Taylor, cell tel. 876/420-5544,

or tour guide Annette Tracy, tel. 876/424-5359, 9am-4pm daily, US$10 includes guided tour and refreshment) is easily one of Jamaica's most beautiful properties, with the most magnificent view of the St. Mary and Portland coast. The property has had a glamorous past, first as the home of the pirate Henry Morgan, and centuries later as a playground for playwright Noël Coward, both of whom were captivated by the stunning view that graces the small plateau. Henry Morgan's house, which dates from the 17th century, has been rebuilt and is now used as the visitors center. It has a small bar and several tables.

Across the lawn, Coward's house remains preserved as a museum essentially as he left it. Downstairs in his studio, an incomplete painting stands on the easel as if he had been interrupted mid-stroke. His famous "room with a view" was inspiration for several works completed in it, and the piano where he entertained his famous Hollywood guests remains the centerpiece in the study. On the lawn outside, a statue of Coward immortalizes his fascination with the view as he holds his cigarette and ponders the northeast coastline. Coward's tomb is at a corner of the lawn.

At the time of Coward's death, the property was left to Graham Payne, who in turn gave it to the Jamaican government, which today leases it to Chris Blackwell, whose Island Outpost manages the attraction. Up to 120 people visit Firefly daily in the high season, while the visits can drop to a trickle during the slower months of the summer and fall.

Other Attractions

Waterfront in a corner of the yard at Ocean Edge Villa, **The Chocolate Box** (cell tel. 876/781-4841, info@oneonecacao.com, www.oneonecacao.com, US$50 pp) offers groups of two to eight visitors the experience of making artisanal chocolate from bean to bar with local cacao connoisseur and chocolate purveyor Nick Davis, whose One One Cacao has won awards from the Academy of Chocolate and is singlehandedly combatting the decline of Jamaica's cacao industry with its world-class product.

The guided farm tour at **Sun Valley Plantation** (cell tel. 876/995-3075 or 876/446-2026, sunvalleyjamaica@yahoo.com, 9am-2pm daily, US$20) includes a welcome drink, coconut water, a cooked snack of ackee and saltfish, and coconut water at the end of the tour. The educational stroll around the farm familiarizes visitors with native crops like sugarcane and banana that have played important roles in Jamaica's economy and the history of the area. Today the farm produces mainly coconuts for the local market. To get to Sun Valley, head inland at the main junction in Oracabessa, passing through Jack's River. After the primary school, continue straight through the junction for about 1.5 kilometers (1 mile). Manager Lorna Binns has trained seven red-billed streamer-tail hummingbirds to come when called by name.

Guests can swim in the pool and bring lunch to enjoy in the picnic area or on the great house veranda at **Brimmer Hall** (tel. 876/994-2309, 9am-4pm Mon.-Fri., US$25 adults, US$10 children), which offers tractor-drawn jitney tours around the plantation and great house. Guides teach visitors about the fruit trees and give a bit of history of the estate, which dates to the 1700s. The house is full of period furnishings and antiques. To get to Brimmer Hall, head east from Port Maria and turn right three kilometers (2 miles) past Trinity on the road toward Bailey Town, continuing about 1.5 kilometers (1 mile) farther.

Food

Chris Café (Main St., Oracabessa, cell tel. 876/861-1611, 7:30am-11:30pm Mon.-Sat., 7:30am-8:30pm Sun., US$8-25) serves local dishes like ackee and saltfish, mackerel rundown, liver and kidney, and curried chicken on a dining deck overlooking the sea. Reservations are recommended.

Susie's (Main St., Oracabessa, cell tel. 876/844-1621, 8:30am-6pm Mon.-Sat., US$3-5) serves local dishes like stew peas, curry goat, and sweet and sour chicken, on a rotating menu.

A local favorite for all manner of fish, lobster, octopus, crab, and shrimp is ★ **Dor's Fish Pot** (Race Course, cell tel. 876/372-4975, 9am-11:30pm daily, US$5-9). The informal open-air dining area overlooks the sea, and a round bar at the entrance serves drinks.

Fresh seafood is prepared at **Conscious Corner Bar** (cell tel. 876/458-1430 or 876/399-2366, by reservation only, 9am-8pm daily), in Rio Nuevo on the fishing beach. It's a popular hangout for locals and cyclists associated with the St. Mary Off-Road Biking Association.

Accommodations

UNDER US$100

Tamarind Great House (cell tel. 876/995-3252, tamarindgreathouse@yahoo.com, US$75-105 d) on Crescent Estate was destroyed by fire in 1987, and then rebuilt and restored as a 10-bedroom colonial-style great house by English couple Gillian and Barry Chambers, who live on the property with their son Gary. Nine attractive rooms have fans and private baths with hot water. Some rooms have private balconies. Furnishings and decor reflect the colonial period. To get to Tamarind House, head inland at the roundabout in Oracabessa along Jack's River Road, keeping straight ahead at the Epping gas station. Continue for about 0.8 kilometer (0.5 mile) past Sun Valley Plantation, keeping left at the broken bridge and continuing up the hill.

High View Cottages (Gibraltar Heights, tel. 876/975-3210, cell tel. 876/831-1975, monica.hucey@hotmail.com, US$60, includes breakfast) is owned by the amiable Colleen Pottinger, who lives in the main house on the property. There are two one-bedroom self-contained cottages with kitchens, private baths with hot water, access to the swimming pool, and Wi-Fi. One cottage has a queen bed and one has two twin beds. An inflatable mattress is available for extra guests (US$30). Additional meals can be prepared on request. The personal attention of its owner and the quiet location on the lush Gibraltar hillside make High View a favorite home away from home for budget-minded travelers. Guests can access the private beach for residents of Gibraltar.

An eight-unit guesthouse overlooking the sea in Oracabessa, **Ocean Edge Villa** (across from Ian Fleming International Airport, tel. 876/350-1276, nicdavis@yahoo.com, US$65 d) has self-contained units with queen beds, private balconies facing the sea, and kitchenettes. Rooms are clean and a great value for the money.

US$100-250

Perched on a cliff overlooking the sea, ★ **Moxons Beach Club** (Stewart Town, moxons_beach_club@flowja.com, www.moxonsbeach.club, tel. 876/975-7023, from US$163 d) is a top-notch boutique hotel. Steps lead down to a pier where kayaks are available for exploring the coast and reefs offshore. Rooms have kings or queens, some with kitchenettes, and fine linens, comfortable mattresses, and Wi-Fi. The restaurant on the property serves a mix of Jamaican and international fare with indoor and outdoor dining areas overlooking the water. The pool deck is found a few steps from the dining area.

A modest three-bedroom property, **Loveland Villa** (Lot 1, Gibraltar Heights, cell tel. 876/833-9142 or 876/564-5114, dpalmer7@gmail.com, US$175 low season, US$200 high season) has a wide veranda for enjoying the panoramic view of the Oracabessa coast. The master suite has a king bed and private bath. Two other rooms each have two single beds

Goldeneye, formerly owned by 007 author Ian Fleming

Tacky's War

On the morning after Easter Sunday in 1760, an enslaved man known as Tacky led a revolt in St. Mary that would reverberate around northeastern Jamaica until September of that year. The uprising became known as Tacky's Rebellion or Tacky's War.

Tacky was an overseer on Frontier Plantation outside Port Maria, giving him the limited freedom necessary to strategize and organize the rebellion at both Frontier and bordering Trinity Plantations. A former chief in his homeland of Ghana, Tacky had the confidence and clout to amass wide support for what was meant to be an island-wide overthrow of the British colonial masters.

Tacky and about 50 of his followers awoke before dawn that morning and easily killed the master of Frontier Plantation before raiding the armory at nearby Fort Haldane, where they killed the storekeeper and took guns and ammunition. The owner of Trinity Plantation escaped on horseback to warn the surrounding estates. But with newfound artillery, the ranks of the rebel army began to swell, and they quickly took nearby Haywood and Esher Plantations and began to celebrate their early success. A slave from Esher plantation, however, slipped away to call in the authorities, and before long a militia of soldiers from Spanish Town and Maroons from Scott's Hall were sent to quell the uprising.

The rebels' confidence had been bolstered by Obeah men (shamans) among their ranks who spread incantations and claimed the army would be protected and that Obeah men could not be killed. This confidence took a blow when the militia, learning of these claims, captured and killed one of the Obeah men. Nonetheless, the fighting would last months and take the lives of some 60 whites and 300 rebels before it was defused. Tacky himself was captured and beheaded by the Maroons from Scott's Hall, who took his head to Spanish Town on a pole to be displayed to dissuade any further resistance.

The legend of Tacky spread across the island, giving inspiration to other resistance movements that would come in the later years of slavery and after emancipation. Many of Tacky's followers committed suicide rather than surrendering, while those who were captured were either executed or sold and shipped off the island. Ringleaders were either burned alive or starved in cages in the Parade in Kingston. It was during Tacky's War that the British authorities first learned of the role African religion played behind the scenes in these uprisings, and Obeah thus became part of the official record with a 1770 law passed to punish its practitioners by death or transportation, at the court's discretion.

that can be joined to make kings and share a bath. The kitchen is fully equipped, and the housekeeper comes daily to cook and tidy up. The villa holds six comfortably and up to eight (US$20 pp after 6 guests). Wi-Fi covers the house; a flat-screen TV in the living room has a DVD player.

GOLDENEYE

A seaside estate formerly owned by 007 creator Ian Fleming, ★ **Goldeneye** (tel. 876/622-9007, U.S. tel. 800/688-7678, info@goldeneye.com, www.islandoutpost.com, from US$620 low season, US$1,150 high season) is where Fleming penned all 14 of the famous spy thrillers. Today it is Jamaica's most exclusive boutique resort. The one- and two-bedroom

lagoon and beachfront villas have full kitchens; the lagoon cottages don't. All units have flat-screens with streaming TV and international cable, music players, and Wi-Fi.

The 26 one- and two-bedroom **Goldeneye Beach Huts** (from US$350 low season, US$760 high season) are raised off the sand, some with lounges and outdoor garden showers and bathtubs. Rooms have custom kings, flat-screen TVs, balconies, and baths with double rain showerheads.

The crown jewel of the property is the five-bedroom **Fleming Villa** (www.theflemingvilla.com, US$6,600 low season, US$8,500 high season), boasting enormous bamboo-framed canopy beds, original furnishings, and indoor and outdoor master baths. Large windows open to the sea breeze and steps lead down from the spacious living room to an outdoor dining area high above the private beach, reserved for villa guests. A poolside lounge features a projection screen and bar.

Meals at Goldeneye are offered à la carte in a casual setting at **Bizot Bar** on Low Cay and at **Gazebo,** overhanging the lagoon. The food is a mix of international comfort dishes and creative embellishments of local Jamaican cuisine. Meals can also be served in the villas. Nonguests may dine on property by making a reservation at least 24 hours in advance.

Water sports activities offered at Goldeneye include kayaking, paddleboarding, snorkeling, fishing, and glass-bottomed boat tours. Goldeneye has evolved in recent years into Jamaica's most exclusive resort community, with several villas owned independently.

In a cottage overhanging the lagoon, **The FieldSpa** (10am-6pm daily) at Goldeneye has open-air treatment rooms hidden behind lush foliage. Massage, meditation, body scrubs, body wraps, bush baths, and facials are among the treatments on offer (from US$130). Homemade concoctions draw on natural ingredients, many grown on the Island Outpost farm at Pantrepant, Trelawny.

Transportation

Minibuses depart from the Transport Centre in the heart of Ocho Rios to Oracabessa throughout the day. Route taxis can also be taken from closer points, including Boscobel to the west and Port Maria to the east.

PORT MARIA

One of the most picturesque towns in Jamaica, Port Maria has a large protected harbor with the small Cabarita Island, also known as Treasure Island, in the center. Originally inhabited by the Taino and later by the Spanish, the island was vulnerable to pirate attacks and fell into the hands of the pirate Henry Morgan until he lost it gambling. In the late 1700s a village began to take shape on the harbor shores, and by 1821 public buildings, including the parish council offices and the courthouse, were built. Port Maria boomed with exports of sugar, rum, indigo, pimento, tropical hardwoods, and coffee, but the town has long since passed its prime. Nevertheless, it still has a strong fishing community and is a commercial center for the surrounding rural districts. Several infrastructure improvements associated with the North Coast Highway project have recently given the town a bit of a face-lift. The Outram

historic ruins at Green Castle Estate

River forms the eastern border of town, beyond which begins a vast wilderness area wrapping around the hilly coastline all the way to Robin's Bay.

Sights

Fort Haldane (unmanaged), or the sparse and scattered remains of it, is located on a road that cuts across the point jutting into the sea, forming the western flank of Port Maria's harbor. The road runs between the Anglican Church and the middle of the bend on the other side of the hill on Little Bay. Two cannons overgrown with brush aim out to sea just past the oldest structure on the premises, a low brick building alongside discarded car parts. The fort was built in 1759 for coastal defense during the Seven Years' War and named after then-governor George Haldane. The property was later a home for the elderly but has since fallen into disuse. The gates to this seldom-visited historical site are typically left ajar and unlocked.

The building that housed the old **courthouse** and **police station** (across from the Anglican church, on east side of town), originally built in 1821, is one of the best examples of Georgian architecture in Port Maria. Much of the original building was destroyed by fire in 1988 but was completely restored in 2002 with funds from the Jamaican and Venezuelan governments. The building is now in use as the Port Maria Civic Center. A plaque by the main entrance dedicates the premises to labor leader and politician Alexander Bustamante.

St. Mary Parish Church was built in 1861 and has an adjoining cemetery with an epitaph dedicated to the Jamaicans who fought in World War I. The **Tacky Memorial** is also located in the church cemetery.

Beaches

Port Maria's anglers keep their boats and bring in their catch at **Pagee Beach.** Outings to Cabarita Island, a great place to explore in true Robinson Crusoe fashion, can be arranged from here by negotiating with the fisherfolk; US$10 pp is a reasonable round-trip fare. Pagee is not a good spot for swimming.

Shopping

If you're planning a stop to check out the old courthouse and Anglican Church, call ahead to see the crafts at **St. Mary Craft Market** (Port Maria Civic Center, by appointment, cell tel. 876/373-7575), featuring work of artists residing in the parish.

Food

Romney's Restaurant Bar & Grill (Llanrumney Square, 5 kilometers/3 miles east of Port Maria, cell tel. 876/849-9106, naturefeelltd@yahoo.com, 8am-10pm daily, US$5-12) serves chicken and pork hot off the jerk pit as well as dishes like fried chicken, cow foot, and steamed or roast fish, along with fresh juice smoothies and juice blends. **Pirates Treats** (Llanrumney Square, 5 kilometers/3 miles east of Port Maria, tel. 876/772-3282, 8:30am-9pm Sun.-Thurs., 1pm-9pm Fri.-Sat.) serves Devon House ice cream and pastries between the jerk grill and bar.

TRANSPORTATION

Port Maria is 30 kilometers (19 miles) east of Ocho Rios on the A3. To get here, head east along the Ocho Rios Bypass and hug the coast, passing Boscobel and Oracabessa along the way. Route taxis leave from the gas station by the clock tower in the center of Ocho Rios for Port Maria as they fill up throughout the day. In Port Maria, route taxis depart for Annotto Bay, passing the turn-off for Robin's Bay.

★ ROBIN'S BAY

One of the most laid-back and picturesque corners of Jamaica, Robin's Bay is entirely different than what's marketed on posters. Robin's Bay is the Treasure Beach of the North Coast, remaining a quiet fishing and subsistence agricultural community with a few lodging options for an easygoing retreat and intimacy with nature. Beginning with Green Castle Estate, a working farm that commands a large swath of land fronting the bay, the area is a small, tight-knit community and has a slow pace that's easy to get used to.

Green Castle Estate

Green Castle Estate (cell tel. 876/881-6279, info@gcjamaica.com, www.gcjamaica.com) is a 650-hectare (1,600-acre) farm producing fruit, vegetables, and flowers. Named after the Irish holdings of one of its earlier owners, several archaeological finds on the property indicate it has been continuously occupied since the time of the Taino. Early English settlement at Green Castle left the iconic windmill that still stands today. Land use has changed from cassava cultivation under the Taino and Spanish to orange, cotton, pimento, cacao, indigo, sugarcane, and then bananas. For centuries the estate was connected with the rest of Jamaica only by sea. Since the 1950s the farm has grown an increasingly diverse mix of fruit crops and more recently organic fruit and orchids. Current ownership has turned the estate into an ecotourism paradise, especially popular for **birding,** and 20 of the country's 28 endemic species can be seen.

Historical sites on the expansive estate include excavated Taino middens dating to 1300, a militia barracks (1834), and the signature coral stone windmill tower (1700).

Estate Tours (US$30 adults, U$10 children) introduce visitors to some of the 120 hectares (300 acres) of certified-organic tree crops and focus on organic coconut oil production and the roughly 2,000 pimento (allspice) trees and cocoa trees. Beef production is also a major activity, with hundreds of cattle roaming the rolling grassy hills. Day passes (US$30) allow visitors to roam free, or contract the services of a guide (US$40 per hour, half day US$120, full day US$180). Guests are offered Jamaican lunch (US$15 adults, US$7.50 children).

Overlooking Robin's Bay with benches for enjoying the view, **Sunrise on the Cliff** (contact Sanchez, cell tel. 876/436-1223, noon-10pm daily) is a bar and grill with a fenced-in lawn and a cook shop preparing steamed, fried, or brown stew fish and occasionally conch soup (US$5-15). The bar serves rum and beer, with stacks of speakers perpetually warming up for the next session.

Shopping

Donald and Belva Johnson are **Clonmel Potters** (Arthur's Ridge, east of Highgate on the B2, tel. 876/992-4495, clonmelpotters@ hotmail.com, call to arrange a visit 9am-5pm Mon.-Sat., US$20-300), working in a variety of local media, from porcelain to terra cotta.

Strawberry Fields Beach

Donald's favorite subject is the female nude, countered by his wife's concentration on organic forms. Both are graduates of Kingston's Edna Manley School of Visual Arts, Jamaica's foremost art college.

Accommodations

★ **Green Castle Estate Great House** (B&B from US$225, 4-bedroom villa US$5,990 weekly, cell tel. 876/881-6279, info@gcjamaica.com, www.gcjamaica.com) is the most luxurious option in the area. There are colonial furnishings in four spacious bedrooms with private baths. An outlying cottage (B&B from US$170, US$3,195 weekly) has an additional four bedrooms, three with their own baths. The swimming pool overlooks the gardens. There is a view of the coast and the Blue Mountains from almost every window and veranda. You're guaranteed to see several species of hummingbird, including the red-billed streamertail, the national bird. All estate tours are included with house rental. Opportunities for farm volunteer work and outreach in the neighboring community of Robin's Bay are sometimes available by request. The estate can accommodate up to 21 guests.

A seafront property with 13 rooms sleeping up to 40, ★ **Strawberry Fields Together Beachfront Cottages and Adventure Tours** (cell tel. 876/337-6127, cell tel. 876/436-6395, U.S. tel. 772/801-6321, info@strawberryfieldstogether.com, www.strawberryfieldstogether.com, US$90-280) sits on seven hectares (18 acres). Cottages have a range of bed sizes and layouts with organic touches like tree-trunk bed frames and natural stone-floor showers. Two small private beaches with fine white sand line idyllic crystalline coves protected by coral reefs. A covered outdoor dining area at the Strawberry Patch Café and Grill has a bar, a pizza oven, and a jerk grill. Wi-Fi covers the entire property. Guests and nonguests can partake in adventure tours, ranging from guided hikes (US$25 pp) and boat rides (US$85) to a black-sand beach, Kwamen Falls, old ruins, and fish roasted over campfire. Snorkeling trips go to Long Reef (US$50).

In a refurbished 400-year-old Spanish fort, **River Lodge** (tel. 876/995-3003, riverlodge@cwjamaica.com, www.river-lodge.com, US$32-50 pp, includes breakfast and dinner) has rooms inside the fort that complement a pair of cottages. From River Lodge, vast unspoiled wilderness stretches along the coast almost to Port Maria, where waterfalls and black-sand beaches are best reached by boat with the local fisherfolk.

Getting There and Around

The best way to reach Robin's Bay is by **route taxi** (US$1) or a **private charter** (US$10) from Annotto Bay. Most accommodations offer pickups from the airport or nearby parishes. Getting around in Robin's Bay often requires long waits before a route taxi passes. If you're driving from Ocho Rios or points farther west, head east into St. Mary on the A3 along the coast through Tower Isle, Boscobel, Oracabessa, Galina, and Port Maria. The road diverges from the coast east of Port Maria, winding through coconut groves before meeting the coast again just west of Annotto Bay. The turn off the A3 for Robin's Bay is marked by a sign two kilometers (1.2 miles) west of Water Valley.

Port Antonio and the East Coast

Port Antonio...........170
Upper Rio Grande
    Valley................188
West of Port Antonio...190
East of Port Antonio....191
Morant Bay 197

Jamaica's easternmost region contains the is-land's least exploited natural treasures. Port Antonio, or "Portie," is a quiet town in the center of Portland Parish's coast, boasting some of Jamaica's most secluded beaches and a handful of other natural wonders.

The world-famous Blue Hole, or Blue Lagoon, where ice-cold spring water mixes with the warm sea, is surreal and reason enough to visit the region. Navy Island, an abandoned little paradise in the middle of Port Antonio's twin harbors, is surrounded by coral reefs and sandbars. Steep, lush hills rise from a coastline dotted with beaches, inlets, and mangroves. Reach Falls is a nature-lover's paradise, where local guides take visitors by the hand along paths only they can see along the slippery river bed. In Bath, natural hot springs are reputed to cure almost any ailment.

Highlights

Look for ★ to find recommended sights, activities, dining, and lodging.

★ **Blue Hole:** Also known as the Blue Lagoon, this freshwater spring wells up in a protected cove and mixes with the warm salty sea, creating a blurring effect that enhances the magical hue (page 176).

★ **Winnifred Beach:** Locals gather at the people's beach to enjoy sand, sun, and some of the best fried fish and conch soup around (page 177).

★ **Rafting the Rio Grande:** Cruise gently downstream through unspoiled wilderness (page 188).

★ **Boston Beach:** Some of the best waves for **surfing** in the northeast are a stone's throw from Portland's famed jerk pits (page 193).

★ **Long Bay Beach:** Palm trees are likely to be your only company on this two-kilometer (1.2-mile) stretch of white sand and strong surf (page 194).

★ **Reach Falls:** The island's most exciting waterfalls carve through a lush valley dotted with caves and crystal-clear pools (page 195).

★ **Bath Hot Springs:** Purported to cure all manner of diseases, the hot springs at Bath provide rejuvenating relaxation (page 198).

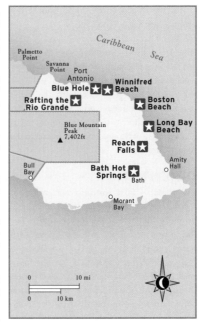

When one of these destinations occupies top priority on your daily agenda, life seems to flow at the right speed. Perhaps the languid pace of this side of the island is just meant to be, and as a visitor, you won't miss the crowds.

PLANNING YOUR TIME

Some say Port Antonio is a place time forgot. It's definitely an easy place to fall in love with, and despite the slow pace, it's hard to be bored. You'll want no less than three days for all the main sights without feeling rushed, but if you go at the beginning of a trip to Jamaica, it's possible you won't want to see anything else.

Port Antonio is small enough to fit in two main activities in a day. Folly Mansion makes a good morning jaunt, when the sun lights up the side facing the sea, and is nicely complemented with an afternoon at the beach. The dusk hours are best spent on a bench at Errol Flynn Marina with a Devon House ice cream cone in hand.

Rafting on the Rio Grande, snorkeling around and exploring Pellew Island, and splashing around in the rivers and at Blue Hole are all great affordable ways to spend a day. If you're planning to head into the higher reaches of the Rio Grande Valley, it will take at least a day there and back with a hike to the falls near Moore Town, and at least three days round-trip to hike with Maroon guides to the historical site of Nanny Town, higher up in the Blue Mountains.

ORIENTATION

The town of Port Antonio is easy to get around on foot with the farthest-flung sights no more than a few kilometers apart. For the natural attractions east of town, you will need to jump in a route taxi or two, charter a cab, or have your own rental car. The main road (the A4) along the North Coast passes through Port Antonio, but twists and turns before emerging on the other side of town. Approaching from the west, the A4 first becomes West Palm Avenue, then West Street going through the center of town, joining Harbour Street in front of Royal Mall, which later becomes Folly Road, and then once again, simply the main road (the A4). Harbour Street and William Street together form a one-way roundabout circling the Courthouse and the Parish Council.

Titchfield Hill, the old part of town, sits on a peninsula across a narrow channel from Navy Island that separates East Harbour from West Harbour. Titchfield has several interesting gingerbread-style buildings and a few guesthouses, with Fort George Street, King Street, and Queen Street running the length of the peninsula parallel to one another. In the heart of town, most of the action is on Harbour and West Streets, where the banks, a few restaurants, and Musgrave Market are located. From Harbour Street, West Avenue starts again, wrapping around a residential district and becoming East Avenue before reuniting with the Main Road, at this point called Allan Avenue. Red Hassell Road, which is the delineator between East and West Palm Avenues, is the route to the Rio Grande Valley.

East of Port Antonio along the coast is a series of hills dropping sharply down to coves and bays, which help delineate the districts of Anchovy, Drapers, San San, and Fairy Hill. Farther east is Boston and then Long Bay. The most popular beaches, including San San, Frenchman's Cove, and Winnifred, are all located on this stretch of coast east of town, as is Blue Hole. Reach Falls is about 40 minutes east of Port Antonio, just past Manchioneel.

SAFETY

Port Antonio is not as sprawling as some of Jamaica's other cities, and thus hustlers are less prevalent. Nonetheless, normal precautions should be taken: avoid lonely stretches of road at night, stick to well-lit areas, and don't tempt hotel staff by leaving cash or valuables lying around.

Previous: Reach Falls; the deep turquoise waters of Blue Hole; Boston Bay

The East Coast

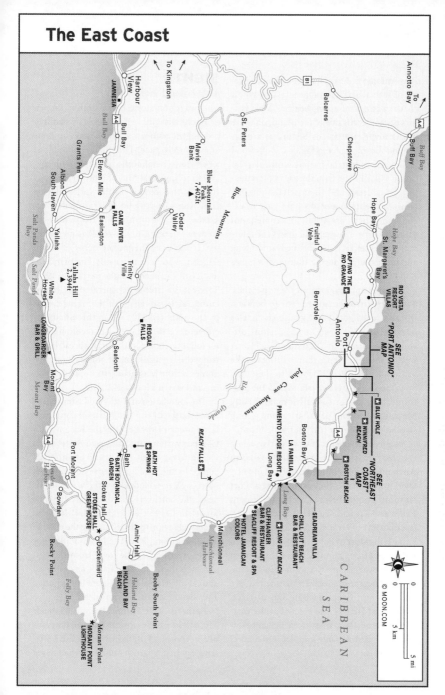

To Annotto Bay

Annotto Bay

Harbour View

To Kingston

JAMNESIA

Bull Bay

Balcarres

Buff Bay

B1

Chepstowe

St. Peters

Mavis Bank

Grants Pen

Eleven Mile

Albion

South Haven

Easington

CANE RIVER FALLS

Cedar Valley

Blue Mountain Peak 7,402ft

Blue Mountains

Hope Bay

Fruitful Vale

Hope Bay

St. Margaret's Bay

RIO VISTA RESORT VILLAS

RAFTING THE RIO GRANDE

Port Antonio

SEE "PORT ANTONIO" MAP

Yallahs

Trinity Ville

Yallahs Hill 2,394ft

White Horses

LONGBOARDER BAR & GRILL

REGGAE FALLS

Seaforth

Berrydale

Morant Bay

Morant Bay

A4

Port Morant

REACH FALLS

Bath

BATH HOT SPRINGS

BATH BOTANICAL GARDEN

STOKES HALL GREAT HOUSE

Bowden

Stokes Hall

Amity Hall

Duckenfield

HOLLAND BAY BEACH

Rocky Point

Booby South Point

Manchioneal Harbour

Manchioneal

Boston Bay

PIMENTO LODGE RESORT

LA FAMILIA

Long Bay

CLIFFHANGER BAR & RESTAURANT

SEACLIFF RESORT & SPA

HOTEL JAMAICAN COLORS

CHILL OUT BEACH BAR & RESTAURANT

LONG BAY BEACH

SEADREAM VILLA

Long Bay

John Crow Mountains

BLUE HOLE

WINNIFRED BEACH

BOSTON BEACH

SEE "NORTHEAST COAST" MAP

A4

CARIBBEAN SEA

Morant Point

MORANT POINT LIGHTHOUSE

Folly Bay

Bowden Harbour

Rio Grande

Salt Ponds Bay

Salt Ponds

Bull Bay

A4

Buff Bay

0 5 km

0 5 mi

© MOON.COM

Port Antonio

Port Antonio is the capital of Portland, a parish of spectacular natural beauty, Old World charm, and one-of-a-kind beaches. Most visitors never see this side of the island, unaware of the town's illustrious history as a playground for the rich and famous. Hollywood actors and industrial barons built their vacation villas in San San, the area's most auspicious address, and their heirs, alongside Kingston's elite, many of whom have weekend homes here, are apparently content not to see throngs. The area still draws the international jet set, recently hosting Daniel Craig and his entourage during filming of a James Bond film.

The area's primary draws are its beaches. Two marinas offer safe harbor to boaters, where a scuba outfit and a sailboat charter operator can be hired for excursions offshore. Fishermen at Shan Shy Beach, just west of town, are more than willing to take visitors across West Harbour in their "canoes" to explore Navy Island and the surrounding reefs for a small sum, and Folly Mansion is a fine destination for a long stroll along the East Harbour waterfront.

The main road east of town curves along the coast, passing a few waterfront villas in Anchovy Gardens immediately east of Folly Oval, which marks the eastern edge of Port Antonio proper, before coming to Trident Hotel and Trident Castle, Turtle Harbour, the districts of Drapers, San San, and then Fairy Hill. Most of Port Antonio's preferred lodging options and the area's three most popular beaches are found on this stretch of coast, beginning with Frenchman's Cove and San San Beach in San San district, where Blue Hole is also located at the eastern end, and then Winnifred Beach below Fairy Hill district, one kilometer (0.6 mile) farther east.

SIGHTS
Titchfield Hill

The heart of historic Port Antonio, known as **Titchfield Hill,** is best visited by strolling around the peninsula, which takes an hour at a leisurely pace. Titchfield Hill today is a run-down neighborhood dotted with several buildings that hint of more prosperous times, with decorative latticework and wide front steps leading up to wraparound verandas. The **Demontevin Lodge** (21 Fort George St., tel. 876/993-2604) is an example. It was once the private home of David Gideon, who became custos, the principal justice of the peace for the parish, in 1923. Today it is a tired hotel operated under unenthusiastic management that rents rooms by the night (US$30) and in three-hour increments (US$15), but it's not recommended for lodging. Its decorative gingerbread house ironwork, reminiscent of old sea captains' homes on the Massachusetts coast, is striking and worth a look.

The foundation and scattered ruins of the **Titchfield Hotel,** built by banana boat captain Lorenzo Dow Baker of the Boston Fruit Company, stand across Queen Street from Ocean Crest Guest House and are now occupied by the Jamaica Defense Force, which patrols Navy Island across the water. At its peak, the hotel was a favored watering hole for celebrities like Bette Davis, J. P. Morgan, and Errol Flynn, the latter buying the place in addition to Navy Island and the Bonnie View Hotel, overlooking the town from the best perch around. The Titchfield was destroyed and rebuilt several times before it was gutted and abandoned after Flynn's death.

At the tip of the Titchfield peninsula stands **Titchfield School,** constructed on the ruins of **Fort George.** Built by the English to defend against Spanish reprisals that never

Port Antonio Coastline

Inset:
- MUSGRAVE MARKET
- POLICE STATION
- THE ITALIAN JOB
- BUS STATION
- WEST ST.
- HARBOUR ST.
- GIDEON AVE.

Map labels:
- To Hope Bay, Buff Bay, Antonio Bay, and St. Mary
- A4
- FIRST AND LAST BAR & RESTAURANT
- SHAN SHY BEACH
- Crab Point
- DICKIE'S BANANA (BEST KEPT SECRET)
- WEST PALM AVE.
- Bryan's Bay
- CARIBBEAN SEA
- RICE PIECE RD.
- HALLS AVE.
- Anoto River
- BOUNDBROOK WHARF
- BOUNDBROOK MARINA
- Port Antonio
- Old Marina
- West Harbour
- Navy Island Beach
- Navy Island
- ERROL FLYNN MARINA
- SEE INSET
- TITCHFIELD HOTEL RUINS
- QUEEN ST.
- KING ST.
- TITCHFIELD HIGH SCHOOL
- DEMONTEVIN LODGE
- IVANHOES
- GIDEON AVE.
- WEST ST.
- To Mupper Rio Grande Valley, Rafting, And Moore Town
- WEST PALM AVE.
- West Town River
- THE VILLAGE CRAFTS CENTRE
- Carder Park
- East Harbour
- A4
- ALLAN AVE.
- YI YAAD
- ANNA BANANNA
- RAMATULLAH'S
- To San San, Boston, Long Bay and St. Thomas
- FOLLY LIGHTHOUSE
- Folly Point
- Woods Island
- FOLLY RUINS
- Folly Beach
- © MOON.COM
- 0, 0.25 km, 0.25 mi

materialized, Fort George didn't see any action, but it operated until World War I. It had walls three meters (10 feet) thick and embrasures for 22 cannons, a few of which are still present. Nobody manages this historic site, making it free and accessible anytime.

Bonnie View

Another dilapidated former Errol Flynn property is the **Bonnie View Hotel** (Bonnie View Rd.), no longer in operation. The view is among the best in town. To get here, take the washed-out Richmond Hill Road directly across from the Anglican Church on the corner of West Palm and Bridge Streets. Bonnie View is not a managed attraction, and there is no cost to have a look, as long as no one is around to make reference to the sign on property that states "All sightseers must pay US$3 (J$150)," which doesn't compute for today's exchange rate and dates the effort. Bonnie View makes a good early-morning walk from town for some aerobic exercise. The steep road up is passable in a car with low clearance if you drive slowly and avoid the deepest potholes.

Marinas

With 32 berths, **Errol Flynn Marina** (tel. 876/993-3209 or 876/715-6044, www.errolflynnmarina.com, 8am-5pm daily) welcomes transient vessels (under 50 feet US$0.95 per foot per night, over 50 feet US$1.75). Metered electricity and water are available. A well-laid-out and planted promenade along the waterfront has benches. A swimming pool and Wi-Fi are available for marina guests, and an internet café (US$4 per hour) is open to nonguests. A Devon House ice cream parlor and a bar serving food are found within the gated complex, and the scenic waterfront makes a romantic spot for an evening stroll. A private beach faces Navy Island. The park along the waterfront (7am-11pm Mon.-Fri., 7am-midnight Sat.-Sun.) is open to nonguests, as is the beach, marina, and bar; the docks and pool are reserved for marina guests. The Errol Flynn Marina has 24-hour security, and a gate to the dock opens with a guest access card.

About a kilometer (0.6 mile) from the clock tower next to the old train station, now home to the Portland Art Gallery, across from CC Bakery, **Port Antonio Marina** (8:30am-5pm daily) offers docking at lower rates with metered water, electricity, and showers, but no security after 4pm. Marina guests have access to showers and laundry 24 hours a day with an access card.

Errol Flynn Marina

Folly Mansion

Just east of Port Antonio along Allan Avenue, a left onto a dirt road before the cricket pitch follows the edge of East Harbour out to Folly Point Lighthouse. A right turn after the cricket pitch along a grassy vehicle track through a low scrub forest leads to **Folly Mansion** (unmanaged), a free and always accessible attraction on government-owned land. Built by Connecticut millionaire Alfred Mitchell in 1905, the 60-room mansion was once the most ostentatious building in Jamaica. Apparently, the cement used in the construction was mixed with saltwater, which weakened the structure and eroded the steel framework, causing almost immediate deterioration. Nonetheless, Mitchell lived part-time in the mansion with his family until his death in 1912, before the house was abandoned in 1936.

On the waterfront in front of the pillared mansion is the humble little **Folly Beach,** which faces small Wood Island, where Mitchell is said to have kept monkeys and other exotic animals. The beach is swimmable, but care should be taken as the sea floor is not even, and parts are covered with sharp coral. The area is also known to have strong currents on occasion.

The name Folly predates the ill-fated mansion in **Folly Point Lighthouse,** built in 1888. The name is said to refer to onetime landowner and Baptist minister James Service and his frugal ways. The lighthouse stands on a point extending along the windward shore of East Harbour and is not generally open to the public, but the property manager is known to let visitors in on occasion. A track sometimes too rutted and muddy for a vehicle with low clearance runs along the water's edge between the lighthouse and the mansion.

Navy Island

Originally called Lynch's Island, Navy Island is a landmass slightly larger than Titchfield Hill, about 0.75 kilometer (0.5 mile) long with an area of about two hectares (5 acres). It protects Port Antonio's West Harbour with a large sandbar extending off its western flank. The island was once slated for development as the town of Port Antonio, but the British Navy acquired it instead as a place to beach ships for cleaning and repairs. A naval station was eventually built, and later Errol Flynn bought the island and turned it into an exclusive resort. Today Navy Island is owned by the Port Authority, which has claimed for decades to be planning its redevelopment. A private bid for the land put together by a consortium of local landowners was blocked by the authority, which seems wary of ceding control despite doing nothing with it, to the dismay of many.

The island has no services, but it's a great place to tromp around and explore, and the Jamaica Defense Force Officers on patrol there are friendly enough to visitors. **Alvin Butler** (cell tel. 876/809-6276) can arrange visits to the island with local fishers (US$20 pp, US$30 with lunch) from Shan Shy Beach, just west of Port Antonio, adjacent to his restaurant, Dickie's Banana, a.k.a. Best Kept Secret.

Other Sights

Boundbrook Wharf is the old banana-loading wharf just west of town, facing Titchfield on the opposite side of West Harbour. While not as busy as in the banana-boom days of the late 1800s, the wharf continues to be used on occasion. It's a good 20-minute walk from town. Just north of the entrance to the wharf, a sandy lane leads off the main road to a beach, where boats are tethered in front of the small fishing community.

BEACHES

On Bryan's Bay, **Shan Shy Beach** charges no entry fee and is home to a beach complex run by Donovan "Atto" Tracey (tel. 876/394-1312). An open building has a billiards room with two tables. One of the less frequented beaches in Port Antonio, Shan Shy is a good place to take off on snorkeling or fishing excursions, which can be

Portland's Banana Boom

The global banana trade, a multibillion-dollar industry, has its roots in Portland and St. Thomas. American sea captains George Busch and later Lorenzo Dow Baker, who arrived in 1870 on the 85-ton *Telegraph*, established a lucrative two-way trade, bringing saltfish (cod), shoes, and textiles from New England, where the bananas sold at a handsome profit. Baker was the most successful of the early banana shippers, forming the Boston Fruit Company in 1899, which later became the United Fruit Company of New Jersey, which went on to control much of the fruit's production in the Americas. As refrigerated ships came into operation in the early 1900s, England slowly took over from the United States as the primary destination, thanks to tariff protection that was only recently phased out.

With the establishment of the Jamaica Banana Producers Association in 1929, smallholder production was organized, a cooperative shipping line established, and the virtual monopoly held by United Fruit was somewhat broken. In 1936, the association became a shareholder-based company rather than a cooperative due to near bankruptcy and pressure from United Fruit. It was this example of organized labor that gave Marcus Garvey the inspiration for a shipping line to serve the African diaspora and bring commerce into its hands. In the 1930s, Panama disease virtually wiped out the Jamaican banana crop, hitting small producers especially hard. Banana carriers and dockworkers were at the fore of the labor movements of 1937-1938 that led to the formation of Jamaica's trade unions and eventually the establishment of the country's political parties.

arranged through Atto or **Alvin Butler** (cell tel. 876/854-4763 or 876/869-4391, US$20-50) of Dickie's Banana. The beach is located five minutes west of town at a sharp curve in the main road.

Around the bend in **White River,** Lucky Star Cookshop and Bar overlooks another angler's beach. It's a favorite cool-out spot for local men, who are often found in the evenings playing poker and dominoes.

FRENCHMAN'S COVE

Frenchman's Cove (tel. 876/993-7270 or 876/564-9779, www.frenchmanscove.com, 9am-5pm daily, US$10), about four kilometers (2.5 miles) east of town along the A4, is a tired resort with a block of hotel rooms (from US$133, including breakfast) in the Great

House and six standalone "villas" (US$194), with dated furnishings and sparse amenities that tend toward rustic. There is little to complain about when it comes to the lush grounds, where a cool meandering river meets a wide sandy beach with gentle surf. The beach and deep cove are well protected from the open water, but the sea floor drops off steeply within 10 meters (30 feet) of the shoreline, so weak swimmers should use caution. Otherwise, it's a great swimming beach, and visitors love the rope swing hanging over the shallow river on the western flank. The beach is staffed with waiters offering drinks and burgers, jerk chicken, fish, and lobster (US$5-30).

SAN SAN BEACH

About 500 meters (550 yards) to the east, **San San Beach** (10am-4pm daily, US$10)

1: Navy Island **2:** Folly Mansion

is at the base of the gentle hill sloping up from the sea that encompasses San San district, where many of the area's most luxurious villas are found. The fine-sand beach hugs a cove next to Alligator Head facing Pellew Island. The reef around Pellew Island is in decent shape, with plentiful small fish, brain coral, and fan coral. The reef extends eastward to the mouth of Blue Hole, protecting a string of luxury villas overhanging the water. This is another prime beach that sees few visitors. A restaurant and bar on the western side of the beach has nothing to offer beyond restrooms in sore need of an upgrade.

Pellew Island is a private island, given, as the legend has it, by industrial magnate and famed art collector Hans Heinrich Thyssen-Bornemisza to supermodel Nina Sheila Dyer, one of his many brides, as a wedding gift. Dyer committed suicide five years later in 1965, and Thyssen-Bornemisza himself died in 2002. There are no organized tours of the private island, but fishers and seafaring entrepreneurs from the small beach adjacent to Blue Hole take visitors over to explore and snorkel along the reefs (US$20 pp round-trip).

★ BLUE HOLE

Blue Hole is also commonly referred to as the Blue Lagoon, thanks to a 1980 Randal Kleiser film of that name starring Brooke Shields. This Blue Lagoon has no relation to the film, though locals sometimes make an erroneous connection. Portland's Blue Hole is Jamaica's largest underground spring-fed lagoon at 55 meters (180 feet) deep. It's in a large protected cove along the coast where warm tidal water mixes with freshwater welling up from below, creating a blurring effect as the two meet. At one time, Robin Moore, author of *The French Connection*, owned much of the land surrounding the lagoon; today his cottage lies in ruins. A restaurant and bar overhanging the lagoon has been closed for years. Local investors are reportedly waiting on government to improve road infrastructure in the parish before reopening these venues.

In the meantime, this natural gem with its magical turquoise waters is an unmanaged attraction, for better or worse, leaving the environs to a handful of craft vendors insistently hawking their goods along the beach to anybody who arrives for a dip. A trip to Port

Pellew Island in the San San district

Antonio would be incomplete without jumping into Blue Hole, with its cool refreshing water. Rafters and fishers tout tours on their boats around the lagoon and along the coast to Pellew Island. Some haggling may be required before you get on the boat; US$20 pp is a fair price for an hour on the water.

Blue Hole is less than one kilometer (0.6 mile) east of San San Beach and Pellew Island, its entrance on the left by the row of villas just past the well-marked turnoff for Goblin Hill heading east. Turn onto the lane off the main road behind the villas and continue down to the small parking area along the beach where bamboo rafts and fishing boats are tied up on the shore.

★ WINNIFRED BEACH

Known as "the people's beach" because it is the only free public beach in the area, **Winnifred Beach** is in a wide, shallow, white-sand cove one kilometer (0.6 mile) east of Blue Hole in Fairy Hill district. It attracts a nice mix of locals and adventurous tourists. It's also a great spot for conch soup and fried fish. Food and beverages are sold by a slew of vendors, but the best food is prepared at **Cynthia's**, on the western end, which serves mouthwatering fried fish and lobster with rice-and-peas (US$20).

Named after the daughter of Quaker minister F. B. Brown as a resting place for missionaries, teachers, and the respectable poor, Winnifred has remained decidedly local, thanks perhaps to the trust that once managed the area. It had provisions ensuring locals could access and enjoy the beach, though they now typically solicit a donation upon arrival (usually US$2-3). The state-owned Urban Development Corporation, based in Kingston, controls the land around the beach and has proposed selling it to hotel developers. Local resistance to such proposals has thus far been successful at keeping Winifred Beach in the public domain to be enjoyed by all.

The rocky road down to the beach has two access points from the main road (the A4). The best route cuts through a housing scheme

on the ocean side of the road less than 0.75 kilometer (0.5 mile) east of Dragon Bay. Turn north into the scheme directly across the road from Jamaica Crest, followed by a quick right in front of the "Neighborhood Watch" sign. Follow the street around to where it meets the washed-out road in a T and turn left, continuing through the forest down to the shore. This route avoids the worst part of the road that descends off the main road next to Mikuzi.

RECREATION
Water Sports
Diving excursions from Errol Flynn Marina are run by **Lady G'Diver** (contact Steve or Jan Lee Widener, tel. 876/715-5957, cell tel. 876/995-0246 or 876/289-3023, www.ladyg-diver.com). Port Antonio's waters are quieter than those off Ocho Rios and Montego Bay, and the fisheries tend to be in better shape. Wall diving along vertical reefs or rock ledges is especially popular, as the currents are minimal with good visibility, sometimes stretching as far as 75 meters (250 feet). Lady G'Diver offers a wide range of packages and programs, from basic PADI certification to master courses. The most basic is the two-dive package (US$100, including equipment), followed by a four-dive package (US$180).

The Lark **Cruises** (contact Captain Carolyn Barrett, cell tel. 876/382-6384, www.barrettadventures.com) offers seven-day (US$5,000 for up to 4 people) cruises out of Port Antonio on *The Lark*, a 40-foot Jeanneau Sloop, and on *Wind Horse*, a 42-foot Catalina (US$8,000 per week). Provisioning is at the guests' expense; captain and cook are included.

Cycling
A popular downhill biking tour is run by **Blue Mountain Bicycle Tours** (121 Main St., Ocho Rios, tel. 876/974-7075, www.bm-toursja.com). The office is in Ocho Rios, but those staying in Portland can catch the bus in Buff Bay before it heads inland to ascend the B1 into the Blue Mountains to the starting point of the downhill ride.

Tennis

Nonguests can use the hotel's hardtop tennis courts (US$15 per hour, including rackets and balls) at **Goblin Hill** (San San, tel. 876/993-7443 or 876/630-1540). The court could use a resurfacing, but nonetheless it's a great spot for a set or two.

ENTERTAINMENT

Port Antonio is no haven for club-goers, but there are a few good venues that hold regular club nights throughout the week, and a couple others that host occasional parties and live performances. Several times a year, stage shows are set up around the area, with Somerset Falls and Folly Oval the preferred venues for large concerts. The Portland Jerk Festival was once held annually in July, and while promoters have taken a hiatus in recent years, it's sure to see a return at some point. In the meantime, the Boston Jerk Festival, held the first week in July, has picked up the slack in Boston Bay, which claims to be the original home of jerk, 15 minutes' drive east of Port Antonio.

Nightclubs

A longstanding nightclub that has been on again, off again over the years, **Roof Night Club** (11 West St., contact Stacy, cell tel. 876/388-3854, cover US$5) is a cozy second-floor venue with wooden floors that gets packed when it's "on," opening at 11pm Saturday and knocking off around 4am.

Serving a lunch and dinner menu (10am-11pm Mon.-Thurs., 6am-midnight Fri.-Sat., 6pm-2am Sun.) that includes sandwiches, pasta, burgers, and fries, **Posh Nightclub** (23 West St., contact Cristalee McFarlane, cell tel. 876/844-3298, cover US$10) is bumping on weekends (10am-4am Fri.-Sat.), and is the place to go on Friday night.

Port Antonio's top nightclub is **Cristal Night Club** (19 W. Palm Ave., contact Peter Hall, cell tel. 876/288-7657, peter-jhall13@gmail.com, 11am-10pm Mon.-Wed.,

11am-11pm Thurs.-Sat., cover US$10), featuring Roadblock Thursdays, a weekly party bringing a street-dance vibe to the car park out front from 5pm-midnight, with a sound system outside before the party moves indoors until 4am. Seafood Friday (5pm-11pm) is a weekly event featuring music and discounted seafood dishes.

Bars

Serving drinks and finger food like burgers, pizza, salads, and fruit by the pool, **Marybelle's Pub on the Pier** (Errol Flynn Marina, tel. 876/413-9731, bellmar_bell92@yahoo.com, noon-10pm daily, US$4-16) offers customers complimentary Wi-Fi.

Irie Vibes (shop 10, West Harbour Plaza, by KFC, contact William Saunders, cell tel. 876/375-4495, noon-close Mon.-Sat., 4:30pm-close Sun. and holidays) is a popular bar with two pool tables overlooking West Harbour; drinks run US$1-5.

Popular seaside watering hole **Jus Booze** (Craft Village, cell tel. 876/285-2523 or 876/869-9370, 11am-11pm daily, later on weekends) has Ladies' Night on Thursday, burgers and booze on Friday, and live music every other Saturday.

Tortuga Lounge Jamaica (Fern Cliff Rd., Williamsfield, tel. 876/390-0118, www.tortugajam.com) is a self-described organic lounge at The Fan villa serving music, spirits, and finger food in an open-air deck overlooking Turtle Crawle Bay.

Festivals and Events

The weekend before the carnival season finale, **Marbana** (www.marbana.com, US$120) is an exclusive all-inclusive party held at Frenchman's Cove noon-7pm on Easter Sunday. The event features top soca selectors (DJs), carnival dancers in full regalia, and fire jugglers, all contributing to "Jamaica's Ultimate Beach Club Experience."

One of Jamaica's most popular annual fishing contests, held the last week in October, **Port Antonio International Marlin Tournament** (contact Ron DuQuesnay, tel. 876/927-0145, cell tel. 876/909-8818, rondq69@gmail.com, www.jamaicasports-fishing.com, entry US$100 pp plus boats 20-30 feet US$500, plus US$18 per foot up to 50 feet, US$22 per foot over 50 feet, including a slip at Port Antonio Marina, ice, water, and electricity) draws anglers from across Jamaica and overseas. Put on by the Sir Henry Morgan Angling Association, the event kicks off with the Canoe Tournament mid-week, in which local fishers set the bar, before the Main Tournament Thursday-Saturday, with the prize-giving ceremony on Sunday.

SHOPPING

Across from the square in the heart of Port Antonio, **Musgrave Market** (6am-6pm Mon.-Sat.) sells fresh produce toward the front and down a lane on one side. The deeper you go toward the waterfront, the more the market tends toward crafts, T-shirts, and souvenirs, including jewelry, clothing, and other Rasta-inspired crafts.

Art and Crafts

A veteran woodcarver with decades in the business, **Rock Bottom** (cell tel. 876/844-9946) was once based at Musgrave Market but has since relocated fittingly to the Craft Village (1 Allan Ave.), where he hawks his own artistry and that of select peers alongside a handful of other vendors. **Mek Yah Craft & Things** (shop 7, Craft Village, tel. 876/488-0319, 8am-10pm daily) sells crafts, carvings, T-shirts, towels, paintings, and customized knitted swimwear made by Port Antonio local Sudan Thompson, who runs the shop.

Inside the old railroad station by the Port Antonio Marina on West Street, about 10 minutes' walk from the Main Square, is **Portland Art Gallery** (9am-6pm Mon.-Sat.). Hopeton Cargill (cell tel. 876/882-7732 or 876/913-3418), whose work includes landscape paintings, portraits, and commercial signs, is the gallery director. **Philip Henry** (tel. 876/993-3162, philartambokle@hotmail.com) is a talented artist who has prints, portraits, and

sculpture for sale in his small home studio. Call or email to set up an appointment.

Books and Music

Hamilton's Bookstore (27 West St., contact Avarine Moore, tel. 876/993-3792, 9am-6:30pm Mon.-Sat.) has a small but decent selection of Jamaican folk books and cookbooks. **A&G Record Mart** (4 Blake St., contact Janet, cell tel. 876/488-1593 or 876/427-8766, 10am-5pm Mon.-Sat.) has a great selection of CDs, DVDs, LP singles and complete albums, 45s, and 33s. Gospel, R&B, dancehall, reggae, soul, soca, and calypso are well represented.

FOOD

Breakfast and Cafés

Great breakfast and sandwiches are at **Yosch Cafe** (Craft Village, 1 Allan Ave., East Harbour, tel. 876/993-3053, majumidb@yahoo.com, 9am-10pm Mon.-Sat., 1pm-10pm Sun.), on a wooden deck on the waterfront.

Devon House I Scream (Errol Flynn Marina, tel. 876/993-3825, 9am-11pm daily) is an ice cream parlor conveniently located at the marina, with benches outside along the waterfront, serving Jamaica's leading national ice cream brand; avoid the tubs that have thawed and refrozen. Devon Stout and Rum Raisin are two popular signature flavors.

Get a milk shake or a smoothie made from frozen local fruit at **C&S Smoothie Bar & Kitchen** (shop 2, Craft Village, cell tel. 876/299-1394, 8am-9pm Mon.-Sat., noon-9pm Sun., US$5-20), also serving Jamaican dishes like ackee and saltfish, baked beans and saltfish, and porridge for breakfast, as well as vegetarian dishes, steam fish, baked chicken, pasta, and roti with curry goat throughout the day.

Jamaican

About 1.5 kilometers (1 mile) west of town center, **Dickie's Banana** (Bryan's Bay, cell

---

1: work by Rock Bottom, one of Port Antonio's veteran wood carvers **2:** hearty fare at Soldier's Camp **3:** Painter cooking lobster at Cynthia's on Winnifred Beach

tel. 876/809-6276, by reservation, US$25 pp), named "Best-Kept Secret" by the *Jamaica Observer* newspaper, serves five-course dinners featuring the proprietor's inventive cuisine, offering fish, chicken, goat, lobster, or vegetarian dishes in a roadside shack at a deep bend in the road on the western edge of town.

Jamaican favorites like fried chicken, curry goat, and stewed pork are served at **Nix Nax Centre** (16 Harbour St., across from Texaco, tel. 876/993-2081, cell tel. 876/329-4414, 8am-8pm Mon.-Sat., 2pm-8pm Sun., US$4-8). Ackee with saltfish and stewed chicken are served for breakfast daily.

Seafood and meat items are at **Wi Yard Anna Banana** (7 Folly Rd., tel. 876/542-1497, 11am-11pm daily). Fish costs about US$12 per pound, and pepper shrimp (highly recommended) is US$16 per pound. There's a happy hour (6pm-7pm Fri.) and a selector playing music to keep patrons entertained.

The funky Port Antonio roadside snack bar and restaurant **Woody's Low Bridge Place** (Drapers, tel. 876/993-7888, noon-11pm daily) is run by Charles "Woody" Cousins and his charismatic wife, Cherry, serving satisfying homemade burgers (US$4-6), including the full house, with mincemeat and ripe plantain. A vegetarian burger is prepared using natural fresh ingredients, including callaloo. More substantial Jamaican meals are prepared to order for small groups. Try the homemade ginger beer (US$4).

Seafood

Downstairs from Cristal Night Club, **Roots 21 Bar & Kitchen** (19½ West Palm Ave., cell tel. 876/288-7657, 11am-11pm Mon.-Sat., from US$10) specializes in seafood, serving curry coconut and steamed snapper with bammy and fried plantain (US$15) in addition to jerk chicken.

Wilkes Cuisine Seafood Restaurant & Bar (8 Folly Rd., Port Antonio, cell tel. 876/378-5970, wilkscuisine16@gmail.com, 10am-9pm daily) serves seafood dishes as well as chicken, beef, and pork.

★ **Cynthia's** (Winnifred Beach, tel. 876/347-7085, 876/506-0767, or 876/562-4860, phylislodge90@gmail.com, 9am-6pm daily) serves the best fish, lobster, and chicken, accompanied by vegetables, rice-and-peas, and festival along with a variety of vegetarian dishes (US$7-15), at the best value.

Soldier's Camp (83 Red Hassell Rd., tel. 876/451-2095, cell tel. 876/351-4821, food from 3pm daily, bar 10am-9pm daily), better known as Soldji's, draws a healthy cross-section of locals and visitors on Wednesday and especially Friday nights for deliciously seasoned janga (crayfish) as well as jerk chicken, pork, and curry goat. Special orders can be arranged on any other night.

International

Pizza made to order with 15 different topping options and baked in a gas oven is at **Chenel's Pizza** (28-A West St., cell tel. 876/440-0968, 11am-8am Mon.-Thurs., 11am-10pm Fri.-Sat., US$5-20).

Golden Happiness (2 West St., tel. 876/993-2329, 11am-8;30pm Mon.-Sat., 2pm-9pm Sun., US$4-7) prepares the best Chinese food in town at a great value. Understated ambience in the restaurant makes it a great option for takeout.

Launched by Gianmaria Pedroli, a native of northern Italy who came to vacation in Portland and fell in love with the area, cozy restaurant **The Italian Job** (29 Harbour St., cell tel. 876/573-8603, theitalianjobjamaica@gmail.com, noon-10pm Tues.-Sat., US$7-20) has pizza, salads, calzones, lasagna, carbonara, and seafood spaghetti.

Fine Dining

The menu at **Mille Fleurs** (Hotel Mockingbird Hill, tel. 876/993-7134 or 876/993-7267, breakfast 8am-10:30am daily, lunch noon-2:30pm daily, dinner 7pm-9:30pm daily, entrées US$25-40) changes daily, serving creative Asian, European, and Jamaican dishes that emphasize local fresh ingredients, like jerk meat with papaya salsa or a pimento-roasted steak with rum-honey glaze alongside grilled banana or pineapple. Reservations are strongly advised.

Creative dishes and a catch of the day are on offer at ★ **The Veranda** (Trident Hotel, tel. 876/633-7100, reservations required for nonguests, 7am-10am breakfast, noon-4pm lunch, 7pm-9pm dinner daily, US$20-50). On Saturday the hotel's semi-formal **Mike's Supper Club** boasts live cabaret music and specials that include whole lion fish, jerk pork, curry goat, and a Portland seafood platter. Regular entrées include grilled rack of lamb, spinach and mushroom ravioli, surf and turf, and mutton vindaloo.

Vegetarian

An ital shack on the beachfront marked by a yellow picket fence on East Harbour, **Survival Beach Restaurant** (Allan Ave., contact Oliver Weir, cell tel. 876/590-5357, 8am-10pm daily, US$10-20) has vegetarian food, jelly coconut, and ital juices served at reasonable prices.

ACCOMMODATIONS

Port Antonio pioneered Caribbean tourism targeting the upper crust, and the area's reputation as a high-end destination of the adventurous elite has been sealed with the proliferation of luxury villas and boutique hotels dotting the hillsides and waterfront east of town. Budget accommodations are concentrated closer to town. High rates in the area's boutique hotels make a stay in one of the many staffed villas affordable by comparison for families and small groups.

Under US$100

Five rustic self-contained cottages and one three-bedroom house (US$60 for 2 people, US$30 per additional person) are at **Mango Ridge** (Somers Lane, tel. 876/275-7222, mikeodonnell39@yahoo.com, from US$40 d). Each unit has its own bath with ambient-temperature showers, foam double beds, and Wi-Fi. The property is a thin 0.4 hectare (1 acre), stretching up the hill in the Somers Town area, overlooking the center of Port Antonio, a 10-minute walk away. The kitchenettes in each unit have two-burner stoves, a mini fridge, and a sink. Congenial proprietor Michael O'Donnell is always at hand to help guests find their way around town.

Seven-room **Drapers San Guest House** (Drapers, tel. 876/993-7118, carla-51@cwjamaica.com, www.draperssan.com), on the easternmost side of Drapers district, has a few rooms with shared baths (US$33, including breakfast) and a few with private baths (US$75). Two newer rooms offer a step up: Rasta Cottage (US$85) is self-contained with a private bath and a veranda, and the other "high-end" room (US$65) is in the main building, with its own bath and a shared veranda. Drapers San owner Carla Gullotta is an avid reggae fan and helps arrange trips to stage shows and cultural heritage sights and events.

Recently rebuilt and redecorated after a devastating fire, **Search Me Heart** (Drapers, cell tel. 876/453-7779, www.searchmeheart. com, US$60-70, including breakfast) is a comfortable and clean three-bedroom cottage. The resilient Italian expat owner has created a serene ambiance with hardwood floors, whitewashed walls, and the occasional brightly colored lamp shade. The most economical room has one double, one twin (US$60), a queen, and the largest, a king; all rooms have a ceiling fan and a private bath with hot water. The queen and the king have private patios.

US$100-250

A large building with 35 rooms in a variety of configurations, **Bay View Eco Resort** (Dolphin Bay, tel. 876/993-3118 or 876/622-3245, www.bayviewecoresort.com, US$167-181) sits above Turtle Crawle Bay, just east of Trident Castle, about five minutes' drive east of Port Antonio. Bed-and-breakfast and all-inclusive packages are offered. Rooms are comfortable and airy, with TVs, air-conditioning, balconies, and private baths with hot water. The hotel's restaurant serves typical Jamaican food for breakfast, lunch, and dinner.

On a gentle slope in the San San district overlooking San San Beach, ★ **Goblin Hill** (tel. 876/993-7443 or 876/630-1540, reservations@goblinhill.com, www.goblinhill.com.com) is a good option for families and couples. The hotel features 12 spacious one-bedroom units (from US$223 low season, US$319 high season) and the equally spacious two-bedroom duplex units (from US$392 low season, US$476 high season) that are a good value, some with views of San San Bay at a slightly higher rate. The two-bedroom duplex suites have large master bedrooms on the side overlooking the sea with a king bed and a second bedroom with two twins overlooking the garden on the second level. Downstairs, the living room opens on an outdoor patio leading to the rolling lawn. Interiors are less extravagant than at some neighboring villas, but Goblin Hill boasts a large swimming pool and tennis courts and is within easy walking distance of the beach and Blue Hole, and guests are provided passes to the beach at Frenchman's Cove. Wi-Fi reaches throughout the property. Each unit has a dedicated cook-housekeeper.

Over US$250

In the hills above Drapers, with a breathtaking view of Dolphin Bay, Trident Castle, and Blue Mountain Peak, ★ **The Fan** (contact Nino Sciuto, tel. 876/993-7259, cell tel. 876/390-0118, info@thefanvilla.com, www.thefanvilla.com, from US$250 low season, US$350 high season) is a private villa that rents two guest apartments. The grand suite, located on the top level, has a king bedroom, a large living room that fits an extra bed if needed, a kitchen, and a balcony. The junior suite, on the lower level, has a double bed and a couch that can be turned into an extra bed if needed. A jetted tub that fits up to six is available for guest use on a deck outside. Meals are prepared to order at additional cost by the housekeeper. The Tortuga Bar on property hosts low-key parties on Friday night.

1: views from Goblin Hill 2: Birdie'ill Island Villa

Port Antonio's most luxurious boutique property is **Trident Hotel** (U.S. tel. 800/300-6220, www.thetridenthotel.com, from US$816), featuring 13 oceanfront suites in one- and two-bedroom units with retro furnishings and creature comforts that include wet bars, 46-inch TVs, private terraces, and Bluetooth sound systems. Amenities include king beds, rain showerheads, and private plunge pools. Mike's Supper Club is a cabaret lounge open each Saturday that welcomes nonguests to dine on well-executed meals (entrées US$26-50) accompanied by live jazz. Every other meal on property is served at the Veranda restaurant.

Hotel Mockingbird Hill (Drapers, tel. 876/993-7134 or 876/993-7267, reservations@hotelmockingbirdhill.com, www.hotelmockingbirdhill.com, Nov.-July) has pleasantly decorated garden view (US$246 low season, US$316 high season) and sea view (US$296 low season, US$366 high season) rooms with ceiling fans and mosquito nets. Wi-Fi is available throughout. Solar hot-water systems, locally minded purchasing practices, and minimal-waste policies have earned Mockingbird Hill a well-deserved ecofriendly reputation. With stunning views of both the Blue Mountains and Portland's coast, it's hard not to love the place. Several large dogs can often be seen tagging along behind the innkeepers. To get to the hotel, take a right immediately after Jamaica Palace and climb for about 200 meters (650 feet); the entrance in on the left.

A recording artists' paradise where Les Nubians, No Doubt, India Arie, Amy Winehouse, and Tom Cruise have taken working vacations, **Geejam** (San San, tel. 876/993-7000 or 876/633-7000, reservations@geejam.com, www.geejamhotel.com, from US$550 low season, US$650 high season) sits on a low hill overlooking San San Bay and consists of the main house with three bedrooms, three cabins dispersed across the property, and a one-bedroom suite below the recording studio. Inside the huts are TVs, sound systems, and minibars. Wi-Fi covers the entire property. Mattresses are comfortable, linens soft and clean, and there's hot water. Two cabins and the suite have steam rooms. The main house, a bona-fide villa, has a stylish pool out front. The recording studio is at the lower reaches of the property, a deck with a whirlpool tub crowning its roof. The studio has all the latest gear and oversize windows overlooking the water. While the property is specifically designed as a recording retreat for a band-size group rentals, the whole place (US$5,650 low season, US$6,700 high season) is also suited for couples and other kinds of retreats. Geejam is a 10-minute walk from Frenchman's Cove and San San Beach, with the Blue Lagoon also a stone's throw away.

On Wilk's Bay between Frenchman's Cove and Alligator Head, accommodating up to 20 guests in all, **Wilk's Bay** (contact owners Jim and Mary Lowe, cell tel. 876/471-9622, reservations@wilksbay.com, www.wilksbay.com, US$320-690 low season, US$420-960 high season) has 10 bedrooms in a three-bedroom villa, a one-bedroom cottage, two one-bedroom apartments, and two two-bedroom apartments. Each unit is staffed with its own housekeeper-cook. The property has a pebbly private beach, a wharf extending into the bay, and a swimming pool. Bedrooms have air-conditioning, high ceilings, mahogany woodwork, and louvered windows.

In the dense forest hugging the eastern banks of Blue Hole, **Kanopi House** (tel. 876/632-3213, U.S. tel. 800/790-7971, info@kanopihose.com, www.kanopihouse.com, US$250-600) is an assortment of six tree houses, on stilts with French doors leading to wide balconies, louvered windows, and exposed wood interiors. Spacious sitting areas have bamboo and wicker furniture; bedrooms have king beds. The cottages are naturally cool in the shade of the forest, with ceiling fans rather than air-conditioning, and do not have TVs. Each cottage has an outdoor grill. Meals are prepared by request, but there's no restaurant on the property. To get here, take a left off the driveway leading into Dragon Bay. Guests have use of snorkeling gear and kayaks and unfettered access to the Blue Lagoon.

Villas

Port Antonio's villas command stunning views from the lush, rolling hills or along the waterfront and tend to be far less pricey than those in Ocho Rios and Montego Bay. The string of villas overhanging the coast near the entrance to Blue Hole are some of the most coveted in Jamaica, perfectly situated between San San Bay and Blue Hole, two of the area's top attractions.

Yvonne Blakey represents many of Port Antonio's finest accommodations through **Island Villas** (2 West St., cell tel. 876/276-7019, www.islandvillasjamaica.com). She can find the right villa for a range of budgets, including Birdie'ill, Bolt Hole, Belmont, Blue Aqua, and Déjà Vu. **Villas with Class** (www.villaswithclass.com), run by Nino Sciuto, offers booking services for many of the area's villas and runs a community-oriented site featuring the area's attractions and services.

One of the premiere villas in the area, with six bedrooms sleeping up to eight adults and six children, ideally located near the mouth of the Blue Lagoon with a clear view of Pellew Island and Alligator Head, ★ **San Bar** (tel. 876/930-6738, bookings@windjammerjamaica.com, www.sanbarjamaica.com, US$12,600 weekly low season, US$18,480 weekly high season) boasts an oversize hot tub on the deck, tropical decor, and several balconies. Cable TV, broadband, and a sound system keep guests plugged in.

Steadfast, stately ★ **Norse Hill** (tel. 876/347-6168, www.norsevillas.com, US$4,800 weekly low season, US$6,300 weekly high season) is built in the style of an alpine chalet, with a commercial-grade kitchen, three large bedrooms, and dedicated staff. Three bedrooms on the second floor have large tiled baths and oversized mirrors. The fourth bedroom downstairs has two queen beds and a sleeping loft for kids. Verandas look out over the pool and gardens and, beyond that, the sea. Amenities include internet access, a collection of Asian art and European furnishings left by the original owners, and an expansive terraced botanical garden overlooking San San Bay, with pathways crisscrossing the hillside. An enormous ficus tree shades a bench with a stunning view of the sea.

INFORMATION AND SERVICES

Portland Parish Library (1 Fort George St., tel. 876/993-2793) offers free internet access on a bank of computers.

Banks

Banks with ATMs outside are **Scotiabank** (3 Harbour St., tel. 876/993-2523) and **FirstCaribbean** (4 West St., tel. 866/743-2257). For currency exchange, try **Kamal's** (12 West St., tel. 876/993-4292, 8:30am-9pm Mon.-Thurs., 8:30am-10:30pm Fri., 8:30am-11pm Sat., 9am-6pm Sun.) or **Kamlyn's Supermarket and Cambio** (19 Harbour St., tel. 876/993-2140; 12 West St., tel. 876/993-4292, 8:30am-5pm Mon.-Thurs., 8:30am-6pm Fri., 8:30am-5pm Sat.).

Postal Services

For shipping services, **DHL** operates through local agent **True Venture Western Union** (shop 6A, West Harbour Plaza, 22 West St., tel. 876/993-3441, 9am-5pm Mon.-Sat.).

Police and Medical Emergencies

Port Antonio Police (tel. 876/993-2546) are located at 10 Harbour Street, and **San San Police** (tel. 876/993-7315) are at the base of San San Hill. **Port Antonio Hospital** (Naylor's Hill, tel. 876/993-2426) is run by well-reputed doctors Terry Hall and Jeremy Knight. **Dr. Lynvale Bloomfield** (32 Harbour St., cell tel. 876/417-7139) has a private general practice in town, and **Dr. Tracey Lumley** (22 Boundbrook Crescent, tel. 876/993-2224 or 876/339-0024) is also a well-regarded local physician. **Modern Dentistry** (9 West Harbour Plaza, tel. 876/715-5896, cell tel. 876/860-3860, info@modern-dentistry.de), run by German expat Eric Hudacek, is an expert dentist with a smart, well-equipped office overlooking Navy Island, attracting patients from across Jamaica and even abroad.

GETTING THERE

Port Antonio is served by **route taxis** from Buff Bay (US$3) to the west and Boston (US$2) and Morant Bay (US$5) to the east. **Minibuses** leave twice daily for these areas from Market Square. **Taxis** gather in Market Square and in front of the Texaco station on Harbour Street. Most guesthouses and hotels arrange transportation from Kingston or Montego Bay airports; Kingston is the closer international airport, about 2.5 hours away.

The quickest route from Kingston (the A3) passes over Stony Hill and then through Castleton, St. Mary, and Broadgate before hitting the North Coast at a roundabout just west of Annotto Bay. The A4 begins at the roundabout, running east through Port Antonio and then following the northeast coast, turning south near the eastern tip of the island and then back westward toward Kingston. The latter route is every bit as scenic, but the time and distance are greater. Count on dodging potholes for at least three hours from Port Antonio to Kingston along the east coast. It's about two hours from Kingston to Port Antonio through Broadgate, most of the time on a winding road that hugs the banks of the Wag River with views of steep grassy slopes dotted with bamboo stands. A windy mountainous route (the B1) passes over Hardwar Gap in the Blue Mountains before descending to the coast in Buff Bay. The descent from Hardwar Gap to Buff Bay follows a very narrow road, in most places hardly wide enough for one car. Make liberal use of the horn going around the sharp corners.

Knutsford Express (tel. 876/971-1822, www.knutsfordexpress.com) offers coach service from Port Antonio to points throughout Jamaica, connecting in Ocho Rios. **TimAir** (tel. 876/940-6660) and **AirLink Express** (tel. 876/940-4870) serve Ken Jones Aerodrome, 10 minutes west of Port Antonio, with charter flights from Kingston, Oracabessa, Montego Bay, and Negril.

GETTING AROUND

The town of Port Antonio is compact enough to get around comfortably on foot. For any of the attractions east, west, and south of town, jump in a route taxi or hire a private charter. Route taxis congregate by the Texaco station on Harbour Street for points east, and in Market Square for points west and south. It's easy to flag down route taxis along the main road if they're not already packed. Expect to pay around US$2 to points east along the coast as far as Boston.

Chauffeur Andre Thomson's **Fisher Tours** (cell tel. 876/488-0319) offers reasonable rates on transfers to and from Kingston airport (US$140) or on excursions to places like Reach Falls (US$20 pp). Andre's van holds eight.

Upper Rio Grande Valley

Nestled between the Blue Mountains and the John Crow Mountains south of Port Antonio are the culturally rich communities of the Upper Rio Grande Valley. These include the farming communities of Millbank and Bowden Pen and the Maroon community of Moore Town. Footpaths like the Cunha Cunha Pass trail lead deep into the lush rainforest of the park and provide an opportunity to see a host of native bird species, and maybe even the rare and endangered giant swallowtail, the largest butterfly in the western hemisphere. The best way to get to know this area is by contacting the Maroon Council to learn from the people who have staked out this land as their own for centuries.

★ RAFTING THE RIO GRANDE

A much-touted attraction operating along the banks of the wide and gentle Rio Grande, **Rio Grande Rafting** (tel. 876/993-5778, 9am-4pm daily, US$90 per raft for up to 2 people) has 73 licensed captains assigned to guests using a roster system. Ignore the hustlers who tout unlicensed tours by the roadside as

beautiful Rio Grande Valley

you cross the Rio Grande heading toward Port Antonio and along the roadside in Berrydale. Unlike the tours offered by these hustlers, the official government-sanctioned tour is insured and provides tickets, armbands, cushions, and life vests along with an assigned captain.

To reach the start of the tour, take Breastworks Road from Port Antonio, keep right on Wayne Road in Breastworks past Fellowship, and keep right following the signs to Berrydale. The raft ride ends in St. Margaret's Bay, by the mouth of the river at Rafter's Rest. Transportation is not included in the cost of rafting. To get to Moore Town, take a left over the bridge at Fellowship Crossing. A shorter tour (US$80 for 2 people) begins at Rafter's Rest and heads upriver for 45 minutes and back, with a stop to swim. Raft captains typically stop at Belinda's cook shop (US$5-10), which serves Jamaican staples such as fried chicken with rice-and-peas, curried crayfish, and *bussu* (snail); you can order in advance when you book a trip.

MOORE TOWN

The stronghold of Jamaica's Windward Maroons, led by Colonel Wallace Sterling since 1995, Moore Town is a quiet community along the banks of the Rio Grande, about an hour's drive south of Port Antonio. Prior to the election of Colonel Sterling, the Moore Town Maroons were led by Colonel C. L. G. Harris from 1964, and before him Colonel Ernest Downer from 1952.

Colonel Wallace Sterling (cell tel. 876/898-5714, US$30 pp) can organize B&B-style homestays in the community, as well as hikes to Nanny Town (US$100 pp for guides, food, and shelter) farther up into the mountains, a two- to three-day hike round-trip. If you don't bring your own tent, guides will use materials from the bush to make shelter at night. Along the way you're likely to pick up a few basic Maroon words like *medysie* (thank you). If you are unable to reach Colonel Sterling, Moore Town Maroon **Council Secretary Charmaine Shackleford** (cell

tel. 876/421-5919) can also help arrange home-stay visits and guides.

The Maroons have maintained their customs throughout the years, with drumming and ceremonies, as well as remnants of their language, a mix of West African tongues brought by enslaved people who belonged to the Ashanti, Fanti, Akan, Ibo, Yoruba, and Congo groups, among others.

Sights

The final resting place of Nanny, the legendary Maroon leader and Jamaica's first national heroine, is **Bump Grave** (donation). It's the principal attraction in Moore Town; a plaque and monument recall her glorious leadership and victory over British forces that tried unsuccessfully to conquer the Maroons in the first Maroon war of 1734. Several other attempts to conquer the Maroons followed but were as futile as the first. Bump Grave is fenced off, but the gate can be opened by the caretaker of the school located across the road. Call to alert the colonel (cell tel. 876/898-5714) or Maroon Council Secretary Charmaine Shackleford (cell tel. 876/421-5919) of your arrival to ensure someone is around to open the gate.

Within an easy hour's walk from Moore Town is **Nanny Falls,** a small waterfall. Ask any local to indicate where the trail starts, just above Nanny's grave. There is also a longer alternative route, about three hours round-trip, if you're looking for more of a workout. The colonel can help arrange a guide (US$15).

The **Moore Town Maroon Cultural Centre,** a newly built addition to the community, is a growing museum and exhibition space for the preservation of Maroon heritage. Young people from the community, as well as visitors, are taught to make and play drums and the *abeng,* a traditional Maroon horn used to communicate over great distances. The *abeng* is said to have struck fear into the hearts of the British, who were never able to conquer the Maroons. Craft items, toys, and a range of items that represent Maroon culture will be produced here, and the center will have an adjoining gift shop and restaurant to accommodate visitors. The cultural center is a work in progress. As Colonel Sterling said of the project, "We are looking at a living thing rather than strictly an exhibition of the past."

Getting There and Around

Locals take route taxis, which require long waits in the clock tower square; however, the remoteness of Moore Town makes taking route taxis an inadvisable mode of transport for travelers. Route taxis come infrequently, and there's a risk of being stranded.

Barrett Adventures (contact Carolyn Barrett, cell tel. 876/382-6384, www.barrettadventures.com) offers transportation to and from the Blue and John Crow Mountains from across Jamaica, as well as a hiking expedition from the Portland side or from Kingston. **Fisher Tours** (cell tel. 876/488-0319) is a local charter taxi operator in Port Antonio led by Andre Thompson, who takes visitors on excursions throughout the parish and provides transfers across the island.

West of Port Antonio

The main road (the A4) west of Port Antonio runs along the coast, cutting inland occasionally through several small towns, including St. Margaret's Bay, Hope Bay, and Buff Bay, before reaching the border with St. Mary, just east of Annotto Bay. The region is characteristically lush, with fruit vendors and intermittent roadside shops. Apart from Somerset Falls, on the eastern edge of Hope Bay, the area is devoid of developed attractions, but the sparsely populated coastline itself is enticing. Adventurers looking for secluded beaches find great opportunities for exploring around Orange Bay.

From Buff Bay, the B1 heads inland, climbing past Charles Town into the Blue Mountains, affording great views. This is the route on which Blue Mountain Bicycle Tours operates.

ST. MARGARET'S BAY AND HOPE BAY

The quiet seaside village of St. Margaret's Bay is notable principally as the end point for the rafts coming down the Rio Grande. Hope Bay is a short distance away.

A few minutes' drive west of Port Antonio is **Somerset Falls** (Hope Bay, tel. 876/913-0046, 9am-5pm daily, US$15), a lovely botanical garden and waterfall. The main attraction, the falls, is reached by a rowboat staffed by a guide, who runs the oars. Guests can jump overboard and enjoy a natural shower beneath the falls and swim around in the cool river water. A large artificial pool provides an alternative to swimming in the river. There's also a waterslide feeding into its own pool. The bar and restaurant serves jerk chicken, jerk pork, burgers, and hot dogs. Somerset Falls also serves as a venue for occasional events, including live music.

Across the street by the mouth of the Danny River, **Likkle Portie** (contact manager Rose Stephens, cell tel. 876/403-7147, 10am-5pm daily, US$7-25) has a seafood grill serving roast, steamed, and fried fish, accompanied by bammy and festival in the style of Little Ochie, a South Coast favorite.

Accommodations

★ **Rio Vista Resort Villas** (eastern bank of the Rio Grande, tel. 876/993-5444, riovistavillaja@jamweb.net, www.riovistajamaica.com, US$90-200) has two-bedroom cottages, a one-bedroom honeymoon cottage with a spectacular view up the Rio Grande (US$155), and four single rooms. The Room with a View is perhaps the nicest cottage, with a private balcony overlooking the river and an inviting king bed. To get here, turn right up the hill just around the corner after crossing the Rio Grande heading east.

CHARLES TOWN

Some five kilometers (3 miles) above Buff Bay along what used to be an old Maroon bridle path up the Buff Bay River (now known as the B1) is the Maroon community of Charles Town. The **Maroon Museum** (free) located at **Asafu Yard** has artifacts and crafts of Maroon heritage. There's an adjoining commercial kitchen producing Jamaican cassava cakes. Cassava is a gluten-free staple starch used since the time of the Taino people and known locally as bammy.

The late Charles Town Maroon Colonel Frank Lumsden is succeeded by the **Maroon Council** (cell tel. 876/445-2861, www. maroons-jamaica.com), which welcomes visitors and leads community tours and hikes (US$20 pp) to Sambo Hill, the ruins of an 18th-century coffee plantation, Grandy Hole Cave, or Old Crawford Town, an old Maroon Village where Quao settled his people after the first Maroon War in 1739. The late colonel formed a group of drummers who perform Koromanti drumming and dance.

A country-style lunch (US$12 pp) of traditional dishes like crayfish rundown (not to be missed) and saltfish rundown accompanied by boiled green banana and ground provisions (yam, coco, dasheen, pumpkin) can be arranged at **Quao's Village,** a bit farther upstream, where Keith Lumsden (cell tel. 876/440-2200) manages a swimming hole and rustic restaurant attraction. The spot is named after Maroon warrior Captain Quao, the Invisible Hunter, who, alongside Jamaica's first national hero, Nanny of the Maroons, fought off the British to assert his people's autonomy from the colonists.

Buff Bay police station (9 1st Ave., tel. 876/996-1497) is located opposite the Adventist Church.

Food

On the east side of town, **G&B Jerk Centre** (contact Glen Ford or Kenroy Ford, cell tel. 876/859-5107, 10am-midnight daily) is the best spot for a roadside bite of jerk pork (US$20 per pound) or chicken (US$5 per quarter pound).

Getting There and Around

Points between Port Antonio and Annotto Bay can be reached via **route taxi or microbus** for under US$5. Route taxis typically run between the closest population centers, and you will have to string together several legs for longer distances. Most route taxis also offer charter service, where rates are not regulated and have to be negotiated. A chartered car between Port Antonio and Hope Bay shouldn't cost more than US$20, with a chartered trip from Port Antonio to Buff Bay or Charles Town around US$50 for two people.

East of Port Antonio

The region east of Port Antonio is dominated by the eastern ridges of the Blue and John Crow Mountains, which run northwest to southeast and taper down to the coast near Hector's River. The John Crow Mountains are some of the least visited territory on the island, and even the coast in the area, which varies from fine sandy beaches to windswept bluffs, sees few visitors. A few minutes' drive east of Port Antonio, Boston is a quiet community said to be the original home of jerk. Long Bay has but a handful of budget and mid-range lodging options serving the trickle of backpackers and adventurous travelers who come to enjoy the undeveloped Long Bay Beach, nearby Reach Falls, and a quieter side of Jamaica. All the larger communities east of Port Antonio are found along the A4, better known as "the main road" by locals.

Northeast Coast

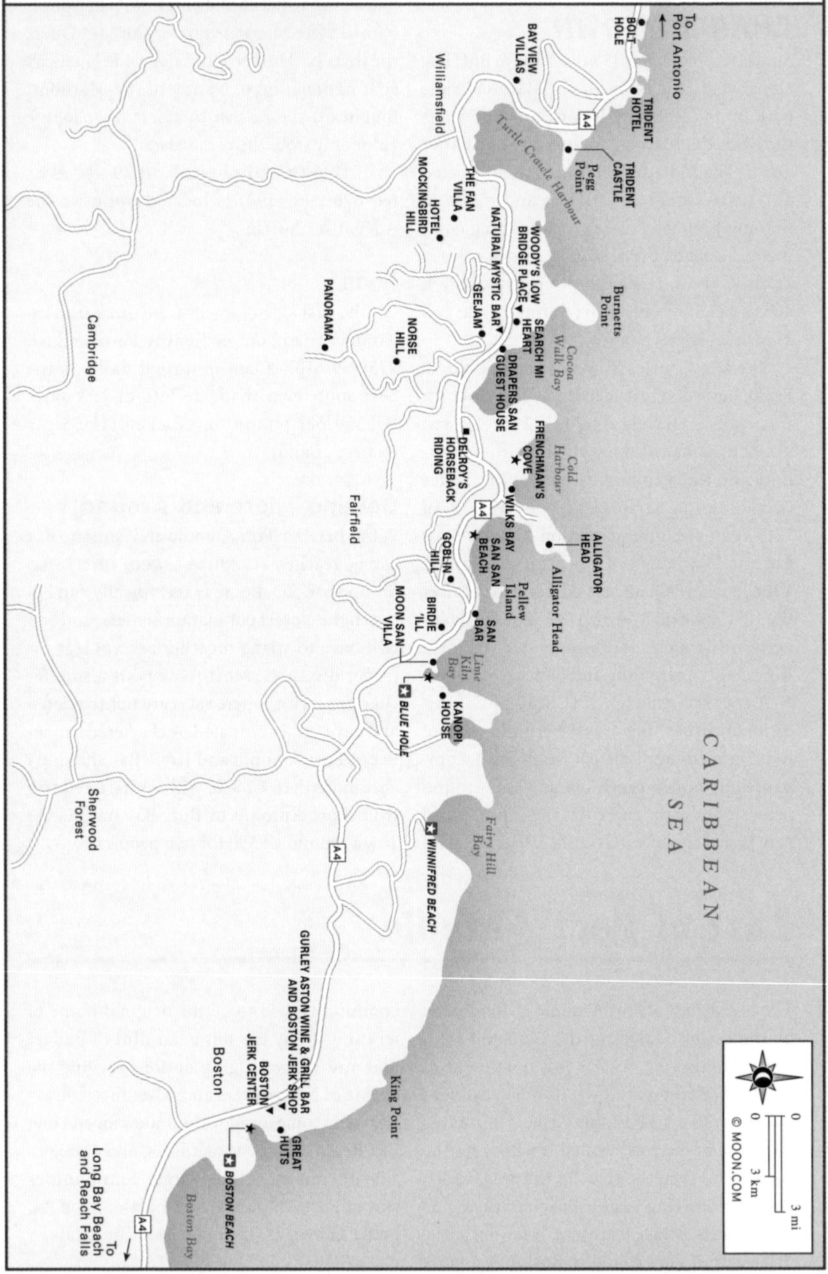

To Port Antonio

Williamsfield

BOLT HOLE

BAY VIEW VILLAS

TRIDENT HOTEL

A4

TRIDENT CASTLE

Pegg Point

Turtle Crease Harbour

Burnetts Point

THE FAN VILLA

HOTEL MOCKINGBIRD HILL

NATURAL MYSTIC BAR

WOODY'S LOW BRIDGE PLACE

SEARCH MI HEART

GEEJAM

DRAPERS SAN GUEST HOUSE

Cocoa Walk Bay

PANORAMA

NORSE HILL

DELROY'S HORSEBACK RIDING

FRENCHMAN'S COVE

Cold Harbour

Cambridge

Fairfield

WILKS BAY

A4

GOBLIN HILL

SAN SAN BEACH

ALLIGATOR HEAD

Pellew Island

Alligator Head

MOON SAN VILLA

BIRDIE 'ILL

SAN BAR

SAN SAN

Lime Kiln Bay

BLUE HOLE

KANOPI HOUSE

Sherwood Forest

Fairy Hill Bay

A4

WINNIFRED BEACH

CARIBBEAN SEA

GURLEY ASTON WINE & GRILL BAR AND BOSTON JERK SHOP

King Point

Boston

BOSTON JERK CENTER

GREAT HUTS

BOSTON BEACH

Boston Bay

To Long Bay Beach and Reach Falls

A4

N

0   3 km
0   3 mi

© MOON.COM

BOSTON

Boston was bustling in the early years of the banana trade, when it took the name of the North American city that made it prosperous for a brief period. Located eight kilometers (5 miles) east of Port Antonio, Boston can be reached by route taxi from Port Antonio (US$3) or by chartering a private car (US$20). The community is the alleged home of Jamaica's famed jerk seasoning, but the **Boston Jerk Centre** has been overrun with pesky vendors seemingly unaware that their relentless harassment of patrons has damaged the area's reputation. A dozen or so jerk vendors' stalls and bars jostle for business when prospective patrons appear, while others insist you buy their noni juice, said to have aphrodisiacal properties and to improve overall performance; still others simply beg for money, giving the place a raucous and seedy ambiance.

Beyond the annoyances, there are also serious inconsistencies in the quality and pricing of food at Boston Jerk Centre. Weekends, when it gets busier, are the best time to go if you must eat here, as during the week the meat can sit on the grill until it goes cold. Fish is also served, but this is not the best place for it. If you do order fish, size it before it gets cooked and understand what you will pay before. The best time to eat jerk is during the annual Portland Jerk Festival (July), when the multitudes don't let the meat sit around for long.

★ Boston Beach

On a picturesque bay with turquoise waters, **Boston Beach** (US$3) sees more locals than foreign visitors, especially on weekends. Boston Bay can have a decent swell suitable for surfing and is the only place around where you can rent boogie boards and surfboards from a small shack manned by proponents of the sport (contact Ramon Ricketts, cell tel. 876/528-2884, US$20 per hour, US$50 per day).

Food and Accommodations

Savory jerk chicken and pork and fresh seafood are served in a hassle-free environment at ★ **Gurley Aston Wine & Grill Bar and Boston Jerk Stop** (Boston Bay, cell tel. 876/849-7853, be.rhone@yahoo.com, 10am-10pm Sun.-Thurs., 10am-midnight Fri.-Sat.).

A stylishly rustic option in the heart of Boston, **Great Huts** (8-10 Boston Bay, at the end of the lane that begins at the Jerk Centre, cell tel. 876/353-3388 or 876/993-8888, www.

rustic accommodations at Great Huts

greathuts.com, US$35-266 d) offers Bedouin-style tents, breezy cottages, and tree houses made of wood, bamboo, zinc, and canvas, recreating an African-Amerindian village vibe. Fabrics and masks cover doorways and walls. Modern amenities like fans, mosquito nets, mini fridges, and plumbing accent the open-air environment. The weekly cultural show on Saturday evening includes lounge classics from the 1950s and Kumina-inspired drummers and dancers recounting Jamaican history with energetic rhythms and sensual movements. Fig Tree House is the best room, with a stunning view of Boston Bay from the queen bed and bathtub. African Sunrise has panoramic views out to sea in cozy quarters up two flights of ladders. Sea Grape is roomy and has a private cliff-top bathtub. The property is not for the physically challenged; loose stone pathways and stairs abound. Wi-Fi is available in the central building, where basic meals are served. A simple breakfast is included.

LONG BAY

Located 20 kilometers (12 miles) east of the town of Port Antonio, Long Bay can be reached by route taxi or chartered car. The community is a sleepy fishing village with little in the way of economic activity beyond a gas station and a few bars and cook shops. A few low-key lodgings have sprung up over the past decade, serving the trickle of off-the-beaten-track travelers who arrive seeking the quieter side of Jamaica.

★ Long Bay Beach

Long Bay Beach is one of the most picturesque and unspoiled beaches in Jamaica. Lined with coconut palms, the beach is also known for its occasional swell and draws surfers from nearby Boston Bay as well as the die-hard Mystic crew from Jamnesia in Bull Bay, St. Andrew. It's also known to have dangerous riptides and a rocky seafloor to the western side; caution is always advised.

Food

Transplants from Bologna, Italy, run ★ La Familia Restaurant (Pen Lane, tel. 876/913-7843, cell tel. 876/892-2195, lafamiliajamaica@gmail.com, by reservation only, US$15-35), serving the best lasagna, tagliatelle, and ceviche. Pizza and bread are baked in a conventional gas oven.

Cliffhanger Restaurant & Lounge (Ross Craig, Kensington District, Portland, cell tel. 876/860-1395, portland.cliff.hanger@gmail.com, 5 kilometers/3 miles southeast of Long Bay, noon-10pm Fri.-Sat., noon-9pm Sun., US$11-50) serves seafood, specializing in lionfish five different ways: with wine and beer, escoveitch, coconut sauce, curried, and jerk. Oxtail, curried goat, fried and stewed chicken, and vegan fare are served.

Accommodations

Six basic rooms at La Familia Resort and Restaurant (Pen Lane, tel. 876/913-7843, cell tel. 876/892-2195, lafamiliajamaica@gmail.com) include three with a shared bath (US$40), three with private baths (US$60), and a small apartment (US$65) with a private bath. Enrico is a promoter and selector of Vinyl Club Jamaica and hosts Vinyl Sunday in front of Natural Mystic Bar in Drapers.

Lloyd Edwards returned from an engineering career in England to launch ★ Pimento Lodge Hideaway Resort (tel. 876/913-7982, cell tel. 876/533-5860 or 876/882-5068, www.pimentolodge.com, from US$155), with three room categories with four-poster king and bamboo-frame beds, louvered windows, and breezy verandas. Nonguests can make reservations to dine at the property.

A three-story boutique hotel about five minutes east of Long Bay, Seacliff Resort & Spa (Ross Craig, Kensington District, Portland, tel. 876/435-9739 or 876/863-0933, cell tel. 876/860-1395, seacliff2000@gmail.com, www.seacliff-jamaica.com, from US$160, includes breakfast) sits at the top of a cliff overlooking the sea 24 meters (80 feet) above the crashing waves. The rooms all have private baths, hot water, cable TV, Wi-Fi, and ocean views.

★ REACH FALLS

In a beautiful river valley in the lower northeast foothills of the John Crow Mountains, **Reach Falls** (tel. 876/276-8663, www.udcja. com, 8:30am-4:30pm Wed.-Sun., US$10 adults, US$5 under age 12), sometimes spelled Reich Falls, cascades down a long series of falls that can be climbed from the base far below the main pool, where the developed attraction is based. Start at the bottom and continue far above the main pool to get the full exhilarating experience. To climb the full length requires about two hours, but if you stop to enjoy each little pool, it could easily consume a full day. A dirt road about one kilometer (0.6 mile) before the parking area leads down to the base of the falls.

To get to Reach Falls from the main road (the A4), head inland by a set of shacks one kilometer (0.6 mile) east of Manchioneel, up a picturesque winding road. A large sign for "Reach Falls" marks the turnoff. Unofficial guides often congregate at a fork in the road, where you stay left to get to the falls. The guides are in fact indispensable when it comes to climbing the falls from far below, as they know every rock along the riverbed, which is quite slippery in places. As always, get a sense of what your guide will expect for the service up front; US$10 pp is the going rate. Leonard "Sendon" Welsh (cell tel. 876/488-0661) and Byron Shaw (cell tel. 876/463-9568) are recommended seasoned guides and great company.

The government's lease on the property extends from a little below the main pool to a little above it, and unofficial guides will be turned away from the main waterfalls area on either side of the leased land when the attraction is officially open (Wed.-Sun.). **Mandingo Cave,** which is found farther up the river, is not currently part of the official tour offered but can visited with local guides.

Long Bay Beach

Morant Bay

St. Thomas parish holds an important place in Jamaican history. In the early colonial period, its mountainous terrain provided sanctuary to the enslaved people who escaped and formed the Maroon settlements of eastern Jamaica. Later, it became an important sugar- and banana-producing region under British rule. When slavery was abolished but the formerly enslaved were not permitted advancement in society, the parish erupted in a rebellion that gave birth to Jamaica's labor rights movement.

At the center of what was once some of Jamaica's prime sugarcane land, Morant Bay is a laid-back town with little action beyond the central market. Between Morant Bay and Port Morant, 11 kilometers (7 miles) to the east, there are a couple of basic lodging options that make a convenient base for exploring the seldom visited rivers and valleys that cut across the southern slopes of the Blue Mountains, as well as the isolated beaches and Great Morass on Jamaica's easternmost tip.

Route taxis and minibuses run the 60 kilometers (37 miles) between Port Antonio and Morant Bay (US$10), passing through the communities of Boston, Long Bay, and Manchioneel, and can be flagged down anywhere along the way provided they are not already jam-packed.

If you are continuing on toward Kingston, the road west of Morant Bay toward Kingston hugs the coast, passing through dusty communities where jerk vendors and a few shops mark the centers of the action. This is an area most people just pass through. One point of interest along the way is **Reggae Falls.** Formed by a manmade reservoir along the Morant River, it is an unmanaged attraction with a shallow pool at the bottom of the dam where you can swim behind the waterfalls

and are likely to have the place to yourself. To get to Reggae Falls, turn left at the roundabout immediately after crossing the Morant River heading east. Head north inland, passing Bogle High School until reaching the community of Hillside. From there the winding road follows the river, traversing it in places, through a cattle farm, ending near the base of the falls, where you can park and walk a few hundred meters to the base of the dam. A 4WD vehicle makes the going easier, but cars with low clearance can also make it.

REACH FALLS TO PORT MORANT

Tucked into the northeast corner of Duckenfield, an active sugarcane plantation that occupies the easternmost land in Jamaica, **Holland Bay** is an isolated cove with a desolate beach that is heavily littered but beautiful nonetheless, with fine white sand and crashing waves. To get here, head straight east from the village of Golden Grove through the Duckenfield Sugar Plantation. A 4WD vehicle is essential in the rainy season, but otherwise not needed.

Morant Point Lighthouse can be reached by continuing past Holland Beach. It stands at Jamaica's easternmost point. Cast of iron in London, the 30-meter-tall (100-foot) lighthouse was erected in 1841 by Kru people, indentured African workers brought to Jamaica in the post-emancipation period.

Built by Luke Stokes, a former governor of the island of Nevis, **Stokes Hall Great House** is near Golden Grove. Stokes came to Jamaica shortly after the conquest of the island by the British. Like many of the early houses, it was built in a strategic location and was securely fortified. The great house was destroyed in the 1907 earthquake and today stands in ruin. It is currently owned by the Jamaica National Heritage Trust but is not managed. Turn south at the main intersection

1: Pimento Lodge Hideaway Resort **2:** fresh Jamaican snapper at Cliffhanger Restaurant and Lounge

Paul Bogle and the Morant Bay Rebellion

In 1864, Paul Bogle was the founding deacon at the Native Baptist Church in Stony Gut, St. Thomas, a village at the base of the Blue Mountains about eight kilometers (5 miles) inland from Morant Bay. A black pride ethos was a central element. Baptist churches in Jamaica provided an alternative philosophy to the Anglican Church, representative of the suppressive mandate of the white planter class and government. In the post-emancipation period, most people were denied voting rights, justice, and civil rights. While the white ruling class controlled the legislature and the economy, the poor felt subjugated and left to fend for themselves. Petty crime rooted in widespread poverty was severely punished by local authorities who represented the landowners.

Bogle used the church as a base to gather support for a militant resistance movement. On October 7, 1865, Bogle and some followers staged a protest at the Morant Bay courthouse, disputing severe judgments made on that day. When a standoff with the police came to blows, arrest warrants were issued against 28 of the protesters. Bogle and 400 followers confronted the militia in Morant Bay; during the ensuing violence, the courthouse was burned and the custos was killed, along with 18 deputies and militiamen. Fighting spread, and several white planters were killed, kidnapped, or injured. Fear of a general uprising grew, prompting Governor Eyre to declare martial law and dispatch soldiers from Kingston and Newcastle. The Windward Maroons were also armed

in Golden Grove and follow the main road past a high school until you reach an overgrown access road to Stokes Hall on the right. It is unmarked, so you may have to ask a local if you get lost.

Overgrown and forgotten, **Port Morant** once busily exported barrels of sugar, rum, and bananas. Today there is an oyster operation on the eastern side of the harbor bordering the mangroves. The oyster-growing zone, which reaches down to Bowden across the bay, is protected from fishing and serves as a spawning area. Several people keep their fishing boats on the waterfront and can be contracted to tour the mangroves and visit the lighthouse on Point Morant.

BATH

The town of Bath was erected using government resources and had a brief glamorous history as a fashionable second-home community for the island's elite. The splendor was short-lived, however, and the town quickly declined to become a backwater—as it remains today.

★ Bath Hot Springs

The hot springs are located 50 meters (165 feet) north of the **Bath Hotel and Spa** (tel.

876/703-4345, US$70-85, including private bath sessions twice a day), which is about three kilometers (2 miles) up a precariously narrow, winding road north of the town of Bath. An easy-to-follow path leads to the springs, where water comes out from the rocks piping hot on one side and cold on the other. There are massage therapists on hand who use wet towels to give an exhilarating albeit exorbitantly priced treatment (typically around US$14). These masseurs are either lauded or despised by visitors and can be quite aggressive in offering their services from below the gate of the hotel. Their technique involves slopping hot towels over the backs of their subjects.

Formally called The Bath of St. Thomas the Apostle, **Bath Mineral Spring** was discovered in 1695 by a man named Jacob who had escaped enslavement on the estate of his owner, Colonel Stanton. Jacob found that the warm waters of the spring healed leg ulcers that had plagued him for years. He braved possible punishment to return to the plantation to relate his discovery to Stanton. In 1699 the spring and surrounding land were sold to the government, and in 1731 the area was developed and a small town was built.

The Bath Hotel and Spa has traditional Turkish-style tiled tubs as well as more after offering their services, and they ultimately captured Bogle, bringing him to a swift trial and death sentence in Morant Bay. Gordon was also implicated in the rebellion, taken to Morant Bay, and hanged. Martial law lasted over a month, during which time hundreds were executed by court martial and over 1,000 houses were burned by government forces. Little regard was given to differentiating innocent from guilty.

The Morant Bay Rebellion pushed Britain to discuss the blatant injustices in its colony. The independent legislature was dissolved, and Jamaica became a crown colony under the direct rule of England. In the following years, colonial rulers ushered in more egalitarian measures that lessened the power exerted by the landed elite.

Paul Bogle and George William Gordon were considered troublemakers and expelled from the national psyche through the remainder of the colonial period. At independence, their memory was rekindled as Jamaica began to contemplate its identity. Bogle and Gordon were declared national heroes in 1969. Today, the Morant Bay Rebellion is remembered during National Heritage Week and Heroes Weekend, which coincides with the anniversary of the uprising, the second week in October.

modern whirlpool tubs. There are three rates for nonguests, depending on how many are enjoying the tub: US$5 for one person, US$8 for two, or US$12 for three. All rates are for 20-minute intervals.

The hotel has an on-site restaurant (8:30am-5:30pm daily, US$8.50-10). Meals are served throughout the day and range from rotisserie chicken to curried shrimp.

Bath Botanical Garden

Bath Botanical Garden was established by the government in 1779 and is the second-oldest garden of its kind in the western hemisphere (one in St. Vincent dates from 1765). The garden retains little of its former glory as a propagation site for many of Jamaica's most important introduced plants, including jackfruit, breadfruit, cinnamon, bougainvillea, and croton. A stand of royal palms lines the road by the entrance, and a two-century-old *Barringtonia* graces the derelict grounds.

From the western side of Bath, a road runs north to Hayfield, where a well-maintained 8.8-kilometer (5.5-mile) trail provides an alternate route over the John Crow to the Rio Grande Valley. If you're heading to Portland,

head east along the Plantain Garden River to where the main road east of Bath hits the A4, a few kilometers west of Amity Hall.

Food and Accommodations

On a quiet surfing beach in Roselle, St. Thomas, between White Horses and Morant Bay, ★ **Longboarder Bar & Grill** (Roselle, cell tel. 876/427-0408, thelongboarderja@gmail.com, kitchen midnight-8pm Tues.-Sun., US$8-30) serves fresh snapper, lobster, and burgers beachfront. A couple of surfboards (US$25 per day) are available to rent.

Getting There

Points between Kingston and Morant Bay along the coast are served by JUTC buses departing from the Transport Centre in Half Way Tree for around US$1. For points farther east or around the coast, a private driver or route taxis are necessary. Taxis and minibuses depart from the square in Morant Bay for Bath and Manchioneel as they fill up, costing less than US$5. Similarly, route taxis and minibuses depart Port Antonio for Morant Bay throughout the day, departing as occupancy allows.

Kingston and the Blue Mountains

Sights 205
Entertainment 218
Shopping. 229
Recreation 232
Food 235
Accommodations 246
Information and
    Services 249
Transportation. 251
Around Kingston. 253
The Blue and John Crow
    Mountains. 263

Kingston is the heartbeat of Jamaica, a city teeming with excitement, driving the island's culture and economy.

Arts and entertainment play an important role in everyday life, with countless recording studios and their up-and-coming artists competing to make the next hit tune. Art galleries abound, and theaters fill to capacity for Jamaica's unique brand of outrageous slapstick comedy in theater productions known as roots plays. Hardly a week goes by without an internationally acclaimed reggae singer hosting a concert to celebrate a birthday or album launch. Bars and nightclubs throb with pounding bass, and dances routinely take to the street; a car wash, parking lot, or tenement yard turns into a dance hall somewhere in the city every night of the week.

Highlights

Look for ★ to find recommended sights, activities, dining, and lodging.

★ **Tuff Gong Recording Studio:** Bob Marley's production base offers a tour that includes a visit to the studio, record-printing shop, gallery, and herb garden (page 209).

★ **National Gallery:** At the crown jewel of the Institute of Jamaica, visitors can view Jamaican art from its roots to the present day (page 210).

★ **Devon House:** Take a tour of the home of George Stiebel, Jamaica's first black millionaire. It's one of the finest estates in Kingston (page 216).

★ **Bob Marley Museum:** The spirit of Jamaica's most revered son has been preserved his former residence at 56 Hope Road (page 216).

★ **Hope Gardens and Zoo:** Kingston's largest green space contains a meticulously maintained Chinese garden and Jamaica's largest zoo (page 217).

★ **Lime Cay:** Once a haven for buccaneers, this idyllic beach comes alive on weekends with swarms of locals living it up island style (page 254).

★ **Hellshire:** An assortment of fried fish and lobster shacks crowd this popular weekend spot. Spend an afternoon relishing the rustic chic scenery with the locals (page 262).

★ **Craighton Estate Blue Mountain Coffee Tour:** This informative tour combines

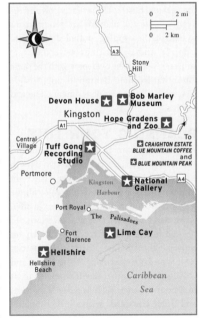

history, delicious coffee, and a walk through the fields of a working farm (page 265).

★ **Hike Blue Mountain Peak:** Set out early to reach the top for sunrise and Jamaica's best view (page 273).

Only a small fraction of leisure travelers to Jamaica visit Kingston, and the populace goes about its business refreshingly indifferent to tourism. Those who do visit tend to be devotees of Bob Marley, drawn to the museum and other cultural sights. Through the year, the capital city celebrates food, visual and performing arts, carnival, and national pride, with events spanning days, weeks, or entire months. There's plenty to do in Kingston even when there's no major event on the calendar, and those who don't visit the capital city miss the epicenter of the island's pulsating nightlife and culture.

While much of Kingston is crowded with uninspiring architecture, Georgian gems dot the urban sprawl, and greenery is everywhere. The foothills of the Blue Mountains hold the city in a semicircular embrace, and nothing beats the higher elevations for respite from the heat and bustle. The serene vistas and diverse wildlife and plantlife are good reasons to take on the winding, potholed roads into Upper St. Andrew. Looking out over the city at sunset, it's easy to be overcome with the same vibes that led Buju Banton to sing, "magic city, magic lights, magic moments, magical heights."

PLANNING YOUR TIME

All the important historical and cultural sites can be seen in a rush with two days in Kingston. A longer stay is in order if you want to adopt the local pace and fully enjoy all the sights, food, and nightlife the city has to offer.

Most of the historical sights downtown can be seen in one day. Attractions uptown are conveniently concentrated in **New Kingston, Half Way Tree,** and along **Hope Road,** and will consume another day if you wish to fit in **Devon House, Bob Marley Museum,** and **Hope Gardens,** with a little shopping and eating in between. The noteworthy attractions in Spanish Town can all be seen in a few hours and combine well with an afternoon at

Fort Clarence or at Hellshire beaches, which offer a maze of fried-fish and lobster shacks.

Kingston's nightlife is worthwhile almost any day of the week, with stage shows and parties held weekly at one venue or another. There are "sessions" almost every night, and the most popular street dances are held on weeknights. Theater performances are held several nights a week.

A few days in Kingston sets the stage for a nice break in the **Blue Mountains**. All the accommodations in the Blue Mountains can arrange transportation to and from town; once there, hiking trails abound, and hummingbirds flit on the cool mountain air. At least a couple of nights should be allocated to the Blue Mountains, especially for serious hikers, birders, or coffee connoisseurs.

ORIENTATION

The parish of Kingston encompasses what is referred to as Downtown, as well as the Palisadoes, a 16-kilometer-long (10-mile) thin strip of land that runs from the roundabout at Harbour View to the tip of Port Royal. Metropolitan Kingston is often referred to as the Corporate Area and is divided into two regions, referred to by Kingstonians as Uptown and Downtown. The junction at **Cross Roads** is the dividing line between Downtown and Uptown.

Downtown Kingston comprises the historical city center spanning outward from St. William Grant Park in a grid bound by Harbour, North, East, and West Streets. The city soon overgrew these boundaries, with ramshackle residential neighborhoods springing up on every side. Over the years, some of these areas have seen zinc shacks replaced by homes of better stature, as well as government low-income apartments and row houses, often referred to as tenement yards. Most of the buildings in the area below **St. William Grant Park,** or the **Parade,** as it is known, are commercial, with limited middle-income

---

Previous: Chronixx; statue of the conquering lion at the Bob Marley Museum; sunrise from Blue Mountain Peak

Kingston and Vicinity

© MOON.COM

0
0   5 km
0   5 mi

COLBECK CASTLE ★

Old Harbour

Gutters

Gallows Harbour

ST. JOHN'S ANGLICAN CHURCH ★

★ MOUNTAIN RIVER CAVE

A2

Hartlands

ST. JOHNS RD

2000

Linstead

A1

B2

A1

Bog Walk

Sligoville

2000

Spanish Town

"SEE SPANISH TOWN" MAP

Salt Island Lagoon

Central Village

CAYMANAS GOLF & COUNTRY CLUB

KINGSTON POLO CLUB

Rock Hall

RED HILLS RD

Old House Point

TWO SISTERS CAVE ★

HELLSHIRE BEACH

Hellshire Beach

WAVES BEACH

THE BOARDWALK

FT. CLARENCE BEACH

Fort Clarence

PRENDY'S ON THE BEACH/SHORTY'S

OLD NAVAL HOSPITAL

FORT CHARLES

GRAND PORT ROYAL HOTEL

GLORIA'S (BOTTOM)

GLORIA'S (TOP)

Y-KNOT

PEBBLES BEACH

Port Royal

Drunken Man's Cay

South Cay

Maiden Cay

Lime Cay

LIME CAY

The Palisadoes

NORMAN MANLEY INTERNATIONAL AIRPORT

ROYAL JAMAICA YACHT CLUB

Kingston Harbour

Hunts Bay

MUNICIPAL BLVD

PORTMORE

DYKE RD

MANDELA HWY

WASHINGTON BLVD

TUFF GONG RECORDING STUDIO

A1

NATIONAL GALLERY

KINGSTON

DEVON HOUSE

BOB MARLEY MUSEUM

NEITA'S NEST

MAJESTIC SUSHI & GRILL

Stony Hill

A3

BLUE MOUNTAIN COFFEE TOUR

CRAIGHTON ESTATE

HOPE GARDENS AND ZOO

WINDWARD RD

"SEE METROPOLITAN KINGSTON" MAP

Newcastle

B1

SEE "THE BLUE AND JOHN CROW MOUNTAINS" MAP

SEE "THE BLUE AND JOHN CROW MOUNTAINS" MAP

John Crow Peak 5,750ft

A4

Bull Bay

LITTLE COPA

JAMNESIA

Cane River Falls

Bull Bay

BOBO HILL

CARIBBEAN SEA

housing in high-rise buildings near the waterfront. A nascent renaissance has brought redevelopment to Downtown Kingston in recent years, with several new corporate headquarters buildings going up and the Oceana Hotel being revived along the waterfront, across Ocean Boulevard from new restaurants and bars at the renovated Victoria Pier.

Actually in the parish of St. Andrew, **Uptown Kingston** includes most of the bustling commercial areas of town. Uptown is an urban and suburban sprawl with little order, the result of economic development after independence. The two most developed commercial areas are the hubs of **New Kingston,** immediately north of Cross Roads, and **Half Way Tree,** just east of New Kingston. **Hope Road,** where several sights are located, runs east from Half Way Tree Square, before becoming Old Hope Road in Liguanea and ending at the roundabout in **Papine** on the eastern edge of town.

Half Way Tree Road is also a major thoroughfare. It starts at Cross Roads, turning into **Constant Spring Road** as it runs north of Half Way Tree Square, and continues to the northernmost edge of town, where it becomes **Stony Hill Road,** later turning into the **A3**

and leading to the parish of St. Mary and the North Coast via the community of Broadgate.

The Blue Mountain foothills flank the entire city, forming a constant backdrop. Along with a handful of high-rises in New Kingston, the hills provide the best natural landmarks for orientation in the city. Kingston's most affluent residential neighborhoods hug the hills. From Papine, Gordon Town Road leads into the Blue Mountains. A left at The Cooperage, by the bus stop in Industry Village, leads along the well-paved but at times narrow and winding B1 road north over Hardwar Gap toward Buff Bay and the North Coast. Continuing straight on Gordon Town Road leads to Gordon Town, while a right turn in Gordon Town Square leads to Mavis Bank and the ascent toward the upper reaches of the **Blue Mountains.**

SAFETY

Kingston is a city of nearly one million people, the vast majority living in poverty. Keep in mind that people will say and do just about anything that gives them the opportunity to eat. While some may use physical intimidation to get what they want, a more common occurrence is for someone to pretend to know you or yell aggressively from across the street,

busy street market in urban Kingston

"Come here!" When you get the feeling that an advance of this sort may lead to an uncomfortable situation, go with that instinct. It helps to keep petty cash on hand to ease tensions when strategically necessary. If you're driving, there's almost always someone nearby to direct your parking and then volunteer to watch your car. When you return, the helpful volunteer will expect a tip. While you don't need to be intimidated by these everyday occurrences, a bit of change or a small bill will put you in good stead.

Crime and violence certainly exist in Kingston, although visitors are unlikely to encounter it. Exercise particular caution when visiting Cassava Piece, downtown (including Trench Town, Tivoli Gardens, and Arnett Gardens), Grants Pen, Standpipe, and Spanish Town. Don't make the mistake of making political statements or getting involved in any way as a visitor, like wearing an orange People's National Party (PNP) T-shirt while walking through Tivoli Gardens, one of the city's most notorious ghettos and a stronghold for the Jamaica Labour Party (JLP). These garrison communities can flare up in violence, usually demonstrated by residents barricading the streets in one of the only displays of power they can muster. Should you be unfortunate enough to be caught in Kingston under these circumstances, avoid going downtown and discuss safety with locals. The U.S. embassy is typically the first to sound an alarm, issuing travel advisories anytime such a situation arises.

Generally, foreigners only make crime news when they have tried to exit the country carrying drugs. Stick with the right locals in the right places and Kingston will be no more dangerous than any other big city in the developing world where wealth and poverty coexist.

Sights

Kingston's main attractions relate to Jamaica's history, heritage, and culture as opposed to the natural features on the north and west coasts. Most of the historical sights, as well as those associated with the Institute of Jamaica, are located Downtown. With a few notable exceptions, the more popular hangouts as well as most restaurants, bars, clubs, and shopping plazas are located Uptown. As Jamaica's music scene has decentralized, thanks in large part to technological advances, the Downtown production studios of yesteryear that controlled the industry, like Sir Clement "Coxsone" Dodd's World Disc, or his even more successful Studio One, have been replaced by scores of modern studios scattered around the residential suburbs, often based at the homes of the artists and producers who run them.

DOWNTOWN

Jamaican art pioneer Edna Manley was honored with a re-creation of her sculpture *Negro Aroused* on Ocean Boulevard along the waterfront at the end of King Street. It's as good as any place to begin a tour of Downtown. Along Ocean Boulevard, anglers casually reel in their lines and children jump off big concrete blocks into the choppy waters of Kingston Harbour, undeterred by the dirty runoff streaming all around. It's a great place for an afternoon stroll or to watch sunsets over the Hellshire Hills.

Another option for exploring Downtown is with **Olde Jamaica Tours** (contact Juliet Gordon, tel. 876/755-3488, cell tel. 876/362-9319, oldejamaica@yahoo.com, www.oldejamaicatours.com, from US$50 pp). Specializing in historical structures around the Corporate Area, the tours visit Holy Trinity Church, the

Metropolitan Kingston

0   0.5 mi

0   0.5 km

© MOON.COM

RED HILLS RD

BIG SHIP

MANNINGS HILL RD

GROSVENOR
GALLERIES

CONSTANT SPRING
GOLF CLUB

KNIGHTSDALE DR

MICHAEL'S RESTAURANT
& COFFEE SHOP

CONSTANT SPRING RD

PRICESMART

RED HILLS RD

WHITEHALL AVE

NORMA'S

Molynes
Gardens

WHITE
BONES

FLAMES
PRODUCTION

LEE'S FOOD FAIR &
LEE'S FAMILY PHARMACY

SCOTIABANK

TROPICAL
CHINESE

SOVEREIGN
CENTRE

WASHINGTON BLVD

MACAU GAMING
LOUNGE & BAR

DUNROBIN AVE

Olympic
Gardens

ALL STAR
THURSDAYS

Eastwood
Park

WALTHAM PARK RD

MOLYNES RD

REGGAE
HOSTEL

N COCKBURN RD

SEE
"UPTOWN
KINGSTON"
MAP

CONSTANT SPRING RD

HOPE RD

SPANISH TOWN RD

HAGLEY PARK RD

Richmond
Park

Maxfield
Park

MAXFIELD AVE

LYNDHURST RD

TUFF GONG
RECORDING STUDIO

ETHIOPIAN
ORTHODOX
CHURCH

SPANISH TOWN RD

Hunts
Bay

PORTMORE - KINGSTON CAUSEWAY

SEE
"DOWNTOWN
KINGSTON"
MAP

CULTURE
YARD

MARCUS GARVEY DR

NORTH ST

ORANGE ST

DAWKINS DR

St. William
Grant Park

Kingston
Harbour

NATIONAL GALLERY

KING ST

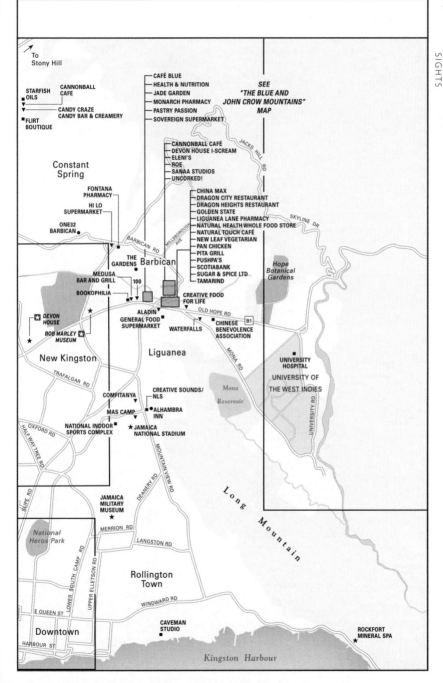

To Stony Hill

STARFISH OILS
CANNONBALL CAFE
CANDY CRAZE
CANDY BAR & CREAMERY
FLIRT BOUTIQUE

CAFÉ BLUE
HEALTH & NUTRITION
JADE GARDEN
MONARCH PHARMACY
PASTRY PASSION
SOVEREIGN SUPERMARKET

SEE "THE BLUE AND JOHN CROW MOUNTAINS" MAP

Constant Spring

FONTANA PHARMACY
HI LO SUPERMARKET
ONE32 BARBICAN

CANNONBALL CAFÉ
DEVON HOUSE I-SCREAM
ELENI'S
ROE
SANAA STUDIOS
UNCORKED!

JACKS HILL RD

SKYLINE DR

CHINA MAX
DRAGON CITY RESTAURANT
DRAGON HEIGHTS RESTAURANT
GOLDEN STATE
LIGUANEA LANE PHARMACY
NATURAL HEALTH WHOLE FOOD STORE
NATURAL TOUCH CAFÉ
NEW LEAF VEGETARIAN
PAN CHICKEN
PITA GRILL
PUSHPA'S
SCOTIABANK
SUGAR & SPICE LTD
TAMARIND

BARBICAN RD

MILLSBOROUGH AVE

THE GARDENS
Barbican
MEDUSA BAR AND GRILL
100
BOOKOPHILIA

Hope Botanical Gardens

DEVON HOUSE
BOB MARLEY MUSEUM

ALADIN
GENERAL FOOD SUPERMARKET
WATERFALLS

CREATIVE FOOD FOR LIFE

OLD HOPE RD

B1

CHINESE BENEVOLENCE ASSOCIATION

New Kingston

Liguanea

MONA RD

UNIVERSITY HOSPITAL

UNIVERSITY OF THE WEST INDIES

TRAFALGAR RD

Mona Reservoir

UNIVERSITY RD

OXFORD RD

COMFITANYA
CREATIVE SOUNDS/NLS

MAS CAMP
ALHAMBRA INN

NATIONAL INDOOR SPORTS COMPLEX

JAMAICA NATIONAL STADIUM

HALF WAY TREE RD

MOUNTAIN VIEW RD

Long Mountain

SLIPE RD

JAMAICA MILITARY MUSEUM

DEANERY RD

National Heros Park

MERRION RD

LANGSTON RD

LOWER SOUTH CAMP RD

UPPER ELLETSON RD

Rollington Town

WINDWARD RD

E QUEEN ST

Downtown

HARBOUR ST

CAVEMAN STUDIO

ROCKFORT MINERAL SPA

Kingston Harbour

Downtown Kingston

PENN ST
PRICE ST
CROOKS ST
ASQUITH ST
FRENCH ST
WILLIAMS ST
SLUPE PEN RD
DRUMMOND ST
ORANGE ST
KING ST
NEW NORTH ST
GARRICK LN
MARK LN
EAST ST
LOCKETT AVE

CONNOLLEY RD
DAMES RD
PRINCE OF WALES ST
PRINCE ALBERT ST
NATIONAL HEROES CIR
HITCHEN ST
GT GEORGE ST
ANDERSON RD
ARNOLD RD
HANNAH ST
NORTH AVE
CAMPBELL RD
CONRAD LN
CENTRAL AVE

HEROES CIRCLE ★

National Heroes Park

Sabina Park
EMERALD RD

NORTH ST
CHARLES ST
BEESTON ST
OXFORD ST
LOVE LN
LUKE LN
BOND ST
SPANISH TOWN RD
HEYWOOD ST

■ THE GLEANER COMPANY

SHAARE SHALOM SYNAGOGUE ★

HOLY TRINITY CATHEDRAL ★

NORTH ST
SOUTH CAMP RD
TEXT LN
BLAKE RD
BLAKE RD

GORDON HOUSE ★
★ JAMAICA NATIONAL HERITAGE TRUST

LIBERTY HALL ★
■
MARCUS GARVEY COMMUNITY CENTRE
THE WARD THEATRE ■

BA BETA KRISTIAN CHURCH OF HAILE SELASSIE I ★

RUM LN
SMITH ST
JAMES ST

N PARADE
COKE MEMORIAL METHODIST CHURCH
JUBILEE/ CORONATION MARKET ■
W QUEEN ST
Saint William Grant Park
W PARADE
E PARADE
★
EAST QUEEN ST

BECKFORD ST
S PARADE
LAWS ST

PRINCESS ST
ORANGE ST
KING ST
TEMPLE LN
CHURCH ST
DUKE ST
JOHNS LN
GEORGES ST
RUM LN
BARRY ST
HIGH HOLBORN ST
FLEET ST
LOWER SOUTH CAMP RD
MCWHINNEY ST

PECHON ST
EAST ST
TOWER ST
INSTITUTE OF JAMAICA ■
MAIDEN LN
GOLD ST
WATER LN
POTTERS ROW

MOBY DICK RESTAURANT ▼
F & B DOWNTOWN ■
HARBOUR ST

KINGSTON CRAFT MARKET ■
DIGICEL ■
PORT ROYAL ST
★ ☆ NATIONAL GALLERY
OCEAN BLVD
■ BANK OF JAMAICA

Kingston   Harbour

0   200 yds
0   200 m

© MOON.COM

Jewish synagogue, St. Andrew Parish Church, East Queen's Street Baptist, Coke Methodist, Cots Kirk, and Spanish Town Cathedral, among many other sights of interest.

Coin and Notes Museum

The free **Coin and Notes Museum** (Bank of Jamaica, Nethersole Place, between East St. and Duke St., tel. 876/922-0750, ext. 2108, 9am-4pm Mon.-Fri., free) provides a history of money in Jamaica from the time when goods were bartered to the present. The in-between period saw the circulation of coins from many countries, including Spain and Mexico. Curators have a wealth of knowledge to share with visitors.

★ Tuff Gong Recording Studio

Operating as living proof that a recording artist can own his music and be in control of his legacy, **Tuff Gong Recording Studio** (220 Marcus Garvey Dr., tel. 876/937-4216 or 876/923-9383, www.tuffgong.com) was started by Bob Marley as a struggling artist, much like the one depicted by Jimmy Cliff in Perry Henzell's film *The Harder They Come*. He was subject to the producer-artist relationship that made voicing the next tune an economic imperative rather than a carefully planned and executed project. When Marley built Tuff Gong Recording Studio, he seeded an empire that continues to earn millions of dollars per year. Today the studio operates as Marley's legacy, with his children Ziggy, Stephen, and Cedella in charge. The studio offers a guided tour, where visitors can see the entire music production process, from the recording studio to the record-pressing factory next door. The studio can also be booked for recording (US$50 per hour), with instruments and a sound engineer included. A small record shop on-site sells CD, LPs, and other Tuff Gong paraphernalia.

Culture Yard

A project developed by the Trench Town Development Association, **Culture Yard** (6-8 1st St., off Collie Smith Dr., contact Clifford "Ferdie" Bent, tel. 876/572-4085, 8am-6pm daily, US$10) offers a museum tour based around Bob Marley's former home. Visiting Culture Yard is a decent excuse to see the slums of **Trench Town,** which have retained the dire conditions that gave birth to songs like "Concrete Jungle" and "No Woman No Cry," even if the cost for a look-around feels more like charity than a great value. The area is marked by a large mural of Marley, visible

Buju Banton at Sumfest

from Spanish Town Road. Visiting Culture Yard is safe, but the communities in and around Trench Town remain explosive, so it's not a good idea to go wandering off on your own.

The Trench Town Development Association was established to carry out projects to benefit the community. Another successful community venture has been the **Trench Town Reading Centre** (Lower 1st St., contact Christopher Stone, tel. 876/546-1559, stonec@kasnet.com, www.trench-townreadingcentre.com), which welcomes donations of books.

St. William Grant Park

The Parade, also known as **St. William Grant Park,** was a popular congregation ground for a host of labor leaders, including William Grant, Marcus Garvey, and Alexander Bustamante, who spoke regularly before large audiences in the decades preceding independence. Originally a parade ground for British soldiers, the park divides King Street into upper and lower regions. The park was recently refurbished to rid it of a sullied reputation after years of neglect, and it is certainly more pleasant today than just a few years ago. Once called Victoria Park, it was renamed in 1977 to honor William Grant for his role in Jamaica's labor movement. Grant was a follower of Marcus Garvey and joined forces with Alexander Bustamante in championing workers' rights. In 1938, both he and Bustamante were arrested for fomenting upheaval among the early trade unions. In the early 1940s, Grant broke with Bustamante's Industrial Trade Union and drifted into poverty and obscurity. Nevertheless he was given the Honor of Distinction in 1974, three years before his death, for his contribution to the labor movement, which paved the way for Jamaica's independence. The "St." preceding his name is for "sergeant," attributable to his service in the military or as a militant member of the United Negro Improvement Association.

Kingston Parish Church

Kingston Parish Church (tel. 876/922-6888) stands on the corner of South Parade and King Street. It was rebuilt in 1911 after the earthquake of 1907, which virtually flattened all of downtown. It is a replica of the original with the addition of a clock tower. The original had stood since reconstruction after the earthquake of 1692. Inside there are several pieces of Jamaican art and a few statues gifted by the Chinese (Our Lady at the High Altar) and Lebanese (Saint Thomas) governments.

Coke Church

The most prominent building on East Parade, **Coke Church** (tel. 876/922-2224) stands on the site of the first Methodist chapel in Jamaica. The present structure was rebuilt after the 1907 earthquake, replacing the 1840 original named after Thomas Coke, who founded the Methodist missions in the British Caribbean. It is one of the few buildings of brick construction in Kingston.

Institute of Jamaica

The **Institute of Jamaica** (IOJ, Main Bldg., 14-16 East St., tel. 876/922-0620 or 876/922-0626, ioj.jam@mail.infochan.com, http://instituteofjamaica.org.jm, US$4, students free) was founded in 1879 by Governor-General Anthony Musgrave to encourage "Literature, Science, and Art," as the letters on the main building's facade read. The institute's several divisions include the National Gallery, National Library, and the Museum of History and Ethnography. The IOJ publishes an excellent series called *Jamaica Journal,* which delves into a range of topics, from dancehall music to sea sponges off Port Royal to national heroes. It's a great way to get a glimpse at the introspective side of the Jamaican people.

★ NATIONAL GALLERY

The **National Gallery** (12 Ocean Blvd., tel. 876/922-1561, 10am-4:30pm Tues.-Thurs., 10am-4pm Fri., 10am-3pm Sat., US$3 adults, students free) is the go-to place for a concise overview of Jamaican art, from Taino artifacts and colonial art dating to Spanish and English rule, to pieces charting the development of Jamaican intuitive and mainstream expression. Temporary exhibits feature works by contemporary artists, live performances, and installations. The works at the National Gallery reflect Jamaica's landscapes and people. Artists in the permanent collection include Mallica "Kapo" Reynolds, Barrington Watson, Albert Huie, Carl Abrahams, John Dunkley, and Edna Manley.

THE NATURAL HISTORY DIVISION AND THE MUSEUM OF HISTORY AND ETHNOGRAPHY

The **Natural History Division** is the oldest division of the IOJ and is housed adjacent to the Institute's main building on the ground floor. The **Museum of History and Ethnography** (10 East St., 8:30am-5pm Mon.-Thurs., 8:30am-4pm Fri., US$4 adults, US$3 students, US$1 under age 13) features temporary exhibits at its headquarters, ranging from colorful examples of contemporary Jamaican life to historical commemorations of events and movements in Jamaican history.

The **Museum of Jamaican Music** is a new development envisioned as part of the IOJ's museum network and dedicated to conserving Jamaica's musical history. Presided over by the IOJ's Museum of Ethnography under the leadership of director and curator Herbie Miller (cell tel. 876/476-6575), the museum supports research into and documentation of all aspects of Jamaican musical history. A temporary exhibit in the ethnography division of the Institute features a display containing musical memorabilia.

THE JAMAICA MILITARY MUSEUM

The **Jamaica Military Museum** (Up Park Camp, contact Michael Anglin, cell tel. 876/926-8121, jmmlib@gmail.com, 10am-4pm Wed.-Sun., US$1 adults, US$0.50 children) is a collaborative effort between the Jamaica Defense Force (JDF) and the staff of the Museum of History and Ethnography,

showcasing Jamaica's military past, starting with the Taino and the Spanish-Taino encounter, with a few old tanks and uniforms on display from the British period, to the present JDF uniforms and medals.

LIBERTY HALL

The latest addition to the IOJ is **Liberty Hall** (76 King St., tel. 876/948-8639, www.libertyhall-ioj.org.jm, info@libertyhall-ioj.org.jm, museum 10am-4pm Mon.-Fri., US$1 adults, US$0.50 children). The rehabilitated building was Marcus Garvey's base of operations in the 1920s and today has a small reference library with a wealth of knowledge related to Garvey and his teachings. Liberty Hall houses a multimedia museum and resource center as well as continuing Garvey's vision with programs for local youth. Garvey's influence on the Jamaican psyche is profound. Liberty Hall, just a few blocks up from St. William Grant Park and the Ward Theatre, a hotbed of Jamaica's labor movement, is the best place to grasp his importance as a founder of pan-Africanism.

AFRICAN-CARIBBEAN INSTITUTE OF JAMAICA

The **African-Caribbean Institute of Jamaica** (ACIJ, 12 Ocean Blvd., tel. 876/922-4793 or 876/922-7415, acij@anngel.com.jm, 8am-4:30pm Mon.-Thurs., 8am-3:30pm Fri.) has a mandate to "collect, research, document, analyze, and preserve information on Jamaica's cultural heritage, through the exploitation of oral and scribal sources." The ACIJ has a memory-bank program in which oral histories are recorded around the country and then transcribed, as well as an active publications program featuring the *ACIJ Research Review*. There is a small library at the office where the Institute's top-notch academic publications can be browsed and purchased. The ACIJ has a tradition of collaboration with individual researchers and institutions. Projects have included studies of traditional religions like Kumina and Revival, and research on the Maroons.

National Heroes Park

National Heroes Park occupies 30 hectares (74 acres) below Cross Roads on Marescaux Road within the large roundabout known as **Heroes Circle.** The roundabout surrounds what was once the city's main sporting ground, later becoming the Kingston Race Course. The park was also the site of several important historical events, including Emancipation Day celebrations on August 1, 1938; the jubilee celebrating Queen Victoria's reign in 1887; and the free Smile Jamaica concert where a wounded Bob Marley offered the people of Kingston a 90-minute performance in defiance of his would-be assassins in 1976. Heroes Park is also said to have been the battleground where warring factions from East and West Kingston would face off in organized skirmishes.

At the southern end of the park, **Heroes Memorial** commemorates Jamaica's most important historical figures and events. Black Nationalist Marcus Garvey rests here, as does labor leader Alexander Bustamante, who formed the Jamaica Labour Party, and his cousin Norman Manley, who founded the opposition People's National Party. Norman's son Michael Manley, who gave the country its biggest communist scare for his closeness with Cuba's Fidel Castro, is also interred here. Paul Bogle and George William Gordon are honored for their role in the Morant Bay Rebellion, which was at the vanguard of Jamaica's civil rights movement in the post-emancipation period.

Recent icons laid to rest at Heroes Memorial are the cultural legend Louise Bennett, referred to lovingly by Jamaicans as "Miss Lou," who died in 2006; Olympic gold medalist Herbert Henry "Herb" McKenley, interred in 2007; Gladys Bustamante, wife of JLP founder Alexander Bustamante, in 2009; and in 2014, former Governor General Howard Felix Hanlan Cooke, as well as his wife, Ivy Sylvia Lucille Cooke, in 2017.

1: Paul Bogle memorialized in National Heroes Park 2: a busy street corner in Kingston 3: Devon House

Headquarters House

Home of the Jamaica National Heritage Trust, which oversees the country's heritage sites, **Headquarters House** (79 Duke St., tel. 876/922-1287, 8:30am-4:30pm Mon.-Fri., free) dates from 1755 and is a good example of Georgian architecture. Merchant Thomas Hibbert built the house in a contest to see who could construct the most ornate edifice to impress a local woman. There's a nice gallery on the ground floor with antiquities. It is also called Hibbert House; the Jamaican Parliament was housed here until it outgrew the small confines of the main chamber.

The Ba Beta Kristian Church of Haile Selassie I

On Oxford Street in front of Coronation Market, the **Ba Beta Kristian Church of Haile Selassie I** is worth a visit for its colorful service on Sunday afternoons. Women must cover their heads, wear dresses, and sit on the right side of the aisle. Men should not cover their heads. The church sponsors community initiatives as well as the Amha Selassie basic school located next door.

Trinity Cathedral

Center stage for several important national events, **Trinity Cathedral** (1-3 George Edly Dr., tel. 876/922-3335, service 8:30am Sun., mass 5:30pm Mon.-Fri.) is where Archbishop Samuel Carter is buried. Michael Manley's funeral—attended by Fidel Castro and Louis Farrakhan, among others—was held here. The original mosaic tile on the north wall has been uncovered, and a Spanish restoration team is set to restore the rest of the mosaic walls, which were painted over in white. Caretaker Craig Frazer leads tours of the building and points out interesting details. A generous tip is sure to make the pious young man even more devout.

UPTOWN
Emancipation Park

At the corner of Knutsford Boulevard and Oxford Road is **Emancipation Park** (tel.

Uptown Kingston

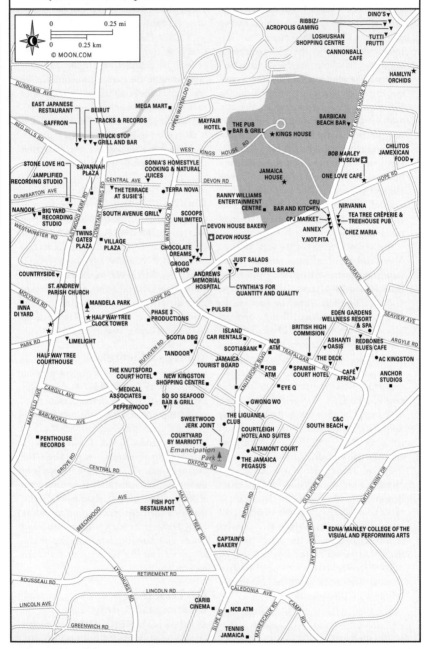

0   0.25 mi

0   0.25 km

© MOON.COM

DINO'S

RIBBIZ/
ACROPOLIS GAMING

LOSHUSHAN
SHOPPING CENTRE

TUTTI
FRUTTI

CANNONBALL
CAFÉ

HAMLYN
ORCHIDS

EAST JAPANESE
RESTAURANT

BEIRUT

MEGA MART

BARBICAN
BEACH BAR

SAFFRON

TRACKS & RECORDS

MAYFAIR
HOTEL

THE PUB
BAR & GRILL

KINGS HOUSE

TRUCK STOP
GRILL AND BAR

WEST KINGS HOUSE RD

CHILITOS
JAMEXICAN
FOOD

STONE LOVE HQ

JAMPLIFIED
RECORDING STUDIO

SAVANNAH
PLAZA

SONIA'S HOMESTYLE
COOKING & NATURAL
JUICES

BOB MARLEY
MUSEUM

JAMAICA
HOUSE

ONE LOVE CAFÉ

CENTRAL AVE

DEVON RD

NANOOK

BIG YARD
RECORDING
STUDIO

THE TERRACE
AT SUSIE'S

TERRA NOVA

RANNY WILLIAMS
ENTERTAINMENT
CENTRE

CRU
BAR AND KITCHEN

NIRVANNA

DUMBARTON AVE

SOUTH AVENUE GRILL

SCOOPS
UNLIMITED

CPJ MARKET

TEA TREE CRÊPERIE &
TREEHOUSE PUB

WESTMINSTER RD

TWINS
GATES
PLAZA

VILLAGE
PLAZA

DEVON HOUSE BAKERY

DEVON HOUSE

ANNEX

CHEZ MARIA

Y.NOT.PITA

COUNTRYSIDE

ST. ANDREW
PARISH CHURCH

CHOCOLATE
DREAMS

GROGG
SHOP

JUST SALADS

DI GRILL SHACK

INNA
DI YARD

MANDELA PARK

ANDREWS
MEMORIAL
HOSPITAL

CYNTHIA'S FOR
QUANTITY AND QUALITY

HALF WAY TREE
CLOCK TOWER

PHASE 3
PRODUCTIONS

PULSE8

EDEN GARDENS
WELLNESS RESORT
& SPA

LIMELIGHT

HALF WAY
TREE
COURTHOUSE

SCOTIA DBG

ISLAND
CAR RENTALS

BRITISH HIGH
COMMISION

ASHANTI
OASIS

REDBONES
BLUES CAFE

TANDOOR

SCOTIABANK

NCB
ATM

THE DECK

AC KINGSTON

THE KNUTSFORD
COURT HOTEL

JAMAICA
TOURIST BOARD

FCIB
ATM

SPANISH
COURT HOTEL

CAFÉ
AFRICA

ANCHOR
STUDIOS

MEDICAL
ASSOCIATES

NEW KINGSTON
SHOPPING CENTRE

SO SO SEAFOOD
BAR & GRILL

EYE Q

PEPPERWOOD

GWONG WO

PENTHOUSE
RECORDS

SWEETWOOD
JERK JOINT

THE LIGUANEA
CLUB

C&C
SOUTH BEACH

COURTYARD
BY MARRIOTT

COURTLEIGH
HOTEL AND SUITES

ALTAMONT COURT

Emancipation
Park

THE JAMAICA
PEGASUS

FISH POT
RESTAURANT

EDNA MANLEY COLLEGE OF THE
VISUAL AND PERFORMING ARTS

CAPTAIN'S
BAKERY

CARIB
CINEMA

NCB ATM

TENNIS
JAMAICA

876/926-6312 or 876/968-9292, emanpark@ cwjamaica.com), where two figures stand resolute, cast in bronze, their bodies thick and steadfast, their heads proudly lifted to acknowledge the rectitude of the long struggle for freedom and silently praying for guidance in a new era. The work, titled *Redemption Song,* was the winner of a competition to give the newly constructed Emancipation Park a meaningful headpiece. It was controversial because its creator, Jamaican sculptor Laura Facey (www.laurafacey.com), is light-skinned, and also because the figures are naked and the man could be considered well-endowed. Some people wanted the sculpture immediately removed, and Facey was the talk of the island for weeks. In the end, artistic freedom prevailed, and the sculpture was kept in place.

Redemption Song and the controversy that surrounded it reflect the deep wounds slavery left on Jamaica and the rest of the world. Emancipation Park is among the best-maintained public spaces in Kingston, perfect for reflecting on the past, relaxing on one of the many benches, or just taking a stroll. Events are held frequently on a stage at the center of the park and next door at the Liguanea Club or on top of the NHT Building.

Half Way Tree

Half Way Tree is both the capital of St. Andrew Parish and a neighborhood within Kingston itself. The bustling commercial area seen today is a far cry from its rural days when it was a popular rest stop for travelers between Kingston and Spanish Town. Several historical sites are wedged among the concrete and strip malls. The **clock tower** at the junction of Half Way Tree, Hope, Constant Spring, and Hagley Park Roads was erected in 1913 as a monument to Britain's King Edward VII. It's the symbol of Half Way Tree.

Also called Half Way Tree Church, **St. Andrew Parish Church** (free) is one of the oldest Anglican churches on the island. The present church has a foundation that dates from 1692, when the earthquake destroyed the previous structure. One of the first U.S. consuls

to Jamaica, Robert Monroe Harrison, brother of U.S. President Benjamin Harrison, is buried here along with his wife. Philip Livingston, a Jamaica-based merchant and son of one of the founding fathers of the United States, was married in the church. Outside there's an old, poorly maintained cemetery.

Adjacent to the Parish Church, the **Half Way Tree Courthouse** is a good example of Georgian architecture, dating from 1807. The front of the building is covered with latticework, presumably to keep out the heat as a form of early air conditioning. The building has been repaired and altered several times to fix storm damage, while it miraculously escaped damage during the 1907 earthquake. The courthouse has seen formerly enslaved people obtaining their certificates of freedom as well as agricultural society meetings, and after 1920 legal proceedings were no longer held here. Until the mid-1980s the building was a branch of the Institute of Jamaica called the Junior Centre, which hosted skills-training courses. The courthouse was listed as a Jamaica National Heritage Trust site in 1957, and in 1985 it was declared a National Monument. Meanwhile the structure suffered neglect and decay.

One important trial held at the Half Way Tree Courthouse was that of Alexander Bedward, a popular folk hero and founder of a Native Free Baptist sect known as Bedwardism, in 1921. Bedward was an early Black Nationalist who spoke out against the religious and government authorities of the day. For this he was committed to Bellevue asylum until his death in 1930.

The **Ethiopian Orthodox Church** (McDonald Lane) was founded in Jamaica in 1972. This is the state church of Ethiopia to which Haile Selassie I belonged. The church has an awkward relationship with Rastafarians in Jamaica; many of them have been baptized as Ethiopian Orthodox, including Bob Marley's children. To this day, the construction remains incomplete, with little more than a foundation in place. Its construction has been held up by a lack of cosmic alignment and a lack of togetherness in the Rasta community, according to Rasta elder Kojo and many others who share his view. Meanwhile, many inside the Ethiopian Church scorn Rastas for considering Haile Selassie a God.

Kingston's **Hindu Temple** (114b Hagley Park Rd., tel. 876/994-0788) holds events for all the major Hindu holidays, including Ganesh Puja and Diwali. Local Hindus attend in heavy numbers on Sunday morning.

★ Devon House

Still one of Kingston's finest homes, **Devon House** (26 Hope Rd., Great House, tel. 876/929-6602 or 876/929-0815, devonhouse-jamaica@cw.com, guided tours 9:30am-4:30pm Mon.-Sat., last tour 4pm, reservations required Sat., US$10 adults, US$8 under age 12) is a source of pride for the city. The mansion was constructed in 1881 by Jamaica's first black millionaire, George Stiebel, who made his fortune in Venezuelan gold. Some of the city's predominantly white elite of the day were less than happy to be outdone by a black man; it is said that Lady Musgrave—wife of Governor-General Lord Musgrave, who founded the Institute of Jamaica—actually had a road built (Lady Musgrave Rd.) so she wouldn't have to bear the humiliation of passing the spectacular mansion that humbled even her husband's residence. Until 1983, Devon House was home to the National Gallery. Today it is furnished and decorated with a range of English, French, and Caribbean antiques as well as some reproductions. The courtyard behind Devon House is full of boutiques and restaurants.

★ Bob Marley Museum

In Bob Marley's former residence at 56 Hope Road, just north of New Kingston, the house has been turned into the **Bob Marley Museum** (tel. 876/630-1588, www.bobmarley-foundation.com, US$25 adults, US$12 ages 4-12), a shrine to the man and his music, with rooms full of newspaper clippings and personal effects. Tours (1 hour, 9:30am-4pm Mon.-Sat.) are by knowledgeable guides who recount with ominous effects the night Marley was shot by political operatives, narrowly escaping with his life. Around back, there's a gift shop and a gallery with rotating exhibitions. A comfortable cozy theater is a great place to catch a movie. A presentation on Marley is part of the tour, and the theater is used occasionally for touring international film festivals. **One Love Café,** on one side of the main gate, has light bites and fresh juices.

Hope Gardens

Marley's Land Rover sits under a protective carport in the other corner of the yard in front of a wall plastered with Wailers photos. Photos are not allowed inside or behind the main building that houses the museum.

King's House

King's House (Hope Rd. at Lady Musgrave Rd., tel. 876/927-6424, kingshouse@kingshoue.gov.jm, visits scheduled by request) has been the home of the Governor-General since the capital was moved from Spanish Town in 1872. Jamaica's ceremonial head of state is appointed by the British monarch for six-year terms. King's House was formerly the residence of Jamaica's Anglican bishop. The original building was destroyed in the 1907 earthquake and rebuilt in 1909. The grounds have nice gardens that can be toured; email to schedule a visit. Jamaica House, just south of King's House on the same grounds, is now the location for the Prime Minister's offices and is closed to the public.

★ Hope Gardens and Zoo

Founded in 1873 and managed by NGO the Nature Preservation Foundation, **Hope Botanical Gardens** (Hope Rd., 6am-6pm daily, free, parking US$1.50) is a great place to hang out in the shade of a Bombacacea tree or picnic on the grass. The diverse collection of exotic and endemic plants isn't as well labeled as it could be. Hope Gardens was named after Major Richard Hope, who once owned the estate. The gardens span 8.5 hectares (21 acres) on the Liguanea Plain. Visitors to Hope Gardens should make time to tour the magnificent Chinese Gardens, gifted by the Chinese government and completed in 2016. The design adheres to feng shui and is adorned with symbols of Chinese culture, including a massive sculpture made of rare Lingbi stone. Of special note is the sizable lily pond, featuring an island in the shape of Jamaica. Guided tours (US$1) of the Chinese Garden are offered. A band shell features occasional performances, and parties are regularly held on the lawns. **Hope Zoo** (tel. 876/927-1085, 10am-4pm daily, US$15 adults, US$10 ages 3-11) is located within Hope Gardens, boasting a lion, monkeys, a few birds, alligators, and iguanas.

AROUND KINGSTON
University of the West Indies

The **University of the West Indies** (UWI, Mona Rd. and University Rd., www.mona.uwi.edu), in the quiet residential neighborhood of Mona, is worth a visit. The campus sits at the base of the Blue Mountains and has extensive rolling lawns with interesting ruins of the old Mona Estate aqueduct and a beautiful mural created by Belgian artist Claude Rahir with the help of UWI students. The cutstone University Chapel by the main entrance is an excellent example of Georgian architecture. It was transported block by block from Gales Valley Estate in Trelawny at the bidding of Princess Alice, first chancellor of the University. The former sugar warehouse was given a new life at UWI, its interior decorated with materials from all the countries the university has served. The coats of arms of these countries are inlaid in the chapel ceiling.

Castleton Botanical Gardens

Along the main Kingston-to-Annotto Bay road (the A3), just over the border from St. Andrew, **Castleton Botanical Gardens** (Castleton, St. Mary, tel. 876/942-0717, free) is still one of the nicest parks in Jamaica, despite having suffered years of neglect and recurring hurricane damage. Castleton was established in the 1860s and planted with 400 species from Kew Gardens in England. It remained an important introduction point for ornamental and economically important species, including scores of palms as well as poincianas and the large Bombay mango variety. One of the most interesting specimens in the gardens is the screwpine (*Pandanus tectorius*), which sends down aerial, or stilt, roots; another is the poor man's orchid, not a true orchid, which has become ubiquitous around the island. Other economically important tree species still growing at the gardens are the Burma teak and West Indian mahogany.

Entertainment

Many Jamaicans love a good party, or "session," as they call it, and Kingston has the most consistent and varied nightlife to support partygoers and dance enthusiasts. Don't be alarmed if someone approaches within intimate distance for what is known as a slow "wine," or sexually suggestive dance, in a club or at a street dance. But it's not just "wining" that Kingston offers. While still less than cosmopolitan in terms of its entertainment offerings (you won't find an opera house), the city does support a wide array of cultural and artistic forms, from modern dance to art and theater. Of course, music touches everybody, and Kingston's nightclubs deliver a raw celebration of music on dance floors as much as in the streets.

There's no need to hurry in Jamaica, as everything inevitably starts late, especially nightlife. Family-oriented and cultural entertainment generally starts earlier in the evenings, 7pm-10pm. Few people go out to a nightclub before midnight, and clubs don't typically fill up until 2am-3am. Street dances start particularly late and can be quite boring until a sizeable crowd gathers and people start showing off their moves amid pan-chicken vendors, enormous speakers, wafting ganja smoke, and the rising sun. Expensive all-inclusive parties maintain an exclusive crowd with ticket prices in the range of US$100. These parties have become quite popular, with the Frenchman's parties the vanguard of Kingston high society chic for its food and select crowd. UWI and University of Technology campuses host parties somewhat regularly.

LIVE MUSIC

Hardly a week passes without some kind of concert for an album launch, talent show, or birthday celebration. Young artists following in the footsteps of reggae legend Bob Marley compete to chant down Babylon with the freshest lyrics. Kingston's vibrant nightlife is a world unto itself, with clubs, parties, and stage shows that entertain well into the morning almost any night of the week.

Live music and stage show performances in Kingston are not as frequent or varied as one would expect given the prominent role music plays in Jamaican life and the prolific music production in town. Nonetheless, there are a handful of venues that feature somewhat regular acts. Stage shows are held routinely, and there are large events held during Jamaica's carnival season, known as Bacchanal, at **Mas Camp** on Arthur Wint Drive. Parties begin in February and continue every Friday until the climax of the carnival season in April.

Legendary old-school roots reggae artists **Chinna Smith** (6 St. Andrew Park, tel. 876/906-0194, earlflute@yahoo.com, US$10 pp contribution) and his Inna De Yard Band welcome visitors to join for rehearsals and host regular jam sessions on Friday.

Redbones Blues Café (rooftop at R Kingston Hotel, 2 Renfrew Rd., tel. 876/978-8262 or 876/978-6091, redbonesmanager@gmail.com, www.redbonesbluescafe.com, noon-11pm Mon.-Fri., 6pm-11pm Sat.) hosts live music on a regular basis, as well as occasional poetry readings and art exhibits.

What began as an informal gathering of "bredren" devotees of roots reggae and dub, preferably emanating from vinyl, **Kingston Dub Club** (contact Gabre Selassie, cell tel. 876/815-1184, sholintemple@gmail.com, www.kingstondubclub.com, 8pm-2am Sun.) has developed into Kingston's weekly pilgrimage to Skyline Drive, where the home of Rockers Sound Station torch bearer Gabre Selassie is transformed into Kingston's preeminent culture yard. The terraced hillside

1: Sizzla performing at MasCamp 2: dancers at Bacchanal Fridays 3: Koffee performing alongside other up-and-coming female artists at Skyline Levels

fills with a motley mix of old school Rastas, young hipsters, and flag-waving disciples, all gathered to relish the fresh and ancient sounds mixed together by the host and his endless entourage of guest selectors (DJs) and artists. Nowhere can a more authentic roots reggae scene be found on any given Sunday night. A few vendors sell books and ital food. A spacious deck with a bar overlooks Kingston's glimmering lights. The stacked boxes begin pumping early in the evening and don't go quiet until the wee hours, when, if you're not moving to the beat, it can get a bit chilly, and a sweater or a light jacket can come in handy.

Rance Chambers is responsible for keeping the disco ball spinning and the good vibes flowing at **Comfitanya Lounge & Restaurant** (169 Mountainview Ave., on Creiffe Rd., tel. 876/978-3517, comfitanya@ aol.com, 11am-4:30pm Mon.-Thurs., 11am-11pm Fri.-Sat., bar 2pm-11pm daily, no food Sun.), which serves local dishes like fried chicken with rice-and-peas, oxtail, curry goat, and vegetarian dishes like steamed veggies in a low-key bar frequented almost exclusively by locals. Live bands perform 9:30pm-1am Saturday and holidays. The bar has a pool table (free on Fri.). A DJ spins on Monday and Thursday-Friday. A movie night on Tuesdays streams comedy and action films.

House of Dancehall (6 Cargill Ave., tel. 876/665-0565, 4pm-midnight Tues.-Thurs., noon-2am Fri.-Sat., main@houseofdancehall. com, www.houseofdancehall.com) hosts occasional live performances and regular club nights on weekends.

FESTIVALS AND EVENTS

Several annual events are worth being in Kingston for, including those that take place during **Reggae Month** in February, when tribute concerts are held for King of Reggae Bob Marley, at the Bob Marley Museum, and Crown Prince Dennis Brown, along the waterfront. The *Jamaica Observer* Food Awards are held in late May.

Bacchanal (www.bacchanaljamaica.com), the organization that took up the mantle of Jamaica Carnival and popularized it, builds the vibes with regular events from February to the April climax, when mas bands take to the Kingston streets.

In early June, Pulse Global (38-A Trafalgar Rd., tel. 876/960-0049, www.pulseworld360. com) hosts the annual **Caribbean Fashion Week** (CFW). Events are held at numerous venues around the capital but mostly at Pulse's Villa Ronai in the suburb of Stony Hill.

The first weekend in March is **Jamaica Blue Mountain Coffee Festival** (www. jamaicacoffeefest.com) at Newcastle. Showcasing Jamaica's coffee culture, crafts, and music, the two-day festival includes a not-to-be-missed Lunch at Belcour Lodge (www. belcourpreserves.com) on Sunday and is held concurrently with the **Misty Bliss** (www.jcdt. org.jm) music festival at Holywell. A two-day event held the second weekend in March, **Jamaica Rum Festival** (www.jarumfestival. com) brings together the island's rum brands for tastings, demonstrations, food, dominoes, and music. Performances have featured Agent Sasco, Aidonia, and Wayne Marshall.

Held in late March, **Jamaica's Girls and Boys Championships,** better known as **Champs,** is an annual track and field meet that sees Kingston's hotels booked with fans from home and abroad who come out to watch the competition. The energy at the National Stadium is palpable, with fans screaming and waving for their schools. Held over the course of a week in mid-June, **Kingston on the Edge (KOTE) Arts Festival** (kingstonon-theedge@gmail.com) hosts a series of exhibits showcasing up-and-coming artistic talent from across the island in art studios and gallery spaces across the city.

Brainchild of larger-than-life fashionista, food critic, and *Observer* lifestyle editor Novia McDonald-Whyte, the *Jamaica Observer* **Food Awards** festival (tel. 876/926-7655, about US$100) celebrates excellence in culinary presentation. Held the last Thursday in May, it affords patrons an opportunity to taste what's new and different in Jamaica's

Carnival in Jamaica

celebrating Carnival in colorful costumes

Carnival was pioneered in Jamaica by students at the University of the West Indies (UWI), who recreated the fetes of their home countries in what continues today as UWI Carnival. Music legend Byron Lee and his cohorts held the first Mas Festival during a week in April 1990. **Bacchanal Jamaica** (www.bacchanaljamaica.com) was formed 10 years later by the pioneering mas bands Revellers, Raiders, and Oakridge Boys as the local organization that would promote carnival. This group of diehards had been making the pilgrimage to Port of Spain, Trinidad, year after year before starting their own bands and developing events that begin in February and build to Easter, when the soca party overtakes Kingston's streets.

The success of Bacchanal Jamaica spurred the emergence of competing bands **Xaymaca** (www.xaymacainternational.com) and **Xodus** (www.xoduscarnival.com), giving participants options to "pick a band and play mas." In addition to the main events in Kingston, Jamaica's carnival season also features parties on the beach outside Ocho Rios. The main events are staged by the mas bands, but several offshoots are held throughout the carnival season and beyond, among them **I Love Soca** (www.ilovesoca.com), BYOB Cooler Fete, and Soca vs. Dancehall.

food industry, with over 60 booths showcasing the country's scrumptious offerings, from the tried-and-true jerk sauces, rum, and Blue Mountain coffee to more exotic offerings. The event is held on the east lawns of Devon House.

One of the best times to be in Kingston for culinary pleasure is **Kingston Restaurant Week,** staged the second or third week in November by *The Jamaica Gleaner* and SSCO Event Management (tel. 876/978-6245, cell tel. 876/564-1700). Prices are slashed by up to 50 percent, and participating venues offer patrons new creations in an attempt to cultivate customer loyalty. The weeklong program has extended to other locations across Jamaica, with participating restaurants now spanning the island, especially in Ocho Rios and Montego Bay.

Beyond the lively weekly nightlife line-up, Kingston is home to a dizzying number of parties, some of them held annually, some held several times a year. **Frenchmen** (www.frenchmenparty.com) is a trailblazing promotion team that has been staging all-inclusive parties for decades, with a series of fetes at the

Crucial Reggae

Most people know Jamaica by its legendary musical king, Bob Marley, who brought international attention to the island. Bob's legacy left an unquenchable thirst for reggae across the globe, paving the way for countless musicians to follow in his wake.

The following is not an exhaustive list of reggae releases but rather a few essentials for any reggae fan's collection and some of my favorites. In the United States, one of the best sources for reggae albums is **Millions of Records** (www.millionsofrecords.com), which has an excellent online catalog of full albums and singles. **Reggae Fever** (www.reggaefever.ch), based in Switzerland, is another good source, as is **Discogs** (www.discogs.com).

SKA

An up-tempo genre that emerged as Jamaica's musical response to the sounds emanating from the US in the roaring 50s, ska became the soundtrack of exuberance for the island's newfound independence in the early 1960s.

- The Skatalites, *Return of the Big Guns*, 1984
- Prince Buster, *FABulous Greatest Hits*, 1993
- Toots & The Maytals, *Funky Kingston*, 2013

ROCKSTEADY

Rocksteady grew out of ska as the offbeat guitar, bass line, and drums were slowed down to let the music breathe, making room for lyrics that stirred romance and revolution.

- Delroy Wilson, *Mr. Cool Operator, 1977*
- Alton Ellis, *Get Ready for Rock Reggae Steady*, 1999
- John Holt, *The Tide is High: Anthology 1962-1979, 2001*

ROOTS REGGAE

Roots reggae put Jamaica on the global stage. Bob Marley, Peter Tosh, and Bunny Wailer attained superstar status introducing the world to a militant message based on the works of Marcus Garvey and Haile Selassie I, who promoted self-determination, African pride and unity.

- Bob Marley and the Wailers, *Songs of Freedom Box Set*, 1992
- Burning Spear, *Marcus Garvey*, 1975
- Dennis Brown, *Milk and Honey*, 1978

DANCEHALL

Born of the streets, dancehall refers to the venue in which it was originally enjoyed. The most popular genre of music in modern Jamaica features lyrics delivered in the imitable "deejay" style, which varies from singing to melodic rapping over up-tempo rhythms with themes typically reflecting struggle, defiance and sexuality.

- Vybz Kartel, *King of the Dancehall*, 2016
- Popcaan, *Forever,* 2018
- Agent Sasco, *Hope River,* 2018

CONTEMPORARY ONE DROP

A roots reggae renaissance has emerged in Jamaica with the rising popularity of a young cadre of artists who draw from the rich lyrical and rhythmic heritage of the country's reggae greats,

Aidonia performs at MVP

eschewing the "slack" lyrics that have come to dominate dancehall in favor of more positive and uplifting message music.

- Chronixx, *Chronology*, 2017
- Protoje, *A Matter of Time*, 2018
- Damian Marley, *Stony Hill*, 2018

BEST PLACES TO HEAR LIVE MUSIC

- Nowhere can a more authentic roots reggae scene be found on any given Sunday night than at the **Kingston Dub Club** (contact Gabre Selassie, cell tel. 876/815-1184, sholintemple@gmail. com, www.kingstondubclub.com, 8pm-2am Sun.). The terraced hillside fills with a motley mix of old school Rastas, young hipsters, and flag-waving disciples, all gathered to relish the fresh and ancient sounds mixed together by the host, Gabre Selassie, and his endless entourage of guest selectors and artists.

- **Chinna Smith** (6 St. Andrew Park, Kingston, tel. 876/906-0194, earlflute@yahoo.com, US$10 pp contribution is customary) and his Inna De Yard Band, legendary old school roots reggae artists, welcome visitors to sit in on rehearsals and participate in jam sessions typically held on Fridays.

- **Bourbon Beach** (Norman Manley Blvd., Negril, tel. 876/957-4432, info@bourbonbeach-jamaica.com, www.bourbonbeachnegril.com) features live music on Monday, Tuesday, and Saturday nights with up-and-coming acts from all over Jamaica.

- For two nights each July, **Reggae Sumfest** (Montego Bay, www.reggaesumfest.com), a.k.a. the "Best Reggae Show on Earth," delivers the top up-and-coming and legendary stars of Jamaica.

- The most popular annual music event held on the North Coast is **Rebel Salute** (www. rebelsalutejamaica.com). Held the Friday and Saturday closest to January 15, it draws thousands of reggae fans from Jamaica and abroad, and typically features the more conscious artists of the genre. Hard-core artists from the dancehall can reinvent themselves for a night as they reveal their more progressive side.

Sound Systems and Street Dances

Sound systems fostered the development of Jamaican music. Starting out as little more than a set of speaker boxes on wheels, the sounds would set up in different places to feed a thirst created by the advent of radio in 1939, which brought American popular music, whetting Jamaica's appetite for new sounds. Jamaica's musicians responded by bringing traditional mento and calypso rhythms to the R&B and pop tunes the people were demanding, ultimately giving birth to ska, rocksteady, reggae, and dancehall. Historically the voice of the street dance, Jamaican sound systems have grown into clubs and stage shows, replacing the African drums of yesteryear.

A sound generally comprises a few individual selectors (DJs) who form a team to blast the latest dancehall tunes using equipment ranging from a home stereo at maximum output, for those just starting out, to the most sophisticated amps operated by the veterans. Selectors will record dub plates, personalized hit tracks with the most popular artists, to up their sound and get ratings from the crowd. Sound clashes pit one sound against the other, each showing off their dub plates recorded through the years, like medals earned in battle.

Street dances have historically played an important role in providing entertainment and an expressive outlet for Kingston's poorest. Dances are held for special occasions like birthdays, funerals, and holidays. Many started as one-off parties but are so popular they became established as regular weekly events. Typically a section of a street or a parking lot is blocked off to traffic, and huge towers of speakers are set up. Street dance venues are safe spaces where people come to enjoy, decked out in their flashiest clothes (jackets and fancy shoes for men, skimpy skirts and tops for women) to drink a Guinness, smoke a spliff, and flex their moves to the latest tunes.

Street dances face a constant threat from police, who have a mandate to shut down music in public spaces at midnight during the week and at 2am on weekends. Promoters complain that this doesn't allow them to recoup their investment, and that street dances reduce crime by giving the youth a free venue, but such claims often fall on deaf ears. Despite the challenges, dedicated party promoters keep at it and struggle through, even if they have to change venues or even take their dance on the road. Some of the most popular dances around town include:

- **Mojito Mondays** (South Avenue Plaza, Half Way Tree), which attracts serious dancers to bust their moves in the parking lot by Susie's

- **Uptown Mondays** (Savannah Plaza, Half Way Tree, cell tel. 876/468-1742), put on by Whitfield "Witty" Henry

- **Boasy Tuesdays** (6 Cargill Ave.), run by dancer and promoter extraordinaire Blazey (cell tel. 876/507-7254 or 876/354-0130)

- **Nipples Tuesdays** (Waterhouse, cell tel. 876/488-5062)

- **Weddy Weddy Wednesdays** (Stone Love HQ, Burlington Ave., Half Way Tree)

height of carnival season (Rise Up, Blocko and Bazodee) in late March or early April, for Heroes Weekend (Breakfast Party, Nitecap and Foreplay) in October, and on New Year's Day (Climax). A team of promoters that calls itself **The Network Jam** (thenetworkjam@ gmail.com) hosts a series of parties around Easter, Heroes Weekend, and Christmas, including Day Break breakfast parties. **Bikini Sundays** (cell tel. 876/381-1281, marjohno@ hotmail.com) parties are typically held on the Kingston waterfront four times a year.

a lively dance crowd at Wet Sundaze

- **Vinyl Thursdays** (Nanook, 80 Burlington Ave., Half Way Tree)

- **All-Star Thursdays** (Olympic Way, Waterhouse)

- **Beer Mug Fridays** (Market Place, Constant Spring Rd., Half Way Tree)

- **Fridays at the Devon** (Reggae Mill, Devon House, Half Way Tree)

- **MVP Fridays** (Pulse8, 38-A Trafalgar Rd., tel. 876/906-6465), which features established dancehall and reggae acts of today and yesteryear

- **Wet Sundaze** (Auto Vision car wash, 8 Hillview Ave., tel. 876/968-9952)

- **Early Sundays** (Grants Pen Ave., Grants Pen, contact Kirk Ferguson, cell tel. 876/849-5889)

- **Bounty Sundays** (Moscow Rd. Waterhouse, contact Marcia Pryce, cell tel. 876/402-4902), the weekly dance endorsed by dancehall legend Rodney "Bounty Killa" Pryce

- **Kingston Dub Club** (Skyline Dr., tel. 876/815-1184), hosted at the hilltop home of roots reggae selector Gabre Selassie of Rockers Sound Station

BARS AND NIGHTCLUBS

An open-air bar at the Pulse Global complex, **Puls8** (38-A Trafalgar Rd., tel. 876/906-6465) hosts a couple of weekly parties, including Pepperseed and MVP Fridays, the latter featuring top contemporary and throwback dancehall and reggae artists.

Nanook (80 Burlington Ave., Half Way Tree, tel. 876/285-3659, Thurs.-Sat.) is a bar and open-air venue that hosts Vinyl Thursdays, among other events that include poetry readings, live art, and music.

Outdoor bar and nightclub **Club Escape** (24 Knutsford Blvd., tel. 876/960-1856, 24 hours daily, US$6 men, US$5 women after 9pm Fri.-Sat.) often has heated dominoes games in the early evenings, plus a mix of music that includes hip-hop and reggae. Lunch (11am-4pm Mon.-Sat.) has items like chicken, oxtail, curry goat, and pepper steak (US$3.50-5). Light items like kebabs and grilled and jerk chicken are served until 3am.

Fishing nets hang from what was once the roof of an auto garage at **The Deck** (14 Trafalgar Rd., tel. 876/978-1582, richard@ thedeck.biz, from 4:30pm daily), a large venue with a boat motif. There are a few billiards tables and a decent bar food menu (US$4-15). Friday's after-work jam is popular, and weekend nights are generally busy, when music blares and patrons are occasionally inspired to dance.

One of the most popular Uptown bars in Kingston, **Regency Bar & Lounge** (Terra Nova, 17 Waterloo Rd., tel. 876/926-2211, 11am-midnight Sun.-Fri., 11am-2am Sat.) caters to guests of the Terra Nova hotel and well-heeled locals. It's one of the most expensive watering holes in town, but scrumptious appetizers are worth splurging for. Try the duck *pissaladière* or the lobster tempura appetizers. The over-the-top interior, reminiscent of a Victorian noble's lair, is complemented by more modest furnishings in the open-air courtyard, surrounded by tropical foliage. The Regency offers live music on Wednesday, endless cocktails on Thursday, a club party vibe on Friday, Latin night on Saturday, and oldies on Sunday.

An open-air bar sharing space with Opa! Greek Restaurant & Lounge (www.opajamaica.com) outside in the courtyard, **Reggae Mill Bar** (Devon House, cell tel. 876/550-2000) is turned into a pro bono art gallery on Wednesday for local artists. Two nights later, Reggae Mill is transformed once again into Kingston's premiere party venue for Fridays at the Devon, regularly attracting A-listers to the VIP section and a solid crowd throughout.

A bar with turntables, old-school reggae on the speakers, and lava lamps, **East Japanese Next Door** (adjacent to East Japanese

Restaurant, Market Place, 67 Constant Spring Rd., tel. 876/960-3962) is serving Kingston's best Japanese food from the full-service sushi bar and restaurant next door. Don't miss Beer Mug Fridays, when patrons pack the venue and spill out into the courtyard outside with guest selectors spinning reggae and dancehall from every era.

Macau Gaming Lounge & Bar (28 Lindsay Crescent, tel. 876/925-6395) has a large gaming lounge on the ground level and an open-air bar upstairs serving light food and dinner items.

A popular watering hole within the Acropolis gaming lounge at Barbican Centre, **Ribbiz Ultra Lounge and Restaurant** (Acropolis, Barbican Centre, cell tel. 876/410-7637, noon-3am Mon.-Thurs., noon-5am Fri.-Sun.) draws a regular crowd of well-watered Uptown Kingstonians, some of them such regular patrons they consider it their second home. Proprietor Ribbi Chung is almost always on location, nursing a rum and building the vibes. Ribbiz hosts themed parties for each day of the week, the crowd favorites being Big People Sundays; Mixology Mondays, featuring various selectors; and 2-for-1 Thursdays for women.

Owned by Caribbean Producers Jamaica, one of the island's leading food and beverage importers and distributors, **Cru Bar & Kitchen** (71 Lady Musgrave Rd., tel. 876/633-5975, cell tel. 876/579-9362, 4:30pm-12:30am Tues.-Fri. 7pm-2am Sat.) is a go-to hangout for young professionals, who stop by the rooftop watering hole in droves on their way home from work. Especially popular on Friday evenings, Cru boasts a smart modern ambiance with premium drinks, wines from the CPJ portfolio, and finger food.

100 (100 Hope Rd., tel. 876/665-3238, contact@islandbet.com, 24 hours daily, kitchen closes midnight Sun.-Thurs., 4am Fri.-Sat.) is a gaming lounge, restaurant, and bar with an open-air thatch-roofed bar and nightclub (8pm-2am Fri.) upstairs that hosts live music on occasion.

Waterfalls (160 Hope Rd., tel.

The Life and Legacy of "Miss Lou"

The life of Louise Bennett Coverley (1919-2006) spanned an evolution in the identity of the Jamaican people. Born in Kingston, she was raised in the pre-independence tumult of Jamaica's emerging Labour Movement, whose leaders were agitating for racial equality. Miss Lou became an outspoken poet, social commentator, and performer at an early age, converting thick patois—considered at the time the language of the illiterate underclass—into a national art form and a source of pride. Miss Lou began publishing books in Jamaican Creole in the early 1940s before pursuing opportunities in London to further her performance career. She brought Jamaican folk culture to media and stages around the world, giving voice to a nation yearning for independence and a new identity.

Jamaican folk culture is based overwhelmingly in African traditions, and in bringing her stories and poems into performance and literary forms, Miss Lou validated an integral part of the country's heritage that had for centuries been scorned. With her warmth and lyrical genius, Miss Lou dispelled the taboo associated with this rich heritage. When Jamaica gained its independence in 1962, Miss Lou's popularity was further cemented as an ambassador for the country's identity in the new postcolonial era. Miss Lou was a founding member of the Little Theatre Movement and was instrumental in the development and popularity of the performing arts in Jamaica.

876/977-0652 or 876/622-5167, www.waterfallsjamaica.com) is a banqueting facility that does functions and opens as a nightclub (9pm-3am Thurs., US$7) for oldies featuring the Merritone Disco sound of the late Winston "Merritone" Blake, carried on by his brother Monty, with a mixture of reggae, calypso, and hip-hop from the 1960s to modern times. It's one of the few places in Kingston that catches the vibe of a 1960s dancehall, with the crowd skanking to ska, rocksteady, R&B, and reggae classics well into the night. The cover charge includes complimentary soup.

One of the top nightclubs in Kingston for weekend parties, **Skydweller Ultra Lounge** (7-9 Ardenne Rd., tel. 876/627-4262, 7am-1am Mon.-Thurs., 7am-4am Fri., noon-4am Sat., 5pm-1am Sun.) is especially packed on Friday nights. The kitchen whips up breakfast, lunch, and dinner, with Jamaican and continental fare until 10pm and finger food until 1am.

PERFORMING ARTS
Theater

Jamaica has a vibrant tradition in theater, pantomime, and spoken word performances, with annual shows and competitions sponsored by the **Jamaica Cultural Development Commission** (www.jcdc.org.jm). Events are held throughout the year but come to a head during the weeks around Emancipation and Independence in early August. Jamaica's theater scene includes occasional classic productions, dramas written by local playwrights, and roots plays, a unique brand of slapstick presented in a mix of English and thick patois, Jamaica's local dialect.

Little Theatre Movement, the Little-Little Theatre, and the **National Dance Theatre Company** (4 Tom Redcam Ave., tel. 876/926-6129, www.ltmpantomime.com) share a theater on the edge of Downtown. **Dance Theatre Xaymaca** (dancetheatrexaymaca@gmail.com) also performs here in late October. Plays run throughout the year; call for details on performances. Pantomime performances run December 26 to early May, with school plays after that. The National Dance Theatre performs July-August. Henry Fowler, Rex Nettleford, Barbara Gloudon, Louise "Miss Lou" Bennett, Oliver Samuels, and Ken Hill are some of the founding members of Jamaica's Little Theatre Movement.

The **Louise Bennett Garden Theatre** and the **Ranny Williams Entertainment Centre** (36 Hope Rd., tel. 876/926-5726, hrd@jcdc.gov.jm, www.jcdc.gov.jm) host occasional plays and concerts as well as bingo, book launches, and barbecues a couple of times a month. **Phillip Sherlock Centre for the Creative Arts** (UWI Mona, tel. 876/927-1456) puts on dance and theatre productions, including those of the student dance society. **Ward Theatre** (North Parade, Downtown, tel. 876/922-0360 or 876/922-0453) holds occasional plays, pantomimes, and special events.

Pantry Playhouse (2 Dumfries Rd., tel. 876/960-9845, US$15 -20) features comical productions throughout the year in a quaint outdoor setting in the heart of New Kingston. Plays usually run for three months, and performances are generally held Wednesday-Sunday. The outdoor amphitheater at **Edna Manley College of the Visual and Performing Arts** (1 Arthur Wint Dr., tel. 876/754-8830) hosts poetry readings at 7:30pm the last Tuesday of every month; regular dance performances are held in the indoor theater next door.

Dance

A full-time dance company that travels frequently and does "edutainment" projects in schools across the island, **The Ashe Company** (contact director Conroy Wilson, tel. 876/960-2985 or 876/997-5935, asheperforms@gmail.com) has regular performances throughout the year. **Movements Dance Company** (Liguanea, contact director Monica Campbell, cell tel. 876/999-7953, maccsl@cwjamaica.com) is one of Jamaica's most dynamic and versatile dance companies. Both traditional Jamaican and Caribbean rhythms inform the company's repertoire. The schedule of performances climaxes each year with the annual Season of Dance in November. The company also travels abroad to perform. **Dance Theatre Xaymaca** (dancetheatrexaymaca@gmail.com) is one of Kingston's leading troupes, performing seasonally at the Little Theatre.

Comedy

Brainchild of Jamaica's leading comedian Christopher "Johnny" Daley, **Johnny Live Comedy Bar** (Phoenix Theatre, 8 Haining Rd., cell tel. 876/566-9017, 8pm-11:30pm Tues., cover US$10) has regular shows every Tuesday and occasional special events on other nights.

GAMBLING

Gambling became legal in Jamaica in 2012 as part of large new resort developments, but "gaming" was never restricted for those over age 18. Video Gaming Machines are found throughout the island thanks mostly to Supreme Ventures, with several locations in Kingston to play the odds against a computer. The most popular gaming lounges uptown include **100** (100 Hope Rd.), **Acropolis** (Loshusan Plaza, 29 E. Kings House Rd., tel. 876/978-1299, 1pm-1am Mon.-Thurs., 1pm-3am Fri.-Sat., 10am-1am Sun.), **Monte Carlo Gaming** (Terra Nova Hotel, 17 Waterloo Rd., tel. 876/926-2211, 11am-4am Mon.-Fri., 11am-6am Sat.-Sun.), and **Treasure Hunt Gaming** (14-15 Trinidad Terrace, tel. 876/929-2938, 24 hours daily).

Caymanas Park (racing@cwjamaica.com, www.caymanasracetrack.com) is a horse track recognized as one of the best in the Caribbean. Races are held on selected Wednesdays and Saturdays, with the occasional Monday race, and are usually well attended. Admission ranges US$0.50-4, depending on seating. A large network of OTB sites offer simulcast races from around the world when races aren't on at Caymanas.

Shopping

Kingston is full of shopping plazas and strip malls. Half Way Tree has the highest concentration of shops in Jamaica, along the stretch of Constant Spring Road running between Hope Road and Market Place.

ART STUDIOS AND GALLERIES

Located upstairs from the unassuming framing shop Herman runs on the ground floor, **Amai Craft** (shop 27, Red Hills Trade Centre, 30 Red Hills Rd., tel. 876/920-9134, vanasherman@gmail.com, 10am-5pm Mon.-Fri., 10am-2pm Sat.) specializes in paintings by Jamaican, Haitian, and Cuban intuitive, or self-taught, artists.

Grosvenor Galleries (1 Grosvenor Terrace, Manor Park, tel. 876/378-5807, grosvenorgallery@cwjamaica.com, 10am-5pm Tues.-Sat.) has contemporary art exhibits and occasional craft fairs that bring artists and craftspeople from around Jamaica. An on-site café (11am-7pm Mon.-Fri., 10am-6pm Sat.) serves salads, sandwiches, and smoothies with outdoor seating.

Island Art & Framing (Orchid Village, 20 Barbican Rd., tel. 876/977-0318, islandart@cwjamaica.com, www.iafjamaica.com, 10am-6pm Mon.-Sat.) sells a wide variety of local and imported arts and crafts and paintings by an array of talented contemporary artists.

Sanaa Studios (25 Barbican Rd., behind Burger King, tel. 876/977-4792, info@sanaastudios.com, www.sanaastudios.com, 10am-5pm Mon.-Sat.) offers classes in ceramics, drawing, painting, art photography, and jewelry making. A small gallery has a steady flow of exhibits featuring student art and an end-of-year art bazaar. Drop-in rates are US$40 for three-hour sessions.

NLS (190 Mountain View Ave., contact executive director Deborah Anzinger, tel. 876/927-7931, cell tel. 876/406-9771, www.nlskingston.org, by appointment only) is a contemporary visual arts gallery associated with recording studio and production house Creative Sounds, on the same premises.

Housed in a uniquely designed apartment building commissioned by A. D. Scott in the 1960s, **The Art Centre** (202 Hope Rd., across from the University of Technology, tel. 876/927-1608, artcentre.ja@gmail.com, 9am-5pm Mon.-Fri., 10am-4pm Sat., free) has colorful murals adorning the interior walls and art displayed on the upper two levels as part of the building's permanent collection. The gallery uses the ground floor space for occasional temporary exhibits.

DEVON HOUSE SHOPS

The courtyard at **Devon House** (26 Hope Rd., at Trafalgar Rd.) is home to an assortment of boutiques, pastry shops, and restaurants. **Starfish Oils** (tel. 876/908-4763, www.starfishoils.com) is one of Jamaica's leading cottage industries, producing soaps, oils, and candles as compact gift items or for everyday use. These products are provided in many of Jamaica's high-end hotels. Starfish also has an outlet in Manor Park Plaza. **T's and Treasures** (shops 3 and 4, tel. 876/632-2961, 11am-7pm Mon.-Sat., 4pm-7pm Sun.) sells books on travel and culture, cultural DVDs, paintings, souvenirs, apparel, and trinkets. **Things Jamaican** (shops 12-14, tel. 876/926-1961, www.thingsjamaicanstores.com, 9am-8pm Mon.-Fri., 10am-8pm Sat., noon-8pm Sun.) sells crafts, books, and creative gift items, all made in Jamaica.

CLOTHING AND ACCESSORIES

Mutamba (tel. 876/387-4112 or 876/320-1209, by appointment only), a clothing line developed by outspoken Jamaican Pan-Africanist dub poet Mutabaruka and his wife, Amber, is popular for its minimalist, chic aesthetic.

Bridget Sandals (90 Hope Rd., tel.

Caribbean Fashion Week

Jamaica's contribution has been central to a bourgeoning Caribbean fashion industry, and during the first half of June, **Pulse Global** (38-A Trafalgar Rd., tel. 876/960-0049, www.pulseworld360.com) hosts the annual Caribbean Fashion Week (CFW) event, now considered one of the most important fashion trends on the planet. The week is filled with fashion shows, parties, and some of the world's most striking women clad in creative attire designed by imaginative talent. It's definitely one of the best times of year to be in Kingston.

Pulse has found great success in attracting a corps of young model hopefuls, mostly from Jamaica, and giving them a chance on the world stage. The most successful have been featured in *Sports Illustrated* and *Esquire* (Carla Campbell), *Vogue* (Nadine Willis and Jaunel McKenzie), and *Cosmopolitan* (Sunna Gottshalk). The younger generation of models includes Alicia Burke (Ralph Lauren, Bobbi Brown, Gucci, Laura Mercier), Francine James (*Vogue, Elle,* Bobbi Brown, Modern Luxury) and Jeneil Williams (*Vogue,* H&M, Macy's, *Allure,* Gap).

Model Kayla Innis rocks Jafrican at Pulse 360's Caribbean Fashion Week at Villa Ronai in Stony Hill above Kingston.

CFW events are held at numerous venues around the capital but mostly at Pulse's Villa Ronai in the suburb of Stony Hill. Fashion Week attendees descend on Kingston amid the tangible buzz created by an invasion of models, fashion media, and increasingly, designers from the United States and Europe coming to catch a glimpse of the latest unabashed creations spurring trends across the globe.

876/968-1913, www.bridgetsandals.net, 10am-6pm Mon.-Sat., US$80-150) sells thong, strappy, and open-toe sandals. The unique and tasteful handcrafted leather footwear for women has a tremendous following. Founder Bridget Brown and son Jonathan Buchanan run the shop.

Lee's Fifth Avenue (Tropical Plaza, Half Way Tree, tel. 876/926-7554, www.leesfifthavenue.com, 10am-7pm Mon.-Sat., 11am-4pm Sun.) sells quality trendy brand-name clothes.

Loran-V Boutique (shop 2, Northside Plaza, 26 Northside Dr., off Hope Rd., tel. 876/977-6450, loran_v_swimwear@yahoo.com, 9am-5pm Mon.-Fri., 10am-2pm Sat.) makes swimwear and light apparel on-site for men and women, with a handful of women at sewing machines churning out well-designed bikinis and trunks.

Kerry manwomanhome (18 South Ave., tel. 876/929-1969, www.kerrymanwomanhome.com) is one of Kingston's top boutiques for locally produced garments, jewelry, and books for him and her. Kerry-Ann Clarke, the fashion aficionado proprietor, is a graduate of Parsons School of Design.

Sobelio Boutique Shop (Sovereign North, cell tel. 876/631-2114 or 876/779-2885, sobelioboutique@gmail.com) sells casually elegant free-flowing dresses dubbed fun, flirty, and fabulous.

Swiss Stores (107 Harbour St., tel. 876/922-8050) sells a wide selection of watches and jewelry, duty-free for visitors.

BOOKSTORES

Kingston Bookshop has several locations around town (70-B King St., tel. 876/922-4056; 74 King St., tel. 876/922-7016; Pavilion Mall, 13 Constant Spring Rd.; shop 6, Boulevard

Shopping Center; shop 2, The Springs, 17 Constant Spring Rd.) that carry Jamaican and Caribbean titles as well as imports. It's also a major force in Jamaica's textbook market. Downtown stores operate 9am-5pm daily; Uptown stores 9am-6pm daily.

Bookland (53 Knutsford Blvd., New Kingston, tel. 876/926-4035, 10am-6pm Mon.-Fri., 10am-4pm Sat.) has the best selection of Caribbean and Jamaican books and magazines, as well as souvenirs.

Sangster's Book Stores (several locations, tel. 876/758-6840, info@sangstersbooks.com, www.sangstersbooks.com) is another major chain with several locations around town. See their website for their many locations.

With a great selection of books and magazines, **Bookophilia** (92 Hope Rd., tel. 876/978-5248, 11am-8pm Mon.-Thurs., 11am-9pm Fri., 10am-7pm Sat., noon-5pm Sun.) also has a small kiosk in the corner of the cozy shop that serves Blue Mountain coffee, tea, cookies, and muffins (US$1-3). The signature drink is the Gingerbread Chai Latte (US$3). A world-beat night is held 6pm-9pm the last Friday of every month. Bookophilia lures first-time customers with a free cup of coffee.

Bolivar Bookshop & Gallery (1-D Grove Rd., tel. 876/926-8799) is a nice boutique with a small art gallery and more rare books than can be found at the other bookstores in town.

Headstar Books and Crafts (54 Church St., tel. 876/922-3915, headstarp@hotmail.com) is an Afrocentric bookshop run by Brother Miguel.

RECORD SHOPS

Rockers International Records (135 Orange St., www.rockersinternational.com, 9am-4pm Mon.-Sat.) specializes in reggae and has CDs and LPs, 33s, and 45s, with the latest domestic singles and imports. The shop is run by Addis Pablo, son of the late, great Augustus Pablo.

A holdout from a bygone era when vinyl was the norm, **Cap Calcini** (58 Dunbarton Ave., cell tel. 876/268-4651, 8am-6pm Mon.-Sat.) has thousands of vinyl 45s and 33s sold at wholesale prices with both vintage and contemporary recordings, leaning toward oldies. The vast majority of the shop's sales are exported to feed a growing demand for that vintage reggae sound only a record can produce. The limited local market benefits from this brick-and-mortar outlet, where patrons can don a pair of headphones and sample the sounds before making a purchase.

Music Mart (8 South Ave., tel. 876/926-4687, www.musicmart.biz, 9:30am-5pm Mon.-Thurs., 9:30am-6pm Sat.) sells CDs, DVDs, and instruments, including traditional Jamaican Maroon gumbe and Rasta base, fundeh, and akete drums.

Derrick Harriott's One Stop Record Shop (shop 36, Twin Gates Plaza, Constant Spring, tel. 876/926-8027, derrickchariotharriott@hotmail.com, 10am-6:30pm Mon.-Sat.) has a good selection of oldies as well as the latest LPs and 45 singles.

Tad's International Records (Unit 40, Trade Centre, 30-32 Red Hills Rd., tel. 876/929-2563, tadsrecordinc@cwjamaica.com, tadsdigidis@gmail.com, www.tadsrecord.com) has an extensive catalog of reggae from the early days of Gregory Isaacs, Dennis Brown, and John Holt, and more contemporary Terry Linen, Cecile, Teflon, Anthony B, and Vybz Kartell.

ARTS, CRAFTS, AND GIFTS

A good place for authentic Jamaican arts and crafts is **Craft Cottage** (Village Plaza, 24 Constant Spring Rd., tel. 876/926-0719, 9:30am-5:30pm Mon.-Thurs., 9:30am-6pm Fri.-Sat.).

For souvenirs, the **Crafts Market** (Ocean Blvd. and Port Royal St., 7am-6pm Mon.-Sat.) features some authentic Jamaican crafts as well as an ever-increasing slew of trinkets, T-shirts, and towels imported from China.

The open-air **Market at the Lawn** (10am-5pm last Sun. every other month) is held on the north lawn of Devon House (26 Hope Rd.) and features a variety of food, fashion, art, and craft vendors. Contact Kaili McDonnough-Scott (cell tel. 876/585-7233, thelawnkingston@gmail.com) for more information.

Original Bamboo Factory (Caymans Estate, Spanish Town, tel. 876/746-9906 or 876/869-6675, hamilton1@cwjamaica.com or bamboojamaica@gmail.com, www.originalbamboofactory.com) has what you need if you're in the market for bamboo furniture or just want to see how it's put together. The bamboo factory also offers low-key tours (US$10 pp).

Fusing together starting at West Parade and running along West Queen Street and Spanish Town Road to Darling Street, **Jubilee and Coronation Markets** are worth a visit to browse the stalls, renowned for touting the best bargains in town on produce and just about anything else. It's not the place for high-end gear, but the experience is gritty Jamaica at its best—with all the accompanying smells. While it's most comfortably enjoyed accompanied by a local, there is no danger to going unaccompanied as long as you can handle unsolicited attention from hagglers seeking a sale. If you're a woman, it's guaranteed the market men will approach you with romantic interest.

Recreation

Kingston has plenty of options to get some exercise, with hiking, golf, tennis, and even surfing all within 20 minutes of the city center.

The National Stadium hosts the most important sporting events on the island, including the home games of the national soccer teams **Reggae Boyz** (www.thereggaeboyz.com) and **Reggae Girlz** (www.reggaegirlzfoundation.com), as well as track and field events. Next door at the **National Arena** and the **Indoor Sports Centre,** several trade shows and events are held. For more information contact the **Jamaica Football Federation** (20 St. Lucia Crescent, tel. 876/929-0484 or 876/929-8036, jamff@hotmail.com).

Sabina Park, located Downtown on South Camp Road, hosts home games for the West Indies cricket team (www.windiescricket.com). The **Jamaica Cricket Association** (tel. 876/967-0322 or 987/922-8423, jcacricket@hotmail.com, www.jamaicacricket.org), based at Sabina, controls the sport on the island.

GOLF

Kingston's most reputable golf course is **Caymanas Golf & Country Club** (Mandela Hwy., tel. 876/746-9772 or 876/746-9773, www.caymanasgolf.com, greens fees US$50 Mon.-Fri., US$55.50 Sat.-Sun. and holidays, cart US$22.50), west of town. Designed by Canadian architect Howard Watson in 1958, the course features elevated greens with lush fairways cut through limestone hills. The views from the tees are excellent, with guango trees providing natural obstacles and occasional shade. A restaurant and bar on-site welcome members and nonmembers alike.

Constant Spring Golf Club (152 Constant Spring Rd., tel. 876/924-1610, csgc@cwjamaica.com, greens fees US$45Mon.-Fri., US$50 Sat.-Sun., cart US$20) is a more humble par-70 course in the middle of Uptown Kingston. Built by Scottish architect Stanley Thompson in 1920, the short, tight course is challenging, with an excellent view at the 13th hole. Clubs (US$35) are available from the pro shop (tel. 876/924-5170) and a caddy costs US$13.50. Canadian National Railways built a magnificent hotel just below the course, parallel to the 18th hole fairway, which was long ago converted into the Immaculate Conception High School, one of Kingston's most prestigious.

RACKET SPORTS

Kingston has a very active tennis scene with a great mix of short-term visitors, expats, and locals meeting on the courts.

Across from the Courtleigh Hotel, **Liguanea Club** (80 Knutsford Blvd., tel. 876/926-8144, liguaneaclub@cwjamaica.com) has squash, billiards, and tennis, plus an outdoor swimming pool. Nonmembers can use the tennis facilities for US$30 per hour. This is the most popular racket club in Kingston, with well-maintained courts, an excellent on-site restaurant, and affordable accommodations.

Formerly the Jamaica Lawn Tennis Association, **Tennis Jamaica** (2A Piccadilly Rd., court bookings Sheron Quest, tel. 876/929-5878 or 876/906-5700, www.tennisjamaica.org, 6am-6pm daily, US$4.50 per hour 6am-4pm, US$6.70 per hour 4pm-6pm) has courts and can set up partners. The organization sometimes holds tournaments. Heading toward Cross Roads on Half Way Tree Road or Old Hope Road, turn onto Caledonia Avenue at the light and then take a right onto Marescaux Road. After you pass the National Water Commission on the left, take the next right at the front entrance of L. P. Azar, a textile store. The courts are at the end of the road.

The **Jamaica Pegasus** (81 Knutsford Blvd., tel. 876/926-3690, ext. 3023, or ask for the tennis court, US$14 per hour day, US$19 per hour night) has well-maintained lighted courts. Court fees cover a lesson for a single player, or the court for you and your partner. Tennis rackets (US$10) are included in some lesson fees.

POLO

The **Kingston Polo Club** (contact Lesley Masterton-Fong Yee, tel. 876/381-4660 or 876/922-8060, or Shane Chin, tel. 876/952-4370, chinrcpolo@yahoo.com) is located on the Caymanas Estate west of town off Mandela Highway. It can be reached by taking the same exit as for the Caymanas Golf & Country Club, about 100 meters (330 feet) west of the turnoff for Portmore. The Kingston Polo Club season runs early January to early August and is host to some of the highest-handicap polo played on the island, starting with the ICWI international women's team, ICWI 18 goal, and the NCB High International 15 goal tournament in May. Matches are held at 4pm Wednesday and 10am Sunday.

horse racing at Caymanas Park in neighboring Portmore

WATER SPORTS

Kingston's waterfront is finally coming to life with the refurbishment of Victoria Pier, bringing a third outpost of Gloria's from across the Harbour in Port Royal and a few lively bars. It's still no place for a swim, given the polluted waters of Kingston Harbour, but there are plenty of places beyond the harbor for a dip, including Port Royal, Cane River Falls, beaches along the coast east of town, Lime Cay, Fort Clarence, and Hellshire. Lime Cay and Fort Clarence have the cleanest stretches of sand in the area, though Fort Clarence is at times covered by Sargasso seaweed.

Surfing

If you're looking to catch some waves, don't miss **Jamnesia Surf Camp** in Bull Bay, where the most active members of the tight-knit **Jamaica Surfing Association** (tel. 876/750-0103, www.jamsurfas.webs.com) congregate. The association has raised the profile of Jamaican surfing in a commendable fashion, organizing events and contests at home and competing overseas with a national team. The family of patriarch Billy Wilmot continues to make waves in the sport. His daughter Imani Wilmot is featured in the 2019 documentary *Surf Girls Jamaica,* which chronicles how surfing is being used to empower young women in the community.

Boating

The **Royal Jamaica Yacht Club** (Palisadoes Park, Norman Manley Blvd., tel. 876/924-8685 or 876/924-8686, rjyc@flowja.com, www.rjyc.org.jm), located on the eastern side of Kingston Harbour between the Caribbean Maritime University and the international airport, holds regular regattas and yacht races. Yachters arriving in Jamaica should stay on their vessels once docked until cleared by quarantine, customs, and immigration officials.

Slips can accommodate vessels of up to 50 feet, while the visitors' dock can accommodate larger vessels. Fees are US$1.50 per foot for the first six days and US$1 thereafter; electricity, water, and fuel are charged according to usage. If you want to sign on as crew, make your interest known at the club. Yearly membership costs US$350. Visiting boats can moor in the harbor for US$12 per day (for two people, and US$2 for each additional crewmember) to use the club facilities, which include restrooms with showers, a swimming pool, a restaurant and bar, and Wi-Fi.

Sail Jamaica (contact instructor Scott

Royal Jamaica Yacht Club sailboat

Clarke, cell tel. 876/579-5291, scottsailtt@ gmail.com) offers sailing excursions on boats of varying sizes, from dinghies to an 87-foot sloop, available for day sails and charters (half-day from US$400).

Fishing

Local anglers go out to the California Banks, about 16 kilometers (10 miles) offshore from Port Royal. Nigel Black operates **Why Not Fishing Charters** (cell tel. 876/995-1142) from Grand Port Royal Hotel's marina. Other fishing expeditions can be arranged with Anthony DuCasse at **DuRae's Boat Sales** (18 Rosewell Terrace, tel. 876/905-1713, duraes@cwjamaica.com), a longtime supplier of powerboat parts, or his son Jody (cell tel. 876/383-8830).

SPAS AND FITNESS

The Jamaican hospitality industry is making a concerted effort to brand Jamaica as a premier health and spa tourism destination. In Kingston there are a few good options when it comes to affordable pampering.

Isabelle's Day Spa (Orchid Village, Barbican Rd., tel. 876/970-0025, reservations advised) is a highly recommended pampering parlor offering rigorous massage therapy as well as nail, skin, and makeup services.

Pandora Day (24 E. Kings House Rd., cell tel. 876/553-4720, pandoradayspa@ gmail.com, reservations required) offers facials, waxing, massage, Blue Mountain Coffee body scrubs, and salon and teeth whitening services.

Eden Gardens Spa (39 Lady Musgrave Rd., tel. 876/946-9981, 9am-6pm daily) offers facials, body massage, full body scrubs and wraps, oxygen therapy, and more (US$60-120).

Jencare Skin Farm (82 Hope Rd., tel. 876/946-3494 or 876/946-3497, jencarejender@yahoo.com) is a slightly more upscale day spa that offers complete bodywork, from nails (US$31) to facials (US$43) and massage (US$50). You can also get a haircut (US$10).

Just west of the Carib Cement factory, **Rockfort Mineral Spa** (Florizel Glasspole Hwy., tel. 876/938-6551, 7am-5:30pm Tues.-Sun., US$2.50 adults, US$1.50 children) has one of Kingston's few public swimming pools adjoined by a bathhouse. On the remains of a British Fort from which it gets its name, the baths are fed by mineral water from the Dallas Mountains. A large swimming pool outside is complemented by enclosed whirlpool tubs available for 45-minute sessions (US$14-31). The tubs are heated with electric heaters; by 10am, they're hot and ready for use. Additionally, the spa has a stress-management center offering 45-minute massages (US$35) and reflexology sessions (US$25).

Food

If there's anything to demonstrate that Kingston has a bona fide cosmopolitan side, it's the food. The city's offerings reflect the country's motto, "Out of Many, One People," with Indian, Chinese, and African influences deeply entrenched. Recent Lebanese and Japanese immigrants have also made their mark at a few recommendable restaurants. Of course, Jamaica's traditional fare, including jerked meats and seafood specialties, can also be found in abundance in Kingston. The price for a filling meal varies according to the venue, with traditional Jamaican staples available for as little as US$5.

DOWNTOWN
Bars, Restaurants, and Cafés

Besides selling watches and jewelry duty-free for visitors, **F&B DownTown** (Swiss Stores, 107 Harbour St., tel. 876/922-8050, www.fnbdowntown.com, 9am-5pm Mon.-Sat., US$9-20) has a refreshing café serving eggs to order and pancakes for breakfast, and for lunch, chicken teriyaki and shrimp salads, soup, sandwiches, and entrées that include pasta dishes, steak, and oxtail.

A waterfront bar that woos the Uptown crowd Downtown, **Ribbiz Ocean Lounge** (ground floor, Victoria Pier, Ocean Blvd., tel. 876/457-3121, noon to midnight daily) is more bar than restaurant, with indoor and outdoor seating. It gets bumping on weekends.

Gloria's Seafood City (Victoria Pier, Ocean Blvd., tel. 876/619-7905, 11am-10:30pm daily) is a branch of a long-standing fish restaurant based in Port Royal. Patrons don't come for quick service, but the fish, best enjoyed fried with spicy escoveitch sauce or steamed with okra, is worth the wait. Other menu items include lobster and shrimp, served in garlic sauce or jerked, with sides of bammy, festival, or rice-and-peas.

A takeaway location with much the same menu of traditional Jamaican fare as the original in Vineyard Town (6 Vineyard Rd., cell tel. 876/930-2112, US$8-12), **M10 Bar & Grill** (Victoria Pier, Ocean Blvd., 7am-4pm Mon.-Fri.) is a popular local eatery, with curried goat, oxtail, and fried chicken in an informal atmosphere. The menu changes daily. Breakfast items at Victoria's Pier include steamed callaloo, cabbage and ackee, and curried chicken liver or kidney. Lunch dishes include sweet and sour pork, fried chicken, curried goat, and cow foot and beans (from US$5).

Moby Dick Restaurant (3 Orange St., at Port Royal St. and Harbour St., tel. 876/922-4468, 10am-5:30pm Mon.-Sat.) is a landmark establishment and the best place to grab lunch Downtown. Moby Dick specializes in curry dishes accompanied by roti, with an ambience reminiscent of India: The cashier sits on a raised structure by the entrance with an overseer's view of the dining area. Seafood like shrimp and conch (US$15) as well as terrestrial staples like goat (US$10) are served with fresh fruit juices (US$3).

NEW KINGSTON

Cafés

Michael's Juice Garden (cell tel. 876/310-7948, 8am-8pm Mon.-Thurs. 8am-6pm Fri., 9am-5pm Sun., US$3-6) serves freshly blended natural juices, coconut water, ackee and saltfish, chicken wraps, and cheese and tuna sandwiches. Juices are seasonal and include june plum, soursop, star fruit, and otaheite apple.

24/7 Café (lobby at the Pegasus Hotel, Knutsford Blvd., tel. 876/926-3690, 24 hours daily, US$5-10) serves rotating soups like fish or red pea, salads, breakfast bagels with smoked marlin or salmon, paninis, wraps, chicken pot pie, and homemade fries. Coffee with scones, cookies, muffins, and cheesecake are sure to satisfy any sweet tooth. Wi-Fi is complimentary for customers.

The atmosphere is relaxing and cozy at **Cannonball Café** (shop 1, 3M Bldg., 20-24 Barbados Ave., tel. 876/754-4486, 7am-6pm Mon.-Fri.), which serves coffee, pastries and sandwiches (US$6), and dishes like beef lasagna (US$10), quiche (US$10), and salad (US$6). Try the scones with sweet cream and jam (US$5) with natural juices (US$4) or cappuccino (US$5). Wi-Fi is complimentary for customers.

Spanish Court Café (lobby at Spanish Court Hotel, 1 St. Lucia Ave., tel. 876/926-0000, 7am-11pm daily, US$5-10) serves pumpkin bisque, salads, sandwiches, paninis, and desserts like brownies, pudding, cheesecake, chocolate cake, and truffles. Wi-Fi is complimentary for customers.

Jerk

Sweetwood Jerk Joint (Emancipation Park, tel. 876/906-4854, sweetwoodja@yahoo.com, 11:30am-10pm Sun.-Thurs., 11:30am-midnight Fri.-Sat.) serves jerk pork (US$20 per pound), sausage, chicken (US$5 per quarter), lamb, conch, and roast fish, prepared on a coal-fired pit smoked with sweet wood and seasoned with scotch bonnet peppers.

Pepperwood (2 Chelsea Ave., tel. 876/906-0602, 11:30am-10pm Sun.-Wed.,

Kingston Street Food

While it is sometimes said that Jamaica's national dish is fried chicken from KFC, there are a host of authentically Jamaican fast-food joints to compete for that title, like Tastee Patties, Juici Patties, Island Grill, and Captain's Bakery. In fact, only a few international franchises have been able to survive in Jamaica; both McDonald's and Taco Bell were unable to stay viable. Others, like Domino's Pizza, Pizza Hut, Popeye's, and Subway, do relatively well in a few locations around town. Pan chicken, patties, and loaves have traditionally been the food of choice for Jamaicans on the go.

Pan chicken vendors set up all over town from evening until the early morning. Some of the best spots in town for real hot-off-the-grill pan chicken include the line of vendors on Red Hills Road just beyond Red Hills Plaza, heading toward Meadowbrook and Red Hills. You can also whiff the pan chicken as you approach Manor Plaza in Manor Park on the upper reaches of Constant Spring Road in the evenings. A few dependable **jerk vendors** hawk their fare in the evenings on the corner of Northside Drive and Old Hope Road by Pizza Hut, and they have a devoted following. Jerk pork (US$8.50 per pound) is sold on one side of the plaza and jerk chicken (US$3.50 per quarter) on the other.

11:30am-11:30pm Thurs.-Sat., US$4-8) serves jerk chicken and pork, accompanied by sides of festival, roasted breadfruit, sweet potato, and yellow yam. Steam roast fish fillet is also served in aluminum foil off the grill, along with spicy chicken and pork sausage.

Jamaican

The Pantry (2 Dumphries Rd., tel. 876/929-6804 or 876/929-4149, thepantry52@yahoo.com, noon-3pm Mon.-Fri., US$3-5) is a roadside takeout cook shop popular for lunch among the corporate crowd of New Kingston, serving Jamaican staples like fried chicken, brown stew fish, and curry goat.

International

Café Africa (2 Trafalgar Rd., cell tel. 876/828-4144, cafeafricaja@gmail.com, 9am-9pm Mon.-Thurs., 10am-10pm Sat., 11am-7pm Sun.) specializes in African dishes, both vegetarian and meat. The spot is also the de facto base for the United Negro Improvement Association, now presided over by the restaurant's proprietor, Stephen Golding, on the site of Marcus Garvey's original office of the Pan-African unity organization. A bust of Garvey stands at the site, commemorating the national hero.

Meat and Seafood

Celebrity chef sister duo Michelle and Suzanne Rousseau, made famous in their local food television program *Two Sisters and a Meal*, run ★ **Summerhouse at The Liguanea Club** (80 Knutsford Blvd., tel. 876/926-8144, liguaneaclub@cwjamaica.com, breakfast 7am-10:30am daily, lunch noon-3:30pm daily, dinner 7pm-9:30pm Wed.-Sat.). The setting has changed little since a young Sean Connery stopped off for a martini in the film *Dr. No*. The farm-to-table kitchen harnesses fresh local ingredients and Caribbean flavors. Don't pass up the homemade gnocchi, pappardelle, and salads. Summerhouse pushes the bar higher for destination dining in Jamaica and leaves the most demanding palate satisfied.

Serving steamed or fried fish, various shrimp dishes, curry or stewed conch, and lobster in season (US$20-23), **Phoenix Lounge at So So Seafood Grill & More** (4 Chelsea Ave., tel. 876/968-2397, 11am-midnight Mon.-Thurs., 11am-2am Fri., 11-1 Sat., 2pm-midnight Sun., from US$15) has finger food and a pleasant ambience with strings of lights and a little waterfall, reggae on the speakers. *So So* is a patois phrase that means "mostly." Crab night is Wednesday, and Campari specials are Friday, when a DJ plays music from 6pm.

★ **Redbones Blues Café** (Rooftop at the R Kingston Hotel, 2 Renfrew Rd., tel. 876/978-8262 or 876/978-6091, redbonesmanager@gmail.com, www.red-bonesbluescafe.com, noon-11pm Mon.-Fri., 6pm-11pm Sat.) has great food, ranging from linguine (US$17) to grilled lobster (US$50). The bar and lounge brings the spirit of New Orleans to Jamaica and is a dependable spot for live music. Events like album or book launches, fashion shows, poetry readings, and jazz or reggae performances are held virtually every week.

Asian

Dragon Gate (12 Trinidad Terrace, tel. 876/906-1288 or 876/906-1388, 11am-9pm Mon.-Sat., noon-9pm Sun., from US$7) has excellent fried fricassee chicken and rice, chow mein, curried shrimp, and chicken and broccoli.

Vegetarian

A vegan restaurant capable of convincing meat lovers to give up the flesh, ★ **Kushite's Vegetable Cuisine** (Eden Gardens, 39 Musgrave Rd., tel. 876/631-9101, thecateringkushites@gmail.com, from US$10) has entrées like North African hummus salad, pesto zucchini pasta, refried bean wraps with plantain chips, and London-style no-fish-and-chips.

HALF WAY TREE

Cafés

Well-prepared entrées, natural juices, and homemade pastries, while not inexpensive, are worth the cost at **Susie's Bakery & Coffee Bar** (shop 1, Southdale Plaza, behind Popeye's on Constant Spring Rd., tel. 876/926-2791, 9am-midnight Mon.-Fri., 7:30am-midnight Sat.-Sun., dinner from 6:30pm daily). The menu includes seafood penne, steak, and lamb chops (US$20-29). Indoor seating by the deli and a fresh salad bar complement the elegant courtyard seating next to the outdoor bar, with a lively schedule of theme nights throughout the week.

The only Jamaican franchise outlet of the Trinidad-based chain, **Rituals Coffee House** (shop 5, Village Plaza, tel. 876/754-1992, www.ritualscoffeehouse.com, 7:30am-7pm Mon.-Thurs., 7:30am-7:30pm Fri., 8am-9pm Sat., 10:30am-5:30pm Sun.) is a coffee shop serving espresso, lattes, cappuccinos, tea, pastries, pastas, salads, and sandwiches (US$3-10).

Jerk

The bar is open during regular business hours at **Jo Jo's Jerk Pit and More** (12 Waterloo Rd., tel. 876/906-1509 or 876/906-1612), which does lunch (Mon.-Wed.) with

East Japanese Restaurant

Jamaican staples, a grill day (noon-10pm Thurs.) that features barbecued ribs, homemade burgers, steaks, lamb and chicken, and the Jerk Pit (noon-10pm Fri.-Sat.), which serves jerk chicken, pork, lamb, and conch in addition to soups and sandwiches. The most popular nights are Tuesday (up-and-coming band night), Thursday (Karaoke night), and Saturday, which features the house band.

Truck Stop Grill & Bar (shop 9c, Market Place, 67 Constant Spring Rd., 3pm-midnight Sun.-Thurs., 3pm-2am Fri.-Sat., tel. 876/631-0841) is a popular bar and informal jerk joint with outdoor seating on barrel stools serving jerk chicken or pork (US$4-7); steamed, fried, or roasted fish; and jerk or garlic lobster (US$16 per pound). A beer costs around US$3.

Jamaican

Grog Shoppe Restaurant and Pub (Devon House, 26 Hope Rd., tel. 876/906-7165 or 876/908-4310, www.grogshoppejm.com, 11am-9pm Mon.-Sat., US$17-50) has a broad menu of soups, appetizers, and mains with Jamaican classics and comfort food done right. Try the smoked marlin salad on a fan of papaya followed by oxtail, curry goat, or fried escoveitch fish from the local menu, or more exotic dishes like grilled salmon with a brown sugar citrus ginger glaze.

Half Way Tree's best and most authentic sit-down eatery is **Sonia's Homestyle Cooking & Natural Juices** (17 Central Ave., tel. 876/929-2435, 7am-5:30pm Mon.-Fri., 7:30am-5pm Sat., 8am-5pm Sun., US$5-7.50), for Jamaican dishes like fried chicken, curry goat, and oxtail. Natural juices (US$1-2) like guava, cucumber, and soursop vary based on seasonal availability. The menu changes daily.

International

Just west of the junction of West Kings House Road and Constant Spring Road, the **Courtyard at Market Place** (67 Constant Spring Rd.) has become the premier international food court in Kingston. ★ **East Japanese Restaurant** (shops 50-51, tel. 876/960-3962, 5pm-10pm Tues., noon-10pm Wed.-Sun.) has authentic sushi at competitive prices (US$25 pp for a full meal) and an ambience that Jamaicanizes the traditional Japanese aesthetic. The food mixes a heavy dose of convincing traditional sushi, sashimi, and teriyaki with innovative Jamaican takes. Proprietor Taka is arguably the most successful restauranteur in Jamaica, with five restaurants in Kingston.

Saffron Indian Restaurant (shop 37 Market Place, 67 Constant Spring Rd., tel. 876/926-6598, 11:30am-10pm Mon.-Sat., 1pm-9:30pm Sun., US$20-30) serves North and South Indian dishes as well as Asian fusion, from grilled fish to tandoori shrimp and malai tikka chicken, accompanied by naan and parotha. **China Express** (shop 53, Market Place, tel. 876/906-9158 or 876/906-9159, noon-9:30pm Sun.-Thurs., noon-10pm Fri.-Sat.) has decent Chinese food in a cavernous setting. Items on the menu range from wonton soup to Cantonese lobster (US$34). It's a popular lunch location. **Dragon Court** (6 South Ave., tel. 876/920-8506, 11:30am-9:30pm daily) serves decent Chinese food ranging from chicken dishes (US$7) to lobster (US$29) and dim sum on Sunday.

With a massive pizza oven imported from Italy, it would be hard to find a more authentic pie in Kingston than at **La Pizzeria** (Devon House, 26 Hope Rd., tel. 876/906-7165 or 876/908-4310, US$8-16), an offshoot of the Grog Shoppe manned by Italian-Jamaican Max Pronel. Toppings range from classic margherita to jerk chicken and ital, topped with callaloo and ackee.

With an extensive wine list and well-trained staff providing attentive service, ★ **Opa! Greek Restaurant and Lounge** (Devon House, 26 Hope Rd., tel. 876/631-2000, cell tel. 876/550-2000, info@opajamaica.com, www.opajamaica.com, US$10-30) serves traditional dishes like moussaka, spinach spanakopita, souvlaki meat skewers, lamb shank, and inventive dishes mixing in Jamaican ingredients. The Reggae Mill bar at the same location hosts Fridays at the Devon, an open-air session that consistently draws a large crowd for a mix of hip-hop and dancehall.

Meat and Seafood

South Avenue Grill (20-A South Ave., tel. 876/754-1380) serves a blend of Jamaican and American food with an alleged Italian touch. The ambience is relaxing with open-air seating by a reflecting pool. The bar makes a decent margarita. Prices range from inexpensive, for a quarter chicken (US$6.50), to a bit pricey, for steak or lobster (US$26). **The Terra Nova Hotel & Suites** (17 Waterloo Rd., tel. 876/926-2211) has a lunch buffet popular with the business crowd. Sunday brunch (11am-4pm Sun., US$30) is also a hit with locals of means.

★ **Steak House on the Verandah** (Devon House, tel. 876/616-8833, noon-10pm Mon.-Sat., US$15-30) overlooks the central courtyard at Devon House, serving a varied menu that includes starters like tempura shrimp, chicken wings, pumpkin bisque, grilled salmon, rosemary herbed chicken breast, and fettuccine fungi alfredo, and of course tenderloin, rib-eye, and filet mignon grilled to perfection. Lighter items include Philly cheese steaks, burgers, and barbecue chicken sandwiches.

HOPE ROAD TO PAPINE
Cafés and Delis

The Deli at CPJ Market (71 Lady Musgrave Rd., info@cpjmarket.com, www.cpjmarket.com, 7am-8pm Mon.-Sat., US$8-15) serves soups and salads, sandwiches, pasta dishes, pastries, and coffee with indoor and outdoor seating and complimentary Wi-Fi. The market sells imported specialty foods, beer, and wine.

The atmosphere is relaxing and cozy at **Cannonball Café** (7am-7pm Mon.-Fri., 8:30am-7pm Sat., 9am-5pm Sun.), which has locations at Barbican Centre (shop 5, 29 E. Kings House Rd., next to Loshusan Supermarket. tel. 876/946-0983) and at Sovereign North (shop 8, tel. 876/970-1532).

The cafés serve sandwiches (US$8) and dishes like beef lasagna (US$10), quiche (US$10), and Greek salad (US$6) in addition to coffee (US$4), pastries, scones (US$5) with sweet cream and jam, and juices (US$4). Wi-Fi is complimentary for customers.

Serving Jamaica Blue Mountain Coffee, ★ **Café Blue** (shop 1A, Sovereign Centre, tel. 876/978-7790, cafebluesov@coffeetraders.com, www.jamaicacafeblue.com, 7am-8pm Mon.-Fri., 8am-5pm Sat.-Sun.) has pastries and light savory food and offers patrons complimentary Wi-Fi. Try the smoked marlin sandwich and rum cake paired with the Blue Mountain Fog (iced coffee with Sangster's Rum Cream).

Jamaican

One Love Café (Bob Marley Museum, cell tel. 876/630-1588, 9am-4pm Mon.-Sat., US$6-8) serves sandwiches, chicken, fish, veggie burgers, wraps, shakes, and smoothies.

★ **Chillin' Restaurant and Serengeti Bar** (Hope Zoo, Hope Rd., tel. 876/630-7183, admin@chillinrestaurant.com, www.chillinrestaurant.com, 4pm-11pm Tues.-Sat., from US$10) serves Jamaican staples like jerk chicken, jerk pork, pork chops, almond and pineapple crusted salmon, and oxtail served with rice-and-peas, sweet potato croquettes, seasoned fries, ripe plantain, and salad. Finger food includes chicken strips, wontons, and wings. Lush foliage encompasses the restaurant and bar at the center of the zoo, recreating a jungle atmosphere. A selector spins on Friday, and an amphitheater hosts occasional live performances.

International

On the top floor of a multiuse building, ★ **Sora Japanese Sky Cuisine** (9-11 Phoenix Ave., tel. 876/649-0131, 11:30am-11pm Mon.-Thurs., 11:30am-midnight Fri.-Sat., US$11-30) offers indoor seating with

---

1: masterful creation from Summerhouse at The Liguanea Club 2: a female black-billed streamertail hummingbird 3: Chillin' Restaurant and Serengeti Bar

Sweet Spots

Jamaican sweet potato pudding

HALF WAY TREE

- **Chocolate Dreams** (shop 2, Devon House, 26 Hope Rd., tel. 876/927-9574, www.chocolat-edreams.com.jm, 10am-7pm Mon.-Thurs., 11am-9pm Fri.-Sat., 2pm-8pm Sun.) retails delectable chocolate treats. All the chocolate treats are produced at the factory at 9 Roosevelt Avenue (better known as Herb McKinley Ave.), where there's also a retail store.

- **Scoops Unlimited** (Devon House, 26 Hope Rd., tel. 876/929-7028 or 876/926-0888, 11am-10pm daily, cones US$2-5, containers US$3.50-10) serves Devon House I Scream, which most Jamaicans rate as the country's best. It gets quite busy on Sunday, with a long line out the door into the courtyard.

- **Devon House Bakery** (next to Scoops Unlimited, Devon House, 26 Hope Rd., tel. 876/968-2153, 9:30am-6pm Mon.-Thurs., 9:30am-8pm Fri.-Sat., 11:30am-8pm Sun.) sells cakes, cookies, brownies, and pastries, as well as delicious flaky gourmet patties filled with chicken, fish, shrimp, or lobster (US$4-8).

HOPE ROAD TO PAPINE

- **Pastry Passions** (49A Hope Rd., Half Way Tree Transport Centre; Sovereign Centre, tel. 876/927-9105, pastrypassionshome@gmail.com, www.pastrypassions.com, 10am-9pm Mon.-Sat., 2pm-9pm Sun.) serves excellent pastries and coffee.

- **Tutti Frutti** (shop 1D, Barbican Centre, next to Loshusan, 29 E. Kings House Rd., tel. 876/946-9664, tuttifruttija@gmail.com, noon-10pm Mon.-Thurs., 10am-11pm Fri., 11am-11pm Sat.-Sun.) sells frozen yogurt and sorbet with a world of toppings by the pound in cups and cones. Another location can be found in the food court at Sovereign Centre.

UPPER CONSTANT SPRING TO STONY HILL

- **Candy Craze** (shop 1, Upper Manor Park Plaza, tel. 876/924-4881, sweetmsja@gmail.com, 11am-9pm Mon.-Thurs., 11am-10pm Sat., noon-10pm Sun.) sells ice cream and bulk candy.

- **Tutti Frutti** (Manor Centre, tel. 876/924-7077, tuttifruttija@gmail.com, noon-10pm Mon.-Thurs., 10am-11pm Fri., 11am-11pm Sat.-Sun.) sells frozen yogurt and sorbet in cups and cones with toppings by the pound.

air-conditioning and outdoor seating alfresco with views of the Blue Mountain foothills toward the northeast and New Kingston to the south. Delectable sushi rolls and sashimi are served in an enjoyable atmosphere with attentive service.

Lebanese restaurant **Chez Maria** (shop 3, 80 Musgrave Rd., tel. 876/927-8078, cell tel. 876/430-3822, chezmaria@cwjamaica.com, www.chezmaria.webs.com, 11:30am-10pm Mon.-Sat., noon-9pm Sun.) makes its own pita bread and decent Italian staples. Lebanese favorites include tabbouleh salad and hummus as well as entrées (US$9-18) like kebabs, shawarma, filet mignon, shrimp, and lobster.

Traditional Lebanese dishes at **Y.not.Pita** (71 Lady Musgrave Rd., tel. 876/927-7482, ynotpita@hotmail.com, 8:30am-9pm Mon.-Fri., 9am-9pm Sat., 9am-5pm Sun., US$5-15) include soups and salads, falafel, and hummus with pita chips as well as Jamaican and Mexican-style chicken, jerk, and curried chicken wraps.

Pita Grill (Orchid Village, 20 Barbican Rd., tel. 876/970-4571, www.pitagrilljamaica. com, 24 hours daily, US$5-11) is a Lebanese-leaning fast food joint serving munchie-killers like ham and cheese sandwiches, Philly cheese steak sliders, hot dogs, buffalo wings, and Middle Eastern traditional fare like beef kibbeh, tabbouleh, pita chips, and falafel. Pita Grill's breakfast wraps and pancakes help get the morning started right.

Aladin (shop 14, Liguanea Plaza, cell tel. 876/632-3711 or 876/528-9552, 10am-10pm daily, US$10-20) specializes in Lebanese food with falafel, hummus, tabbouleh, and kebabs.

Tea Tree Creperie (Unit 2, 80 Lady Musgrave Rd., tel. 876/978-7333, info@ teatreecreperie.com, www.teatreecreperie. com) serves sweet and savory crepes, coffee, tea, and spirited concoctions.

Chilitos (88 Hope Rd., tel. 876/978-0537, 11am-10pm Mon.-Thurs.) is a self-described "Jamexican" restaurant serving quesadillas, tacos, and burritos as well as mixed drinks. Taco Tuesday is the most popular night to visit, when tacos are just US$2.

★ **Uncorked!** (shop 2, Sovereign North, 29 Barbican Rd., tel. 876/632-5500 or 876/970-3406, delicious@uncorkedjamaica.com, www. uncorkedjamaica.com, 10am-10pm Mon.-Sat., 11am-7pm Sun., US$9-35) is a wine and cheese bar that has evolved into a full-fledged bistro with patrons spilling out onto the curb. The wide selection of wines, olives, and cheeses from around the world form the foundation for a varied Mediterranean menu. Bruschetta,

"Jamexican" tacos at Chilitos

pan-seared almond-crusted goat cheese, citrus garlic muscles, and baked brie are starters, with grilled flatbreads filled with meats, veggies, cheeses, or chipotle shrimp. Salads, burgers, paninis, and a creative rotation of specials round out the offerings.

Asian

In a modern plaza just off Hope Road, **Nirvanna Indian Fusion Cuisine** (shop 1A, 80 Lady Musgrave Rd., tel. 876/927-9077, www.nirvanna-jamaica.com, lunch 11am-3pm Sun.-Wed., 11am-3pm Thurs.-Sat., dinner 6pm-9:30pm Sun.-Wed., 6pm-10:30pm Thurs.-Sat., US$10-27) is decidedly high-end, with a white onyx bar imported from the motherland as its focal point. Booths and table seating cater to groups of various sizes. The menu features traditional Indian dishes as well as Asian fusion and creative renditions of local seafood.

A north Indian-Chinese fusion restaurant with smart, modern decor, **Tamarind** (shop 28, Orchid Village, 18-22 Barbican Rd., tel. 876/977-0695 or 876/702-3486, www.tamarindindiancuisine.com, 11am-9:30pm Mon.-Thurs., 11am-10pm Sat., 5pm-9:30pm Sun., US$12-30) has a delectable menu prepared by chefs from Delhi. The offerings include mutton biryani, spring rolls, fish Szechuan, noodles, fried rice, fish tikka, and the Tamarind tandoori platter of assorted kebabs.

The typical menu at **China Max** (shop 27, Orchid Village, 18-20 Barbican Rd., tel. 876/927-1888 or 876/927-1388, 11am-9:30pm Mon.-Sat., 12:30pm-9:30pm Sun., US$3-25) includes wontons, soups, shrimp, chicken, pork, fish, and lobster dishes. Try the delish whole crispy fried snapper with rice.

Jade Garden (shop 54-59, Sovereign Centre, tel. 876/978-3476, jadegarden.ja@gmail.com, noon-10pm Mon.-Sat., 11am-9pm Sun., US$12-40) serves MSG-free Chinese food with dishes like Peking duck, roast pork, and the signature pimento steak. Cantonese dim sum is a popular house specialty.

★ **Pushpa's** (Northside Plaza, tel. 876/977-5454 or 876/977-5858, www.

pushpa-ir.com, 11am-10pm daily, US$4-6.50) is by far the best restaurant in the complex and among the best Indian restaurants on the island, serving a mix of north and south Indian dishes, including *idli* on Sundays. Lunch specials include chicken dishes like *moghlai*, vindaloo, and *kurma*; vegetarian dishes like eggplant curry as well as mutton, shrimp, and fish are served either curried, fried, or vindaloo.

Meat and Seafood

The best place in town for rib fingers, tips, spare, and baby back ribs is ★ **Di Grill Shack** (9-11 Phoenix Ave., tel. 876/968-0125 or 876/960-4210, digrillshack@gmail.com, noon-9pm Mon.-Thurs., noon-10:30pm Fri.-Sat.). Chicken, fish, and lobster dishes are also served. The outdoor setting is pleasant for downing a beer with friends. Takeout and delivery are also offered.

Vegetarian

Jamaica Juice (shop 14, Sovereign Center tel. 876/354-2000, askdrjuice@jamaicajuice.net, www.jamaicajuice.net, 10am-9pm Mon.-Thurs., 10am-9:30pm Fri.-Sat., noon-8pm Sun., US$3-5) serves fresh juices, smoothies, and food items, most notably chicken or chickpea roti.

★ **New Leaf Vegetarian** (shop 6, Lane Plaza, 121 Old Hope Rd., tel. 876/977-2358 or 876/977-5243, newleafvegetarian1@gmail.com, www.newleafvegetarian.com, 11am-6pm Mon.-Sat., US$5-10) specializes in Trinidadian-style *doubles*—mild curried chickpeas wrapped in flatbread with spicy sweet cucumber relish and chutney—but the flavor doesn't stop there. Delicious creations include *chile sin carne*, falafel platter, and ackee bammy pizza, with fresh fruit blends and vegetable juices to wash it down.

UPPER CONSTANT SPRING

Cafés

Cannonball Café (Manor Centre, Manor Park, tel. 876/969-3399, 7am-7pm Mon.-Fri.,

9am-5pm Sat.-Sun.) prepares sandwiches (US$5), beef lasagna (US$9), quiches (US$9), and salad (US$7), in addition to coffee (US$3), pastries, scones (US$3.50), and juices. The atmosphere is relaxing and cozy; wireless internet is offered free for customers.

Jamaican

Michael's Restaurant & Coffee Shop (141B Constant Spring Rd., tel. 876/969-24037, 9am-7pm Mon.-Sat., 9am-4pm Sun.) serves Jamaican staples for breakfast, lunch, and dinner to a loyal clientele. It's your best bet in town for ackee and saltfish, boiled banana, and yam for breakfast any day of the week. Lunch items include fried or baked chicken, curried goat, and oxtail. The menu rotates daily.

Legendary cook shop ★ **Norma's** (31 Whitehall Ave., tel. 876/931-0064, ktapita@gmail.com, 8:30am-4:30pm Mon.-Sat.) has some of the best local fare, serving staples like curry goat, oxtail, and stewed chicken for takeout. You won't find better value in all of Jamaica; lunches come in small (US$4) or large (US$5-8). Seasonal juices (US$2-3) like carrot and orange, june plum, otaheite apple, and carrot punch are made fresh daily. Fish and shrimp are sometimes prepared. Call in advance to find out what's on the menu and to make sure it "nah sell-off" yet. The kitchen, around back, is filled with industrial pots and a flurry of activity.

Jerk

Next to the Constant Spring Golf Club, **PeppaThyme** (152 Constant Spring Rd., tel. 876/630-8131, noon-9pm Sun./Tues., 11am-11pm Wed.-Sat., closed Mon.) is a jerk pit serving jerk chicken (from US$5) and pork (from US$6) accompanied by festival, breadfruit, and rice-and-peas. The large open-air venue has a number of circular thatch-roofed eating areas and a large bar.

Seafood

In a great setting with fish tanks, nets, and strings of lights, **White Bones** (1 Mannings Hill Rd., at Constant Spring Rd., tel. 876/925-9502, 11:30am-11pm Mon.-Sat., 2pm-10pm Sun.) has excellent seafood to match. Appetizers start at US$8.50 and include raw or grilled oysters, soup du jour, and salads. Entrées include snapper fillet (US$20) and grilled snapper burger (US$12). The popular all-you-can-eat crab buffet (US$20) is on Thursday.

International

Tropical Chinese (Mid Spring Plaza, 134 Constant Spring Rd., tel. 876/941-0520, noon-10pm daily) serves entrées like chicken (US$8.50), shrimp with cashew nuts (US$16), steamed whole fish (US$28.50), lobster dishes (US$23.50), eggplant (US$7), seafood (US$17), and stewed duck (US$14). Tropical also has a branch at Barbican Centre.

Built on the success of Taka's East Japanese Restaurant, ★ **Majestic Sushi & Grill** (Villa Ronai, Old Stony Hill Rd., tel. 876/960-3594 or 876/564-1334, noon-10pm Tues.-Thurs. and Sun., noon-11pm Fri.-Sat., US$12-40) shares the top ranking for Japanese food in Jamaica. Decor and ambiance include low comfy lounge couches complementing table seating and a separate dining room next to the sushi bar. Lunch hour tends to be quiet, making it a good venue for business meetings.

Accommodations

Kingston is not known for its luxury rental villas or five-star hotels. Nonetheless, comfortable and affordable options abound. Most business travelers tend to stay in New Kingston or Half Way Tree for easy access to the corporate district. Spanish Court, The Courtleigh, and Terra Nova are business traveler favorites. For those with more down time, it may make sense to seek quieter options in residential neighborhoods or on the edge of town. Don't expect a lot of amenities for less than US$100. The higher end of the spectrum pushes US$300 for suites at a few hotels.

The outlying communities of the corporate area in St. Catherine don't have much in the way of inviting accommodations, with a strip of pay-by-the-hour dives along Port Henderson Road, commonly known as Back Road, in Portmore, and a few similar establishments in Spanish Town. None of these are recommended for a good night's sleep.

Airbnb has been widely embraced in Jamaica, with abundant inventory on offer throughout. The baseline standard is quite low, however, and prospective guests should be careful to stay at properties that have sufficient reviews to instill confidence.

Under US$100

A favorite among backpackers for its proximity to Half Way Tree, **Reggae Hostel** (8 Burlington Ave., tel. 876/920-6528 or 876/968-1694, www.reggaehostel.com, from US$25 pp shared room) is affordable and has a communal vibe where budget travelers meet, hang out, and explore the city. The hostel has private and shared bunk rooms with common kitchen and bath facilities.

Mayfair Hotel (4 Kings House Close, tel. 876/926-1610, mayfairjamaica@gmail.com, www.mayfairja.com, from US$70 for 2 single beds or 1 double), tucked away in the heart of Half Way Tree near King's House, has

41 units in a hotel block and in four stand-alone houses, each with five bedrooms sharing a common entrance and living area. Rooms have air-conditioning, hot water, and cable TV. On a large lawn there's a decent-size swimming pool, an independently run Jamaican restaurant, and a bar called The Pub. Nonguests are welcome to use the pool (US$5).

US$100-250

Jamaica Pegasus (81 Knutsford Blvd., tel. 876/926-3690, US$171 s or d, US$215 junior suite, includes breakfast) is a favorite for visiting and local bureaucrats and hosts local government and private sector functions in some of the largest conference facilities and ballrooms in town. A beautiful pool, a 24-hour deli, and tennis courts round out this premier New Kingston property.

A no-frills hotel and racket club in the heart of New Kingston, **The Liguanea Club** (Knutsford Blvd., tel. 876/926-8144, www.theliguaneaclub.com, from US$140) has rooms with kings, doubles, or twins, air-conditioning, en suite baths, cable, desks, and mini fridges. The courts are in good shape, as is the pool. In-house guests can use the tennis courts at no charge; nonguests pay US$30 per hour. On the veranda downstairs, **Summerhouse** is an excellent restaurant serving Caribbean fusion cuisine featuring local ingredients for breakfast, lunch, and dinner. The bar, where 007 stopped by for a martini in the first James Bond film, was recently refurbished, leaving it plush, cozy, and inviting.

Across from the Liguanea Club, **The Courtleigh Hotel & Suites** (85 Knutsford Blvd., tel. 876/929-9000, courtleigh@cwjamaica.com, www.courtleigh.com, US$207, presidential suite US$550) is a popular business hotel next to the Jamaica Pegasus. Rooms are modern, with mini fridges, cable TV, air-conditioning, and a 24-hour gym. Wi-Fi and continental breakfast are included.

The Knutsford Court Hotel (16 Chelsea Ave., tel. 876/929-1000, www.knutsfordcourt.com, from US$124) is situated within easy walking distance to New Kingston restaurants, bars, and nightclubs. The hotel offers amenities like a 24-hour business center, a gym, meeting rooms, two restaurants, and a bar. The rooms have standard amenities like phones and cable TV. Two townhouses in the courtyard have the property's best suites.

A good value is **Altamont Court** (1 Altamont Terrace, tel. 876/929-4497, altamontcourt@cwjamaica.com, www.altamontcourt.com, from US$142), where 57 standard rooms come with two doubles or one king. The Alexander Suite is a spacious and luxurious room with an expansive bath that has a tub and a separate shower. Wi-Fi is included in all rooms; there's a computer for guest use in the business center, which has three meeting rooms. A restaurant by the pool serves breakfast, lunch, and dinner.

Designed with extended stays in mind, every room above the standard category at **R Hotel Kingston** (2 Renfrew Rd., tel. 876/968-6222, info@rhotelja.com, www.rhotelja.com, from US$160 d) comes with a kitchenette, a balcony, and Wi-Fi. Flat-panel TVs have premium channels, and solar hot water, locally produced furnishings, and views of the hills, urban skyline, and Kingston Harbour provide an eco-friendly experience. Redbones Blues Café on the roof adds great food and a showcase for Kingston's vibrant arts scene. The busy calendar of events includes musical performances, poetry readings, and book launches.

Evocative of Miami, ★ **Spanish Court Hotel** (1 St. Lucia Ave., tel. 876/926-0000, www.spanishcourthotel.com, from US$180) is a chic and clean boutique hotel and with attentive service. Rooms are well appointed, with flat-screen TVs, warm and cozy decor, and comfortable bedding. It's a favorite of visiting businesspeople. The Spanish Court Cafe serves coffee, pastries, and light savory fare; the restaurant on the opposite side of the lobby serves well-executed meals for breakfast, lunch, and dinner. Both welcome nonguests.

A stylish boutique hotel operating as a bed-and-breakfast, **Eden Gardens Wellness Resort & Spa** (39 Lady Musgrave Rd., tel. 876/946-9981 or 844/446-3336, US$193-385) has wellness and business facilities a few

Spanish Court Hotel

blocks from the bustle of New Kingston in Liguanea. It has large, comfortable suites with functional desks and kitchenettes. Wireless internet is included, and the property has conference facilities, a pool, and a restaurant.

A nice boutique hotel with a country feel, **Alhambra Inn** (1 Tucker Ave., tel. 876/978-9072 or 876/978-9073, alhambrainn@cwjamaica.com, US$110 for 2 double beds, US$120 for 1 king, US$20 per extra person) is across Mountain View Avenue from the National Stadium and a five-minute drive from New Kingston and Downtown. Twenty spacious rooms with comfortable sheets and a lush courtyard make the inn a cool option where the air-conditioning is barely necessary, even in the summer. Bring soap and shampoo. Wi-Fi is available in the courtyard.

In a quiet and green setting in the heart of Liguanea, **The Gardens** (23 Liguanea Ave., tel. 876/927-5957, mlyn@cwjamaica.com, www.gardensjamaica.com, 1-bedroom US$105, 2-bedroom US$200) has seven two-bedroom townhouses. The townhouses have spacious living-dining rooms and full kitchens on the ground floor, with a master and second bedroom upstairs, each with a private bath. Guests can rent a single bedroom of the two-bedroom units for the lower rate. Wireless internet reaches most of the property. Air-conditioning and cable TV are in all bedrooms.

One32 Guest House (132 Barbican Rd., tel. 876/969-6439, cell tel. 876/816-5233, one-32jamaica@gmail.com, US$120-180) has two cozy self-contained studios, each suitable for up to two guests, and two two-bedroom apartments, accommodating up to four, giving the property maximum capacity of 12. A deck out back has a love seat, a dining table, a jetted tub, and a plunge pool.

Over US$250

A 130-room property catering to business travelers, **Courtyard by Marriott** (1 Park Close, facing Emancipation Park, tel. 876/618-9900, www.marriott.com, from US$440) has guest rooms with a king or a pair of queens, desks, flat-screen TVs, air-conditioning, and Wi-Fi. The pool deck and bar are on the second floor overlooking the park. Meeting rooms, a large open-format lounge and dining area, and its central location make the Courtyard an easy sell.

A second Marriott property in Kingston is **AC Hotel Kingston** (38-42 Lady Musgrave Rd., U.S. tel. 888/236-2427, from US$280), with rooms that include a complimentary minibar, bath amenities, and Wi-Fi, in addition to the plush bedding, air-conditioning, plasma TVs, and functional work desks.

Terra Nova All Suite Hotel (17 Waterloo Rd., tel. 876/926-2211, www.terranovajamaica.com) has comfortable rooms (US$207) with two double beds, junior suites (US$261) with minibars, executive suites (US$331) with whirlpool tubs and a bit more space, and three royalty suites (US$686) with balconies. Internet is included. Terra Nova has a great lunch buffet (US$22) with a different theme each day, and it offers one of the best Sunday brunch buffets (US$28) in town, with a mix of international and local food. The Regency Bar on the ground level is popular.

Information and Services

INFORMATION

The **Jamaica Tourist Board** (64 Knutsford Blvd., tel. 876/929-9200, www.visitjamaica. com, 8:30am-4:30pm Mon.-Fri.) has a small library with staffers available to assist with information on Jamaica's more popular attractions. The **Jamaica National Heritage Trust** (79 Duke St., tel. 876/922-1287, www. jnht.com) is located Downtown in the historic Headquarters House. The Trust can provide information on Heritage sights across the island. The **Survey Department** (23 Charles St., tel. 876/922-6630 or 876/922-6635, ext. 264, patricia.davis@nla.gov.jm) sells all kinds of maps.

Post Offices and Parcel Services

Post offices are located downtown (13 King St., tel. 876/858-2414, www.jamaicapost.gov. jm), Cross Roads (tel. 876/364-6316), and Half Way Tree (118 Hagley Park Rd., tel. 876/364-6119). Shipping services are available through **DHL** (19 Haining Rd., tel. 876/920-0010) and **FedEx** (40 Half Way Tree Rd.; 75 Knutsford Blvd., U.S. tel. 888/463-3339).

Telephone and Internet

The **Jamaica Library Service** offers internet access free of charge at all branches. The **Public Library** (Main Branch, 2 Tom Redcam Rd., tel. 876/928-7975 or 876/926-3315, ksapl@cwjamaica.com, www.jls.gov.jm) has a decent collection and allows visitors to check out books by leaving a deposit. Internet is available free of charge at a handful of computer terminals.

    Digicel (14 Ocean Blvd., tel. 876/619-5000) offers island-wide wireless cards for laptops on its plans. GSM SIM cards can be bought at any of its retail locations around town. **FLOW** (tel. 876/926-9700, U.S. tel. 888/225-5295) has a similar USB modem for US$65 and offers unlimited prepaid plans by intervals of 24

hours (US$5), weekly (US$15), or monthly (US$45), and plans for US$10 per month for 50 MB, US$15 for 100 MB, or US$25 per 1 GB.

POLICE AND IMMIGRATION

Police stations are located at Half Way Tree (142 Maxfield Ave., tel. 876/926-8184), Downtown Kingston Central (E. Queen St., tel. 876/922-0308), and Constant Spring (2-3 Cassava Piece Rd., tel. 876/924-1421). **Immigration** (8 Waterloo Rd., tel. 876/754-7422) is responsible for granting extensions of stays or processing the paperwork for visas.

HOSPITALS AND MEDICAL FACILITIES

UWI's **University Hospital** (Papine Rd., Mona, tel. 876/927-1620) has a good reputation and is probably the best public hospital in Jamaica. **Tony Thwaites** (University Hospital, Mona, tel. 876/977-2607) is UWI's private facility. **Andrews Memorial Hospital** is located at 27 Hope Road (tel. 876/926-7401, emergency tel. 876/926-7403). **Medical Associates Hospital and Medical Center** (18 Tangerine Place, tel. 876/926-1400) is a private clinic with a good reputation. It also has a pharmacy at the same location.

    Eye Q Optical (shop 10, Lower Manor Park Plaza, tel. 876/925-9298; Courtleigh Corporate Center, 8 St. Lucia Ave., New Kingston, tel. 876/906-1493) is the best spot in town to get your eyes tested or pick up a pair of prescription glasses.

Pharmacies

Andrews Memorial Hospital Pharmacy (tel. 876/926-7401, 8am-10pm Mon.-Thurs., 8am-3:30pm Fri., 9:30am-3:30pm Sun.) is at 27 Hope Road. **Liguanea Drugs and Garden** (134 Old Hope Rd., tel. 876/977-0066) and **Lee's Family Pharmacy** (86-B

Red Hills Rd., tel. 876/931-1877) are two other local pharmacies. **Fontana Pharmacy** (Barbican Square, tel. 876/946-2630, www. fontanapharmacy.com, 8am-10pm Mon.-Sat., 9am-9pm Sun.) is a large-format drugstore for prescriptions and a wide array of personal care products and basic groceries. **Monarch Pharmacy** (shop 23, Sovereign Centre, 106 Hope Rd., tel. 876/978-3495) fills prescriptions and sells personal care items, household products, and trinkets.

MONEY

ATM withdrawals are usually the most convenient way to get cash, but foreign transaction charges and poor exchange rates are drawbacks. Depending on the amount you are changing, a few dollars lost in fees and rates can be worth the convenience. All the major banks will cash traveler's checks, but lines are typically long, slow-moving, and overwhelmingly frustrating.

Western Union (main office 2 Trafford Place, tel. 876/926-2454) has offices all over the island, including in Kingston (Cross Roads, 20 Tobago Ave., New Kingston); Hi-Lo in Liguanea Plaza; BluMenthal in Lower Manor Park Plaza; and in Pavilion Mall (shop 30 upstairs, and Super Plus downstairs, Constant Spring Rd., Half Way Tree).

Currency Exchange

The best exchange rates are at **FX Traders** (U.S. tel. 888/398-7233), which has *cambios* at Cross Roads FSC (13 Old Hope Rd., 9am-5pm Mon.-Sat.); shop 7, Boulevard Super Centre (45 Elma Crescent, 9:30am-5:30pm Mon.-Sat.); King Street FSC, Woolworth Building (83 King St., 9am-5pm Mon.-Fri., 9am-3:30pm Sat.); K's Pharmacy, shop 17, Duhaney Park Plaza (10am-6pm Mon.-Fri., 10am-5pm

Sat.); Pavilion FSC, shop 30, Pavilion Mall (Constant Spring Rd., 9am-5pm Mon.-Sat.); and Park View Supermarket (7 Chandos Place, Papine, 8:30am-7pm Mon.-Thurs., 8am-8pm Fri.-Sat.).

Banks

Scotiabank has branches with ATMs Downtown (35-45 King St., tel. 876/922-1420), Cross Roads (86 Slipe Rd., tel. 876/926-1530), Liguanea (125-127 Old Hope Rd., tel. 876/970-4371), New Kingston (2 Knutsford Blvd., tel. 876/926-8034), Portmore (lot 2, Cookson Pen, tel. 876/989-4226), Bushy Park (tel. 876/949-4837), and UWI (tel. 876/702-2518). Some Scotiabank ATMs, namely at Barbican Centre and in New Kingston, allow you to withdraw U.S. dollars in addition to local currency.

First Caribbean has branches with ATMs in New Kingston (23-27 Knutsford Blvd., tel. 876/929-9310), Downtown (1 King St., tel. 876/922-6120), Half Way Tree (78 Half Way Tree Rd., tel. 876/926-7400; Twin Gates Shopping Centre, tel. 876/926-1313), Liguanea (129 Hope Rd., tel. 876/977-2595), and Manor Park (Manor Park Plaza, tel. 876/969-2708).

Sagicor Bank has branches with ATMs Downtown (134 Tower St., tel. 876/922-8195), New Kingston (17 Dominica Dr., tel. 876/960-2340), Half Way Tree (6C Constant Spring Rd., tel. 876/968-4193; Tropical Plaza, 12 Constant Spring Rd., tel. 876/968-6155), and Liguanea (Sovereign Centre, 106 Hope Rd., tel. 876/928-7524).

NCB has branches with ATMs Downtown (37 Duke St., tel. 876/922-6710), Cross Roads (90-94 Slipe Rd., tel. 876/926-7420), New Kingston (32 Trafalgar Rd., tel. 876/929-9050), and Half Way Tree (Half Way Tree Rd., tel. 876/920-8313).

Transportation

GETTING THERE
By Air

Norman Manley International Airport (KIN, tel. 876/924-8546, www.nmia.aero) is located on the Palisadoes heading toward Port Royal, east of Downtown. Domestic flights leave from a small terminal by the cargo area, reached by taking a left off the boulevard leading to the main terminal before reaching the roundabout. The airport has flights from North America on **Air Canada** (www.aircanada.com), **American** (www.aa.com), **Delta** (www.delta.com), **JetBlue** (www.jetblue.com), **Spirit** (www.spirit.com) and **WestJet** (www.westjet.com), and from Europe on **British Airways** (www.ba.com). The regional carriers flying to Kingston are **Aerogaviota** (www.aerogaviota.com), **Caribbean Airlines** (www.caribbean-airlines.com), **Cayman Airways** (www.caymanairways.com), **Copa Airlines** (www.copaair.com), and **InterCaribbean** (www.interCaribbean.com).

AirLink Express (Domestic Terminal, tel. 876/940-6660, reservation@flyairlink.net, www.intlairlink.net) offers charter service between any two airports or aerodromes on the island. **TimAir** (Domestic Terminal, tel. 876/952-2516, timair@usa.net, www.ti-mair.net) also offers air taxi service to Negril, Treasure Beach, Boscobel (St. Mary), Ken Jones (Portland), and Montego Bay.

Ground Transportation

The **Knutsford Express** (18 Dominica Dr., tel. 876/960-5499 or 876/971-1822, www.knutsfordexpress.com) is popular with Jamaicans and visitors alike, offering the most comfortable coach service between Kingston, Ocho Rios, and Montego Bay, with two or three daily departures from each city. New Kingston-Montego Bay (departs 6am, 9:30am, 2pm, and 5pm Mon.-Fri., 6am, 9:30am, and 4:30pm Sat., 8:30am and 4:30pm Sun., US$20

prepaid, US$23 day of travel) buses run between the parking lot behind New Kingston Shopping Centre and Pier 1 in Montego Bay. The trip lasts four hours, depending on traffic. There are few places you can't get to with the coach service; check the site for the latest destinations, and book online for discounted rates.

Buses ply routes around town and between Kingston and major points on the eastern side of the island. The main bus terminals for routes out of Kingston are the **Transport Centre** (tel. 876/754-2610) in the heart of Half Way Tree and the **Parade Downtown**. Buses depart throughout the day to Port Royal (US$0.50), Spanish Town (US$1), Bull Bay (US$0.50), Morant Bay (US$1.50), Mandeville (US$3), Port Antonio (US$3), Ocho Rios (US$3), Savanna-la-Mar (US$7), Montego Bay (US$6), and Negril (US$8).

Route taxis and **minibuses** depart from the roundabout on upper Constant Spring Road in Manor Park for destinations due north and at the roundabout in Papine for destinations in the Blue Mountains. Route taxis or minibuses depart for Kingston from virtually every city or town in the surrounding parishes and from parish capitals across the island. Route taxi fares are typically slightly higher than buses on the overlapping routes but don't typically connect faraway points.

GETTING AROUND
On Foot

Jamaicans who walk around Kingston generally don't do so by choice, day or night, and are ridiculed as "walk foots" by their fellow citizens. It's mainly due to the prestige of driving, and more importantly, the heat that pedestrians suffer. Traffic safety concerns around town are generally exaggerated, and being in a vehicle stopped at a light offers little protection anyway. There is really no better way to get to know the layout of some of the more congested areas like Downtown around the Parade, Knutsford Boulevard's Hip Strip, and around the center of Half Way Tree than to go on foot. Beyond that, route taxis and public buses are the best way for those without a car to get around.

By Bus

Jamaica Urban Transit Company (www.jutc.com, US$1-3) operates buses in and around the Corporate Area. Routes are extensive, but service and schedules can be daunting. Covered street-side bus stops are scattered along all the major thoroughfares throughout the city, and the more people that are gathered, the sooner you're likely to see a bus. This is definitely the most economical way to get around, and the yellow buses even offer service to and from the airport.

By Taxi

Route taxis are the most popular means of transportation across Jamaica, and apart from careening around corners and making sudden stops without using indicators, they tend to be relatively safe; kidnappings or muggings by taxi drivers are unheard of on the island. White Toyota Corollas, known locally as "deportees" or "Kingfish," tend to be used as shared taxis that can be stopped anywhere along their route, provided there's room to squeeze in another passenger. Route taxi rates are regulated (www.ta.org.jm), so drivers don't usually attempt to rip off unsuspecting passengers. Ask another passenger what the fare is if you're in doubt.

For trips around Kingston, call a dispatch service rather than trying to charter a route taxi if you're not traveling along a normal route taxi trajectory. Fares with dispatch services are assessed by distance rather than with a meter; ask for the "stamp," or fare, when booking a pickup so you know exactly what the trip will cost.

On Time Taxi (12 Burlington Ave., tel. 876/926-3866, cell tel. 876/309-8294 or 876/881-8294, www.ontimetaxijamaica.com) is Jamaica's leading dispatch taxi service, with countless affiliated drivers and usually the quickest response to pickup requests. **Gadgepro Taxi & Tours** (tel. 876/765-0200, cell tel. 876/434-3050 or 876/437-2021, gadgeprotrading@yahoo.com) also offers reliable service in well-maintained vehicles. **City Guide Taxi** (tel. 876/969-5458) is a decent and dependable service, offering airport pickups and service around Kingston and beyond. **Gevani's Transport** (Darlington Ave., cell tel. 876/448-2118, gevanitransportinc@gmail.com) offers VIP service in Wi-Fi enabled Mercedes Benz sedans with premium bars and drivers in a bow tie and jacket.

By Car

Rental cars tend to be very expensive across the island, but they are unfortunately indispensable when it comes to independently exploring remote areas. For the upper reaches of the Blue and John Crow Mountains, a 4WD vehicle is necessary. Pervasive potholes in the cities don't really warrant a 4WD. Check with your credit card company to see if it covers insurance.

Unlicensed rental operators abound. While they may be cheaper (US$50 per day) than more reputable agencies, there is less accountability in the event that anything goes wrong. These private rentals don't take credit cards, often want a wad of cash up front, and usually don't offer insurance. These informal agencies are best avoided.

Listed rates do not include insurance or the 16.5 percent GCT (sales tax). Insurance is typically US$15-40 daily, depending on coverage. A deposit is taken for a deductible when customers opt for anything less than full coverage. The use of select gold and platinum credit cards obviates the need to purchase insurance from the rental agency. Check with the establishment for their policies.

Island Car Rentals (17 Antigua Ave., tel. 876/926-5991; Norman Manley Airport, tel. 876/924-8075, icar@cwjamaica.com, www.islandcarrentals.com) has a wide range of vehicles from a Toyota Yaris (US$44 low season,

US$55 high season) to a Suzuki Grand Vitara (US$99 low season, US$109 high season).

Budget (53 S. Camp Rd., tel. 876/759-1793; Norman Manley Airport, tel. 876/924-8762, U.S. tel. 877/825-2953, budget@jamweb.net, www.budgetjamaica.com, 8am-4:30pm Mon.-Fri., 8am-10pm daily) has a range of vehicles from a Yaris (US$60 low season, US$75 high season) to a VW Passat (US$95 low season, US$120 high season).

Around Kingston

Kingston is the best base for exploring the metropolitan area, from Spanish Town to Greater Portmore, the Palisadoes, and even upper and eastern St. Andrew. Spanish Town, once the colonial capital, has an old iron bridge and historic square that are worth a quick visit but little else to keep visitors. The beaches of Greater Portmore, namely Fort Clarence and Hellshire, are the most popular in the Kingston area, the latter known for its seafood shacks and throngs on weekends. A few beachfront venues in the vicinity, like The Boardwalk and Waves Beach, are alternatives offering shade and seaside bars for a small entry fee.

Communities east along the coast include Harbour View and Bull Bay. The Palisadoes, a 16-kilometer (10-mile) stretch from the roundabout at Harbour View to the tip of Port Royal, is home to the Royal Jamaica Yacht Club, the Marine Research Institute, Norman Manley International Airport, Plumb Point Lighthouse, Port Royal, and, just offshore, a couple of cays popular with boaters and Sunday bathers.

The community of Harbour View, to the north and east of the roundabout at the base of the Palisadoes, was built on the site of Fort Nugent, originally constructed by a Spanish slave agent, James Castillo, and later fortified by Governor Nugent in 1806 to protect the eastern approach to Kingston Harbour.

PORT ROYAL AND THE PALISADOES

Part of Kingston parish, the Palisadoes is a thin stretch of barren sand, brush, and mangroves; it acts as a natural barrier protecting Kingston Harbour, with Port Royal at its western point. After Lord Cromwell seized Jamaica for Britain from the Spanish in 1655, Port Royal grew in importance, as the town's strategic location brought prosperity to merchants based there. The merchants were joined by pirates and buccaneers, who created one of the busiest and most successful trading posts in the New World. Imports included enslaved people, silks, silver, gold, wine, and salmon, while exports were mostly rum, sugar, and wood.

The British collaborated with the pirates as insurance against the Spanish, who were thought to be seeking revenge on the island's new colonial masters. The outpost flourished, with a local service economy growing alongside its bustling maritime commerce until June 7, 1692, when a massive earthquake left 60 percent of Port Royal underwater, immediately killing 2,000 people. Eight hectares (20 acres) supporting the principal public buildings, wharves, shops, and two of the town's four forts disappeared into the sea. Aftershocks rattled the city for months. In 1703 a fire devastated what remained of Port Royal, sending most survivors across the harbor to what soon grew into the city of Kingston. The town also sustained significant damage in the earthquake of 1907, and then again during Hurricane Charlie in 1951.

Sleepy Port Royal is worth a visit. The village is hassle-free and small enough to stroll leisurely around in a few hours. Scuba trips can be arranged from the Grand Port Royal Hotel. On weekends the square comes alive with a sound system and an invasion of Kingstonians, who come for the fish and beach just offshore at Lime Cay. Port Royal was the epicenter of the transatlantic slave trade until the devastating earthquake of 1692 sank most of the city. It has been nominated for UNESCO World Heritage status by the government of Jamaica and is on the tentative list.

Plumb Point Lighthouse

Protecting the approach to Kingston Harbour, **Plumb Point Lighthouse** was built in 1853 and has gone dark only once, during the earthquake of 1907. Sitting on a point named Cayo de los Icacos, or Plumb Tree Cay (a reference to the coco plum by the Spanish), it is constructed of stone and cast iron and stands 21 meters (70 feet) high. Its light is visible from 40 kilometers (25 miles) out at sea. The beach immediately west is known for its occasional good surf, as is the shoreline between Plumb Point and Little Plumb Point. The area is also known for its strong currents, however, and surfers should use caution. The lighthouse itself is not accessible to the public.

Fort Charles

The most prominent historical attraction in town and the most impressive, well-restored fort in Jamaica, **Fort Charles** (tel. 876/967-8438, 9am-4:45pm daily, US$10 adults, US$5 ages 3-17) was built in 1656 immediately following the British takeover and is the oldest fort on the island from the British colonial period and one of the oldest in the New World. Originally it was named Fort Cromwell after Oliver Cromwell, who was responsible for designing the strategic takeover of Jamaica, which was meant to give Britain control of the Caribbean. The fort was renamed in 1662 after the British monarchy was reinstated under Charles II. Fort Charles sank one meter (3 feet) during the earthquake of 1692.

Admiral Horatio Nelson, lauded as Britain's all-time greatest naval hero for his victorious role in the 1805 Battle of Trafalgar, spent 30 months in Jamaica, much of it at Fort Charles when the island feared a French invasion; he spent the tense period pacing and nervously scanning the horizon from what's now referred to as Nelson's Quarterdeck, a raised platform along the southern battlement. On the inside wall of the fort is a plaque advising those who tread Nelson's footprints to remember his glory.

Also within the walls of Fort Charles is the Grogge Shop, where sailors once enjoyed their spirits, and a nice little exhibit managed by the Museum of History and Ethnography, with period artifacts, old maps, and information about Port Royal and its glorious and notorious inhabitants.

★ Lime Cay

Just big enough to sustain some vegetation, **Lime Cay** is a paradisiacal islet about one kilometer (0.6 mile) offshore and 15 minutes by boat Port Royal. The windswept spit can draw a crowd on weekends, especially Sunday, and is worth a visit to take in the local scene. Launches leave for Lime Cay on weekends from Y-Knot Bar and from Grand Port Royal Hotel (US$10 pp round-trip); you can get there any day of the week, but the boat captains tend to ask a slightly higher price if there are only a few passengers. The beach is popular for sunbathing and swimming, and on weekends, Uptown Kingstonians cruise over in their boats from the yacht club, drop anchor, blast music, drink, and splash around. Storm swells can submerge Lime Cay entirely, which has kept it in its natural state, looking much the same way it did when Jimmy Cliff took his last stand here in the final scene of the film *The Harder They Come.*

Other Attractions

Built in 1725, **St. Peter's Church** replaced earlier churches on the site destroyed by the 1692 earthquake and then the 1703 fire that again ravaged Port Royal. On display inside are several period items. In the churchyard is the tomb of Lewis Galdy, one of the founders of St. Peter's, who miraculously survived the

---

1: Fort Charles 2: Bobo Hill, home to the Bobo Shanti house of Ras Tafari

EE BLACK MAN NOW!!
RICA FOR US BLACK PEOPLE
VERSHAL PEACE IS TO FREE
BLACK PEOPLE

1692 earthquake after being swallowed by the earth and spit out by the sea, where he was rescued. The tomb is inscribed with the complete legend of Galdy, who went on to become a local hero.

McFarlene's Bar is the oldest tavern in Port Royal, constructed in the 1800s, and one of the few buildings to withstand Hurricane Charlie in 1951. Unfortunately the pub no longer operates. The **Old Gaol** (jail, Gaol St.) was once a women's prison. **Giddy House** sits half-submerged at an awkward angle in the earth behind Fort Charles. It was built in 1888 as an artillery store by the British Navy, but the earthquake of 1907 left the building skewed as a reminder that dramatic seismic events can humble vicious buccaneers as easily as the world's foremost navy.

The oldest prefabricated cast-iron structure in the western hemisphere, the **Old Naval Hospital** was built in 1818 on the foundation of an earlier hospital, using enslaved labor under the direction of the Royal Engineers of the British Army. The hospital went out of use in 1905 before getting a new lease on life as the Port Royal Centre for Archaeological and Conservation Research in 1968. Seventeen hurricanes have not fazed the structure, nor did the earthquake of 1907 do it any harm.

Food

With two locations, ★ **Gloria's Seafood Restaurant** ("Bottom," 1 High St., tel. 876/967-8066, managed by Cecil; "Top," beachside, 15 Foreshore Rd., tel. 876/967-8220, managed by Angela) is a must for anyone who appreciates seafood (US$10 for a fried fish and bammy). Service can be slow with the crowds that swarm in, especially on Friday evenings and after church on Sunday. Gloria's does some of the most dependable and delicious fried escoveitch fish. Both Gloria's locations have a laid-back setting good for unhurried meals with a view of the water.

Accommodations

The only lodging option in Port Royal is **Grand Port Royal Hotel, Marina & Spa**

(tel. 876/967-8494, cell tel. 876/833-6321, grandportroyal@gmail.com, www.grandportroyal.com, from US$117, including continental breakfast buffet). It has a mix of recently refurbished and antiquated rooms, all with air-conditioning and cable.

Slip fees at the hotel marina are reasonable at US$1 per foot per day, plus taxes, similar to rates found across the island. Water, electricity, and laundry services are available. The hotel was built on the former naval shipyard. A scene in the 1962 James Bond film *Dr. No* was shot here. Small boats depart from the marina throughout the day for Lime Cay (US$10 adults, US$5 children).

Getting There

JUTC buses leave from the Parade (route 98, US$1), or hire a **taxi** (US$25). **Route taxis** between Downtown and Port Royal run sporadically, leaving once filled with passengers. The ferry service, which once brought passengers from downtown Kingston to Port Royal, has unfortunately been discontinued.

BULL BAY

Bull Bay is a quiet fishing community, 15 minutes east of Kingston along the A3. It has a long beach that lacks fine sand but also lacks crowds. It is a nice place for a dip, and the surf is decent for water sports at times. The community is perhaps best known for reggae artist and Jamaican surfing champion Billy "Mystic" Wilmot, who runs an irie surfing guest house on the beach, and as home to the Bobo Shanti (Ashanti) House of Ras Tafari, which has its base at nearby Bobo Hill.

Sights

About 1.5 kilometers (1 mile) before reaching Bull Bay, a sign for **Cane River Falls** (US$3) marks a left turn off the main road onto Greendale Road by Nine Mile Square. The falls themselves are not impressive, but they do have some interesting historical significance. Nevertheless, it's a nice place to relax and get some food with the sound of the water, which varies from a bubble to a roar depending on recent rainfall.

Just before Bull Bay at Seven Mile, on the main road east of Kingston toward St. Thomas, **Cane River** meets the sea. The river is formed by the Barbeque and Mammee Rivers, among smaller tributaries that run down the northern slopes of the Dallas Mountains. The falls were once the stomping ground of Three Finger Jack, a legendary Robin Hood-like cult figure who terrorized the planter class with kidnappings for ransom and murder. Almost 200 years later, the falls became a favorite cool-off spot for Bob Marley, who sang "uppa Cane River to wash my dread / upon a rock I rest my head" in the song "Trench Town."

Bobo Hill (top of Weise Rd., Nine Mile, Bull, contact Priest Daniel Samuel, cell tel. 876/422-3471) is home to the Bobo Shanti, or Bobo Ashanti, House of Ras Tafari. Known for their hardline interpretation of Marcus Garvey's teachings, the Bobo have been popularized by many dancehall artists who proclaim an affiliation. Paramount to Bobo philosophy and lifestyle are the ever-present themes of self-confidence, self-reliance, and self-respect. The Bobo can often be seen around Kingston, their locks carefully wrapped in a turban, peddling natural-fiber brooms, one of their signature crafts. At the center of the Bobo philosophy is the holy trinity between Bobo Shanti founder Prince Emmanuel Charles Edwards, who is said to have carried the spirit of Christ; Marcus Garvey, the prophet of the Ras Tafari Movement; and Haile Selassie I, the Ethiopian emperor who is their King of Kings. Women visiting the camp are asked to wear a dress or skirt below the knees and a head wrap, in accordance with the traditional dress code.

Leonard Howell, recognized as the first Jamaican to proclaim the divinity of Haile Selassie I, founded a commune at the inception of the movement in Pinnacle, St. Catherine, similar to the community found today at Bobo Hill. Despite popular belief to the contrary, the Bobo are among the most open and welcoming of the various Houses of Ras Tafari. While it will not be appreciated if you turn up unannounced to sightsee at their commune, sincere interest is well received, and they routinely open their home and hearth to visitors from around the world. Some visitors stay several days with them to share food and partake in their ritualized lifestyle. To reach the camp, turn left on Weise Road right after a bridge about 1.5 kilometers (1 mile) past the center of Bull Bay. A contribution of at least US$10 pp for the guidance is customary.

Surfing

Located in the community of Eight Mile, just before reaching Bull Bay, **Jamnesia Surf Camp** (look for the surfboard sign right after the driveway beside AB&C Groceries, next to Cave Hut Beach, tel. 876/750-0103, cell tel. 876/545-4591, www.jamnesiasurf.com) is Jamaica's number-one surfing destination. It's run by Billy "Mystic" Wilmot, of Mystic Revealers fame, and his family. They are great hosts for a surf vacation and offer the widest variety of boards for rental, as well as complete surf vacation packages. Rates start from US$15 for two to pitch your own tent. Three camp rooms (US$35 s, US$45 d) have bunk beds, and three bungalows have double and bunk beds (US$45 s, US$55 d). Nearby apartments can also be rented through Jamnesia. Six-night packages include room, two meals daily, a surfboard, and a shuttle to the breaks. Breakfast (US$4), lunch (US$6), and dinner (US$8) are offered at Shacks, the rustic restaurant on the property.

Jamaica has two good surf seasons: summer (June-Sept.) and winter (Dec.-Mar.). The fall and spring seasons may or may not have surf, but the room rates are lower off-season and open to negotiation. The property also features a skateboard bowl for when the water is flat, and the kids have set up a gully a short distance away like a skate park.

Entertainment

Little Copa (Eight Mile, contact Ian Hudson, cell tel. 876/845-3418, ianhudson348@yahoo.

com) is a roadside bar and nightclub that hosts a regular "Young People Tuesday" party as well as occasional functions and club nights.

Wickie Wackie Beach (contact Ronnie Jarrett, cell tel. 876/864-6188, Nine Mile) is a private home turned live music venue in Nine Mile since the 1940s, when a nightclub stood on the beach. Today the venue hosts occasional parties, like the Fat Tyre Festival and the Wickie Wackie Music Festival (US$10) the first week of December. One room is available for rent to short-term visitors (US$60).

Jamnesia Sessions are held at Jamnesia Surf Camp starting around 9pm every other Saturday and feature up-and-coming musicians.

ST. CATHERINE

With over a 500,000 people, the parish of St. Catherine is Jamaica's second-most populous. Spanish Town, the sedate parish capital, was Jamaica's center of government until the British bureaucrats relocated to Kingston in 1872. Originally founded as Villa de la Vega or St. Jago de la Vega by the Spanish, the city was named Spanish Town after the British takeover in 1655.

Spanish Town and surrounding communities like Old Harbour and Freetown have grown rapidly with housing schemes that respond to demand for low-income housing for first-time homebuyers and are essentially bedroom communities for Kingston. Most activity in Spanish Town today revolves around the two malls and bus park along Burke Road. Mandela Highway has heavy traffic between Kingston and Spanish Town during weekday rush hours (7am-9am and 4pm-7pm).

Spanish Town

Known simply as "Spain" or "St. Jago" on the street, the city has a rich heritage but has largely been left to decay. The old part of the city is well organized in a grid with Spanish Town Square at its center. There's little activity in the historic part of the city; the hustle and bustle is around the commercial plazas along Burke Road and the bus park, where

route taxis and buses depart for Kingston, May Pen, Mandeville, Linstead, and Ocho Rios. Still, Spanish Town has impressive facades and is home to Jamaica's national archives. The oldest Anglican Church outside of England is within a five-minute walk of the square.

SIGHTS

Spanish Town Square was laid out by Jamaica's first colonial rulers as their Plaza Mayor. It's surrounded by the burned remains of the Old King's House, destroyed by fire in 1925, on its western side, opposite the court house; the Rodney Memorial, to the north; and behind it, the National Archives. The Old House of Assembly, now the parish administration offices, with the courthouse upstairs, is the only building facing the square that's still in use.

In the Old King's House complex on Spanish Town square, the **People's Museum of Craft and Technology** (tel. 876/907-0322, 9am-4pm Mon.-Thurs., 9am-3pm Fri., US$1.50 adults, US$0.50 children) began as a Folk Museum in 1961 and was refurbished in 1997 when Emancipation Day was declared a national holiday. The exhibit has indoor and outdoor sections with carriages, early sugar- and coffee- processing machinery, and a variety of other colonial-period implements.

On the northern side of Spanish Town Square, the **Rodney Memorial** was erected in homage to British Admiral George Rodney, who prevented what was seen as imminent conquest by an invading French and Spanish naval fleet led by Admiral de Grasse in 1782. The memorial is housed in a spectacular structure with a European palatial look and gives a nice facade to the National Archives housed just behind. The statue of Rodney was contracted to one of the most respected sculptors of the day, Englishman John Bacon, who reportedly made two trips to Italy before finding the right block of marble for the job. A panel inscribed in Latin inside Rodney's octagonal "temple" tells of Rodney's victorious sea battle, which

Spanish Town

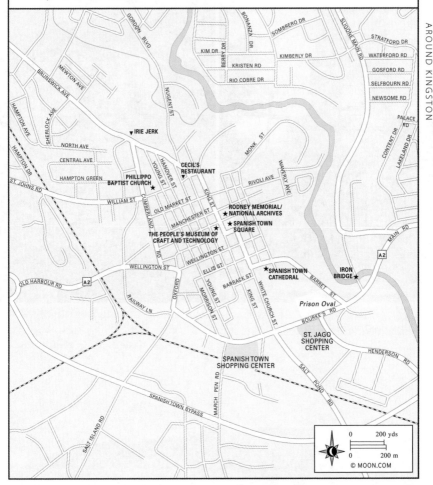

restored some dignity to Britain, recently badly defeated by the French-American allies in the American Revolution. Rodney was duly lauded as a national hero. The two brass cannons displayed just outside the statue enclosure were taken from defeated Admiral de Grasse's flagship, *Ville de Paris.*

On the site of the Roman Catholic Red Cross Spanish Chapel, originally built in 1525 and run by the Franciscans, stands **Spanish Town Cathedral,** or the Anglican Cathedral Church of St. James. Cromwell's Puritan soldiers destroyed the Spanish chapel along with another on the northern end of town known as White Cross, run by Dominicans. The church has been destroyed and rebuilt several times through a series of earthquakes and hurricanes. It became the first Anglican cathedral outside England in 1843, representing the Jamaican diocese. It's also the oldest English-built foundation on the island, after Fort Charles in Port Royal.

Several monuments of historical figures are found inside and in the walled churchyard.

Better known as Phillippo Baptist Church, **Spanish Town Baptist Church** (Cumberland Rd. and Williams St.) is a few blocks northwest of the square. The church was built in 1827 on an old artillery ground and later went on to play an active role in the abolition movement. Abolitionist Reverend James Murcell Phillippo arrived in Jamaica in 1823 and later established the church with help from freed slaves. On the night of emancipation in 1838, when local authorities granted Jamaica's slave population full freedom, 2,000 freed slaves were baptized in the church. There is a tablet in the churchyard commemorating the act of emancipation, which was celebrated there after the proclamation was read in front of Old King's House.

Cast in England and shipped in prefabricated segments, the **Iron Bridge** over the Rio Cobre was erected on the eastern edge of Spanish Town in 1801. Today it is used as a pedestrian crossing and is in a poor state of preservation. Designed by English engineer Thomas Wilson, it was the first prefab cast-iron bridge erected in the western hemisphere.

Taino wall paintings were first uncovered in 1897 at **Mountain River Cave** (caretaker Monica Wright, tel. 876/705-2790), located 21 kilometers (13 miles) due northwest from the roundabout at the beginning of St. John's Road on the western edge of Spanish Town. After leaving an Uptown suburb, St. John's becomes Cudjoe's Hill Road as you pass through red earth hills on the way to Kitson and then Guanaboa Vale, the stomping ground of Juan de Bolas. A few kilometers beyond a beautiful old church, pull over at Joan's Bar & Grocery Shop, marked by a painted facade reading Cudjoe's Cavern.

Monica will indicate the trailhead that leads down a steep hill across the meandering Thompson's River and up the facing bank through cacao and passion-fruit stands to where the small cave is caged in against vandals. The cave itself is shallow and unspectacular, but its paintings are interesting; it's easy to make out a man with a spear, a turtle, some fish, and a few women. The paintings are said to be authentic, given the ash and bat guano mix used, supposedly a typical medium for the earliest Jamaican artists. The highlight of this attraction, apart from the well-preserved petroglyphs, is the beautiful walk through lush forests and Thompson's River, which has a large pool upstream and a waterfall downstream from the crossing, fitting for a cool dip.

FOOD

Irie Jerk Centre (21 Brunswick Ave., tel. 876/749-5375, 24 hours daily) serves fried and jerk chicken (US$2 per piece, quarter chicken US$4), pork (US$10 per pound), and beer to wash it down (US$2). Irie also cooks curry goat, porridge, and soup. A small food court with some decent lunch options is at **St. Jago Shopping Centre,** which is also the location of **Nature's Vitamins, Herbs & Wellness Centre** (tel. 876/984-1305, US$2), serving vegetarian patties, sugar-free pastries, and natural juices.

Spanish Town's most-lauded restaurant is ★ **Cecil's** (35 Martin St., tel. 876/984-2986 or 876/984-2404, 10am-10pm Mon.-Sat., noon-8pm Sun., US$4-12). The late Cecil Reid was a chef at a number of other restaurants for years before opening his own place in 1983. Menu items have a decidedly Asian lean, with chop suey, chow mein, fried rice, and more typical curry dishes, beef, chicken, and lobster. Beer and fresh juices are US$2.

SERVICES

St. Catherine Parish Library (tel. 876/984-2356, 9am-6pm Mon.-Fri., 10am-5pm Sat.), across from Spanish Town Cathedral, offers free internet access on a few computers.

GETTING THERE AND AROUND

Spanish Town is served by Kingston's JUTC with **buses** from Half Way Tree Transport

---

1: Spanish Town Cathedral 2: Colonel's Cottage at Belcour Lodge 3: Hellshire Beach

Centre and the Parade Downtown departing every 10 minutes on routes 21 and 22. Private Coaster buses arrive and depart from bus stops a few paces down Molynes Road, across Eastwood Park Road from the Transport Centre. They charge just over US$1 one-way. **Route taxis** ply all major roads in Spanish Town and can be flagged down, charging anywhere from US$0.75 to US$1.75 around town.

If you're driving, the most direct route to Spanish Town is along Spanish Town Road or Washington Boulevard to Mandela Highway. Stay to the right at the first roundabout. You'll see the Old Iron Bridge on the right just after crossing the Rio Cobre as you enter town. Take a right at the stoplight at the gas station immediately thereafter to reach the historical sites surrounding Spanish Town Square or to pass through town for Linstead, Moneague, Walkerswood, and Ocho Rios. Heading straight at the stoplight leads to the commercial district after passing Prison Oval.

To reach Old Harbour, head west from Spanish Town along the bypass, following well-marked signs at the second roundabout along Old Harbour Road, which leads southwest through vast tracts of sugarcane fields.

Fort Clarence Beach Park

Fort Clarence Beach Park (cell tel. 876/364-3628, 10am-6pm Wed.-Fri., 10am-6pm Sat.-Sun., US$2, US$1 under age 13) is a popular 13-hectare (32-acre) beach park with showers, portable toilets, and a ramshackle kitchen cooking up fried fish and soup. The beach has lifeguards on duty and a cordoned swimming area.

Waves Beach

Family-friendly private **Waves Beach** (contact Lisa Golding, cell tel. 876/364-0182, wavesbeach@icloud.com, 10am-10pm Mon.-Fri., 8am-10pm Sat.-Sun., US$2 adults, US$1 under age 13) is a few lots west of Fort Clarence Beach Park, offering a seaside restaurant and bar with a covered dining area. The restaurant serves a variety of seafood dishes, including conch soup; fried, curry, and

brown stew fish; lobster, and shrimp. Patrons are offered complimentary Wi-Fi and showers, as well as secure parking.

The Boardwalk

A few lots west of Fort Clarence Beach Park, **The Boardwalk** (contact proprietor Roger Davis, cell tel. 876/404-0078, US$3 adults, US$1 under age 12) is a restaurant and bar with its own strip of beach. The admission gets you a bit of shade under wooden umbrellas and rustic nailed-together lounge chairs—watch out for the rusty nails. A kitchen on-site serves soup and fish.

★ Hellshire

Protected by offshore reefs, **Hellshire** (usually free, holidays US$2) is a small public beach with gentle waves where families from Greater Portmore and Kingston congregate on weekends. While beach erosion has diminished the amount of sand, there's still enough beach to swim and the main attraction is the scene, along with fried fish. Speakers are stacked at Prendy's on the far eastern end of the beach by a rocky breakwater, and party-lovers gather round as the day grows old to dance, with plenty of drinking and smoking.

Fish-frying entrepreneurs are highly competitive as they woo hungry diners, and unsuspecting patrons can easily be scammed in search of lunch. As soon as you drive beneath the arch into Hellshire, men will offer parking spaces, and once parked, they'll direct you to the fish stalls where they receive a commission for bringing guests; it's best to keep walking like you know where you're headed. A handful of dependable and honest restaurateurs offer good value, and the lively beach scene is worth a visit.

The sand and water can be littered, but it's generally clean enough to swim despite the fishermen's habit of scaling their catch at the water's edge, and the locals don't bat an eye at the floating plastic bags. Peddlers of every sort eke out a living at Hellshire, from the man selling customized bamboo vessels to the ganja, jewelry, and bootleg CD vendors and the pony handler who gives tame rides down the short stretch of beach for a couple of bucks. Don't be alarmed by constant solicitations; it's just part of Hellshire's color. Sadly, Hellshire Beach is struggling with significant beach erosion. Over the past decade the wide swath of sand that stretched the entire length of the coast in front of the fish shacks has disappeared, leaving only a small patch on the easternmost end of the beach today.

FOOD

Highly recommended ★ **Shorty's** (contact proprietor Judith Ewers, cell tel. 876/586-3623 or 876/323-1915, 9am-10pm Mon.-Thurs., 9am-10pm Fri.-Sat., 6am-11pm Sun.) has dependable brown stew, snapper (US$15 per pound), and lobster (US$15 per pound) in season, accompanied by bammy and festival. It's always best to call ahead to put in your order to ensure minimal waiting time.

An honest and dependable seafood restaurant, **Prendy's on the Beach** (cell tel. 876/575-6057 or 876/575-6063, prendysonthebeach@yahoo.com, 9am-9pm Mon.-Thurs., 8am-11pm Fri.-Sun., US$11-15 per pound) serves fried (US$11 per pound), steamed, garlic, brown stew, roast, curry, and jerk fish, plus conch, lobster, shrimp, and king crab, with two festival sides included. A location at Hi-Lo in Portmore Pines Plaza offers prix-fixe meals (3pm-10pm Fri.-Sat., US$10). DJ Marlon

of Exstasy Sound plays a mix of reggae, dancehall, and hip-hop all day Sunday.

Fifteen minutes up the road is the backyard Chinese seafood restaurant ★ **Di Dragon** (173 Armada Way, Portmore, cell tel. 876/630-7665 or 876/590-4486; 2pm-10pm Mon.-Thurs., 2pm-11pm Fri.-Sat., 2pm-9pm Sun., US$15-25 per pound), complete with alfresco dining on picnic tables overlooking a canal. The kitchen serves up chicken, pork, and vegetarian dishes, including chow mein, suey mein, and fried rice, but the stars of the show are the seafood specialties, especially the lobster and king crab. The salty pepper, black bean, and ginger scallion renditions are ridiculously good. However, the town of Portmore is not Jamaica's leading tourism destination by any means; the outstanding seafood restaurant is only a few blocks from the infamous Fort Augusta Drive, better known as "Back Road," where scantily clad women of the night prowl for tricks all day long. Exercise caution if you choose to venture here.

Two Sisters Cave

A regular hangout for the first Jamaicans centuries ago, the unmanaged **Two Sisters Cave** comprises two large caves, one with a deep pool suitable for swimming, about 100 meters (300 feet) apart down a series of steps. A third, unmanaged cave can be found about 100 meters (300 feet) east of Two Sisters, reached by a footpath descending from the road.

The Blue and John Crow Mountains

The Blue and John Crow Mountains harbor rich biodiversity and played an important cultural role in history, providing refuge to Taino and enslaved Africans fleeing colonial oppressors, transplanted French-Haitian coffee farmers fleeing revolution, and later to Bob Marley, when he sought safety and seclusion at Strawberry Hill following an attempt on his life in 1976. Today the area attracts visitors for its lush and diverse flora, colorful

birdlife, delicious coffee, and crisp mountain air, all of which earned the Blue and John Crow Mountains UNESCO World Heritage Site status in 2015. During much of the year, the peaks cloud over by mid-morning, so it's always a good idea to get an early start for the best views.

Five parishes can be seen from Blue Mountain Peak, Jamaica's highest summit, at 2,256 meters (7,402 feet): Kingston and

The Blue and John Crow Mountains

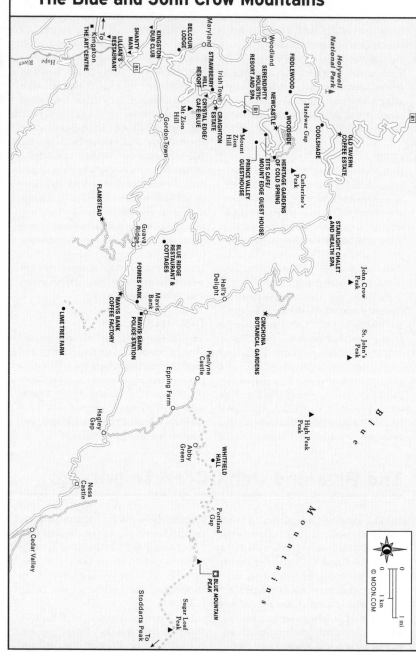

Holywell National Park

To Kingston
THE ART CENTRE
LILLIAN'S RESTAURANT
SHANTY MAN
KINGSTON DUB CLUB
BELCOUR LODGE
Maryland
Woodland
FIDDLEWOOD
B1
Hope River
Hope
B1
STRAWBERRY HILL RESORT
SERENDIPITY HOLISTIC RESORT AND SPA
Irish Town
CRYSTAL EDGE/ CAFE BLUE
CRAIGHTON ESTATE
NEWCASTLE
WOODSIDE
Hardwar Gap
COOLSHADE
OLD TAVERN COFFEE ESTATE
B1
Mt Zion Hill
Mount Zion Hill
Catherine's Peak
HERITAGE GARDENS OF COLD SPRING
EITS CAFE/ MOUNT EDGE GUEST HOUSE
PRINCE VALLEY GUESTHOUSE
Gordon Town
STARLIGHT CHALET AND HEALTH SPA
FLAMSTEAD
Guava Ridge
BLUE RIDGE RESTAURANT & COTTAGES
FORRES PARK
Hall's Delight
Mavis Bank
MAVIS BANK COFFEE FACTORY
MAVIS BANK POLICE STATION
John Crow Peak
St. John's Peak
CINCHONA BOTANICAL GARDENS
LIME TREE FARM
Penlyne Castle
Epping Farm
Blue
High Peak Peak
Hagley Gap
Abby Green
WHITFIELD HALL
Ness Castle
Mountains
Portland Gap
Cedar Valley
BLUE MOUNTAIN PEAK
Sugar Loaf Peak
To Stoddarts Peak

0   1 km
© MOON.COM
0   1 mi

St. Andrew to the south, St. Thomas to the east, Portland to the north, and St. Mary to the east. The range forms a physical barrier to the northeasterly fronts that typically hit the island, giving Portland and St. Thomas copious rainfall compared to the southern coastal plains, where drought is more common.

Irish Town, Hardwar Gap, and Mavis Bank are great destinations for a quick escape from the city, all within an hour's drive. This is where rural Jamaica is at its coolest. The elevation and lush greenery offer welcome respite from the heat of the city. The road up and the rugged terrain are not for the faint of heart, but the prized Blue Mountain coffee, breathtaking views, diverse vegetation, and abundance of native birds are more than adequate rewards.

INDUSTRY VILLAGE TO SILVER HILL GAP

Turning left at the Cooperage onto the B3 leads up a series of sharp hairpin turns that can leave passengers nauseated. The winding road first passes through the lower hills and valleys of Maryland before reaching the principal hamlet along the route, Irish Town. **Irish Town** has as its centerpiece St. Mark's Chapel, a quaint little church reached by a 15-minute walk along a footpath.

St. Mark's Anglican Church

A beautiful old church that sits on a hilltop in Irish Town, **St. Mark's Anglican Church** is a great destination for a short hike from Strawberry Hill. As you arrive at the junction in Irish Town where the driveway to Strawberry Hill leads up to the left, the chapel looms up ahead.

Mt. Zion Hill

A Rastafarian farming community is based in a squatter settlement known as **Mt. Zion Hill** (to request a visit call Priest Dermot Fagan, cell tel. 876/868-9636). The carefully maintained trail and fence along the path up the hill demonstrates the respect given to Priest Dermot Fagan, referred to simply as "the priest" by his followers, who rank in the range of 50-odd adults and children living at Zion Hill. Fagan has established His Imperial Majesty School of Bible Study and Sabbath Service, with a small yurt-like structure at the entrance to the community serving as its chapel. The small community follows primarily an agrarian life, growing food and herbs and selling roots wine around town to bring in a little cash. There are several people who espouse the school's teaching but live in town rather than on Zion Hill.

Fagan advocates a total rejection of the system that has separated humankind from direct reliance on our labor and the food we can provide for ourselves. He warns of an even greater divide between humanity and its sustenance through the impending mass implantation of micro-biochips. The Mt. Zion Hill community has established itself as one of the more colorful, albeit apocalyptic, Houses of Rastafari.

Strawberry Hill

Boutique hilltop resort **Strawberry Hill** (tel. 876/944-8400, www.islandoutpost.com) is an assortment of guest cottages that hug steep hillsides, with an infinity pool, a restaurant, and a bar at the core. Designed by renowned Jamaican architect Ann Hodges in contemporary Georgian style with gingerbread fretwork and white wooden railed balconies, the property welcomes nonguests to enjoy the view (US$20), spa treatments, and food and drink, unless there's a function being held. Don't miss the collection of gold and platinum albums hanging on the walls in the boardroom below the restaurant, recalling the illustrious career of music producer Chris Blackwell, founder of Island Records and the hotel chain. It's well worth a visit for a luxurious afternoon or evening.

★ UCC Craighton Coffee Estate

Owned by Japan-based Ueshima Coffee Company, **UCC Craighton Coffee Estate** (Irish Town, tel. 876/929-8490, cell tel.

Jamaican Coffee: Cultivating an Industry

Coffee is one of 600 species in the Rubiaceae family, understood to have its center of origin in what is today Ethiopia. The plant's beans and leaves are believed to have been chewed by the earliest inhabitants and later brewed by ancient Abyssinians and Arabs, the latter credited with originating the global coffee trade. Jamaica's relationship with the revered bean dates to 1728, when a former governor introduced coffee of the Typica cultivar to his Temple Hall estate in upper St. Andrew. Its cultivation was formalized in earnest with large plantations covering hundreds of hectares established in the nearby Blue Mountains by an influx of planters fleeing Haiti in the years leading up to the neighboring country's 1804 independence. By 1800, there were 686 coffee plantations in Jamaica, with exports totaling 15,199 tons.

These early planters discovered that the intact plantation economy and the cloud forest climatic conditions were conducive to lucrative coffee production. The misty climate allowed the coffee berries to ripen slowly, a process said to grant the end product its smooth, full-bodied flavor, free of bitterness. The bumper earnings of these early plantations were short-lived, however, deteriorating when global demand subsided and competition increased from other colonies imposing lower taxes. The abolition of slavery and emancipation further challenged Jamaica's large-scale coffee plantations; when labor became more expensive, the country's production deteriorated, and the bean's cultivation was soon dominated by small-scale farmers. By 1850 there were only 186 plantations left in Jamaica, with exports falling to 1,486 tons.

Jamaica's Coffee Industry Board (CIB), established in 1950, was set up to control the quality of the product and participate directly in the production process. The CIB also regulates the coveted Jamaica Blue Mountain Coffee registered trademark, allowing its use only by farms certified by the board in the parishes of St. Andrew, St. Thomas, Portland, and St. Mary, all located at elevations of 610-1,525 meters (2,000-5,000 feet). Obtaining a certification by the CIB as a producer of Jamaica Blue Mountain Coffee is a challenge, especially for small farms. It can take several years, as certification demands scrupulous implantation of the CIB farming practices and production processes.

Coffee produced at lower elevations can also be of high quality, though it doesn't attract the same attention or price as Jamaica's Blue Mountain coffee. Jamaica Prime, Premium Washed, and High Mountain Supreme are some of the names Jamaican coffee is sold under when not originating from the Blue Mountains. There are notable coffee producers in several parishes around

876/292-3774, beddalton@gmail.com, US$25 adults, US$15 ages 6-12) offers a one-hour tour led by leading Jamaica Blue Mountain Coffee connoisseur Alton "Junior" Bedward. The tour features a lecture covering coffee history and cultivation and a walk around the working coffee farm and historic great house, ending at a hilltop gazebo. UCC is a major exporter of Jamaica Blue Mountain Coffee to Japan, the leading foreign market for the prized product.

Old Tavern Coffee Estate

The Twyman family has been growing some of the best Jamaica Blue Mountain coffee since 1968 at their **Old Tavern Coffee Estate** (contact Danna Watt in David

Twyman's Kingston office to arrange a visit, tel. 876/924-2785, cell tel. 876/865-2978, oldtaverncoffee@gmail.com, US$20 adults, US$10 ages 6-12). The estate is run by David Twyman, son of original owners Dorothy and the late, great coffee farmer Alex Twyman. When he's available, Twyman offers visitors an informal coffee roasting and tasting experience with a jaunt through the fields, weather permitting.

Three different roasts are produced from Old Tavern beans: medium, medium dark (Proprietors' Choice), and dark roast. Peaberry beans, oddballs that develop only one side of the normally paired bean, are smaller and have a unique mild flavor that's prized by many.

coffee beans

Jamaica, among them farms in Bog Walk and St. Catherine, at Key Park Estate in Westmoreland, at Aenon Park along the Clarendon-St. Ann border, at Clarendon Park, and in Maggoty, St. Elizabeth.

Jamaica's climate is at once a blessing and a curse for the country's coffee farmers. The high altitude mist nurtures the bean to give it its distinct character, but the country's highest peaks are also most exposed and vulnerable to hurricanes and tropical storms, which can destroy several years' work in one night. The lack of insurance for the industry since Hurricane Ivan in 2004 has made production at many small farms a real gamble. Combating disease is also a constant struggle. Nonetheless, today's coffee industry employs some 50,000 Jamaicans and brings in around US$35 million in foreign exchange each year. Retailing at nearly US$40 per pound in Jamaica and US$50 per pound abroad, Jamaica Blue Mountain coffee's high price keeps the coffee industry viable.

Catherine's Peak

Rising to the right as you drive up to Newcastle from Red Light, **Catherine's Peak** quickly becomes visible, easily distinguishable by the clutter of communications antennae at the summit. The peak is a one-hour hike from the Parade ground at Newcastle, where there is plenty of parking. A rough road goes all the way up, but it becomes impassable to anything but a 4WD vehicle. Jamaica Defense Force soldiers stationed at Newcastle restrict access to all vehicles except those carrying the most trustworthy-looking visitors. It's best to hoof it from Newcastle rather than drive part of the way.

Holywell National Park

Holywell National Park (US$10) sits atop Hardwar Gap, affording a view of St. Andrew Parish to the south and St. Mary and Portland to the north. The birding is excellent in the 50-hectare (124-acre) park, which borders Twyman's Old Tavern Coffee Estate on the north side and is a haven for migratory birds in the winter months. Hiking trails lead to a few peaks, and there's also a loop trail. Birds that can be seen at Holywell include lizard cuckoos, chestnut bellied cuckoos, orangequits, yellow-shouldered grassquits, becards, *Spindalis,* todies, hummingbirds, woodpeckers, and owls.

The graveled 1.2-kilometer (0.75-mile) **Oatley Mountain Loop Trail** is a steep ascent to Oatley Mountain Peak at 1,400 meters (4,593 feet). Three lookout points along the way offer great views of St. Andrew, St. Mary, and Portland. The **Waterfall Trail** is also about 1.2 kilometers (0.75 mile) long, meandering along the mountain edge and then following a stream with a small waterfall at the end. Shorter and less strenuous trails include the 600-meter (2,000-foot) **Shelter Trail,** the 350-meter (1,150-foot) **Blue Mahoe Trail,** and the 630-meter (2,100-foot) **Wag Water/Dick's Pond Trail.**

Food

Owned by the Sharps, who own Coffee Traders and Clifton Mount coffee estate, **Café Blue** (Irish Town, tel. 876/944-8918, www.jamaicacafeblue.com, 8am-6pm Mon.-Fri., 8am-8pm Sat.-Sun.) serves Blue Mountain coffee and pastries and retails local sauces, candles, and soaps.

★ **Crystal Edge** (next door to Café Blue, Irish Town, contact Winsome Hall, tel. 876/944-8053, 8:30am-4pm Sat.-Sun., 10:30am-4pm Tues.-Fri.) serves excellent Jamaican dishes at Jamaican prices. The menu rotates daily, with starters like crayfish or red pea soup and entrées that include oxtail and escoveitch fish. The restaurant is located just before Irish Town where the road starts to level out, sharing a building with Café Blue.

With spectacular views from a wraparound porch, **Strawberry Hill** (tel. 876/944-8400, www.islandoutpost.com, 8am-10:30am, noon-4pm, and 6pm-9pm daily, appetizers US$13-20, entrées US$30-50) has a varied menu of Jamaican and international cuisine. It's by no means a budget eatery, but the ambience will leave you with no regrets for having splurged. Reservations are required for guests not staying on the property. On Sunday there is an all-you-can-eat brunch buffet (noon-3pm).

Overlooking the gardens of Food Basket Farm and the valleys, ridges, and peaks of the Blue Mountains, **Europe in the Summer (EITS) Café** (Mount Edge Guesthouse, just before mile marker 17, approaching

Newcastle, tel. 876/944-8151, foodbasketjamaica@gmail.com, 9am-6pm daily, US$5-30) offers a farm-to-table dining experience in a cozy open-air dining terrace. Entrées include rack of lamb, barrel roasted chicken, and coconut curry veggie stew.

Starlight Chalet (Silver Hill Gap, tel. 876/969-3116, 7am-5pm daily, later with reservations, US$10-25) serves Jamaican dishes at reasonable prices, bakes cakes and pastries from scratch, and prepares natural juices with whatever fruit is in season.

A charming restaurant with indoor and outdoor seating, **The Gap Café** (Hardwar Gap, cell tel. 876/399-2406, 10am-3pm Mon.-Thurs., 10am-5pm Fri.-Sun., US$10-18) serves a rotating home-style menu with items like curried goat, oxtail and beans, and callaloo-stuffed chicken breast. When not shrouded in mist, it boasts spectacular views over Kingston and St. Andrew at 1,280 meters (4,200 feet) elevation. Located three kilometers (2 miles) past the Jamaica Defense Force hill station at Newcastle, the restaurant will stay open longer by reservation. It is said Ian Fleming wrote some of his first James Bond book, *Dr. No,* at the Gap.

Accommodations
UNDER US$100
Mount Edge Guesthouse (just before mile marker 17, approaching Newcastle, tel. 876/367-8191, jamaicanmountedge@gmail.com, from US$45) has four rustic cottages hanging on the edge of a cliff overlooking the farm with single, double, or king beds. Some share a bath and some have private baths. A central building has two private rooms with a shared bath, a living room, and a dining room. A third building has bunk beds for four with adjoining baths. Amenities include hot water, Wi-Fi, a small roadside bar, and a trail to the river. Mountain bikes are available.

On a small coffee farm in Middleton Settlement, ★ **Prince Valley Guesthouse** (cell tel. 876/892-2365, jaqdes@netstep.net, US$35-40 pp) is managed by Bobby Williams and has five guest rooms, each with its own bath. Linens and towels are provided, along with a basic breakfast of coffee and toast. Dinner (US$12 pp) is available by request. A common room has a refrigerator, books, a couch, a work table, and Wi-Fi. The lodging is ideal for backpackers. Bobby offers pickups from the airport (US$100) or Kingston (US$60), or you can take a route taxi from Papine for about US$3. To get there, take the first right after Mount Edge Guesthouse at Bubbles Bar, followed by another right at the first intersection, and then a left after crossing a little ramp.

Holywell National Park provides cabins and tent sites bookable through the **Jamaica Conservation and Development Trust** (29 Dumbarton Ave., Half Way Tree, tel. 876/920-8278 or 876/920-8279, jamaicaconservation@gmail.com, www.greenjamaica.org.jm). Book at least two weeks in advance for a weekend stay in one of three self-contained cabins. Two one-bedroom units (US$50) have an open layout, and one two-bedroom unit is US$70. Campers (US$10) can use the shared showers, toilets, and barbecue pits (US$5) on-site.

The Gap Café (Harwar Gap, cell tel. 876/319-2406) offers a one-bedroom rustic apartment (US$60) containing two twin beds, a private bath, a kitchenette, and a small sitting room.

US$100-250

In an enchanting river valley set amid citrus groves and orchids, ★ **Colonel's Cottage at Belcour Lodge** (Maryland district, contact Robin Lim Lumsden, tel. 876/927-2448, cell tel. 876/383-8942, limlums@gmail.com, US$125) is a small one-bedroom self-contained cottage with a kitchenette that provides for a one-of-a-kind retreat. Belcour Preserves sauces, jams, and marmalades are available for purchase along with the *Belcour Family Cookbook*.

An old coffee estate, **Heritage Gardens of Cold Spring** (just below Newcastle, tel. 876/978-9519 or 876/978-4438, b.eleanor@gmail.com, www.heritagegardensjamaica.com, US$100 for 2, US$20 per additional person) has large barbecues, which are the flat areas where coffee is laid out to dry, hinting at its past as a coffee processing estate, established in 1747 by Irish botanist Matthew Wallen, credited with bringing several exotic plant species to Jamaica, including watercress, dandelion, nasturtiums, and bamboo. The cottage on the property sleeps up to six and has a rustic but comfortable feel with hot water and a cool breeze. The gardens are well cared for, and the entire property boasts spectacular views. The cottage makes a good base for hiking in the western section of the Blue Mountains and is a short walk to Newcastle, where the road up to Catherine's Peak begins.

The quaint retreat **Starlight Chalet** (Silver Hill Gap, tel. 876/969-3070, cell tel. 876/414-8570, www.starlightchalet.com, US$130, includes breakfast) is reached by heading north from Hardwar Gap. Turn right at Section and travel until you reach Starlight Chalet. The 17-room property has several different room layouts, some with one queen, others with two, and two with kings. The original structure, a two-bedroom cottage at the top of the property, has a formal dining room with marble floors, a fireplace, and antique furniture, ideal for small groups looking for a degree of independence. Common areas have satellite TV and Wi-Fi. The kitchen serves a rotating menu of Jamaican fare.

OVER US$250

★ **Strawberry Hill** (Newcastle Rd., tel. 876/944-8400 or 876/619-7872, reservations@islandoutpost.com, www.strawberryhillhotel.com, from US$400) is an exclusive hotel operated by legendary record producer Chris Blackwell's Island Outpost hotel group. There are 13 guest cottages, most doubles, some holding up to four guests, spread over 10.5 hectares (26 acres) hugging steep hillsides covered in bamboo. Inside the wooden cottages, by renowned Jamaican architect Ann Hodges in her minimalist functional design, louvered windows open to panoramic views of lush hillsides and Kingston below. Canopy king beds are shrouded in mosquito nets, and the windows are well screened. The absence of television is a welcome escape from screen life to enjoy the scenery. The Wi-Fi works well and a lounge by the restaurant has a big flat-screen TV if you must tune in. Kitchenettes come with a mini fridge and fixings for tea, coffee, and snacks.

The restaurant and bar are located next to a sprawling lawn. A yoga pavilion faces the Blue Mountain range, and a reflective infinity pool faces Kingston. Below the restaurant, a community room is adorned with the golden discs reflecting the acclaim of Blackwell's career as a record producer. The ayurvedic **Strawberry Hill FieldSpa** is tucked behind thick foliage where holistic rejuvenation dubbed Strawberry Hill Living is administered. Guests are pampered in five indoor-outdoor treatment rooms with aromatherapy, reflexology massage, body scrubs, body wraps, facials, manicures, and pedicures (US$75-185). Packages bundle massage, reflexology, wraps, and facials (US$130-350). The property welcomes nonguests (US$20) to enjoy the view, patronize the restaurant and bar, enjoy spa treatments, and visit the gift shop. Make a lunch or dinner reservation to avoid the entrance fee—it's worth a visit for a luxurious afternoon or evening.

Located 1.5 kilometers (1 mile) past Newcastle, just below Hardwar Gap and Holywell National Park, ★ **Woodside** (tel. 876/977-5020. ext. 253, guangotree@gmail. com, 2-night minimum, 3 bedrooms US$300, 4 bedrooms US$400, 5 bedrooms US$500) is a charming, staffed, colonial-era home on a 12-hectare (30-acre) coffee farm. Woodside is a stylish base for hiking in the park, bird-watching, and exploring the western reaches of the Blue Mountains. The house is impeccable in its old-Jamaica feel and boasts spectacular views, gardens, and a spring-fed pool. There is no better place for a cool escape during Jamaica's hottest months.

MAVIS BANK

Mavis Bank is a sleepy village nestled in a river valley in the shadow of Blue Mountain Peak. Its principal economic foundation for the past century has been the Mavis Bank Coffee Factory, which keeps many of the area's residents employed. The area is a good base for exploring the upper reaches of the Blue Mountains and for birding.

A few homey lodging options around Mavis Bank offer visitors a chance to prepare in relative comfort for the trek up Blue Mountain Peak, a grueling three-hour hike from the trailhead at Abbey Green, reachable by 4WD, or alternatively, a nine-hour hike from Mavis Bank. It's about 16 kilometers (10 miles) from Mavis Bank to Whitfield Hall, which is about 800 meters (0.5 miles) from the trailhead. From the trailhead, it's another 10 kilometers (6 miles) to the peak, with the campground at Portland Gap located a little less than halfway to the summit.

Sights

Right off the Main Road as you reach Mavis Bank from Gordon Town, **Mavis Bank Coffee Factory** (tel. 876/977-8005 or 876/977-8013, www.bluemountaincoffee.com, 8:30am-noon and 1pm-3:30pm Mon.-Fri., US$10 adults, US$5 children) was established in 1923 by an English planter, Victor Munn. As the biggest coffee factory in Jamaica, it has been the economic lifeblood of the area since. Reservations are required for the tour.

The factory is supplied by six of its own plantations and around 5,000 independent farms. Most of the picking is done by local women, who receive about US$50 per box full of berries. Of this, most goes to the farm owner where the berries were picked. The coffee is then left outside to dry for five to seven days, weather permitting, or dried in a giant tumbler for two days if it's too rainy outside. Once dry, the coffee is aged in big sacks for four to six weeks before the outer parchment,

1: Cinchona Gardens 2: views from Lime Tree Farm 3: Strawberry Hill

or hull, is removed and the beans are cleaned and roasted. The whole process takes three or four months from bush to mug. Four grades (peaberry, 1, 2, and 3) are produced, around 80 percent of which is consumed in Japan, with 5 percent going to the United States and 4 percent to the rest of the world. Mavis Bank processes 1.4 million pounds of green beans per year.

A former hilltop plantation turned botanical research station, **Cinchona Gardens** (6am-6pm daily) has a sunken garden modeled after London's Kew Gardens. The cinchona for which the gardens were named was brought from Peru in the 1800s to cultivate for quinine to treat malaria, which was afflicting the enslaved population on the sugar plantations below. Visitors will find a wide variety of lilies, dahlias, conifers, eucalyptus, and orchid species, making it a magical place with spectacular views.

Cinchona Gardens can be reached by turning left at the Anglican church in Mavis Bank, and then descending to cross the Yallahs River at Robertsfield. Keep left at the fork to Cinchona via Hall's Delight, or take the right at the fork to reach Cinchona via Westphalia. Both roads can only be traveled by 4WD vehicle. The bumpy journey takes about an hour from Mavis Bank. Contact the caretaker, Norman Ta (tel. 876/276-0762, normanijtate@gmail.com), who lives nearby. There's no admission fee, but given the gardeners' low government wages, it's advisable for visitors to leave a US$5-10 tip when presented with the visitors' book for signing. Call the caretaker prior to visiting for weather conditions and the best route, as road conditions are in constant flux and one may be better than another at any given time.

An easier route to Cinchona descends from Section above Hardwar Gap. Turn right at Section and descend to St. Peters. In St. Peters turn off the main road to the left toward Chestervale and Clydesdale rather than continuing the descent toward Guava Ridge. At Clydesdale, you'll see barbecues used to dry coffee beans, a water wheel, and an old great house now in ruins that hints at its more glorious past as a coffee plantation. It's a fitting place for camping for those with their own tent. From Clydesdale, an old road leads to Cinchona that takes about 1.5 hours to walk, or it's a bit quicker for intrepid drivers with a 4WD vehicle. The views hold more natural beauty on the route down from Section, but it takes quite a while longer to reach Cinchona.

Flamstead is a historic estate commanding a strategic view of the approach to Kingston Harbour and was used as a lookout point by Jamaica's colonial overlords. During the Napoleonic Wars (1803-1815), it served as a residence for Admiral Rodney and was used as a base for the British army. A plaque on the house there notes that the site helped prove the usefulness of longitude, as first measured using John Harrison's marine chronometer in 1761, by Harrison's son William. The Harrisons would eventually take the prize offered by the British crown for a solution to the problem of measuring longitude in the age of sail.

Tours

Arrow Head Birding Tours (cell tel. 876/260-9006, www.arrowheadbirding.com), led by Ricardo Miller, offers excursions to the best birding spots across the island, including choice locations in the Blue and John Crow Mountains.

Services

In the square in Mavis Bank is the **post office and police station** (tel. 876/977-8004). To venture farther into the mountains, a 4WD vehicle is needed. If you're heading up to Blue Mountain Peak, you can call **Whitfield Hall** (tel. 876/927-0986, cell tel. 876/383-9964, cell tel. 876/878-0514) to arrange for a 4WD vehicle to meet you at the police station, a good place to leave your car under watchful eyes.

THE BLUE AND JOHN CROW MOUNTAINS NATIONAL PARK

Consisting of nearly 81,000 hectares (200,000 acres) in the parishes of St. Andrew, St. Mary, St. Thomas, and Portland, the **Blue and John Crow Mountains National Park** (BJCMNP, tel. 876/920-8278, jcdt@cybervale.com, www.greenjamaica.org.jm, US$20 pp to use the Blue Mountain Peak Trail) covers the highest and steepest terrain in Jamaica. This alpine terrain is one of the two last known habitats for the endangered giant swallowtail butterfly, the second-largest in the world, which makes its home on the northern flanks of the range. Several endemic plant and bird species, including the Jamaican owl, among many others, reside in the park as well, and many migratory birds from northern regions winter there. Among the most impressive of the native birds are the red-billed streamertail hummingbirds—known locally as doctor birds—and the Jamaican tody, the Jamaican blackbird, and the yellow-billed parrot. The Blue Mountains generally are the source of water for the Kingston area, one of many reasons it is important to disturb the environment as little as possible. The BJCMNP has the largest unaltered swath of natural forest in Jamaica, with upper montane rainforest and elfin woodland at its upper reaches.

TOP EXPERIENCE

★ Blue Mountain Peak

The pinnacle of the Blue and John Crow Mountains National Park, **Blue Mountain Peak** can be reached by a variety of means, depending on the level of exhaustion you are willing to endure. Generally, hikers leave before first light from Whitfield Hall at Penlyne, St. Thomas, after having arrived the previous day. For ambitious hikers, there's a 4.5-kilometer (2.8-mile) trail from Mavis Bank to Penlyne Castle, which is pleasant and covers several farms and streams. This option also obviates the need to send for a 4WD vehicle. From Penlyne Castle, follow the road to Abbey Green (3.2 kilometers/2 miles), and from there to Portland Gap (3.7 kilometers/2.3 miles). At Portland Gap a ranger station, sometimes staffed, has bunks, toilets, showers, and campsites. These facilities can be used for US$20-100 by contacting the JCDT, which asks that visitors register at the ranger station. From Portland Gap to the peak is the most arduous leg, covering 5.6 kilometers (3.5 miles). Warm clothes, rain gear, and comfortable, supportive footwear are essential. Blue Mountain Peak is also a mildly challenging three- to-four-hour hike from **Whitfield Hall,** a rustic farmhouse with a great stone fireplace.

From Portland Gap westward along the Blue Mountain range, there are several other lofty peaks along the ridge with far less traffic. These include Sir John's Peak, John Crow Peak, and Catherine's Peak. *Guide to the Blue and John Crow Mountains,* by Margaret Hodges, has the most thorough coverage of hiking trails throughout the national park. Otherwise, local people are the best resource. On a clear day, the view from Blue Mountain Peak is spectacular, with five parishes in sight and views of the Caribbean to the north, east, and south.

Accommodations

Blue Ridge Restaurant & Cottages (Blue Ridge, tel. 876/562-7580, blueridgeja@gmail.com, www.blueridgeja.com, by reservation) offers guests two cottages on a bed-and-breakfast basis. Peacock Cottage (US$110) sleeps two with a king bed, a private bath with hot water, and a private balcony. Butterfly Cottage (US$125) sleeps four with a king bed and a sofa bed in the living room. It has a private bath with hot water and a balcony. The cottages are perched on a steep hillside below the restaurant deck, surrounded by coffee and fruit trees. The cottage balconies face the slopes of the Blue Mountain range. The restaurant aims high with creative appetizers like bacon wrapped plantain served with cilantro cream sauce and signature entrées like chicken pot pie and Blue Ridge pork chops in guava glaze. The spot is very remote and boasts the most spectacular vistas of Jamaica's majestic peaks. The staff is well-trained and attentive.

A small coffee plantation with four tastefully decorated cabins, ★ **Lime Tree Farm** (Tower Hill, cell tel. 876/446-0230, ratcutt@yahoo.com, www.limetreefarm.com, US$285 per couple, includes 3 meals, alcohol not included) overlooks Mavis Bank with a spectacular view of Portland Gap, Blue Mountain Peak, and the Yallahs River Valley. Owned by English expat Rodger Bolton, the property operates as a boutique family-style all-inclusive resort. Excellent home-cooked meals shared around a communal table make Lime Tree Farm a great value. A 4WD vehicle is needed to reach the property; the hosts can arrange transportation from Kingston or Mavis Bank. A trained masseuse offers Swedish massage, and a yoga patio faces the ridges and valleys. Lime Tree offers a number of packages that include lodging, food, and excursions to Blue Mountain Peak, Flamstead, and Cinchona Gardens.

A great option for bird-watchers and hikers, especially for groups, is **Forres Park Guest House** (tel. 876/977-8141, reservations tel. 876/927-8275, mlyn@cwjamaica.com, www.forrespark.com, US$105-200). A two-story main house and four cabins are surrounded by a small coffee farm that attracts many endemic and migratory bird species. The large veranda is a great vantage point, as all three of Jamaica's hummingbirds—vervain, Jamaica mango, and streamertail—frequent the bushes all around the chalet-style house. Rooms have a mountain cabin feel. You won't mind the lack of air-conditioning as nights are pleasantly cool. Hot water is appreciated. Two superior deluxe rooms include a suite with a whirlpool tub and a view of the mountains; the other large room below also has a four-poster king bed and a private balcony that opens to a garden.

A few kilometers Past Hagley Gap, just over the border in the parish of St. Thomas, is **Whitfield Hall** (Penlyne, St. Thomas, tel. 876/927-0986 or 876/878-0514, www.whitfieldhall.com, dorm US$20, room US$55, tent with use of indoor facilities US$10), a beautiful old house and coffee farm that offers rustic lodging in a grand setting with a well-appreciated fireplace to fend off the evening chill. Whitfield is the most common starting point for expeditions up to Blue Mountain Peak via Portland Gap, which generally start in the early morning hours to

the majestic Blue Mountains

arrive at the summit for sunrise, when there is the best chance at taking in a clear view. As the morning progresses, clouds tend to roll in, often obscuring the peaks and valleys. A guide to the peak (US$36 per party) can be arranged. Penlyne is only accessible by 4WD from Mavis Bank. Transportation can be arranged from any point in Kingston (US$100) or Mavis Bank (US$60) for up to six people.

Getting There and Around

The Blue Mountains are accessible from three points: from Kingston via Papine; from Yallahs, St. Thomas, via Cedar Valley; and from Buff Bay, St. Mary, on the North Coast, via the B1, which runs alongside the Buff Bay River. The B1 route is a very narrow road barely wide enough for one vehicle in many places.

There are two main routes to access the south-facing slopes of the Blue Mountain range. The first, accessed by taking a left onto the B1 at the Cooperage, leads through Maryland to Irish Town, Redlight, Newcastle, and Hardwar Gap before the Buff Bay River Valley opens up overlooking Portland and St. Mary on the other side of the range. The second route, straight ahead at the Cooperage along Gordon Town Road, leads to Gordon Town and then, taking a right at the town square over the bridge, to Mavis Bank. Continuing beyond Mavis Bank requires a 4WD vehicle, and you can either take a left

at Hagley Gap to Penlyne or go straight down to Cedar Valley and along the Yallahs River to the town of Yallahs.

Getting to and around the Blue Mountains can be a challenge, even if keeping lunch down on the way isn't. Only for the upper reaches, namely beyond Mavis Bank, is it really necessary to have a 4WD vehicle; otherwise the abundant potholes and washed-out road are only mildly more challenging to navigate than any other part of Jamaica due to the sharp turns.

A hired **taxi** into the Blue Mountains will cost upward of US$50 for a drop-off at Strawberry Hill, and at least US$100 for the day to be chauffeured around. **Route taxis** travel between Papine and Gordon Town (US$3) throughout the day, as well as to Irish Town (US$4); you'll have to wait for the car to fill up with passengers before it departs.

To reach Whitfield Hall, the most common starting point for hiking up to Blue Mountain Peak, 4WD taxis can be arranged by calling Whitfield Hall.

Many travelers find letting a tour operator take care of the driving is the easiest, most hassle-free way to get around the island. One of the most dependable and versatile tour companies on the island is **Barrett Adventures** (contact Carolyn Barrett, cell tel. 876/382-6384). Barrett can pick you up from any point on the island and specializes in off-the-beaten-path tours.

The South Coast

Mandeville............280

North of Mandeville....284

South of Mandeville ...286

Treasure Beach........288

Black River and South
    Cockpit Country 298

The South Coast is the place to get away from

crowded tourist hubs and see some of the country's farmland and less-frequented coastline.

Rather than boasting grandiose or glitzy resorts, this region, covering the parishes of Elizabeth, Manchester, and Clarendon, offers accommodations with rustic charm and unpretentious luxury, with the highest concentration and variety in Treasure Beach. If unwinding away from it all gets dull, there's still plenty to do: YS Falls is one the best waterfall attractions in Jamaica. Appleton Estate welcomes visitors to tour the distillery producing the island's most revered rum. Many swimming holes along the South Coast are visited rarely, even by locals,

Highlights

Look for ★ to find recommended sights, activities, dining, and lodging.

★ **Guts River:** A desolate stretch of coastal road east of Alligator Pond leads to a seldom-visited swimming hole (page 287).

★ **Pelican Bar:** Located on a sandbar about 1.5 kilometers (1 mile) offshore, this is a great place to spend an afternoon snorkeling and eating fresh fish (page 298).

★ **Lower Black River Morass:** As one of Jamaica's largest wetlands, this mangrove and swamp is home to a variety of unique animals and plantlife (page 299).

★ **YS Falls:** This well-managed waterfalls attraction offers swimming, a rope swing, and a heart-thumping zip-line tour high above the river (page 300).

★ **Rum Tasting at Appleton Estate:** Take a tour at the distillery of Jamaica's most popular spirits brand (page 302).

and languid fishing villages dot the coast from Treasure Beach to Rocky Point.

High above the plains, the cool air of Mandeville has been a draw for centuries. It's often referred to as the "retirement capital of Jamaica" for the number of repatriating Jamaicans who call the small city home. Serious birders will find a warm welcome at Marshall's Pen, and foodies will find a handful of noteworthy restaurants and bars, making Mandeville a worthwhile stop for a bite or even an overnight on trips between Kingston and points west. It's not a place that keeps visitors long, though, which makes it an attraction in itself as a major population center representing the "real" Jamaica.

PLANNING YOUR TIME

If your goal is to hit the main sights and take in a bit of South Coast culture, a few days in Treasure Beach and a night in Mandeville is probably sufficient. Treasure Beach is the kind of place many find hard to leave, with a unique feel and windswept natural beauty that gives the area its rough-edged charm. The immediate surroundings of Treasure Beach lend themselves to long walks in Back Sea Side (a wilderness area with tall grass waving in the wind covering sand dunes and a rocky shoreline), hiking in the Santa Cruz Mountains, boat rides, and cautious swimming. The sea in Treasure Beach can be treacherous, with strong tides and undercurrents.

Most people visiting the South Coast choose Treasure Beach as a base, making day trips to surrounding attractions. Treasure Beach is a string of seaside fishing villages along a 10-kilometer (6-mile) stretch of coast from Great Pedro Bluff westward with numerous beaches and coral-lined coves. It has the most varied lodging options on the South Coast, with a low-key, hip vibe, several swimmable beaches, and unique scenery. A few decent lodging options are found farther west outside Black River, but it's not a magnetic destination for most. Mandeville also has a smattering of decent hotels, and for those set on getting as much curative power as possible from the hot baths at Milk River, the attached hotel has basic affordable rooms. For its river tours in the company of exotic birds and alligators and the inimitable Pelican Bar just offshore, Black River is a unique destination worthy of at least a day trip.

SAFETY

Locals in these parishes are less dependent on tourism dollars, so travelers tend to find a welcome respite from the prolific street hustling that can be a nuisance elsewhere on the island. Nevertheless, travelers are best advised to keep their wits about them, to avoid compromising or vulnerable situations, not to keep valuables lying around or unattended while swimming, and not to wander alone on deserted stretches of beach or road at night. Don't draw attention to yourself or trust strangers. When partying, stick with a group.

Beaches along the South Coast are often deserted, and swimming alone is not safe, especially in Treasure Beach, where anglers and even experienced swimmers drown regularly. The current and undertow in all the bays of Treasure Beach can be dangerous, and it's wise to ask the locals about conditions before getting too comfortable in the water. It's also advisable to avoid eating jackfish and barracuda, which can accumulate high concentrations of ciguatera toxin, a heat-stable compound that can cause severe food poisoning.

Previous: YS Falls; firey pepper shrimp; Appleton Estate, home of Jamaica's leading rum brand

The South Coast

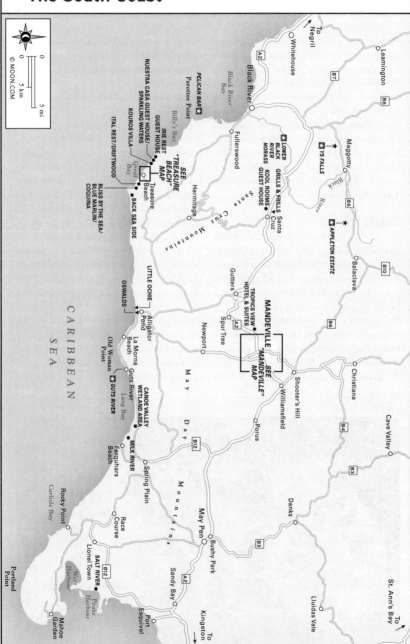

@ MOON.COM

0 — 5 km
0 — 5 mi

CARIBBEAN SEA

Black River Bay

PELICAN BAR

Billy's Bay

NUESTRA CASA GUEST HOUSE/
SPARKLING WATERS

IRIE REST GUEST HOUSE

KOUROS VILLA

ITAL REST/DRIFTWOOD

SEE "TREASURE BEACH" MAP

Parottee Point

Great Bay

Treasure Beach

BLISS BY THE SEA/
BLUE MARLIN/
COQUINA

BACK SEA SIDE

LITTLE OCHIE

OSWALDS

Alligator Pond

La Morna Beach

Old Woman Point

Guts River

GUTS RIVER

CANOE VALLEY WETLAND AREA

Long Bay

MILK RIVER

Farquhars Beach

Spring Plain

Rocky Point

Carlisle Bay

Race Course

SALT RIVER

Lionel Town

West Harbour

Peake Harbour

Portland Point

Mahoe Garden

To Negril

Whitehouse

Leamington

Black River

Fullerswood

Hermitage

LOWER BLACK RIVER MORASS

GRILLS & FRILLS

KOOL ROOMS GUEST HOUSE

Santa Cruz

YS FALLS

Maggotty

APPLETON ESTATE

Balaclava

Santa Cruz Mountains

Gutters

Newport

Spur Tree

TROPICS VIEW HOTEL & SUITES

MANDEVILLE

SEE "MANDEVILLE" MAP

Shooter's Hill

Williamsfield

Christiana

Cave Valley

Porus

M a y   D a y   M o u n t a i n s

May Pen

Bushy Park

Danks

Sandy Bay

Lluidas Vale

St. Ann's Bay

Port Esquivel

To Kingston

Black River

A2

B7

B6

B10

B6

B4

B3

B12

B12

B3

A2

Mandeville

Manchester is Jamaica's sixth-largest parish, much of it at relatively high altitudes with three mountain ranges: the May Day Mountains, the Don Figuerero Mountains, and the Carpenters Mountains, which have the highest peak in the parish at 844 meters (2,769 feet). Any approach to Mandeville, the parish capital, entails a steep climb, fortunately along some well-maintained roads. Caution is advised in navigating the sharp turns and heavy grades, especially along Spur Tree Hill, known as an accident hotspot.

SIGHTS

Mandeville's historic sights are concentrated around the town square, Cecil Charlton Park. These include the **Mandeville Courthouse,** built of limestone using slave labor and finished in 1820. The courthouse had the town's first school on its ground floor. The **Mandeville Jail and Workhouse,** also among the first public buildings in town, is now in use as the police station. Adjacent to the courthouse, the **Mandeville Rectory** is the oldest house of worship and the original

Anglican rectory in Mandeville, having once also served as a tavern and guesthouse, to the dismay of many parishioners.

Bird-Watching at Marshall's Pen

A popular spot for serious birding for many years, **Marshall's Pen** (contact Ann Sutton, tel. 876/904-5454, cell tel. 876/877-7335, asutton@cwjamaica.com) attracts birders to see the Jamaican owl, especially, which can often be seen in its favorite cedar tree. Of Jamaica's 28 endemic birds, 23 have been spotted at Marshall's Pen, with a total of 110 species recorded on the property over the years.

Marshall's Pen was built in 1795 at the latest; the exact date is a mystery. Originally the estate was about 810 hectares (2,000 acres), whereas today it has dwindled to a still respectable 120 hectares (300 acres). The origin of the name is also ambiguous. The present owner is Ann Sutton, widow of the late Robert Sutton, one of Jamaica's foremost ornithologists, who created an audio catalog of Jamaican bird songs that was

a Jamaican Tody at Marshall's Pen

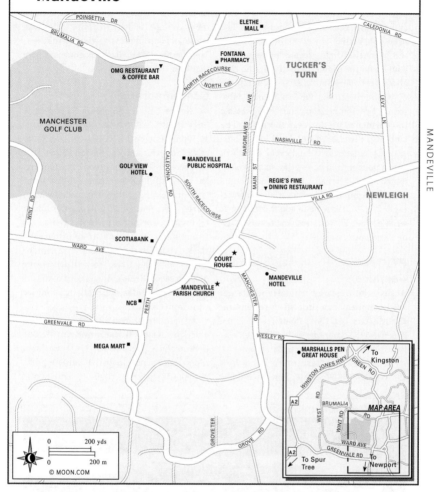

Mandeville

released by Cornell University's ornithology department.

Robert Sutton coauthored *Birds of Jamaica,* the island's best bird guide. Herself an ornithologist and conservationist, Ann Sutton welcomes serious birders to Marshall's Pen, where they will find warm hospitality on a tour of the great house and extensive gardens (by appointment only, minimum 6 people, US$20 pp). Visitors will find orchids, anthuriums, ferns, and other indigenous plants.

NIGHTLIFE

Paris Ville Nightclub (Willowgate Plaza) is the most happening spot in Mandeville, hosting Beer Rave Wednesday, Ladies Night Thursday, After Work Jam Friday, Clubbing Saturday, and Karaoke-Retro Sunday.

RECREATION

The oldest golf course in the western hemisphere, **Manchester Club** (Caledonia Rd., tel. 876/962-2403, manchester_club@hotmail.com) dates to 1865 and remains the least expensive course in Jamaica (greens fees US$30, clubs US$12, caddy US$14 per round). The nine-hole course is well maintained, even if it is not the bright green of more popular courses on the island. Beyond golf, the club also offers tennis on three hard courts, the only squash court on the South Coast, table tennis, a swimming pool, and a billiard table in continuous use for over 100 years. The club also hosts barbecues and luncheons. A golf tournament is held every month in which golfers from across the island participate. The All Jamaica Hard Court Tennis Championship is held each summer, attracting over 200 children and adults over a one-week period. There's a resident tennis coach and a golf professional.

FOOD
Jamaican
Across the highway from Hood Daniel Well Company is a little sit-in restaurant, **Claudette's Top Class** (Spur Tree Hill, tel. 876/964-6452, 8am-4pm daily, US$4-10), a favorite local spot to get curry goat.

★ **All Seasons Restaurant Bar & Jerk Centre** (tel. 876/965-4030, 8am-11pm daily, US$5-20) is considered by many to be the best jerk spot in Manchester, with other typical Jamaican dishes served as well. Perched on the steep slopes of Spur Tree Hill, All Seasons commands an impressive view of southern Manchester and St. Elizabeth, down to where the sky meets the sea.

Contemporary
★ **Regie's Bistro** (37 Main St., entrance on Villa Rd., tel. 876/285-6605, 11:30am-10:30pm Mon.-Sat., US$3.50-40) serves creative Jamaican and Caribbean dishes in a cozy second-floor dining room. The top level has a beautiful outdoor bar area suitable for large groups and parties. The menu includes starters like jerk chicken drumsticks, buffalo wings, shrimp bruschetta, and salad. Sumptuous entrées range from prime aged steaks, chops, and ribs to lobster thermidor and coconut shrimp beignets with pepper jelly dipping sauce. Regie's also has one of the area's best international wine lists, including ice wine from Canada.

An upscale restaurant with marble tables and a sleek bar, **OMG Restaurant & Coffee Bar** (1 Brumalia Rd., tel. 876/962-7251, 7am-10pm Mon.-Sat., brunch 10am-3:30pm Sun., dinner 5pm-10pm Sun., US$10-50) serves a mix

All Seasons Jerk Centre on Spur Tree Hill

of vegetarian and meat dishes with appetizers like calamari al aioli, shrimp margarita, and spring rolls. Entrées range from snapper cutlet pan fried in caper butter to duckling breast. OMG is in Cobblestone Professional Centre, the first set of buildings on Brumalia Road on the left coming up from Caledonia Road.

Chinese

Upstairs from Cash & Carry Supermarket, **Bamboo Garden Restaurant** (35 Ward Ave., tel. 876/962-4515, noon-10pm Mon.-Sat., 1pm-10pm Sun., US$7-30) serves sweet-and-sour chicken, butterfly shrimp, and lobster with butter and cola.

Lucky Dragon Restaurant (shops 9-10, Orange Complex, 5½ Caledonia Ave., tel. 876/961-6544 or 876/867-6720, 11am-10pm Mon.-Sat., noon-10pm Sun., US$2-8) offers dine-in, takeout, and delivery of standard Chinese fare.

Seafood

An urban outpost of the original Little Ochie in Alligator Pond, ★ **Little Ochie Mandeville Seafood Specialist** (beside Nashville Plaza, cell tel. 876/367-6340, 11am-11pm Mon.-Thurs., 11am-late Fri.-Sun., US$7-20) serves fish, conch, and lobster tail. It's the best place in town for seafood, answering the call locals were making for years to bring Little Ochie to them instead of having to make the trek down Spur Tree Hill to the St. Elizabeth coast. Next door, a vendor sells roasted breadfruit, a favorite accompaniment for the seafood.

In the Hopeton district between Kingsland and Hatfield, going up Spur Tree Hill from Mandeville, **Gran's Seafood and Bar** (tel. 876/603-4254, noon-midnight daily, US$7-17) is the best spot on the hill for seafood, including steamed, escoveitch, and fried fish; shrimp; and lobster.

ACCOMMODATIONS
Under US$100

A 62-room hotel near the center of town, **Golf View** (5½ Caledonia Rd., tel. 876/962-4477, golfviewhotelmandeville@gmail.com, www.thegolfviewhotel.com) has standard rooms (US$95) that have a ceiling fan and private baths with hot water. Deluxe rooms (US$110) and a one-bedroom suite (US$120) have air-conditioning, while the sole two-bedroom suite (US$135) does not. The central location is probably the best feature of this hotel. The hotel claims the same address as the Odeon Cineplex but is actually not adjacent, sitting a bit farther down Caledonia Road at the top of Golf View Plaza, bordering the golf course.

The oldest hotel operating in Mandeville is **The Mandeville Hotel** (4 Hotel St., tel. 876/962-2460, reservations@themandevillehotel.com, mandevillehoteljamaica.com, US$63-103). Clean sheets, ceiling fans, air-conditioning, a fridge in some rooms, cable TV, and hot water make this a comfortable option in the heart of town. Bring your own soap and shampoo. Rooms have full, queen, and king beds. There are also junior suites and one- to three-bedroom apartments.

Tropics View Hotel (Wardville District, off Winston Jones Hwy., tel. 876/625-2452, tropicsviewhotel.frontdesk@gmail.com, tropicsview@cwjamaica.com, www.tropicsview.com, from US$70, includes breakfast) offers Wi-Fi throughout, a pool, a gym, a basketball court, and a restaurant and bar. Standard rooms have queen beds and private baths with hot water. Two-bedroom suites (US$125) are also available. A restaurant and bar (7am-10pm daily) by the front gate on the property serves local dishes. Rooms have ceiling fans and no air-conditioning, but it rarely gets hot in Mandeville. Standing fans are available on request.

INFORMATION AND SERVICES
Medical

Hargreaves Memorial Hospital (Caledonia Ave., tel. 876/961-1589) is a private clinic, with many of its staff also working at Mandeville Regional. **Mandeville Regional Hospital** (32 Hargreaves Ave., tel. 876/962-3370) is the largest hospital for kilometers around, with a good reputation.

Money

In Mandeville, both **NCB** (9 Manchester Rd., tel. 876/962-2161; Mandeville Plaza, tel. 876/962-2618) and **Scotiabank** (1A Caledonia Rd., tel. 876/962-2035) have bank branches with ATMs.

GETTING THERE AND AROUND

Mandeville is served by regular **buses** from Kingston and May Pen and regular **route taxis** departing from the square for surrounding destinations including May Pen, Christiana, and Santa Cruz (US$2).

The main road west from Mandeville (the A2) rises over Spur Tree Hill and is infamous as a dangerous stretch to drive—the road plunges from around 600 meters (2,000 feet) elevation to sea level in the span of less than 10 kilometers (6 miles). It is famous for a roadside jerk center with a panoramic view and two curry goat huts, Alex Curry Goat and Claudette's Top Class. From atop Spur Tree Hill, the view of Manchester's lowlands, St. Elizabeth, and Westmoreland is spectacular; the roof deck at All Seasons Jerk Centre

provides a great vantage point to look out over the plains and the Santa Cruz Mountains tapering down to the sea.

One of Jamaica's best thoroughfares is a stretch of toll road known as **Highway 2000.** It begins in Portmore and leads west to rejoin the A2 in May Pen. From May Pen, the A2 climbs to the upper reaches of Manchester, passing Mandeville along the bypass before descending down Spur Tree Hill to the South Coast and extending as far west as Negril. To get from Mandeville to the North Coast, head east toward Kingston and turn north along the descent, following signs for Christiana, and then toward Spalding, Cave Valley, Alexandria, and Brown's Town, the last major population center before reaching Runaway Bay.

From Mandeville, the drive to Kingston takes about 1.5 hours along the toll road from May Pen, with Treasure Beach within 1.5 hours in the opposite direction. Negril, Montego Bay, and Ocho Rios are all about a 2-hour drive, and Port Antonio is another 1.5 hours east of Ocho Rios along the North Coast.

North of Mandeville

To the north of Mandeville, rolling hills ascend toward the town of Christiana, located near the center of the island at the edge of Cockpit Country, the interior so named for its characteristic karst formations that give the hilly countryside a pitted look.

CHRISTIANA

A small community near the highest reaches of Manchester, Christiana is a quiet town with one main drag and a single guest house. The most popular attraction in town is **Christiana Bottom,** a gorge located within walking distance of the town center. Located 20 kilometers (12 miles) from Mandeville, Christiana has little to attract visitors in the town itself. The surrounding area, however

has a few natural attractions and protected areas worth checking out.

Sights
CHRISTIANA BOTTOM

An alluring river valley located below the town of Christiana, **Christiana Bottom** is popular for its Blue Hole, a natural pool fed by underground streams and small waterfalls. There's another waterfall at William Hole, farther downstream. To get here from Mandeville, turn right immediately after the NCB bank on Moravia Road, then take the first left around a blind corner, and then the first right, which leads to Christiana Bottom. Continue past the first left that leads to Tyme Town, and park at the entrance to the second left, a wide path that leads down to the river. Ask for Mr. Jones for a guided tour (US$20) of Blue Hole and William Hole and his farm, where he grows ginger, yams, potatoes, pineapples, bananas, and sugarcane.

GOURIE RECREATIONAL PARK

Located between Christiana and Colleyville, about three kilometers (2 miles) past Christiana, **Gourie Recreational Park** was recently upgraded under a United Nations Development Program with eco-cabins for short-term rentals. To get here, take the first left immediately after passing Bryce United Church, then take the first right until reaching the unmanned Forestry Department station and picnic area. **Gourie Cave,** a highlight of the park, is not actually inside the park but rather about 400 meters (0.25 miles) down the hill to the left of the park entrance. A picnic and camping area near the cave entrance has a hut, tables, and benches. The main trail through the park leads to the community of Ticky Ticky, with excellent views along the way of the Santa Cruz Mountains, Spur Tree Hill, and the historic Bethany Moravian Church.

Gourie Cave is the longest cave in Jamaica and is said to have been used as a hideout by escaped enslaved people. The cave follows the channels of an underground river about one meter (3 feet) deep, depending on how much rain has fallen. If you go north from the main entrance and upstream, you end up on the other side of Colleyville Mountain. A different route leads downstream along the underground river, deep into the earth where there are several caverns along the way. If you're going to explore in the cave, you should monitor the weather and be aware of any rain in the forecast, though the cave is not prone to flooding. It's not wise to venture into the cave alone.

SCOTT'S PASS

The official headquarters of the Nyabinghi House of Rastafari in Jamaica is at **Scott's Pass** (between Toll Gate and Porus), where House of Elders is based. The land was bought by Bob Marley and given to the Binghi for that specific purpose. The community members are for the most part welcoming of visitors, but you may get some evil eyes if you fail to recognize their customs for the Binghi celebrations: women must wear skirts or dresses (no pants) and cover their heads, while men must not cover their heads.

To arrange a visit or learn about the birthday celebrations or other Nyabinghi events

historic Bethany Moravian Church

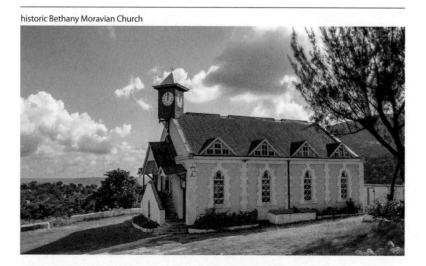

around the island, contact the Rasta in Charge, Paul Reid, known as **Iyatolah** (cell tel. 876/850-3469), or Ras High Vybes (cell tel. 876/486-1724). Arts and crafts are sold throughout the year at Scott's Pass. A small donation toward the maintenance and development of the community at the end of the tour is encouraged.

Roy "Ras Carver" Bent (cell tel. 876/866-7745, rascarver@gmail.com) is a Nyabinghi elder and master drum maker associated with the Scott's Pass order of Rastafari who lives in nearby May Pen. Ras Carver fashions, tunes, repairs, and sells the full line of drums used at Nyabinghi ceremonies. Important **Binghi celebrations** throughout the year include Ethiopian Christmas (Jan. 7), a celebration during Black History Month and Reggae Month (a couple of days in Feb.), commemoration of His Majesty's 1966 visit to Jamaica (Apr. 21), All African Liberation Day (May 25), Marcus Garvey's birthday (3 nights around Aug. 19), Ethiopian New Year (3-7 days starting Sept. 11), and Haile Selassie's coronation (Nov. 2).

The Scott's Pass Nyabinghi community is located one kilometer (0.6 mile) west of the Juici Patty factory in Toll Gate just over the Clarendon-Manchester border. Take the left (heading west) over a small bridge crossing the Milk River on the south side of the road upon entering Scott's Pass and go up the hill, where you'll find the homes of several members of the Nyabinghi community.

South of Mandeville

Jamaica's central southern coast stretches across the parishes of Clarendon, Manchester, and St. Elizabeth. Much of this coastline is rugged and rocky with rough seas. It's a region that sees far fewer tourists than the north and west coasts of the island, drawing visitors who eschew crowded resorts and favor a more low-key community-based tourism experience. The sites south of Mandeville are listed east to west.

CANOE VALLEY WETLAND

Just east of Guts River, **Canoe Valley Protected Area** (Coast Rd., contact rangers Devon Douglas, cell tel. 876/578-9456, or Ucal Whyte, cell tel. 876/874-1422) is a coastal wetlands area full of diverse plant and animal life. The manatees that live in semi-captivity along the river in the park are the highlight. **Rowboat excursions** (US$20 pp) to spot the manatees and snorkel (gear not provided) in the surreal crystal blue waters are offered from the ranger station, a few kilometers south of Milk River. The rangers at the station also offer hikes to remote Taino Caves

(rates negotiable). Turtles and alligators also share the waters; swimmers are advised to be vigilant.

There are a few ways to get to Canoe Valley Protected Area, the best option depending on which direction you're coming from. The most straightforward route is along James Road, which leaves the A2 in Toll Gate, 12 kilometers (7.5 miles) east of the end of the Highway 2000 toll road, following signs for Milk River. It's a straight shot west for 2 kilometers (1.2 miles) before the road turns south for 10 kilometers (6 miles) to Milk River. Turn west on Coast Road 2 kilometers (1.2 miles) south of the square in Milk River. The Canoe Valley Protected Area is 3.5 kilometers (2 miles) west of the junction. Alligator Pond is 16 kilometers (10 miles) farther west along Coast Road, which is heavily potholed and overgrown in places. From the west, turn south at the base of Spur Tree Hill, following signs for Little Ochie, and head straight south to Alligator Pond. From Alligator Pond, turn east for 20 kilometers (12.5 miles) on Coast Road.

★ GUTS RIVER

Guts River (Coast Rd., Manchester) is a crystalline swimming hole about 16 kilometers (10 miles) east along the coast into Manchester from Alligator Pond. The Guts River creates a small pool as it emerges from the rocks with cool, crystal-clear waters purported to have medicinal qualities. The deserted beach nearby is great for a stroll. If you don't have your own vehicle, getting to Guts River requires chartering a taxi or hiring a boat from Treasure Beach or Alligator Pond. Guts River is located 12 kilometers (7 miles) east of Alligator Pond along Coast Road.

ALLIGATOR POND

One of the busiest fishing villages on the South Coast, Alligator Pond has a few popular seafood restaurants. To get to Alligator Pond, turn south at the bottom of Spur Tree Hill (a left coming from Mandeville, a right from Santa Cruz) and continue straight for 18 kilometers (11 miles) until you reach the coast.

On the main fishing beach in Alligator Pond, ★ **Oswald's** (cell tel. 876/381-3535, 10am-11pm daily, fish US$13 per pound, lobster US$25 per pound) serves excellent seafood, including shrimp, lobster, fish, and oysters, along with various sides, in a casual setting.

Seafood emporium **Little Ochie** (tel. 876/610-9692, cell tel. 876/852-6430, little. ochie@yahoo.com, www.littleochie.com, 9am-midnight daily, US$10-30) has a wide range of dishes, including jerk and garlic crab, fish, and lobster. Over 75 seafood recipes are utilized on a daily basis, with lobster cooked 15 different ways, the best of which could very well be the garlic sauce.

The **Little Ochie Seafood Festival** (tel. 876/852-6430, little.ochie@yahoo.com), held the first or second Sunday in July, draws patrons from across the island for the lobster, fish, oysters, and cultural activities that range from traditional dance to popular reggae acts.

JUNCTION

A busy stopover point on the way over the Santa Cruz Mountains, Junction is the closest outpost of civilization to Treasure Beach that has supermarkets and banks. Junction Guest House offers basic accommodations, and a few restaurants serve hearty meals. To reach Junction, turn south on Gutters Main Road off the A2, following signs for Alligator Pond and Junction Guest House across from the Texaco station at the base of Spur Tree

excellent seafood at Oswald's in Alligator Pond village

Hill. Turn right toward the southwest at the second three-way intersection 2.4 kilometers (1.5 miles) from the Texaco station onto Alpart Main Road. Turn left on Nain Main Road at the T intersection after the speed bump, 2.6 kilometers (1.6 miles) from Gutters Main Road. Nain Main Road joins Junction Main Road about 5 kilometers (3 miles) farther south, about 3 kilometers (2 miles) before reaching Junction.

Just before Junction, ★ **Atlantis Seafood** (Junction Main Rd., contact Shay Sinclair, cell tel. 876/409-3373, 10:30am-10pm daily), connected to Lunie's Hot Spot, serves the best seafood in the area, with fish, lobster, conch, crab, and shrimp (US$10-25 per pound). Call ahead to put in your order to minimize wait time.

Junction Oasis Café Restaurant (Main St., cell tel. 876/508-9802 or 876/312-0116, 7am-8pm Mon.-Sat.) serves baked beans and salt mackerel, callaloo and cabbage, kidney and liver, and ackee and saltfish for breakfast and escoveitch fish, curry goat, and chicken prepared many ways for lunch and dinner. Karaoke night on Thursday is a hit with locals.

Heavy's Bar & Grill (between Junction and Bull Savanna) is the hottest club in the area.

Junction Guest House (tel. 876/965-8668, www.junctionguesthouse.com, US$30-150) has basic rooms with fans, private baths, TVs, and air-conditioning. There's also a suite with a kitchen and a veranda.

The best options for groceries are the **Shopper's Fair** (Caledonia Rd., tel. 876/618-1430, 9am-8pm Mon.-Thurs., 9am-9pm Fri.-Sat., 10am-5pm Sun.) and **Intown Super Save Supermarket** (Bull Savannah Main Rd., tel. 876/965-8764, 8am-8pm Mon.-Wed., 8am-8:30pm Thurs., 8:30am-9pm Fri., 8:30am-9:30pm Sat., 9am-8pm Sun.). **NCB** (tel. 876/965-8611) and **Scotiabank** (shop 1, Tony Rowe Plaza, tel. 876/965-8257) have branches with ATMs.

Treasure Beach

Isolated from the rest of the island by the Santa Cruz mountains, which create the area's distinct coastal desert environment by capturing the westbound rainfall, Treasure Beach is a catch-all name for a series of bays and fishing villages that extend from Fort Charles, at the community's western edge, to Billy's Bay, Frenchman's Bay, and Great Bay, on the eastern side. Treasure Beach prides itself on offering a different kind of experience than in Jamaica's more built-up tourism centers. Local ownership of the guesthouses and restaurants is more the rule than the exception, with ample opportunity to interact with everyday Jamaicans beyond being served a cocktail.

Many of the bays have decent swimming areas, but it's best to inquire with locals about the safety of jumping in the water at any particular point until you get accustomed to the area. Remain vigilant of riptides and strong currents.

SIGHTS

As an off-the-beaten-track destination, the main appeal of Treasure Beach is the community itself and the infectious sleepy pace that permeates the area. Despite their laid-back nature, residents of St. Elizabeth pride themselves on being extremely hardworking, from people on fishing boats who spend days out at sea to the farmers who take great care in mulching and watering their crops to fight the perpetual drought. Despite the lack of mass-market tourist attractions along the Treasure Beach coast, there are several worthwhile excursions within an hour's drive, many of which are around Black River. There are also a few notable attractions east of Treasure Beach along the coast.

Less than 16 kilometers (10 miles) east of Treasure Beach along the coast, **Lovers' Leap** (Southfield, tel. 876/965-6887, cell tel. 876/595-2421, 10am-8pm Mon.-Thurs.,

Treasure Beach

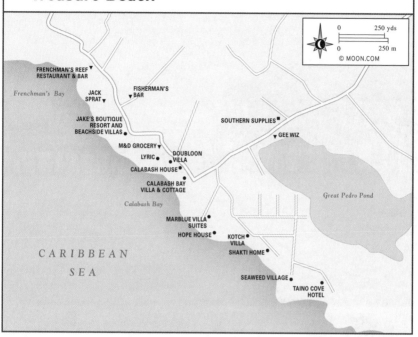

0 250 yds
0 250 m
© MOON.COM

FRENCHMAN'S REEF
RESTAURANT & BAR

Frenchman's Bay

JACK
SPRAT

FISHERMAN'S
BAR

JAKE'S BOUTIQUE
RESORT AND
BEACHSIDE VILLAS

SOUTHERN SUPPLIES

GEE WIZ

M&D GROCERY

LYRIC

DOUBLOON
VILLA

CALABASH HOUSE

CALABASH BAY
VILLA & COTTAGE

Great Pedro Pond

Calabash Bay

MARBLUE VILLA
SUITES

HOPE HOUSE

KOTCH
VILLA

SHAKTI HOME

CARIBBEAN

SEA

SEAWEED VILLAGE

TAINO COVE
HOTEL

10am-10pm Fri.-Sun., restaurant 1pm-close daily) is a 480-meter (1,575-foot) drop to the sea. According to legend, an enslaved couple leapt to their deaths to avoid forced separation by their owner, who was lusting after the woman. As the legend has it, an old woman who witnessed their leap said the moon caught them up in a golden net, and they were last seen holding hands, standing on the moon as it sank over the horizon. A lighthouse was built on the point in 1979 and can be seen from 35 kilometers (22 miles) out at sea. Admission is US$3, or support the bar and restaurant in lieu of admission.

Recent renovations have created a more rustic, natural look and feel, and menu upgrades have brought new life. A selector (DJ) plays a mix of lovers, rock, and reggae from 5pm Saturday, and a live band performs 6pm-8pm Sunday. The crowd is mostly local, with a smattering of international visitors. The menu includes oxtail and beans; curry goat; jerk and fried chicken; fried, steamed, brown stew, or jerk fish; lobster in season; veggie, chicken, and beef burgers; and appetizers of codfish fritters, wings, and fish tea. Vegetarians can try the bean stew. The 30-minute drive from Treasure Beach is worth the view, the fable, and the unique topography of the clifftop location.

BEACHES

Wherever you go in the water in Treasure Beach, it's best to have a companion and to inquire with locals to ensure it is safe. Many have fallen victim to the hungry sea, which can have strong currents and undertows. Treasure Beach has several lovely expanses of golden sand in small coves and wide bays, some of them protected by coral just offshore that creates large wading pools ideal for small children. Other areas not fit for swimming embody the rugged charm that gives the area its distinct appeal.

Frenchman's Beach is great for body surfing when the sea is a little rough, but be sure to watch out for the coral toward the edges of this beach, even in shallow waters. The safest spot to swim is directly in front of Golden Sands Guest House. Calabash Bay Beach is a fishing beach with a large clear sandy area that's good for swimming. The safest spot to swim is in front of Calabash House, west of the lined-up fishing boats. Great Bay has the best beach in the area for unencumbered swimming. Protected from the prevailing easterly winds by Great Pedro Bluff, Great Bay lacks the offshore reefs protecting many of the beaches in Treasure Beach and has a comfortable slope into the sea, with a wide sandy beach. A handful of villas on this beach offer unpretentious comfort at a great value.

Back Sea Side is a wilderness area found inland from Great Pedro Bluff with meadows covered in tall grass that looks like waves as the breeze hits it. A dirt road leads through the area from the eastern end of Great Bay and curves around to the eastern shore of Great Pedro Bluff, where large boulders and coral outcroppings dot the rugged coast. This is not a good place for swimming, but the scenery is beautiful and the area makes for great walks.

RECREATION

People come to Treasure Beach to get a different experience from the bustling tourist hubs of Ocho Rios, Negril, and Montego Bay. Swimming, fishing, long walks, and yoga are the most popular recreational activities.

Dennis Abrahams runs Captain Dennis Adventure (cell tel. 876/435-3779, tel. 876/965-3084, dennisabrahams@yahoo.com), offering excursions and fishing trips to Pelican Bar alone (US$85 for 2 people), to Black River and Pelican Bar (US$140), or to secluded white-sand beaches, where he'll cook up a private seafood meal. Dennis also offers fishing excursions (US$60 per hour).

1: Pelican Bar 2: Treasure Beach

SPAS

Run by Great Bay native herbalist Shirley Genus, Shirley's Steam Bath (tel. 876/965-3820, cell tel. 876/827-2447, smgenus@hotmail.com, open daily by appointment) is a local institution offering 15-minute herbal steam baths along with 30- or 60-minute massage sessions (US$85-100). Joshua Lee Stein's Joshua's Massage & Bodywork (tel. 876/965-0583, cell tel. 876/389-3698, doctorlee85@outlook.com, www.joshualeestein.com, by appointment 9am-5pm daily, 1 hour US$80, 1.5 hours US$115) offers deep and light pressure, gentle movement, and sensitive touch massage therapy on location by appointment.

Jake's Driftwood Spa (Calabash Bay, tel. 876/965-3000, stay@jakeshotel.com, www.jakeshotel.com, US$55-140) offers a mélange of techniques and philosophies from around the world, with treatments that include Swedish, aromatherapy, and tai chi energy massages. The spa uses ingredients sourced in Jamaica, like coffee, wild ginger, mint mocha rum, and lemongrass for body scrubs and facials. Open-air treatment rooms let the ocean breeze and crashing waves enhance the experience and put patrons in relax mode. The spa also offers alfresco yoga sessions.

ENTERTAINMENT

If you're looking for wild all-night parties, Treasure Beach won't cut it. Romantic sunsets and quiet nights are more the norm than live music or blaring dancehall, which is part of the area's allure. Nonetheless, a few venues see regular activity on weekends; most operate as restaurants during the day as much as nightspots. Treasure Beach comes alive for annual events like Calabash Literary Festival and the Hook 'n' Line Fishing Tournament, with bonfires on the beach and roots reggae pumping from sound systems well into the night.

Nightlife

The closest thing to a club in Treasure Beach is Fisherman's Bar (cell tel. 876/379-9780, 10pm-2am daily), with dancehall and roots

Farm-to-Table Dinners at Jakes

The farm-to-table movement hasn't been lost on Jamaica's number-one agricultural community in St. Elizabeth, and the savvy entrepreneurs at Jakes Boutique Resort have wholeheartedly embraced the growing interest in reducing the intermediaries between production and consumption. **Jakes farm-to-table dinners** (www.jakeshotel.com) are held each month at a long communal table on Dool's farm near Southfield. Each month a different guest chef is invited to create a five-course meal using mostly local ingredients. Not for travelers on a budget, the tantalizing flavors and good company will surely be a memorable highlight of any trip to Treasure Beach. Check the website for upcoming dates.

reggae booming. A pool table and domino area around back are popular with locals, while the restaurant out front serves typical Jamaican fare at reasonable prices. The venue occasionally hosts live music.

Festivals and Events

A fun, free event held every other year the last weekend in May or first weekend in June, **Calabash Literary Festival** (www.calabashfestival.org) is at **Jake's** (tel. 876/965-0635, www.jakeshotel.com). The event draws writers, poets, musicians, and attendees from across the Caribbean and African diaspora, as well as featuring some of Jamaica's most accomplished lyricists and authors.

The last weekend in April, **Jake's Jamaican Off-Road Triathlon and Sunset Run** (contact Tamesha Dyght, cell tel. 876/564-6319, anneke@jakeshotel.com) draws Jamaicans from across the island as well as international competitors. The winner typically receives a weekend for two at a sponsoring hotel.

Local NGO **BREDS** (Kingfisher Plaza, Calabash Bay, contact Sean Chedda, tel. 876/965-0748, www.helpinghandsjamaica.com/breds, 9am-5pm Mon.-Fri., 9am-1pm Sat.), sponsored by Jake's, supports the community and promotes sustainable tourism by training lifeguards, including those posted at Frenchman's Beach, one of the area's most dangerous. BREDS organizes Jake's Triathlon and Run as well as the **Hook 'n' Line Canoe Tournament,** held at the Calabash Bay Beach on Heroes weekend (2nd weekend in Oct.).

The popular event starts on Saturday and goes into Sunday, when all the boats come in by noon to weigh their catch. Whoever gets the largest fish by weight wins; any species is fair game. Visitors may participate by renting boats. The modest entry fee (US$7 per boat) ensures the event remains decidedly local. The top prize is usually fishing equipment.

SHOPPING

Run by the Treasure Beach Women's Group, **Treasure Hunt Craft Shop** (Old Wharf Rd., tel. 876/965-3878, tbwgjamaica@yahoo.com, 9am-3pm Mon.-Fri., 9am-1pm Sat.) sells handcrafted items made out of calabash and other local materials. Baskets, gourds, postcards, and the signature Star Light candle holders make nice gift items. Upscale craft and souvenir shop **Callaloo Butik** (Frenchman's District, cell tel. 876/390-3949, 9am-6pm daily) sells clothing, bags, jewelry, beach wraps, baby items, ceramics, and home decor, all of it made in Jamaica.

FOOD

Delroy Brown is the affable proprietor and ital chef at **Gee Wiz Vegetarian Restaurant** (shop 4, Lazza Plaza, Calabash Bay, cell tel. 876/573-5988, 7am-7pm daily, US$6-15), serving fish and veggie food like curry or tomato chunks, pumpkin in coconut sauce, and broad bean stew.

Favorite watering hole and restaurant ★ **Jack Sprat** (adjacent to Jake's, tel. 876/965-3583, 10am-10pm daily, US$8-30) serves fried fish, conch soup, pizza, and

Devon House ice cream, with a large outdoor eating area overlooking the sea. Decked out with retro posters and other paraphernalia celebrating Jamaican rum bar culture and music, Jack Sprat is full of vibes and a go-to spot for locals and visitors alike.

Serving typical Jamaican dishes for breakfast, lunch, and dinner as well as international fare, **Cattleya Restaurant & Bar** (behind Callaloo Boutique, cell tel. 876/291-7584, 7am-7:30pm daily, US$4-12) has a morning menu that includes ackee and saltfish, salt mackerel rundown with fried dumpling, yam and boiled green banana, eggs any style, french toast, and fruit salad. For lunch and dinner, dishes include stew pork, cow foot, stew beef, fried and barbecue chicken, as well as wraps and burgers.

Close to the main gate of Frenchman Bay Beach, **Frenchman's Reef Restaurant & Cocktail Bar** (tel. 876/965-3049, cell tel. 876/428-5048 or 876/861-4917, frenchmansreef@yahoo.com, 8am-4am daily, US$7-20) serves seafood and pizza, as well as burgers, typical Jamaican dishes, vegetarian meals, pasta, and jerk chicken. Natural juices and freshly brewed Jamaica Blue Mountain Coffee complement local and international breakfast offerings. Frenchman's also delivers, accepts credit cards, and offers complimentary Wi-Fi. The cocktail bar is beachside.

Jamaican breakfast dishes like ackee and saltfish, callaloo, and saltfish as well as continental favorites like omelets and eggs done to order are at **Pardy's Coffee Shop** (Frenchman's Bay, cell tel. 876/326-9008, 7am-7pm Mon.-Sat., US$5-20). Lunch and dinner are prepared to order, with items like fish, lobster, and curry goat. Pardy's serves High Mountain coffee and freshly squeezed OJ in season, and you can grab a beer anytime.

Round the Clock Bar (Frenchman's Bay, contact owner Charmaine Moxam, cell tel. 876/378-6690, 6am-1pm daily) is a small grocery shop and bar for basic supplies and drinks, located next to Jake's.

A small roadside restaurant, **Strikie-T** (Billy's Bay, cell tel. 876/319-8929 or 876/592-6478, noon-10pm Mon.-Sat. Nov.-late May) serves jerk chicken (US$8), shrimp coconut (US$11), and garlic lobster (US$18). Strikie-T is run by Christopher Bennet, who spends the summer in Provincetown, Cape Cod, closing this Treasure Beach shop.

ACCOMMODATIONS

The popularity of Treasure Beach as an off-the-beaten-track destination has led to a blossoming lodging market, fueled mostly by wealthy Jamaicans building luxurious weekend retreats. Most guesthouses are remarkably affordable compared to the more highly trafficked destinations in Jamaica, with a basic room for two starting as low US$40. Even villas rent for considerably less than in other parts of the island, starting at US$1,200-2,600 weekly for 2-8 people.

The only time of year it becomes hard to find a room in Treasure Beach is during the Calabash Literary Festival, when those who haven't booked well in advance settle for whatever's available, even staying in Black River, Junction, or as far away as Mandeville, about an hour's drive. **Treasure Tours** (tel. 876/965-0126, treasuretoursjamaica@gmail.com, www.treasuretoursjamaica.com) handles many of the accommodations in the area, with prices and amenities listed on the website. Many of the listings can be booked through Treasure Tours.

Under US$100

Five double rooms with king beds, ceiling fans, en suite baths, and Wi-Fi are at ★ **Lashings Boutique Hotel and Villas** (tel. 876/903-6369, tel. 876/550-1610 or 876/846-4073, villas@lashings.co.uk, www.lashings.co.uk, from US$66). A two-bedroom apartment on the top level has a large outdoor living area and a king bed in each room, one of which can be separated into two twins. A five-bedroom villa (US$500) has one king bed and four queens. Located on a hill in Sandy Bank district overlooking Treasure Beach, the property commands a panoramic view of the sea from Great Bay to Frenchmen's Bay. A large

infinity pool is surrounded by a wooden deck a few steps below the rooms.

With limited electricity supplied by solar panels, **Ital Rest** (contact Frankie and Jean, tel. 876/863-3481, US$40, US$250 weekly) is about as roots as you can get. Smart wood cabins are an easy walk from several sandy coves, and mosquito nets cover the beds. There are no fans or air-conditioning; a communal kitchen on the property is available for guest use. Vegetarian food can be prepared by request.

Jack Sprat Motel (tel. 876/965-3000 or 876/564-3000, cell tel. 876/491-0649, from US$33) offers 32 bunk beds in two communal dorm rooms with lockers for luggage and shared baths. Across the road from Jakes Boutique Resort in the heart of Treasure Beach, the budget accommodations complement the more upmarket cottages and villas on the waterfront. On the second level, three twin rooms have one king bed (US$115), and three quads have one king and two bunk beds (US$178). They are ideal for families on a budget who want more privacy, and rooms include continental breakfast at Jakes. The king beds in the upstairs rooms can be separated to make two twins.

Calabash House (Calabash Bay, tel. 876/818-9830, ees01@earthlink.net, www.calabashhouse.com, US$75 low season, US$85 high season, entire house US$200 low season, US$250 high season) is a four-bedroom villa right on Calabash Bay, one of the best spots for swimming in Treasure Beach. Bedrooms have air-conditioning, with hot water in the baths. A housekeeper tidies up during the day, while a cook can be arranged to prepare breakfast and dinner (additional US$25 daily for 4 people). Two cute mini cottages are in the yard, where there's also a hammock for lazing and watching fishing boats bring in their catch. The house is decorated with shells and mosaics.

1: view from the pool at boutique hotel 77 West 2: room at Jakes Boutique Resort and Beachside Villas

An attractive seafront property located on a quiet windswept stretch of beach along Calabash Bay, **Marblue Villa Suites** (cell tel. 876/848-0001, marblue.andrea@gmail.com, US$79-159) has junior, villa, and honeymoon categories. The well-appointed suites have air-conditioning (for an additional cost), fans, attractive decor, Wi-Fi, and double, king, or queen beds. Sitting areas have day beds overlooking the pool on the property from the veranda or pool deck. The property is self-catering, with kitchenettes in the suites and a communal kitchen for the smaller rooms.

US$100-250

Villa-style guesthouse **Nuestra Casa** (Billy's Bay, tel. 876/965-0152 or 807/624-7667, booking@nuestracasajamaica.com, www.nuestracasajamaica.com, US$200 low season, US$250 high season) has three rooms: two with a double bed, and a third with two twin beds. One room has a private bath, while the other two share a bath. Amenities include ceiling and standing fans and hot water. Dinner is prepared by request. The property also houses a separate self-contained apartment (US$100) suitable for two adults and a small child.

An eight-bedroom boutique hotel located at the far eastern end of Treasure Beach, **Taino Cove** (cell tel. 876/845-6103, www.tainocove.com, from US$100 low season, US$150 high season) has queen or double beds in rooms that overlook the sea and pool area, with tile floors, colorfully painted walls, comfortable linens, and wooden vaulted ceilings in the suites. The large property features a common area on the ground floor of the main building and a pool with an adjacent bar and restaurant.

Thanks to the visionary aesthetic of the family business matriarch, Sally Henzell, ★ **Jakes Boutique Resort and Beachside Villas** (tel. 876/965-3000, www.jakeshotel.com, from US$175) has taken rustic chic to a new level. Plush bedding and elaborate details in the oceanfront rooms and cottages are reminiscent of an Arabian love lair. The honeymoon suites have outdoor showers and sunbathing decks on the roof. Sometimes described as "shabby shacks," the cottages don't neglect the modern essentials, with solar hot water in all rooms. Jake was the owners' pet parrot, but "Jake" is also a generic term Jamaicans often use in jest to call out to a person of light complexion.

A five-unit boutique hotel built on a bluff overlooking a protected cove with shallow water, **77 West** (Billy's Bay, cell tel. 876/469-4828, annabelle77west@gmail.com or jana77west@gmail.com, www.77west.net, US$130) is centered around a four-foot-deep pool surrounded by a large sunbathing deck with the rooms perched a few steps higher overlooking the sea. Rooms have minimalist furnishings and decor, with polished concrete floors, ceiling fans, and air-conditioning. Louvered windows open on three sides to take advantage of the sea breeze. Classic vinyl album covers and reading lamps hang over the bed; queen foam mattresses are comfortable. A bar and restaurant open to nonguests serves breakfast, lunch, and dinner, including crepes, french toast, and eggs any style with bacon and toast, as well as local fare like ackee and saltfish. Stairs lead from the parking area over the dunes to the hotel, and then from the pool deck down to the beach, where the water is waist deep inside the protective reef. A break in the reef allows access to the open sea for unencumbered swimming and snorkeling. Like most of Treasure Beach, rip currents can be dangerous, and it's always best to swim with other people.

Over US$250

"Your Om away from home," as its owner, one of Jamaica's leading yoga instructors, Sharon McConnell, puts it: ★ **Shakti Home** (tel. 876/965-0126, treasuretoursjamaica@gmail. com, www.shaktihomeja.com, US$3,000 weekly low season, US$3,500 weekly high season) is an airy, well-appointed, and tastefully decorated beach house with mosquito nets, fans, and air-conditioning in three bedrooms. The house sits beachfront, overlooking Old Wharf, and includes a great cook and caretaker-gardener. The chef specializes in vegetarian cuisine in addition to traditional Jamaican food. Shakti Home has a beautiful yoga deck with a small infinity pool overlooking the sea that comfortably fits six people, yoga mats included.

Three-story five-bedroom waterfront **Kotch Villa** (cell tel. 876/447-3799, kotchvilla@gmail.com, www.kotch.co) books in its entirety (US$850) or as three self-contained units. The ground floor (US$300) and second-floor (US$400) each have two bedrooms with open-plan kitchen-living room layouts. Each bedroom has a king bed and private bath. The romantic oceanfront suite (US$290) on the third floor has one king bed and private bath, kitchenette, and balcony. All units have air-conditioning, Wi-Fi, and laptop-friendly workspaces. The bottom two floors come with a cook-housekeeper. A cook can be arranged for the third-floor unit (US$35 per day). Natural wood finishes, louvered windows, ceiling fans, wicker chairs, and lamps create an inviting ambiance to complement the unobstructed sea views.

Comfortable four-bedroom **Doubloon Villa** (UK tel. +44/1543-480-612, from US$2,950 weekly) has a small pool and deck overlooking the beach on Calabash Bay. One of the area's premier properties, Doubloon amenities include private baths, a well-equipped kitchen, air-conditioning, complimentary Wi-Fi, and three full-time staff.

On a bluff overlooking the sea, four-bedroom ★ **Kouros Villa** (gillesnegril@hotmail.com, www.villa-kouros.com, 3-night minimum, from US$550, US$3,850 weekly) is built in the whitewashed Greek island style. The villa has three terraces with sea views and a large outdoor space by the infinity pool for alfresco dining. Inside, polished cement floors are etched with wistful spirals. Amenities include wicker furnishings, comfortable mattresses, a kitchen, Wi-Fi, and an entertainment center in the living room.

Exquisitely decorated **Sparkling Waters** (Billy's Bay, tel. 876/965-0126, www.sparklingwatersvilla.com, from US$250) is three modern two-bedroom villas that share grounds with a pool, whirlpool tub, and a gorgeous private beach. Comfortable inviting baths have hot water, and there is satellite TV, stereos, and air-conditioning in the bedrooms, at the top of a spiral staircase. Spacious and comfortable living and dining rooms are downstairs with the kitchen. Wi-Fi is included.

★ **Blue Marlin Villas** (Great Bay, contact Sandy Tatham, cell tel. 876/965-3311, info@bluemarlinvillas.com, www.bluemarlinvillas.com) has two houses for rent on the one-hectare (2.5-acre) beachfront property at the western side of the beach in Great Bay. The villas can be rented together or separately. Wi-Fi covers the property. Blue Marlin (US$2,427 weekly low season, US$3,475 high season) is a four-bedroom, three-bath, single-story villa with air-conditioning and ceiling fans in the bedrooms. Coquina (US$2,044 weekly low season, US$3,475 high season) is a three-bedroom, three-bath, two-story villa with ceiling fans. Both are staffed with a cook-housekeeper, a maid, and a gardener.

INFORMATION AND SERVICES

The Calabash Bay **post office** (10:30am-1pm and 2pm-4:30pm Mon.-Fri.) is located in Kingfisher Plaza, five minutes' walk east of Southern Supplies, where Jamaica National Bank has an ATM. There's also an ATM at Jack Sprat.

GETTING THERE AND AROUND

Treasure Beach is served by frequent **route taxis** from Santa Cruz, direct and via Watchwell (US$2), and from Junction (US$2). If you're driving, there are three routes: From Black River there is a short, direct road along the coast that is rough in places but still passable with a regular passenger vehicle. Turn off the main road toward the sea on a road just past the communications tower heading east of Black River, immediately past the turnoff for Parottee. From Mandeville, take a left at the base of Spur Tree Hill, following signs for Little Ochie, and take a right at the second three-way intersection, following signs for Alumina Partners. At the T junction, take a left and pass the alumina plant, followed by a soft right at the stop sign to continue up the hill, continuing straight through Junction. Continue down the hill, passing through Southfield, and then turn left at the gas station at the four-way intersection in Pedro Cross, following Pedro Plains Road all the way down to Treasure Beach. From Santa Cruz, turn south toward the sea about 1.5 kilometers (1 mile) west of the stoplight on the west side of town. The turnoff is marked by a sign for Jack Sprat.

Black River and South Cockpit Country

An important economic center in years past, especially for the export of logwood and mahogany, Black River is today a quiet backwater parish capital, with the main attraction being the river at the heart of town that serves as the entry point into the Lower Black River Morass. There are a few popular attractions within a half hour's drive, and plenty of forlorn stretches of mediocre beach just east of town along the coast toward Parottee. A few interesting buildings around town are worth a look, most notably Invercauld Great House. The accommodations options for staying in Black River are limited. Most visitors come to town just for the day, either from nearby Treasure Beach, Montego Bay, or Negril.

BLACK RIVER
Invercauld Great House

Along the waterfront between town and the hospital, **Invercauld Great House** is the most striking structure in Black River, with well-preserved Georgian architecture.

The great house was built in 1894 by Patrick Leydon. For many years it was a hotel but has fallen out of use and sits idle within its gated compound. Nevertheless it is an architectural gem and worth a look from outside the gate.

Luana Orchid Farm

On the northern outskirts of Black River, **Luana Orchid Farm** (contact Dr. Bennett, cell tel. 876/361-3252, US$20) offers formal tours by appointment only to check out the 150,000-odd local and foreign orchid plants at the 0.6-hectare (1.5-acre) farm. Bennett has bred several new varieties himself. The farm is along the road between Black River and Middle Quarters, opposite Luana Sports Club and quarry.

★ Pelican Bar

One of the most unique attractions in all of Jamaica, **Pelican Bar** is a ramshackle structure less than 1.5 kilometers (1 mile) from shore on a sandbar off Parottee Point. Run

boat on the Lower Black River Morass

by the charismatic Denever Forbes, who goes by "Floyde" (cell tel. 876/354-4218), Pelican Bar serves drinks and cooks up plates of fish (US$10) and lobster (US$15) accompanied by rice, bammy, or festival. The sandbar is a great spot to spend the day relaxing and snorkeling. The best way to reach the bar is by calling Daniel McLenon, better known as **Dee** (cell tel. 876/860-7277), who offers round-trip shuttle service in his fishing boat (US$10 pp) from Parottee. Other transporters are available and can be seen most times lingering in and around the Frenchman's Bay Beach. Dee leaves from near his yard past Basil's, just after some houses with blue roofs on the right heading south toward Parottee Point. Turn right and park along a little lane that leads to the beach. Call Floyde before heading out to make sure he's around. He keeps hours starting at 9am until the last customers leave in the evening. The bar is closed in bad weather.

★ Lower Black River Morass

The **Lower Black River Morass** is one of Jamaica's largest wetlands, with 142 square kilometers (55 square miles) of mangrove and swamp providing a rich habitat for a variety of animals and plantlife. Turtles and crocodiles are still abundant, although manatees, once relatively common around the mouth of the river, have completely disappeared from this part of Jamaica, now only found in Manatee Hole in Clarendon. It's the largest remaining undisturbed wetland in the English-speaking Caribbean at 7,280 hectares (18,000 acres). The Black River Morass has 113 species of plants and 98 species of animals. The anchovy pear *(Grias cauliflora)* of the Brazil nut family (Lecythidaceae) grows in the morass. Sawgrass, or razor grass *(Cladium jamaicense)*, first described by botanists in Jamaica and thus given the Latin name *jamaicense*, covers about 60 percent of the wetlands area. Sable palm *(Sabal jamaicensis)*, or thatch palm, is another wetland plant abundant in the reserve that was first described in Jamaica.

The crocodiles along the Black River are quite accustomed to being around people, to the point that many visitors think the ones sitting on the river's edge next to the restaurant are tame. While it's not recommended, some people swim in the water with the crocs. It's best to respect their space, however, and not give them the chance to prove they are anything but friendly.

The Black River and the Lower Black River Morass are best accessed by taking one of the river safari tours that start in the town of Black River, where three tours are offered from the river banks on pontoon boats.

Black River Safaris

Charles Swaby's **Black River Safari** (tel. 876/965-2513 or 876/965-0220, jcsafari@hotmail.com, www.jamaica-southcoast.com) has a pontoon boat tour (75 minutes, 9am, 11am, 12:30pm, 2pm, and 3:30pm daily, US$20 adults, US$10 children) up the Black River with a commentary by the captain. Lunch is served at the Paradise Ocean View Restaurant at additional cost.

On the opposite side of the river, **St. Elizabeth Safari** (tel. 876/965-2374, cell tel. 876/361-3252, st.elizabethsafari@gmail.com, US$20 adults, US$10 under age 12) runs with local businessman Dr. Bennett, operating a virtually identical 75-minute tour up the Black River.

Irie Safari (12 High St., contact Lloyd Linton, cell tel. 876/472-4644, 876/834-0262, or 876/877-6222, lintonirie@hotmail.com, 8:30am-4:30pm Mon.-Sat., 9am-3pm Sun.) offers a narrated Black River Safari tour by pontoon boat (70 minutes, minimum 2 guests, US$20 adults, US$10 under age 12). Irie's **Lost River Kayak Adventures** tour (2 hours, single and 2-person trips, US$65 pp) includes the regular safari tour on the pontoon boat before continuing into the upper reaches of the Broad River, which runs east-west into the Black River. The adventure tour outfit has two three-seater, four two-seater, and two single-seat kayaks. Tours venture into the upper reaches, where there are blue holes suitable for swimming, birds that wouldn't be seen from a motorized craft, and happily for wary swimmers, no crocodiles, thanks to the freshwater.

★ YS Falls

One of the most popular attractions in Jamaica is **YS Falls** (ysfalls@cwjamaica.com, tel. 876/997-6360, www.ysfalls.com, 9:30am-3:30pm Tues.-Sun., US$19 adults, US$11 ages 3-15), on the YS Estate. The YS River changes with the weather—normally clear blue, it turns muddy brown when it swells after rain in the mountains. A bar and grill on the property serves jerk chicken, and gift shops sell a wide array of books, crafts, and Jamaica-inspired clothing. Lounge chairs surround two swimming pools, one with colder water, near the base of the falls, and the other slightly warmer, by the picnic area.

A series of three zip lines traverses the falls for a **canopy tour** (US$35 adults, US$20 ages 3-15) operated by Chukka Caribbean. The tour is a rush, to say the least, and perhaps the most exhilarating of Chukka's many canopy tours in Jamaica, given the scenery.

The origin of the name YS is disputed. One version is that it comes from the Gaelic word *wyess,* meaning winding and twisting. Another is that it comes from the last names of the two men who ran the estate in 1684, John Yates and Richard Scott, who branded the cattle and hogshead of sugar with "YS." The original 3,240-hectare (8,000-acre) property has been reduced to 810 hectares (2,000 acres) today, where champion thoroughbred racehorses are bred and Pedigree Red Poll cattle graze the guango tree-lined fields. Sugarcane production was discontinued in the 1960s.

The YS River originates in Cockpit Country and is fed by many springs on its way to meet the Black River. A spring on the estate is the original source of water for the town of Black River, 13 kilometers (8 miles) downstream.

Bamboo Avenue

One of the most beautiful stretches of road in Jamaica, running four kilometers (2.5-mile) from Middle Quarters to West Lacovia, Bamboo Avenue is also known as Holland Bamboo. The stretch is lined with Jamaica's largest bamboo species, the common bamboo *(Bambusa vulgaris),* introduced to the island from Haiti by the owners of the neighboring Holland sugar estate, which once belonged to John Gladstone (1764-1851), father of William Gladstone, who became prime minister of Britain 1868-1894.

famous and beautiful YS Falls

Bamboo Avenue provides shade for several jelly coconut and peanut vendors. On the eastern side of Bamboo Avenue is **Bamboo Ville,** a vibesy jerk center with big pots on open fires. **Middle Quarters** is a community located at the edge of the Black River Morass that's a favorite pit stop for passing motorists. Women line the road calling out "swimps, swimps!" to advertise their spicy morsels of boiled pepper shrimp.

A petting zoo that allows visitors to touch and interact with snakes, baby American crocodiles, iguanas, and birds is **Jamaica Zoo** (Burton District, Lacovia, tel. 876/435-9999 or 876/487-3001, info@jamaicazoo.org, www.jamaicazoo.org, 10am-5pm Sat.-Sun., by reservation Mon.-Fri., US$20 adults, US$10 under age 13). A monkey performs tricks, as does a Labrador retriever. The guided walking tour allows visitors to see the llama, a pair of lions, Amazon parrots, and snakes like boa pythons and boa constrictors, among the 20 species on the farm.

Food

Northside Jerk Centre (5 North St., tel. 876/965-9855, cell tel. 876/275-7694, 7am-9pm daily, US$4-8), a.k.a. Alvin's Fish & Jerk Pork Centre, serves fried, curry, stew, or jerk chicken, stew jerk pork, and curry goat as well as steamed, brown stew, and escoveitch fish.

Tasty Foods (2 Market St., tel. 876/634-4027, 8am-11pm Mon.-Sat., US$2.50-7) serves ackee and saltfish, salt mackerel, chicken, and fries.

The quintessential beachfront bar and restaurant ★ **Cloggy's on the Beach** (22 Crane Rd., tel. 876/471-7766, www.cloggys.com, 10am-midnight daily, US$5-40) serves chicken and seafood dishes, including fish, conch, shrimp, and lobster. This is a great place to kick back and unwind, even if the beach along this stretch out to Parottee Point can get a bit muddied by the mouth of the Black River.

The most interesting restaurant around is **Pelican Bar**, but it requires a boat ride to get here. It's offshore on a sandbar off Parottee Point. Run by Denever Forbes, known as Floyde (cell tel. 876/354-4218), Pelican Bar serves drinks and cooks up plates of fish (US$10) and lobster (US$15) accompanied by rice, bammy, or festival.

Holland Bamboo Curry Restaurant (beside the primary school, cell tel. 876/507-3236, 11am-5pm daily) serves curry goat, curried chicken, fried chicken, roti, and rice-and-peas or white rice.

Irie Vybes Restaurant & Sports Bar (cell tel. 876/363-7242, 10am-7pm daily, US$3-7) is a roadside shop painted red, gold, and green. It's a good bet for fresh-out-the-pot "peppa swimps," cold beer to wash it down, and fresh fruits and vegetables.

Information and Services

The **post office** (35 High St., tel. 876/634-3769) is open 8am-5pm Monday-Friday. **DHL** (tel. 876/965-2651, 9am-5pm Mon.-Sat.) is at 17 High Street. Both **NCB** (13 High St., tel. 876/929-4622) and **Scotiabank** (6 High St., tel. 876/965-2251) have branches with ATMs. The **St. Elizabeth Parish Library** (64 High St., 8:45am-5:15pm Mon.-Fri., 8:45am-3pm Sat.) also offers internet service (US$1.50 per hour).

Getting There and Around

Black River is easily reached by **route taxi** from Sav-la-Mar in Westmoreland (US$3) or from Santa Cruz in St. Elizabeth (US$2). If you're driving, there's a dodgy but interesting road along the coast to Treasure Beach that's much shorter and not too much more potholed than the long way around. To take the coastal route, head over the bridge east of Black River along Crane Road and turn off the main road toward the water after passing the communications tower east of Parottee. A left turn at a Y intersection leads along the coast to Treasure Beach.

SOUTH COCKPIT COUNTRY

The interior of St. James, St. Elizabeth, Manchester, and Clarendon Parishes is rugged terrain, much of it forming part of Cockpit Country, which blankets pitted limestone hills full of caves and underground rivers. As the impassible interior descends to the sea, ridged hills taper down around lush valleys, which have proved some of the most fertile land in Jamaica. The YS and Appleton Estates remain prized lands. The **Nassau Valley,** where Appleton Estate is located, is still heavily planted in sugarcane to feed the healthy rum business.

From Maggotty, the main road (the B6) heads east, skirting a large wetland area fed by the upper reaches of the Black River before rejoining the main South Coast "highway" (the A2) just east of Santa Cruz. From Balaclava, a turn to the north on the B10 leads deep into the interior to Troy and then Warsop, passing by Ramgoat Cave before hitting Clarks Town, Trelawny. North of Clarks Town the road emerges on the coast in Duncans. For extreme adventure-seekers, the **Troy Trail** is a challenging traverse of the most rugged part of Cockpit Country. The trail is best accessed with the help of a guide, which can be set up through the **Jamaica Caves Organization** (www.jamaicancaves.org).

★ Appleton Estate

One of the most popular attractions in Jamaica and well worth a visit, **Appleton Estate** (tel. 876/963-9215 or 876/963-9217, appletonrumtour@campari.com, www.appletonestate.com, tours 9am-3:30pm Mon.-Sat., US$30) is in Nassau Valley. The Appleton Estate Rum Tour takes visitors through the rum-making process from cane to cup. It includes a demonstration of the traditional crushing technique powered by Paz, the resident donkey, and a walk through the distillery and aging room, filled floor to ceiling with oak barrels. The tour ends with a tasting, when guests can sample three of Appleton Estate's premium rums, the Signature, Reserve, and 12-year-old.

The distillery is owned by J. Wray & Nephew, Jamaica's oldest company and most successful spirits group, founded in 1825 and bought by Italy's Campari in 2012. To get to Appleton Estate, turn inland off the A2 toward Maggotty in West Lacovia after passing through Bamboo Avenue from the west, or upon entering Lacovia from the east. Where the road splits, keep right, following well-marked signs for Appleton Estate. An on-site restaurant serves jerk chicken, jerk pork, veggie balls, and fish alongside rice-and-peas and salad (US$15). The tour lasts about an hour.

fisherman on the Black River

The Unconquerable Maroons

Jamaica's Maroons date to the Spanish settlement of the island, when it became accepted that a fraction of the people brought from Africa would perpetually resist enslavement. These so-called "runaways" were termed Cimarrones by the Spaniards, a name later translated into English as Maroon. To name these warriors "runaway" is to diminish the fact that they claimed land in the most remote and mountainous regions of the island and held it against assault. The Spaniards ultimately gave up trying to conquer the Maroons, many of whom it is said descended from the warrior Ashanti people of West Africa. The British would also eventually sign a peace treaty with the Maroons in 1738, the legacy of which has left the Maroons with their sovereignty to this day.

Large Maroon settlements grew in Accompong, St. Elizabeth; in Moore Town in the Rio Grande River Valley; above Buff Bay in Charles Town, Portland; and in Scott's Hall, St. Mary. Today the Maroons are still courted by elected officials who have Maroon lands within their constituencies. While the communities themselves have largely been diluted since emancipation, their warrior spirit has permeated Jamaican society at large, influencing social movements like the Rastafarians, who draw on their experience as rebels against the status quo to present an alternate worldview based on principles that can be traced through the Maroon heritage to Africa.

Accompong

Home of the Leeward, or Trelawny, Maroons, Accompong was named after Achumpun, the brother of the most famous Maroon leader Cudjoe (Kojo), who signed a peace treaty with Great Britain in 1738 that granted his people autonomy from the crown. In exchange for their sovereignty, granted 100 years before slavery was abolished in Jamaica, the Maroons were called on repeatedly to assist the British in suppressing rebellions and to capture escapees and insurgent leaders.

The Leeward Maroons are today led by **Colonel Ferron Williams** (cell tel. 876/790-0867 or 876/893-2321, ferronwilliams302@ yahoo.com), a retired police inspector elected to the leadership position. The colonel will ensure visitors are treated fairly and can arrange community tours (US$20 pp) to important local landmarks, including the cave where the peace treaty was signed in 1738, a burial ground, and the church where English names were doled out to the Maroons after emancipation. A modest Maroon museum holds artifacts dating to the 18th century, among them a pistol captured from the British during the 83-year war before the peace treaty was signed.

The best time to visit is for the annual **Accompong Maroon Festival** (Jan. 5-6), when the village comes alive with traditional Maroon music and dance as well as stage shows more typical of the rest of Jamaica. During the rest of the year it's a great destination for fresh air and taking in the spectacular countryside from a seldom visited corner of St. Elizabeth.

Santa Cruz

A bustling transportation hub more than a tourist destination, Santa Cruz can get congested during the day; if you're passing through, the bypass road around the town center saves a lot of time. Arriving from the east, veer right off the main road at the Y where the road splits at the Total gas station before town. Take the third left to rejoin the main road at the stoplight on the western edge of town. Arriving from the west, follow the reverse route: a left at the first stoplight, and then a right until the road meets the main road at the Total station on the eastern edge of town. The dusty bus terminal parking lot in the heart of Santa Cruz is a good place to catch a route taxi for Treasure Beach, Black River, or Mandeville.

FOOD

Jerk chicken and pork and roast fish (from US$10) are on offer at **Grills & Frills** (New River Rd., cell tel. 876/336-6822, 10am-10pm

Mon.-Sat., US$4-5), along with other Jamaican dishes like fried chicken, curry goat, brown stew chicken, and brown stew pork. **Hinds Restaurant & Bakery** (Santa Cruz Plaza, tel. 876/966-2234, 7am-6pm Mon.-Thurs., 7am-7pm Fri.-Sat., US$4-9) has decent Jamaican dishes liked fried, stewed, and baked chicken as well as oxtail, curry goat, stew pork, and escoveitch fish.

ACCOMMODATIONS

Well-kept **Chariots Hotel** (Leeds, tel. 876/966-3860 or 876/834-5014, US$55-85) has a pool, a Jamaican restaurant, and a bar. Heading west through Santa Cruz, turn left at the stoplight onto Coke Drive, pass Sagicor bank and then NCB, four kilometers (2.5 miles) from Santa Cruz on the road to Malvern. All rooms have private baths, cable TV, air-conditioning, and either two doubles or one king. The more expensive rooms have hot water.

The four rooms at **Kool Rooms Guest House** (just west of the last stoplight in Santa Cruz, cell tel. 876/312-8735, tel. 876/387-9417, vernonbourne@yahoo.com, www.thekoolrooms-guesthouse.com, US$50) have two queens or two doubles in each room with air-conditioning, cable TV, and en suite baths with a tub and shower. Run by roots rock reggae singer Vernon Bourne, a.k.a. Singing Vernon, the guesthouse is a good place for young travelers looking to unwind in the countryside. You're likely to see other popular reggae artists during your stay.

SERVICES

NCB (7 Coke Dr., tel. 876/966-2204) and **Scotiabank** (77 Main St., tel. 876/966-2230) have small branches with ATMs.

Background

The Landscape

The Landscape.........305
Plants and Animals.....307
History 312
Government and
   Economy 315
People and Culture 318
The Arts 322
Sports 326

Jamaica enjoys widely varied topography for its small size, ranging from tropical mountainous regions in the Blue and John Crow Mountains to temperate areas at the higher elevations of Manchester, lush tropical coastline along much of the coast, and near-desert conditions south of the Santa Cruz Mountains in St. Elizabeth. No other island in the Caribbean can boast natural features and attractions in such abundance and close proximity. The most expansive wetlands in the Caribbean, the Lower Black River Morass, for example, is a popular wintering ground for birds from across the continent as well as

crocodiles, while various mountain ranges create distinct ecosystems that support unique species only found in Jamaica.

Land use in Jamaica was the colonial plantation economy for the four centuries following European arrival in 1492, where overseers would control vast tracts of land on behalf of absentee landowners and enslaved people would not be granted title. The plains were coveted for growing sugarcane, while the more mountainous regions produced timber and spices. The birth of the banana industry in 1866 opened up large new areas to plantation agriculture in northeast Jamaica, before a plague virtually wiped out the crop a century later.

After the abolition of slavery in 1834, migration made towns into cities, and the cultural aversion to agriculture and rural life persists today. As you drive across the island you still see vast cane fields in many parishes, with banana and citrus plantations in others. But farming as a way of life has fallen out of fashion, and much agricultural land is left unfarmed.

When the Jamaica Labour Party came to power in 2008 after being in the opposition for 18 years, a renewed emphasis was placed on agriculture as a sector vital to the country's growth and development. Nonetheless, Jamaica has struggled to bring its land-use policies into the modern era to encourage productive use of land, and squatting continues to be a problem. In the greater Kingston area, subdivisions are claiming old cane fields as urban sprawl continues to fan outward, extending bedroom communities in Old Harbour, Spanish Town, and Portmore. Sadly, Jamaica continues to import many vegetables the country could produce itself.

GEOGRAPHY

Jamaica is a relatively small island: 235 kilometers (146 miles) long and 93 kilometers (58 miles) at its widest point, covering 10,992 square kilometers (4,244 square miles). It's slightly smaller than the state of Connecticut. Distances in Jamaica can seem much greater than they really are thanks to mountainous terrain and poor roads. Connectivity is improving, however, with the North-South Highway cutting travel time between Kingston and Ocho Rios to under an hour, and ongoing work improving roads in Westmoreland and St. Thomas.

CLIMATE

Jamaica has a tropical climate along the coast and lowlands, with average annual temperatures of 26-32°C (79-90°F). In the mountains, temperatures can drop down near freezing at night at the highest elevations. Jamaica has two loose rainy seasons: April-June and then later, with heavier, more sustained rains coinciding with hurricane season July-November.

Previous: panorama of Doctor's Cove Beach in Montego Bay

Plants and Animals

In terms of biodiversity, Jamaica is surpassed in the Caribbean only by Cuba, a country many times its size. What's more, Jamaica has an extremely high number of endemic species: plants and animals found nowhere else in the world. Perhaps most noticeable are the endemic birds, some of the most striking of which are hard to miss. The national bird is the red-billed streamertail hummingbird, known locally as the doctor bird, ubiquitous across the island. Other endemic birds, like the Jamaican tody, are rarer, requiring excursions into more remote areas to see.

PLANTS

Agriculture has diminished in importance as tourism, remittances from the diaspora, and bauxite mining took over as Jamaica's chief earners, but the country still depends heavily on subsistence farming outside the largest cities and towns, and most houses have mango and ackee trees in the yard. Coffee is still an important export crop; the Blue Mountain varieties fetch some of the highest prices per pound in the world. In recent years, a growing number of entrepreneurs have begun developing cottage industries based on key agricultural crops, with jams and pepper sauces among the most notable.

The market for Jamaica's niche products is strong both domestically and abroad. It helps that prices within the country are buoyed by heavy reliance on imported foodstuffs, which, while posing a challenge for consumers, means producers can get a fair price for their goods at home. Some of the most notable of these cottage industries include Walkerswood, Starfish Oils, Pickapeppa, and Belcour Preserves. Look for these brands in crafts shops and supermarkets across the island. Many of these small enterprises offer tours of their production facilities.

Jamaica's flora consists of a diverse mix of tropical and subtropical vegetation. Along the dry South Coast, the landscape resembles a desert, while mangrove wetlands near Black River provide a sharp contrast within relatively close proximity. In the highlands of Manchester, temperate crops like carrots,

Ackee, the national fruit of Jamaica

yams, and potatoes, the latter known locally as Irish, thrive.

Fruits

A small to mid-size tree native to West Africa, **ackee** *(Blighia sapida)* was introduced to Jamaica in 1778 when some plants were purchased from a slave ship captain. It is said to have been present earlier, however, owing to an enslaved African who wouldn't relinquish the fruit across the Middle Passage. Ackee must be cooked after it has fully ripened and the pods have dehisced, or popped open; otherwise it is poisonous and can cause illness or death. Ackee is firm until it is boiled, after which it has the appearance and consistency of scrambled eggs. Jamaica's national fruit, it makes up the major part of the national dish ackee and saltfish. On its own, ackee has a benign, mildly bitter taste.

Any number of fruits in Jamaica are referred to by the generic term **apple,** starting with the delicious otaheite apple, whose name is believed to derive from Old Tahiti, linking to Captain William Bligh's expeditions from the South Pacific to the Caribbean in the 18th century. Other apples include star apple, custard apple (sweetsop, soursop), mammee apple *(Mammea americana)*, crab apple (also known as coolie plum), golden apple *(Passiflora laurifolia)*, velvet apple *(Diospyros discolor)*—also known as the Philippine persimmon—and rose apple *(Syzygium jambos)*, used as a windbreak and for erosion control. The imported American or English apple has unfortunately slowly been taking over from the local varieties on fruit stands due to its exotic appeal.

Known commonly in Jamaica as "pear," the **avocado** *(Persea americana)* is a native of Mexico, from where it was taken by the Spaniards throughout the world. The Spanish name, *aguacate,* is a substitute for the Aztec name, *ahucatl.* Avocados are in season in Jamaica August-December, with a few varieties ripening into February. Alligator, Simmonds, Lulu, Collinson, and Winslowson are some of the varieties grown on the island.

The world's largest herb (nonwoody plant), the **banana** *(Musa acuminate × balbisiana)* became an important Jamaican export in the post-Emancipation period, 1876-1927. Jamaica was the world's foremost producer of the fruit then, with Gros Michel and later Cavendish varieties. The banana trade gave rise to Caribbean tourism when increasingly wealthy shippers began to offer passage on their empty boats returning to Jamaica from New England, where much of the produce was destined. In this way Portland, an important banana-growing region, became the Caribbean's first tourism destination, with the Titchfield Hotel, built by a banana baron, exemplifying the relationship between the fruit and the tourism economy that would come to replace it in importance. Several varieties of banana are still grown in Jamaica, including the plantain, an important starch; boiled bananas are a necessary accompaniment in the typical Jamaican Sunday breakfast of ackee and saltfish, callaloo, and dumpling.

Bearing one of the world's most beautiful flowers, **passion fruit** *(Passiflora edulis* var. *flavicarpa)* is delicious juiced alone or with orange.

Ugli fruit is a hybrid between grapefruit *(Citrus paradisi)* and tangerine *(Citrus reticulata)* developed at Trout Hall, St. Catherine. It has a brainy-textured thick skin that is easily removed to reveal the juicy orange-like fruit inside. A few large citrus estates, most notably Good Hope in Trelawny, make this an important export.

Trees, Shrubs, and Flowers

Agave *(Agave sobolifera)* is a succulent, its broad leaves edged with prickles, notable for its tremendous 5- to 10-meter (16- to 33-foot) flower shoots February-April. Bulbils fall from the shoots to develop into independent plants.

Anatto *(Bixa orellana)* is an important dye and food coloring, and was once an important Jamaican export, likely lending its name to Annotto Bay in St. Mary, which was a center of production and export.

Antidote caccoon *(Fevillea cordifolia),* known as sabo, segra-seed, and nhandiroba, is a perennial climbing vine whose fruit has been used for its medicinal and purgative qualities.

Arrowroot *(Maranta arundinacea)* was brought from South America by pre-Columbian populations and used medicinally. Later it was grown on plantations and used as a starch substitute and thickener.

Barringtonia *(Barringtonia asiatica)* is a large evergreen originating in Asia. Its large coconut-like fruit will float for up to two years and root on the shore where it lands. Known locally as the duppy coconut, the tree has been naturalized in Portland, and 220-year-old trees grow at Bath Gardens in St. Thomas.

Bauhinia *(Bauhinia spp.),* known locally as "poor man's orchid," is a favorite of the streamertail hummingbird, or doctor bird, which visits the orchid-like flowers. It grows as a shrub or mid-size tree with pinkish flowers.

Blue mahoe *(Hibiscus elatus)* is a quality hardwood of the Malvaceae family. It grows native in the Blue Mountains and is the national tree.

Ironwood *(Lignum vitae)* is an extremely dense tropical hardwood that produces Jamaica's national flower.

Kingston buttercup *(Tribulus cistoides)* is a low, spreading plant with bright yellow flowers. It's known commonly as "kill backra" because it was thought to have caused yellow fever, which killed many European settlers. It's also called "police macca" because of its thorns, as well as turkey blossom.

Madam fate *(Hippobroma longiflora)* is a poisonous perennial herb with a five-petaled, star-shaped flower used in Obeah and folk medicine. Found along pastures or on riverbanks, it's commonly called star flower or horse poison.

Mahogany *(Swietenia mahagoni)* is still highly valued for its timber and has accordingly been unsustainably harvested since the Spanish colonial period, resulting in dwindling numbers today. Mahogany can still be seen growing, albeit sparsely, along the banks of the Black River, which was originally called Rio Caobana (Mahogany River) by the Spanish.

Sorrel *(Rumex acetosella)* is a cousin of the hibiscus whose flowers are boiled to make a drink popular around Christmas time.

Wild basil *(Ocimum micranthum)* is a wild

iguana

bush used in folk medicine and in cooking, popularly called barsley or baazli.

ANIMALS

Mammals

Jamaica's only surviving indigenous land-dwelling mammal, besides bats, is the **coney** or Jamaican hutia *(Geocapromys brownii)*. Conies are nocturnal and thus seldom seen. The animal is basically a large rodent with cousins inhabiting other Caribbean islands like Hispaniola. Its meat was prized by the Taino people centuries ago, while it is still a delicacy for the mongoose today, which is blamed for pushing it toward extinction. Another threat is loss of habitat, owing to encroaching urbanization of its principal habitats in the Hellshire Hills and Worthy Park of St. Catherine. It is also found in the John Crow Mountains in Portland and St. Thomas.

Commonly seen scurrying across the road, **mongooses** are widely regarded as pests. It is said that all mongooses in the western hemisphere are descendants of four males and five females introduced to Jamaica from India in 1872 to control the rat population on the sugar estate of one William Bancroft Espeut. They soon went on to outgrow their function, eventually being held responsible for killing off five endemic vertebrates and bringing Jamaica's iguanas to the verge of extinction.

Bats

In Jamaica, the term *bat* typically refers to moths. Jamaica has 23 species of bat, known locally as rat bats. Many species of the Bombacaceae family are bat-pollinated, including the baobab, cottonwood, cannonball, and night cactus trees. Bats also go for other pulpy fruits like sweetsop, banana, naseberry, and mango. *Noctilio leporinus,* a fish-eating bat, can be seen swooping low over harbors and inlets at twilight.

Birds

Of the 280 species of birds that have been recorded in Jamaica, 30 species and 19 subspecies are found nowhere else. Of these 30, two are extinct. There are 116 species that use Jamaica as a breeding ground, while around 80 species spend the northern winter months on the island. The **Jamaican tody,** the ubiquitous **"doctor bird"** (Jamaica's national bird, properly called the red-billed streamertail), and the **Jamaican mango hummingbird** are especially colorful species to watch for.

Insects

Jamaica has a wide variety of insects, many of which are unwelcome pests. Apart from **mosquitos,** which can be a nuisance as well as vectors for viruses like chikungunya, Zika, and dengue, insects to be wary of include the occasional **scorpion, fire ants,** and **spiders,** all of which can bite or sting but none of which are lethal.

On the brighter side, Jamaica has an abundance of butterflies and moths, the king among them being the **giant swallowtail butterfly** *(Papilio homerus),* extremely rare and protected as it teeters on the brink of extinction. Once found across the island, the last populations of these butterflies can be found in the Blue and John Crow Mountains in the east and in Cockpit Country in the west.

Reptiles

Jamaica has 26 species of lizards, including the island's largest, the Jamaican iguana *(Cyclura collei),* now protected in the Hellshire Hills and in slow recovery after near extinction on the island due to slaughter by farmers and mongooses. The *Anolis* genus includes seven of the most common species, often seen in hotel rooms and on verandas, their showy throat fan extending to attract females. The largest *Anolis* is the garmani, which prefers large trees to human dwellings. All Jamaica's lizards are harmless.

Six of Jamaica's seven snake species are endemic, and all of them are harmless. Mostly found in remote areas like Cockpit Country, snakes have fallen victim to the fear of country folk, who generally kill them on sight, and to the introduced mongoose, famous

Endangered Fisheries

The spiny lobster is one of Jamaica's most prized culinary delicacies, often prepared grilled, with garlic sauce or with a curry sauce. Lobsters fetch US$10-20 per pound at local grills and restaurants, and as high as US$40 per plate in many tourist establishments. The sustainability of lobster harvesting depends on allowing the creatures a safe period for reproduction, which has been acknowledged in Jamaica by the Ministry of Agriculture and Land with a ban on harvesting April-June. It is crucial that visitors to the island respect this ban to ensure sustainable lobster populations for the future. Some establishments serve what they say is frozen lobster during the closed season, but it's best to avoid ordering it altogether. Conch (Strombus gigas) is also protected from overfishing and has a closed season July-October.

Jamaican waters are also becoming severely overharvested where finned fish are concerned. It's best to avoid buying fresh fish smaller than 15 centimeters (6 inches) unless it's a type of fish that doesn't grow to a larger size, like sprat. The median size of the catch brought in from traditional line fishing and spearfishing in waters close to Jamaica's shores has decreased noticeably over the past decade. The situation becomes clear when snorkeling along Jamaica's coastal reefs, as few large fish can be seen today, and snapper, once common, are increasingly scarce. More recently, as the crucial role of the parrot fish in maintaining coral reef systems has come to be better understood, the government of Jamaica is actively discouraging their consumption.

for its ability to win a fight with the cobras of its native India. The island's largest snake is the yellow snake, with yellow and black patterns across its back. The snake is a boa constrictor, known locally as nanka, which can grow up to 3.5 meters (11 feet) in length.

The nanka is seldom seen, as it is only active at night when it emerges from hiding to feed on bats and rats. Other less impressive snakes include three species of grass snake of the *Arrhyton* genus and the two-headed or worm snake *(Typhlops jamaicensis)*, which burrows below ground with its tail end virtually indistinguishable from its head. The black snake is considered an extinct victim of the mongoose.

Crocodiles are Jamaica's biggest reptiles, and are often referred to on the island as alligators. The American crocodile *(Crocodylus acutus)* is found across the island in swampy mangrove areas like Font Hill Wildlife Sanctuary and the Lower Black River Morass. This is the same species of croc found in Florida and other coastal wetlands of the Caribbean. Crocodiles have a long tapering snout, whereas alligators have a short, flat head.

Sealife
MARINE MAMMALS

Jamaica has no large native mammals on land. The largest mammals are instead marine-based, namely dolphins and manatees, the latter known locally as sea cows. Manatees are endangered and now protected under wildlife laws after having seen their population dwindle due to hunting.

TURTLES

Of the six sea turtle species known worldwide, four were once common, and now less so, in Jamaican waters: the green turtle *(Chelonia mydas)*, the hawksbill *(Eretmochelys imbricata)*, the leatherback *(Dermochelys coriacea)*, and the loggerhead *(Caretta caretta)*. Turtle meat formed an important part of the diet of the Taino and was later adopted as a delicacy by colonial settlers. In keeping with Taino practice, they kept green turtles in large coastal pens known as turtle crawles, to be killed and eaten at will.

History

EARLY INHABITANTS AND SPANISH DISCOVERY

Jamaica was first inhabited by the Taino, sometimes referred to as the Arawak, who arrived from the northern coast of South America in dugout canoes around AD 900. The Taino practiced subsistence agriculture to complement hunting, fishing, and foraging activities, forming mostly seaside settlements from where travel by dugout canoe remained an important mode of transportation.

Upon his arrival on the island in 1494, Italian explorer Christopher Columbus claimed the island on behalf of his financiers, King Ferdinand and Queen Isabella of Spain—in spite of the presence of a large Taino population with whom the Europeans engaged in an easily won battle. The exact point of his arrival is contested; it is likely the explorer landed in Rio Bueno, on the border of present-day St. Ann and Trelawny, where there is freshwater, rather than in Discovery Bay, which he named Puerto Seco, or Dry Harbour, because it lacked freshwater—something historical observers say would have influenced where explorers chose to make landfall.

Jamaica was not deemed of much importance to the Spanish Crown due to its relatively rugged terrain, and more importantly its lack of gold. Spain was more concerned with exploits in Mexico and Central and South America. Neighboring Hispaniola had more gold and was thus deemed more worthwhile, while Cuba, 145 kilometers (90 miles) to the north, was also more important to Spaniards, as its vast arable flat lands were easily settled, and it held a strategic position as the key to the Gulf of Mexico. While Cuba became increasingly important as a transshipment point for gold and other goods from the New World to Europe, Jamaica remained a backwater left largely under the control of Columbus's heirs. Within 50 years of "discovery," the indigenous Taino population, estimated to have been as high as one million at time of contact, was virtually annihilated through forced labor and European diseases to which they had no immunological defenses.

Four early Spanish settlements are known to have been established at Melilla, somewhere on the North Coast; at Oristan, near present-day Bluefields, Westmoreland; at Spanish Town, which grew into the principal city of Santiago de la Vega; and in Yallahs, near today's border of St. Andrew and St. Thomas. These settlements were mainly focused on cattle ranching, while horse breeding was also an important endeavor. Jamaica became a regular provisions stop for Spanish galleons heading to Colombia, among other important goldfields. While a few inland routes were carved out of the tropical rainforest, transportation around the island remained almost entirely sea-based, with the long and navigable Martha Brae River becoming an important route between the North and South Coasts.

The lack of a centralized strategy for settlement and defense left Jamaica extremely vulnerable to attack from other early colonial powers, ultimately leading to an easy takeover by England's naval forces during the rule of Oliver Cromwell. While it was the Spanish who first brought many of the plants that would become key to the island's economy in subsequent centuries, including bananas, sugarcane, and indigo, it was the English who created an organized plantation system—key to effectively exploiting the land and establishing lucrative trade with Europe.

THE ENGLISH TAKEOVER

In 1655, during the rule of Oliver Cromwell, English naval forces invaded Jamaica and easily captured Spanish Town, the colonial rival's capital. The Spanish colony had virtually no defense strategy in place, a fact known and exploited by the English, who distributed vast tracts of land to the officers as a reward for their service. These land grants would form the first plantation estates of the English colony. The former Spanish rulers, led by the last governor, Cristóbal Ysassi, were loath to abandon the island, waging guerrilla warfare and reprisal attacks on the English with the help of loyal Maroons. The Spanish fled to the North Coast or left the island altogether for Hispaniola or Cuba.

Soon after their forces seized Jamaica, the English began a policy of legitimizing the activity of pirates—in effect gaining their allegiance in exchange for allowing them to continue their raids on mostly Spanish ships as privateers instead of buccaneers. The alliance made Port Royal, at the tip of the Palisadoes in Kingston Harbour, into a boomtown, fueled by bustling trade in enslaved people and rum in addition to commerce in luxury goods, some imported from England and beyond, others plundered from victim ships. The pirate Captain Henry Morgan enjoys status in popular culture as someone once considered a criminal but subsequently legitimized and named Lieutenant General of Jamaica in 1663, an appointment often cited by locals as the concretization of corruption as a permanent feature of Jamaican politics. A catastrophic earthquake on June 7, 1692, sank most of Port Royal, adding to common lore that acts of God were the only things to punish criminality and sin.

While the slave trade had been established on the island under Spanish rule, it wasn't until the English set up vast, well-organized sugarcane plantations that enslaved laborers were imported en masse from Africa. Jamaica became the Caribbean's primary transshipment point for enslaved people to other parts of the New World, including the United States, after the British takeover in 1655.

PLANTATION CULTURE AND THE SLAVE TRADE

As an incentive to see Jamaica reach its full potential as a plantation colony, the English offered land not only to those who had been involved in the successful takeover, but also to people from England and other English colonies, most notably Barbados. Vast estates covered thousands of hectares, with many absentee landowners installing overseers to take care of business on the island while reaping the benefits from quiet England. The cultivation of sugar expanded during the 1700s to the point where Jamaica was the world's foremost producer and England's most prized colony. But the economic boom was far from equitable, relying heavily on the slave trade, set up first by the Portuguese and later by the Dutch and English along the Gold Coast, now Ghana, and the Slave Coast, in today's Nigeria. Slavery was not a new phenomenon in Africa, but with the arrival of European traders it was formalized, and raids into the interior began to supplement the prisoners of war who were first exported as slaves. The slaves brought to Jamaica were a mix of different ethnicities, including Coromantee, Ibo, Mandingo, Yoruba, and Congo. Slaves of different ethnic backgrounds and languages were intentionally put together to complicate any potential resistance.

Enslaved laborers were used not only in the fields on the plantations, but also as domestic workers, carpenters, masons, and coopers. The tendency for women around the plantation to give birth to children of lighter complexion helped loosen the hold of the slave system as the moral high ground assumed by the English eroded and the boundaries of race increasingly blurred.

RUMORS AND REBELLION

The 1700s saw Jamaica rise to be the world's greatest producer of sugar and rum, with large estates covering the island's arable land worked by thousands of enslaved people. The runaway slaves, or Maroons, consolidated their autonomy in the country's rugged highland interior, while overseers managed the large estates for their mostly absentee masters.

But the plantation system could not be taken for granted by the British, with a series of slave uprisings stirring the foundations of their booming economy. The rumors of freedom began with Tacky's War in 1760, in which a Coromantee chief known as Tacky, a driver on Frontier Estate in St. Mary, orchestrated an uprising that spread to neighboring estates, and had as its objective the overthrow of the colonial masters throughout the island. Even while the Maroons maintained, and still maintain, aloofness when it came to how they viewed enslaved Africans who accepted their lot, their parallel existence in free communities served as a constant reminder on the plantation that slavery was not unshakable. Free people of color, meanwhile, helped maintain the status quo, breeding a culture of superiority related to their complexion, which is retained in Jamaican society to this day.

With fellow slaves in North America earning or buying their freedom in increasing numbers following the War of Independence, the nonconformists in Jamaica took added encouragement. In 1783 one such freed slave, the Baptist reverend George Liele, arrived in Jamaica to establish a ministry in Kingston that would give birth to the Baptist nonconformist movement on the island as he proceeded to baptize enslaved people in scores. These early Baptists, like nonconformist Methodists, Moravians, and Congregationalists, struck a chord with the masses with their antislavery stance. Liele sought patronage from the Baptist Ministry Society of Great Britain, which responded by sending the first British Baptist Missionary in 1814. For the next 20 years, anti-slavery rumblings grew until Sam Sharpe's rebellion, known as the Baptist War, broke from its intent of carrying out a peaceful strike with several plantations burned to the ground. While the uprising was suppressed by the plantocracy's militia and a British garrison, the British Parliament held inquiries that would lead to abolition two years later.

EMANCIPATION AND THE FALL OF COLONIAL RULE

The abolition of slavery in 1834 preceded a four-year period of "apprenticeship" designed to integrate newly freed slaves into more "sophisticated" jobs, and more importantly, allow the plantation economy to adapt to a labor force that required compensation.

Following the apprenticeship period, however, the plantation owners soon found it difficult to secure workers, as many left the countryside for town in search of alternative livelihoods far from the memory of chains. Soon after emancipation, Jamaica's plantocracy, along with cane growers in places like Trinidad, Guyana, and Suriname, resorted to the importation of indentured Indian and Chinese laborers to work their fields beginning in 1845 through 1921.

The period following emancipation was the cradle for the modern identity of the Jamaican people. It was by no means an easy time, as Jamaica continued to be wrought with oppression and injustice, as evidenced by the Morant Bay Rebellion of 1865. Continued repression and oppression in Jamaica led many ambitious and frustrated young men to seek their fortunes overseas, whether in Panama, where the canal would be built between the late 1800s and the early 1900s, thanks in part to Jamaican labor, or to the United States, where a similar cultural identity was being formed as uprooted Africans became African Americans. Many of these fortune seekers, among them Marcus Garvey, George Stiebel, and Alexander Bustamante, returned with wealth, which afforded them a voice in society that they used to advance the cause of the worker, and ultimately, an independent Jamaica. Suffrage was tied to land ownership until it was universally declared in 1944, one of the many reasons for the ongoing struggle throughout the post-emancipation period.

Jamaica's dark history of forced labor was a natural hotbed of resistance leading to the rise of the country's vibrant labor movement.

"INDEPENDENT" JAMAICA

Jamaica's road to independence was trod with baby steps. In 1938, Norman Manley founded the People's National Party, and Alexander Bustamante formed the Jamaica Labour Party five years later. The first elections with voting rights for all were held in 1944. World War II had a significant impact on Jamaica, with widespread shortages adding to the urgency of rising social and political movements. The 1950s saw waves of emigrants leave Jamaica for England, with the tendency for emigrants to head for the United States increasing when Britain restricted immigration following independence. Many old folks in Jamaica still bemoan the country's independence, recalling the good old days when schools were better and society more proper under the British.

The 1970s were a particularly tumultuous decade in Jamaican society, with the main political parties of the island openly flirting with contrasting ideologies: communism on the part of the People's National Party (PNP) leader Michael Manley, and on the other side, a deeper alliance with the United States by the Harvard-educated leader of the Jamaica Labour Party (JLP), Edward Seaga. Shortages of basic goods, economic uncertainty, and spiraling crime were the issues of the day. Popular culture reflected this notorious period with the enduring image of reggae legend Bob Marley holding aloft the hands of the rival politicians onstage during the musician's One Love Peace Concert at the National Stadium at a time when Marley himself had been the target of assassination attempts. The 2015 Booker Prize winner *A Brief History of Seven Killings,* by Marlon James, covers this period in detail. The troubles of the 1970s and 1980s led many of the elite to flee the island and gave Jamaica a lasting reputation for violence that endures despite the fact that tourism areas were never directly affected.

The past several decades have been characterized by a young nation, still under the Commonwealth system, experiencing growing pains and still as dependent as ever, albeit on different external forces. The flow of remittances from Jamaicans abroad, the health of the global economy, approval of multilateral financial institutions, maintenance of bilateral trade agreements, and uninterrupted royalty payments from foreign mining companies are all vital to Jamaica's economic welfare today. Until Jamaica becomes a net exporter of goods and services and manages to decrease its dependence on imported fossil fuels, it will have a difficult time being truly independent, as today it relies little on its own productivity for survival.

Government and Economy

GOVERNMENT

The Jamaican central government is organized as a constitutional monarchy and member of the British Commonwealth with Queen Elizabeth II as its official head of state. On the island, the queen is represented by the governor-general, who signs all legislation passed by the bicameral Jamaican Parliament. Parliament comprises a Senate and a House of Representatives, known as the Upper and Lower Houses, respectively. Representatives are elected for five-year terms, one from each of the island's 60 constituencies. Of Jamaica's 50 senators, 21 are appointed by the governor-general, 13 on the advice of the prime minister, and eight by the opposition leader. The cabinet consists of the prime minister and a minimum of 13 other ministers, including the minister of finance, who must also be an elected representative in the house, with not more than four cabinet ministers selected from the members of the senate.

Beyond the national government, Jamaica has been organized into parishes of ecclesiastical origin since the arrival of the British, who installed the Church of England as their watchdog and pacifier. The Church of England later became the Anglican Church, whose rectories are still some of the most impressive buildings in rural areas across the island. The 60 federal constituencies are subdivided into 275 electoral units, each of which has a parish councilor in the local government. The Corporate Area, as metropolitan Kingston is known, combines the parishes of Kingston and St. Andrew into one local government entity known as the Kingston and St. Andrew Corporation.

Local representation dates to 1662, when the Vestry system was installed to manage local affairs across the island. The Vestry was composed of clergy members and lay magistrates of each parish and was in effect indistinguishable from the Church of England as far as governance and policy were concerned, as it operated almost exclusively for the benefit of the landed elite. The ruling class of the planters, clergy, and magistrates became known as the plantocracy. After 200 years of the Vestry system, it was abandoned in favor of a system of Municipal and Road Boards following the Morant Bay Rebellion of 1865. During the period when Jamaica was ruled by the Vestry system, the number of parishes increased from seven at the outset to 22 by the time it was abandoned. In 1867, the number of parishes was reduced to the 14 recognized today. In 1886, a new representational system of local government was installed consisting of Parochial Boards, which merged the operations of the Municipal and Road Boards into one entity. A general decentralization occurred during the intermittent period before the Parochial Boards were established, leaving local governments in charge of public health, markets, fire services, and water supply. Following implementation of the Parochial Board system, the oversight of building regulations, public beaches, sanitation, slaughterhouses, and streetlights was also assigned to the local government bodies.

Political Parties and Elections

Jamaica's two political parties, the People's National Party (PNP) and the Jamaica Labour Party (JLP), were founded in 1938 and 1943, respectively, by cousins Norman Manley and Alexander Bustamante. Bustamante was a labor leader who came to some degree of wealth through his travels around Latin America before exploiting the anticolonial sentiment of the day to push for greater worker rights and ultimately Jamaican independence. The PNP held power since the 1980s, instating Portia Simpson-Miler in 2007 before the JLP's Bruce Golding toppled her in 2008. Five years later Sister P was back, beating shoe-in Andrew Holness. Simpson-Miller held power until February 2016, when her party lost by a thin margin and Andrew Holness became prime minister once more.

Election time tends to be tense and tumultuous in Jamaica, when memories of the political violence of the 1970s become fresh again. Kingston's poor neighborhoods bear the brunt of the tension and are often barricaded during elections to prevent opposition loyalists from entering with their vehicles to stage drive-by shootings. One of the lasting effects of the political fractiousness in its heyday is that entire neighborhoods and communities in Jamaica can be fully affiliated with a political party through a collusion of kickbacks, graft, extortion, and intimidation in what has come to be known as garrison politics. Entire sections of town can be awash in green, which is the representative color of the JLP, and other sections in orange for the rival PNP. Passersby with no party affiliation are not typically targeted, but it's best to avoid volatile neighborhoods downtown whenever there's an impending election.

ECONOMY

Jamaica's economy is supported by agriculture, bauxite, tourism, and remittances (in order of increasing importance). The financial sector is closely tied to other English-speaking Caribbean countries, most significantly Trinidad and Tobago, with large regional banks and insurance companies dominating the market. Jamaica has a serious balance of payments problem owing to high external debt dating back several decades. Austerity measures imposed by International Monetary Fund (IMF) restructuring during the political reign of Edward Seaga left little money for education and social programs, a situation which persists today. A new IMF arrangement was brokered in 2010 that imposed a heavy burden on the country, with a two-year public-sector wage freeze accompanied by large government job cuts, but the results of this intervention, as well as a debt swap in 2013, are finally bearing fruit. The country managed to bring its debt-to-GDP ratio below 100 percent in 2018 for the first time in nearly two decades, and a banking sector flush with cash is eager to lend, stimulating construction and home ownership across the island. Universal education has inched nearer with the removal of school fees, but the quality of schools varies widely from district to district, and many old-timers claim education was better under British rule. Failure to guarantee universal education is a serious shortfall of both political parties and has directly impacted productivity. The flip side of the coin sees the country's best educated leaving for higher-paid jobs overseas.

Agriculture

Agriculture remains an important part of Jamaica's economy, if not in sheer numbers then for its role in providing sustenance. Cultivation of provisions as established during slavery persists to some degree in rural areas today, where most households grow some kind of crop, even if it is limited to a few mango and ackee trees.

Sugar production is still ongoing on a handful of large estates across the country, but the end of preferential pricing for Jamaican sugar in England has affected the crop's viability, just as it dampened the prospects for Jamaica's banana industry. Apart from sugar, important export crops include coffee, with the Blue Mountain variety fetching some of the highest prices in the world, along with papayas, yams, peppers, ginger, coconuts, pimentos, and citrus, including oranges and Ugli fruit.

Mining

Bauxite mining and processing in Jamaica is dominated by foreign entities like Russia's RUSAL, Noble Group of Hong Kong, and U.S.-based Noranda. Bauxite is mined across the island, leaving gaping red holes as the telltale sign. Bauxite is converted into alumina before being smelted into aluminum, both processes requiring huge amounts of energy. Jamaica has a serious energy problem in that it is overwhelmingly dependent on imported oil for generating electricity. High global energy prices combined with the global recession and low aluminum prices paralyzed the bauxite and alumina industry in 2009, eliminating a large royalty revenue stream earning foreign exchange for the government. Jamaica remains one of the most important bauxite sources in the world, once ranked third in production of bauxite ore and fourth in alumina production globally, but it requires high aluminum prices and low energy prices to be viable. At its peak in the 1970s, Jamaica's bauxite industry accounted for around 75 percent of the country's export earnings and represented 18 percent of global bauxite production.

Other less important mineral resources found in Jamaica include gypsum, limestone, marble, silica sand, clay peat, lignite, titanium, copper, lead, and zinc. The export of crushed limestone, or aggregates, and limestone derivatives is an important growth industry with several players across the island.

Tourism

Tourism continues to be the primary driver of economic growth in Jamaica. Tourism development in recent years has taken the form of megaprojects that employ large numbers at low wages and keep foreign exchange and profits offshore. There seems to be little interest in seeing tourism dollars distributed more evenly among the population, with the government apparently happy just to collect its general consumption tax for each guest that passes through the mass-market all-inclusive resorts. Despite the government's lack of effort to see tourism revenue benefit more Jamaicans, entrepreneurial Jamaicans see great benefits from tourism, with a slew of niche attractions created and developed to serve this market.

Remittances

As a percentage of GDP contributed by remittances, Jamaica is ranked seventh in the world and fourth in the Caribbean—after the Dominican Republic—with nearly US$2 billion entering the country each year. The "Jamaican Dream," pursued by many who are able, consists of leaving the country to pursue a career abroad for however long it takes to make it, and then returning to Jamaica to live well. Sometimes the required period lasts generations, especially when those left back home are reliant on remittances. In tough economic times, Jamaica is more dependent than ever on expatriates, with large concentrations living in Toronto, New York, Florida, and London.

Distribution of Wealth

Some say there are two Jamaicas, made up of the haves and the have-nots. While the truth is more complex, the fact is that there is a serious cash-flow problem in Jamaica. Competition is strong in larger cities for resources that might otherwise be picked from a tree. Even more overwhelming than the price of local produce from the market are imports, which cover everything else.

With jobs hard to come by for youth, there is a desperate situation for many, especially as prices for groceries and other basic goods keep rising. Add in the fact that it is not uncommon for a man to have several children with more than one woman, and the role of what's termed "social capital" becomes clear. If it weren't for the way Jamaicans help each other out—raising children belonging to a niece or nephew, employing a man around the house who really doesn't do much gardening but clearly has no other prospects—Jamaica would find itself in a far worse state.

This cycle of too many mouths to feed with too little to go around maintains a steep class divide on the island. Education costs money for school fees, books, and uniforms, and with competing interests vying for the limited resources in many cash-strapped homes, school can be a low priority. Without proper education, youth become stuck doing menial jobs or nothing at all, and the cycle continues.

People and Culture

RACE AND CLASS

Jamaica's national motto, "Out of many, one people," reflects the tolerance and appreciation for diversity promulgated from an institutional level. Meanwhile, individuals and communities of Jamaica's myriad ethnic groups keep old prejudices and stereotypes very much alive, usually without malice but still with names that are considered derogatory in other parts of the world. If you find yourself the victim of this kind of stereotyping, try not to be offended. Ethnic divisions and cultural prejudices in Jamaica are a result of a history steeped in confrontation and oppression. Rarely, if ever, do these prejudices lead to conflict or violence.

Historically, race in Jamaican society has been of utmost importance in maintaining the strict class structure, while in contemporary society everything boils down to money. Nonetheless, complexion and ethnic background still often form the basis of an individual's perception of self and place in society. While the island has an overwhelming black majority, other minority groups play an important, even dominant role in the local economy. Chinese and Indians who were brought to the island as indentured laborers following the abolition of slavery became and remain prominent members of society as shopkeepers and traders, even in the smaller communities. Lebanese Jamaicans have also played a significant role in business as well as in national politics. White Jamaicans still own some of the most beautiful and expansive estates.

The British established the precedent of "complexionism" by putting lighter-skinned, or "brown," Jamaicans—often their own progeny—in managerial positions, a self-perpetuating phenomenon that continues today in the nepotism that pervades the political and economic elite. The Maroons, who initially put up fierce resistance to the British colonial government and forced a treaty giving them autonomy and freedom from slavery long before abolition, have been an important source of pride for Jamaicans, even while the issue of their collaboration with the British in suppressing slave rebellions remains something of a cultural taboo. Today Jamaica's African heritage is celebrated in popular music enjoyed across social and economic classes.

RELIGION

Jamaica is listed by *Guinness World Records* for the most churches per square mile. Virtually every religion and denomination on earth is represented on the island, with churches everywhere you turn. A common sight on weekends is large tents set up across the countryside for the open-air services preferred by evangelical denominations. Only those churches that are unique to Jamaica or have played an important role in the country's history are described here, with listings in the destination chapters for those of historical or architectural significance.

Revival

Born as a distinctly Jamaican fusion between Christian and African beliefs during the Great Revival of 1860-1861, Revival today is composed of two different branches: Pukkumina (Pocomania or Poco) and Revival Zion, the former closer toward the African end of the spectrum, the latter incorporating more obviously Christian beliefs and practices. Revivalists wear colorful robes and turbans during energetic ceremonies, during which trancelike states are reached with drumming, singing, and a wheeling dance that is said to induce possession by spirits. Revival has its roots in the Native Baptist and Myal movements that lie at the margins of Jamaica's more prominent Anglican and Baptist churches. Baptist churches were early venues for the emergence of what would become known as the Revival faith. Morant Bay rebellion leader Paul Bogle's church in Stony Gut was one such Native Baptist church, where elements of African worship were incorporated into more typical Baptist practice. Today Revival is closely associated with the Pentecostal denomination, and practitioners will generally attend one of the established churches in addition to observing Revival practices.

Core to Revival philosophy is the inseparability of the spirit and physical worlds. It is based on this belief that Revivalists can be possessed and influenced by ancestral spirits. Revivalists reinterpreted the Christian theme of the Father, the Son, and the Holy Spirit, placing emphasis on the last, which manifests as the "Messenger" attending services and possessing believers.

Baptist Church

Significant in Jamaica for its role in fomenting abolitionist sentiment and fueling revolt, the Baptist church was first brought to the island by a freed American slave, Reverend George Liele, in 1738. Liele was baptized in Savannah, Georgia, before receiving a preacher's license and being ordained a minister. He brought his ministerial prowess to Jamaica, where he attracted large numbers of converts with his abolitionist rhetoric that would prove indispensable in firstly attracting followers and ultimately in bringing about emancipation with the help of the British Baptist Mission, which arrived on the island in 1814. After emancipation, the Baptist Church was instrumental in organizing the free villages that allowed the former slaves a new start after leaving the plantation. The church was also important in promoting education among the former slaves. Three of Jamaica's seven national heroes were Baptists, including rebellion leaders Sam Sharpe and Paul Bogle. Today Baptists remain one of Jamaica's strongest religious groups following their separation from the British Baptists in 1842.

Hinduism

Brought to the island by indentured Indians, Hinduism is still practiced but maintains an extremely low profile within tight-knit and economically stable Indian communities. There is a temple on Maxfield Avenue in Kingston that holds regular services on Sunday.

Judaism

The first Jewish people arrived in Jamaica early in the colonial period during the Spanish Inquisition, when they were expelled by King Ferdinand and Queen Isabella and found refuge in Jamaica—in spite of not being officially allowed in the Spanish colonies. Many of these Jews outwardly converted to Catholicism while continuing to practice their own religion in secret. When the British arrived in 1655 to capture the island from the Spanish, they were aided by the Jews, who were subsequently free to practice their religion openly after the conquest. Sephardic Jews of Spanish, Portuguese, and North African descent were the first arrivals, followed in the 1770s by Ashkenazi who left Germany and Eastern Europe.

Obeah

Essentially the Jamaican version of Voodoo, Obeah plays an important role in Jamaica, evoking fear even among those who don't believe in it. The mysticism and use of natural concoctions that help bridge the physical and spiritual worlds has similar African roots as Santeria or Voodoo found in neighboring Cuba and Haiti. While there are few who practice Obeah as priests or worshippers, its casual practice is a widespread phenomenon evidenced by markings and charms strewn about many Jamaican homes.

Ethiopian Orthodox Church

Brought to Jamaica in 1972, the Ethiopian Orthodox Church was the official state church of Ethiopia. Following Haile Selassie's visit to the island in 1966, he instructed the establishment of a church in Kingston in an attempt to legitimize the Rastafarians with a bona fide institution. Many Rastafarians were drawn to the church, even while it does not recognize Selassie as a divine person beyond his own affiliation with the church and the divinity that would convey.

Rastafari

The name of Ethiopian Emperor Haile Selassie I prior to his coronation was Ras Tafari, Ras meaning Prince, and Tafari Makonnen his given name at birth. When Leonard Howell, a Jamaican follower of Marcus Garvey, saw Ras Tafari Makonnen crowned as Emperor Haile Selassie I on November 2, 1930, he viewed the coronation as the fulfillment of biblical prophecy, more so given the emperor's title, King of Kings, Lord of Lords, Conquering Lion of Tribe of Judah. The original prophecy that foretold of a black man rising in the east is attributed to Black Nationalist and Jamaican national hero Marcus Garvey, who had written a play performed in support of his movement in the United States, from which the now-famous line, "look to the east for the crowning of a black king" was supposedly gleaned. It is interesting to note that Garvey never viewed Selassie as a god or claimed his coronation a fulfillment of prophecy at any point during his turbulent life, but this did not stop Leonard Howell from making the proclamation, which fell upon eager ears among his own followers in rural Jamaica and sparked a global movement that continues to grow today.

Leonard Howell chose an opportune time to proclaim Selassie's divinity. Disillusionment by the masses of blacks descended from slaves was high in the 1920s and 1930s, fueling Jamaica's labor movement and the establishment of the two political parties. The Harlem Renaissance of the 1920s gave blacks in the United States a confidence that was exported to the Caribbean in the form of bold ideas that came to a people that never really forgot Africa. Thanks to the important role Jamaica's Maroons played in preserving African belief systems, and the persistence of Revivalist and Obeah religious practices even within the many Christian denominations that were established on the island, select segments of the Jamaican population were well primed for the proposition that the divine had manifested in an African king.

Nevertheless, these select segments were predominantly poor blacks, essentially social outcasts seen at the time as the dregs of society. Dreadlocks, as the hairstyle became known—to the chagrin of many adherents who scorn the fear and criminality the term "dread" implies—predate the Rasta movement and were effectively a natural occurrence for those who neglected to use a comb. With the conversion to the Rastafarian philosophy among many up-and-coming reggae musicians during the 1960s and 1970s, the faith gained traction in Jamaica, and as the island's music became an increasingly important export, Rasta soon became almost synonymous with reggae, and the philosophy spread around the world. The adoption of the Rastafari philosophy by reggae musicians, with its focus on mental, spiritual, and physical fitness, has become a rite of passage for many, as it was for Bob Marley, who was guided in his faith by Rastafari elder Mortimer "Kumi" Planno. Marijuana was brought to Jamaica by Indian indentured laborers in the years following abolition and was adopted by Rastafarians, who point to the bible in condoning its use. Marijuana has been used by Hindu sadhus, or wise men, for mediation purposes in much the same way for thousands of years.

The Rastafarian movement can be traced directly to the recognition of the divinity of Selassie upon his coronation in 1930, but most Rastafarians assert their faith is far more ancient, going back at least to the Nazarenes mentioned in the Old Testament from whence they derive their aversion to razors and scissors, as well as to the eating of flesh. King Selassie has become the head of the movement by default as the most recent manifestation of divinity on earth, despite his own disagreement with being viewed as a god. But the lineage is traced straight back to the divine theocracy of the Old Testament. Selassie himself was said to be the 225th descendant of King Solomon and the Queen of Sheba. Rastafarians essentially claim the Hebrew lineage as their own and have reinterpreted the Old Testament by identifying Africans as the Israelites of modern times, having been enslaved just like the Jews in Babylon. In effect, Rastafarians espouse a natural lifestyle free of the contamination and corruption of modern society. Repatriation to Africa, whether spiritual or physical, forms a central theme.

Along the movement's course of development, charismatic leaders carved out the many "houses," or denominations, that can be found today across the island, including the Nyabinghi, Bobo Ashanti, and the Twelve Tribes of Israel.

The Nyabinghi invoke the warrior spirit of the African empress Iyabinghi; drum ceremonies that last for days around important dates are a central feature.

The Bobo Ashanti, or Bobo Shanti, is a group based at Bobo Hill in Nine Mile, just east of Kingston along the coast. The Bobo live a ritualized lifestyle away from society, putting emphasis on the teaching of Marcus Garvey and founder Prince Emmanuel. Themes of self-reliance and self-confidence are central to the Bobo philosophy. The group has gained as converts many contemporary dancehall reggae musicians, including Sizzla and Capleton.

Perhaps the most international house of Rastafari is the Twelve Tribes of Israel, founded by the late Vernon Carrington, known by his brethren as Brother Gad. Members of the Twelve Tribes are found across the world, with the denomination having crossed social and economic barriers more than other houses, perhaps due to its Christian lean. The Twelve Tribes of Israel house embraces Christianity and views Haile Selassie I as representing the spirit of Christ.

Another important force within the Rastafarian movement has been that of Abuna, or Rasta priest Ascento Fox, who has made strong inroads in society by establishing churches in Kingston, London, and New York. These churches are used as a base for maintaining a presence in the community and providing an alternative for convicts in the prison systems, where the group does a lot of work.

Rastafarians in Jamaica and "in farin" (abroad) are viewed with a combination of respect and fear to this day. Many Rasta colloquialisms have become everyday parlance in Jamaican society as reggae music grew to a global force recognized and appreciated far beyond the Caribbean, with phrases like "one love," "blessed," and "irie" used commonly even by those who don't claim the faith as their own. Use of marijuana, or ganja, has been legitimized to some degree in society at large thanks to the important role it plays for Rastas as a sacrament.

LANGUAGE

In Jamaica, free speech is held as one of the foremost tenets of society. Nevertheless, using the wrong language in the wrong place can cause scorn, embarrassment, or even murder, and knowing how to speak under given circumstances defines a Jamaican's identity and reveals the layers of a highly classist society. Language use ranges from thick patois to the most eloquent queen's English and generally suggests to which tier of society the speaker belongs. Nevertheless, those raised in Jamaica to speak an impeccable form of English will often flip in mid-conversation to outwardly unintelligible patois. The rich flavor of Jamaica's language is the most apparent expression of feverish pride based on a 400-year struggle that spanned the country's anti-slavery, black power, and independence movements. The rise of the island as a cultural hotspot owes not disparagingly to the influence of Indians, Lebanese, Syrians, Jews, and Chinese, and a remaining smattering of the old white plantocracy.

The Arts

Culture and its expression in many forms put Jamaica on the map and continues to be the major draw beyond the sun, sea, and sand. From its intuitive and trained painters to dance troupes and theater groups, Jamaicans have a robust culture that is full of vibes, and they are proud to express themselves in the latest slang, new dance moves, or in song.

MUSICAL HERITAGE

Music has been an integral element of Jamaican society for centuries—from use of song on the plantation to mitigate the torturous work, to funeral rituals that combine Christian and African elements in the traditional nine nights. Most of the instruments used in Jamaica have been borrowed or adapted from either European or African traditions, while some Taino influence surely occurred before their cultural annihilation.

Today music remains as important and central to Jamaican culture as ever. From the beach resorts to the rural hills, sound systems blare out on weekends into the early dawn hours, with a wide variety of genres appreciated on the airwaves.

Reggae

Most people know Jamaica by its legendary musical king, Bob Marley, who first brought international attention to the island. Marley's music impacted the world far beyond Jamaica's shores and the expatriate communities in London, Toronto, New York, and Miami, serving as a rallying cry for freedom movements the world over, from Zimbabwe to South Africa. Bob's legacy left an unquenchable thirst for reggae across the globe, paving the way for countless musicians to follow in his wake. In recent years, dancehall reggae has gone mainstream internationally, thanks to crossover artists like Shaggy and Sean Paul who emerged in the 1990s. Fast-forward a few decades, and leading pop artists Rhianna and Drake can't put enough Jamaican references in their music to satisfy fans, while DJ Khaled made a point of visiting Buju Banton upon his release from prison to boost his street cred.

Reggae has its roots in ska and rocksteady of the 1950s and 1960s, when radio brought American popular music to Jamaican shores and the country's creative musicians began to adapt American tunes to an indigenous swing. Ska artists, who included the likes of Desmond Dekker, Alton Ellis, Toots and the Maytals, and Bob Marley and the Wailers, transitioned to rocksteady and then reggae as the music and popular culture evolved, ushering in the golden age of reggae in the 1970s, when seminal artists like Jimmy Cliff, Dennis Brown, Ken Booth, Gregory Isaacs, Cocoa Tea, and John Holt made their mark.

When Bob Marley shot to international stardom in the late 1970s, his original bandmates, Bunny "Wailer" Livingston and Peter Tosh, began solo careers, the latter's ending prematurely when he was murdered at home in Kingston in 1987. Peter Tosh was among the most outspoken advocates of marijuana, his philosophy and music earning him the status of a cult hero in Jamaica and around the world.

After a decade of slackness in reggae spanning the late 1980s and early 1990s, several talented artists have managed to capitalize on a resurgence of conscious music by launching successful careers as "cultural" reggae artists in the one-drop tradition, sometimes using original tracks, sometimes singing over of the more popular rhythms of the day or of yesteryear. These include Luciano, I-Wayne, Queen Ifrica, Junior Kelly, Richie Spice, and Fantan Mojah in the early 2000s, and from 2010 onward a young cadre comprising Chronixx, Jesse Royal, Kabaka Pyramid, Jah9, Jah Boukes, and Protoje. A cadre of young female artists inspired by the new wave of conscious artists includes the likes of Lila Iké and Sevana and is indisputably led by a young prodigy from Spanish Town who calls herself Koffee. The youngest among a pool of talented artists who meld reggae and dancehall, alternating between song and the unique Jamaican form known as deejaying with uncanny ease, Koffee has a style reminiscent of industry veterans like the lyrically and melodically masterful Sizzla Kalonji, Agent Sasco, Busy Signal, and Bugle.

Dub, a form of remixed reggae that drops out much of the lyrics, was an offshoot of roots reggae pioneered by King Tubby and others, and led to the dub poetry genre, whose best-known artists include Mutabaruka and Linton Kwesi Johnson.

Dancehall

Still the most popular genre of music in Jamaica, dancehall refers to the venue in which it was first enjoyed. Dancehall music is born of the street, with themes typically reflecting struggle, defiance, and relationships with women. Bounty Killer, Agent Sasco, Voicemail, TOK, Busy Signal, Mavado, Vybz Kartel, Elephant Man, Mr. Vegas, Popcaan, Alkaline, Tifa, and Spice have led the pack in popularity and influence in modern dancehall, while Beenie Man still claims the title "King of Dancehall." Lady Saw is still regarded by many as "Queen of the Dancehall," having inspired the emergence of other female artists of the genre like Lady G, Macka Diamond, Spice, and Tifa, before finding God and turning to gospel music.

Ska and Rocksteady

The origins of ska date to the early 1950s, when Jamaicans began to catch on to popular music from the United States that reached the island via the radio and U.S. military personnel stationed here following World War II. Popular American tunes were played by mobile disc jockeys, the predecessors of today's sound systems, before being adopted and adapted by Jamaican musicians. The emphasis on the infectious upbeat was carried over from mento and calypso, with the trademark walking baseline sound borrowed from jazz and R&B. The birth and popularity of ska coincided with an upbeat mood in Jamaica at the time of independence in the early 1960s, and the lyrics of many ska classics celebrate the country's separation from England. Spearheaded by pioneering producers like Prince Buster, Duke Reid, and Clement "Sir Coxone" Dodd, the genre became a hit, especially among Jamaica's working-class masses. The genre was popularized and taken international by bands like Byron Lee and the Dragonaires, Derrick Morgan, and Desmond Decker.

As ska's popularity began to wane by the late 1960s, the rhythm was slowed down, making way for the syncopated base lines and more sensual tone of rocksteady. A series of hits representative of the genre brought artists like Alton Ellis and Hopeton Lewis to fame with songs like "Girl I've Got a Date" and "Tek it Easy." Made for dancing, rocksteady continued to adapt popular American hits, with rude boy culture and love dominating the lyrics.

Jonkunnu

Pronounced "John Canoe," Jonkunnu is a traditional music and skit-like dance performed primarily at Christmas. The Jonkunnu rhythm is played in 2/2 or 4/4 time on the fife, a rattling drum with sticks, bass, and grater. Dancers wear costumes and masks representing characters like Pitchy Patchy, King, Queen, Horse-Head, Cow-Head, and Belly Woman that act out skits and dance.

The origin of Jonkunnu is revealed in the word's etymology: Jonkunnu is an adaptation of the Ghanaian words *dzon'ko* (sorcerer) *nu* (man), derived from secret societies found on the African mainland. Among the costumes found in Jonkunnu are pieced-together sacks similar to those seen in the Abakua, a secret society in neighboring Cuba that also uses dance and drumming.

In Jamaica, Jonkunnu became associated with Christmastime likely because it was the only real holiday for the slaves in the whole year, during which they would tour the plantation with their music, dance, and skits, typically with headgear consisting of ox horns. At the height of the British colonial period, plantation owners actively encouraged Jonkunnu, and it took on European elements, including satire of the masters, Morris dance jigs, and polka steps. The importance of Jonkunnu declined as it was replaced by the emergence of "set girls" who would dance about to display their beauty and sexual rivalry. Later, following emancipation, nonconformist missionaries suppressed Jonkunnu and the mayor of Kingston banned the Jonkunnu parade in 1841, leading to riots. In the years leading up to Jamaican independence, as the country's cultural identity was being explored, Jonkunnu gained the support of the government, which still sponsors the folk form in annual carnival and other events, as younger generations have little exposure to early forms of music and dance.

Kumina

The most distinctly African of Jamaica's musical forms, Kumina was brought to Jamaica after emancipation by indentured laborers from Congo and remains a strong tradition in Portland and St. Thomas. Kumina ceremonies are often held for wakes and burials, as well as for births and anniversaries, and involve drumming and dancing.

Mento

Jamaica's original folk music, mento is a fusion of African and European musical elements played with a variety of instruments that were borrowed from plantation owners and fashioned by the slaves themselves as the genre developed. A variety of instruments have a place in mento, from stick and hand drums to stringed instruments, flutes, and brass, along with the crucial rumba box, the precursor to the upright bass and bass guitar. Mento was one of the most important foundations for ska, which gave birth to reggae.

FINE ART

The Jamaican art world can be classified broadly into folk artists, schooled artists, and self-taught or intuitive artists. Folk art has been around throughout Jamaica's history, as far back as the Taino, whose cave paintings can still be seen in a few locations on the island, most notably at Mountain River Cave near Kitson Town, St. Catherine. European and African arrivals brought a new mix, with the planter class often commissioning works from visiting European portrait painters, while enslaved Africans carried on a wide range of traditions from their homelands, which included wood carving, fashioning musical instruments, and creating decorative masks and costumes for traditional celebrations like Jonkunnu. The annual Hosay celebrations, which date to the mid-1800s in Jamaica, as well as Maroon ceremonies, are considered living art. Folk art had a formative influence on Jamaica's intuitive artists.

The century after full emancipation in 1938 saw deep structural changes and growing pains for Jamaica, first as a colony struggling to maintain order and then in the tumultuous years leading up to independence. Jamaican art as a concerted discipline arose in the late 1800s, and culminated with the establishment of formal training in 1940. In the early years, sculpture and painting reflected the mood of a country nursing fresh wounds of slavery, with progressive, renegade leaders and indigenous Revival and then Rastafari movements giving substance to the work of self-taught artists.

Edna Manley, wife of Jamaica's first prime minister, Norman Manley, is credited with formally establishing a homegrown Jamaican art scene. An accomplished artist, Edna Manley was born in England in 1900 to a Jamaican mother and English father and schooled at English art schools. On arrival in Jamaica, Manley was influenced by Jamaica's early intuitive sculptors, like David Miller Sr. and David Miller Jr., Alvin Marriot, and Mallica Reynolds, a revival bishop better known as "Kapo." Edna Manley's 1935 sculpture *Negro Aroused* captured the mood of an era characterized by cultural nationalization, where Afrocentric imagery and the establishment and tribulations of a black working class were often the focus. Manley began teaching formal classes in 1940 at the Junior Centre of the Institute of Jamaica, giving the structure necessary for the emergence of a slew of Jamaican painters, including Albert Huie, David Pottinger, Ralph Campbell, and Henry Daley. Her school later developed into the Jamaica School of Art and Crafts, which was ultimately absorbed by Edna Manley College. Several other artists who did not come out of Manley's school gained prominence in the early period, including Carl Abrahams, Gloria Escofferey, and John Dunkley. Dunkley's works consistently use somber shades and clean lines with dark symbolism reflective of serious times, making them immediately recognizable.

Jamaican fine arts exploded in the fervent post-independence years along with the country's music industry, fueling the expansion of both the National Gallery as well as a slew of commercial galleries, many of which still exist in Kingston today. The post-independence period counts among its well-recognized artists Osmond Watson, Milton George, George Rodney, Alexander Cooper, and David Boxer. Black Nationalism and the exploration of a national identity remained important topics for artists like Omari Ra and Stanford Watson, while many other artists, like the ubiquitous Ras Dizzy or Ken Abendana Spencer, gained recognition during the period for the sheer abundance of their work, much of which celebrated Jamaica's rural landscape. In the late 1970s, the National Gallery launched an exhibition series called the Intuitive Eye, which brought mainstream recognition to Jamaica's self-taught artists as key contributors to the development of Jamaican art. Some of the artists to gain exposure and wider recognition thanks to the Intuitive Eye series include William "Woody" Joseph, Gason Tabois, Sydney McLaren, Leonard Daley, John "Doc" Williamson, William Rhule, Errol McKenzie, and Allan "Zion" Johnson.

Sports

The sporting arena has seen many achievements that have been etched in the hearts of Jamaicans, becoming a part of the country's national identity. Jamaica has come to embody the sporting adage of "punching above one's weight," echoed in the local expression "we likkle but we tallawa" (we're little but we're strong), and this has been shown most emphatically in recent times on the sprinting track and during the 2019 Women's World Cup, but also historically on the cricket ovals, boxing arenas, and, to add a bit of pizzazz to the diverse accomplishments, with bobsledders and aerial skiers competing in the Winter Olympics.

Track & Field

For an island nation with modest sporting infrastructure, track and field events have always been a mainstay in schools and communities with participants in organized events as young as primary school age. In fact, arguably the biggest and best attended annual sporting event in the island's calendar would be the Boys and Girls Championships held at the National Stadium for the various high schools, known popularly as Champs. It is this background that fostered the likes of Merlene Ottey, Juliet Cuthbert, Veronica Campbell-Brown, Shelly-Ann Fraser-Pryce, Asafa Powell, and, of course, the inimitable Usain Bolt, who shattered the 100-meter and 200-meter world records. Many gold medalists who have run for other nations were also born and raised in Jamaica, including Linford Christie, Ben Johnson, and Donovan Bailey. The excitement is palpable on the island when its fastest citizens are set to race in a meet anywhere in the world.

Soccer

It's fair to say that the favorite spectator sport of Jamaicans is the "world sport" of football or soccer. The "Reggae Girlz," as the country's national women's team are affectionately called, qualified for the Women's World Cup 2019 in France for the first time in their history, capturing many hearts. Though lacking in major historical exploits before qualifying for the 1998 FIFA World Cup, the Reggae Boyz are viewed with expectant hopefulness by Jamaican sport lovers.

Boxing

Champion boxers who have raised the Jamaican flag include Mike McCallum, Trevor Berbick, and Glen Johnson, while noted boxers Lennox Lewis and Frank Bruno, although representing Great Britain, speak fondly of their Jamaican roots.

Cricket

A nostalgic remnant of British colonialism, cricket is still a ubiquitous sporting activity on any level field throughout the island. Jamaican cricketers play on the regionally federated West Indies Cricket Team (affectionately called "the Windies"), which joins the other island nations of the Caribbean sharing a British colonial past. Though the fortunes of the Windies have drastically fallen since the turn of the 21st century, there was a time when they were the unmistakable rulers of the sport. West Indies cricket did not lose a single international Test series for 15 years from the mid-1970s to the early 1990s. Notable Jamaican cricketers include former Windies captains Michael Holding, Jimmy Adams, and Courtney Walsh, as well as current bad boy of the sport Chris Gayle, who has earned as much of a reputation for his skills on the pitch as for his wild parties.

Essentials

Transportation 328
Visas and Officialdom . . 331
Food 331
Accommodations 333
Conduct and Customs . 334
Travel Tips 335
Sustainable Tourism 337
Health and Safety 339
Information and
    Services 340

Transportation

GETTING THERE
By Air

Montego Bay's **Sangster International Airport** (MBJ) is served by regular commercial flights throughout the year and by seasonal charter flights. International airlines serving Sangster International Airport include Air Berlin, Air Canada, Allegiant, American Airlines, Condor, Delta, Eurowings, Frontier Airlines, JetBlue, Southwest, Spirit, Sun Country, Sunwing Airlines, Thomas Cook, TUI, Virgin Atlantic, and WestJet. Regional flights around the Caribbean are on Aerogaviota,

Caribbean Airlines, Cayman Airways, Copa Airlines, and InterCaribbean, which offers the only regularly scheduled service between Kingston and Montego Bay, from the domestic terminal. International Airlink and TimAir offer domestic charter services, also from the domestic terminal.

Kingston's **Norman Manley International Airport** (KIN) is served by Aerogaviota, Air Canada, American Airlines, British Airways, Caribbean Airlines, Cayman Airways, Delta, InterCaribbean, JetBlue, Spirit, and Virgin Atlantic. British Airways offers flights from London to Montego Bay and Kingston. Sangster International Airport in Montego Bay is the most popular entry point for visitors to Jamaica.

By Sea

Two million passengers per year stop over on **cruise ships,** and their numbers have been growing steadily in the three major ports of call in Jamaica: **Falmouth,** where Royal Caribbean has its own pier, followed by **Ocho Rios** and **Montego Bay.** Port Antonio has a smaller cruise ship pier that sees less than a dozen arrivals per year, and Kingston sees even fewer but is now building a floating pier off Port Royal in a bid to attract cruise lines.

Visitors arriving in Jamaica on **private vessels** have three options to clear customs and immigration: the Montego Bay Yacht Club, the Royal Jamaica Yacht Club in Kingston, and the Errol Flynn Marina in Port Antonio, all of which also have 24-hour security and repair facilities with lifts. There are also marinas with slips in Port Royal, Ocho Rios, and at Drax Hall.

GETTING AROUND

It can be challenging to get around Jamaica on public transportation, and you will likely arrive at your destination a bit frazzled by the congested route taxis and buses, dangerously fast driving, and inevitably loud R&B or dancehall blasting from the speakers. It's important to remind yourself that this is all part of Jamaica's charm.

Public transportation is readily available and very affordable for those who are patient and adventurous. Whether starting your journey in a major urban area or in the middle of the bush, it's always easy to catch a ride by flagging down a minibus or route taxi.

By Bus

The **Jamaica Urban Transit Company** (JUTC, http://jutc.gov.jm) operates in and around Kingston, with bus stops along all the main thoroughfares, with fare at around US$1. The two hubs in Kingston are the Half Way Tree Transport Centre and Downtown at Parade.

Minibuses and coaster buses run between every major city and town and represent the most affordable means of covering long distances across Jamaica, with fares typically no more than US$10, even for the long hauls. Passengers are packed in tight, and these vehicles were not designed for comfort, which can be a problem for those with long legs. **Knutsford Express** (www.knutsfordexpress. com) offers coach service between every major destination in Jamaica and is the most comfortable option and the only scheduled service. Buses depart seven times a day between Kingston and Montego Bay during the week and nine times a day on weekends, with one-way fare around US$30. **Jamaica Union of Travelers Association** (JUTA, www.juta-toursja.com) has cars, minivans, and buses of all sizes in its fleet and offers charter service across the island as well as a great deal on trips between Montego Bay and Negril, which must be booked in advance.

Taxis
ROUTE TAXIS

Arriving with luggage or backpacks to hike up to the road and hail down a route taxi is perfectly feasible in Jamaica, even if it does provide amusement for local people. Most taxis will want to be chartered, however, when you are carrying luggage, and others won't stop. This makes chartering a taxi a good idea.

Route taxis are typically white Toyota Corolla station wagons with the origin and destination painted in small letters on the side by the front doors. These cars can be flagged down from the side of the road anywhere along their route, and when not operating as route taxis, they will generally offer private charters at greatly inflated rates. Haggling is a must when chartering a car, while routes have fixed rates that are not typically inflated for visitors except in highly touristed areas like Negril or Ocho Rios, or at night, when fares increase.

Route taxis run between even the smallest communities and between different parts of town in the larger urban areas. Inevitable drawbacks are the cramped quarters ripe with body odor, blaring music, long waits, and reckless drivers. The clear advantage is the regulated fare of just a few dollars, which can't be beaten for short distances, apart from walking or cycling. Route taxi drivers are quick to offer an exclusive charter to veer off their normal route, a service that costs considerably more than they would charge operating their normal shared taxi service.

CHARTER TAXIS

Chartering a car and driver is the most expensive way to get around, but it takes most of the stress out of a journey around the island. The standard rate of US$100 for the one-hour trip between Montego Bay and Negril is a good indication of typical private charter costs islandwide. Drivers typically charge a premium to go into the Blue Mountains, with the typical fare between Kingston and Irish Town at around US$150 for the two-hour round-trip.

Domestic Flights

InterCaribbean is the only airline to offer regularly scheduled domestic service between Kingston and Montego Bay, at around US$70 each way. Two charter carriers, International Airlink and TimAir, both based at Sangster International Airport in Montego Bay, offer flights between the three major airports and the island's network of aerodromes starting at US$300 for the shortest hop between Montego Bay and Negril for up to two passengers.

Renting a Car

For those who can afford it and have the confidence and experience, a rental car is by far the best way to get around the island, most importantly for independence. Rentals are slightly expensive by international standards and you should expect to pay no less than US$60 per day for a compact car, plus insurance and fuel. Options for different car rental agencies are included in the destination chapters.

Visas and Officialdom

U.S. citizens now require a passport to reenter the United States after visiting Jamaica. U.S., UK, Canadian, and EU citizens do not require a visa to enter Jamaica and can stay for three to six months, although the actual length of stay stamped into your passport will be determined by the customs agent upon entry. For extensions, visit the **immigration office** (25 Constant Spring Rd., tel. 876/906-4402 or 876/906-1304) in Half Way Tree.

EMBASSIES AND CONSULATES

- **Canada** 3 W. King's House Rd., Kingston 10, tel. 876/926-1500 or 876/926-1507, fax 876/511-3491, kngtn@international.gc.ca

- **United Kingdom** 28 Trafalgar Rd., Kingston 10, tel. 876/510-0700, fax 876/511-0737, bhckingston@cwjamaica.com (general), consular.kingston@fco.gov.uk (consular), ukvisas.kingston@fco.gov.uk (visa)

- **United States** 142 Old Hope Rd., tel. 876/702-6000, consularkingst@state.gov (visa and consular), opakgn@state.gov (general)

Food

Jamaican food is reason enough to visit the island. Home-cooked meals are generally best, so it's worth seeking out an invitation whenever possible. The traditional dishes were developed during the era of slavery and typically include a generous, even overwhelming, serving of starch, and at least a token of meat or seafood protein known historically as "the watchman." In recent years pan-Caribbean fusion has caught on as a new culinary trend, with creative dishes added to the traditional staples.

Ackee is a central ingredient of the national dish, ackee and saltfish. The fruit contains dangerous levels of toxic amino acid hypoglycin A until the fruit pods open naturally on the tree, or "dehisce," in horticultural terminology, at which point the yellow fleshy aril surrounding the glossy black seed is safe to eat. Ackee has the consistency and color of scrambled eggs and is generally prepared with onion and rehydrated saltfish.

Bammy is derived from the Taino word *guyami*. A staple for the Taino people, bammy is made from cassava, or manioc, known in many Spanish-speaking countries as *yuca*. In Jamaica, bammy is either steamed or fried and usually eaten as the starch accompaniment to fish.

Bulla is a heavy biscuit made with flour and molasses.

Bun, or Easter Bun, is a tradition that has become popular enough to last throughout the year, so much so that by Easter there is little novelty left. Bun is typically eaten with yellow cheddar cheese.

Callaloo is a spinach-like green often steamed and served for breakfast, either alone as a side dish or sometimes mixed with saltfish.

Curry was brought to Jamaica by indentured Indians and quickly caught on as a popular flavoring for a variety of dishes, most commonly curry goat, but also including curry chicken, conch, shrimp, crab, and lobster. Curry rivals ganja as the most popular contribution from India to Jamaican culture.

Dumpling is a round doughy mass that's either boiled or fried, generally to accompany breakfast. When boiled, at the center there is little difference from raw dough. **Spinners** are basically the same thing but rolled between the hands and boiled with conch or corn soup.

Festival is another common starchy accompaniment to fish and jerk meals, consisting basically of fried dough and corn flour shaped into a slender cylindrical blob.

Fish tea is similar to mannish water except it is made with boiled fish parts.

Food refers to any starchy tubers served to accompany a protein, also known as "ground provisions." The term has its roots in the days of slavery when provision grounds were maintained by slaves to ensure an adequate supply of food.

Ital stew describes any vegetarian soup prepared in the Rasta tradition, but typically refers to the vegan-friendly alternative to stew peas, which would usually include pork. Ital stew made from kidney beans, scotch bonnet peppers, coconut milk, garlic, scallions, onions, potato, flour spinners or dumplings, pimento, thyme and other spices.

Jerk is a seasoning that goes back as far as Jamaica's Taino. The most common jerk dishes are chicken and pork, optimally barbecued using pimento or sweet wood, which gives the meat a delicious smoky flavor complemented by the spicy seasoning made with fiery scotch bonnet pepper, pimento (all spice), ginger, thyme, molasses, scallion, and garlic. Jerk seasoning recipes may differ slightly, but these are the most important ingredients.

Mannish water is a popular broth with supposed aphrodisiac properties made of goat parts not suitable for other dishes (the head, ears, testicles) and cooked with green banana, spinners, and seasoned with pepper and sometimes rum.

Oxtail is a popular dish.

Provisions are an inexpensive and important part of the Jamaican diet. The most commonly consumed starches include rice, yam, cassava, breadfruit, dumpling (fried or boiled balls of flour), boiled green banana, or fried plantain.

Rice-and-peas is the most ubiquitous staple served with any main dish. "Peas" in Jamaica are what the rest of the English-speaking world refers to as beans and usually consist of either kidney beans sparsely distributed among the white rice, or gungo peas, cooked with coconut milk and seasonings.

Saltfish was originally codfish that was shipped from New England in large quantities, with salt used as a preservative. It became a protein staple that helped sustain the slave trade. Despite the widespread use of refrigeration today, saltfish continues to be a sought-after item, even as the stocks of cod have been depleted from the Grand Banks of the North Atlantic and other salted fish has been substituted in its place.

Fresh **seafood** is readily available throughout Jamaica, though fish, shrimp, and lobster are typically the most expensive items on any menu. Fish is generally either red snapper or parrot fish prepared steamed with okra, escoveitch style, or fried. **Escoveitch** fish comes from the Spanish tradition of *escaveche,* with vinegar used in the preparation. In Jamaica, scotch bonnet pepper and vinegar-infused onion is usually served with fried escoveitch fish.

The most common Jamaican lobsters are actually marine crayfish belonging to the family Palinuridae *(Palinurus argus).* Commonly known as the spiny lobster, two species are widely eaten, and, while noticeably different, are every bit as delicious as lobster caught in more northern waters.

Popular breakfast items include **hominy porridge** and **beef liver** in addition to ackee and saltfish, typically eaten on Sunday.

COFFEE

Jamaican coffee is among the most prized in the world, Jamaica Blue Mountain Coffee being the most coveted variety on the island. The Jamaica Blue Mountain Coffee name is a registered trademark, and only a select group of farmers are authorized to market their beans with it. Some of the best Blue Mountain Coffee is grown on Old Tavern Estate. Mavis

Bank Coffee Factory sells under the Jablum brand and is also of good quality.

The annual Jamaica Blue Mountain Coffee Festival is held in Newcastle, near Kingston, the first weekend in March and features barista demonstrations and coffee-infused food and beverages as well as local arts and crafts alongside live musical performances. There are also business workshops geared toward the formation of new industry partnerships.

Jamaica's coffee industry dates to the Haitian Revolution, when many farmers in the neighboring island fled to Jamaica out of fear for Haiti's future prospects. The cloud forests of the Blue Mountains were found to provide ideal growing conditions that allow the beans to mature slowly, giving the coffee its unique, full-bodied flavor.

RUM

Since the days of old when pirates stormed from port to port pillaging and plundering their way to riches, Jamaica has been an important consumer of rum. Rum production in Jamaica was an important component of the colonial economy under the British, and Jamaican rum is still highly regarded today. There are two varieties of Jamaican rum, white and aged. Aged rum has a reddish-brown tint and is smoother than white rum. Jamaica's most comprehensive range of vintages comes from Appleton Estate Jamaica Rum, owned by Italy's Campari and produced by J. Wray & Nephew in the parish of St. Elizabeth and at its Kingston distillery. Worthy Park Estate in St. Catherine has been attempting to rival J. Wray & Nephew's White Overproof Rum with its Rum Bar Rum brand in recent years.

It is said that the number of rum bars in Jamaica is matched only by the number of churches, the two institutions equally ubiquitous in even the smallest hamlets across the island. The annual Jamaican Rum Festival is held in March at Hope Gardens in Kingston, with samplings, food pairings, edutainment, and consumer workshops.

SAUCES AND SPICES

Jamaica has for centuries been a great producer of spices, from pimento, also known as allspice, to scotch bonnet peppers and annatto. The island's historical reputation as a source of flavorings gave birth to several successful brands sold the world over, from Pickapeppa Sauce, produced in Shooters Hill, Manchester, to Busha Browne's Jamaican sauces, jellies, chutneys, and condiments, made in Kingston, and Walkerswood Jamaican Jerk Seasoning, produced in St. Ann. Belcour Blue Mountain Preserves continues this tradition with delicious sweet and savory products to spice up virtually any dish.

Accommodations

BUDGET OPTIONS

As an island with a limited manufacturing sector, Jamaica relies on imports for many basic goods and all the fossil fuels used to power electricity generation and transportation, putting a premium on the economy as a whole. As a result, many visitors find the country to be an expensive destination, where a small bag of groceries can cost more than US$50. Nonetheless, most Jamaicans live on less than US$10 a day, and there are easy ways to shave costs as a visitor on a budget. Airbnb lists many budget accommodations with varying standards in every part of the island. These include hostels with bunk beds, guest houses, and modest apartments as well as a few down-market hotels and even an all-inclusive hotel, Deja Resort, in Montego Bay, in a great location across from Doctors Cave Beach and a no-frills format for under US$100 pp. Budget accommodations under US$50 pp typically offer foam versus spring mattresses, a standing fan rather than a ceiling fan or air-conditioning, and minimal staff and housekeeping services.

HOTELS

The hotel offerings in Jamaica include waterfront boutiques, international flags like Hilton and Holiday Inn, and city hotels catering to a mix of leisure and business travelers in Kingston, Montego Bay, and Mandeville. In resort areas, hotel rates range from under US$100 a night to US$800, and seasonal pricing typically applies. In Kingston, rates range similarly, but there tends to be little to no seasonal variation. The unfortunate reality is that the level of service in Jamaica tends to be poor on the whole, especially at the lower end of the price spectrum.

ALL-INCLUSIVE RESORTS

Jamaica pioneered the all-inclusive formula beginning with three locally owned resort chains: Couples, SuperClubs, and Sandals. The model has since spread the world over. All-inclusive options have grown exponentially in Jamaica over the past two decades with the arrival of several new chains, many of them based in Spain, including Iberostar, AM Resorts, Excellence Resorts, Fiesta Group, Riu, Karisma, Meliá, Grupo Piñero's Bahia Principe, and more recently H10. The well-established homegrown options include Butch Stewart's Sandals and Beaches Resorts, Lee and Paul Issa's Couples Resorts, and their cousin John Issa's SuperClubs brand Hedonism. The quality of the food and beverages varies widely with the price point, and sticklers for top-shelf spirits are often disappointed to find more expensive brands are not

available. Rates at all-inclusive resorts typically range from under US$100 pp per night to over US$400 at the high-end properties.

Many smaller resorts, including several boutique hotels and many villas, have started offering all-inclusive packages. An all-inclusive meal plan can certainly be a good value and will eliminate the hassle of budgeting for food or reimbursing staff for groceries, but it's rarely more economical than buying the food and beverages yourself, especially for more discerning eaters and drinkers.

VILLAS

Jamaica has a long tradition of cultivating a luxury lifestyle, dating to the days when plantation owners, profiting from enslaved laborers, built tremendous great houses designed for relaxation and entertaining. The growth of the villa market has built on that tradition, and the country has a great variety of rentals available, with five-bedroom properties from US$3,500 to US$75,000 weekly, plus food and gratuity. While staying at a villa is by no means a budget option, for a large group or family it can work out cheaper than a boutique hotel or all-inclusive resort. The personalized attention from staff, home cooked meals, and private facilities make the villa option especially compelling.

VACATION RENTALS

Airbnb has given Jamaicans who never participated in the tourism market an opportunity to do so, with an explosion of inventory over the past five years. With low standards in the formal hotel sector as a starting point, visitors booking accommodations through vacation rental sites should pay close attention to the reviews and err on the side of caution.

Conduct and Customs

ETIQUETTE

Manners are taken very seriously in Jamaica, though like anywhere, some make

it abundantly clear they pay no mind to proper etiquette. To a greater extent than elsewhere in the world, etiquette and speech are perceived as directly correlated to upbringing and socioeconomic status. Be aware of the impression you make, especially with language. Cussing, for instance, is scorned by many Jamaicans, especially devout Christians. Others couldn't care less about the impression they make and speak freely and colorfully. Generally speaking, it's considered rude if you enter a room or place of business and don't say "Good morning," "Good afternoon," or "Good evening" before addressing the person in front of you.

Photographing people in Jamaica can be considered rude or intrusive and should only be done after asking permission. That said, media professionals are highly respected, and if you are walking around with a camera, people will often ask you to take their picture, regardless of whether they will ever see it. It makes a nice gesture to give people photos of themselves and is a great way to make friends. Photographing people without asking permission will often result in a request for money. Asking permission often elicits the same response. If the picture is worth it, placate your subject with whatever you think it's worth. Money is rarely turned down.

The explosive proliferation of camera phones and social media hasn't missed Jamaica, and selfie culture has sunk in deep. It's common to see patrons at a bar, club, or even a live performance photographing themselves. That doesn't necessarily mean they want to be photographed by others or have their likeness posted online elsewhere; ask before taking pictures and posting them publicly.

TIPPING

Tipping is common practice in Jamaica to a varying degree of formality, depending on the venue, from leaving a "smalls" for the man who watched your car while you were at the club to more serious sums for the staff at your villa.

Many of the more formal restaurants include a service charge in the bill, in which case any further tip should be discretionary based on the quality of service provided. At inexpensive eateries, tipping is rare, while at the more upscale restaurants, it is expected. The amount to leave for a good meal at a midrange to expensive restaurant follows international standards, between 10 percent and 20 percent, depending on the attention you received.

Most all-inclusive hotels have banned tipping to discourage the soliciting that makes guests uncomfortable. Where no-tipping policies are in place, it's best to adhere to them. At lodging-only hotels, a US$5-10 tip for the bellhop is a welcome gesture.

Staffed villas usually state that guests should leave the staff a tip equal to 10-15 percent of the total rental cost. This consideration should be divided equally among the staff who were present during your stay and given to each person individually.

Tipping is also common practice at spas, where a US$20 bill on top of the cost of treatment for the individual who provided the service will be well received. Tour guides at attractions, even when included in the cost of the tour, greatly appreciate a tip, and the poorly trained will insist on it.

Travel Tips

VOLUNTEER OPPORTUNITIES

While work is often the last thing on people's minds on a trip to Jamaica, volunteering can be an immensely rewarding experience. It inevitably puts visitors in direct contact with real working people as opposed to the forced smiles associated with the tourism industry. Several church groups offer volunteer opportunities, while there are also several secular options.

Dream Jamaica (contact programs

director Adrea Simmons, programs@dream-jamaica.org, www.dreamjamaica.org), one of Jamaica's best volunteer programs, operates summer programs in Kingston that bring volunteer professionals from abroad and connects high school students in career-driven summer programs with the local business community. Dream Jamaica seeks local professionals who can commit four hours per month to mentoring high school students, as well as program coordinators and assistance from Jamaica or abroad for full-time volunteer work over the six week program each summer.

Blue Mountain Project Jamaica (contact service learning program coordinator Haley Madson, U.S. tel. 920/229-1829, www.bluemountainproject.org) is a volunteer organization focused on the Hagley Gap community in the Blue Mountains that places visitors to Jamaica in homestays and coordinates volunteer work in any number of socioeconomic development projects it oversees, like establishing health clinics, art camps, adult education, basic infrastructure, and ecological projects embodying the group's "Educating and Empowering" tag line. Volunteers pay US$79 per night for a minimum of a week, which covers lodging, meals, and transportation. Longer volunteer stints are rewarded with discounted rates.

The **U.S. Peace Corps** (www.peacecorps.gov) is quite active in Jamaica but generally requires an extensive application process, offering no opportunity for spontaneous or temporary volunteer work on the island. Nevertheless, Americans looking to make a contribution to sensible development programs have found Jamaica a challenging and rewarding place to work with the Peace Corps.

ACCESS FOR TRAVELERS WITH DISABILITIES

Travelers with disabilities should not be turned off by the lack of infrastructure on the island to accommodate special needs, but it is important to inquire exhaustively about the facilities available. Most of the all-inclusive resorts have facilities to accommodate wheelchairs, but outside developed tourist areas, a visit will not be without its challenges.

TRAVELING WITH CHILDREN

Despite the common perception that Jamaica is dangerous and fraught with violence, most places on the island are actually perfectly safe, and the country is a fascinating and engaging place for children. Beyond the obvious allure of its beaches, Jamaica has a wealth of attractions that make learning fun, from rainforest and mountain hikes teeming with wildlife to farm tours that offer visitors a sampling of seasonal fruits. The activities available to engage children are endless. What makes the island an especially great destination for families is the love showered on children. Nannies are readily available and can be easily arranged by inquiring at any lodging, not just at those that tout it as a unique service.

WOMEN TRAVELERS

Jamaica is a raw and aggressive society, with little regard for political correctness and little awareness of what is considered sexual harassment in the United States and Europe. Flirtation is literally a way of life, and women should not be alarmed if they find they are attracting an unusual degree of attention compared with what they are used to back home. On the street, catcalls are common, even when a woman is accompanied by her boyfriend or husband; in nightclubs women are the main attraction, and dancing tends toward the sexually suggestive, if not explicit. Both on the street and in the club it's important to keep your wits about you and communicate interest or disinterest as clearly as possible. It is more the exception than the norm for men to persist after a woman has clearly and politely communicated her disinterest.

Jamaica depends overwhelmingly on the tourist dollar, and the authorities generally make an extra effort to ensure visitor safety. Nonetheless, if you are a woman traveling alone, it's best to exercise caution and avoid uncomfortable encounters. Suitors will inevitably offer any and every kind of enticing service: Accept only what you are completely comfortable with, and keep in mind that local men might make romantic advances because they're motivated by financial interest.

GAY AND LESBIAN TRAVELERS

Jamaica is notoriously and blatantly antigay. Many Jamaicans will defend their antigay stance with religious arguments, and many reggae artists use antigay lyrics as an easy sell, often instigating violence against gay men both metaphorically and literally. Some of these artists—like Buju Banton, who had a hit that suggested killing gay people—have toned down their rhetoric following tour cancellations abroad owing to their prejudice, while others, like Sizzla Kalonji, continue undaunted. On the whole, Jamaica is a tolerant society, but as a precautionary measure, it is best for gay and lesbian travelers not to display their sexual orientation publicly.

Sustainable Tourism

COMMUNITY TOURISM

When you visit a foreign country, your money is your most substantive demonstration of support. Jamaica is an expensive place to live, and foreign currency is the chief economic driver. The benefit, or lack thereof, that tourism brings to the island is dependent on where the money ends up. Though rock-bottom all-inclusive packages are an easy way to control your vacation spending, the money that flows to these businesses is not widely distributed. Large resorts often pay their workers a pittance.

Jamaica has gone through several different eras of tourism development dating to the booming banana trade in the late 1800s. Until the 1960s, Jamaica was a niche destination for the wealthy. In the late 1960s and early 1970s, hippies discovered Jamaica, and large groups would tour on motorbikes, reveling in the laid-back lifestyle and plentiful herb. Montego Bay was the upscale destination on the island, with Port Antonio the playground of movie stars and Negril a newly discovered fishing beach. In those days the numbers of visitors were low, and outside Montego Bay, the environmental impact of tourism was negligible.

Then came the all-inclusive resorts, the largest of which, Sunset Jamaica Grande, had 750 rooms by 2006. Since then, several new hotels have been built along the North Coast with over 1,000 rooms. The water resources required by these facilities puts a huge strain on the environment, as does wastewater, which is often poorly or minimally treated before being dumped into the sea. Food at these establishments is often imported rather than sourced locally.

Perhaps the best way to make a positive impact on a visit to Jamaica is by promoting community tourism by staying in smaller, locally run establishments and eating at a variety of restaurants rather than heeding the fear tactics that keep so many visitors inside gated hotels. Treasure Beach in St. Elizabeth is a mecca for community tourism, where a few boutique hotels are far outnumbered by guesthouses and villas, many of them locally owned.

ENVIRONMENTAL ISSUES

Since the turn of 21st century, the Jamaican government has actively sought investment from multinational groups that continue to build new hotels, most under the all-inclusive model. All-inclusive resorts now occupy what were Jamaica's remaining untouched stretches of coastline. The absence of beaches has not inhibited developers from making their own, at incalculable environmental cost to coral reefs and the marinelife they support. When scuba diving and snorkeling along Jamaica's reefs, minimize your impact by not touching the coral.

Bauxite Mining

The bauxite industry is an important foreign exchange earner for Jamaica, but the environmental costs are clear. The Ewarton Aluminum Plant in St. Ann is noticeable by its stench for kilometers around, and from the heights of Mandeville several bauxite mines and refineries scar the landscape. Export terminals built for bauxite coexist with tourism interests in Ocho Rios and Discovery Bay, while their presence on the South Coast is less obvious to most visitors. A surge in aluminum prices and the threat of sanctions against Russia, one of the world's leading producers, has led to new investment in Jamaica's bauxite industry, reviving the country's largest plant, mothballed before the global financial crisis of 2008, under new Chinese ownership.

Litter

Environmental education in Jamaica is seriously lacking. Environmental awareness has only recently been directly linked to the island's tourism economy under a national campaign with "Nuh Dutty Up Jamaica" (Don't dirty up Jamaica) as its slogan. The difference in sanitation and upkeep between the leisure destinations frequented by Jamaicans rather than foreign visitors is marked. Choice spots like Salt River in Clarendon are littered with trash, while other popular local spots like Bluefields Beach Park in Westmoreland make greater efforts to clean up. Regardless of how senseless it may seem to maintain a green stance when it comes to litter in the face of gross negligence on the part of Jamaicans themselves, keep in mind that locals can be influenced by what they see from visitors. Make a point of not trashing the country, even if you seem to be up against insurmountable odds.

Water Table Salinization

Several coastal areas suffer salinization of the water table when water is extracted more rapidly than it is replenished. While Jamaica is fortunate to have high rainfall in the east and abundant water generally, salinization will likely be an increasing problem in drier northwest coast areas, where new all-inclusive resorts are being built. Wherever you end up staying, the best way to lessen your impact on

bamboo rafting on the Martha Brae River

finite water resources is by not taking long showers and by reusing towels during your stay.

Deforestation

Despite the known harm it causes and the ensuing potential for erosion, slash-and-burn agriculture remains the predominant means of smallholder cultivation in rural areas. While significant portions of land have been designated as protected across Jamaica, pressure on the environment, especially around tourism boom towns like Ocho Rios, where little planning preceded the influx of workers from other parishes, is leaving the water supply under threat and causing erosion where forestlands on steep inclines are cut for ramshackle housing settlements.

Overfishing

Jamaican fisheries are threatened by warming waters and overfishing, especially the near-shore and reef fisheries, with seasonal bans on lobster (Apr.-June) and conch (Mar.-Jan.) and prohibitions on spear-fishing. Poor enforcement of these regulations means many restaurants ignore the bans. As fish stocks dwindle, the size of fish being caught is shrinking. Catching small fish before they've reached reproductive age exacerbates the dwindling stock. As a visitor, you can do your part by not ordering lobster and conch when the season is closed and by not buying fish smaller than six inches on the roadside. Brightly colored parrot fish have delicious fleshy meat but should be avoided, given their role as protectors of reef ecosystems. Most of the snapper served is imported, and pelagic blue-water fish like king fish and mahimahi are not under threat to the same extent as reef fish. Billfish caught sportfishing should be released to maintain their population.

Health and Safety

HEAT

Jamaica is a tropical country with temperatures rising well above 38°C (100°F) in the middle of summer. Sensible precautions should be taken, especially for those not accustomed to being under the hot sun. A wide-brimmed hat is advisable for days at the beach, and a high-SPF sunblock is essential. Being in the water exacerbates rather than mitigates the harmful rays, creating a risk for overexposure even while swimmers may be unaware of the sun's effects—until the evening, when it becomes impossible to lie down on a burned back. While many hotels offer air-conditioning, just as many have been constructed with cooling in mind to obviate the need for air-conditioning. Louvered windows with a fresh sea breeze or ceiling fan can be just as soothing as air-conditioning while not putting strain on Jamaica's antiquated and inefficient electrical grid. In the summer months, air-conditioning is a well-appreciated luxury, especially for sleeping. If you are traveling between June and September, consider spending some time in the Blue Mountains, where there's a cool breeze year-round.

SEXUALLY TRANSMITTED DISEASES

Jamaican culture celebrates love, romance, and intimacy. It's not uncommon for men and women to maintain multiple sexual partners, and infidelity is generally treated as an inevitable reality by both sexes. The obvious danger is reflected in the high incidence of STDs on the island, including underreported HIV infection. If you engage in sexual activity while in Jamaica, like anywhere else, condoms are indispensable and the best preventative measure.

CRIME

Unfortunately, criminal acts are a daily reality for a large number of Jamaicans, from petty crimes by the economically marginalized to high-rolling politicians and drug dons who control the flow of capital, illegal substances, and arms on the island. In sharp contrast to other developing nations with high poverty rates, and perhaps contrary to what one might expect, random armed assault and muggings are quite rare. The crimes that are most ingrained are devious petty thievery and systemic corruption. Almost everybody who has stayed in Jamaica for any length of time has experienced the disappearance of a wallet, jewelry, or cell phone. Stay vigilant and take precautions and you will likely have no problem. Most hotels offer safes in the rooms; use them.

BRIBERY

Bribery is officially illegal in Jamaica, and people offering a bribe to an officer of the law can be arrested and tried. It's generally quite obvious when a police officer is seeking a payoff, however. Phrases like "Do something for me nuh," "Gimme a lunch money," or "Buy me a drink" get the message across. Do not take the bait, and never offer a bribe to police unsolicited; there are officers who will take offense, or pretend to, and use the gesture to compound the severity of the offense or increase the sum demanded. It's always best to observe the law. If you're being threatened with a speeding ticket or other road infraction, let the officer write the ticket. Chances are they'll let you off with a warning rather than go through the trouble.

The **Office of Professional Responsibility** (OPR, tel. 876/967-1909 or 876/967-4347) is tasked with routing out corruption in the police force. The office is based in Kingston but has officers across the island. Be sure to take note of the badge number of the officer in question if you are planning to make a report, and always do so anonymously to avoid retribution.

DRUGS

Jamaica has a well-deserved reputation as a marijuana haven. Contrary to what many visitors believe, marijuana is still classified as an illegal drug, but marijuana use and possession of up to two ounces was decriminalized in 2015, and carrying small amounts of ganja is no longer a crime for which you can be arrested. Being in possession of larger quantities without a license is still a criminal offense, however. Possession of under two ounces is still a civil offense requiring fine of less than US$10. Some police officers in resort areas have been known to prey on visitors who are not familiar with the law and threaten arrest if a handsome bribe is not paid. Should you experience such intimidation, remain calm and explain that you are familiar with the laws governing marijuana possession.

Jamaica has a well-deserved reputation as a transshipment point for cocaine originating in Colombia. Crack addiction has been a problem in some coastal communities where cargo inadvertently washed ashore. While marijuana use is tolerated on the island due to its widespread consumption and the widely respected Rastafarian culture, which celebrates its use as a sacrament, there is no valid reason to use cocaine or any other hard drug in Jamaica, despite the inevitable offers you'll get on a walk along Seven-Mile Beach in Negril.

Information and Services

MONEY

Prices throughout the book are converted to U.S. dollars as the best indicator of cost.

Most establishments not heavily trafficked by tourists perform most transactions in Jamaican dollars. In tourist hubs like Negril,

Montego Bay, and Ocho Rios, as well as in establishments catering largely to foreign visitors, menus will show prices in U.S. dollars. The U.S. dollar tends to be more stable and is worthwhile as a currency of reference, but most establishments will not use the official or bank exchange rate and set their exchange rate considerably lower as a means of skimming a bit more off the top. It usually pays to buy Jamaican dollars at a *cambio*, or currency trading house, for everyday transactions. While walking around with large amounts of cash is never advisable, carrying enough for a night out does not present a considerable risk. Credit cards, accepted at well-established businesses, typically incur foreign-transaction fees of 3 percent that will show up on your statement alongside each transaction.

The best way to access funds in Jamaica is by using an ATM with your normal NYCE, Maestro, or Cirrus debit card. "Express kidnappings" (where victims are taken to a cash machine to withdraw the maximum on their accounts) are not especially common in Jamaica, but be cautious when using an ATM to ensure you're not being watched or followed. The minimal effort involved in canceling a debit card makes the ease of 24-hour access worth the risk of losing it or getting it stolen. Taking large amounts of cash to Jamaica is not advisable. Scotiabank offers Jamaican and U.S. currency from many of its ATMs; foreign bank fees run around 6 percent of the amount withdrawn.

ELECTRICITY

Jamaica operates on 110 volts, similar to the United States, and uses U.S.-style plugs and sockets, but electricity is at 50 hertz rather than 60 hertz like in the U.S. and Canada. The frequency difference typically only causes a problem for devices with a motor, though some electronic devices are also affected. Most electronics are designed to adapt automatically. Power outages are frequent in some areas, but seldom at the resorts. Most tourism establishments have backup generators.

COMMUNICATIONS AND MEDIA
Telephones

The proliferation of internet service in Jamaica has led to voice over internet protocol (VoIP) telephony replacing traditional land lines. The cellular providers Flow and Digicel operate on GSM networks and sell prepaid SIM cards. Both have roaming agreements with carriers in the U.S. and elsewhere, but unless you've signed up for a roaming service, fees tend to be high, and it's more economical to buy a prepaid SIM card locally (US$5) if you have a GSM phone. Prepaid phone credit is sold in increments as low as US$0.50.

The 876 area code must be dialed for calls within the country; to call abroad from a Jamaican phone, dial 1 before the area code as you would in the United States or Canada, or 011 and then the country code if dialing elsewhere overseas.

Radio

Jamaica has some great radio stations, and it's not just reggae you'll find on the airwaves. Radio stations of note include RJR 94 FM, Power 106 FM, Irie 107.5 FM, Fame 95.7 FM, Zip 103 FM, Hits 92 FM, and SunCity 104.9FM. Radio Mona 93 FM broadcasts from the University of the West Indies at Mona and Mello. Radio 88.1 FM broadcasts from Montego Bay.

Radio broadcasting in Jamaica dates from World War II, when an American resident, John Grinan, gave his shortwave station to the government to comply with wartime regulations. From wartime programming of one hour weekly, the station quickly expanded to four hours daily, including cultural programming. Radio had a key impact on the development of Jamaican popular music in the 1940s and 1950s as the only means of disseminating new musical styles coming mainly from the United States.

Television

Jamaica's main television stations are Television Jamaica (TVJ, www.televisionjamaica.com), formerly the Jamaica Broadcast

Corporation (JBC); CVM (www.cvmtv.com); Reggae Entertainment Television (RETV); and Jamaica News Network (JNN, www. jnnntv.com). In 2006, TVJ acquired both JNN and RETV, consolidating its leadership in both news and entertainment programming on the island. Hype is an entertaining competitor to RETV, with music video countdowns, artist interviews, and the latest happenings in the local music industry and party scene.

MAPS AND VISITOR INFORMATION

GPS devices provided by car rental agencies and apps like Google Maps and OpenStreetMap generally afford the best directions and orientation, though some of the more obscure roads may not appear or may be incorrectly identified. The city maps sold by the National Land Agency are less detailed and lack many road names. The Land Agency does have good topographical maps, sold for US$7 per sheet. Twenty sheets cover the whole island, and the maps can be obtained on CD. Tourism-oriented business brochures are available free of charge at the chamber of commerce offices in Ocho Rios, Montego Bay, and Negril.

WEIGHTS AND MEASURES

One of the most frustrating things in Jamaica is the lack of a consistent convention when it comes to measurements. On the road, where the majority of cars are imported from Japan and odometers read in kilometers, many of the signs are in miles, while the newer ones are in kilometers. The mixed use of metric in weights and measurements is also a problem complicating life in Jamaica, with "chains" (20 meters/66 feet) used commonly when referring to distances, liters used at the gas pump, and pounds used for weight.

TIME

Jamaica is on Greenwich mean time minus five hours, which coincides with North America's eastern standard time in winter and central time in summer. Jamaica doesn't change time for daylight savings.

Resources

Glossary

Glossary 343
Suggested Reading 347
Internet Resources 349

Jamaican patois is a creative and ever-evolving English dialect rooted in the mélange of African and European cultures that together make up Jamaica's identity. Irish, English, and Scottish accents are clearly present, as is the influence of Spanish, with many words also of African origin. Patois carries a thick and warm lilt that can be very difficult to understand for those unaccustomed to hearing it. After relaxing your ears for a few weeks, however, Jamaican talk begins to make perfect sense.

Babylon: used by Rastafarians to refer to any evil and oppressive system; also used to reference the police

badman: a thug or gangster

badmind: corrupt mentality; a scheming person, as in, "dem badmind, e-e-eh?" (can be used as a noun, adjective, or verb)

bakra: a plantation overseer, often used to express resentment toward someone acting in an authoritarian manner

baldhead: used by Rastafarians to refer to non-Rasta black persons, in a derogatory sense if they consider them anti-Rasta

bangarang: when hell breaks loose

bankra: basket (of West African Twi origin)

bare: uninhibitedly, solely; as in, "That boy is giving me attitude, bare attitude."

bashment: a party; celebration; any form of excitement

batty: backside or derriere

battyman: a gay man

big up: used to show respect; a shout-out, as in, "big up to all mi fans;" (used mostly as a verb but also as a noun)

blenda: blender; a mixed-up situation rife with confusion

blessed: can be used as a greeting, shortened from proclamations like "Blessed love!"

blood: used as a greeting between close friends considered like family, as in "wha'apen blood?"

blouse and skirt: an exclamation, similar to "Wow!"

bly: a chance or opportunity; to be let off the hook

bombo claat: an expletive; sometimes used without the "claat" as a less vulgar exclamation

boops: a man or woman who is only in a relationship for material gain; a user (as in, "boops you out")

boots: condom

brawta: an extra something thrown into a deal when the haggling is done; a bonus

bredda: brother; used in referring to a close friend, as in "Yes, mi bredda!"

bredren: brethren; used when referring to a close friend, as in "mi bredren dem"

brownin: a light-skinned black woman

bruk: broken or broke, meaning not having any money

bruk out: to let loose and be free

buck up: meet or run into someone

buddy: male genitalia

bulla: a heavy biscuit made with flour and molasses

buss: burst or bust out, as in a career break

bway: a boy

cha: a versatile exclamation that can indicate disgust or astonishment; also written "cho"

chalice: a water pipe used to smoke ganja

chi chi: a termite

clash: a battle; often used in the context of a sound clash, where different sound systems or artists face off

collie: marijuana

copacetic: usually shortened to copacet: cool, nice, criss

cotch: to rest or lean up against; to brace something, as in the tire of a car to keep it from rolling; also used to say where you stay or spend the night

craven: greedy

crawle: pen, likely derived from the corral where animals were kept, such as a hog crawle or turtle crawle

criss: nice (crisp)

dads: used as a show of respect, as in "Yes, mi dads"

dawta: when used by Rastafarians, can refer to any young woman

deejay: a dancehall rapper

degge-degge: small or flimsy, as in "$5 for this degge-degge roll?!"

deh: to be at, as in "wheh yuh deh?"

deh pon: doing or thinking about doing, as in "Mi deh pon a part-time work"

dehso: there; over there

don: from the Italian usage, a honcho or area leader

downpress: to suppress (a play on the word oppress, where the "op" which sounds like up is changed to "down")

dread: a derogatory term used for someone who wears locks; also used to describe hardship, as in "The time getting dread."

duppy: a ghost

e-e-eh: an inflection used at the end of a phrase to denote a casual query of consensus, as in "It's pretty, e-e-eh . . . " ("It's pretty, isn't it?")

endz: a home or somewhere where someone spends a lot of time, like a hang-out spot, as in "Mi deh pon di endz."

face: to demonstrate interest

flex: used negatively, to show off or profile; used positively, to relax or take a trip

forward: come or arrive, as in "Mi soon forward."

front: genitalia

galiss: a womanizer

ginnal: a con artist or hustler, either male or female

give bun (burn): to cheat (on your spouse)

grind: pelvic gyrations central to popular dance; also interchangeable with having sex

groundation: a Nyabinghi session of drumming that can last for days, usually held around a significant date in the Rasta calendar, such as Selassie's birthday or Ethiopian Christmas

gwaan: go on, as in "Wha gwaan?" ("What's going on?")

gweh: go away, as in "Gweh nuh, tek weh ya self!"

gyal: girl; tends to be construed as somewhat derogatory

haffi: have to, must

herb: marijuana

higgler: a trader in the market; also small-scale importers who bring goods to sell in Jamaica from Panama

high-grade: top-quality marijuana

hush: an expression of sympathy

I and I: the Rastafarian substitute for "me," referring to the individual's inseparability from the divine creator

idren: used like "bredren"

irie: to feel nice or high

ital: natural, derived from "vital"

jacket: a child born outside an established relationship that is obviously from a different father

Jah: Rastafarian term for the Almighty, derived from Jehovah in the Old Testament

John crow: turkey vulture, buzzard (*Cathartes aura*)

jook: to stick; to prick; to knock; a jooking stick is used to knock ackee or mangoes off a tree.

junjo: mold or fungus; also a type of mushroom once used as a meat substitute

leggo: let go; leave alone

likkle: little, as in "a likkle more" for "See you later."

lyme: to hang out; also used as a noun for a laid-back gathering or party

macca: thorn, as in "Di macca jook mi." ("The thorn pricked me.")

mampy: a heavy-set woman

massive: shortened formed for a large gathering of people or a collective, as in "the Kingston massive"

mawga: meager; skinny; thin

medi or medz: meditation, as in to "hold a medi" or "hold a medz"; to ponder or meditate on something

"Mi credit run out": what people will say when they place a phone call before hanging up so that the recipient will have to call back and pay for the call

natty: a person who wears dreadlocks in their hair

nuff: enough, or a lot

nyam: to eat, as in "Mi a nyam some food" ("I'm going to eat"); thought to be derived from a West African word

Obeah: Jamaican black magic or Voodoo

par: hang out with, shortened from spar

pickney: a child; children; derived from piccaninny

pop-down: tired; destroyed; shabby; disheveled, referring to a place or person

pum pum: female genitalia

raahtid: an exclamation, such as "Wow!"

raas: a versatile expletive, referring to your behind

ragamuffin: a serious dude, used in referring to a true soldier, Rasta thug, or rude boy

ramp: a Jamaican pronunciation of romp; to play with, as in "Mi nah ramp wid dem people!"

ram-up: rammed or ram-packed with people

ras: from Amharic, meaning "prince," as in Ras Tafari

rat-bat: a bat; *bat* alone usually refers to a moth.

reason: to converse; hold a discussion; a reasoning

red: used in reference to people of a ruddy complexion, typical of the people in St. Elizabeth parish

respect: a greeting or acknowledgment of appreciation

riddim: rhythm

roots: used about drinks, refers to herbal tonics and potions; used about music, refers to something original: roots reggae is the early form of the music, considered the most traditional and authentic.

rude boy: a badass, as popularized by Jimmy Cliff's character in the film *The Harder They Come*

runnings: the way things operate, as in "Him don't understand di runnings roun' yahso."

screw face: an expression of bitterness

selector: a disc jockey

sell-off: exclamation derived from *sold out*, as in something in high demand; used in the context of something that's immensely popular, as in "Di dance sell-off!"

sensi, sensimilla: marijuana, adapted from Spanish *sin semilla,* meaning without seeds

session: party

set girls: rival groups of female dancers who would sing and dance and compete in matching costumes against other such groups during the colonial period

sistren: a sister, the female version of "bredren" (brethren)

skank: to dance, especially to ska music

skettel: a prostitute

skylark: to laze away one's days rather than work or go to school

slack: loose; degrading; debauched, as in "pure slackness a gwaan."

soon come: used to say, "I'll be there in a bit" or "I'll be back in a bit." This is a very loose phrase, and could mean in a few minutes, days, or years.

sound system: often referred to as simply a "sound"

spliff, skliff: a marijuana cigarette or joint

stageshow: a musical concert typically featuring performances by many artists

stoosh: snooty, uptown

swimps: shrimp

tek: to take

tun up: turn up, meaning "great" or "on fire"

unnu: you (plural), "one" in the third-person sense

up: a term used to voice solidarity or support

vex: (can sound like "bex" in the Jamaican pronunciation) upset, angry

wine: wind; gyrating, sexually suggestive pelvic motion at the heart of the bumping and grinding seen in a typical dance club

wood: male genitalia

wuk: work, as in "wuk mi a wuk." Also used in a sexual sense, as in "you wuk mi out."

wutless or wukless: worthless

yahso: here, as in "Yahso mi deh." ("I am here.")

yard/yaad: home, as in "Mi deh mi yard" ("I'm at home"); also used to refer to Jamaica

yuzimi: "You see me?" as in "Do you understand?" or "Do you see what I'm saying?"

Zion: the holy land, as referred to by Rastafarians

Suggested Reading

HISTORY

Besson, Jean. *Martha Brae's Two Histories: European Expansion and Caribbean Culture-Building in Jamaica.* University of North Carolina Press, 2002.

Bryan, Patrick E. *Jamaica: The Aviation Story.* Arawak Publications, 2006. An interesting account of aviation and the role air travel has played in Jamaica's modern history.

Buckley, David. *The Right to Be Proud: A Brief Guide to Jamaican Heritage Sites.* Neil Persadsingh, 2005. This book covers select sites from those listed by the Jamaica National Heritage trust. It is a good coffee-table book with interesting details.

De Lisser, Herbert G. *White Witch of Rose Hall.* Humanity Press, 1982. A fantastic account of Annie Palmer, rooted in much historical truth. This is a great quick preparatory read for a visit to Rose Hall Great House near Montego Bay.

Goldman, Vivian. *The Book of Exodus: The Making and Meaning of Bob Marley and the Wailers' Album of the Century.* Three Rivers Press, 2006. An excellent account of the years surrounding Bob Marley's launch into international stardom with great anecdotes and lots of good context on the tumultuous 1970s.

Gottlieb, Karla. *The Mother of Us All: A History of Queen Nanny, Leader of the Windward Jamaican Maroons.* Africa World Press, 2000. The story of Nanny, Jamaica's most prominent Maroon leader and only national heroine.

Pariag, Florence. *East Indians in the Caribbean: An Illustrated History.* An illustrated look at the arrival of East Indians in the Caribbean basin, focused on Jamaica, Trinidad, and Guyana.

Price, Richard. *Maroon Societies: Rebel Slave Communities in the Americas.* Johns Hopkins University Press, 3rd ed., 1996. An interesting look at the parallel development of Maroon societies in a number of Latin American countries.

Senior, Olive. *An Encyclopedia of Jamaican Heritage.* Twin Guinep Publishers, 2003. An A-to-Z of things, people, and places Jamaican and their historical relevance. An indispensable quick reference for scholars of Jamaica.

LANGUAGE

Adams, L. Emilie. *Understanding Jamaican Patois.* LMH Publishers, 1991. An introductory guide to Jamaican patois and phrases.

Christie, Pauline. *Language in Jamaica.* Arawak Publications, 2003. An academic examination of the significance of language in Jamaica as it relates to history, class, and prejudice.

Reynolds, Ras Dennis Jabari. *Jabari Authentic Jamaican Dictionary of the Jamic Language, Featuring Patwa and Rasta Iyaric, Pronunciation and Definitions.* Around the Way Books, 2006.

LITERATURE

Banks, Russell. *Rule of the Bone.* Minerva, 1996. An engaging novel that traces the growth of a somewhat troubled American youth who ends up in Jamaica.

Bennett, Louise. *Anancy and Miss Lou.* Sangster's Book Stores, 1979. A must-have among Miss Lou's many printed works. The Anancy stories are folk tales rooted in

Jamaica's African heritage. Miss Lou brings them to life in a book appreciated by children and adults alike.

Figueroa, John. *Caribbean Voices: An Anthology of West Indian Poetry: Dreams and Visions.* Evans Bros., 1966. This book is a good representative of Figueroa, one of the grandfathers of Jamaican literature.

Fleming, Ian. *Dr. No.* Jonathan Cape, 1958. Fleming's first James Bond novel features his adopted island prominently and sealed his legacy as the greatest spy thriller author of all time.

Henzell, Perry. *Cane.* 10a Publications, 2003. A novel about a white slave from Barbados who becomes a member of the planter class and owner of the largest plantation in Jamaica. While the book is fiction, it accurately portrays class dynamics and gives an excellent sense of the brutal reality that characterized the colonial period.

Kennaway, Guy. *One People.* Canongate Books, 2001. A hilarious look at the idiosyncrasies of the Jamaican people.

Marlon, James. *A Brief History of Seven Killings.* Riverhead Books, 2014. A novel that explores the 1976 assassination attempt on Bob Marley with insightful context about the political climate in Jamaica.

McKay, Claude. *Selected Poems.* Dover Publications, 1999. Many of McKay's poems are written in colorful dialect ranging in theme from clever critiques on political and economic ills to love poetry.

McKenzie, Earl. *Boy Named Ossie: A Jamaican Childhood.* Heinemann, 1991. Earl McKenzie, who grew up in the years leading up to independence, is one of Jamaica's most respected literary figures.

Mutabaruka. *The First Poems/The Next Poems.* Paul Issa Publications, 2005. Mutabaruka's definitive collected printed works, spanning many years of his career.

NATURE AND THE ENVIRONMENT

Fincham, Alan. *Jamaica Underground.* University Press of the West Indies, 1998. An essential guide to the sinkholes and caves of Cockpit Country. Diagram and plates of cave layouts complement anecdotal accounts and exploration logs.

Hodges, Margaret. *Guide to the Blue and John Crow Mountains.* Natural History Society of Jamaica. Ian Randle Publishers, 2nd ed., 2007. Edited by expert naturalist Margaret Hodges with chapters written by several members of Jamaica's Natural History Society, this book improves on the much-in-demand and out-of-print first edition, *Blue Mountain Guide,* published in 1993. This is an essential guide for travelers looking to get intimately acquainted with Jamaica's most spectacular national park, for which the Jamaica Conservation and Development Trust is seeking UNESCO endorsement. The book is divided into six regions, making it especially practical for devising day-trip excursions.

Iremonger, Susan. *Guide to the Plants of the Blue Mountains of Jamaica.* University Press of the West Indies, 2002. A handy guide to the flora of the Blue Mountains.

BIRDING

Downer, Audrey, and Robert Sutton. *Birds of Jamaica: A Photographic Field Guide.* Cambridge University Press, 1990. A good guide to Jamaica's birds.

Raffaele, Herbert, et al. *Birds of the West Indies.* Princeton University Press, 2003. This is the best bird guide for the Caribbean basin, with excellent plates.

FOOD

Burke, Virginia. *Eat Caribbean Cook Book.* Simon & Schuster, 2005. Easily among the best Caribbean cookbooks on the market. Burke makes essential recipes easy to put together with widely available ingredients.

Lumsden, Robin. *Belcour Cookbook: Jamaican, French and Chinese Family Recipes for Entertaining.* Belcour Preservatives, 2014. This autobiographical culinary masterpiece can't be recommended enough, tracing one of Jamaica's most prominent families across oceans and generations in food.

Quinn, Lucinda Scala. *Jamaican Cooking.* Wiley, 2006. A selective cookbook with some excellent recipes for those seasoned in Jamaican cooking.

SPIRITUAL

Barrett, Leonard E. *The Rastafarians.* Beacon Press, 20th anniversary ed., 1997. A comprehensive study of the Rastafarian movement.

Bender, Wolfgang. *Rastafarian Art.* Ian Randle Publishers, 2004. Bender covers the contribution of Rastafarian philosophy to Jamaican contemporary art.

Bethel, Clement E. *Junkanoo.* Macmillan Caribbean, 1992. An in-depth look at Jonkunnu, a fascinating dance and music style closely associated with Jamaica's folk religions and performed for a few celebrations throughout the year, notably at Christmastime.

Chevannes, Barry. *Rastafari: Roots and Ideology.* University of West Indies Press, 1995. One of the best assessments in print of the Rastafarian movement, Chevannes is the top academic authority in Jamaica on the faith, having studied and lived amongst Rastas throughout his career.

Hausman, Gerald. *The Kebra Negast: The Lost Bible of Rastafarian Wisdom and Faith from Ethiopia and Jamaica.* St. Martin's Press, 1st ed., 1997. Considered the Rasta bible by many adherents, this is a must-have resource book for those with deep interest in the faith.

ESSENTIAL PERIODICALS

Jamaica Journal, published by the Institute of Jamaica (IOJ), is a great easy-to-read academic publication highlighting different aspects of Jamaican culture and heritage.

The Jamaican Magazine is an excellent periodical published by the University of Technology. Each edition highlights a different parish.

Internet Resources

TRAVEL INFORMATION

Jamaica Tourist Board
www.visitjamaica.com
The official website of the Jamaica Tourist Board, smartly designed and easy to navigate.

NEWS

The Jamaica Gleaner
www.jamaica-gleaner.com
Jamaica's most widely circulated daily, aligned center-left.

The Jamaica Observer
www.jamaicaobserver.com
The island's second most popular, pro-business newspaper, owned by Gordon "Butch" Stewart.

The Star
www.jamaica-star.com

Jamaica's daily entertainment tabloid, published by the Gleaner Company, is chock-full of gossip and trash talk, making for good entertainment and little news.

Loop Jamaica
www.loopjamaica.com
A news portal owned by mobile phone carrier Digicel.

FLIGHT INFORMATION

Norman Manley International Airport
www.nmia.aero
Norman Manley is Kingston's international airport. The site has useful information, including airlines and flight schedules.

Sangster International Airport
www.mbjairport.com
Montego Bay's international airport receives the majority of the island's visitors. The airport's website provides complete travel information, from arrivals and departures to shopping and food options.

ECOTOURISM

Jamaica Environment Trust
www.jamentrust.org
Education, advocacy, and conservation are the pillars of this crucial NGO. The membership organization welcomes volunteers and contributors for projects aimed at protecting Jamaica's natural resources.

Jamaica Caves Organization (JCO)
www.jamaicancaves.org
JCO is the most active scientific exploratory organization on the western side of the island, researching the caves and sinkholes of Cockpit Country on a continual basis. The JCO sells maps and can arrange guides for those with an interest in serious exploring through Jamaica's deepest caves and backcountry.

Jamaica Conservation and Development Trust (JCDT)
www.jcdt.org.jm
The JCDT is in charge of the Blue and John Crow Mountain National Park and is the go-to organization for matters related to hiking and staying at the park.

Southern Trelawny Environmental Agency (STEA)
www.stea.net
A regularly updated site dedicated to coverage of the activities of the STEA, which include the annual Yam Festival. The site also contains resources for exploring the Trelawny interior and contracting guide services.

MUSIC AND ENTERTAINMENT

Irie FM
www.iriefm.net
Jamaica's most popular reggae station, Irie broadcasts on 107.5 and 107.9 FM as well as over the internet.

Sun City Radio
www.suncityradio.fm
Station 104.9 FM is the voice of Portmore, representing "fi di Gaza" with music, information, news, artist interviews, and more.

Skkan Media
www.skkanme.com
An entertainment site covering parties across Jamaica.

Bob Marley
www.bobmarley.com
The official Bob Marley family website, with bios on individual family members, merchandise, and news. Most of the Marley progeny have their own sites as well.

Reggae Entertainment
www.reggaeentertainment.com
A site dedicated to the reggae industry, with entertainment news and downloads.

ART AND CULTURE

Panache
www.panachejamagazine.com
A Caribbean fashion, beauty, and lifestyle magazine with print and online editions.

Buzz Caribbean
www.buzzzmagazine.com
A lifestyle and entertainment magazine with an online edition mirroring its print copy.

Index

A

accessibility: 336
accommodations: 333-334; see also specific place
Accompong: 303
Accompong Maroon Festival: 303
adventure sports: Blue Hole Mineral Spring 35;
      cliff jumping 37; Good Hope plantation 114;
      Mystic Mountain 124; Ocho Rios 130; as a top
      experience 13, 25, 37
African-Caribbean Institute of Jamaica 211
agriculture: 317
air travel: 328-329, 330
Alligator Pond: 286, 287
alligators: 286
all-inclusive resorts: 334
animals: 310-311
Appleton Estate: 22, 302
Aquasol Theme Park: 82
architecture: Falmouth 106; Half Way Tree
      Courthouse 215; Headquarters House 213;
      Invercauld Great House 298; Kenilworth 62;
      University of the West Indies 217; see also
      estates
art and crafts: general discussion 322-326;
      Jamaica Giants 66; Kingston 229, 231; Kingston
      on the Edge (KOTE) Arts Festival 220; Montego
      Bay 91; National Gallery 210-211; Negril 44;
      Port Antonio 180; see also crafts
Asafu Yard: 24, 191
ATMs: 19, 341
ATV rides: 67, 114

B

Ba Beta Kristian Church of Haile Selassie I: 213
Bacchanal: 132, 220, 221
backpacking: 189, 191, 302
Back Sea Side: 22, 291
Bamboo Avenue: 300-301
Bamboo Beach Club: 129
Bamboo Ville: 301
bananas: 175
banking: general discussion 19, 341; Kingston
      250; Mandeville 284; Montego Bay 102; Negril
      57; Port Antonio 187
Baptist Church: 319-320
Baptist Manse: 106
Baptist Theological College: 113
The Barracks: 62
bars: Kingston 224-227; Montego Bay 88; Negril
      41; Ocho Rios 130; Port Antonio 179
Bath: 198-199
Bath Botanical Garden: 199
Bath Hot Springs: 198
Bath Mineral Spring: 198
bats: 310
bauxite mining: 338
beach clubs: 180
beaches: Bluefields Beach 68; Boston Beach 193;
      Broughton Beach 65; Duncans 111; Falmouth
      107; Half Moon Beach 60; hidden 26-28;
      Hopewell 62; Long Bay Beach 194; Montego
      Bay 82-83; Negril 35-36; Ocho Rios 129;
      Oracabessa 158; Port Antonio 173-176, 177;
      Port Maria 163; Priory 147; Runaway Bay 148;
      Spanish Town 262; as a top experience 14, 27;
      Treasure Beach 298
Bellefield Great House: 23, 80
Belmont: 26, 28, 68-70
Belmont Crab Festival: 68
Bent, Roy "Ras Carver": 286
best-of itinerary: 20-22
biking: Fat Tyre Festival 158; Ocho Rios 130; Port
      Antonio 177
Binghi celebrations: 286
Birch Hill: 62
birds: 310
bird-watching: Blue and John Crow Mountains
      16, 272; Bluefields 68; Forres Park Guest
      House 274; Green Castle Estate 164; Holywell
      National Park 267; Marshall's Pen 280;
      Montego Bay 86
Black Power movement: 148
Black River: 22, 28, 298-301
Black River and South Cockpit Country: 298-304
Black River Safaris: 299
Blackwell, Chris: 158, 265
Bloody Bay: 36
Blue and John Crow Mountains: 263-275
Blue and John Crow Mountains National Park: 273
Bluefields: 68-70
Bluefields Beach: 27, 28, 68
Bluefields Great House: 68
Blue Hole: 176
Blue Hole Gardens: 20-22, 23, 26, 66
Blue Hole Mineral Spring: 15, 20, 26, 35, 177
Blue Hole River: 128
Blue Lagoon: 176
Blue Mahoe Trail: 268
Blue Mountain Peak: 15, 28, 274
The Boardwalk: 262

boating: Alligator Pond 287; Black River Safaris 299; Canoe Valley Protected Area 286; Kingston 234; Pelican Bar 299; for transport 329
Bob Marley Mausoleum: 155, 157
Bob Marley Museum: 22, 24, 157, 216
Bob Marley sights: general discussion 156-157; Bob Marley Mausoleum 155; Bob Marley Museum 216; Cane River 257; National Heroes Park 213; Nine Mile 155; Scott's Pass 285; Trench Town 209; Tuff Gong Recording Studio 209
Bobo Ashanti House: 321
Bobo Hill: 24, 257
body surfing: 291
Bogle, Paul: 198
Bonnie View: 172
Bonnie View Hotel: 172
Boston: 193-194
Boston Beach: 27, 193
Boston Jerk Centre: 193
Boundbrook Wharf: 173
boxing: 326
Braco Rapids Adventures: 25, 113
BREDS: 292
bribery: 340
Brimmer Hall: 159
Broughton Beach: 65
budget accommodations: 333-334
Buff Bay police station: 191
Bull Bay: 24, 256-258
Bump Grave: 189
Burchell Baptist Church: 80
Burwood Beach: 25, 26, 27, 107
bus travel: 329
Butler, Alvin: 173, 175
butterflies: 273

C
The Cage: 80
Calabash Bay Beach: 291
Calabash Literary Festival: 292
Calby's River Hidden Beauty: 25, 128
camel rides: 127
camping: 61, 272
Cane River: 257
Cane River Falls: 24, 256
Cannabis Cup Jamaica: 43
Canoe Valley Protected Area: 286
Cap Calcini: 24, 231
Cardiff Hall Property Owners Association: 148
Caribbean Fashion Week: 220, 230
Carnival: 221
Castleton Botanical Gardens: 217
catamarans: 130

Catherine's Peak: 267
caves: Gourie Cave 285; Green Grotto Caves 153; Mandingo Cave 195; Mountain River Cave 261; Two Sisters Cave 263; Windsor Great Cave 115
Champs: 220
Charles Town: 24, 191
children, traveling with: 336
chocolate making: 159
Chris Café: 22, 159
Christiana: 284-286
Christiana Bottom: 284
Chukka Caribbean: 25, 26, 87, 114
churches: Falmouth 106-107; Irish Town 265; Kingston 210, 213, 215; Montego Bay 80; Port Royal 254, 256; Prospect Plantation 127; Rio Bueno 113; Spanish Town 259, 261; St. Mary Parish Church 163
Cinchona Gardens: 28, 272
Cinnamon Hill Great House: 81
Clarendon: 24, 286, 301
classes, social: 318-319
cliff jumping: 13, 25, 37, 130
climate: 306
clothing: 19
Clydesdale: 272
Cockpit Country: 16, 26, 114-116, 298-304
coffee: general discussion 266, 332-333; Blue Mountains 16, 266; Jamaica Blue Mountain Coffee Festival 220; Lime Tree Farm 274; Mavis Bank Coffee Factory 270; Old Tavern Coffee Estate 266; UCC Craighton Coffee Estate 265
Coin and Notes Museum: 209
Coke Church: 210
Columbus Park: 154
comedy clubs: 228
communications: 341
community tourism: 337
consulates: 331
contemporary one drop: 222
Coronation Market: 22, 213
Coward, Noël: 158
crafts: David Pinto's Ceramic Studio 115; Falmouth 108; Fern Gully Art Studio 134; Kingston 229; Maroon 191; Montego Bay 91; Negril 44; Ocho Rios 133; Oracabessa 157; Port Antonio 180; Port Maria 163; Robin's Bay 164; Treasure Beach 292
Craft Village: 22, 180
Craighton Estate: 22, 265
cricket: 326
crime: 340
Cristal Night Club: 22, 179
crocodiles: 299
cruises: 83, 177
Crystal Edge: 28, 268
cuisine: general discussion 331-332; Belmont Crab

Festival 68; dessert 242; highlights 29; *Jamaica Observer* Food Awards 220; Kingston Restaurant Week 221; Kingston street food 237; Little Ochie Seafood Festival 287; as a top experience 12, 29; Trelawny Yam Festival 90; Westmoreland Curry Festival 66
cultural centers: 78, 189, 211
culture: 318-322
Culture Yard: 22, 24, 157, 209
Curry Festival: 66
curry goat: 29, 182, 282

D

dance: Accompong Maroon Festival 303; Asafu Yard 191; Jonkunnu 324; Kingston 224, 228
dancehall music: 222, 323
David Pinto's Ceramic Studio: 115
Day-O Plantation: 20, 89, 96
Dead End Beach: 74, 82
deforestation: 339
Demontevin Lodge: 170
Devon House: 22, 216, 229
disabilities, access for travelers with: 336
Discovery Bay: 153-155
distilleries: 302
diving: Montego Bay 84; Negril 36, 37; Ocho Rios 129; Port Antonio 177; Port Royal 253; Runaway Bay 149
Doctors Cave Beach: 20, 23, 27, 74, 82
Dolphin Cove: 123
Dolphin Cove Negril: 62
dolphin encounters: 62, 123
Dolphin Head Eco Park and Trail: 62
Dolphin Head Mountains: 62
downtown Kingston: food 235-236; sights 205-213
Drapers San Guest House: 24, 183
Dream Weekend: 41
driving: 330
drugs: 340
drumming: 191, 286
Dump-Up Beach: 83
Duncans: 26, 111-112
Dunn's River Falls: 16, 22, 122

E

economy: 316-318
electricity: 341
emancipation: 314
Emancipation Jubilee: 147
Emancipation Park: 213-215
embassies: 331
Encounter Program: 123

endangered fisheries: 311
English colonization: 312-313
entertainment: Montego Bay 88-90; Negril and the West Coast 41-43; Ocho Rios 130; Port Antonio 179; Treasure Beach 291-292; *see also* specific place
environmental issues: 337-339
Errol Flynn Marina: 172
estates: Bellefield Great House 80; Cinnamon Hill Great House 81; Flamstead 272; Good Hope plantation 114; Greenwood Great House 105; Hampden Sugar Estate 106; Invercauld Great House 298; Kenilworth 62; Oracabessa 159; plantation culture 313-315; Prospect Plantation 127; Rose Hall Great House 81; Seville Great House 147; Tacky's War 161; tours 81; Tryall 62; Whitehall Great House 35
Ethiopian Orthodox Church: 215
etiquette, social: 334-335

F

Fairfield Theatre: 20, 90
Falmouth: 106-109
Falmouth All Age School: 107
Falmouth Courthouse: 107
Falmouth Heritage Renewal: 106
Falmouth Heritage Walks: 107
Falmouth Presbyterian Church: 107
family activities: Dolphin Cove 123; Hope Gardens and Zoo 217; Jamaica Swamp Safari Village 107; Jamaica Zoo 301; Kool Runnings Waterpark 38; Mystic Mountain 124; Rotary Club of Negril Donkey Races 43; travel tips for families 336
Fantasy Beach: 147
farm tours: 159
Far Out Fish Hut: 26, 106
fashion week: 220
Fat Tyre Festival: 158
Fern Gully: 133
Fern Tree Spa: 21, 87, 100
festivals and events: 17; Kingston 220; Montego Bay 90; Negril and the West Coast 43; Ocho Rios 132; Port Antonio 179
The FieldSpa: 21, 161
fine art: 325
Firefly: 22, 158
Fire River: 146-147
Fishermen's Beach: 129
fishing: Alligator Pond 287; Bluefields 68; Glistening Waters 110; Hook 'n' Line Canoe Tournament 292; International Marlin Fishing Tournament 83; Kingston 235; Montego Bay 84; Negril 38; Pellew Island 176; Port Antonio International Marlin Tournament 179; Port

Maria 163; Runaway Bay 148; Savanna-la-Mar 65; Treasure Beach 291
Flamstead: 272
Flavours: 148
flora: 307-310
flowers: 308
Flynn, Errol: 172
Folly Beach: 173
Folly Mansion: 24, 173
Folly Point Lighthouse: 173
food: *see* cuisine
Forres Park Guest House: 28, 274
Fort Charles: 254
Fort Charlotte: 62
Fort Clarence Beach Park: 262
Fort Dundas: 113
Fort George: 170
Fort Haldane: 163
Frenchman's Beach: 291
Frenchman's Cove: 22, 27, 175
Frenchmen: 132, 221
fruits: 308

G

Gallery Joe James: 113
Gallery of West Indian Art: 23, 91
gambling: 228
ganja: 43
gardens: Bath Botanical Garden 199; Blue Hole Gardens 66; Castleton Botanical Gardens 217; Cinchona Gardens 272; Hope Gardens and Zoo 217; King's House 217; Luana Orchid Farm 298; Shaw Park Gardens 125; Turtle River Falls & Gardens 127; Turtle River Park 127
Garvey, Marcus: general discussion 148-149, 314; birthplace of 119; Bobo Hill 257; Heroes Memorial 213; Liberty Hall 211; and the Rastafari movement 320, 321; statue 147; St. William Grant Park 210; United Negro Improvement Association 237
gear: 19
geography: 305-306
geology: 114
Georgian Society: 106
Giddy House: 256
Glistening Waters: 109-111
Gloria's Seafood City: 22, 24, 236
Gloria's Seafood Restaurant: 24, 256
glossary of terms: 343-346
Goblin Hill: 24, 179
go-karts: 40, 82
Goldeneye: 161
golf: Kingston 232; Mandeville 281; Montego Bay 86; Negril 41; Ocho Rios 130; Runaway Bay 149; Tryall 64

Good Hope plantation: 114
Gourie Cave: 285
Gourie Recreational Park: 285
government: 315-316
government offices: 102
Grant, William: 210
gratuities: 335
The Great Weekend: 132
Great Bay: 22, 27, 291
Great Huts: 24, 193
Green Castle Estate: 164
Green Grotto Caves: 22, 153
Green Island: 60-61
Greenwood: 26, 105-106
Greenwood Great House: 22, 105
Guangos Jerk: 22, 67
Guts River: 287

H

Half Moon Beach: 23, 26, 60
Half Way Tree: 215, 238-240, 242
Half Way Tree Courthouse: 215
Hampden Sugar Estate: 106
Harlem Renaissance: 148
Harmony Cove: 26, 27, 111
Headquarters House: 213
health: 339-340
heatstroke: 339
Hellshire Beach: 24, 262
Heroes Circle: 213
Heroes Memorial: 213
high season: 17
hiking: 19; Bluefields 68; Blue Mountain Peak 16, 273; Catherine's Peak 267; Cockpit Country 115; Holywell National Park 267; itinerary 26-28; Lucea 62; Mayfield Falls 66; Moore Town 189; South Cockpit Country 302
Hinduism: 320
Hindu Temple: 216
Hip Strip: 20, 89, 252
historic sights: Bluefields Great House 68; Brimmer Hall 159; Columbus Park 154; Devon House 216; Falmouth 106-107; Flamstead 272; Fort Charles 254; Fort Charlotte 62; Fort Haldane 163; Green Castle Estate 164; Headquarters House 213; Heroes Circle 213; Liberty Hall 211; Mandeville 280; Moore Town 189; Mountain River Cave 261; Museum of History and Ethnography 211; Ocho Rios Fort 123-124; Port Antonio 170; Port Royal 253; Richmond Hill Inn 78; Rio Bueno 113; St. Catherine 258; Tacky's War 161
history: 312-315
Holywell National Park: 28, 267, 269
Hook 'n' Line Canoe Tournament: 292

Hope Bay: 190
Hope Gardens and Zoo: 217
Hope Road: 240, 242
Hopewell: 62-64
horseback riding: Montego Bay 87; Negril 40-41; Ocho Rios 130; Rio Bueno 113; Runaway Bay 149; Yaaman Adventure Park 127
hotels: 334
The HouseBoat Grill: 20, 23, 95
Howell, Leonard: 320-321
hurricane season: 17

I

I Love Soca: 221
independence: 315
Indoor Sports Centre: 232
insects: 310
Institute of Jamaica: 210
International Marlin Fishing Tournament: 83
Internet resources: 349-350
Invercauld Great House: 298
Irish Town: 265
Iron Bridge: 261
Island Lux Beach Park: 20, 23, 36
Island Records: 158
itineraries: 20-29
Iyatolah: 286

J

J-22 International Regatta: 83
Jack Sprat Motel: 22, 295
Jacob Taylor Bathing Beach: 111
Jake's Driftwood Spa: 21, 291
Jakes farm-to-table dinners: 292
Jake's Jamaican Off-Road Triathlon and Sunset Run: 292
Jamaica Blue Mountain Coffee Festival: 220
Jamaica Caves Organization: 302
Jamaica Cricket Association: 232
Jamaica Football Federation: 232
Jamaica Giants: 66
Jamaica Military Museum: 211
Jamaica Observer Food Awards: 220
Jamaica Rum Festival: 220
Jamaica's Girls and Boys Championships: 220
Jamaica Swamp Safari Village: 107
Jamaica Tourist Board: 18, 102, 249, 349
James Bond Beach: 158
Jamnesia Sessions: 24, 258
Jamnesia Surf Camp: 24, 25, 257
jazz: 132
jerk: 29
jerk seasoning: 193

Jonkunnu: 324
Judaism: 320
Junction: 287-288
The Jungle: 23, 41

K

karst topography: 114
kayaking: Black River 299; Falmouth 107; Negril 36; Rio Bueno 113
Kenilworth: 62
King's House: 217
Kingston and the Blue Mountains: 200-275; accommodations 246-248; Blue and John Crow Mountains 263-275; entertainment 218-228; food 235-245; highlights 201; information and services 249-250; maps 203; orientation 202; planning tips 16, 202; recreation 232-235; safety 204-205; shopping 229-232; sights 205-217; spas 21; transportation 251-253
Kingston Dub Club: 24, 218
Kingston on the Edge (KOTE) Arts Festival: 220
Kingston Parish Church: 210
Kingston Restaurant Week: 221
Kingston street food: 237
kiteboarding: 25, 84, 107
Kiyara Spa on the Cliff: 21, 56
Knibb Memorial Baptist Church: 107
Konoko Falls: 24, 28, 125, 125-127
Kool Runnings Waterpark: 38
Kumina: 324

L

language: 322, 343-346
Lark Cruises: 74
laser tag: 40
Lash: 295
Laughing Waters: 27, 129
LGBTQ+ travelers: 337
Liberty Hall: 211
lighthouses: 35, 173, 254
Likkle Portie: 190
Lime Cay: 27, 254
Lime Tree Farm: 28, 274
literary festivals: 292
Little Ochie Seafood Festival: 287
Long Bay: 194
Long Bay Beach: 27, 194
Long Bay Beach Park: 36
Lover's Leap: 288-289
Lower Black River Morass: 299
low season: 17
Luana Orchid Farm: 298
Lucea: 61-62

Luminous Lagoon: 109-110
Luminous Lagoon Tours: 110
Luna Sea Inn: 28, 69

M

Mahogany Beach: 129
mammals: 310
Mammee Bay: 144-146
manatees: 299
Mandeville: 16, 280-284
Mandeville Courthouse: 280
Mandeville Jail and Workhouse: 280
Mandeville Rectory: 280
Mandingo Cave: 195
Manley, Norman: 315
manners: 334-335
Manning's School: 66-68
maps: 342
marathons: 43, 292
Marbana: 179
Margaritaville: 20, 23, 41, 88
Margaritaville Beach: 129
marine life: 311
markets: Falmouth 108; Montego Bay 91; Ocho Rios 133; Port Antonio 180; Port Maria 163
Marley, Bob: 156-157
Maroon Council: 191
Maroon Museum: 191
Maroons: 189, 303
Marshall's Pen: 280
Martha Brae River: 109
Mavis Bank: 28, 270-272
Mayfield Falls: 20, 23, 66
McFarlene's Bar: 256
measures: 342
media: 341
medical services: Kingston 249; Mandeville 283; Montego Bay 102; Negril 57; Port Antonio 187
Mento: 325
Middle Quarters: 22, 23, 301
military museum: 211
mining: 317, 338
Miss Lily's at Skylark: 20, 23, 44
Miss Lou: 227
Miss T's Kitchen: 22, 134
Misty Bliss: 220
Mobay Proper: 20, 93
money: 340-341
money museum: 209
Montego Bay and the Northwest Coast: 20, 22, 25, 72-116; accommodations 98-102; beaches 82-83; east of Montego Bay 104-113; entertainment 88-90; food 93-97; highlights 73; information and services 102; itinerary 74; maps 75-77; North Cockpit Country 114-116;
orientation 74; planning tips 16, 77; recreation 83-88; safety 78; shopping 91-93; sights 78-81; spas 21; transportation 103-104
Montego Bay Cultural Centre: 74, 78-80
Montego Bay Yacht Club: 90
Moore Town: 189-190
Moore Town Maroon Cultural Centre: 189
Morant Bay: 197-199
Morant Bay Rebellion: 198
Mt. Zion Hill: 265
mountain biking: 158
Mountain River Cave: 261
Mt. Zion Hill: 265
Museum of History and Ethnography: 211
Museum of Jamaican Music: 211
Musgrave Market: 180
music: general discussion 322-325; Accompong Maroon Festival 303; Binghi celebrations 286; Emancipation Jubilee 147; itinerary 23-25; Kingston 16, 218-220, 223; Marbana 179; Montego Bay 89, 90; Museum of Jamaican Music 211; Negril 41, 43; Ocho Rios 132; Port Antonio 180; Rebel Salute 152; stores 93; as a top experience 12, 156, 224
Mystic Mountain: 22, 124

N

Nanny Falls: 189
Nassau Valley: 302
National Arena: 232
National Gallery: 22, 24, 210-211
National Gallery West: 78
National Heroes Park: 213
National Museum West: 78
National Stadium: 232
Natural History Division: 211
Navy Island: 173
Negril and the West Coast: 20, 23, 263; accommodations 49-57; beaches 35-36; entertainment 41-43; food 44-49; highlights 31; information and services 57; maps 33, 34, 36; Northeast of Negril 59-64; orientation 32; planning tips 16, 32; recreation 37-41; safety 34; shopping 44; sights 35; Southeast of Negril 65-71; spas 21; transportation 58-59
Negril Lighthouse: 35
Negro Aroused: 205
New Kingston: 236-238
nightlife: clothes for: 19; Kingston 218-227; Mandeville 281; Negril 41-43; Ocho Rios 130-132; Port Antonio 179; Runaway Bay 149; Treasure Beach 291-292
Nine Mile: 155-157
Norman Manley International Airport: 329
Norman Manley Sea Park Beach: 35

North Cockpit Country: 114-116
Nyabinghi House of Rastafari: 24, 285, 321

O

Oatley Mountain Loop Trail: 267
Obeah: 320
Ocean Boulevard: 22, 205
Ocho Rios and the Central North Coast: 24, 117-165; Discovery Bay 153-155; highlights 118; maps 120, 121, 122; Nine Mile 155-157; Ocho Rios 122-143; planning tips 16, 119; Runaway Bay 148-153; safety 120-121; spas 21; St. Mary Parish 157-165; west of Ocho Rios 143-148
Ocho Rios Bay Beach: 129
Ocho Rios Fishing Village: 24, 135
Ocho Rios Fort: 123-124
Ocho Rios Jazz Festival: 132
Office of Nature: 36
Olde Jamaica Tours: 205
Old Folly: 154
Old Fort Bay: 144-146
Old Gaol: 256
Old Hospital Park Beach: 83
Old Naval Hospital: 256
Old Steamer Beach: 83
Old Tavern Coffee Estate: 28, 266
One Love Café: 216
One Love Trail: 28, 129
One Man Beach: 83
Oracabessa: 157-162
orchids: 298
overfishing: 339

P

packing: 19
Pagee Beach: 163
paintball: 40
Painted Negril: 43
the Palisadoes: 253-256
Papine: 240, 242
Paradise Park: 67
parasailing: 38
Passport Immigration and Citizenship Agency: 18
passports: 18
patties, Jamaican: 29, 242
Pearly Beach: 129
Pelican Bar: 22, 298, 301
Pellew Island: 176
People's Museum of Craft and Technology: 258
performing arts: 90, 227-228
Peter Tosh Memorial Garden: 23, 68
pharmacies: 102, 249
phone services: 341

Pier 1: 20, 23, 93
Pineapple Cup Race: 83
La Pizzeria: 22, 239
planning tips: 16-19
plantation culture: 313-315
plantations: see estates
plants: 307-310
Plumb Point Lighthouse: 254
police services: 249
politics: 315-316
polo: 233
Port Antonio: 22, 24, 170-188
Port Antonio and the East Coast: 166-199; beaches 173-176; east of Port Antonio 191-196; highlights 167; maps 169, 171; Morant Bay 197-199; planning tips 16, 168; Port Antonio 170-188; safety 168; Upper Rio Grande Valley 188-190; west of Port Antonio 190-191
Port Antonio International Marlin Tournament: 179
Port Antonio Marina: 172
Portland: 175
Port Maria: 162-163
Port Morant: 198
Port Royal: 24, 253-256
postal services: 187, 249
Priory: 147
Prospect Plantation: 127
Puerto Seco Beach Club: 154
Pulse Global: 230
Pushcart Restaurant and Rum Bar: 20, 23, 48
Pushpa's: 24, 244

QR

Quadrant Wharf: 154
Quao's Village: 191
racial issues: 318-319
radio: 341
rafting: 109, 128, 188-189
Rastafarian culture: general discussion 320-322; Ba Beta Kristian Church of Haile Selassie I 213; Bobo Hill 257; Mt. Zion Hill 265; Rastafari Rootz Fest 43; Scott's Pass 285; Stepping High Festival 43
Rastafari Rootz Fest: 43
Reach Falls: 24, 195
reading, suggested: 347-349
Rebel Salute: 132, 152
record stores: 231
recreation: Kingston 232-235; Montego Bay 83-88; Negril and the West Coast 37-41; Ocho Rios 129-130; Port Antonio 179; Treasure Beach 291; see also specific place
Reggae Boyz: 232
Reggae Girlz: 232

Reggae Horseback Riding: 22, 40
Reggae Marathon, Half Marathon, and 10K: 43
Reggae Mill Bar: 24, 226
Reggae Month: 220
reggae music: general discussion 323; best albums 222-223; Island Records 158; Marley, Bob 156-157; Rebel Salute 132, 152; Reggae Month 220; Reggae Sumfest 78, 90; Western Consciousness 43
Reggae Sumfest: 16, 90
religion: 319-322
remittances: 318
reptiles: 310
resources, Internet: 349-350
Revival: 319
Richmond Hill Inn: 78, 98
Rick's Café: 25, 37
Rio Bueno: 112-113
Rio Bueno Anglican Church: 113
Rio Bueno Baptist Church: 113
Rio Grande River: 188-189
Robin's Bay: 163-165
Rockhouse Spa: 21, 55
Rocklands Bird Sanctuary and Feeding Station: 86
rocksteady: 324
Rodney Memorial: 258
Rose Hall Great House: 20, 23, 74, 81
Rotary Club of Negril Donkey Races: 43
Royal Swim: 123
rum: 302, 333
Runaway Bay: 148-153
Runaway Bay Public Beach: 148
running: 326

S

Sabina Park: 232
safety: 339-340
sailing: Kingston 234; Montego Bay 83; Ocho Rios 129
St. Andrew Parish Church: 215
St. Ann's Bay: 146-147
St. Catherine: 258-263
St. James Parish Church: 80
St. Margaret's Bay: 190
St. Mark's Anglican Church: 265
St. Mary Parish: 16, 157-165
St. Mary Parish Church: 163
St. William Grant Park: 210
salinization: 338
Sam Sharpe Square: 74
Sangster International Airport: 328
San San Beach: 175
Santa Cruz: 303
sauces: 333
Savanna-la-Mar: 20, 65, 66-68

Scotchies: 20, 23, 29, 94
Scott's Pass: 23, 285
sculpture: 66
seafood: 282
sealife: 311
season, travel tips by: 17
Seven-Mile Beach: 20, 27; accommodations 49-54; beach 35; food 44
Seville Great House: 147
sexually transmitted disease: 339
Shackleford, Council Secretary Charmaine: 189
Shan Shy Beach: 173
Sharkies: 148, 150
Shark Program: 123
Sharpe, Sam: 80
Shaw Park Gardens: 125
Shelter Trail: 268
Shorty's: 24, 263
S Hotel Jamaica: 23, 99
shrubs: 308
Silver Sands: 26, 27, 111
Silver Sands Beach: 111
ska: 222, 324
Skydweller Ultra Lounge: 24, 226
slavery: 161, 261, 313-315
snorkeling: Glistening Waters 110; Montego Bay 84; Negril 36, 38; Ocho Rios 129; Pelican Bar 299; Pellew Island 176; Shan Shy Beach 175
soccer: 326
social customs: 334-335
Somerset Falls: 190
sound systems: 224
South Coast: 21, 276-304; Black River and South Cockpit Country 298-304; highlights 277; Mandeville 280-284; maps 279; north of Mandeville 284-286; planning tips 16, 278; safety 278; south of Mandeville 286-288; Treasure Beach 288-297
South Cockpit Country: 301-304
Southern Trelawny Environmental Agency: 115
The Spa at The Caves: 21, 56
Spanish Bridge: 128
Spanish colonization: 312
Spanish Town: 258
Spanish Town Baptist Church: 261
Spanish Town Cathedral: 259
Spanish Town Square: 258
The Spa Retreat: 21, 56
spas: general discussion 21; Bath Hotel and Spa 198; Kingston 235; Montego Bay 87; Strawberry Hill FieldSpa 270; Treasure Beach 291
spelunking: 115
spices: 333
sports: 326-327
Stepping High Festival: 43

Sterling, Colonel Wallace: 189
Stony Hill: 242
Strawberry Hill: 265, 269
Strawberry Hill FieldSpa: 270
The Strawberry Hill Field Spa: 21, 269
street dances: 224
sugar estates: *see* estates
The Sugar Mill: 20, 95
Sun Valley Plantation: 159
surfing: general discussion 25; Boston Beach 193; Bull Bay 257; Kingston 234; Long Bay Beach 194
sustainable tourism: 337-339
Swallow Hole Fisherman's Beach: 148
Swim Adventure: 123
swimming: Bluefields Beach 68; Blue Hole Mineral Spring 35; Blue Hole River 128; Dunn's River Falls 122; Frenchman's Cove 175; Good Hope plantation 114; Jacob Taylor Bathing Beach 111; Lime Cay 254; Rio Grande River 189; Treasure Beach 288, 291; Turtle River Falls & Gardens 127; Windsor Great Cave 115

Trelawny Parish Church of St. Peter the Apostle: 107
Trelawny Yam Festival: 90
Trench Town: 209
Trench Town Reading Centre: 210
Trinity Cathedral: 213
Tropical Bliss Beach: 83
Troy Trail: 115, 302
Tryall: 62-64
tubing: 128
Tuff Gong Recording: 157
Tuff Gong Recording Studio: 22, 24, 209
Turtle River Falls & Gardens: 127
Turtle River Park: 127
turtles: 311
Twelve Tribes of Israel: 322
Two Sisters Cave: 263

T

Tacky's War: 161
Taino people: 164, 261, 312
Tamarind: 24, 244
taxis: 329
telephone services: 341
television: 341-342
tennis: 179, 233
Tensing Pen: 23, 26, 55
theater: 90, 227-228
theft: 340
tipping: 335
Titchfield Hill: 170
Titchfield Hotel: 170
Titchfield School: 170
Tmrw Tday Festival: 43
top experiences: 11-15; adventure sports 13, 25, 38; beaches 14, 27; Blue Hole Mineral Spring 15, 35, 177; Blue Mountain Peak 273; cliff jumping 37; cuisine 12, 29; Dunn's River Falls 122; music 12, 156, 224; waterfalls 11, 122, 125
Tosh, Peter: 68
tourist economy: 317
track and field: 326
transportation: general discussion 328-330; Kingston 251-253; Mandeville 284; Montego Bay 103-104; Negril 57-58; Ocho Rios 142; Port Antonio 187-188; Treasure Beach 297; *see also specific place*
Treasure Beach: 16, 22, 288-297
trees: 308
Trelawny: 25, 74, 77

UV

UCC Craighton Coffee Estate: 265
University of the West Indies: 217
Upper Constant Spring: 242, 244
Upper Rio Grande Valley: 188-190
uptown Kingston: 213-217
vacation rentals: 334
vaccinations: 18
vegetation: 307-310
villas: 334
visas: 18, 331
visitor information: 57, 342
volunteering: 335-336

WXYZ

Wag Water/ Dick's Pond Trail: 268
Walter Fletcher Beach: 82
waterfalls: Cane River Falls 256; Christiana Bottom 284; Dunn's River Falls 122; Konoko Falls 125-127; Mayfield Falls 66; Nanny Falls 189; Reach Falls 195; Rio Bueno 113; Somerset Falls 190; as a top experience 11, 122, 125; Turtle River Falls & Gardens 127; YS Falls 300
Waterfall Trail: 268
waterparks: 38
water sports: Kingston 234-235; Montego Bay 83-86; Negril 36, 37-38; Port Antonio 177; Puerto Seco Beach Club 154-155; *see also specific sport*
water table salinization: 338
Waves Beach: 262
wealth distribution: 318
weights: 342
West End Negril: accommodations 54-57; food 46-49
Western Consciousness: 43

Westmoreland Curry Festival: 66
Westmoreland Interior: 66-68
Wharf House: 20, 98
Whitehall Great House: 35
Whitehouse: 70-71
White River: 22, 28, 175
white-water rafting: Martha Brae River 109; Negril
    37; Ocho Rios 130; Rio Bueno 113
Whitfield Hall: 273, 274
wildlife: 310-311
wildlife encounters: Blue and John Crow
    Mountains 263; Blue and John Crow
    Mountains National Park 273; Canoe Valley
    Protected Area 286; Jamaica Swamp Safari
    Village 107; Konoko Falls 125; Lower Black

River Morass 299; Lucea 62; Ocho Rios 123
Williams, Colonel Ferron: 303
Windsor Great Cave: 115
windsurfing: 107
Winnifred Beach: 22, 177
women travelers: 336
Woodside: 28, 270
Xaymaca: 221
Xodus: 221
Yaaman Adventure Park: 127
YS Falls: 22, 28, 300
Zest Restaurant: 23, 49
zip lines: 25; Black River 300; Good Hope
    plantation 114; Mystic Mountain 124
zoos: 217, 301

List of Maps

Front Map
Jamaica: 4–5

Discover Jamaica
The West Coast: 33
West End: 34
Negril Beach: 36

Montego Bay and the Northwest Coast
The Northwest Coast: 75
Montego Bay: 76
Montego Bay Detail: 77

Ocho Rios and the Central North Coast
The Central Coast: 120–121
Ocho Rios: 122
Ocho Rios and Vicinity: 124–125
Runaway Bay: 150–151

Port Antonio and the East Coast
The East Coast: 169
Port Antonio Coastline: 171
Northeast Coast: 192

Kingston and the Blue Mountains
Kingston and Vicinity: 203
Metropolitan Kingston: 206–207
Downtown Kingston: 208
Uptown Kingston: 214
Spanish Town: 259
The Blue and John Crow Mountains: 264

The South Coast
The South Coast: 279
Mandeville: 281
Treasure Beach: 289

Photo Credits

Trips to Remember

TRIP OF A LIFETIME

ANGKOR WAT

TOM VATER

TRIP OF A LIFETIME

GALÁPAGOS ISLANDS

ICELAND

JENNA GOTTLIEB

TRIP OF A LIFETIME

MACHU PICCHU

STAN GODE

MOROCCO

NEW ZEALAND

JAMIE CHRISTIAN DESPLACES

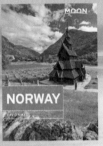

NORWAY

DAVID NIKEL

TRIP OF A LIFETIME

PATAGONIA

WAYNE BERNHARDSON

PRAGUE, VIENNA & BUDAPEST

ROME, FLORENCE & VENICE

ALEXEI J COHEN

ZION & BRYCE

W. C. McRAE & JUDY JEWELL

Epic Adventure

MOON

Drive & Hike

APPALACHIAN TRAIL

THE BEST TRAIL TOWNS, DAY HIKES, AND ROAD TRIPS IN BETWEEN

TIMOTHY MALCOLM

MOON

ROUTE 66

Road Trip

JESSICA DUNHAM

MOON

YELLOWSTONE TO GLACIER NATIONAL PARK

Road Trip

JACKSON HOLE, CODY, THE GRAND TETONS & THE ROCKY MOUNTAIN FRONT

CARTER G. WALKER

AMALFI COAST
With Capri, Naples & Pompeii
LAURA THAYER

ARUBA

BAHAMAS
MARIA LAURINE MOYLE

BAJA
Tijuana to Los Cabos
JENNIFER KRAMER

BELIZE
LEBAWIT LILY GIRMA

BERMUDA
ROSEMARY JONES

COSTA RICA

DOMINICAN REPUBLIC

FIJI

FLORIDA
JASON FERGUSON

HAWAII
KEVIN WHITTON

JAMAICA

MAUI
With Molokai & Lanai
KYLE ELLISON

PUERTO VALLARTA
With Sayulita, Guadalajara, Nayarit & Guadalajara
MADELINE MILNE

YUCATÁN PENINSULA

Embark on an epic journey along the historic Camino de Santiago, stroll the top European cities, or chase Norway's northern lights with Moon Travel Guides!

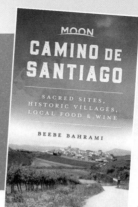

MOON
CAMINO DE SANTIAGO
SACRED SITES, HISTORIC VILLAGES, LOCAL FOOD & WINE

BEEBE BAHRAMI

MOON
AMALFI COAST
WITH CAPRI, NAPLES & POMPEII
LAURA THAYER

MOON
BARCELONA & MADRID
JESSICA JONES

MOON
CROATIA & SLOVENIA
SHANN FOUNTAIN ALTIOUR

MOON
EDINBURGH, GLASGOW & THE ISLE OF SKYE

MOON
FRENCH RIVIERA: NICE, CANNES, MONACO & ST-TROPEZ

MOON
ICELAND
JENNA GOTTLIEB

MOON
IRELAND
CAMILLE DEANGELIS

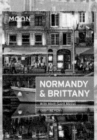

MOON
NORMANDY & BRITTANY
With Mont-Saint-Michel
CHRIS NEWENS

MOON
NORWAY

MOON
PORTUGAL

MOON
PRAGUE, VIENNA & BUDAPEST

MOON
PROVENCE

MOON
ROME, FLORENCE & VENICE
ALEXEI J. COHEN

GO BIG AND GO BEYOND!

These savvy city guides include strategies to help you see the top sights and find adventure beyond the tourist crowds.

OR TAKE THINGS ONE STEP AT A TIME

MOON JAMAICA
Avalon Travel
Hachette Book Group
1700 Fourth Street
Berkeley, CA 94710, USA
www.moon.com

Editor: Rachael Sablik
Acquiring Editor: Nikki Ioakimedes
Series Manager: Kathryn Ettinger
Development Editor: Jay Cooke
Copy Editor: Christopher Church
Graphics Coordinator: Scott Kimball
Production Coordinator: Scott Kimball
Cover Design: Faceout Studios, Charles Brock
Interior Design: Domini Dragoone
Moon Logo: Tim McGrath
Map Editor: Albert Angulo
Cartographer: Andrew Dolan
Proofreader: Deana Shields
Indexer: Rachel Kuhn

ISBN-13: 9781640490925

Printing History
1st Edition — 1991
8th Edition — February 2020
5 4 3 2 1

Front cover photo: Dunn's River Falls, © Doug Pearson, Getty Images
Back cover photo: Beach at Jamaica Inn, © Oliver Hill

Printed in China by RR Donnelley.